LETTERS OF
MARSHALL
McLUHAN

LETTERS OF
MARSHALL
McLUHAN

SELECTED AND EDITED BY

Matie Molinaro   Corinne McLuhan   William Toye

TORONTO   OXFORD   NEW YORK

Oxford University Press

1987

CANADIAN CATALOGUING IN PUBLICATION DATA

McLuhan, Marshall, 1911–1980
Letters of Marshall McLuhan

Includes bibliographical references and index.
ISBN 0-19-540594-3

1. McLuhan, Marshall, 1911–1980 – Correspondence.
2. Authors, Canadian (English) – 20th century –
Correspondence.* I. Molinaro, Matie. II. McLuhan,
Corinne. III. Toye, William. IV. Title.

P92.5.M24A4 1987   001.5′092′4   C87-09411-X

1 2 3 4 - 0 9 8 7

Printed in Canada by
John Deyell Company

Contents

List of Illustrations

Preface I

BY MATIE MOLINARO

In 1948, during the Toronto appointment of United States Consul General H. Earle Russell, the American colony was small enough for consular executives to treat the "members" as family at the occasional small dinner party. At a dinner given by the consular official Charles Johnson, and his wife Florence, my husband Giulio Molinaro and I met Corinne and Marshall McLuhan for the first time. This was two years before I established my literary agency and three years before the publication of McLuhan's first book, *The Mechanical Bride*. I remember that the dinner conversation was largely a McLuhan monologue about advertising and comics, particularly Li'l Abner. With my limited experience, and complete lack of clairvoyance, I was surprised that he could be entranced by subjects so far removed from what I expected an English professor's interests to be. None of us at that dinner realized that we were being exposed to early McLuhan probes.

Over the years Giulio and I followed his career with great interest, but as I do not seek out clients, it did not occur to me to discuss literary representation with Marshall McLuhan. In the autumn of 1969, however, I returned from Europe to find several urgent messages from him. He had decided that he needed a media agent and I had been recommended to him by a leading New York advertising executive. Thus began a friendship, and a good working relationship, that lasted for the rest of his life. Over the ten years from 1969 to the time of his stroke in September 1979, Corinne, Marshall, Giulio and I spent a lot of time together — dinners and theatre, movies, visits, studying *The Inferno*, and walks around Wychwood Park and our farm in Sandford. In fact the McLuhans bought the farm next but one to ours.

Three weeks after Marshall McLuhan's death Corinne wrote to me asking if I would continue to look after all business matters concerning the literary estate to which she was now sole heir. Two months later she wrote again asking me to include Marshall's personal papers in the properties that needed special attention, since she had begun to receive enquiries about their final disposition. Thus my connection with McLuhan's work was extended for another seven years.

When the University of Toronto decided to close the Centre for Culture and Technology in 1980, Corinne was asked to remove as quickly as possible all of McLuhan's personal papers. Much of the material was in filing cabinets and half of these were sent to the basement at Wychwood Park while the other half went to the basement of Eric McLuhan's house. From my work on other collections of literary papers I knew that dampness and acids could destroy them. In July 1981, therefore, I urged Corinne to start a new index and a new inventory since those kept so well and faithfully by Marshall's secretary, Margaret Stewart, had been lost in the turmoil following her illness and Marshall's stroke. The task was monumental and Corinne could not possibly handle it alone. I offered to help and I well remember the first day, just a few days before Marshall's birthday, when we began this new voyage of discovery.

The papers that were especially important to Marshall had been stored in boxes in the closets and cupboards of his study on the third floor of the house in Wychwood Park. Although reading his letters in his study almost made us feel his presence and prolonged Corinne's grief, his absence was most acutely felt on the many occasions during the sorting, cataloguing, and filing when we longed to ask him the meaning of indecipherable handwritten notes. Once begun, the task was *not* half done by any means. It was soon obvious that the papers, to be studied and filed efficiently, should all be in one place. By the end of August several further approaches about acquiring them made such a move more urgent.

Through the good offices of Ian Mang, Corinne McLuhan's attorney, and a bank manager whose name we never learned, we were given a floor of a small bank building downtown. Promising us that we would not be obligated to them in any way, representatives from the Public Archives of Canada in Ottawa offered to move all of the papers from Wychwood and Eric's house to the bank. I began to work double shifts: from early morning to mid-afternoon in my own office; then, after calling for Corinne, working another six to eight hours or longer with her at "the bank". This went on almost daily, summer and winter, for nearly three years.

The very first file I had worked on at Wychwood was marked "A Guide to Chaos", which in the circumstances seemed a good place to start. We soon learned that each file had to be thoroughly examined because few of them contained what their labels promised. (For instance, "A Guide to Chaos" was a guide to nothing. It contained 85 reviews of *The Mechanical Bride*: 80 from the United States, three from Canada, and two from England.) For easier handling the material in the filing cabinets was gradually transferred to 225 boxes.

Early in 1982 a team of American evaluators was sent up to look at the papers. Since their evaluation was to be based somewhat on the size of the collection, team members counted every sheet of paper in every envelope of letters and every manuscript. That is how we learned that we had sifted through over 800,000 pieces of paper—100,000 pages being letters. From this collection of notes, letters, manuscripts, theses evaluated, annotations, records, honorary degrees, we chose 1,500 letters that to us seemed the most interesting part of the papers. Arranged properly, we felt, they would constitute the autobiography that McLuhan never even dreamed of writing.

By January 1984 the letters were in very good order and an index to the rest of the material had been prepared. For a little while we knew what was in each of the 225 boxes! Although the papers were ready to be sold, we had not quite finished making the selection for a projected book of letters because Corinne had fallen and broken her hip. When we managed to reach an agreement for the sale of the papers to the Public Archives, Corinne was pleased that Marshall's work and records would remain in Canada. Even though McLuhan had become a citizen of the world, he always remained fiercely Canadian. Most of the papers were moved to Ottawa in mid-February, but through the generosity and compassion of Dr Wilfred Smith, then Dominion Archivist, and Mr William Ormsby, Director of the Ontario Archives, ten boxes of letters were kept in the Ontario Archives building so that upon her recovery Corinne and I could go back and finish the letter selection.

By the autumn of 1985 we had four volumes of letters and had made a summary of every year of McLuhan's life from the Cambridge years forward. What we desperately needed then was an editor who would understand that we wanted the world—those who were familiar with his works and those who would be introduced to him by these letters—to see Marshall McLuhan as he explained himself, his beliefs, and his ideas. How fortunate we were that William Toye developed an enthusiasm for this project that soon equalled and perhaps at times surpassed our own! We are grateful to him for making this tribute to Marshall McLuhan a reality.

Preface II
and Acknowledgements

BY WILLIAM TOYE

In November 1985 Matie Molinaro and Corinne McLuhan presented me with a very large selection of Marshall McLuhan's letters, which had clearly been compiled objectively and was generously representative. It had been made from a much larger collection they had assiduously brought together and deposited in the Public Archives of Canada (recently renamed the National Archives of Canada). I proceeded to reduce their own selection in keeping with the extent of the single volume of letters that Oxford projected. While this was being done, other letters were acquired—mainly those to Father Walter J. Ong, and those written to McLuhan's mother immediately after his marriage and during his 1939-40 year at Cambridge University. A representative selection of these letters was added, along with several letters from the collection in the Archives and a few others contributed by donors.

The selection that follows was chosen for biographical reasons; for illuminating McLuhan's intellectual development and interests; for containing statements of his ideas, along with clarifications and elaborations of them; for providing pertinent information; for documenting his epistolary relationship with well-known people; or (particularly in the early period) for being bridges to other letters. The overall intention was to make a selection that would convey, within limitations of space, the educational background, personal qualities, family life, influences, thought, developing ideas, friendships, and later life of McLuhan in as much detail as his letters provide.

My annotations and commentaries should be read in the knowledge that I never had the privilege of meeting Marshall McLuhan (though I heard and saw him on radio and television). These additions are in three forms. (i) Introductions to the periods 1911-36, 1936-46, and 1946-79 are intended to provide a biographical background for the letters that follow. (ii) Occasional italicized passages preceding letters appear as explanations of, or introductions to, subjects or correspondents that have particular significance in the context of the letters. (iii) The footnotes documenting or clarifying references (which may sometimes seem to identify or explain what is common knowledge) have been written with the thought that as the letters embrace, and will interest specialists in, many disciplines, an expert in one may know little about others; and that for young readers many topical and other references could very well be mysterious.

Several editorial points might be kept in mind in reading these letters:

Transcriptions of the early handwritten letters match the originals—with their occasional misspellings and vagaries of punctuation, including McLuhan's omission of the apostrophe in possessives—in order to retain their immediacy and personality.

Most of the early letters are undated, or merely record the day of the week. However, the postmark on an envelope, or the context of the letter, sometimes indicated the time of writing, and references in McLuhan's diary for 1935–9 often provided exact dates. All presumed dates or periods appear in square brackets.

Beginning with the letter to Edward S. Morgan of May 16, 1959, the letters were dictated and typed (though most of the letters to Father Walter J. Ong that follow were handwritten). To increase the readability of typed letters, alterations have been made in typographic style (such as italicizing book titles) and anomalies of spelling and punctuation have been corrected, since (in spite of the pleas of his secretary, Mrs Margaret Stewart) McLuhan usually did not read these dictated letters before signing, swept up as he was by his many other activities. As signatures do not appear in most of the copies, they have not been simulated.

Beginning on August 4, 1963, copies of letters either have no heading, and were presumably written at St Michael's College, or bear the photocopied heading "Centre for Culture and Technology". These places of origin have not been recorded repeatedly: unless otherwise indicated, all letters from here on issued from the University of Toronto.

The editorial supplement to these letters could not have been written without the help of a great many people. My first expression of thanks must go to Corinne McLuhan, who gave me access to her husband's library and exercised never-ending patience in providing information concerning family and other matters, and in giving me addresses of some of McLuhan's friends with whom I corresponded. She, and Marshall McLuhan's literary agent, Matie Molinaro—who contributed her own knowledge generously and objectively, and prepared the Index with Corinne McLuhan's assistance—provided some corrections of factual detail in the annotations.

In the early stages of my research, Professor Giulio Molinaro very kindly obtained for my use library books from the University of Toronto (and on occasion gave guidance in his field of Italian literature to his forgetful former student). The research eventually required the help of an assistant, and this role was expertly filled for nearly a year by Andrew Hewitt—a recent graduate of Bishop's University, Lennoxville, Quebec, and an M.A. student at the University of Toronto. His contribution was immense, and much appreciated. His friend Kevin Halligan, an undergraduate at St Michael's College, also assisted me.

I am grateful to Maurice McLuhan for talking with me in person and by phone about his brother's early life, and to Marshall McLuhan's elder son Eric, who has been most supportive.

This collection of letters has itself brought about a large correspondence. With one or two exceptions everyone I wrote to replied—not only with requested information, but often expressing pleasure in assisting the publication of Marshall McLuhan's letters.

I thank the following recipients of letters from Marshall McLuhan for responding to my enquiries most helpfully: Claude Bissell (who generously provided information about McLuhan at the University of Toronto in the 1960s, in letter form and in conversation), the late Morton Bloomfield, Harry J. Boyle, Edmund Carpenter (whose many letters from New York vividly conveyed his friendship and association with McLuhan), John Culkin, Barry Day, Lionel Elvin, Gerald Mason Feigen, Marshall W. Fishwick, Robert Fulford, Philippe Dean Gigantes, Michael Hornyansky, William Jovanovich, Frank Kermode, J.G. Keogh, William Kuhns, Hugh T. Lane, Thomas Langan, Gershon Legman, Father John W. Mole, Mother St Michael, Father Walter J. Ong (who patiently answered a great many questions by letter and phone), David Riesman, Tony Schwartz (who, in a phone call from New York, put on the line a tape of McLuhan making several observations), R.J. Schoeck, R. Murray Schafer, Ernest Sirluck (with whom I had several long and useful conversations), Harry J. Skornia, David Staines, George Steiner (who very kindly permitted the quotation from his comments on *The Gutenberg Galaxy* on page 329, note 2), Brian Stock, John Wain, Sheila Watson and Wilfred Watson (both of whom wrote long and helpful letters), and D. Carlton Williams.

I am also grateful to the following people mentioned in the letters who answered my enquiries: Pauline Bondy, Elizabeth Trott Cera, Christopher Cornford, J. King Gordon, Barrington Nevitt, Joseph T. O'Connor, Evelyn Shrifte, Richard J. Stanbury, Donald F. Theall (who elucidated several concepts for me, including the idea of "secret societies"), and Guy R. Turgeon.

For various forms of assistance I am indebted to Leslie Armour, University of Ottawa (who helped me with several philosophical annotations), Osmond Beckwith, Arthur I. Bloomfield, Gale Carrithers, David Clandfield, William Dendy, Marianne Fizet, David Gerard, Thomas Howarth, Elizabeth M. Knowles, John Lennox, Hugh MacCallum, Thelma McCormack, Father M.B. McNamee, Jean Milner (who provided me with an invaluable computer print-out of all the recipients in alphabetical order, with dates of their letters), Ellie Plimack, Omar Pound, Mrs John Reid, Gavin Ross, George Sanderson (a friend of McLuhan's, and editor of *The Antigonish Review*, who was helpful in many ways), Allegra Snyder (who gave me permission to quote—on page 308, note 1—from a letter written by her father, Buckminster Fuller), R.E. Sproule, Jean van der Tak, Maria Tippett, Elmer Von Felt, Robert Weaver, Ronald S. Wilkinson (Manuscript Historian, The Library of Congress), Richard Virr, and Marcia Willison.

I am grateful to archivists and others at universities McLuhan was associated with for providing me with information: The Reverend Frederick Black, St Michael's College, University of Toronto, who patiently answered many phone enquiries; Dr Helen Canada, Saint Louis University; The Reverend C.G. Heath, Assumption University; Sandra Raba, Trinity Hall, Cambridge University; C.A. Santoro, the University of Manitoba; and Bernard Schermetzler, the University of Wisconsin-Madison.

To the National Archives of Canada, where the McLuhan Papers are kept in meticulous order, I am deeply indebted—particularly to David Enns, the knowledgeable and efficient custodian of the McLuhan Papers, and to his colleague Anne Godard—for extending the greatest possible assistance during my three visits there. David Enns responded to numerous requests by phone and provided me with many photocopies.

I owe thanks to four Oxford colleagues who worked on the letters: to Barbara Mendelson and especially to Phyllis Wilson, both of whom checked the original transcriptions against the early handwritten letters and made corrections; to Rhoda Rubinoff, who retyped many letters and notes; and to my fellow editor Patricia Sillers.

Grateful acknowledgement is made to the Cornell University Library for the letters to Wyndham Lewis; to the Collection of American Literature, The Beinecke Rare Book and Manuscript Library, Yale University, for two letters to Ezra Pound dated December 18, 1954 and January 22, 1957; to the Lilly Library, Indiana University, for the other letters to Ezra Pound; to the University of Toronto Archives for the letter to Harold Adams Innis; to Margaret Deaver Brown for the letter to E.K. Brown; to Robert Fulford for the letter to the *Toronto Star* of July 4, 1978; to Margaret W. Giovanelli for the letters to Felix Giovanelli; to Father Walter J. Ong for the letters to him; to Dr Ernest Sirluck for the letter to him of February 21, 1973; and to the Right Honourable Pierre Elliott Trudeau for permission to reprint his letter to Corinne McLuhan, which appears at the end of this collection. Unless otherwise indicated, all handwritten letters and all copies of typewritten letters are in the National Archives of Canada, Ottawa. The McLuhan Papers there bear the call number MG 31, D 156.

I wish also to acknowledge with thanks permission to quote from the writings of Wyndham Lewis and Ezra Pound:

For quotations from Wyndham Lewis's letters to Marshall McLuhan: the Library Board of Cornell University Library.

For quotations from Wyndham Lewis's books: Omar Pound and The Wyndham Lewis Memorial Trust.

For quotations from Ezra Pound's letters to Marshall McLuhan, and from Pound's *Make It New* and *A Visiting Card*: copyright © 1987 by the Trustees of the Ezra Pound Literary Property Trust. Used by permission of New Directions Publishing Corporation, agents.

For quotations from Ezra Pound's *Guide to Kulchur*: copyright © 1970 by Ezra Pound. All Rights Reserved.

For a quotation from Ezra Pound's *ABC of Reading*: copyright 1934 by Ezra Pound.

All the above Pound material is reprinted by permission of New Directions Publishing Corporation and Faber & Faber Ltd.

Introduction
1911–1936

Marshall McLuhan's Canadian antecedents went back three generations on his father's side and five on his mother's. William McLughan of County Down, Ireland, settled with his family in Essa Township near Alliston (Ontario) in 1849—changing the spelling of his name to McLuhan when he came to Canada. His son James bought a lot in Luther Township and became a pioneer farmer and eventually Reeve and Justice of the Peace. In 1908 he and his wife and seven children—one of whom was Herbert Ernest McLuhan (1879–1967), Marshall's father—left their home in Mount Forest, Ontario, to homestead in the West, buying a farm in the future District of Creighton, Alberta. On the maternal side John Hall, from Bristol, settled in Annapolis County, Nova Scotia, before 1790. His great-grandson Henry Seldon Hall was the father of Marshall McLuhan's mother Elsie Naomi (1889–1961). Henry Seldon moved west in 1906 to a rented log cabin and farm south of Mannville, Alberta, in the same District of Creighton where the McLuhans lived. Elsie Hall, who had been teaching school in Nova Scotia, followed her parents in 1908 and became the teacher in the Creighton school. She boarded with the McLuhan family and so met Herbert McLuhan, whom she married on December 31, 1909.

In 1911 Herbert and Elsie McLuhan moved to Edmonton, where Herbert went into real estate with three partners. Their son Herbert Marshall was born on July 21, 1911, and a second son, Maurice Raymond, in 1913. Elsie's father and brothers, Ray and Reg, enlisted when the Great War broke out and Herbert McLuhan enlisted in 1915. Elsie and her sons lived throughout the war with her mother on Rosedale Avenue in Winnipeg. When Herbert was discharged, he and his family settled in Winnipeg, where he became an insurance agent for North American Life.

A sociable, kindly, unsuccessful businessman, Herbert McLuhan had married an intellectually bright, demanding, but also generous woman. She was ambitious for her sons and placed great importance on their being well educated; she was heard to say that she would like them to grow up to be presidents of universities. When Marshall failed Grade 6 in Gladstone Public School, she went to the principal and arranged for his conditional acceptance into Grade 7 at Earl Grey Junior High. There he flourished under an English teacher, Miss Muir, who aroused his interest in books and guided him as he began a regimen of omnivorous reading that was to become a lifelong habit. At this time he also began to build things: model sailboats and crystal radio sets. While attending Kelvin Technical High School for Grades 10 and 11 he built a vacuum-tube radio for distant signals; played hockey and baseball; and was a regular church-goer, attending Nassau Baptist Church, half a block away from his home, and its Bible Class.

Meanwhile Elsie McLuhan, who had become dissatisfied with her husband and her marriage, looked outside for fulfilment. In 1921 she enrolled in, and completed, the first-year English course at the University of Manitoba. She also took elocution lessons and thus found a *métier* that satisfied her creative urge: she discovered that she could hold the attention of an audience as an elocutionist and monologuist and began to give recitals locally. In a memoir, "Class of '30", which appeared in the University of Manitoba *Alumni Journal* (Spring 1980), Charles Rittenhouse, who knew Marshall and Maurice McLuhan as boys, remembers how "Their pretty mother used to take time off to tell stories to the neighborhood kids, and I used to sit at her feet, enthralled by her voice, eyes, and graceful hands. When I was older, I heard her do monologues at concerts. Sheer delight!" In 1922 Elsie McLuhan arranged tours for herself, to the east and then to the west, leaving her family in the hands of a housekeeper. After 1933 she never returned to Winnipeg. She divided her time between Toronto and Detroit performing, directing plays, or teaching.

Marshall thereupon entered into a mainly epistolary relationship with his mother, writing her sometimes several times weekly. His letters to her, which are a kind of diary of his activities and reading, are suffused with warmth and affection, kindled partly by distance, partly by the mutual support and admiration each offered the other—she for his educational attainments and he for his mother's forays into acting and directing. (Years later, on July 28, 1947, his mother wrote to him in part: "It was grand to hear your voice today but I still want to write a line for you to have on your birthday. You have been such a joy and comfort to me—your work your family and just you—being yourself. You have been always, so considerate about writing, when you were in England and now these past few weeks when I have needed to know you thot of me—") Apart from spending the summers of 1937 and 1938 with his mother, he saw her infrequently as an adult until she was in her mid-sixties when, following a stroke, she went to live with or near him and his family for the last years of her life.

In 1928 McLuhan enrolled in Engineering at the University of Manitoba but realized he had made a mistake and switched to English Literature the next year. He embarked on, and enjoyed, an intensive curriculum. His courses included the History of Literature; Chaucer and Spenser; Shakespeare; Milton; Restoration and Eighteenth-Century Literature; Victorian Poetry and Prose; Elementary Old English, Middle English and Advanced Old English; Drama; Non-Dramatic Literature of the Sixteenth and Seventeenth Centuries; American, Contemporary English, and Canadian Poetry; Masterpieces of European Literature (including Homer, Plato, Virgil, Dante, Montaigne, Cervantes); Nineteenth-Century Prose; and the History of Criticism in England. The names of his professors crop up in his early letters: Aaron J. Perry, William Allison, R. Fletcher Argue, A. Lloyd Wheeler, P.L. Carver. He also took courses in History under Noel Fieldhouse, in Philosophy under Rupert Lodge, and in Social Psychology under Henry Wright.

In the McLuhan Papers in the Public Archives of Canada are two diaries for 1930 and 1931. The first of these documents on every daily page his activities.

interests, thoughts, and feelings: on the last day of 1930 McLuhan writes with satisfaction: "This completes a volume of approx. 60,000 words (6 words a line, 27 lines, 365 pages)." The second diary, not as full, is less personal in content; much of it is devoted to quotations from his reading—of Shakespeare, Carlyle, Chesterton, Leibniz, Johnson, Dryden, Webster, Macaulay, *et al.*—which he indexed at the back.

"Each day the question is suggested to me. What am I going to do . . . I think it is safe to follow strongly natural inclinations. Never a prof. tho." (January 8, 1930)

"I would not like to teach but . . . here again I place implicit faith in my Maker." (February 14, 1930)

"An illuminating lecture on the development and technique of modern advertising . . . the appeal is always to some powerful feeling in man: fear, pride, sex, wealth, ambition etc. Fifty years hence, if they have not proceeded to more absurd extremes, a volume of 1930 slogans and advertising tricks would make more interesting reading than anything that has appeared in this generation." (March 26, 1930)

"To them [his male friends] the most absorbing topic . . . is sex and women . . . Personally I wish that my sex instinct was nil if such were possible." (April 8, 1930)

"I realize what I missed in not having a sister. I cannot appreciate a girls viewpoint. I don't get on with them." (April 10, 1930)

"Found the Cicero very hard going so got at it early. One hour a chapter. My eyes began to get sore." (April 28, 1930)

"5 minutes ago I completed my index of literary references on Macaulays essays, plus a note of any particularly striking statement or description." (May 11, 1930—he began this index on May 8.)

"I like the poetry of Chaucer Spenser Sh[akespeare] Milton but neither their biographies or times. I dislike the poetry of the Restoration and after till we come to Wordsworth but find the times of great interest. From Wordsworth on both the poetry and the times are of equal interest. (By poetry I mean literature.)" (July 14, 1930)

"[On his birthday] Mother gave me a fine shirt a pair of pajamas and Gibbon's Decline and Fall . . . Most certainly I shall read it. First I shall skip through Herodotus and thus prepare the ground." (July 21, 1930)

"During the last three months I have read something from him [Shakespeare] nearly every day. I have chosen Spenser to fill his place for daily perusal, then Milton, then Dryden, then Pope." (July 22, 1930)

"Looking back I can say that my literary knowledge has been increased, my standards of real manhood raised, my standards of domestic affection set, my self-conceit dispelled, and this and much more the result of a careful perusal of the faithful account of a great man's life [i.e. Macaulay's]. I cannot help but feel that the study of men of all sorts and their deportment in the multifarious situations of life is infinitely more effective as a guide to life than such a general

precept as 'Love thy neighbour' 'Forgive them that despitefully use you.' "
(August 14, 1930)

"He [Professor Allison] paints the Yale & Harvard outlook in what (for me)
are dreary colors. He spoke of the necessity of being able to read Latin French
and German at sight. Felt rather depressed about the cramming that it entailed. It
looks like Oxford or Cambridge for me." (November 19, 1930)

"20 years hence I shall read this accdunt and think that those were 'the good
old days'"(December 30, 1930). An annotation on this entry two years later
reads, "Looking at them on Jan 30 1933 I can say they were 'bloody awful' . . .
the best is yet to be, thank God."

"Great God Almighty during the coming year enable me to live among my
fellows in such a manner that we may find it mutually beneficial; "what in me is
dark, illumine, what is low raise and support" that I may by personal example
benefit the lives of others. May my daily life become more and more an expression
of Thy self in me . . . ; above all teach me to pray. Teach me the true function of
prayer gracious Father even as it was perceived by Thy glorious Son. Amen and
amen." (January 1, 1931)

"I have reason to be elated to-day. I received back [from Professor Fieldhouse]
my 2nd History essay with the following note: 'This is that very very pure thing,
a student's essay, which I can finally say I enjoyed reading. Excellent Work!' It
was worth two weeks work to earn a compliment from the fastidious Fieldhouse."
(February 23, 1931)

Writing in his diary McLuhan could be sententious, pietistical, critical of others, given to bouts of self-evaluation and discouragement; and his industrious
engagement with literature seems predominantly solemn. But these traits—not
unusual in the confessional outpourings of an inward-looking intellectual nineteen-
year-old—can be set against the details he provides of his day-to-day life, which
convey another McLuhan: an active and sociable person who was by no means a
reclusive bookworm. On January 1, 1930 he reports having hosted a New Year's
Eve party: "Bill Al and I with the girls . . . Got B[abe] under mistletoe." Over
the holiday he went skating, tobogganing, played hockey, and visited with friends.
Workouts at the YMCA several times a week and church-going were part of his
routine throughout the year, but now his church attendance alternated between
hearing the Sunday-evening sermon preached by Dr Leslie Pidgeon at Augustine
United and by Dr S. W. Kerr at Knox United Church. He does chores around the
house, buys birthday gifts for his parents, helps his brother with homework—
while very much feeling the effects of his parents' estrangement. Over two summers in 1928–9 he built a small cat-rigged sailboat, with Bill Jones and Tom
Easterbrook, to plans given him by another friend, Jim Rainey. "After lunch
went sailing. It was such a glorious day and the boat will be on the water such a
short while longer that it really is worth dropping a few hours of studying to
have memories of lovely fall afternoon" (September 10, 1930). Perhaps money
pressures at home had made him write: "Decided *I must sell the* boat $150 or
even $100" (February 17). He carefully records his expenses: "Skating lunch

.collection $1.60" (February 4). "Paint for boat $2.00" (March 25). "Macaulay's History $1.50" (March 28). He earned five dollars in September at the Hudson's Bay Company department store for working as a salesman in "the great overcoat sale". He reflects on morality and religion and talks about these things with friends: "2 or 3 of them were science men and they were airing some odd views on evolution. They did not believe in it. I finally . . . whaled into them on the matter of 'laws' and God's identity with them. I soon discovered they were the most dogmatic orthodox individuals that I had ever run into . . ." (December 4). Every night before bed he reads some Shakespeare and a few chapters of the Bible. G.K. Chesterton and Thomas Babington Macaulay are his literary heroes, but in 1931 he discovers Thackeray ("Thak. is a wonder . . . I am going to read everything of his", January 25, 1931) and Robert Louis Stevenson. He considers specializing in nineteenth-century English literature. He also reads Emerson, Santayana, Nietzsche, Anatole France, and many more authors. He complains of eyestrain (October 27, 1930) and writes of Macaulay: "I often marvel that his eyes never trouble him. I can never study more than 5–6 hrs. a day" (August 13, 1930).

Charles Rittenhouse (who later became head of the Theatre Department of the Montreal Protestant School Board), when he was visiting Winnipeg from Montreal in 1932, recalled how Marshall "came over to talk about graduate schools and teaching. . . . He had a manuscript with him—'just some ideas'—and hesitatingly asked if I would read it. I was highly flattered. The next night we sat on the verandah again. I told him gravely that I was unable to finish his essay; it was too incoherent, too wordy, and far too abstract. 'Would you help me to correct it?' he asked. 'You're going to teach English this fall.' At that moment I missed one of the really golden opportunities of my life. 'I can't,' I said. 'I don't know what on earth you're trying to say. Anyway I don't think you're cut out to be a writer.' I don't remember the words I used, of course, but those are near enough. However, I can still see the steady look he gave me and the little smile with which he thanked me. He was always a very polite boy. Then he took his manuscript and left."

The summer of 1932 was spent in England. With Tom Easterbrook, McLuhan left Montreal on a cattle boat in June and bicycled to many of the Cathedral towns (a copy of Palgrave's *Golden Treasury* among his belongings), staying at Youth Hostels in the early days of that movement. After spending time in London they returned home in September. Some twenty long letters describe their travels in great detail. (Only two examples are included here: one describing the voyage over and a short letter written from Canada House, London.)

McLuhan received his BA from the University of Manitoba in 1933 and stayed on to earn his MA in 1934, with a thesis on George Meredith. In the meantime he had applied for, and received, an IODE Postgraduate Scholarship for study in a British university. He chose Cambridge.

Trinity Hall, Cambridge, was a fortunate choice for McLuhan. "It was like going home," he once said, "the place I had grown up imagining was my headquarters." Whatever his professors and friends privately thought of this mid-western Canadian, there is no indication in McLuhan's letters that he had any difficulty in adjusting to the fellowship and academic demands of the ancient university. His letters suggest that he could not get enough of what it had to offer. What we now know to be an important element of Cambridge life in the thirties—many brilliant students, particularly at Trinity College, were Communists—receives scant but disapproving notice in letters of February 7 and May 17, 1935.

McLuhan filled his life happily with lectures, course papers, rowing (he was always proud of the oar he won in a bumping race), friends, films and plays, trips, constant reading—and writing letters home. He took courses from Mansfield Forbes, F.R. Leavis, F.L. Lucas, Quiller-Couch, I.A. Richards, Ernest de Selincourt, and E.M.W. Tillyard, among others, and heard lectures and readings given by Lord David Cecil, R.W. Chambers, C. Day-Lewis, Bonamy Dobrée, Sean O'Casey, Dorothy Sayers, Arthur Waley, Charles Williams, and Dover Wilson. He got closer to his hero G.K. Chesterton, subscribing to *GK's Weekly*, joining the Distributist League, which Chesterton promoted, listening to him on the radio, and attending a Distributist dinner in London at which the great man spoke. Beginning on January 1, 1935 McLuhan's activities are noted in a five-year diary—a present from the mother of his Winnipeg friend Marjorie Norris—which contains four lines for each day. Until the end of 1939 McLuhan dutifully made an entry almost daily.

After living in lodgings for his first year he moved into college on October 1, 1935. "The room is new and redolent of oak. The running water and basin are a treat. Great luck to have. . . . Good to be alive." A few days later (October 13) he wrote: "How I enjoy the bells and the Backs by moonlight!"

Authors and works McLuhan read for pleasure included Jacques Maritain and *The Little Flowers of St. Francis*, a reflection of his serious interest in Roman Catholicism; T.S. Eliot's criticism ("an inspiration") and his *Murder in the Cathedral* ("really a very important bit of work. Surely he can give us more."); Virginia Woolf's *A Room of One's Own, Mrs Dalloway, To the Lighthouse* ("exquisite"); Joyce's *Ulysses* (August 6, 1935: "Reading Joyce *very* slowly."); Hemingway's *A Farewell to Arms*; F.O. Matthiessen's *The Achievement of T.S. Eliot* (he read it "with deep excitement"); Edmund Wilson's *Axel's Castle*; the poems of Ezra Pound; R.W. Chambers' *On the Continuity of English Prose from Alfred to More* ("very exciting"); William Empson's *Seven Types of Ambiguity* ("found it excellent"); Wyndham Lewis's *Time and Western Man* ("very much excited" by it); Aldous Huxley's *Do What You Will*; John dos Passos' *The 42nd Parallel*; and Thomas Wolfe's *Of Time and the River* ("it produces agonies in me. It is the *thing* unredeemed by art.") On the eve of his graduation in June he was reading Hopkins, Eliot, and Pound.

He also went to the theatre (seeing Chekhov's *The Seagull*, Shaw's *The Apple Cart*, Congreve's *The Way of the World*, Ruth Draper in her monologues, Eliot's *Murder in the Cathedral*, Ibsen's *Rosmersholm* and *The Master Builder*), and saw numerous foreign films along with American films (Greta Garbo in *Anna Christie*, Wallace Beery in *Viva Villa!*, Victor McLaglen in *The Informer*, Charles Laughton in *Ruggles of Red Gap*, Mae West in *Goin' to Town*: "Could not help but admire her open declaration and conduct of sex-war. She has brains but not more art than is popular"; the next day, October 20, 1935: "Wrote an article on Mae West.")

The only stated unhappiness in McLuhan's two years at Cambridge came towards the end when, in spite of his unceasing essay writing and prodigious reading, he was overcome with depression as he prepared for his final examinations. April 22, 1936: "The blankness and uncertainty of the future, the mass of work before me and dwindling possibility of doing well plus disappointments etc have reduced me so low that I have become externally very cheery! I never felt so sick of work." April 27: "Sweating plugging with magnificent futility—my mind feels drugged." May 5: "If only I had these last 2 years to do over! From the point of view of study I have made little of them. I have not yet recovered from Manitoba U."

He was successful, however, and his immediate future was not a blank. June 18: "Got a two-one [a high second-class degree]—both relieved and dissatisfied." He received his Cambridge BA on June 23. And he had been offered, and accepted, a one-year appointment at the University of Wisconsin. After a holiday in Ireland, McLuhan left Cambridge on July 20 for London, where he stayed until August 2. He travelled in Germany until August 11 and then sailed for Quebec and home.

Dear Mother:

Thursday

Well I was initiated to the writings of mr Bernard Shaw last evening when we attended a very admirable performance of Pygmalion presented by the University. I certainly wish that you had been there to criticize the acting. There could be very little said against it. One didn't feel for an instant that it was an amateur performance. But regarding Shaw himself: I was very agreeably surprised. He has looked at life with a very penetrating & somewhat disapproving eye. I should think that he deserves one of the highest places among English dramatists, after Shakespeare. As far as comparing him with that paragon of mortals, the very quintessence of human clay, why it is of course absurd. Shaw has studied life and reduced his observations to pithy and valuable aphorisms; Shakespeare held up the mirror to life itself. Nothing further need be said in comparison, the difference is as great as between sublime genius and clever brilliance. I shall certainly get thru Shaw at the first opportunity. They are changing the whole English course

The handwritten opening of the letter opposite, half size.

1931

To Elsie McLuhan

[Winnipeg]
Thursday [February 19, 1931]

Dear Mother:

Well I was initiated to the writings of Mr Bernard Shaw last evening when we attended a very admirable performance of Pygmalion presented by the University. I certainly wish that you had been there to criticize the acting. There could be very little said against it. One didn't feel for an instant that it was an amateur performance. But regarding Shaw himself: I was very agreeably surprised. He has looked at life with a very penetrating if a somewhat disapproving eye. I should think that he deserves one of the highest places among English drama- tists, after Shakespeare. As far as comparing him with that paragon of mortals, the very quintessence of human clay, why it is of course absurd. Shaw has stud- ied life and reduced his observations to pithy and valuable aphorisms; Shakes- peare held up the mirror to life itself. Nothing further need be said in comparison, the difference is as great as between sublime genius and clever brilliance. I shall certainly get thru Shaw at the first opportunity.

They are changing the whole English course from beginning to end. I cannot help but think that the revision should have started with the staff. I am so utterly disgusted and impatient with both Argue and Allison that I should never enter their classes had I not the idea of the scholarship in the back of my head.[1] It is necessary to get a lineup on the examinations however. Next year I shall throw myself into Philosophy during the term and leave the English for the summers. I shall certainly attend very few lectures in English. By the way I have a competitor (one at least) for the scholarship. He is Bill Morton the editor who is but one mark behind me.[2] I have been weak on the Shakespeare this term and must buckle down. Argue is such a big-hearted, blustering, fidgety, erratic hay-seed that it is impossible to work for him. I spent 2 hours reading Hamlet this morning. I never enjoyed anything so much. What power! What tremendous genius! A won- derful cure for conceit and ambition. The weather is wonderful. We are all in

---

[1]Robert Fletcher Argue (1877–1962) was then an Assistant Professor, later Professor, in the Department of English, University of Manitoba. Dr William Talbot Allison was Professor of English and head of the Department during the 1931–2 session.

[2]This was the Rhodes Scholarship to Oxford University, which was won in 1932 by W.L. Morton (1908–81), the editor of *The Manitoban*, a university periodical. (On November 13, 1930 Morton had asked McLuhan to take on the assistant editorship. McLuhan was tempted but decided against it, preferring to concentrate on his studies.) Morton later had a distinguished career as a professor of history at his *alma mater* and as a leading Canadian historian.

great health, tho 90% of those one meets have the most disgusting colds. I still weigh 141 lbs! We received the candy but put it away for awhile. Got the papers OK, also the wee book which promises to be work [*sic*] a perusal. Keep well

Lots of Love

1932

The letter that follows contains the first of many references to Gilbert Keith Chesterton (1874–1936), the celebrated English man of letters, author of works of fiction, poetry, biography, history, belles lettres, literary criticism, and polemics. McLuhan was greatly influenced by Chesterton's books in his student years. He had discovered Chesterton the previous summer when he read What's Wrong With the World *(1910), a collection of 49 pithy reflections on society. Though wide-ranging in its concerns, the book has a religious undertone. In a typical paradox Chesterton states that "The Christian ideal has not been tried and found wanting. It has been found difficult, and left untried", and he expresses a strong antipathy to Calvinism: "The difference between Puritanism and Catholicism is not about whether some priestly word or gesture is significant and sacred. To the Catholic every other daily act is a dramatic dedication to the service of good or of evil. To the Calvinist no act can have that sort of solemnity, because the person doing it has been dedicated from eternity, and is merely filling up his time until the crack of doom." Chesterton converted to Roman Catholicism in 1922.*

To Elsie and Herbert McLuhan

[Montreal][1]
Friday Evening [June 1932]

Dear Mother and Dad:

Well we have had a pleasant 24 hours since mailing the last letter. We had a fine rest last night and slept in this morning. By this means we need get but one meal ourselves. It has been a cold rainy day. Yesterday was a dusty windy day. Its predecessor was hot and sultry. In short we have had a lot of exceptional weather for Montreal.

---

[1]McLuhan and Tom Easterbrook were in Montreal awaiting the sailing date of the cattle boat that would take them to England for a bicycle tour. A life-long friend of McLuhan's, William Thomas Easterbrook (1907–85) became a well-known scholar and Professor of Political Economy at the University of Toronto.

There is an old chap in the house here who tries to be very sociable. He is an old athlete and lives entirely in the past. We have managed to be quite studious. Tom [Easterbrook] has just finished a book on England and the English by Price Collier.[2] I intend to save it for the cattle boat where we shall have lots of time. There is very little work to the job.

After the rain let up for a while at 1 PM. we walked downtown (about 2 miles) and picked up our passports. Thence we proceeded straight towards Mount Royal and visited the art galleries which were charging admission to-day. We shall look through them to-morrow. Since a further shower of rain was impending we hastened into a library (there are only 2 in Montreal) and each sat down with a book of G.K.C[hesterton]'s and spent a very pleasant 2 hours. Then home in time for supper and then up to reading and talking. I have finished Goethe's autobiography (Vol I) and am considerably puzzled by the man Either he has misrepresented himself or he was a much smaller man than he is generally acceded to have been. The German people were in his time and are now flirting with barbarism. He was in every sense a barbarian.

Before it slips from my mind let me urge you to send in the following proposition to the Tribune Believe it or not contest: G.K. Chestertons "Short History of England" [1917] does not contain a single date. That should win you a dollar bill. It is perfectly true.

You probably know that Mr Norris gave me $5 wherewith to purchase a souvenir[3] I may use it for books and antiques etc. and will of course remember them.

I need hardly impress on Dad that I shall need another $40 se[n]t to me in London say 3 or 4 weeks hence. We shall have no occasion to break into our travelling checks till we arrive in England

Limestone is used copiously in Montreal skyscrapers; but it is a stone that is as homely as concrete to which indeed it bears a great resemblance. The Tyndale limestone is vastly superior in appearance to anything we have seen. The girls of Winnipeg, as we were aware, are equally superior in beauty. The women of Montreal are the plainest that it has ever been my lot to see. Especially are the French girls an ugly, lanky, gaunt-cheeked, pout-lipped lot.

I have not written Red yet but you can send him my letters after Al [Bolton,] Bill [Jones] and the Easterbrooks have had them.[4] I think it advisable that he should not be away much longer

Lots of Love   Marshall

---

[2]Price Collier, *England and the English from an American Point of View* (1909).

[3]Mr Norris was the father of McLuhan's friend Marjorie Norris; see page 17, note 4.

[4]"Red" was the family nickname of McLuhan's younger brother Maurice (see page 25). "Al" is Al Bolton, a close boyhood friend of McLuhan's. He became an executive of Air Canada and died in 1957. Bill Jones, a fellow student and University of Manitoba friend, became a high-school teacher in Toronto. Mr and Mrs W.J. Easterbrook were Tom's parents.

To Elsie, Herbert, and Maurice McLuhan

[Salford, Eng.]
Friday [June] 18? [17]/ 32

Dear Mother, Dad, and Red:

Well it is rather difficult to start. I recommend Tom's letter to you by way of details. I shall like Hamlet's "daggers" speak of them but use none. Only by observing chronology can I hope to write straight ahead.

We walked down with our stuff on Thursday morning arriving just in time to avoid a heavy rain that never let up from that moment till 4 or 5 days later. We got thro the Red Tape by 9.30 and got on board and to work. There were 14 of us, and 488 cattle. We had to capture and tie each one of them. That done (about 4 hrs work) we emerged and watched the scenery thro the drizzle. Meals are not bad, but they are not balanced. Meat gravy and potatoes and soup 3 times a day but no desert [*sic*]. I find it a great privation not to drink [the] tea or coffee. I have tried but have come to detest the taste of both. I shall never be able to drink them even if inclined to do so.

Well it is now Sat. morning 9 AM We get up at 4.30 A.M. water all the cattle by pail then haul up 20 or so bales of hay from the hold, then 20 or 30 sacks of feed. After which we feed the hay then go up and wait for breakfast which comes along at 7. We are divided up into groups of 3 and each have 1/4 of the cattle to feed. After breakfast (8 AM) we clean up all the alley ways and troughs then bed the cattle, then give them each a pail of oats. This takes till 9.30 Then we are finished until 2 PM At 2 we water and feed and then are free for the day. Dinner is at 11.30 AM Supper at 4.30 P.M. The trouble with the meals is there monotony. There is never a prelude nor apologue [*sic*] to any of them. If we had each subscribed 50¢ at the 1st the cook says we would not only have had more meat and gravy (which by the way is very tasty, there being several varieties of meat) but we should have had pie or fruit etc. every meal. We never thot to take anything aboard with us in the fruit line. Had we got away from Montreal when we should have done, we would have had about 10 lbs of Tom's cakes and my cookies for the boat. Since we had spent approx $24 between us in Montreal we did not feel warranted in stocking up again.

Well as far as the boat trip is concerned I have only to say that nothing short of dire necessity could ever again put me aboard an ocean liner of any sort for any port. There is nothing quite so boring. People are just sufficiently sociable to waste your time. There are passengers aboard here (1st class, $85 return) Of course we had filthy weather. The sailors were kicking too. They said that you often had a better crossing in January. Wednesday last was our 1st fine (partially) day. It was the 1st time we saw the sun. At the present writing just off the north coast of Ireland with a 9 hour run at 15 mph to Liverpool the weather is simply glorious and we are in the worst part of the Atlantic Ocean ie. the infamous Devil's Hole. That has been the way so far. Everything contrary to expectation and natural conditions.

I was violently seasick on the 2nd day out (we saw the Empress of Australia in dock at Quebec Thursday night and passed the Empress of Britain Friday at 3 AM. We saw a full rigged ship this morning and are now passing a tramp from Norway with a deckload of lumber. We shall see many boats to-day) Well I was seasick till Tuesday to such an extent that I could neither eat nor stand erect (while working) That was 3 1/2 days It was simply terrible. At a modest computation I vomited 150 times. On Tuesday morning I felt a bit better, had a dose of castor oil from the steward and then a good Samaritan hooked a couple of apples for us. We were fairly famished for fruit and drinks. The water on board is rotton [*sic*] and no water is good for one while seasick. What we (Tom was almost as bad as I) missed was any sort of quiet or cleanliness. Seasickness between sheets or in a deck chair with ginger ale and crackers would not be too bad, but to lie in a smoke-filled noisey [*sic*] little bunk room while the gang clamored and gloated over the extra rations which our sickness meant— well it was not so hot. It was too bitterly cold to be outside a moment, and while working below decks in the stuffy bovine atmosphere it was simply unutterable. Anyway the castor oil and the apples brought us around rapidly (the sickness had run its course anyhow) and soon we were yelling for our share of the grub with the rest although the rough weather continued till Thursday. It is not likely that we shall be sick on the way back regardless of the weather. But we paid dearly for our immunity. Just to give you an idea of how peculiarly rotton was our luck and how malicious was Fortune I might say that the Empress of Australia reported perfect weather 300 miles behind us while the S.S. Silicia reptd perf. [weather] 200 miles ahead. We remained in that little disturbance center for over a week our cloud by day and pillar of fire by night[1] Instinctively I feel that our luck has changed. We are sailing into Manchester (where it rains every day in the year) with perfect weather. We are to unload our cattle to-night at Birkenhead 10 P.M. Thence we proceed via canal to Manchester. We cannot leave the boat till Sunday afternoon, which is the time we get there. The canal trip will be a scenic treat, the boys say. Of the 14 men we are the only Canadians. There is one Australian artist and globe trotter The rest are Scotch and English. Not a bad gang. There are some who enjoy argument but having had too little opposition at their respective Labor Unions and Home Towns Tom and I are curing them rather effectively Writing has been impossible on deck, and out of question below, till the present moment It is now practicable in both places but the men are all on deck so here am I below. I have managed to read considerable of [Alexander] Pope. (about 300 pages of his polished condensed couplets) The little blue books[2] have been doing the rounds of the cabin. I have read only one of them—[Edgar Allan] Poe's Tales. I find them amusing, interesting, curiosities, any thing but exciting or absorbing. It must be remembered that he practically created the short story and the detec-

[1] "And the Lord went before them by day in a pillar of a cloud, to lead them the way; and by night in a pillar of fire, to give them light." Exodus 13:21

[2] Perhaps the pocket-sized volumes of the World's Classics series, published by the Oxford University Press.

tive story at one stroke. His successors have in many instances improved on him.

Well we have worked quite hard to day. It is now 7.30 and we are just taking on the pilot at the mouth of the Mersey. Ireland was the 1st land we saw. This morning we passed a Northern island within 3 miles The Isle of Man was our next view. We have had glorious weather. The crew say they never saw anything like it in this part of the water. During the afternoon we heaved 450 bales of hay from the hold to the deck and at 10 PM to-night we shall toss them onto the dock at Birkenhead while the cattle are being unshipped.

I have just this instant returned from watching the pilot clamber over the side. Our boat stopped dead to receive him—1st time since Quebec. He boarded from a stubby seaworthy little power boat which put out from the pilot ship anchored near by. We have been racing into port with a small steamer from India. It passed within a 1/4 mile of us while we were stopped.

Everyone on board is in high spirits since the pay checks and beer are imminent. I got 2 or 3 pictures of the gang and cooks and foremen but shall be sparing in that line in the next few weeks.

We feel assured that our money will easily last 2 months since everyone regards 4 shillings a day as ample. ie for each of us There is a reassuring consistency in opinion on this head. I am becoming quite elated now as the hours slide by, but Manchester is a filthy hole to land in. Once on our bikes we shall be out of it in an hour into the lake country.

Sunday 3 P.M.

I am writing from the Jutland's Sailor's Rest in Salford—a suburb of Manchester. We got into Liverpool last night at 10 sharp and had landed the cattle and hay in an hour. We were right at the busy part of the waterfront. The downtown section extends right to the riverfront and we could see the double decker street cars dashing along. Dozens of brightly lighted ferries fussed back and forth across our bows carrying people and diminutive autos. We got tired and cold watching and went below at 12 and to sleep a little later. Since starting the cruise I have been eating late lunches along with the rest. The effect has been a series of vividly real and rather logical and consequential dreams. At one time I endured all the agonies of a marriage ceremony; at another I was the dictator of the destinies of the small remnant of the human race after an international catastrophe—and so on. That my stomach has not been out of order I gather from the rather enjoyable rather than otherwise effect of these dreams. However that is now all over. From now on we are going to eat 2 good meals a day (25¢ each) and a small lunch if necessary. Our first meal ashore in England is still agreeably situated in the upper reaches of my digestive tract—Lamb, cauliflower, potatoes, and a brown duff plus pie for desert [*sic*] (and milk) I ate the cauliflower because it has been long and far between since I have had any vegetables. It cost us 10 d (ie 20¢ which I shall hereafter write / 10 and leave you the pleasure of converting it into Canadian currency. Shillings are indicated thus: 10/)

Well I got up this morning at 5.30 to watch the scenery. We were in the canal by then—Cheshire on our right, Lancashire on our left. It was a fine day, tho a bit cold, and till 6.30 the scenery was fine—hills, trees, pastures, buildings, gardens, flowers, and birds. After that things assumed the well known Manchester aspect—dull red brick and metal bldgs long lines of railroad tracks etc. The last pleasing scene was at 6.30—a man wife and their boy all in hiking gear starting off down a lane with fishing tackle and a lunch basket.

It was 11 AM when we finally docked at Salford; and another dreary restless hour e'er the customs men had finished with us and had given us back our passports. Tom, myself, and another chap set off with Art Thompson, (one of the sailors, and a fine fellow) for our present address, where we were assured good meals at a reasonable prices [*sic*] and a bed and bath for 1/. All was as promised— and further he has undertaken to show us to good clothing stores tomorrow and to a good bike shop.

We should have had an awkward time with our Travellers' checks and Canadian currency due to getting in on Sunday had it not been for our sailor friend. He stays regularly at The Rest and easily got credit for us till to-morrow. I have had 1 1/2 hrs sleep and am now going to turn to my article on the Summer occupations of Amer. + Canad. U. students. I have written it once roughly. I shall now re-write and may perhaps do so again before submitting it to the Manchester Guardian to-morrow. You would be surprised at the amount of effort required to sit down to write any kind of an article. Moreover Tom's temperament is even more averse to it than my own. The amount of writing we shall accomplish may ∴ prove negligible. I think that the train and boat trip as a cattleman sees them would make an interesting little article for the Guardian, and if so we shall alter it sufficiently to send it home. If not we shall send it home as it was presented to them. This will keep us in Manchester all day to-morrow. We hope to make an early start Tuesday morning. Apart from the writing we might have started to-morrow afternoon

To Elsie, Herbert, and Maurice McLuhan

Visitors' Writing Room
Canada House
Trafalgar Square
London, S.W. 1
[Wednesday, July 13, 1932]

Dear Mother, Dad, and Red.

I feel as though I had been sitting on the front veranda waiting to be called to supper, for I have just set down the Winnipeg Tribune I have read about 2 weeks of papers (June 25 to July 5) and feel au courant with Manitoba affairs once more.

I am writing in the reading room of Canada house. It is 3 P.M. Wednesday the

13th of July and I am looking out of the window at Nelson's monument in Trafalgar Square. About 3 hours ago Professor Carver left us in Westminster Abbey where he had spent an hour with us and then proceeded to an appointment but not before inviting us to dinner at 7 P M to-morrow.[1] From the Abbey we proceeded to the Thames embankment and the Houses of Parl. Then after getting some fruit and a couple of buns each we walked down Birdcage Walk thro St James Park to Buckingham Palace We ate our lunch in the Park and came back to Canada House to sign the visitor's book. Hence we are going to the National art Gallery then to St Martin's [-in-the-Fields] church and then to a counter luncheon where we may indulge in a hot meal, then along Charing Cross Road and thence home.

I should not omit reference to the brief visit we made to No 10 Downing St. this morning The street is about 150 feet long, the particular bldg. is of most ordinary brick and looks like a cheap apartment house We are going to have an interesting and a busy week in London but I believe a week will be plenty. We will be longing for the open country before long.

London is not like other cities and lives up to the usual impressions one has of its individuality; but for all that[,] traffic and pavement are not the most ideal of surroundings. What is particularly refreshing about London architecture is its breadth and flatness, which give it an imposingly substantial effect and is easy on the neck.

I believe I shall seal this now, or rather, since stamps are expensive I shall put another letter in with it first. Then I shall send a line to Bill [Jones].

Lots of Love
Marshall

[1]Patrick Longworthy Carver had been an Assistant Professor in the English Department of the University of Manitoba from 1930 to 1932 and then returned to England.

In the issue of Tuesday, May 16, 1933 of the Winnipeg Evening Tribune, *it was announced that "University gold medals in the arts and science honors course were awarded to Stanley E. Brock, William T.J. Easterbrook, Max Finegood, Gertrude Phyllis Gracey and Herbert M. McLuhan." This was the culmination of McLuhan's undergraduate studies and his attainment of a B.A. degree from the University of Manitoba. He then concentrated on his M.A.*

1934

To Elsie McLuhan

Dear Mother:

Just one more play to read: The Winter's Tale. I [am] completing The Tempest having 1st done MacBeth with some care to-day. I must then devote a day to general reading on Shak. Sunday I shall review Chaucer; Monday, prepare Beowolf which I write Tuesday. Next comes Chaucer, then skip a day and then Spenser and Shakespeare. It is a huge amount of material that I have compassed in the past month since dropping my thesis.[1] What infinite delight there is in Shakespeare, however. I have not had any dull moments except with the incredible pedants who crawl all over him with their microscopes and fine combs, and then write up their "discoveries" with a mixture of stupid dullness and childish delight that is almost interesting. How I have tried to individualize and picture some of them. You see I am using the Arden Shakespeare and each play is prefaced & edited by a different scholar. It is fun to see the fur fly when they "reject with wonder the suggestion of Mr. . . ." or speak of the "unmitigated trash and baseless speculation that has obscured the obvious truth of this question for so long . . ." I stick to Coleridge,[2] and shall do all my life so far as Shakespeare is concerned. Even Mrs Jameson[3] is not to be recommended (except to producers) because her interpretations are too long-drawn and serve rather as a substitute for the text than a stimulus thereto.

Well Red has dined but little at home for 2 weeks. We can expect a huge food bill in the event of any fracture of amity or split of concord between Zelma and him.

Marjorie will soon be through[4] she has not the knack in studying Literature, yet. Mr Norris writes a commercial law exam to-morrow. He has worked too hard for his speedy convalescence.

Now for a walk before bed. Jack is not to have a goitre operation. I had an interesting letter from Tom. Bundles of Love from Marshall

---

[1]That is, since finishing his M.A. thesis, "George Meredith as a Poet and Dramatic Parodist".

[2]Lectures on Shakespeare given between 1808 and 1818 by Samuel Taylor Coleridge (1772–1834) and published as *Shakespearean Criticism* (2 vols, 1907).

[3]Anna Brownell Jameson (1794–1860) achieved considerable respect in her day as a Shakespearian scholar for her *Characteristics of Women* (1832), later known as *Shakespeare's Heroines*. She was also the author of *Winter Studies and Summer Rambles in Canada* (1838).

[4]Marjorie Norris—whose parents were friends of the McLuhan's—was McLuhan's girl-friend at this time and there was an "understanding" between them. When McLuhan went to Cambridge, letters and Marjorie's knitted gifts sustained their platonic relationship until 1936 when it ended. See page 85, note 1.

Having been disappointed in his hopes for a Rhodes Scholarship, McLuhan applied for (in October 1933) and won the renewable IODE Post-Graduate Scholarship of $1600, "for post-graduate study in any British University", in 1934-5. (McLuhan thought that Professor Perry, who was on the IODE awards committee, would oppose his application because he sensed McLuhan's dislike of him as a teacher. McLuhan's father therefore visited Perry and, to Perry's surprise and pleasure, assured him of his son's admiration.) McLuhan chose Cambridge, a university that represented high academic attainment to his mother, and was accepted by Trinity Hall. He was also awarded one of two University Travelling Fellowships ($400).

To Elsie, Herbert, and Maurice McLuhan

[Cambridge, Eng.,
October 4, 1934]

Dear Everyone:

[*Added later:*] This letter should have gone 2 days ago but was mislaid in my folder. Oct 6/34

Well I'm back again. Two things have occurred to me about expenses. The £20 (sent by now) is for the most part returnable and I made the mistake of estimating college[1] dinners during the 8 weeks of vacation between now and May 10. I think that will give me back $20 but (only too likely) it will be absorbed by some unforeseen expense.

Now about my rooms. I have a bath and toilet to myself (in practice) and a bedroom, bright, airy, and well furnished beside it. You see I am Odams 1st boarder and everything has been newly decorated and set up.[2] He plans to keep in touch with things by that means Speaking of residence—there are only 70 able to live in the Hall out of 225 so it is not unnatural that I should be out. My general room is really the front parlor with 3 built out windows [*sketch*] facing the street. Now Magrath is a blind street and since there are no lanes in Cambridge I face the back wall of the Houses on Hartford That means privacy and lack of distracting sights or sounds. By the way tell Fred and Eliza that I shall write them shortly. The room is 12 × 12—light paper 3/4 way up then white plaster with base [*sic*] relief design. There is a fine bright (light grey with red design) woolly rug covering 6 inch oak boards. There is a good fireplace— white enamel wood mantlepiece topped by candlesticks and a silver-framed mirror. There is a new desk with a brass inscribed "presentation to W H Odams by his fellow servants Trinity Hall, on retirement March 1934. It is dark stained

[1]McLuhan was enrolled in Trinity Hall, Cambridge, founded in 1350 (not to be confused with Trinity College, founded in 1546).

[2]McLuhan lived first in the house of Mr and Mrs W.H. Odams at 29 Magrath Avenue. Mr Odams was a retired porter of Trinity Hall.

solid one inch oak and will age nobly. There are 2 small stands (flowers) a coal container disguised as a cabinet an excellent writing & study chair with a round upholstered back shaped: [*sketch*]. There is a small chesterfield & a big chair to match, a drop-leaf mahogany table and 2 chairs (upholstered seats) to match. Then a book case and the dish & food cabinet being the centre section of his rowboat. Nor yet am I crowded at all. Some of the wall pictures are OK the most are ridiculous—being 2 "attacks of Mamalukes [*sic*] and what looks like a Jewess in a richly beaded robe (the beads being actually superimposed) swimming under a tree. These 3 are about 3' x 2' and can be replaced when I find some old prints or etchings I can use whatever I get in my college rooms next year. Oh yes, on top of my desk in an oval frame 11" x 9" is a beautifully mounted crest of Trinity beside the arms of Cambridge. I shall keep an eye open for something of the kind for you. It is quite worth having.

I went around to the Hall yesterday afternoon—I am going to send you a large scale map of Cambridge when I have made myself familiar with it. The colleges are well indicated—looked in at St Johns (now under repairs as is our own) and then Trinity [College]. Then our own. Quod intervallo! What a contrast. We are indeed a Hall rather than a college. We have no splendid chapel or cloisters. However I had a chat with [Wansbrough] Jones (who is not my English tutor but a general overseer)[3] and then Crawley[4] the History man (both in their 30's) and now I await Mr Elvin, my English tutor but who may tutor me only in a general fashion.[5] Apparently lectures are rather common at Camb. I may have 10 hrs a week. Then I have at least 2 essays to prepare for tutorials. I cant see Elvin till Saturday. I went and bot a shilling guide to Cambridge giving many details briefly. It was very luxurious to be able to wander into a college[,] look at any part and wander out knowing that you could take 2 years to become familiar with every portion. I wont say much about them until I have a better grasp of them. I shall take some snaps and perhaps take one or 2 of each college so as to have a completely personal record tho I can buy such a set of pictures. I went to "Hall" last night (a supper is a "hall"). I got very wet in my grey going thither and found about 9 sitting all dead quiet. There were as many waiters. Well 1st a plate with a slice of mellon (everything is served on dinner plates) a piece of bread (no butter) beside it—then a bit of fish—then fricasséd chicken, potatoes & cauliflower then apricot tart & cream—I took no ale (it being extra Odams tells me). So we arose scarcely having murmured and departed into the night. It won't be so bad when term commences Monday.

I'm just back from "hall" again and may sign off to-morrow night. It was muchly better to-night, there being about 40 present. In term there are 2 "halls". Senior sit last and I shall likely be among them. There was soup, fish, chicken, roast pota-

---

[3]O.H. Wansbrough-Jones, now Sir Owen Wansbrough-Jones, was a Fellow of Trin. all and Tutor, 1930–46, and lectured in colloid science. He looked after Marshall's personal well-.

[4]Charles William Crawley was a Fellow (now an Honorary Fellow) of Trinity Hall from 1924 to 1966. He wrote *Trinity Hall: The History of a Cambridge College 1350–1975* (1976).

[5]See page 21, note 1.

toes, marrow, and a marangue for dessert. The last is round, crispish, sweetish with whipped cream in the center. There was more noise and chat. It is wonderful to go out into empty streets—they are very narrow and not too crooked—and hear great bells striking solemnly all about you. The atmosphere more than you would suspect and quite what you could imagine provided all is at peace within you. I was more easy to-night. I was out strolling with my guidebook this afternoon and suddenly recalled that G.A. Chase, (who got me into Trinity Hall) now President of Selwyn College was not far from me.[6] We had a fine chat, and since it began to pour, a longer one than was warranted, and tea thrown in. Gad, but do these people know how to live over here! Even the poorest make it an art. (But yes: there are already new items of expense—light and fuel which may come to $45 by May 10—the light is nearly $10 a term! No wonder the streets are lit by gas.

Walking home scenes are different than ours. You see beer mugs in front of men in The Red Cow, The Boars Head, The Mitre, etc. They are all low buildings and look cosy—then the odd pair of students idling over tea in a little 2 table shop. There is no restaurant trade even in London to any extent. These people believe in eating at home.

I have written Al [Bolton], Herklots and Mrs McQuillan to-day.[7] Spence, Kirkconnell, Perry, Wheeler etc. will have one as soon as term begins and I have something to tell them.[8]

I have to be in by 10 or be fined 6/6. Moreover my windows have to be locked because the proctors travel around to all lodgings to test their integrity. Each college has a proctor or more and together they constitute a Univ. police force. They wear gown and bib and are called bullies (once bulldogs)

I am sorry to say that the chicken leg which I took from the soup has gone mouldy and hence out my window. I thot that it might dry out but it was wrapped up in my grip too long.

Oct 6/ What a pity that I forgot to post this. I have been reading the complete English exams for 1933—that is the English Tripos—I am going to send Prof. Wheeler a copy. They would slay Perry. It is a joy to read them—I shall have a 1st or burst—but there is a huge deal of work—exciting, joyous work ahead of

[6]The Rev. G.A. Chase (d. 1971) had been Dean, Senior Tutor, and Vice-Master of Trinity Hall, which he had recently left to become Master of Selwyn College, Cambridge; he later became Bishop of Ripon.

[7]Canon Herklots of St Luke's Anglican Church, Winnipeg, led a youth group that McLuhan attended as an undergraduate. Mrs L. McQuillin was Provincial Educational Secretary of the IODE (Imperial Order Daughters of the Empire), which had provided the scholarship that enabled McLuhan to attend Cambridge.

[8]Dr W.J. Spence was Registrar of the University of Manitoba, 1910–47. Dr Watson Kirkconnell (1895–1977) taught English, and later Classics, at Wesley College, Winnipeg, from 1922 to 1940. A notable linguist and prolific scholar, he later became President of Acadia University, Wolfville, Nova Scotia (1948–64). Professor A.J. Perry was head of the English Department, University of Manitoba. Dr Arthur Lloyd Wheeler (1898–1970) joined the staff of the English Department of the University of Manitoba in 1932 as an Assistant Professor.

me. For instance: "write the minutes of an imaginary debate between Burke and Godwin on the present state of Europe" Burke the great conservative (1732–97) Godwin the radical (1760–1824).[9] You see what is involved? "Is it possible for tragedy to flourish at a period when hero-worship and poetic speech are either unfamiliar or uncongenial to the majority of theatre-goers?" Discuss this with special reference either to modern drama in general or to the work of 2 of the following: Strindberg Tchekov Pirandello, Eugene O'Neill. again: "Tragedy is only possible to a mind which is for the moment agnostic or Manichean." Discuss why "knowledge" of philosophy will prove useful in the highest degree—it remains to master French. Now I must send this off and then for a snap in cap & gown.

Heaps of Love for all
from Marshall

[9]The birth and death years of Edmund Burke and William Godwin, are, respectively, 1729–97 and 1756–1836.

To Elsie, Herbert, and Maurice McLuhan

[Cambridge]
Oct 6/11 pm [1934]

Dear Mother, Dad, and Red:

I must commence to ration you very soon if I am to do anything but write letters. This morning I saw Mr Elvin, my English tutor.[1] We shall hit it off perfectly—he is obviously able keen and informed—a young man however, about 35, and just married. I saw Wansb.-Jones 1st and he had not your letter or hadn't opened it so its all right awhile.) You see the Eng. faculty is young and has scarcely anyone over 45 except Quiller-Couch who is about 80.[2]

Elvin thought I could do the degree in a year if I wished to, but said he could tell in a month. It would leave me free to do an M. Litt my 2nd year or to start a Phd. However.

I then commenced a preliminary snapshot tour and took 12 snaps which I shall have with the previous 4 on Monday. It costs 36¢ for 8 here and 42 at home. It costs 3¢ for copies and 4¢ at home so you see I can just as well have it done here.

I ordered my grey trousers (they are a bit darker and much tougher stuff than my flannels—will last years and I can save these for summer.) I shall let the coat

[1]Lionel Elvin (b. 1905). a Fellow of Trinity Hall from 1930 to 1940 and McLuhan's Tutor. He went on to become Principal of Ruskin College in Oxford, Director of the Education Department of UNESCO, and Professor of Education, London University, 1956–8, then Director of its Institute of Education until 1973. He is now Professor Emeritus of London University and Honorary Fellow of Trinity Hall.

[2]Sir Arthur Quiller-Couch (1863–1944)—the prolific author of fiction, verse, criticism, etc., published under the pseudonym "Q"—was 71 in 1934; he had been given the chair of English at Cambridge in 1912. McLuhan took several courses from him, including one on Aristotle's *Poetics*.

go because I got back my brown suit to-day ($2.00) and there is a heap of wear in the coat yet. I shall need shoes and hat plus long underwear ($1.00) and the odd tie and shirt. The shirts are considerably different here. They are in style the equivalent of Harris Tweeds.

Now there is a new item of expense—Lectures cost $30 a term. I simply have to pay that tho the number of lectures I attend may be few. There are many other faculties whose lectures I can hear having paid that sum. Its a corker though.

Well I have bought all my china and cutlery—about $1.50 viz. cup[,] saucer[,] tea plate, dinner plate, milk jug, butter dish, (all same pattern on cream base) water jug, 2 glasses[,] small knife[,] fork[,] spoon, large of same, bread knife and teapot. Then I got enough food for 2 or 3 days. I made my supper to-night for 16¢—I had ham & egg pie, tomatoes, tea milk hovis, raisin bread, cookies, honey etc. I am so glad I like tea. You can take many things cold if *it* is hot. I never had such perfect absence of awareness of digestion. When I commence rowing I shall be in the best shape I ever was—shall be preposterously healthy. I sleep like a top and am never tired these days, so judge for yourselves.

I am just returned from 10.30 service at Kings College Chapel. I wrote Fred and Eliza just before starting out. On the way I snapped St John's Avenue at the back of the [St John's] college and Trinity [College] library and bridge. After church I got the main St. J's tower and then Mr & Mrs Odams and Mick and then myself in hat and gown. The last I'm doubtful of. I had the cap too far back—it is a cursed rig—too heavy entirely. I am going to get my own lunch and dinner. When I commence rowing I am going to bring home a bit of steak for lunch.

Well the service was very fine—the choir beautiful—one of the best in England it is said—but it was high church and bewildering to me. I shall be more at ease later on. To-night I shall hear Mr Chase at our own Chapel.

To-day I am going to devote to letters to Perry Wheeler Allison Spence Kirkconnell etc.

It will be wonderful to be able to show you around this place Mother.[3] By the way I noticed a lady's name in the BBC programme, to read Merlin and the Gleam.[4] Mr Odams says it is not very common. I don't get any invitations to hear their radio or to sit at their table when I buy my meal from them. However I think it as much their compliance with form as anything else. I may come to eat Sunday dinner with them in time. I'll wait till I see how the land lies. I think I would learn more to eat with them, tho they are not very classy. They regard me as "one of the gentry."

I think to get a very cheap wrist watch. No vests are allowed without trousers to match, and it is hard to carry mine (not having watch pockets in English trousers or my flannels.) Don't you think my watch is a bit too good in any case, for constant wear. I can have it always.

Mr Odams has looked me up a good bike, 3 speed, big frame, only 30/ = $7. I

---

[3]Mrs McLuhan never did visit Cambridge or travel overseas.
[4]*Merlin and The Gleam* (1886), a poem by Alfred, Lord Tennyson.

can get about the same for it if I find it necessary to have a lighter wheel when I'm travelling in the long vac. Now it costs 30/ to rent a wheel for one term and they are really quite necessary when you consider how far apart lectures often are and libraries and the boat house. I shall send the map shortly because I am becoming familiar with it now. The guidebook I shall send when I have annotated it a bit and been around to all places therein described with it in hand. Will send pictures to-morrow.

Heaps of love from
Marshall

To Elsie, Herbert, and Maurice McLuhan

[Cambridge]
Oct 14/34

Dear Mother, Dad, and Red:—

Speaking as a thin-blooded Canadian I can say that I'm the only person in Cambridge who hasn't had a fire in his room up to date. It is a bit cooler to-day and I think I'll have one to-night. What fun to eat beside an open grate in the afternoon and then sit before it. Thats what I've been doing in Mr Wilkinson's rooms at the Hall. He is one of the Hesperides[1] and had in a St John's man and two more Hall men—all last year—Law, History and Modern Languages were represented. They are honors men doing their course in 3 years. Is this place stimulating or not,—well after 1/2 an hour they were writing down my bon mots for the College magazine—pray for me or I shall disintegrate with conceit. It was a great time believe me—But I have a terrific advantage of years and reading over these lads. They lent me several books I have been wanting a long time.

We walked around to the famous Union[2] buildings in a while where Myers (St Johns) proposed me as a member (by signature) If I pay the other £5½ before Dec 15 I am a life member not only of the Union but automatically of many others: Oxford, Dublin, Edinburgh, Durham, Harvard, Sidney (Aust.), Hart House Toronto, Capetown, McGill Union Montreal. That is I have full privileges in all these places for life.

Well now for a bit of supper and then work for my essay for Elvin.

I'm reading Granville-Barker[3] on the production of Shak[espeare], Mother. Speaking of the soliloquy he maintains that Shak uses it to screw up the tension of the action in a second or so—then something that should interest you "For a

[1]On October 11, McLuhan attended his first meeting of the Hesperides, the Trinity Hall Literary Society, named after a volume of poems (1648) by Robert Herrick, who graduated from Trinity Hall in 1617. The Society no longer exists.

[2]The Union Society, or Cambridge Union, for students—part club and part debating society.

[3]Harley Granville-Barker (1877–1946), whose influential Prefaces to twelve Shakespeare plays were published between 1927 and 1947.

parallel to its full effectiveness on Shakespeare's stage we should really look to the modern music-hall comedian, getting on terms with his audience—recalling, those of us who happily can, Dan Leno[4] as a washerwoman, confiding domestic troubles to a theatre full of friends, and taken unhindered to their hearts." A find and an idea, is it not? You could do it splendidly It would be away ahead of the intimate tone of the office-boy. You could do it in Irish or plain Canadian.

Oct 15/ Worked on my 1st essay most of to-day. Some of our lectures are excellent—best yet to come. Got my new trousers at last—real class—will need long underwear shortly I fear. Am at the moment enjoying my 2nd fire. It is a very warm grate indeed. So glad it isn't gas as are some. Had tea with Capt Bowen of the Royal Engineers—He is only 19—looks 28—Anglo Indian—sent to school here—fine fellow.

I was a bit late finishing my essay, but it went over very well I think—of course I disagreed very profoundly with Elvins view. Why in the nature of damnation does no one else take the rather considerable trouble of mastering the philos. of which GK is an exponent! It is a social (not faddish) philosophy based on a completely adequate religion. Cambridge and Oxford are cliquish rather than social in their thought and are the birthplaces and spawning ground of every sort of fad—However Elvin and I shall get along very well, I know.

Oct 16 Now I heard Mr Forbes[5] of Clare this morning who lectures ostensibly on "metre rhyme, rhythm, and the reading (aloud) of poetry with spec. ref. to the ages of Pope and Wordsworth." It was the biggest intellectual treat of my life. He is about 40 and while queer in appearance and manner very likeable. I long to know him and shall do before long—There were 200 there to-day. By December there will be not more than a dozen Elvin tells me. But the man is wonderful—so excited about his subject that he is almost incoherent—He wears an aura of scholarly enthusiasm, but never tires of delightful gibes at the bilge given out by his fellow lecturers here—"they set out to cover ground—I shall cover no ground—I shall teach you to dig, in the most fertile parts." However, by "ground" he means "course" He skipped over a 1001 things to-day—D.H. Lawrence, Galsworthy, Eliot, Rylands, Cowper, Burns,—oh yes. With 15 minutes to go he said "now I want to devote the rest of my time to Burns because of the peculiar value belonging to an understanding of how his poems should be read"—that was the last that was said of Burns, because he remembered T.S. Eliot lecturing on Burns in that room a few years before and so we had much uproarious gossip. There is great variety in tone and accent among lecturers

---

[4]Dan Leno (1860–1904), famous star of the English music hall and pantomime.

[5]Professor Mansfield Forbes (1889–1935), Fellow of Clare College, had contributed greatly to the founding of the English Faculty (sometimes called the English School) at Cambridge and enlisted I.A. Richards and F.R. Leavis, among others, as fellow teachers. McLuhan studied under him in the last year of Forbes' life. On May 21, 1936, he wrote in his diary: "Forbes is a great loss—he had such splendid energy and capacity for direct experience." See *Mansfield Forbes and His Cambridge* (1984) by Hugh Carey.

here. They are never as extreme as the youth of the place. But all of them try to read poetry—Forbes hasnt started yet—and do it only respectably. That is firmly (doggedly determined to weigh scrupulously each syllable) and without any transitions of manner to suit the poem. I'm not quite sure if this standard way is justifiable or not. In any case it lags miles behind your interpretation Mother, and I simply must get a background of technique. The only advice given here about reading poetry aloud is to "read slowly"—good as far as it goes.

I would love to have a suit (coat and vest) to match my new trousers. Talk about class!

Oh yes Mr Salt[6] goes to Elvin with me. He is deformed (undersized) and unhealthy, but has a normal face and head that are well developed.

Had tea with Mr Chib—a Punjabi Hindu to-day. He is at Emmanuel and had in a Downing man. He has a good head and a well-stocked mind. We learnt a great deal about Indian history and politics in 3 hours.

After Hall I proceeded to the debate which was undoubtedly below the par that may be expected. Oh, woe is me—they had GKC[hesterton] last year!

Oct 17.   I have not yet decided what courses to take, or whether to do the Tripos in one or 2 years. So I have no criterion for selecting my lectures and I am sampling them all. There are 20 lecturers, and 33 lectures a week. I hope to attend no more than 8–10—it breaks the day badly—Hoping to hear again soon.

All Love from Marshall

[6]Walter Salt, a fellow student and friend, was crippled with tuberculosis of the spine, though he was always cheerful. He had won an extramural scholarship given annually by the University to outstanding students in evening classes who had not completed their secondary schooling. He died in 1936.

The letter below contains the first advice, of numerous examples to follow, from Marshall to his brother Maurice (b. 1913)—called "Red"—about his reading. Maurice had attended the University of Manitoba from 1930 to 1932 and was at this time enrolled in the general arts course at Victoria College, University of Toronto. After graduating he attended Emmanuel College, University of Toronto, and was ordained as a United Church minister in 1943. In various charges in Manitoba, and in churches in Ottawa and Windsor, Ontario, his clerical skills and empathy with people served him well, until he decided to resign as a minister in 1962. From 1969 to 1972 he was a research associate for his brother at the Centre for Culture and Technology, often substituting for him as a speaker. Maurice then spent twelve years as a teacher at Sheridan College, Oakville, until his voluntary retirement in 1984.

To Elsie, Herbert, and Maurice McLuhan

[Cambridge]
Oct. 19/20 34

Dear Mother and Red and Dad:

I was out in an 8[1] for the 1st time yesterday. Just prior to our setting out the Newnham[2] 8 moved past (the girls) tho for no particular reason, since nobody hit the water at the same time even when at all! However I regretted laughing a few minutes later, when in the full tide of agonizing uncoordination. It was much better to-day. Ours is a very inexperienced 8 and is usually tilted to one side or the other, making it difficult to row. Last night at hall I ate a large and appetizing plate of "veal" only to learn that it was rabbit! What a man! Nothing is impossible now.

Elvin advised me to join the English Club of the University. It is 5/(bob) a term—we get 5 excellent lectures for that, from eminent men in every sort of walk, or interest. The 1st is to-night—Dobré [sic] on the idea of the conflict in modern drama.[3]

I bought a Trinity Hall sweater to-day—12/6 = $3. It is a fine heavy sweater with sleeves, big V front and is white (ribbed) with black trimming at the V and bottom. I can wear it under my coat any time, but had to have one if I was to be out with the crew. Marjorie's sweater is in a class by itself here—I like it immensely, and it excels by reason of its individuality. It is not loud. Only dullish garb is accepted here. Where men predominate, and are not either fascinating to, or fascinated by, some woman you will inevitably find unconventional garb.

Enclosed is a raffle ticket that cost me 15¢ on the cattle boat. It is part of a card which read "Muir's Cattle Feed". It might have won me an excellent cigarette lighter!

Oh yes Mother—regarding the Washerwoman number—you would naturally hesitate to assume a brogue—might the negro do? I'm afraid that negro psychology would not have enough in common with our own for the purpose.

Well, I've been to hear Dobrée—He was not a revelation—neither a powerful mind nor a vivid character—simply an efficient military chap with an unresonant voice. His theme was that conflict in drama was simply a means of holding attention. At its best it would grow from the opposition of ideas for which the characters and their interplay would be midwives. The function of this—the serious drama—was to clarify and prepare the way for sounder action. Dobrée is

---

[1]In the first weeks of October, college boat clubs begin to train novice oarsmen for races at the end of each term. There are eight oarsmen in a racing boat (usually known as a shell or an eight).

[2]Newnham College for women.

[3]Cambridge-educated Bonamy Dobrée (1891–1974) was by this time the author of *Restoration Comedy* (1924) and *Restoration Tragedy* (1929)—there was no more recent publication by him on Restoration drama. He became Professor of English at the University of Leeds (1936–55) and a well-known literary scholar.

noted for his mastery of mod. drama. He has just prod. a book on restoration drama. Everyone writes books here—not many of them worth reading either.

Oct. 20   Well I had a much more pleasant time in the 8 to-day and perspired from physical, not mental strain! They say rowing puts weight on those who take it up. In any case, it can't take any off this lad.

At 5.15 I attended a lecture in honor of the tercentenary of the death of Sir Edward Coke (the great Elizabethan and Jacobean advocate, jurist, and parliamentarian). A lecture was given by Sir Wm Holdsworth[4] at Oxford (head of Law school) who was introduced by Trevelyan.[5] I was surprised to find T.'s features lightly cast, tho finely moulded. He looks not unlike [Prime Minister] Ramsay MacDonald. Holdsworth's appearance conveys my idea of the walrus in Alice in Wonderland—tho the walrus has a decidedly more intellectual cast of head in my opinion. His little head is put further out of perspective by a huge moustache. The lecture was very much a jurist's "summing up" but interesting to me as betraying the prejudices common throughout English legal tradition.

I bought some fruit on the way home and had 1/2 a pound of beefsteak (exquisitely done) with a 3d. tin of peas, for supper.

T'was Thursday morning I got your letter Red—what a treat it was! I note a great development of expression and of clearness in statement. Of course this is in some measure acquired through writing, but more largely due to having something to say and clearly perceiving what it is.

I am sending GK's Weekly[6] to Al (each week)—incidentally hoping that he'll pay a nickle a week on it, and he will send it on to you. You must read it carefully because parts, at 1st uninteresting, will become so. (Save them carefully, please).

It is great to hear that you [Red] are established at Toronto "U". During the few hours I helped you I realized what a mistake I had made in not having given you a similar assistance before—that is, instead of general exhortation, to have forgotten my own work for a few days (at first) and plunged right into yours. You have an excellent English course, I think. We have all the books except: [Tobias] Smollett, [Samuel] Rich[ardson], and [Laurence] Sterne. The Pref. to Shak. is in the Harvard Classics—so with Burke, Bunyan.[7] I have Vol. I of Addison in Everyman—keep your eye peeled for 2nd hand copies of 2 & 3 & 4.[8] It is an excellently printed edition. I don't think you need buy the novels, unless at a snap. (Oh, yes, I have Johnson's "Lives"[9] with me, so you neednt search). I think in philos. you'll find my "Roger's Students Hist. of Phil." excellent.[10] Do

---

[4]Sir William Holdsworth (1871–1944), Vinerian Professor in English Law, Oxford University.
[5]G.M. Trevelyan (1876–1962), Regius Professor of Modern History at Cambridge.
[6]*G.K.'s Weekly*, edited by G.K. Chesterton from 1925 until his death.
[7]Samuel Johnson's *Preface to Shakespeare*, selections by Edmund Burke, and John Bunyan's *The Pilgrim's Progress* are all contained in the 50-volume Harvard Classics (1910).
[8]The writings of Joseph Addison (1672–1719) in the Everyman's Library.
[9]Samuel Johnson's *The Lives of the Poets* (1779–81).
[10]A.K. Rogers, *Student History of Philosophy* (3rd ed., 1932).

you slog bravely at the French until you can read it with pleasure. I can see that to master another language is in a sense "to have another soul". Moreover it assists your mastery of your own in the case of French, as well as opening to you the mind of the greatest European people. You must not take yourself too seriously as regards results at the U. (By the bye Read Thackeray's English Humourists of the 18th cent. [1853] for that period—we have it). You have got the most needful thing—namely an incipient perception of the nature of mental growth—once you feel your thoughts on the move don't worry about the tempo or pace of U. standards—you have a life time ahead of you. Books like the Everlasting Man[11] will do much to start you—that work is an Encyclopedia with the facts or padding left out—when you come to a word like Manichee or Houmousian or Arius or Athanasius,[12] do you go to the Brittanica [*sic*] (not merely the dictionary) and carefully look up everything not only the 1st time you read it but the 2nd time. (You can't expect to win much grasp in the first reading.) Look up something of Roman and Greek history; for instance, The Punic Wars, and see the difference between "impartial" lifeless writing and the writing of a thinker and a poet [Chesterton] with a serious and comprehensive belief about the nature of life. I'll continue this after I've mailed this 1st part.

Love to you all in the
meantime from Marshall

[11] *The Everlasting Man* (1925), G.K. Chesterton's response to H.G. Wells's *Outline of History* (1920). Divided into two parts—the story of mankind and a study of Christ—it is Chesterton's interpretation of the meaning of history, with Christ as its central figure, as well as a defence of Christendom, which for Chesterton took the form of the Roman Catholic Church.

[12] "Manichee", "Arius", and "Athanasius" appear in Part II, Chapter IV, of *The Everlasting Man*. *Homoousian* (also spelled *homousian*) is the adjectival anglicized form of *homousios* (Gk.), the doctrine that the Father and the Son are alike in substance.

To Maurice McLuhan

[Cambridge]
Oct 20/21 [1934]

Here I am again:

It has been beautifully warm again You should see the brilliance of the ivy on the colleges now! quite up to the maples. My room is full of flaming flowers—astorcans(?)—apparently the bloom all winter. Mr Odams commenced to pick a nice 3rd crop of green peas to-day! The moon is nearing the full and the marbled clouds about it remind me that down along the backs[1] and on the bridges and in the gardens are coigns [corners] affording unrivalled beauty. However I must save all that, for my time is badly broken by lectures, rowing, and "halls". Now and then it occurs to me to wonder what those I.O.D.E. people are "brew-

[1] Grounds on the Cam at the back of some Cambridge colleges.

ing up"; also why Marjorie hasn't written since that readdressed letter from Selby St. I think she was waiting to reply to my 1st letter from England.

Good to hear of you reading Pepys Red. He should be read only in short stretches—about 15 minutes—Don't be too sure that you have "nailed him" Read Stevenson's (R.L.) fascinating study of him (In "Men and Books")[1] I always wanted to read Sir W[alter] Scotts article on Pepys but could not get it in Winnipeg. So go you to the library and try to find it. Get the habit of looking up all sorts of books of the 16th, 17, 18, and 19th centuries when reference has been made to them. Spend a few minutes considering their size and the general scope of the contents. Get the habit of looking at the date and edition. Now you have an excellent chance to extend your knowledge of Macaulay in this 18th century course—He has essays on Milton & Dryden & Johnson. The one on Sir Wm Temple leads you into the period and gives you Swift and Pope, then re-read the wonderful "Addison" and go thru "[Leigh] Hunt's Comic Dramatists."[3] These, with Thackeray,[4] will give you a thorough background which unlike the texts you will be referred to, will be of excellent literary quality itself. I thoroughly recommend however that you give main emphasis to the actual course—unlike me—for it is obviously sufficiently extensive, and interesting.

Now concerning your intention to read further concerning Catholic ideas respecting images and doctrine—you need go no further than the succinct and admirable little volume by Father Darcy entitled "Catholicism".[5] Mervin Sprung told me of it.

It is simply astonishing about your new job! You thoroughly deserved to have it, and will find it a source of profit and experience (the latter, I think, unpleasant in a sense) What a pleasure to have your own pocket money!—concerning clothes—flannels are the only thing for college, and whether they are worn at Toronto or not you may be sure that they are absolutely in order. Tell the curious that you have a br[other] at Camb[ridge]! Dont try to keep them pressed, and save up to have a Harris tweed coat made to wear with them. Dont buy a vest because only sweaters are in order with flannels (and plus fours also). Then in the summer you can have a pair of plus fours made to match the coat. Another don't!—Bill Shaver is the very embodiment of unrestrained undisciplined extracurricular activity—stand clear!

Concerning your Philos. I have "Bakewell's Sourcebook of Ancient Philos"[6] and the [Nichomachean] Ethics of Aristotle—Dont bother with [Will] Durant. I brought [Plato's] the republic here. Would that I had all my books. I need them (and many more) constantly for reference. If you wish to set aside 25¢ a week to send me to buy you books of your own, I think you might have reason to congrat. yourself later on. There are wonderful buys to be had here constantly.

[2]Robert Louis Stevenson, *Familiar Studies of Men and Books* (1882).

[3]These are all references to essay-reviews in Volumes I (Temple) and II of the *Critical & Historical Essays by Thomas Babington Macaulay* (Everyman's Library, 1907).

[4]William Makepeace Thackeray, *The English Humourists of the Eighteenth Century* (1851).

[5]The Rev. M.C. D'Arcy, *Catholicism* [1928].

[6]Charles M. Bakewell, *Source Book in Ancient Philosophy* (1907).

Good heavens! how long did I say that £10 would last? The bike and trousers knocked it hard—only 4½ left! I think to postpone joining the union (£2) till next term when I may be able to pay the whole £7½ (if I get the I.O.D.E. [cheque]) or else stay clear of it. Its advantages are not unltd. by any means.

Oct 21st The enclosed half penny is simply for your curiousity—being new. I have had several 1934 shillings but kept them for obvious reasons.

Another thought occurs concerning your English course—Red: Read Dowden on [Edmund] Burke (Edward Dowden). The chapter occurs in a book dealing with the beginning of the Romantic period in thought and prose. Look up D's works and you will soon guess which volume contains it. The chapter is short and beautifully clear.[7] Chesterton (Whats Wrong with the World, beg. of Part V) suggests that there is an atheistic strain in Burke—In taking his stand against the French Rev. which "appealled [sic] to the idea of an abstract and eternal justice" Burke uses the new mod. argument of evolution. "Each people practically got, not only the tyrant it deserved, but the tyrant it *ought* to have." . . . "man said Burke in effect[,] must adapt himself to everything like an animal."[8]—then follows [in Dowden] a note on [Laurence] Sterne. There is a good note on [Samuel] Johnson & [Joseph] Addison Pt II, 3; and one on the 18th cent. Pt III, 5. It is a great help to introduce principles of evaluation into your factual acquaintance with a period. Don't read a lot *about* your texts however. You can do that much later. For instance too much has been written about Johnson. There is nothing to say *about* him. There he is—enjoy him! Remember this about the 18th century:—It was the most civilized (in the strict social sense) time since the Athenian heyday. It was a complete and self-contained world. You will come most readily to appreciate its virtues through the Spectator papers.[9] Don't suppose that the 19th century was an advance on the 18th simply because of certain shining names.

I have just come from lunch with Mr Crawley (my personal tutor) Wansborough-Jones is my formal tutor and Elvin my study tutor. Crawley is quite the most pleasant personally and Elvin is a close 2nd. Crawley is quiet (about 35) frank—a little nervous if blinking is an indication—and smiling when attentive but not too much so. His wife looks much older (she too is a grad.) but because she is manifestly unwell—Extremely likeable however. There are 2 children—John only a few months and Mary 2½. Mary is very beautiful indeed. [Of] other guests, there were 3—His nephew, Ricardo—a Hall man till last year and a young lady, now a junior Hist. tutor at Girton,[10] (very plain, very superior) and lastly a blonde; charming, [a] Dubliner—a science grad from Trinity now doing research in Camb.

---

[7]Edward Dowden, *The French Revolution and English Literature* (1897): Chapter III: "Anti-Revolution: Edmund Burke".

[8]Gilbert K. Chesterton, *What's Wrong With the World* (1910), pp. 257–8.

[9]*The Spectator*, a London periodical conducted by Sir Richard Steele and Joseph Addison from March 1, 1711 to December 6, 1712. The papers were edited for the Everyman's Library by G. Gregory Smith: *The Spectator* (1907).

[10]Girton College, Cambridge, for women.

in natural science. What a beautiful home and grounds and garden! Over their low walls you can see the Backs on one side and have St Johns playing field on the other. They have roses blooming yet and will have till January! Walnut, quince and other trees—3 century elms, rose trees (climbing) and otherwise and a spacious lawn. Conversation seldom expands among Englishmen—It is curious that the great majority, here, have very small mouths. They not only appear but often are restrained & compressed. Now to work on my Samuel Butler essay Am reading [Samuel] Butler's Erewhon and the Way of All Flesh.

Love to you all, from Marshall.

P.S. What fun about Rags "the old man"[11] I would send a letter to you in Wpg. Dad only think it would miss you.

[11]"Rags" was the family dog.

To Elsie, Herbert, and Maurice McLuhan

[Cambridge]
Oct 22/34

Dear Mother and Dad and Red:

How I long to hear more from you, and that you are all in excellent health and spirits. Before I forget, Red, don't slight your Ethics course if it is to be Greek and Roman in emphasis. Those old writers are fascinating and represent the nē plus ultra of purely human achievement. They explored all the limits of merely human possibility and wisdom. Read always with a succinct summary at hand. For instance you might lose yourself in Marcus Aurelius without a definite notion of the Stoic position.[1]

What an ass was I not to take my camera to the opening.[2] I missed my only opportunity to have a picture of the King & Queen and Stanley Baldwin.[3] It was a perfect morning—bright and warm. I was at the grounds—but we could tell when the "progress" from the station commenced by the burst of all the college chimes—they have continued to play in succession all day. Baldwin was present because he is the present Chancellor. It was great to see the garb of the heads of the colleges—they wear beefeater hats. The Chancellor spoke and then the King (inside) and we were given it via marconiphone, as they call their amplifiers.

I had a good pull on the river to-day and then went out in my whiff.[4] Finished my essay this A.M. and am now attempting to finish "The Way of All Flesh".[5]

All love from Marshall.

[1]Marcus Aurelius (121–180), Roman emperor and Stoic philosopher, whose precepts were collected in his *Meditations*.

[2]The opening of the new University Library.

[3]George V and Queen Mary. Stanley Baldwin, then Chancellor of Cambridge University, began his third term as Prime Minister the next year.

[4]A two-oared shell—a sculling boat—for one person.

[5]The novel (1903) by Samuel Butler (1835–1902).

To Elsie, Herbert, and Maurice McLuhan

[Cambridge]

Fragment November 3 [1934]

Will you inquire the cost of life membership privileges of Hart House,[1] Red? It will affect my ideas about joining The Camb. Union, which in itself, is of little use to me. It is a splendid spot to entertain friends and visitors but that is of small moment to me. It gives one full privileges in the Oxford union however which by itself cost double what ours does. I think that is because there are more than twice as many men at Cambridge (about 9000!—far too many) but the town is laid out to serve them and you would never place the estimate so high on the strength of a practical guess. Speaking of visitors—it is very pleasant on Saturdays and Sundays to see the mothers, sisters and sweethearts perambulating the streets and colleges with their sons, brothers, lovers. Many the excellent hamper must come up with them.

Despite the fact of the Peacock exam this morning,[2] I went to hear the great Dover Wilson[3] last night—I went to see, I staid to listen—and, remain unconverted. His appearance is a libel even on Shakespearean commentators—for that he is, and one of the "greatest". He is tall and shamefully stooped, (about 50 yrs old)—has a large head and face and neck, on a pigeon chest which only criminal indifference to his body could have left so undeveloped. His feature[s] are loosely strung together suggesting that they were selected and arranged with the same rigorous eye to light and symmetry as the critical footnotes on one of his pages! The effect is soullessly bookish. His manner of delivery is harsh, emphatic, and unnecessarily impatient in irrelevant matters. When he has to mention American and German professors his gorge fairly rises and one wishes one had an umbrella. His paper was excellent: "The make-up of Hamlet"—his psychol. make up—briefly he stated: Hamlet is not a real person, not a consistent psychological creation but simply a portion of the tissue of the play. Shak. published his plays upon the stage and would have been amazed at the critical ingenuity of readers. Hamlet's character is simply a means of developing a total dramatic effect—one of tremendous brooding mystery. Therefore his "madness" and his antic-disposition are a problem Shak. never meant us to understand as the drama is actually played. And so with the reasons for his procrastination. After bringing H's character into discredit and low worth he suddenly rehabilitates him with almost a single magic stroke. It is his greatest artistic triumph—

---

[1]Hart House accommodates the athletic, social, and dining facilities of students (at this time male only) of the University of Toronto, where Maurice McLuhan was a student.

[2]Thomas Love Peacock (1785–1866) was the author of many books, including the satirical novels *Nightmare Abbey* (1818) and *Gryll Grange* (1861). Marshall had just sat for the Latham Prize. See next letter, note 1.

[3]Dover Wilson (1881–1969), Shakespeare scholar who co-edited (with Sir Arthur Quiller-Couch) the plays in the New Cambridge Shakespeare series and whose books include *The Essential Shakespeare* (1932).

the duel scene—of tremendous interest to the Elizabethans—the process of the duel has not been appreciated. Laertes anticipates the signal and wounds Hamlet. H. drops his [,] wrests his untipped sword from him and ironically points to L. to take it up. *Then* he runs L. through. (This is undoubtedly superior to a mere exchange during a scuffle)

Well the Peacock paper was not nearly of the calibre of the English tripos [examination] questions. It required fact fact fact and much quotation from memory. Moreover it was too long. I shall hear in a week, or so. Meantime I have made a very solid acquaintance with a man whose work had an amazing and pervasive effect on Meredith and which in itself is quite as pleasant to read—[4] It is in reality much more pleasant but not as great in scope or as deeply conceived as Meredith's. There is no hurry for Red to read Peacock because he requires considerable in the way of information and developed literary taste for his proper enjoyment.

Since the exam I have tried to catch up [on] other reading and commence to read for my essay this week on Earle,[5] Overbury[6] and Butler[7] as sketchers of character. The description of queer individuals and of representatives of permanent social types became a popular literary form in the 1st part of the 17th century—Sir Roger[8] a century later is in the tradition, which flowered forth into the novel.

Guy Fawkes day is Monday and the children have been very active in the streets. There are dozens of effigies of poor old Guy toted about in small carts, doll's carriages etc. He is accompanied by a dozen or so urchins who clamour to all and sundry for "a penny for Guy F." They wait outside the colleges at Hall time as well.

I have been heavy on books this week but have now nearly a full bookcase to show for 15 shillings at most. To-day I got good copies of: "Butlers Analogy & Sermons"[9] "Thackeray's Humourists", "Carlyles Essays",[10] [Victor] Hugo's poems and Chateaubriand's Atala en Amerique[11] etc. (in French) for 4¢ a vol. Also The Tempest, and Seneca translated. Many of these volumes have been held up until very recently at 1/ or 2/ shillings.

[4]That is, the work of Thomas Love Peacock. (Meredith married Peacock's eldest daughter Mary Ellen, who left him for another man eight years later.)

[5]John Earle (?1601–65), whose *Microcosmographie* (1628) was a collection of character sketches.

[6]Sir Thomas Overbury (1581–1613), the author of the poem *A Wife*, published posthumously in 1614, to which "Characters" were added in later editions, some of which John Earle responded to in his *Microcosmographie*.

[7]Samuel Butler (1612–80), author of the mock-heroic poem *Hudibras* (published in three parts between 1663 and 1678), whose *Characters and Passages from Notebooks* were edited and published in 1908.

[8]Sir Roger de Coverley, a fictional English gentleman described by Richard Steele and Joseph Addison in their essays in *The Spectator* (March 1711–December 1712).

[9]*Sermons on Human Nature* (1726) and *The Analogy of Religion, Natural and Revealed, to the Constitution and Course of Nature* (1736) by Joseph Butler (1692–1752)—works that earned for Butler a permanent place in the history of philosophy.

[10]Thomas Carlyle's *English and Other Critical Essays* (Everyman's Library, 2 vols. 1915).

[11]François-René Chateaubriand's *Atala* (set in Louisiana), first published in 1801.

Well, you may imagine my excitement after posting my last letter to you when the mail had brought Mother's picture (much wondered at by Mr Odams et famille they have maintained the "true English reserve") to return from Hall to find letters from Dad, Marjorie and Mother again, and the 5£ therewith. It was my 1st from Dad whom I shall write to at Winnipeg.

Do not hesitate, Mother, to be forthright and authoritative in your talk to the English-speaking union. You can speak with authority, yet not as the scribes. I would elaborate the theme that elocution has suffered, more than singing, from its seeming proximity to common parlance. Point out that excellence therein is as far removed from the flowers and intonations of rhetorical oratory (with its narrow compass of tones and showy emphasis) as is excellence in poetry (with its organic relation or interdependence *between content and tone and metrical patterns.*) from the easy swing of doggerel. Forbes believes that nearly all faults in the reading of poetry proceed from *"pathological* (ie. a mania for) *acceleration"*. Use that phrase. He is wrong of course, in his emphasis.

I am sorry that Aunt Ethel should be involved but I know it is an impossible load for you and Dad. She shall have no regrets. Don't worry about my ability to stand the rowing. They dont [*words obscured by fold*] very hard and in any case I am comparatively knit or set physically. I shall be on my guard. Don't bother to mount the snaps until the albums come from Winnipeg. Then use "corners" and the backs may be read. A 3rd angel may ultimately hallow my room. Marjorie (of whom I have no photo) hints she may have one taken. I think your costume portrait is quite a little triumph of taste and beauty.[12] It is good to hear of Red working hard—it is really a great treat to be alone and free when studying. How I would like to have Rags to lie by my fire. What a fine old doggy odour he has. I love it beyond even that of horses! The enclosed jokes are from Marjorie's clippings.

Sunday—I am about to write Kirkconnell a very presentable letter so will cut this off here.

A delightful thing occurred the other night when I was in the midst of "Maid Marian".[13] The radio picked up a concert of Purcell's old English airs rendered on the old instruments—in this case a flute of "oaten stop". The music is indescribably exquisite at any time, but I was "in" Sherwood Forest at that time. I have just written out (very hastily) what I believe a just modern version of some celebrated verses:

> This orgy now is ended. These mad hustlers
> As I foretold you, were all bluff and
> Are shown to be air, even hot air:
> And like the baseless credit of their business
> Their sign-capped towers and raucous newspapers,
> Their film temples, great Hollywood itself,

[12]A photograph that Elsie McLuhan had taken for a publicity flyer. It is reproduced on page 89.
[13]A medieval romance (1822) by Thomas Love Peacock.

And all that it doth breed on shall dissolve,
And like an insubstantial pageant faded
Leave not a rack behind. They were such stuff
Screen-stars are made on and their feverish life
Is quieted now in sleep.[14]

I go to tea with Mr and Mrs Dean at 4.30—then chapel, then Hall, then work.[15]

Love for all from Marshall

[14]A parody of Prospero's speech in Act IV of *The Tempest* ("Our revels now are ended. . . .").
[15]Henry Roy Dean, M.D. (d. 1961), was Professor of Pathology and Master of Trinity Hall (1929–54).

To Elsie, Herbert, and Maurice McLuhan

[Cambridge]
Nov 9/11.30 P.M. [1934]

Dear Mother, Dad, and Red:

Well you can now perceive what all my hasty study of Peacock was for.[1] Even if I had not been successful I would have been a big gainer thereby. It is going to be pleasant laying out that money to-morrow morning. Next term the subject is "Percy's Reliques"—also a closed book to me, hitherto.[2] I feel that if I pick off a few such prizes that I can go ahead more leisurely with the GK article, which will be a knockout when complete—it will be for a more advanced stage what the Macaulay article was for a previous period. It resembles the Macaulay article in being born of a mighty enthusiasm that has necessarily perverted my judgement; and I shall no doubt be much the better for getting it off my chest. I will send you a list of the books that I buy.

This week has been very full, commencing Sunday with tea at the Masters Lodge. Tuesday I went to Wallace Beery in Viva Villa with Bowen—it was a stirring picture excellently produced.[3] We had supper at B's rooms afterwards and a good time generally.

Wednesday, I heard glorious old "Q" lecture, for the first time.[4] He is a splendid figure (nearly 80) but his voice is beginning to quaver a bit—a real old Cornishman—nothing professorial or "intellectual" in his bearing or features. His theme was, fittingly enough, the history of the Cambridge Eng. course [,] its aims hopes and shortcomings.

That night I went to the Hesperides where a Hall fellow gossiped on Goethe.

[1]McLuhan had won the Latham Prize, which was endowed by a former Master of Trinity Hall, Henry Latham, for competition through a written examination on a set book in English literature.
[2]*Reliques of Ancient English Poetry* (3 vols, 1765), an anthology edited by Thomas Percy (1729–1811).
[3]Wallace Beery (1886–1949), a leading film actor of his time, had one of his greatest roles as Pancho Villa in *Viva Villa!* (1934), an account of the Mexican revolution.
[4]"Q" was the pseudonym of Sir Arthur Quiller-Couch (see page 21, note 2).

Thursday called me to dinner at 8 with Elvin who I was surprised to discover is newly married. Mrs. Elvin is young (25) tall, fair graceful, dignified, beautiful, gracious, refined in every sense—yet an American from California. I take it that her father is an ambassador for they have been here 4 years.[5] There were 2 others: Louis Clarke (elderly debonair man of the world—anthropologist at the Hall)[6] and a young German "putting in" 11 years around Europe until his father's firm wants him.[7] An unusually fine evening, you may be sure.

The same day I ordered a Harris tweed coat—it is between a fawn and a grey (no thats not it for it is brownish) and is about an inch thick and will last me forever—*but*, it is expensive—£2—but so vastly ahead of the £1½ suit that I was perhaps unduly influenced. The vest & plus fours will cost £2 also when I require them—I tell you, I felt that this wonderful cloth might make me look like a man, but I may be wrong. In any case it is classy and will *never* wear out.

Mr Ifor Evans (a London U. prof in Eng) spoke to the Eng. Club to-night. I had the profitable if uncomfortable experience of listening to myself. He has the same ingrained prejudices about the ends and uses of life, the same dogmatism, and considerably more capacity, I think.

Tomorrow night I am going to make my 1st appearance at the famous Festival Theatre (repertory comp[any]) where Strindberg's "Father" is playing. Will write again soon. Hope to hear from you soon too.

Lovingly, Marshall.

[5]Margaret Elvin's father was minister of the First Unitarian Church in San Francisco.
[6]Louis Clarke, a Fellow of Trinity Hall, was curator of the Museum of Archaeology and Anthropology until 1937, and then became Director of the Fitzwilliam Museum in Cambridge.
[7]Heinz Tannhauser, a fellow student. See page 77, note 3.

To Elsie, Herbert, and Maurice McLuhan

[Cambridge]
Nov 10/34 6.30 P.M.

Dear Mother, Dad, and Red:-

There is no evidence of winter here now except the fact that the winter ocean service seems to have commenced—5 letters in one mail! 2 from Mother, my *second* from Red, one from Al and one from Marjorie.

I forgot to tell you that Halloween is not an English but a Scotch day. They know nothing of it here. But to-day (poppy-day) is a big occasion in Cambridge. There is a lively contest among the colleges to collect the largest amount of money. The devices are infinite and laughable. Trucks with bands (and crooners singing into amplifiers!) and students holding out small hoop nets for pennies— single men dressed as Jews, Shieks [*sic*], (excellently and gaudily got up) Africans (in shorts) everything, sideshows, sidewalks portrait painters, weight-guessers,—nobody escaping from their urgent iteration. Alas for pretty girls—

the celibate frosh protected by disguise and the occasion seemed to regard them as the only persons suffering from an excess of pennies.

Well I ordered my books this morning. Unfortunately the college arms stamp (which goes on the outside) costs 6 pence a volume—I have ordered 18 volumes and have 4 shillings credit.

1st, all of Q's lectures = 9 volumes including his book on Shakespeare and an earlier work "From a Cornish Window"[1] I shall send them to Red as soon as I have read them and am able to dispense with them. They are an education all by themselves.

2nd, Longinus on the Sublime

3rd Blake complete works

4th Oxford Concise Dict. (new ed. one week old)

5th Cassells French Dict

6th Keats in Oxford [Standard Authors] edition

7th GK's miscellany (a big volume of extracts from the 1st 500 issues of GKs Weekly

8th Short Talks with the Dead—[Hilaire] Belloc

9th The Craft of Fiction—Percy Lubbock—will send to Red if it seems likely to be of assistance to him

10th, Son of Woman by Middleton Murry, which is a detailed biography of D.H Lawrence but also an important document for our century. [*Crossed out, with the notation:*] "I've decided not to buy it".

I have inquired about the Winchester Prizes for elocution—there are 2 prizes of £20 and £10 and usually about 30 entries. It comes off in May, by which time I may feel sufficiently audacious to enter. We read sight passages from Shakespeare, Old & New Testaments, the Prayerbook, and from Donnes Sermons (the set book this year) There is an annual £20 prize at the Hall for an essay on a set subject in (usually modern) Eng. Literature. I think I can get it next year. Meantime I *am*, more or less gritting my teeth with the idea of writing my exams this year. It is a big order and if I dont feel sure of a 1st I shall have to drop the notion, because I can't do Phd work without one. I feel that I must have a Phd from here if anywhere—it would be ridiculous to go to America for one unless a good fellowship was offered. I have had an opportunity to take the measure of the Cambridge dons and can say that they are not superhuman by any means. But they have exceptional advantages here.

My life is sufficiently occupied here you may be sure, but it is amazing what one can do in a buoyant mood even between rowing, teas, halls, and lectures morning and evening. Everything being on the spot makes a huge diff. The wheel [bicycle] saves me an hour or more a day—a great deal. The weather is "winter". That is, often damp, misty, but never colder than 40°. I prefer it a great deal to our winter I must say.

[1]Sir Arthur Quiller-Couch, *Shakespeare's Workmanship* (1918) and *From a Cornish Window* (1928).

Al [Bolton] writes that Jim['s] "Rainey" died of blood-poisoning—bitten by another dog.[2]

I enjoyed your letter a very great deal indeed Red and have been tickled to hear how you are plunging in and beginning to tussle with and enjoy poetry and thought. It requires much of such discipline before one begins to reap the greatest pleasures and rewards from mental experience. Simply rest assured despite fluctuations of enthusiasm that sooner or later (sooner, if you are reasonably persistent) you will "arrive". Let me recommend that you resist the almost irresistible temptation to underline and annotate your own and others' books. It is a disease that left ugly marks on many of *my* books and which I realize was quite profitless and pointless. But I know the power of the impulse. A minute tick (✓ or .) at rare intervals is the utmost that later developed taste will endorse.

Keep "Come to Think of It"[3] when Brock[4] gives it to you. I told him I wanted it especially for the article to encourage him to get busy.

I think you will find all your French texts (except Beaumarchais) among [Joe] Hilts's books. I'm sure of it.

Strangely enough I started Milton just as you did: in the fall, reading aloud the sonnets and minor poems on the bank of the Red River. I think you improved on that. Now, the fact of determined irreverence of behaviour in chapel at Milton's day was simply an expression of that black mood of pessimism which abhorred art and the "works of man". It was not simply the stark insensibility of youthful high-spirits, but the deliberate intention of Puritan low-spirits. Don't forget to read Macaulay on Milton and I have heard that Mark Pattison's volume in the Men of Letters is one of the best things on him.[5]

Here is what Grierson (a very able critic) says (1921) of him [Milton]:

> The greatest English poet [indeed] of the century was, or believed himself to be, a philosophical or theological poet of the same order as Dante. Paradise Lost was written to be a justification of the ways of God to men, resting on a theological system as definite, and almost as carefully [articulated] in the De Doctrina Christiana (Milton's own) as that which Dante accepted from the Summa of Aquinas. And the poet embodied his argument in a dramatic poem as vivid[ly] and intensely conceived . . . as the Divina Commedia. But in truth Milton was no philosopher. The subtleties of theological definition and inference eluded his rationalistic [get that word, Red—it does not imply much ability to reason] practical, tho[ugh] idealistic mind. He proved nothing. The definitely stated argument of the poem is an obvious begging of the question. What he did was to create or give a new definiteness and sensible power to, a great myth, which through him [his poem], continued for a century or more to dominate the mind and

[2]Jim Rainey's dog "Rainey".

[3]G.K. Chesterton, *Come to Think of It* (1930).

[4]Stanley E. Brock, a fellow gold medalist at the University of Manitoba and winner of a Rhodes Scholarship to Oxford.

[5]Macaulay's essay (1825) on Milton in Volume II of the *Critical & Historical Essays by Thomas Babington Macaulay: Volume One* (1907) in the Everyman's Library; Mark Pattison, *Milton* (1875; 1925).

imagination of pious Protestants without many of them suspecting the here-sies which lurked beneath the imposing and dazzling poem in which was retold the Bible story of the fall and redemption of man.[6]

Now I can heartily recommend GK's book on St Thomas as being of use to you in your philosophy.[7] He deals with Plato and Aristotle and their influence on Christendom—incidentally there is a very clear exposition of their theories of knowledge (how we know and know we *can* know) You are quite right in read-ing Robinson on these men. Take a look at Caird's Hist. of Anc. Philos.[8] I found him exceptionally clear but perhaps he is more exhaustive than you have time for. In any case these ideas are not simple. I remember what difficulty I had. I never understood the importance or meaning of Plato and Aristotle until I read Kant a year later. Memorize certain key ideas so that you can turn them over in your mind. It is useful broadly to distinguish Pl. and Arist as tending towards Bhuddism and Christianity respectively. Plato was an oriental in mind (and many believe in blood) Artistotle heartily accepts the senses just as Browning did, and says

> "Let us not always say
> 'Spite of this flesh to-day
> I strove, made head, gained ground upon the whole!'
> As the bird wings and sings,
> Let us cry 'All good things
> Are ours, nor soul helps flesh more, now, than flesh helps
> soul.' "[9]

And that is why great Aquinas accepted Aristotle into Christian theology.

Your little question "By the way, what is justice", is a poser. It is an open question whether Plato answered it. But certainly he refutes certain perennials views of it. As for that fusty old rationalist [Herbert] Spencer—don't puzzle yourself about him. As a philosopher and thinker he is less than nothing.

I think I said before Red that we have Walton's lives and angler[10] and Miltons Prose.

I saw an excellent French film yesterday with Bowen. He has had me to tea 4 times so I took 2 lbs of grapes this time. I'm not keen to entertain *yet*. Moreover my rooms are further out than most.

Well I got my "jacket extraordinaire" yesterday.[11] It fits perfectly and is a joy to see and wear. The color is fawn with a slight tendency to be brown. It weighs as much as 2 ordinary coats. One pity is that if I'm to match it in plus 4's and vest

---

[6]From the Introduction (p. xv) to *Metaphysical Lyrics and Poems of the Seventeenth Century: Donne to Butler* (1921) by Herbert J.C. Grierson.

[7]G.K. Chesterton, *St. Thomas Aquinas: the Dumb Ox* (1933).

[8]Unidentified.

[9]Stanza 12 of "Rabbi Ben Ezra" by Robert Browning.

[10]*The Compleat Angler; or the Contemplative Man's Recreation* (1653) by Isaak Walton (1593–1683), who also wrote a series of biographies (of John Donne, George Herbert *et al.*) known as *Walton's Lives*.

[11]The Harris Tweed overcoat.

I must put a deposit (10/) on them right away else the cloth (which is hand made and dyed and not matched) will be used up and another stock put up. The deposit will hold them till after Xmas.

Yesterday we went into training for the Fairbairn Cup races which take place next Friday.[12] Last night the training diet was fish & lemon mutton brussell sprouts etc Then a huge fruit desert [*sic*] followed by 2 poached eggs on toast and 1/2 a pint of beer. Its lots of fun. One wonders where it goes.

I must get this away this A.M. But last night there were letters (2) from you Mother and a delightful one from Red. These I will answer later. But you are undoubtedly harrassed Mother. What an ass is Wansborough[*sic*]-Jones. The figures I sent from the bursar (which I have not kept) were absolutely reliable. No guarantee above $500 is necessary—W-J. must have been thinking of lodgings as well. In any case ignore it. My whole year will be just under $1000 so plan on it.

I dont think it possible for you to keep up that pace very long—you must retrench your energies and consider that your health is your principal and interest.

The weather is warm but misty. Well I am off to Forbes—will write to-morrow.

Lovingly Marshall

[12]The Fairbairn Cup Races were timed boat races over a full course of the Cam (River). In 1934 Trinity Hall entered three boats in the race.

To Elsie, Herbert, and Maurice McLuhan

[Cambridge]
Thursday Dec 6/34

Dear Mother Dad and Red

It is sometime since I heard from you—however I have been too busy to note how long. Do you know, I have not lit my fire for 5 days. It has been about 55–60° with occasional rain—Early October weather, and not at all Xmas-like. Yes, speaking of Xmas I have been worried by the problem of gifts. I bought 3 calendars one of which I am sending to you. They were 2/6 each. One is for Mr & Mrs Norris (I'm sending Miss Campbell a card), and the other is for Mrs McQuillan, who deserves much more. Now I have been able to discover nothing for Marjorie except a bracelet that is too expensive (22/6) When I mentioned the antique shops here she asked me to look for: a locket, a bracelet or a letterbox. Well all 3 are rather scarce, tho a casual glance at the shop would give you the idea that there were wagon-loads of such things. The only suitable bracelet that Mr Whittaker has is one of gilded-silver (½ an inch wide—hinged sections) with bright red (opaque) stones mounted prominently. It is Hungarian workmanship of about a century ago. It has real distinction, but is expensive, I know. Consider however, my sweater, and heaven knows what in preparation. I will look for something else for a day or two. I don't wish to send a book and obviously am not qualified to select ephemeral articles of wear. Now I have not thought of buying you people anything, because I am going to be put to it for cash very soon. My expenses may mount a bit during vac since I must cater my own dinners. I think to visit Oxford at Xmas, and go when Odams wants these rooms—about the 19th. Now that I think of Margery B's invitation to Derbyshire for Jan 5 however, it would be foolish to break up my studies by leaving here before Jan 1st. From Oxford I can proceed to Derbyshire—by bike, using the Hostels. But there will be extra room rent from Dec 12 till Jan 1st to pay in Cambridge. I shall get a cheaper rate than during term of course.

Now Odams bill should be paid before the end of the month. I gave you a pretty good idea of its size did I not? The college bill will reach you Jan 1st and must be attended to quickly—also to save 10 shillings discount—for I cannot continue residence if it is not paid.

Ah, here is Odams with my tea (5.10 every day) and slice of sponge-cake. For these he will accept nothing. And here is the postie with a letter from you Mother, saying you have heard of the Latham prize. I did not submit an essay but "sat" in a competitive (3 hour) exam.

To-morrow afternoon (lectures over now) I am going to commence work at the French required books, with wee Salt. I have got out a big stack of books from the library, which I can keep through the vac. My studies this term have been largely devoted to the 1st part of the 17th century—a strange period to me. Donne, Crashaw, Herbert, Vaughan, Traherne, Walton, Davenant, and the Cavalier poets—then Thos Browne etc. It is a rich, various, courtly, learned, mellow, rural-loving period, and quite the most civilized in English history.

Of late I have been wayfaring among the work of T.S. Eliot. He is easily the greatest modern poet, and just how great he is remains to be seen, because he has not produced his best yet. However the poems I am reading (ed. Faber & Faber: "Poems 1909–1925") have the unmistakable character of greatness. They transform, and diffuse and recoalesce the commonest every day occurrences of 20th cent. city life till one begins to see double indeed—the extremely unthinkable character, the glory and the horror of the reality *in* life yet, to all save the seer, *behind* life is miraculously suggested. (Eliot is an anglo-Catholic, a theologian and philosopher, and one of the best critics who ever wrote in English) Now there is something ineffably exciting in reading a man, a genius and a poet, who has by the same stages, in face of the same circumstances, (he is an American) come to the same point of view concerning the nature of religion and Christianity, the interpretation of history, and the value of industrialism. There is scarcely a modern "intellectual" who has the background of opinion necessary to enjoy Eliot—yet they have one and all heralded him and ranted about him; while he has necessarily been amused by their efforts to show that his poetry "dispenses with *all* creeds and beliefs"!

I came across this section from a recent poem in a volume of criticism by Miss Sitwell:[1]

"The "Triumphal March" is the presentation of the poor world that is waiting for the coming of Christ—for the great coming—and that is given, in His stead, Caesar, the king of the world." These are a few lines quoted from it by Miss Sitwell

> So many waiting, how many waiting? What did it matter, on such a day?
> ["and the[n] the terrible march onward in place of Him, of"]
> "5,800,000 rifles and carbines,
>   102,000 machine guns,
>   28,000 trench mortars,
>   53,000 field and heavy guns
> I cannot tell how many projectiles, mines and fuses,
>   13,000 aeroplanes,
>   24,000 aeroplane engines,
>   50,000 ammunition wagons
>   11,000 field kitchens
>   1,150 field bakeries.
> What a time that took. Will it be he now? No
> [But now at last he comes—but]
>   There is no interrogation in those [his] eyes."

Then comes a typical cry from Eliot. He has an uncanny capacity to hang all the terror of eternity on a common phrase or word.

> . . . . . "Please, will you
> Give us a light?
> Light
> Light."

How I wish I could read you some of these Mother! Eliot is an extremely careful and conscientious artist in words and metre and rhyme. His poems all hit a pitch (as the above) that is consistently developed or played upon. Now it is my firm belief that if you had the time to study carefully some of his poetry and some of Yeats and Gerard Manl[e]y Hopkins, (whose poems I bought with the last of my prize money) you could take the élite London by storm. There is a persistent and really irresistible drive, here, for the right reading *aloud* of poetry, and there is no one to do it. This "desire" is limited to leisured cultivated classes and to university circles. I do not say that the above poem on mod. civilization would thrill an Ontario audience but I am not sure that it wouldnt. Most people are sufficiently conscious of the crucial condition of morals, belief, hope, government, and the future of society, to enable them to be moved by an adequate reading of such a poem. (I will cite others later, when I have studied them a bit more) He

[1]The poem is T.S. Eliot's "Coriolan: Triumphal March" and it is discussed in *Aspects of Modern Poetry* (1934) by Edith Sitwell (1887–1964), p. 140. The sentence quoted actually begins: "And in this great poem we have as I see it, the presentation of the poor world . . . ". In the extracts that follow, the lines in square brackets are interpolations by Miss Sitwell.

has many shorter poems (30 lines) that you could start with as an experiment. But there is really an amazing opportunity for you Mother to break with the outworn idea of an elocutionist as a pre-movie entertainer and to use *your art* to focus attention on really great modern art. You would be GIVEN the air by the B.B.C. after a successful rendering [of] such poems. Unfortunately, you are, I know, too busy to give Eliot, (for instance) the attention he requires. You see, he is using different rhythms than you are accustomed to. But, they are not used as arbitrarily as Browning's and they are not as hard. Moreover his poems, like B's, use the method of dramatic monologue with its swift ranging over every sort of experience. But Eliots "consciousness" is not that of a lover, a count[?], or a distinct individual—it is *impersonal* and universal and instead of ranging over *individual* associations he ranges over all history and all modern society, but with a miraculous relevance and effectiveness. Meantime get the one volume of poems I cited *and* "The Poetry of T.S. Eliot" [1932] by Hugh Ross Williamson which will give you a really clear succinct approach. I think you need read only the 1st 5 chaps. and leave "The Waste Land" alone completely unless you are keenly interested and confident of the possibiltics [*sic*] for yourself of the shorter poems.

Now for some items that you mention: I have paid Odams nothing except for coals and breakfasts for which I owe nothing

I feel disinclined to apply for the Ottawa bursary before next year when I shall have more strength in my position. It seems likely that I will be permitted to count next year as a Phd year even if I dont write this spring. That means putting in one year here after my degree and then finishing my Phd work in Canada if I wish. Now the Ottawa bursaries are designed for research, and until I am a Phd aspirant I haven't a chance. Moreover they are granted in Feb–March so next year would not be too late, and I *might* get the IODE extended.

GK's "miscellany" (accent "cell") is a lark,[2] I wish I could send it but have not read it yet. eg.: "(Mr Middleton Murry records that his book "On Reading "God"", records his farewell to God)

> Murry on finding le Bon Dieu
> Chose difficile à croire
> Illogically said "Adieu"
> But God said "Au Revoir".
> GKC.

It contains contributions from many besides GKC.

You will be grieved to hear that the tux has not yet been donned. People wear baggy flannels on such occasions as I have mentioned. I will try to get Salt to take some pictures of me—Odams is not very adept.

[2]*GK's: A Miscellany of the First 500 Issues of* GK's Weekly *with an Introduction by G.K. Chesterton* (1934). The squib that follows concerns the prominent literary critic John Middleton Murry (1889–1957), who, after the death in 1923 of his wife Katherine Mansfield, discovered God; his books in this period included *God* (1929).

It is good to think that your weather is also behaving. The winter does not appear here till January I am told.

You speak of my grounding! Wow! I never felt so helplessly futile and ignorant before. I have an exact knowledge of nothing. When I really get a grip on English I shall be in a position to understand other arts much more readily. My mind is a ferment these days—boiling with new ideas and experience. I must keep it so for years yet, if I am to be worth anything as an educator. Believe me I would vastly prefer dairy-and-orchard-culture to this intense mental culture. The latter is not easy and its results are less certain.

Red, send the enclosed article to Al [Bolton] at your pleasure. It is full of meat. If you have read the Everlasting Man you will find it simple enough.

To think of Rags getting excited over my good fortune! Hope Dad gets down [to Toronto] for Xmas—

Lovingly
Marshall

To Maurice McLuhan

[Cambridge, December 1934]

Dear Red

If you ever want to learn anything about D.H. Lawrence refer to Middleton Murry's "Son of Woman".[1] The 1st 40 pages gives you an excellent summary, *and* revelation of the man. It is the story of one with an extraordinary tenderness and love and who was afraid of this great power in himself, and sought "fulfilment" in sex. Actually, he was one of [those] rare men who are born "eunuchs for the Kingdom of Heaven's sake"; but who, having no religious education, (like all the English poor, from whom he came) and becoming the unconscious victim of modern psychological quackery, denied and frustrated his great spiritual capacity for dedication and leadership. Sex was for him an attempt to get oblivion and forgetfulness of the great urgent forces that terrified him. He was a true modern man in his fear of anything bigger than himself.

In the London Illustrated News of Nov 8 or 15 GK has an article on modern psychology.[2] The copies at the college are withdrawn during vac so I can't send it to you—But he simply points out that an ornithologist studying a bird may appear to be a queer bird, but he does not identify himself with the goose that he chases. But in psych. the confusion arises from the fact that the thing which is being studied is also the thing studied. The psych. forgets that a man does know

[1]*Son of Woman: The Story of D.H. Lawrence* (1931) by John Middleton Murry (1889–1957).

[2]Towards the end of 1905 Chesterton began a weekly column, "Our Notebook", for the *Illustrated London News*, which he kept up (with interruptions) for thirty-one years. This article—which appeared on December 8, 1934—was prompted by Hugh Kingsmill's attempt at a psychological interpretation of Charles Dickens's life and works in *The Sentimental Journey* (1934).

some things about a man long before he is cloven in 2 and one 1/2 becomes a psych.ist and the other a psycol.al problem. When he plunges into the dark sea of the subconscious he forgets that there is such a thing as the broad daylight of human nature. You will remember Coleridge saying that "Shak keeps to the main highway of the human affections." GK continues: "It attributes an irrational talismanic power to single words and memories and wallows in the idea of wild things that appear in action without ever sans ever having passed through thought . . . I can suggest that GBS became a socialist economist because he nearly swallowed a penny when he was a child."[3]

So you have Xmas tests to attend to? Do you find it easier to assimilate the years work as a whole when it is not split by finals at Xmas? Here of course you write finals ("the tripos" it is called, and "collections" at Oxford) only at the end of your work, though there are preliminaries at the end of the 2nd year to give you an idea of your status.

I never know whether to write Dad in Wpg or not. I can't help but suppose he will be in Toronto before it reaches him—distance hath power to pervert the judgement—

Your letters are always welcome but do not consider my enjoyment of them an adequate reason for spending time at them which you can ill afford.

I expect the GK's [*Weekly*] to be kept carefully Red. You will find them very attractive I think. Marjorie does, and Al too, I expect. But I have heard from him but once. In describing the renovations at 507 he said our furnace "that old smoke signal" had been replaced. By the way, Marj. writes that Mrs Young has become a blushing bride and is now Mrs Keracher residing at Argyle.[4] Apparently there were infinite showers for her (even in November). I am delighted to hear of the event.

I should not recommend you to push your music for 2 or 3 years. The mental discipline and the enlarged capacity for enjoyment that 3 years of steady wayfaring amidst ideas and masterpieces, will give to you, will enable you to continue with more effect than if you spend limited time in too many pursuits.

Speaking of the internationalization of the radio GK. said that all this was possible when almost for the 1st time the nations had nothing to say. Many men have radios both in and out of college, but they confess that they are not thinking of a first.

Let me recommend to you the letters of Dorothy Osborne (1650–3).[5] I have only read them recently after having entertained the desire from the time I read Macaulay's account of her (she became the wife of Sir Wm Temple) in his essay

[3]In this passage Chesterton is writing about "the dim and groping new psychology, with its irrational talismanic power in single words or memories, or its wallowing in the idea of wild things that appear in action without having passed through thought. . . . I can suggest Bernard Shaw became a Socialist economist because he nearly swallowed a halfpenny when he was a child. . . ."

[4]Mrs Young was Herbert McLuhan's housekeeper.

[5]Dorothy Osborne (1627–95) married the statesman (Sir) William Temple (1628–99) in 1654; these letters, written to him between 1652 and 1654, were available in the Everyman's Library (1914).

on her husband.[6] They (the letters) illuminate a time just prior to [Samuel] Pepys, but belong to the world of the cavalier gentlemen. If you were thinking of a gift for Zelma they would prove very acceptable. They are neither long nor numerous, and may be had in Everyman. (They are love letters by the bye.)

You must also read some of Cobbett—see what the library has—His "Advice to Young Men" or his "Rural Rides" will prove extremely interesting.[7] His style is a marvel of unadorned grace and force. His attitude to life is that of the English yeomanry, of GKC and the Distributists.[8]

But Macaulay can teach you much, and especially has the power of showing history to be an affair of personalities rather than of vague tendencies and economic forces.

By the way, I have spent all my last £4 and £1 that I borrowed from Salt. But more, and how hard-earned it is I know, will be here soon, I expect.

I have a book on the Craft of Fiction [1921] by Percy Lubbock which I may send to you if I think it would be of use in your novel course Would that I had Rags here to lie by my fire. I enjoyed even the smell of him.

Well, I could write endlessly, but it would be pointless, just now, so au revoir mon frère,

As ever, Marshall

P.S. Induce Mother to send Dad *all* my letters if he is going to be "detained" any longer![9]

[6]"Sir William Temple", in the *Critical and Historical Essays of Thomas Babington Macaulay: Volume I* (Everyman's Library, 1907).

[7]*Advice to Young Men* (1829) and *Rural Rides* (1830) by William Cobbett (1763–1835).

[8]Distributism was an impractical political theory that advocated, among other things, that the nation's property, especially its land, should be distributed among the people and that the work of craftsmen in local workshops should replace mass production by industry. The Distributist League was founded in 1926 and Chesterton's *G.K.'s Weekly* became its official organ. (Its faltering subscription list was substantially increased thereby.) Chesterton's articles on Distributism in *G.K.'s Weekly* were collected in *The Outline of Sanity* (1926).

[9]Herbert McLuhan kept being "detained" from joining his wife in Toronto. Maurice McLuhan was living in the same rooming house on Selby Street as his mother.

To Elsie McLuhan

[Cambridge]
Monday [December 17, 1934] after lunch

Dear Mother:

It is good to know that you are enjoying the enviable society of Red and Rags. In some ways it would be difficult to conceive of two more deeply contrasted individuals. But, then, as you know, Browning has no more profound conviction than that of the absolute sanctity of human difference.

It is amusing to reflect that I got my cable from Dad some hours before you were awake, heaved a great sigh, and turned back to the glorious business of sleeping My previous failures did doubtlessly disgust me, but I saw wherein I was partly to blame in demanding to high a standard *from others*. It was a lesson in human nature and human weakness that may prove to have been timely and valuable. As for myself, I have too firm a conviction of my superiority, to do other than take "fortune's buffets and rewards with equal thanks!"[1] I am far too independent—so much so, that applause "deserved" means nothing and undeserved, it arouses my scorn.

Mr Odams has been suffering with a cold and Mrs Odams says she "misses her housemaid". He fetches my things in and out etc.

Had a lovely row to-day, and think to take a lunch and paddle about 12 miles down to Clay Hithe. Seven miles in an hour gives you 15 minutes of rest and is easy pulling.

I have just encountered a remark of T.S.Eliot that suggests returning sanity in the realm of human values.

> Poetry is a superior amusement: I do not mean an amusement for superior people. I call it an amusement, an amus[ement] pour distraire les honnêtes gens, not because that is a true definition, but because if you call it anything else you are likely to call it something still more false. If we think of the nature of amusement then, poetry is not amusing; but if we think of anything else that poetry may seem to be (eg., a criticism of life, a religion, moralizing, director of politics, etc) we are led into far greater difficulties[2]

For my part I confess I can enjoy poetry more when I go to it without thinking of all Shelley's rhapsodical claims for it. It falsifies the value of ordinary living to claim that all those who have never read a line of poetry are outcasts, unwashed and unregenerate. Let us consider it simply "as excellent words in excellent arrangement and excellent metre".[3] And if it comes to mean much more for *us* so much the better. But do not arrogate universality of sanction for a personal emotion. Faith, and it do not stand to reason.

Someone pulled out the plug and the Cam is almost dry to-day. So I cannot take my trip to Clay hithe.

Mrs Weeks replied very quickly and would appear to be an eminently satisfactory person. Her rates are *very* cheap for this country—1£ a week for bed and breakfast! I shall know where to go hereafter. But how I detest making such arrangements. Here, Mrs Robb has done the scouting for me.

Thurs 20 [December]
I am now installed with one of Odams married daughters, where I shall stay until Jan 2. Then I shall move back the few things I have brought before setting out

[1]"A man that fortune's buffets and rewards/Hast ta'en with equal thanks." *Hamlet*, III, ii, 72.
[2]T.S. Eliot, *The Sacred Wood* (1920), from the Preface to the 1928 edition, pp. viii–ix. The beginning of the third sentence correctly reads: "If we think of the nature of amusement, then poetry is not amusing; . . ." The parenthesis at the end is McLuhan's interpolation.
[3]Eliot, loc. cit., p. ix.

[on a bicycle trip] for Derbyshire. I am only a 1/4 mile from Odams and can get my mail very easily; while my new situation is exceedingly neat and agreeable.

I just remembered to send Aunt Ethel [McLuhan] a card and note. I had sent Pidgeon a card.[4]

My head is teeming with ideas for the GK article which will be written on a sudden shortly. I have kept jotting down separate notions as they came from all sorts of reading I have been at lately, so the longer it waits the better it will be. I intend to send it to the mgr of GK's Weekly before sending it to Canada, to have any criticism or suggestion he can offer. To be quite frank, I hope to use it as a means of meeting GK. Whatever else comes of it, cash or fame is dross.

If you want a whale of a novel to read, get his "Man Alive".[5]

The French progresses at the rate of 100 lines of [Molière's] Tartuffe a day. Would that I had an advanced grammar. I shall pick one up I expect.

Love for all of you
from Marshall

[4]Dr Edward Leslie Pidgeon (1873–1946) was a friend of Elsie McLuhan's while he was minister of St Augustine Presbyterian Church, Winnipeg (1915–25); he then became minister of Erskine United Church, Montreal, and Marshall visited him there on his way to Cambridge. He was the brother of Dr George C. Pidgeon, minister of Bloor Street United Church, Toronto (1915–48).

[5]G.K. Chesterton, *Manalive* (1912).

1935

To Elsie, Herbert, and Maurice McLuhan

[Cambridge]
8.30 PM Wed. Jan 16/35

Dear Mother Dad and Red:

Within one hour I have been 3rice blessed. 1. I heard GK for the 1st time on the wireless 2. I had read about 50 pages of the life of the wonderful (poet) Gerard Manley Hopkins (1844–89) when 3. the Xmas box arrived.[1] The latter was in excellent order and now contains, alas, somewhat less of its delicious contents. Everything in it is quite remarkably fresh, and is now in no danger of going stale. It was ever so welcome and a most *sensible* and joysome offering.

GK. reviews books over the B.B.C. fortnightly. He sounds like a wheezy old

[1]Perhaps *Gerard Manley Hopkins* (1930) by G.F. Lahey.

[2]Hill had been Marshall and Maurice McLuhan's Scoutmaster.

Colonel and often reminded me of Hill.² Every now and then, however, he seemed to annul the concentric pressure of the encircling and stifling flesh and then for a phrase or so came words in clear pleasing English. However the accent was exceedingly English—a fact for which I was prepared, but nonetheless disconcerting after having lived with him so long in a Canadian accent. I will always remember the shock I received when Emerson described Macaulay's voice as being English par-excellence. It was a great blow to think that I had read and worshipped him as tho he spoke perfectly good Canadian! Belloc notes many differences of rhythm and intonation between us, besides vowels *and* an incipient consonantal change. He says the American drops his voice at the end of phrases, and puts more syllables into his words, giving them a staccato metallic effect. Of course that is not new to you nor to me.

I enclose a clipping that might be interesting to keep. It is surely good news to think that strange pair will end their days in rather more easefulness. I hope he may live to enjoy it many years.

I expect my college account money will arrive in a day or so. They are exceedingly strict. Our Bursar is one of the nosiest, most officious, and detested would-be-tyrants in Cambridge. He is a study for Dickens.

The Latham prize subject this term is "Percy's Reliques" (that is a collection, of Old English Ballads). Even if I'm successful there is only £2 permitted to me. It is worth trying for, obviously. Moreover the Reliques are exceedingly interesting and pertinent to my studies.

Lectures commence to-morrow and so does the rowing. I'm in excellent condition.

Now I'm off to put this in to-nights post and then will commence the struggle to resist further onslaughts on the red-wrapped tin-box.

> Love for you all and Rags
> from Marshall

To Elsie McLuhan

> [Cambridge]
> Friday noon Jan 18[1935]

Dear Mother

I have just cabled, and was dreadfully sorry to have to do it. They are really quite strict, or appear to be. It occurred to me that I should send it to Dad, but his address would have cost about 3 shillings alone. I also thought you might be out of town, but I knew Red could wire Dad. You should have received The Bill before the New Year. I suspect you did not, and in any case there is no fault in the matter, except a regrettable lack of cash. I shall write Aunt Ethel very soon. Certainly, I think a loan the most sensible thing, and unavoidable. As it is the constant stress caused by my *heavy* expenses has been far too much already. I have forgotten whether Spence said this 2nd $200 was forthcoming early in Jan or Feb. I think the latter. I had intended to have him send it to you but don't remember doing so.

I received a very entertaining letter from Wheeler which I'll pass along to you when it is answered.

By the way I hope you did not discover anything abrupt in my omission to sign the cable. At 4½ d a word I did not see that "Love, Marshall" mattered. Perhaps I was wrong. Certainly I was if you didn't regard it in that light.

Salt and I are to receive supervision from Mr Angus in Greek Tragedy.[1] He is a classic don at the Hall and of visage and dimensions good to see. I make no doubt that he is a Scot, tho successfully metamorphosed. You see there is a Greek Tragedy section in our Tragedy paper.

Richards is conducting mass experiments in the criticism of prose extracts this term.[2] He hands out sheets with the extracts, and gives us 20 minutes. He produced a huge volume by this method using poems, and made the "great" discovery that nobody admired or was repelled from anything for any "good" reason. I have some doubts about the method of giving *one* poem of any person as a test. A really cultivated taste might hit the nail most all the time, but uncultivated people can enjoy many things in a *volume* by one writer, where the merits of his craft and ideas and feelings are permitted to permeate the consciousness from a 1000 different angles. Richards is a humanist who regards all experience as *relative* to certain conditions of life. There are no permanent, ultimate, qualities such as Good, Love, Hope etc. and yet he wishes to discover objective, ultimate[ly] permanent standards of criticism. He wants to discover those standards (what a hope!) in order to establish intellectualist culture as the only religion worthy [of] a rational being and in proportion to their taste for which all people are "full sensitive, harmonious personalities" or "disorganized, debased fragments of unrealized potentiality". When I see how people swallow such ghastly atheistic nonsense, I could join a bomb-hurling society.

I feel as badly as you about the silver-wedding gifts from 569.[3] They can't

---

[1]C.F. Angus was Classics Fellow of Trinity Hall.

[2]I.A. Richards (1893–1979), the Cambridge-educated authority on linguistics and co-founder of Basic English. (McLuhan took a course on the Philosophy of Rhetoric from him.) A Fellow of Magdalene College and Lecturer in the English Faculty, he left Cambridge for Harvard University in 1940 but returned in retirement. His *Practical Criticism: A Study of Literary Judgement* (1929) — based on the results of presenting unsigned poems to students and asking for their written comments— revolutionized the teaching and study of English literature. Richards is also associated with the New Criticism. Influenced in part by the writings of Ezra Pound and T.S. Eliot, it emphasized not the biographical/social background of a work, or its narrative organization, but an analysis of the text itself through its nuances of language and thematic organization. Other critics mentioned in these letters who practised some form of the New Criticism are F.R. Leavis and William Empson (a student of Richards) in England and Yvor Winters, Cleanth Brooks, and Allen Tate in the U.S. There is a letter to Richards on page 355.

[3]Elsie and Herbert McLuhan had recently attained their silver wedding anniversary but didn't want to mark it in any special way and did not want gifts, which Marjorie Norris's parents had given them. 569 was the street number of the Norris house.

afford it, and what's more have been buying wedding gifts at a frightful rate for some months past. They certainly finished up the year with a bang. I think, therefore, you must simply reconcile yourself to the idea of Marjorie as a daughter-in-law. It is the *least* you can do in return for a plethora of gifts.

Your "hunch" that I should inquire about certain matters for you is a subtle and belated reminder that I should have started long ago. It is reasonable that being on the spot I should be able to discover something useful. I shall set about it without delay. But surely June, July and August is not the most promising season—it is, however, true that there are many amateur theatricals in the summer. It is London that is "dead".

The sweater, knitted by Mrs C.,[4] was from Marjorie and with her photo was my Xmas present. Which reminds me of another puzzle. What happened to my calendars? Neither you nor the N's [Norrises] have acknowledged their receipt. But I am greatly relieved about the "Q" books.[5]

What a selfish old epicure is Rags! To think "Q" bored him! I'm sure if he could talk, he would have justified his preference for Red's bed in good anti-intellectualist terms.

I await word of the performance of As You Like It with real eagerness. What a chore it is to deal with such material. Perhaps it is less trying than attempting to satisfy a crowd of egocentric professional actors, however.

The French paper is being dealt with this term by [Jack] Roach of the French faculty. He has started with Molière. What a treat it is simply to follow the text as he reads it in French. I'm sure I could pick up a great deal that way. Each day the privative sense of incompleteness due to not having Greek and Latin grows in me. It is hard for one like me, so deeply interested in the roots and beginnings of things, to be without means of access to the great fount and reservoir of our own civilization. I am determined however to master French.[6]

How rapidly my ideas have been shifting and rearranging themselves to make room for others! My difficulty is to keep up with myself. I can see that I would perhaps have done better to have taken History to teach, not only because my faculty is scarcely literary, but because English Literature is a foreign literature, more alien to America and Canada every day. I have long said that, but can I now see the *how* and *why*. It is quite as alien as French and I shall always teach it from that assumption and so save many younkers[7] the rude awakenings consequent upon glib acceptance of officially encouraged and systematic hypocrisy.

I have so much to do, and so must leave this for now, and send my warmest love to all

Marshall.

[4]Perhaps a relative of Marjorie Norris.

[5]McLuhan had sent calendars home for Christmas. He also sent a set of small books by Quiller-Couch that for a time appeared to be lost.

[6]McLuhan never became orally fluent in French, though he learned to read it well.

[7]"younker" is an archaic word (originally Dutch or German) for "young gentleman" from which "youngster" developed.

To Elsie, Herbert, and Maurice McLuhan

[Cambridge] Thurs. Jan 24/35

Dear Mother and Dad and Red

Old "Q" hasn't come into action yet but Ernest de Selincourt delivered his 6th lecture on Wordsworth to-day.[1] It is increasingly clear to me that Wordsworth was little more than an English and poetical Rousseau. We feel vaguely dissatisfied with his whole treatment of life and things simply because his basic assumptions in those matters were equally queer. He supposed mankind not only *good* but infinitely potential.

My nose is almost without a symptom and is fast clearing up. I shall commence rowing Monday—But it is time, time time, here. Forbes referred rather slightingly to Ruth Draper this morning. I must sound him in the matter—not for his personal opinion alone but for others'. He also referred to Chesterton thus: "You have seen him haven't you? Why he isn't adult." Now Forbes is of course a "broadminded" modern sceptic who has put his shirt on psychoanalysis. Personally I would prefer the hickory bush.

To-night I went to Angus for supervision in Euripides. Salt didn't turn up and we drifted into a 100 channels of discussion. He is a Baptist clergyman of the modernist wing and a few years ago made a lecture tour of the Canadian Baptist Theological colleges, including Brandon. We had an interesting time. By the way he says the atmosphere of Acadia is pleasant, unAmerican (the rest of Canada he thot quite American) but stagnant. I have borrowed some books from him— modern novels! With ancient Greek settings.

Tuesday night I saw Jew Suss.[2] It is quite worth seeing but very much intended for too wide a taste. Veidt isn't given a fair chance for his powers at all. Of course it is pure propaganda.

By the way when this reaches you my pocket money will be quite gone I can always put off Odam's wee bills. I dont quite know about the college account or whether you got my cable.—ie whether you were in town. It is such a pity. I have written Aunt Ethel recently, and have Kirkc[onnell], Spence, Wheeler and others to deal with right away.

Mrs Norris sent me a very nice letter indeed, and sends me regularly more of the [Winnipeg] Free Press than I have time to read.

In talking to Potts[3] about a Phd (he is the head of the board of post grad. studies) he thought I could get credit on my MA for one year's research and

---

[1]Ernest de Selincourt (1870–1943), a Wordsworth scholar, had been professor of poetry at Oxford (1928–33) and was at this time editing *The Letters of William and Dorothy Wordsworth* (6 vols, 1933–9).

[2]*Jew Süss* (1934), a British-made film starring Conrad Veidt—directed by Lothar Mendes and based on a novel, *Jud Süss* (1925), by Leon Feuchtwangler—was a satire on the pointlessness of race distinctions.

[3]Professor L.J. Potts was a Fellow of Queen's College and a specialist in Restoration comedy. McLuhan took a course from him on English Satire.

would have to spend one year here after graduation and one more where I liked—if satisfactory facilities were available. But he did recommend 2 years for the tripos. Had I finished the French before coming up, and not looked at rowing etc. it might have been feasible. As it is, it is not.[4]

Now to post this with all speed
and, love from Marshall

[4]McLuhan did take the tripos at the end of his second year.

To Elsie, Herbert, and Maurice McLuhan
[Cambridge, February 1?, 1935]

Dear Mother, Dad and Red

You will be interested to hear that my weight has disregarded the previous restriction of 145 and risen to 151 (stripped). Ordinarily I do not weigh myself, since the result varies so little and the facts at best are so unpleasant. It is a fact which increases my pleasure in rowing. The weather has returned to its preternatural pleasantness. When a cold day occurs everyone seems quite cheery and calls it "more seasonable". That is using the word properly.

As a handbook on Philosophy with especial regard to its historical development I strongly commend Maritain's "Introd. to Phil." to you Red.[1] He is the greatest living French thinker and is one of the foremost students and interpreters of Aquinas. Like most French texts it is a marvel of lucidity and order. I have read or dipped into numerous histories (all of which supposed Augustine and Aquinas were spoofers) and which therefore misunderstood everything that happened in society and philosophy after them. It is for his sympathy in this matter, as well as his general account that I recommend him to you as certain to prove most coherent and stimulating. Lodge[2] is a decided Platonist and I learned [to think] that way as long as I was trying to interpret Christianity in terms of comparative religion. Having perceived the sterility of that process, I now realize that Aristotle is the soundest basis for Xian doctrine.

It is most gratifying that we have a well-equipped English library—I speak of the one separate from the Big library which probably contains all extant Literature—the day that a new book comes off the press it appears in our library, provided it is related to the English faculty. It is difficult to exaggerate the importance of having recent, and even ephemeral, thought and expression beside the enduring pieces of the past. Not only does it awaken the comparing and judging faculties, but it teaches the necessity of constantly new expression and interpretation of old truth. There is scarcely a member of the English faculty who has not written several books on standard themes in our Lit. There is the

[1]*Introduction to Philosophy* (1932), by Jacques Maritain (1882-1973), translated by E.I. Watkins. For Maritain, see page 137, note 9.

[2]Professor Rupert Lodge (1886-1961), head of the Department of Philosophy, University of Manitoba.

other danger, of course, and it is one that has overtaken most people of the "intellectual" variety in England—the neglect of direct acquaintance with their literature. They can scarcely keep up with books *about* these books.

My position in regard to English Literature is altering rapidly. I have discovered that having in previous courses sampled numerous bits of it, I came to certain conclusions about them which really discouraged a further expansion of interest. I have discovered the utmost reluctance to open Keats or Shakespeare, partly because a growing dissatisfaction tells me not where to begin, but largely because of an unconscious reluctance to disturb my previous judgements about them. I have recently, in this new atmosphere, dissolved the old incrusted opinions (even where they were "correct" but none the less sterilizing) and obtained a fresh receptivity which is the thing most difficult to maintain in America. I had thought that I at least was not being victimized by our insane methods of abstracting certain men from the living context of English history and considering them as classics per se. I had not escaped, though would have done in later life, I hope. But I can see most clearly *why* the obtaining of a degree in America means literally the *end* of education. It is simply because the mode of presenting any matter oversimplifys it, so that when a young mind has dwelt on it for a very limited time, its possibilities are exhausted for him. Willy nilly, his "education" is finished. He has a set of clearly defined conceptions about everything he has studied and is left with the curious impression (I felt it myself) that if in later life he should desire to improve the use of his leisure by re-reading Wordsworth, the best way would be to start by re-reading the succinct and "accurate" (too accurate) remarks taken down in notes as an undergraduate.

Once more the gigantic training dinners are being bolted by us rowin men. The disadvantage is that the table is exclusively reserved for us, and there is a consequent limitation of one's company

I have practically all the work yet to do for the Latham [Prize] and have only to-day and to-morrow. In reading some of the exquisite parodies and skits of Max Beerbohm I met this image in a blank verse play on Savonarola.

> I thought I was of sterner stuff . . .
> Lo! My soul's chin recedes, soft to the touch
> As half-churned butter. Seeming hawk is dove,
> And dove's a gaol-bird now. Fie out upon't![3]

Now to the instant task—with love

Marshall

[3]From Act IV of the short play "Savonarola" in the parody "'Savonarola' Brown", included in *Seven Men* (1917), a collection of stories by Max Beerbohm (1872–1956).

To Elsie, Herbert, and Maurice McLuhan

[Cambridge]
Tuesday 11 PM [February 5, 1935]

Dear Mother Dad and Red:

I went to a flick to-night after Hall. The Latham test was held from 5 till 7.45 I messed it up rather badly. Just couldn't do anything about it. I was rowing till 3.30 and cramming from 4 till 5. I left the reading till a bit too late. However it was certainly not wasted time. The picture[1] to-night was German—based on an actual episode of 1906 when a poor down-trodden persecuted pillar-to-post ex-convict bought an officer's uniform, commandeered a troup of soldiers, entrained them to Copenek and arrested the mayor and his secretary. The world rocked with laughter. You will prob. recall the incident. Odams did. But what a country! What a drab-soulled lot of bureaucrats!

Wednesday
Wow! but Ive a lot to do. Had a fine letter from Tom [Easterbrook] to-day. It did me good. Then, the $200 came too. I had to cash it with the £ [note] at 491 when it was 478 a short time ago. The check should have been turned into pounds before being sent on under those conditions.

I have had 2 letters from you Red and will write you about Plato and Arist[otle] in a day or two. Plato was of course a Puritan in his artistic views [,][2] and his philosophy when fully developed as by the 15th cent Augustinian monks (of whom Luther was one) leads definitely to the Calvinist position.[3]

The weather has been mild but uncertain of late—a great gale whipped up the Cam this afternoon and we shipped considerable water. Due to constant changes, illness, etc. our crew has been steadily worsening—so we don't anticipate the races with any pleasure. They commence on the 20th I believe.

The arms on the knocker which I sent are the Hall arms—the crescent on a shield. In reading the Reliques I learnt that they are the same as the arms of the Percy (Hotspur etc) family.[4] Of course they derive from the Crusading days. I must attempt to discover the connection in the matter of the arms.

I must give you another snatch from Max Beerbohm's "Seven Men". They are all figures of the Art for Art's Sake 90's.

[1]*Der Hauptmann von Köpenick* (The Captain from Köpenick), 1931, based on the comedy (1931) by Carl Zuckmayer (1896–1977).

[2]In certain of Plato's *Dialogues* all figures and images, including works of art, are said to be falsehoods because they deceive people by giving the appearance of being real. For McLuhan this brought to mind the suppression of art by the Puritans.

[3]The thread of influence may be indicated as follows. The doctrine (*anamnesis*) that the truth is remembered from another life and is therefore within us was held by Plato and developed, by way of Neo-Platonism, by Augustine: if truth = God, then God is within us; the belief that God is within the elect is central to Calvin.

[4]There is no resemblance between the arms of Trinity Hall (Sable, a crescent within a border ermine) and those of the Percy family (Or, a lion azure; ancient: azure, a fesse of five fusils or).

"Milton had a dark insight." [And again,] "I can always read him in the reading-room."

"The Reading-room?"

"Of the British Museum. I go there everyday".

"You do? I've only been there once. I'm afraid I found it a rather [rather a] depressing place. It—it seemed to sap one's vitality."

"It does. That's why I go there. The lower one's vitality the more sensitive one is to great art. . . . "

This person published a book of poems and Max "gives" us one or 2 of them:

To a Young Woman

Thou art, who hast not been!
    Pale tunes irresolute
    and traceries of old sounds
    Blown from a rotted flute
Mingle with the noise of cymbals rouged with rust,
Nor not strange forms and epicene
    Lie bleeding in the dust,
    Being wounded with wounds.
      For this it is
    That in thy counterpart
      Of age-long mockeries
    Thou hast not been nor art![5]

Max has a most delicate sense of atmosphere and can create minor marvels in that kind, with words. I say minor, partly because of the attention he attracts, quite consciously, to the words themselves, and partly because he understands the most effective sphere for exercising his Talent.

Now for a word about your play Mother: I was very proud to think about it and hope it establishes you more solidly, and higher, among the hoighty-toighty Torontonians. $100 will be very welcome, no doubt, but scarcely commensurate with your labours. I shall speak to Forbes about Ruth Draper to-morrow,[6] having been absent from his lectures for some time.

Marjorie's 14th scarf was addressed to me—It is fawn with black for a cross pattern—a very nice bit of work I think.

I fear I must not spend any more time writing about so little.

With love for all—Marshall

P.S. Had also a note from Yuill[7] who hopes to get over here next year. Did you know Prof Perry etc is coming this summer? Bill Jones has sent me nothing I have sent him 2 cards—not a letter as far as I remember. He phoned Marjorie when he was home at Xmas.

---

[5]From "Enoch Soames", included in Beerbohm's *Seven Men*.

[6]Ruth Draper (1884–1956), an American actress who performed dramatic monologues that she herself wrote and whose many tours in the United States, England, Canada, and elsewhere made her internationally famous. McLuhan's mother, herself a monologuist, was naturally very much interested in her.

[7]George Yuill Loughead was a friend of McLuhan's at the University of Manitoba.

To Elsie, Herbert, and Maurice McLuhan

[Cambridge]
Thursday 10.30 PM
Feb 7/35

Dear Mother, Dad, Red:

Having just returned from the Divinity School where "Q" recommenced his course on The Poetic[s] of Aristotle, I wish to set down certain facts while they are fresh. There was just one other chap with me and so we were able to be a very chatty trio. The Poetics were soon side-tracked when illustrating the theory of the punctum indifferens in Shakespeare—ie. the idea that in all art there is a point of rest in the midst of surrounding conflict. Horatio in Hamlet[,] Kent in Lear etc. The last led us to ask whether the fool played a similar part in maintaining the salutory mean of sense and sanity. Then "Q" gave us a "frantic" (he called it, and justly) theory about the fool in Lear. He appears only when Cordelia is off stage (both parts prob. acted by some boy "star")[.] he brings missives from Cordelia, and when Lear holds the dead Cordelia in his arms he calls her "my poor fool" (or sumpin like it) The idea is that Kent is in on the secret. When the fool meets the wild "Tom O Bedlam" Edgar he goes quite hysterical etc. We had a lot of fun mauling this idea. Before leaving I asked "Q" if he had ever met Meredith—Yes he had spent an afternoon with him.[1] The Sunday after the performance of Barrie's 1st play, "Q", Barrie and Conan Doyle entrained for Box Hill. Barrie had *all* the papers and was reading the accounts of his plays [*sic*]. Meredith had not lost the use of his legs at that time (it must have been in the late 90's [*sic*]) and walked around his garden with "Q" "teaching" him a lot. At dinner "Q" was engaged in conversation with M's daughter, and shielded her from her fathers wrath when he saw that she had *cut*! flowers for the dinner table. Meredith was occupied in illustrating Napoleon's campaigns to Doyle with knives forks and salt cellars. He said M had exquisite manners. Leslie Stephen turned up, having lost his return ticket to London (no great matter for that stalwart hiker) "Q" said he has a number of letters from M.

Now I'm for bed.

Feb. 8.

I omitted to say that "Q" overheard Meredith singing snatches of an Italian opera. If I go any further I shall become snobbish.

I was surprised (genuinely) and elated in an amused fashion to learn that I had won the Latham [Prize] again. (£2) I had, I am still certain, written very badly. I shall not buy all my books at once.

---

[1]The following anecdote of Quiller-Couch concerns the novelist George Meredith (1828–1909); Sir James Barrie (1860–1937) and his first play *Richard Savage*, which was first performed in 1891; the novelist Sir Arthur Conan Doyle (1859–1930); and Sir Leslie Stephen (1832–1904), a man of letters who was a friend of Meredith's (and the father of Virginia Woolf).

[In margin of 1st page]
Wednesday night I went with Bowen to the Festival to see Tchekov's "Seagull", a typically Slav drama, full of mystic wryness and poignancy *and* symbolism. It was very good entertainment however.

I "sat in" to hear Prof A E Housman lecturing on the Odes of Horace this morning.[2] He is the author of Shropshire Lad etc. His outer semblance doth (somewhat) belie his soul's immensity. He is small and lightly made—a smallish high head unadorned by hair—a smooth sweep of pale delicate-skinned cheek—a white (not wide) moustache He speaks quietly with remarkable clarity of tone and precision of phrase. His lectures are notorious for their dry ruthless scholarship and attention to text. Tell Tom that I shall not only find out about C.R. Fay but go to hear him (He lectures in Economic History)[3]

Angus told Salt and myself an amusing story about [A.W.] Verrall, the great classical don of the last generation. He was Trinity lecturer and used to lecture the hour after [R.C.] Jebb the prof. of the dept. He would attend Jebb's lecture (there was a classical don in Housman's [lecture] writing shorthand this morning) and listen to Jebbs division and destruction of a play of Euripides. Then addressing his own class (largely the same as Jebb's) he would say: "You have heard Prof Jebb say that the Antigone falls into two parts utterly uncorrelated? I will ask you to believe with me (speaking in a treble ending in an inarticulate scream) that he is wrong!" Then followed a ruthless analysis.

I spoke about Ruth Draper to Forbes. He said she jammed her houses in London Oxf and Camb.—That she made a mistake in attempting to perform in a large room (when she did). But that her ability to hold an audience for 2 hours he considered very remarkable. He said she was effective in light pieces but quite unsatisfying in serious numbers. This may prove useful to you. I am sure that the English would revolt at Jim and John—I dont know about the Leetle Red C.—because they are ashamed of emotion, tho far from unemotional.[4] They love [Stephen] Leacock They like impersonations—would appreciate Negro and French Canad. numbers. Forbes was impressed by Ruth D's capacity to present "two or three different people" (consecutively). I must find out some more. A couple of my cattle-boat friends (Bruce Marshall of Regina stud. agricult at Oxford) are descending upon me Sunday and want me to Cicerone them a bit. It will do me good, because I have learnt very little about the colleges as yet.

Richard's read aloud my (annonymous) comments on one of his "prose passages for practical criticism" to-day, with approval. He reads many and much

[2]A.E. Housman (1859–1936), author of *A Shropshire Lad* (1896), had been appointed professor of Latin at Cambridge in 1911.

[3]Professor C.R. Fay, of King's College, specialist in economic history and the Co-operative Movement.

[4]Two of Elsie McLuhan's "numbers": "Jim and John" was a sentimental poem, of unknown authorship, about two brothers; "The Red Canoe" is a poem by William Henry Drummond (1854–1907), whose dialect verse dealing with French-Canadian *habitant* life was very popular at the turn of the century and later (the phrase "leetle red canoe" recurs).

fun we have at the expense of various unknowns. Went to tea with Wade[5] where he produced a notorious Communist organizer of St Johns. We had a whale of a time and Wade was hugely entertained. Then I went with him to Mr Loke's rooms (a wealthy Chinese) and we played ping pong. Now I shall attempt to give Red a few hints for his essay. Oh yes, anent the engravings: I got them from Whitaker and wish one to be sent on to Marjorie—They are well worth 3/6 apiece and the Hall is a rare subject. Keep whichever you prefer.

You will be pleased to hear that I got a very good shirt—at least $2.50 in Canada—for 5 bob. I shall get plus four socks etc right away.

[Ends here. Additional page(s) missing?]

[5]Donald William Wade (b.1904), a fellow student. Later a solicitor and a Liberal MP (1950-64), he became Lord Wade in 1964 when he was made a Life Peer.

To Elsie McLuhan

[Cambridge]
Friday A.M. Feb 22 [1935]

Dear Mother:

It has been much too long since I wrote to you—but what a life it is during the Lent bumping races! This is the 3rd day—to-morrow is the 11th and last race. Any crew making 4 bumps (and ipso facto going up 4 places) is presented with its oars. We have made 2 bumps—the 1st easily, the second (due to our excitement and initial demoralisation) with more difficulty. The next two, if made, will be even harder, since the crews are better, the higher they are in the division.

Our practice is to lunch together in one of the men's rooms at the Hall—this has the disadvantage of producing incipient hysteria and unrestrainable prophetic optimism. We then go to the boat house at 1.30 and paddle down (3 miles) to our starting positions. It is awful waiting for the 4 minute, the one minute and the final guns—simply awful. The boats are spaced only 150 feet apart and so a good start means a great deal

It was a rare bit of luck for our crew to get in the Times. That sheet is worth keeping, I'm thinking. Unfort. our stroke and cox are excluded and you can see how close a call I had.[1] The picture was taken about 5 seconds before we bumped the Fitzbilly rigger. At the moment the picture was taken I happened to be the only man in a rowing position—not that I always am!—but the others are simply ludicrous. We make up in strength what we lack in ease and rhythm.

Did I tell you the books I ordered with the Latham money?

Yeats' Collected Poems

[1]The Stroke is the oarsman sitting at number 8 in the boat, at the stern end, who sets the time for the other oarsmen; the Cox (coxswain) is the short man who steers the boat and shouts instructions to the crew. McLuhan won an oar for this bumping race—a trophy that he kept and prized.

> Keats' Letters (2 vols)
> Jonson's Plays 2 vols
> Ezra Pound's XXX Cantos
> Fowler's The King's English—(Grammar & usage)
> Eliot's Collected Poems

I had only 40 shillings credit of course—cash is not given.

I was much amused by Mrs Odams' elaborate epistle—no doubt you appreciated the shrewd analysis of my character, and the subtle sidelights thrown thereon.

I have been neglecting lectures this week, but enjoyed reading [J.M.] Synge's plays and produced a fairly decent essay for Elvin.

It was good to hear of you enjoying yourself at the "As You Like It" party. You did send me a programme right enough.

Thanks so much for the 5 pounds. I shall deposit it, right away, now having an account.

I heard from Ed and Herman[2] recently and received the London address of their brother Charles.

Ask Red to send me Moliere's Tartuffe[,] Racines Athalie, Beaumarchais' "Marriage [*sic*] de Figaro" if any of them are among Joe Hilts French books.

I must read French hard this vac, but will wait till summer to visit France. I think 2 weeks in Oxford (studying and scrounging about could be done *very* cheaply)

I have been trying to write some articles—heavens what happens to time here—it is telescoped, annihilated.

Lovingly Marshall

[2]Ed and Herman Robeneck, who were Russian-born, had made friends with McLuhan in the summer of 1931 when he sailed his boat off the Fort Rouge shore of the Red River.

To Elsie McLuhan

[Cambridge]
Sunday [24 February 1935]

Dear Mother:

Well Ross Pratt[1] was able to discover for you only so much as is written on this card. There is nothing helpful thereon—just the usual pessimism of a 3rd rate professional.

Now regarding the races—Friday we chased Clare [College] the whole way with about a 1/4 length between us—we lost a length or more at the start. It was a gruelling time. Our stroke was not very well and we were ∴ unable to pick up our time sufficiently to catch them early.

[1]Ross Pratt (b. 1916), Winnipeg-born concert pianist and teacher who studied at the Royal Academy of Music, London, from 1934 to 1939, the year he made his recital debut at Wigmore Hall.

Nobody had fully recuperated yesterday and we had Jesus V[2] behind us who had been improving every day. However we hoped to get Clare early. (The crew we had chased the day before) It so happened that there was a poor crew in front of them yesterday and they caught them before we could get them. We, enfeebled after our spurt suddenly saw Jesus V swoop down upon us at Grassy,[3] and our labours were o'er. Had we had a heavy head wind yesterday we would have got Clare easily (our crew is best in a gale) and the crew in front of them were nothing at all. However it was a great time.

There was a banquet after Hall for which we dressed and wore our blazers (mine is well cut and will be must [*sic*] serviceable with my cream flannels. The Boat Club blazer is cream with black edges. The dinner cost 7/6 and was not worth it I assure you. There were speeches some of which achieved a length of several phrases ending with a toast to something or other. Our coach sent us each a pint of champagne and 3 of us shared a bottle of Moselle wine. I was not sufficiently affected even to forget that I was very tired. After much scrawling on one another's menus we sallied forth to Jesus grounds where they were burning an eight, to celebrate their retention of the headship of the river. Our 1st boat got out of the 2nd division into the 1st again.

I have returned from my 1st attendance at the University Sermon (2.30 PM) in Great St. Mary's.[4] Guess who I went to hear! The grim old Dean Inge and no other![5] I sat in the gallery, not 20 feet from him. The 2 proctors sat below me in full dress. They came in each bearing a large volume suspended from their hands by a brass chain—the rules and reg.s of the Univ. I believe. It is the custom of each don to stand with his head bowed into his cap before seating themselves in their upholstered pews.

Inge has a high voice and speaks not too carefully—often dropping a syllable. His face is an expressionless mask of stern lineaments and unpleasant texture. His sermon (40 mins) was on St Pauls title to be considered orthodox. He scouted the idea that Paul was ever executed. He read what he himself had written for he often hesitated over his hand-writing.

I shall write Spence using the poor old Dean as a theme—Have written an article "Distributism[6] and Communism" for a new Cambridge fortnightly "Apes and Angles [*sic*]."

Ever so much love

for you all

from Marshall

---

[2]The fifth boat of Jesus College.

[3]On the Cam, about a mile and a half downriver from the boat-houses.

[4]St Mary the Great, the University church.

[5]W.R. Inge (1860–1954), Dean of St Paul's Cathedral, was first called "the gloomy dean" by the *Daily Mail* in 1911 for his pessimistic view of society.

[6]See page 46, note 8.

To Elsie, Herbert, and Maurice McLuhan

[Cambridge, February 27, 1935]

Dear Mother and Dad and Red:

I received word from the 3rd person of this trinity which shall be duly answered. The 2nd person has told of office broils between Beill and Weir. The first person blandly asks if I shall be rowing against Oxford. I can only retort that though I am not (and will not) [be] in the Varsity 8 I am in the Times. I'll swear many would pay the amount of my expenses to appear on the same sheet even in dishabille [*sic*]. And as for the concomitant sounds of the bumping race Noyes (noise) is not adequate. It is a case of "the eight bravely rowing beneath the roar of the guns" and the splash of excited folk who insist upon riding their bikes into the river.

It is indeed amusing to think of Rags, the one-man hound, aloof, stoic, arrogant, now subsiding into the veriest sop for gentle attentions. I, who have never set myself so rigorous and simple a code as he followed, yet hope to avoid the abyss of itch-scratch bliss.

The other evening I called on Mr R.L. Russell[1] of Christs after I had learnt that he was the 3rd subscriber to GK's in this town. He is about 30, and has his Phd in Agriculture. He hopes to take up a post at Oxford very shortly. We had a very interesting time talking over the prospects and possibilities (2 widely diff. things, unfort.) of subsistence farming in England. Great Britain is now 40% self-sufficing and could easily be made 80% [ditto marks = self-sufficing], he says, by small proprietor cultivation. Large scale cultivation, he says, is only less productive than it is ugly and degenerating.

I wrote a paper comparing Racine's Athalie with [Milton's] Samson Agonistes which I discussed with Elvin this week. I have been working at a couple of articles for "Apes and Angles [*sic*]" a new college magazine. Heaven's how the time disappears.

I was fairly bowled over by discovering that the Boat Club banquet had cost 9/6. It is a grotesque figure for what we were given

Heard GK on the wireless again to-night. Will turn to the completion of my article on him as soon as term ends. If it is accepted I will feel impelled to further essays and efforts.

To-night we had Ernst Freud, (the son of the notorious Viennese Jewish psychologist) at the Hesperides. He is an architect and his theme was "mod arch. in Eng—question mark." He is a consistent functionalist himself, placidly accepting modern materialism as the basis of his craft. He told some good stories—1st in apologizing for his English he told of a Czech football team that toured England with considerable success. Its captain was the mayor of the town from which they came and was exceedingly proud of his English. At a banquet held for them one night he made an oratorical effort to which the English captain replied as

---

[1]A.G. Russel in the Diary (though the name is spelled with two l's both here and in the letter of May 16).

follows: "We have long admired the Czechs as sportsmen, and held their country in high regard for its colourful and various achievements. But there is now another bond which may be said to unite us for your speech is in some respects not unlike English."

Freud said "I had the misfortune to be interviewed by a journalist on arriving in England. After explaining my views with care I read in the paper "Psycho-Architect would revolutionize architecture" The "psycho" being a glance at his paternity.

One of many remarks was that recent architecture is attempting to break down the division between the house and the out-of-doors by means of the new sort of doors and windows. The idea of the house as centred around the hearth was gone. Central heating makes people more interested in windows—

Love for all Marshall

To Elsie McLuhan

[Cambridge]
Thursday March 7/35

Dear Mother:

I have pondered your observation that I "am not the John Bull type" with a great deal of relish. In point of fact, I had suspected as much for some time past. Perhaps more interesting still is, that John Bull isn't either. The figure of John Bull is the burly front behind which the subtle, arrogant, Englishman, shame-facedly conceals a poetic and sentimental nature.

To-day has been very full—I took 4 lectures—have been attending many to make up for those I missed during the week of the Races. At four Chib, my Hindu friend and Wade and Salt came up for tea. I had tea cakes and buns, and Mrs Odams (who lends me her best china) provided me with a fresh sponge cake and macaroons. With much gusto I produced my new 7lb tin of Jamaica honey—we heard much about India and the English methods of ensuring the degradation and "loyalty" (to Britain) of the Princes. They are taken from their homes at the age of 7 and kept in special British schools for 10–12 years. Here they are carefully taught and encouraged in the pursuit of golf cricket and women. They are taught a cooked version of English history and none of their own. Chib says that there are only 4 (of 100's) princes who would retain their position if the British army was withdrawn for a week.

At 7 I met Hugh Lane[1] at the Hall and we went to the Waffle for supper—it is a modern "antique shoppe" done in Dutch style—Here I actually had maple syrup on my waffles. Thence to the Cosmop where "Reka" (Young Love) a splendid

---

[1]Hugh Lane (b. 1914), a fellow student at Trinity Hall who entered the Indian Civil Service and then became Bursar of Rossall School, Fleetwood, Lancashire (1950–75). He and McLuhan kept in touch and last met in 1974 at Eric McLuhan's wedding in England.

Czech film of modern peasant life [was playing].[2] It is set amidst beautiful valley scenes, and is miles from the mushy unconcocted emotional sprawling that the title might suggest. The film standards of the continent are much higher than English or American standards. The screen is seriously regarded as a new artistic genre with laws and possibilities of its own.

I have been deeply impressed by Epsteins newly exhibited statue of Christ. It is "Ecce Homo".[3] The intense and terrible nature of the expression strikes first. (after the early novelty and grotesqueness has been surmounted) The body is puny and passive. All attention is directed to the face, to the eyes the mouth and chin. The head is very broad and low, the eyes strained with indescribable anguish and meaning—the nose long and powerful, the lips heavy and protuberant, the chin as broad as the chest, calmly asserting that "all things are given unto me". The low, broad, head expresses limitless power and practical intensity. The mouth is not simply revolting as it would be in the face of man. But set in a face of such unbelievable power and profundity it is a voluminous commentary on the text "tempted in all things as we were". It is not a negro but a Hindu mouth. At least it is common to the features of the majority of the Hindus in Cambridge (there are 9000 in Great Britain but only 125 here! You would swear the place was overrun by them) Set this great interpretation beside the figure of Bhudda. Those idols of a philosopher-god, who treated the flesh as a disease to be exterminated, display a hideous hill of flesh surmounted by an expression of sickly placidity. I do not believe that Epstein has done justice to his subject; but mere audacity and unfeeling agnosticism could not produce such a deeply stirring figure. It is worth all the sermons preached since the sermon on the mount. It should be enough to erect each several hair upon the heads of infinite clergymen and christians who have "offered their complacency to Christ".

It is an amazing fact that Will Rogers[4] is as unknown here as Ripley.[5] His "Handy Andy" is advertised as "the humorous wit and wisdom of Handy Andy"—his name does not appear! The average Englishman moves at a level of taste and feeling which often make me think that he has not only made the industrial revolution but deserves it. However, I am judging England by the 6th generation of the trodden victims of a hideous tyranny. Another side of the picture may be seen in our new Combination Room,[6] where, in sharp contrast to any possibility of

[2]The Cosmopolitan was a cinema specializing in foreign and experimental films. The title of the Czech film *Reka* (1934) means literally "The River".

[3]In his diary entry for this day, immediately after mentioning having seen *Reka*, McLuhan wrote: "Am much interested in Epstein's 'Ecce Homo'." So it seems as though he saw it in a newsreel. This large stone sculpture by (Sir) Jacob Epstein (1880–1959)—an impression of Christ, known also as "Behold the Man" (1935)—was displayed at the Leicester Galleries, London, in March 1935. Though it received much abusive criticism, as well as appreciation by a few art critics, it is considered the strongest of all Epstein's large stone carvings.

[4]Will Rogers (1879–1935), popular American comedian of stage and screen who adopted the persona of a cowboy philosopher to deliver homespun satirical comments on life.

[5]Robert L. Ripley (1893–1949), American cartoonist and radio personality who syndicated "Believe It or Not", a popular newspaper feature that presented amazing facts in cartoon form.

[6]The Junior Combination Room (Common Room).

such a thing in America, good manners and easy conversation and humour prevail. A man may (often does) order coffee for his friends to be served before the fire—(there is a fire in each end of the room—good rugs and deep chairs—oak panelling and beams)—Think of great burly rugby men relaxing over a cup of tea in America! Squash is a favourite game here.

H N Brailsford—a noted socialist—addressed the Hesperides on Voltaire, last Wednesday. He has just completed a book [*Voltaire*, 1935] on the subject (Home Univ. Library). His talk was rotten. He has simply gone stale on the subject, and has not read around it further than his Marxist interests have led him to do.

Enjoyed Red's last letter which I will answer in a week. Term ends Friday! I have done much more this term and written fewer letters. I am reminded by a deal of reading to abbreviate this one. Will you please send it (with the enclosed clippings) to Marjorie who can pass it on to Dad. Perhaps it would be best to reverse that order.

Love for you all from
Marshall.

P.S. Had such a jolly letter from Aunt Ethel.

To Elsie, Herbert, and Maurice McLuhan

[Cambridge]
Sunday 11 PM
March 30 [31, 1935]

Dear Mother, Dad, and Red

It is very inspiriting to read these words from the pen of the greatest English-speaking poet and the clearest-headed critic of literature writing in our time (T.S. Eliot):

> What chiefly remains of the new freedom is its meagre impoverished emotional life; in the end it is the Christian who can have the more varied, refined and intense enjoyment of life; which time will demonstrate. . . . [p. 10] The World is trying the experiment of attempting to form a civilized but non-Christian mentality. The experiment will fail, but we must be very patient in awaiting its collapse; meanwhile redeeming the time: so that the faith may be preserved alive through the dark ages before us; to renew and rebuild civilization, and save the world from suicide. [p. 32][1]

How much more courageous realistic and honest to say "the dark ages before us", than to gibber cravenly in Wellsian fashion of vulgar Utopias. Eliot is an Anglo-Catholic.

Monday night [April 1]. Late last night I commenced "The Turn of the Screw" [1898] by Henry James—a comparatively short story of indescribable horror

[1]T.S. Eliot, *Thoughts After Lambeth* (1931).

and loathesomeness. It is a tale of how two small children, angelic, beautiful, precocious, become obsessed by 2 foul spirits. Everything is wrapped in terrible vagueness, and the hints of diabolical cleverness. Another tale which I have just set down is "Juan in America" [1930] by Eric Linklater. It towers above sloppy work like "Eng. their England!" by reason of its beautiful language and a light satiric touch, deft and sure; and it will be most readable even a century hence. I was invited to supper by Mr and Mrs Willison (the G.K. fan) last Thursday and took it with me to entertain them with some snappy American dialogue. They had a very tasty supper for me, and we had a most pleasant evening. It is, as literature, something between Swift's Gulliver and Fielding's Tom Jones. Juan is a lineal descendant of Don Juan There are no morals in the book, but there is no pornographic pruriency.

Saturday [Friday] night I went with Turgeon[2] to a play at the Festival "The Blind Goddess" (Justice) by the Communist Ernst Toller.[3] Turgeon came up to lunch to-day and we chatted anent a 1000 things until 7 P.M. So he had tea as well—a very intelligent lad, but as greedy for pleasure, wealth etc as he is able. He is however a devout Catholic, interested in theology and history.

Hope the money for Odams will come soon. I shall just manage my week with what I have. If the day is reasonably fair I shall leave at 8 AM to-morrow. The railway fare is likely very little—I havent inquired. But I rather enjoy the freedom of cycling. One is eminently one's own boss then, independent of the schedule of others.

I had 3 letters from Marjorie to-night, one from Ed and Herman [Robeneck], and one from Dad and one from Wheeler. Prof Perry has been relieved of the headship of the dept and a very young chap [E.K. Brown] is apparently the elect. I cant understand the delay in M's letters which were posted over a week apart. The GK article—ignoble me—is not done yet, but much more has been written. It *shall be complete* before term commences. The French has been coming slowly. Turgeon talks a bit to me now and then—they have a baffling way of merging all words in a monotonous tone whose polished and continuous articulation presents no corner or grip-hold to the English ear.

Having written Marj. and Al rather longish letters I must skimp you this time, but will give you 1st preference—as you deserve—next time. My mail will be sent on—Believe me most affectionately

Marshall

[2]Guy Turgeon (b. 1916), who had been a pre-med student at McGill University, was studying Natural Sciences at Cambridge. He graduated in 1937, returned to McGill, and obtained his M.D. in 1940. He practises medicine in La Mirada, California. About the McLuhan he knew at Cambridge, Dr Turgeon has written: "His conversation was liberally sprinkled with paradoxes, and I was not too surprised to find quite a few of them in the writings of G.K. Chesterton, to which he steered me."

[3]*Die blinde Göttin* (1932) by Ernst Toller (1893-1939), a German poet and dramatist and exponent of Expressionism who committed suicide in the USA on hearing of the outbreak of the Second World War.

To Elsie, Herbert, and Maurice McLuhan

[Cambridge]
Friday—May 16 [17, 1935]

Dear Mother, Dad, and Red:–

Last night when I had returned from Fritz Lang's "M" at the Cosmop (a German thriller—the story of the Druseldorf (?) child-murderer) I heard a nightingale on the wireless.[1] It was performing in some Surrey garden and was given temporary precedence over a jazz-band which played in the background! However the song was unbelievably rich and full—strangely unlike what I expected. It is an unhurried song, low in tone, lasting about 3 seconds—maybe 5, with a slightly longer interval.

Was at a tea at Newnham yesterday at Miss B's rooms. She had her tutor in and some others. Apparently there are some Canadians there who "I simply must meet" in the tutor's phrase.

This afternoon, after our "outing" I called for tea with Dr and Mrs (also Dr.) Leavis. He is the editor of "Scrutiny", a highbrow English Journal, and a ci-devant (ie. former) lecturer of the English faculty. By nature, an uncompromising idealist, tactless, impatient, vain and affected, he soon clashed with old "Q" and went "out".[2] However he does considerable supervising and has "open house" for his pupils on Friday afternoons. [A.G.] Russell, the GK. enthusiast, is a close friend of Leavis and a contributor to his quarterly. He urged me to go, but was not there himself. I was soon in argument with a nest of Communists. They have nothing else around here. Leavis is not a Communist.

Last night after Hall I went to the 1st of four lectures on monetary reform. It was given by that doughty old scrapper Arthur Kitson.[3] He is himself a wealthy

---

[1] The famous German film *M* (1931) was based on actual child killings in Düsseldorf and starred Peter Lorre.

[2] The influential literary critic F.R. Leavis (1895–1978) taught English literature at Cambridge from 1927 to 1964. The occasion of McLuhan's visit was an "open house". In the financial crisis of 1931 his appointment as Assistant Lecturer was not renewed, though he continued in the English Faculty as supervisor or tutor and in due course became a full Lecturer. Leavis introduced rigorous standards and a new seriousness into English criticism, employing in his critical discourse not only toughness but sometimes animus towards works, writers, and critics that to him bespoke mediocrity or feeble intellect; he inspired both devotion and antagonism. His *New Bearings in English Poetry: A Study of the Contemporary Situation* (1932), which attacked Victorian and Georgian verse (it is easy to imagine his clashing with Quiller-Couch, editor of *The Oxford Book of English Verse*, 1900), reflected the influence of T.S. Eliot's views on poetry; later books altered the course of English criticism in arguing for the central importance of great fiction. Leavis was the chief editor of, and frequent contributor to, the periodical *Scrutiny*, which was mainly devoted to criticism and appeared in 19 issues from 1932 to 1953. He and his wife—Q.D. Leavis (1906–81), who was also a scholar of English literature—had both been students of I.A. Richards at Cambridge.

[3] Arthur Kitson (1859–1937) was an inventor—among his many inventions was the Kitson incandescent light used in lighthouses—and a monetary reformer who had been president of the Banking and Currency Reform League. He visited Canada and the United States as a young man and is said to have been one of the founders of Mimico, west of Toronto.

manufacturer with plants in nearly every country and he *knows* the bankers to a man. He told many amusing stories—one in particular of how Ramsey MacDonald [*sic*] used to come to him (after the war) for ideas about money. Kitson said I found he had a very thick head on more subjects than one but I could not make him see that money was not "*intrinsically* valuable".

Had a splendid lecture (the last of 6), from Potts of Queens, on [Edward] Gibbon. Altho only in his middle 30's he has a peculiar capacity for endearing himself despite a very high pulpit and a very up-to-date and over-sized lecture room. He has a look of rather good-natured surliness, speaks slowly and with many long gaps (not in the middle of his sentences). Everything is amazingly lucid, condensed, martialled. After 2 or 3 sentences he seems to efface himself— hides his face in his hands stares at the desk, then emerges effortlessly to deliver some more.

(Saturday) To-day is the alumni day at the Hall. The old boys were clambering around the Boat Club and we had one of them rowing 4 in our boat—wish we could have kept him.

In a few minutes I am going to the Festival to see Shaw's "On the Rocks". The Willison's will be there. All Love for you

from Marshall.

[No complimentary opening]

[Cambridge]
Sunday June 2nd/35

Well, GK *was* at the dinner![1]

I had seen his pictures, heard his voice, and thought his thoughts, and knew what to expect. But I was not prepared for his quick, light-blue eye, or the refinement and definition of his features. He has much that reminds me of R.B. Bennett,[2] but a larger head, and as I say, finer features. His hair is not very long but it curls up at the back of his head—like his light moustache, it is quite white. His bulk is unexaggerated by accounts He is 6 feet 2 or 3 and much thicker (at the equator) that [*sic*] he is wide at the shoulders, or elsewhere. His voice is not tiny or high-pitched but it is not very powerful. He holds himself quite erect when he stands—necessarily he moves slowly, and because he is GK, he imparts a sense of largesse, ample humour, tolerance, and significant dignity to the necessity

---

[1]On Saturday, June 1, McLuhan and his friends the Willisons (see note 4 below) went to London to attend an afternoon meeting of the Distributist League and a dinner afterwards, at which Chesterton spoke. (McLuhan wrote in his diary: "Surprised by the refinement of his features and his quick, small light-blue eyes.") This appearance by Chesterton was almost exactly a year before he died on June 14, 1936.

[2]Prime Minister of Canada (1930–5).

which nature has laid upon him. His eye and head and face might easily, in a more portable figure, have been consonant with the speedy active agitator and leader. His brother was such a man (without GK's genius but most of GK's abiity and character) and was slain at the very end of the war, after insisting upon leaving the hospital before he was well.[3]

Mrs Chesterton was not able to come because she had strained her back by a slight fall. But Miss Dorothy Collins, his red-haired secretary was with him. (All his stories have red- or auburn-haired people somewhere about) She is about 35–40, very lively and efficient and pleasant.

GK. made several short speeches at various times. His chair was directly opposite an emergency exit and he feigned each time he rose that the morbid grip of the prepensive suggestion which he was sure was in our minds had tightened on his mind. At 10.15 when he rose to go he announced that he had conquered the morbid desire to fling himself through the emergency exit and would content himself with breaking several stairs as he departed in the usual manner. He urged us to go on with our songs and recitations (which we did) and hoped that his departure would occasion only a geographical deficiency (which it did).

We (Mr & Mrs W.[illison])[4] took the 1 o'clock train and had to pay 7 bob because we had missed the 12.30, the excursion. We had some lunch on the road—how unbelievably ugly was our approach to London by way of Bethnal Green. What slums! We took the tube to Temple bar and were soon at "The George" (a very fine old Inn in the very heart of London). We were just opposite St Clement's The Dane—the church that Dr Johnson attended—St Pauls was close by and we visited it after the afternoon business of the Distributist League was done.

[*No closing*]

[3]Cecil Chesterton (1879–1918).
[4]In a letter of January 2(?) McLuhan mentioned visiting R.E.S. Willison (1908–83)—he and his wife became known to McLuhan as Ted and Kath—who was the organizer in Cambridge for the Distributist League. McLuhan wrote: "It was a great pleasure to meet a man who was sympathetic and conversant with GK's point of view—a man who not only had most of his and [Hilaire] Bellocs books, but had a framed photo of GK hanging in his study! We had a great time."

To Elsie McLuhan

[Cambridge]
Saturday June 8 [1935]

[*No complimentary opening*]

Well Well, Marjorie has decided to wait till next year since she has only enough to keep her here a month at present. From my point of view this is quite satisfactory, tho naturally disappointing. Not only may I hope to have more money next summer, but my exams will be done and I will feel more justified in taking a holiday. I am really in an unpleasantly unsettled state of mind at present. I don't feel at all confident that I shall have a job at the end of my work here. I must make some applications—but how? Here, I have only Elvin for a reference since my work has brought me in contact with him alone. Next year I shall take no lectures, thus saving £18. I shall devote the additional time to reading and perhaps pay for a term or 2 of additional supervision. I may even persuade Elvin to give me up to some one else for a term.

But what about applications for jobs? If I am going to France to study French at all (or for any purpose) I think I shall go soon after the 15th. David (a French lawyer here) has his home near Grenoble (where I shall go) and has invited me for a visit.[1] Several chaps I know were there last summer at the classes and thought themselves repaid. But board is high—£9 for a month—room & board—and £3 for the school, besides other expenses. Fares are reduced 40% from here to Paris to Grenoble. I hope to meet some French chap who is willing to travel on foot or bike and arrange to pair up and so get around somewhat. In such an event I might stay only briefly at the school. However such prospective uncertainty of objective, mode, [and] expense is very trying for me and I feel like staying here all summer. If only I had not to learn any French (I could study it here almost as well) but could amble across to Calais from Dover and rent a motorbike with some other chap and start off through France Spain and Italy with a tent.[2]

The Willisons are off to-day for the first week of their holidays. The second they will take later on (in their car) and I hope that they may go to Scotland and that I shall accompany them (sharing expenses) They would probably use Youth Hostels. There is an excellent chain up there in the lake country. (Loch Lomond etc)

They spoke once, apropos of nothing, of having a boarder. I might stay with them part of the summer. I could prob. stay here for 25 bob a week (dinner only, provided) The fact is that I *might* get it cheaper elsewhere but cheapness is not all when there is work to be done. I hate changes. I seem to get nothing done in the midst of the most favourable routine. I shall have neither lectures nor rowing next year however—I can always go sculling when I need it.

The point is that I had better have some ready cash immediately—about £20 in case some particularly fine opportunity offers at the end of term. It had best be wired as soon as possible. I have £2 in hand and £6 in the bank. I shall write immediately to discover what Youth Hostels exist in Europe.

I no longer feel that imperative diffidence which resolved that I should spend

[1]René David had been a very young Professor of Law at the University of Grenoble, from which he took a leave of absence to attend Cambridge. He became a Professor of Comparative Law at the Sorbonne. McLuhan did not go to Grenoble.

[2]On the night of June 30 McLuhan, with his Winnipeg friend Stewart Robb (who was at Oxford), sailed from Harwich for Belgium to begin a European sojourn to improve his French. After nearly two weeks in Brussels and Bruges, McLuhan travelled to Boulogne-sur-Mer, France, where he stayed with Mme Devin and her family—in the company of some Americans who were also learning French—and attended two weeks of classes. For reasons of space his letters about this episode could not be included here.

all my time studying. I am ready to work partly because my studies have equipped me for some jobs, and partly because I am eager for some mundane experience simply that I may use it as a weapon to call the bluff of the "practical", "no-nonsense", cads and grafters who have put us where we are. If ever there was a red-hot revolutionist c'est moi at this moment.

If I felt no vocation in this direction I could think of no more pleasing alternative than to take a 30 acre orchard-dairy farm in the Maritimes.[3] I would not sell an ounce of anything I grew if I could trade it in the village or with a neighbor for any needed article. Buying and selling is the deadly curse of our civilisation. Agriculture would be a blessed haven compared with the pursuit of the dregs of a departed culture amidst the rags and ends of our up-rooted modern lives. As soon as I have a job I intend to purchase such a small farm (near the sea) which shall have a worthy tenant who shall pay no rent beyond partly providing board and lodging for me and my family (if any) during holiday months. But my idea is not merely sentimental. If property (in adequate amounts) has any value or rhyme or reason it is to provide the bases and bulwarks of liberty. If my writings are such as to procure my removal from whatever job I have[—]a likely prospect[—]I shall show that while a man cannot *afford* to be honest while a wage-slave in a city he can be honest while he has an independent property. [William] Cobbett in prison was provided with food from his own farm[1]—but King Gordon having tread on the toes of McGill plutocrats has to depend on charity.[5] The world has become so base, so utterly indifferent to honour and valiancy that the only way to keep one's head above water at all is by an untiring heroism. It is obviously better to-day to perish nobly, knowing wherefore one strikes, than to endure ignobly the bonds of luxury and ease *and* silence.

[Ends here. Additional page[s] missing?]

[3]The idealism and mood of this passage reflect McLuhan's reading of Chesterton's articles on Distributism in *GK's Weekly*.

[4]The prolific English journalist William Cobbett (1763–1835), writing in support of the Radical interest in his *Political Register*, was imprisoned for two years for attacking the use of flogging in the army.

[5]King Gordon (b. 1900)—the son of the Presbyterian minister Charles W. Gordon, of Winnipeg, who was also the popular novelist Ralph Connor (pseud.)—accepted in 1931 the chair of Christian Ethics at United Theological College in Montreal (United Church of Canada), which was near the McGill campus but not part of that university. For being involved in the formation of the League of Social Reconstruction (1932), and in a church group that became known as the Fellowship for a Christian Social Order, he came under criticism by members of his college board. In 1933 he was notified that his chair was being discontinued for financial reasons, and his many supporters raised $1500 a year as a salary if the College would reinstate him. He was rehired for the 1933–4 term, but a renewal under this arrangement was refused. The affair was known to McLuhan through much newspaper comment, particularly in Winnipeg. Gordon went on to a successful career as an editor, a United Nations staff member, and a teacher.

To Elsie McLuhan

[Cambridge]
Thursday A.M. [September 5, 1935]

Dear Mother:

Your alarm about my "religion-hunting" traits which you assume to be inherited from the most questionable part of my ancestry, is largely unfounded. Letters are of course fatal things when it comes to imparting a situation with its shades of emphasis. I need scarcely point out that religious enthusiasm (in which I am lamentably weak) has rarely directed the erratic and leaping feet of the inebriated one along the slow and arduous path that leads from a meeting-house to the Church—I mean the Catholic and universal Church, the visible body of Christ. Now religion-hunting even in its worst phases is yet a testimony to the greatest fact about man, namely that he is a creature and an image, and not sufficient unto himself. It is the whole bias of the mind that it seek truth, and of the soul which inspires our very life, that it seek that which gave it. The great difficulty about Truth is that it is not simple except to those who can attain to see it whole. The very definition of an enthusiast is that he has seized *a* truth which he cannot and would not if he could, relate to other truths of life. He is invariably unsympathetic and lacking in humanity. I have some elements of enthusiasm which have been more than occupied in hero-worship—eg Macaulay and Chesterton. Them days is gone forever but I shall always think that my selection of heroes was fortunate. Both were calculated to suppress effectively any tendency I had towards harping on *one* truth at a time. You may be sure that I shall make no inconsiderable step about entering the Roman communion—I shall probably take some years, because I am completely uneducated for the step. I am not even serious enough to be "contemptuous" of the probable effect on my worldly prospects. I believe they would not be altered save for small colleges originally of religious origin—perhaps Acadia, certainly Wesley. The Provincial U.'s would be indifferent, religion being at such an ebb in our land at present as to be considered a negligible factor. However I will not be a Catholic when I come to apply for posts. And I am waiting advice from Wheeler at present regarding what U's in Canada and U.S.A. to apply to, and *how* to apply to them. I therefore implore you to put aside your apprehensions. Religion is a personal matter and I shall not be visibly altered—tho I could wish for countless improvements—by such a change. The Catholic religion is the only religion—all sects are derivative. Bhuddism and similar oriental philosophies and mythologies are not religions in any sense. They have no covenants and no sacraments and no theology. The very notion of "comparative" religion is ridiculous. Now the Catholic religion as you may be able to check in your own experience of it is alone in blessing and employing all those merely human faculties which produce games and philosophy, and poetry and music and mirth and fellowship with a very fleshy basis. It alone makes terms with what our sects have hated and called by ugly names—eg carnal which is delightfully near to charnel. The Catholic church does not despise or wantonly mortify those members and faculties which Christ deigned to assume. They are henceforth holy and blessed. Catholic culture produced Chaucer and his merry story-telling Canterbury pilgrims. Licentious enthusiasm produced the lonely despair of Christian in Pilgrim's Progress—what a different sort of pilgrim! Catholic culture produced Don Quixote and St. Francis and Rabelais. What I wish to emphasize about them is there [*sic*] various and rich-hearted humanity. I need scarcely indicate that everything that is especially hateful and devilish and inhuman about the conditions and strain of modern industrial society is not only Protestant in origin, but it is their boast(!) to have originated it. You may know a thing by its fruits if you are silly enough or ignorant enough to wait that long. I find the fruits and the theory of our sects very bitter. Had I not encountered Chesterton I would have remained agnostic for many years at least. Chesterton did not convince me of religious truth, but he prevented my despair from becoming a habit or hardening into misanthropy. He opened my eyes to European culture and encouraged me to know it more closely. He taught me the reasons for all that in me was simply blind anger and misery. He went through it himself; but since he lived where much Catholic culture remained and since he had genius he got through it quicker. He was no fanatic. He remained an Anglo-Catholic as long as he was able to do so (1922)[1] His wife became a Catholic a few years later.

You ask about Marjorie and her folks—they know my mind very well. Marjorie is quite agnostic and would probably become a Catholic—In any case her reactions to Protestant morals and the dull dead day-light of Protestant rationalism which ruinously bathes every object from a beer parlour to a gasoline station, are my reactions. You see my "religion-hunting" began with a rather priggish "culture-hunting". I simply couldnt believe that men had to live in the mean mechanical joyless rootless fashion that I saw in Winnipeg. And when I began to read English Literature I knew that it was quite unnecessary for them so to live. You will remember my deep personal enjoyment of "Tom Brown's Schooldays" in grade 8. It brought me in contact with things for which I was starved—things which have since disappeared from England. All my Anglo-mania was really a recognition of things missing from our lives which I felt to be indispensable. It was a long time before I finally perceived that the character of every society, its food, clothing, arts, and amusements are ultimately determined by its religion—It was longer still before I could believe that religion was as great and joyful as these things which it creates—or destroys. Look at the Bedouins the Arabs and Turks. Spain would have looked like Morocco if it had not expelled the Moors. There would have been no Don Quixote.

In writing to Red as I did I not unnaturally forgot that he never has experienced any reaction to the culture in which he was reared—not one in a million does be it in China or Peru—*My* hunger for "truth" was sensuous in origin. I wanted a material satisfaction for the beauty that the mind can perceive. I still

[1]1922 was the year of Chesterton's conversion to Roman Catholicism.

do. Unfortunately very few do. But I cannot but think that whether they do or not they would be happier and more profitable servants if they felt otherwise. That is putting it mildly; for there is a true and eternal pattern for human life which the "progress" mongers wot not of. Blessed are they that find and follow that pattern. I never saw it more clearly described from the fact than in Balzac's "Country Doctor".[2] I believe some of the Russian novelists adhere to it. All art is an attempt to realise it. It emanates from God himself. There is a vast gulf between the virtue of Faith and dogmatic conviction. The latter is harsh intolerant feverishly restless and utterly unlovely. And yet Faith is merely the first means of grace not in itself implying any spiritual attainment whatever. When you suggest that "a life of service" is superior to membership in the Church of Christ you say only what every Protestant conscious of exclusion from that membership says. It implys that the map of the universe was not radically altered by the Incarnation and Ressurrection [*sic*]. It is like saying 2 and 2 makes 3. I long to serve and I know that in this muddled world there are so many opportunities that one need not worry lest one is left idle and useless.

> The world is so full of a number of *things*,
> I'm sure we should all be as happy as Kings.[3]

The deepest passion in man is his desire for significance. Significance in clothes, in labour, in gesture. It is the most frustrated passion where men are huddled together and taught to admire luxury. A life of service implies that one is serving something that is in [the] position of Lord and worthy of service.

> But good grows wild and wide,
> Has shades, is nowhere none;
> But right must seek a side
> And choose for master one. (Hopkins)[4]

The Americans serve "service". Like the rest of the world they have smothered man in men and set up the means as an end. It does not speak so well for your discrimination as for your affectionate fears that you should confuse my position with the evangelicism of which you have had experience. Nor do I believe that I am being unfair to Red in pointing out to him that there is an alternative which if he does not honestly face now he cannot but regret when increasing knowledge of that alternative and bitter experience with his present sect shall have mingled in later years. I have an uneasy suspicion Mother that you regard the United Church [of Canada] as an almost respectable profession in which oratory and humanitarian rhetoric can win the applause of good solid prosperous folk. You view with horror the idea of introducing religion into those auditoriums so well

---

[2] A translation of Honoré de Balzac's *Le Médecin de campagne* (1833), part of his *Comédie humaine*.

[3] Robert Louis Stevenson, "Happy Thoughts".

[4] Gerard Manley Hopkins, "On a Piece of Music" (stanza 7). The last line correctly reads: "And choose for chieftain one."

designed to exclude it. Let me tell you that religion is not a nice comfortable thing that can be scouted by cultivated lecturers like the Pidgeons. It is veritably something which, if it could be presented in an image, would make your hair stand on end. Hence the fate of those poor uneducated undisciplined devils who stumble upon some of its "horrors" (they cannot administer the sacraments to themselves nor to their followers) while remaining inaccessible to its resources. Such was Bunyan and countless others. It is no wonder that men unable *thus* to see God and to live, quickly rationalise their beliefs as has happened in all the older Protestant sects. Men must be at ease in Zion if they are to pay more than a flying visit. The 17th cent. Protestants abandoned the world and the flesh to the Devil and packed up for Zion. They found the climate their [*sic*] impossible and returned to earth only to discover that the Devil had been making hay. That is the origin of predatory laissez-faire commerce:

> Industrialism establishes a state of slavery more corrupting than any previously known in the world because the master is not a man but a system, and the whip an invisible machine. With this it is impossible to enter into any but inhuman relations, and in such an inversion of humanity all the instincts become perverted at their source   Osbert Burdett.[5]

There are two points to be cleared. First I shall not rush into the Church where even angels tread reverently. Therefore my worldly prospects will continue just as they are. Second, I wish to take no unfair advantage of Red. No matter what he decides in the matter, I wish only to present the matter at a time when it should be faced. Since I cannot discuss it with him in person I recommend that he pursue this course: As soon as he can discover what Protestantism is and in what points it cannot possibly agree with Rome, let him lay these points before a Churchman (ie. a priest) and let him discuss them with him. Let him then present the Churchman's replies to Dr Pidgeon or any theologian of the Protestant Communion and see what is retorted in the matter. Maurice [Red] has chosen to become a minister in the Church of Christ.[6] There can be no question of a career in such a choice. Abnegation is its definition. Such a choice unaccompanied by apostolic vows of chastity and poverty becomes almost meaningless. This whole question can be decided by reasoning, provided one is not loath to employ reason. But the matter decided (whichever way) affects the destiny of the soul. Let us leave it for now.

I have been most pleased with the snaps. I think you are getting a stummock Mother! Rags looks good to me. How I would like to have him here a while.

Last Sunday I was to the Willison's for dinner at 1. Then we listened to Elgar's 1st symphony on their gramophone and chatted and read around their fire till tea, after which we went to church. The 1st time I have been to *church* (outside of chapel) since I came. It was (evensong) [at] St Clement's, which is "Very

---

[5]Osbert Burdett, *The Beardsley Period: An Essay in Perspective* (1925), p. 268.

[6]Maurice had decided to enrol in Emmanuel College, University of Toronto, and become a minister of the United Church of Canada.

High".[7] In the course of a brief sermon I was ashamed to be told that there were 2 St Augustines (one of the 6th and one of the 8th centuries). The 2nd was the one who came to England. The 1st the great theologian and author of the Confessions. We went to the Fellow's garden at the Hall afterwards which we had entirely to ourselves. It was a lovely night and I wished heartily that you were here then to enjoy it. It is clear that the presence of 25 or 30 great parks and gardens in close but hidden proximity raises each one to a higher power of peace and beauty than merely one could impart. I am going to write 2 or 3 articles for The [Winnipeg] Free Press which even if published wont fetch me a penny I fear—"Cambridge in Vacation Time" is already written. Monday I had supper with the Crawleys. Last night went to see East Lynne played at the Festival.[8] Since there was a large town audience they did not give it the burlesque touches that students demand. But it was funny enuf. Think what fun some of our "serious" sex problem plays will provide for the next generation!

This morning I had 2 teeth filled—cant be helped. This afternoon I spent watching the town regatta. Jim Odams got beaten in sculling—close race. Ted and Kath [Willison] are in London looking for a house and have left me their key so that I can go to listen to Elgar's 1st Symphony on their radio. It is a Promenade concert from London directed by Sir Henry Wood—6 weeks of the best music every year.[9] It starts in 10 minutes so I'm off. Will read over there.

I feel utterly ashamed to think of using your thrice-earned money—well something *shall* be done before long. This next year will offer some relief for you—I mean the scholarship. I feel very badly to think of having caused you pain by my words and thoughts—you must know that I love you all more dearly every year—

Marshall

[7]St Clements, a parish church of Cambridge.

[8]A dramatization of the melodramatic and sensational romance (1861) by Mrs Henry Wood (1814–87).

[9]The English conductor Sir Henry Wood (1869–1944) founded in 1895 the popular summer programs of Promenade Concerts in London.

To Elsie McLuhan

[Cambridge, December 11, 1935]

Dear Mother

Some more ideas for material for your pupils occur. You must read Mark Twains "Innocents Abroad" [1869]. You are sure to find 1st rate stuff in it. What about the Fence White-washing from Tom Sawyer [1876]? In "Innocent . . .["] you will read "they spell it Vinci but pronounce it Vinchy. Foreigners spell much better than they pronounce." You will read how Twain was mistaken for the Prussian historian Mommsen on one occasion. "We have the same hair", he explained "but on examination it was found that the brains were different." I really think that you should have one number consisting simply of well-told anecdotes—for yourself. There is quoted (2 pages long) in Bergson's essay on "Laughter"[1] (near the end I think) a marvellous bit of Twain in which he is being interviewed by a reporter. The reporter sees a picture and [*sic*] the wall and asks "wasn't that your brother Bill?" Twain proceeds to become mysterious and ends. by explaining that he and his brother were twins and that they got mixed in the bath one day and so he can never hope to be sure whether it was Bill or himself that died (later). It is really a perfect bit of fooling that would make [a] very popular 4 minute recitation

If you have any pupils who have any capacity for Irish brogue you will find in the plays of Synge (they are only 300 largely printed pages) great treasure for your needs. It is most important that they should be chanted in definite rhythm which he intended (and about which you can read in Yeat's [*sic*] essays on Synge) and which holds life at a distance and thus permitting the expression of the most vehement passion without any loss of dignity or beauty. In The Shadow of the Glen, The Playboy and Deirdre you will find considerable passages of dialogue which either one or 2 people could undertake.[2] I am giving Synge and "To the Lighthouse" [1927] by Virginia Woolf to Marjorie this Xmas. The latter work is an exquisite novel rivalled by its predecessor "Mrs Dalloway" [1925] only.

I have met a very interesting chap recently. He is a Hall man—a German Tannhauser by name[3] He is a Bavarian speaking English perfectly and French equally well. He is slight but handsome refined, quick of mind and motion. His grandfather established an art business in Berlin which his father has much expanded. His father "discovered" Picasso and the families are intimate. He will carry on the business which means travelling the world over once or twice a year. Actually he looks French rather than German and detests Prussians.

Am listening to Henry Purcell's opera "King Arthur" as I write—it is 8:30 P.M. Wednesday Dec. 11. It is a 17th cent. piece recently unearthed, and very good it is.

Lorna Doone has been broadcast as a play in 2 parts—adapted by Louise Drury— might save you some trouble, but don't think it has been published.

I haven't any idea how my finances stand, but think I have spent rather less than last year—nothing for clothes or bike to date and less on food—about the same on books.

[1]*Laughter* (1911) by Henri Bergson (1859–1941), a translation of *Le Rire: essai sur la signifi-cance du comique* (1900).

[2]The plays of John Millington Synge (1871–1909) include *In the Shadow of the Glen* (1903), *The Playboy of the Western World* (1907), and *Deirdre of the Sorrows* (1910). W.B. Yeats wrote the Prefaces to Synge's *Poems and Translations* (1909) and *Synge and the Ireland of His Time* (1911). McLuhan wrote in his diary on December 9: "Reading glorious Synge out on the River".

[3]Heinz Tannhauser, son of a well-known New York art dealer (who left his collection of Impres-sionists to the Guggenheim Museum), read English literature at Cambridge, then attended Harvard Art School. He joined the U.S. Air Force and was killed shortly before the war ended. McLuhan had previously met him in November 1934: see page 36.

Finally wrote to Pres. Smith,[4] and Dr [E.K.] Brown[5] at Manitoba (Brown is the new English head). I would go there like a shot, I'm afraid, if I got the chance. I could not endure the thought of spending my life there, but until these times are past. . . However I must now concoct a circular letter and have it typed. A year or so in the States would be useful experience and I should welcome it—apart from the necessity of working at a Phd while in their universities. But I hope to get East sooner or later—I want the sea and also to be within a practicable distance from Europe.

Well here is Sunday evening. Tannhauser and myself are the only men in college and I shall be the only one to-morrow night. I go to London Tuesday.

When I got up at noon to-day I found a note from Mr Crawley on my breakfast plate inviting me to lunch—I had just time to go and decline it (and accept an invitation to tea). Because I had invited Tannhauser and A R Humphreys to lunch. The latter, just back from 2 years at Harvard, is now on the English staff here. I gave them mock turtle soup (6d.) ham and tomatoes plus buttered eggs (1/6) cherry pie (1/3) coffee (2d.) and cigarettes (4d.)—a very good lunch it was for about a dollar (for 3 people). Humphreys had had me to lunch and paid 2/6 for me. And then we had our own time, the fire, the radio, and books handy for reference.

I went to tea with [the] Crawley's at 4.30 and it shure rained while I was on my way. I must buy a hat and a pair of shoes—the shoes I have *will* not wear out. Last night at one AM it snowed a bit. It is a queer feeling to be alone in a big college at night, especially where there has been so much activity a little while before. I have Bowen's radio and hear many good things—Philip Snowden on Keir Hardie on Friday Desmond McCarthy on Samuel Butler Thursday etc

I have much to do concerning my scholarship application and Thesis subject etc before Tuesday. I am consulting with H.S. Bennett on the matter.[6] Am in the best of health and spirits. It has been a bit too cold for the river and there is no fire in the Boathouse—I have missed it.

My rooms [in college] give me infinite content Certainly I have no right to be as fortunate and happy—but shall probably have enough of thin times hereafter to level up so that I shall die neither more nor less felicitous than common men.

Hope you have *such* a Christmas

Best of Love from
Marshall

---

[4]Sidney Smith (1897–1959), President of the University of Manitoba, 1934–44; he would later be President of the University of Toronto (and thereafter Secretary of State for External Affairs).

[5]See next letter.

[6]H.S. Bennett (1889–1972), a Life Fellow of Emmanuel College, Cambridge (Librarian, 1934–59), was the author and editor of many books on English history and literature. McLuhan had taken courses on Literary Life and Thought, and Seventeenth-Century Verse, from Mrs. Bennett.

To E.K. Brown[1]

Trinity Hall   Cambridge
December 12/35

Dear Dr. Brown,—

I wish merely to introduce myself as one of the products of some of the leanest years of the Manitoba English Department. The last year was somewhat relieved by the presence of Dr Wheeler but I had directed my energies to philosophy, and did my best work for Professor Lodge.

I say it without affectation, your appointment to the chair of English, or rather your acceptance of the chair, cheered me a great deal. Nor had any thought of even applying for a position at Manitoba occurred to me. I don't think the thought of any position would have occurred to me as soon as this but for the shock of the suicide of a near friend of mine—a splendid fellow—who found idleness and dependence intolerable.[2] But I have suddenly realised that I have no connections whatever in the East or elsewhere, and that eight years at University is long enough to be a weight on the family.

Frankly, I am quite keen about teaching although, until I came to the Cambridge English School,[3] my principal qualification was a boundless enthusiasm for great books, great events, and great men. Dr Richards and Dr Leavis have proved to be a useful supplement and corrective to that attitude. But it is probably the attitude rather than the supplement by which Dr. Wheeler remembers me.

I did not read French at Manitoba but have somewhat supplied that deficiency since that time—there being a French paper in the English tripos and I am a very sincere admirer of French literature and thought. Remy de Gourmont and Jacques Maritain are my principal contacts with "recent" French thought. If only in view of the French stimulus behind Yeats and Joyce, James, Pound, [Edith] Whart[on], Eliot, I should agree that the French and English literatures cannot be studied profitably in isolation—not in their fullest intent.

I have been advised, and feel personally the desire for some practical teaching experience before undertaking any research. I should be very happy indeed to work under you and Dr. Wheeler.

You probably know all about the very exciting and thriving time that the Cambridge English School is experiencing. Dr Richards has been a great stimulus, even to his opponents (!), and the easy accessibility of Willey, Tillyard, Lucas and Leavis (editor of Scrutiny) makes for an intellectual variety that not even my

---

[1]E.K. Brown (1905–51) was Chairman of the Department of English, University of Manitoba (1935–7). Later, while teaching at Cornell and the University of Chicago, he wrote several distinguished works of literary criticism, including *On Canadian Poetry* (1943), which won a Governor General's Award.

[2]McLuhan's Winnipeg friend Gerry O'Connell committed suicide in Toronto on November 4, 1935.

[3]The English Faculty.

wildest hopes had prefigured.[4] We have recently had an extra bit of excitement provided by the Clark lectures of R.W. Chambers.[5] He is lecturing on the foundations and continuity of English prose, and has set aside one hoary hypothesis after another—and laid the hapless Wycliffe in the dust![6] He has shown not only that several of W.'s contemporaries wrote better prose and made better translations, but that the best that W. did was the work of his secretary.

Miss Spurgeon's book has aroused more amusement than excitement I fear.[7]

It may save you inquiry if I say that I did my M.A. thesis on George Meredith (under severe anathema as "bogus poet and prose writer" up here, and perhaps not unjustly so).

I am very sincerely yours

H M McLuhan

Margaret Deaver Brown

[4]Basil Willey (1897–1978), E.M. Tillyard (1889–1962), and F.L. Lucas (1894–1967) all lectured in the English Faculty of Cambridge, though none were Fellows of McLuhan's college. For Leavis, see page 67, note 2.

[5]R.W. Chambers (1874–1942), Professor of English Literature at University College, London, and a much-published scholar. McLuhan became friendly with him and called on him in London.

[6]The English theologian and reformer John Wyclif (c. 1330–84) condemned the abuses of the Church, attacked orthodox Church doctrine, especially transubstantiation, and was condemned as a heretic. He instigated the first complete English translation of the Bible.

[7]*Shakespeare's Imagery* (1935) by the American critic Caroline Spurgeon (1886–1942) was the first detailed study of its subject.

1936

To Elsie McLuhan

[Cambridge, January 13, 1936]

Dear Mother

I forgot to put this in my earlier note to-day: 1) Send Burpee 2 copies of my Dalhousie article when you get the lot.[1] Send me half a dozen and Dad half a dozen and keep the rest or do what you will with them; 2) unearth from my

[1]McLuhan's much-worked-on Chesterton article, "G.K. Chesterton: A Practical Mystic", appeared in the *Dalhousie Review* (January 1936). He received his copy on January 27. "Burpee" was likely Lawrence J. Burpee (1873–1946), President of the Royal Society of Canada and the author of many books of Canadiana.

papers my MSS. copy of Chap IV of my MA thesis and send it to me (in an envelope) I think to use it as an essay (to be submitted along with the tripos exam papers.

Henry Moore, the IODE man from Moncton N.B. came up to see me to-day.[2] He is huge, flabby, pasty—an engineer. Hates it here. Sees nothing of Cambridge life. He used the IODE invitations however and spent 3 weeks in big country houses—gratis. I could have done that last year, but not me this year. Jerry Riddel took such invites—you bet. He got a free trip to Italy as guest of one family. However here am I.

Ian Jackson (next door) is back from Switzerland (skiing)—What a tan! Apparently it is a very innocuous sport—no danger. He nearly split laughing at the antics of beginners—like himself.

I had intended to tell you that John Gielgud spoke his Romeo lines as tho he was thinking about them and as tho he were enjoying the innumerable ambiguities and cross references by sound and meaning that Shakespeare used to enrich the texture of his verse.[3] He did not intone his lines (all the time) or rattle them off or affect a dulcet sweetness of rhythm. He paused on a word now and then where some shade of meaning demanded slowness or where the latent meaning required some gesture, some steps, some "impromptu" and "spontaneous" physical expression or flick at some other person on the stage. Shak. knew the men he was writing for and he expected ("all art is collaboration") a great deal from them in order to carry across to the audience the deal of stuff he packed into his lines. Have you used "Q"'s and Dover Wilson's New Cambridge Shak. ed. at all. I haven't been through it but it contains a great deal that is unconventional and stimulating for a producer. They emphasise the delicate melancholy vein of sentiment that is interwoven with the rollick.

They give a good glossary and a stage history and the best notes obtainable. However it is not one of the difficult plays. Granville-Barker has notes on its production I believe.[4] The enveloping paper to this note has no partic point of interest!

Lovingly
Marshall.

[2]Henry Moore was at Cambridge on an IODE scholarship, like that of McLuhan's. The two men eventually became friends.

[3]McLuhan had seen this famous long-running production of *Romeo and Juliet* on December 18. It was directed by the distinguished actor John Gielgud (b.1904) who also alternated the roles of Romeo and Mercutio with Laurence Olivier.

[4]Harley Granville-Barker (1877–1946), English stage director who published five series of Prefaces to Shakespeare's plays, beginning in 1927, that contained a producer's notes.

To Elsie McLuhan

[Cambridge]
Sunday April 12 [1936]

Dear Mother,—

Judging from some excerpts I believe you might find some excellent material in Max Beerbohms "Zuleika Dobson"[1911]. She may merely be a character in a story of a diff. title but could easily be traced because Max is an exquisite and not a voluminous writer: "Zuleika Dobson was not strictly beautiful. Her eyes were a trifle large, and the[ir] lashes longer than they need have been. The mouth was a mere replica of Cupids bow . . . No apple-tree, no wall of peaches, had not been robbed, nor any Tyrian rose-garden, for the glory of Miss Dobson's cheeks. Her neck was imitation marble. Her hands and feet were of very mean proportions. She had no waist to speak of."

I dont know (Owen?) Merediths aux Italiens but imagine that it is very daring of you to say a good word for them these days![1]

Regarding your use of Phelan[2] on my behalf, I am of course not exactly elated. But there was nothing disreputable in the proceeding. I think there is latent in my mind a fear to exert myself fully on *any* occasion lest I should have to admit the result to be my *best*; and that best not good enough. I have a strong sense of superiority that is utterly incomensurate with my abilities—by superiority, I mean superior *ability to do*, not superiority of personal value. It is the fact that goads me on when a 100 invitations of diversion, which would be welcomed by more pleasant people, vainly offer themselves. My very ordinary mind having been stimulated somewhat beyond the ordinary by whatever queer motives, soon had to admit that there was no merely personal or even human end to which such effort was owing—the utter transience and confusion of human affairs at their stablest being evident even to casual curiosity. Most people admit the natural growth of religious consciousness at this point—a growth usually blighted by various demands and sophistications of social life. You perceive no doubt some gruesome analogy between Roy and myself.[3] An innate distaste for spiritual perversion and incontinence would have kept me neutrally agnostic forever unless

---

[1]George Meredith spent a brief period in Italy as a war correspondent in 1866; Italy shocked world opinion in 1935 when Mussolini's troops invaded Ethiopia.

[2]Father Gerald B. Phelan (1892–1965), whom Elsie McLuhan knew, was at this time Professor of Philosophy at St Michael's College, University of Toronto, and in the School of Graduate Studies. He was President of the Pontifical Institute of Mediaeval Studies from 1937 to 1946, the year he moved to the University of Notre Dame. On January 29, 1936 (diary) McLuhan had been "immensely gratified by a note of appreciation (of my GK article)" from Phelan. Elsie McLuhan had perhaps offered to speak to Father Phelan about the possibilities of a teaching position for Marshall after he graduated from Cambridge. Later in the year Phelan would have a preliminary role in McLuhan's conversion to Roman Catholicism—a goal towards which McLuhan was moving when he wrote this letter. To his brother Maurice he had written on April 11: "Had I come into contact with the Catholic Thing, the Faith, 5 years ago, I would have become a priest I believe."

[3]McLuhan's Uncle Roy (McLuhan) was a Jehovah's Witness.

there had come opportunities for knowledge of things utterly alien to the culture—the grim product of a life-denying other worldliness—that you know I hated from the time that I turned from our pavements and wheels to boats and sails.

I could never have respected a 'religion' that held reason and learning in contempt—witness the 'education' of our preachers. I have a taste for the intense cultivation of the Jesuit rather than the emotional orgies of an evangelist—or a poet like Shelley and even Browning in part.

I quite realise Red's difficulty—but I am far from increasing it by criticising *now*, before he has even begun his 'theology' courses. I dont pretend to superior reasoning powers in these matters. I simply *know* of certain *things* which I didnt know 2 years ago and which you have never had an opportunity to know.

I was skipping through Morton's "In His Steps"[4] (what a sickening title!) after dinner today—(A very good dinner of cauliflower, roast fowl, Yorkshire pudding etc plus Xmas pudding!) I certainly found the *information* fascinating but am out of patience with Morton's journalistic trick of giving you the exact colour tone and amount of emotion with each *thing* that confronts him. It is like a cinema where you are the most passive of passive receptacles until you 'cat' over some particularly fulsome slab of stuff. When I came to his good samaritan stuff with the starving dog, I "catted" (i.e. puked) It was simply awful. You feel as tho he really could not distinguish between a spiritual being and an animal—a result of spiritual disorder and derangement. Had he reported this from France it would not have been so bad. But on *that* soil where the fact of the terrible spiritual stature of man is present in the mere reference and description—It was awful!

Almost as bad was his absurd journalistic presence at the ceremony of the Black Monks on the roof of the Church of the Holy Sepulchre. The more beautiful or wonderful the *thing* (and things alone, not emotions about things, are wonderful) the more inevitably remote and inadequate is Morton to its comprehension. He never knows when to have done with reporting raptures. But there is no need for me to enumerate the undeniable body of excellent stuff (almost entirely cribbed from better writers whom his readers are never likely to consult) which stands outside my strictures.

Jean Farquhar's death is very bad news—a tragic family indeed.[5]

It is very selfish of me not to take time to comment on your own very interesting doings lately. I am most pleased at the pleasure and acknowledgements you receive. Occasionally I catch an oblique glimpse or illumination of Canadians, or some vivid memory is aroused and, I must confess, that at such times my heart sinks at the task awaiting the educator. But education is really 90% domestic in nature. The mere formal educator cannot transform the radical modes of life of which he is usually only too natural a product. My life in Canada will be a

[4]This book was *In the Steps of the Master* (1934) by H.V. Morton. The title McLuhan gives was that of a bestselling inspirational novel by Charles M. Sheldon, *In His Steps: What Would Jesus Do* (1896). The references conform to passages in Morton's travel book.

[5]The Winnipeg lawyer Jean Farquhar was a family friend.

continual discontent. My task as a teacher will be to shake others from their complacency—how is it possible to contemplate the products of English life (ie. Literature) without criticising our own sterility—

> We are the unfruitful fig-tree
> A land so prosperous to men and kine,
> That which were which, a sage could scarce define![6]

Believe me dear Mother, most lovingly

Yours
Marshall

[6]Unidentified.

To Elsie McLuhan

[Cambridge, June 1936]

Dear Mother,—

Ask Pidgeon if there is any chance of my finishing my Camb. Phd at McGill if I do the 1st year here. I could get a £50 or £60 grant here for next year but no more.

I have not turned down Wisconsin but dont know how they will react to my suggestion to commence my Camb. Phd. there this year.[1] If they dont like it and Pidgeon cant be sure of a job for me next year (after one year's research here with Dr R.W. Chambers) then I'm off to Wisconsin to do their degree. A degree there means 3 years— but my expenses will be covered, and I haven't the nerve to be dependent any longer—unless Pidgeon has a job for me!

Dont write such long letters Mother—dont try to equal me! I know what time and energy they require. A note every week and [a] half or so will do. Get some rest.

Lovingly
Marshall

[1]On February 6 McLuhan had received an offer from the University of Wisconsin for a one-year appointment as a Graduate Assistant at a salary of $860. He eventually accepted this and arranged to begin work on his Cambridge Ph.D. thesis while there.

To Elsie McLuhan

[Cambridge]
Tuesday, June 23 [1936]

Dear Mother,

I am now a BA Cantab—I, simultaneously with 3 others—we were presented in batches of 4—holding a finger of the praelector's right hand with our right hand, was presented to the vice chancellor, in Latin. Then our names were read out separately and we knelt before the V. Ch's chair with hands held prayerwise. He laid his hands on mine and received me into the Univ. in the name of the Father Son and Holy Ghost—a relic of medieval barbarism!

I enclose the "bands" which are worn over our white ties. The cord of the hood rests under the bands. I had borrowed a hood from a chap I know.

Marjorie hasn't turned up yet—the weather is superb—Cambridge is *very* beautiful. It makes such a difference to be in college in the heart of it.

I shall be here for a few days yet. Want to finish some reading. Have been doing a great deal of work, but liking it, and knowing that little will be done in July and August.

Spent a very pleasant evening with John and Elfreida Allen last night—was 10 mins after 12 getting back! My *last* night and my first time late! Grant the porter didnt report me and so saved me 5 bob.

Don't feel "lettery" Mother—have a bit of patience. Am I fed up with mental uncertainty and vagueness!!!! etc.

Lovingly   Marshall

To Elsie McLuhan

[Cambridge]
Sunday [June 28, 1936]

Dear Mother,—

My third day with the Allens on Milton Road. We get along *very* well. They are extremely agreeable and interesting people. Finally got my packing done. Marjorie is in Belfast: we are going to the Lakes for a week or so very soon.[1] We [he and the Allens] are just off for a picnic with bathing suits. We will take a punt up towards Grantchester. It would be such fun for you!

---

[1] On July 4 McLuhan took a night boat to Belfast and was met the next morning by Marjorie Norris and her Uncle Albert. By this time their romantic feelings for each other had cooled—the trip to the Lake District never took place—but they spent ten days together in Belfast and Dublin, and met again in London shortly before McLuhan left England.

Tuesday AM I have just refused tea at 11 Downing Street with Mrs Neville Chamberlain.[2] Not the least bit interested

I have been having a splendid time with the Allens. They are good fun and very intelligent and well educated—widely travelled. Mrs Allen—Elfreida Hiebert is MA Harvard (Jack is Phd Toronto)—has German degrees as well. Heavens how we have talked. Jack is very keen on affairs. They were 2 years in the States before coming here. How they hated it.

Starting July 15 there is a congress of Empire U. presidents in Camb. The Allens know several—including [President Sidney] Smith of Manitoba and Wallace of Queens[3] and we are going to entertain them a bit—take them out on the river etc and play politics. So I expect to spend 2 weeks in the Lakes with Marj then come back here for "politics" then go to the continent. By that time I will have the Wisconsin reply and my mind will be settled—or my fate.

I certainly dont intend to cost you another penny. I have plenty of ideas for articles and will write one per quarter from now on. It is one of the best ways of consolidating one's reading and ideas in any case.

Margot Asquith is an intolerable ass—her 'wit' the most strained and tinny that ever mortal sat up to prepare.[4]

How Red works—God what a country, what a religion. . . .

Had a letter from Tom and one from Dad. Tom will get along because he . . . doesnt make stodgy people uncomfortable. I am going to tear the hide right off Canada some day and rub salt into it.

How fortunate I have been with friends—never without them, and always the best in the world. Yet I never feel dependent on any. Dont *need* any. Men are always *really* alone. That is why society is so necessary—

Best love Mother dear

Marshall

[2] The wife of the Prime Minister. McLuhan received a calling card from Mrs Chamberlain, with the words "At Home/Tuesday, July 7th, 4 to 6 p.m."—three days after he had planned to leave for Belfast—and a typed note from her secretary, saying that if he arrived at 4 Mrs Chamberlain would show him the "Cabinet Room and also the Chancellor's Room at the Treasury".

[3] Robert Charles Wallace (1881–1955), Principal of Queen's University, Kingston, Ontario (1936–51).

[4] An enquiry by McLuhan's mother doubtless elicited this description of Margot Asquith (1864–1945), widow of a former Prime Minister and a leading figure in London society, known for her wit.

McLuhan left England on August 2 and travelled in Germany until August 11, when he sailed from Bremen for Quebec, arriving there on August 26 and in Toronto by train the next day. He remained there until September 2, visiting his mother—who was head of the drama department of the Von Kunitz Academy— and Tom Easterbrook. After spending eight days in Winnipeg he left for Madison, Wisconsin, arriving on September 17. The following day he was signing in freshmen at the University.

Herbert and Elsie McLuhan
displaying Herbert Marshall at
4 months.

Marshall and Maurice
McLuhan with their father
in Montreal, 1917.

Maurice and Marshall McLuhan, *c.* 1921.

Marshall and Maurice McLuhan, and Ed Robeneck,
among the boats on the shore of the Red River, 1928.

Elsie McLuhan in the 1920s.

ELSIE McLUHAN

*Reader and
Impersonator*

Elsie McLuhan's publicity flyer.

Marshall McLuhan's University of Manitoba
graduation photograph, 1933.

One of the bumping races on the Cam in February 1935. McLuhan is the second man facing the Cox.

The Trinity Hall rowing team. McLuhan is in the middle of the back row.

Introduction
1936-1946

McLuhan had been hired by the University of Wisconsin as a 1936–7 Graduate Assistant in the English Department; his salary was higher than expected, $895. Apart from a letter to his brother Maurice that discusses at great length W.R. Sorley's *Moral Values and the Idea of God* (1918)—it has not been included—no letters from this period survive. But some facts and impressions can be gleaned from brief entries in McLuhan's five-year diary.

The courses McLuhan taught cannot today be identified by the University, but he worked with a "Lower Group" and a "Middle Group", marked their themes conscientiously, while hating this task ("Absolute agony for me to grade—feel like a hangman"—January 27, 1937), and on January 15 was "grateful for many expressions of enthusiastic praise from my Middle Group". Two years later (on January 28, 1939) Professor Helen C. White of his Department wrote, in support of McLuhan's application to the Royal Society of Canada for a government bursary to complete his doctoral thesis on Thomas Nashe at Cambridge, that she had been "much impressed not only by his brilliance of mind, but by the breadth of his interests and of his contacts with what was going forward in England as well as in this country. There is no question that he made the most of his time at Cambridge and came over to us keen and resourceful, ready to share an unusual background. He is an enthusiastic and a hard worker, and I am sure he can be counted upon to do well the thesis upon which he has settled. I very cordially recommend him."

In McLuhan's diary his teaching duties at Wisconsin are given a minor place—he was apparently handling them easily. He mainly notes the books he is reading and other activities: film-going, skating in winter, frequent socializing with friends. Among the people he saw often were Professors Ruth Wallerstein (whom he always calls "Miss Wallerstein"), a Renaissance specialist; Madeleine Doran (see page 293, note 2), Shakespeare scholar; and two fellow Graduate Assistants who were also Ph.D. students: John Pick (see page 108, note 7) and Morton Bloomfield (see page 473, note 1). Of the books McLuhan read that have a later significance in his letters, there are diary notations on Wyndham Lewis's *Tarr* (which he began "with much relish"); Ezra Pound's *Letters* and *ABC of Reading* ("Wish I had read it 7 years ago at least"); James Joyce's *Ulysses*, which he read for the second time; and Yeats's *Collected Poems*. He also took early-morning German classes; read poetry aloud with friends, whom he often met for talkative inexpensive suppers; and attended informal cocktail and dinner parties. His mother visited him from April 11 to 13, 1937.

Two significant events in McLuhan's personal life occurred while he was at Wisconsin. He and Marjorie Norris formally terminated their friendship. And

McLuhan became a Roman Catholic, a conversion he had been moving towards for some time. On November 26, 1936 he wrote his mother's friend Father Phelan of St Michael's College, Toronto, saying that he would like to be admitted to the Church. On his Christmas visit to his mother in Toronto, McLuhan saw Phelan several times and submitted to a strict questioning about his beliefs and devotion. When he returned to Madison he began to attend Sunday Mass (at which he felt "more at home" on March 7) and to take instruction from Father Kutchera. On March 23 "Fr. Phelan wrote me most kindly and will offer Mass for me when I am received." McLuhan was duly received into the Church by Father Kutchera on March 24, 1937, with his friend John Pick as godfather. (This diary entry is outlined in red.) The next day he took his first communion in the college chapel.

McLuhan applied for an appointment at Saint Louis University, a Jesuit institution, on April 13, 1937. (Father Phelan sent a letter in support.) On April 19 Saint Louis asked him to name a salary; and on April 24 McLuhan learned that he had been hired as an Instructor in English. On June 24 he arrived in Vancouver to spend the summer with his mother in Sidney, Vancouver Island, during which time he made several enjoyable visits to Victoria. He returned to Winnipeg on August 19. On September 9 he left for St Louis.

McLuhan found St Louis "quite a livable place apart from the noise and dust", and moved in with the Gerardots at 4343 McPherson Avenue. His courses in his first two semesters at Saint Louis were Freshman English (which he taught every year), The English Renaissance, Shakespeare's Comedies, Reading and Discrimination, and Studies in Milton. On September 21 he met his Shakespeare class at the University and held a seminar ("All will be well. I believe I can keep ahead of them!"), and on September 28 he got five theses started—quizzing, on October 5, an MA thesis on John Donne. On October 13 he enjoyed "puffing the 'Scrutiny' approach to literature" and on November 2 he wrote that he was becoming "quite keen about getting Leavis across to my classes." He gave a lecture on medieval poetry on November 23 and on October 4, 1938 he gave a public lecture on More's *Utopia*. On November 4, 1938 Father McCabe, the head of the English Department, told him that he could take a leave of absence any time (to continue his doctoral studies) and stay at Saint Louis University as long as he wished. On May 9 he held his first Ph.D. chairmanship. Other courses he taught—in 1938–9 and from 1940 to his departure from Saint Louis in 1944—included English Literature to 1775, a seminar on the Renaissance: 17th Century, Studies in the History of Literary Criticism; Poetry and Life; The Study of Literature; The Victorian Novel; Practical Criticism; The Appreciation of Literature; Studies in English Renaissance Literature: Poetry to Milton. McLuhan's closest friends in St Louis were colleagues: Bernard Muller-Thym, who taught philosophy, and (beginning in 1940) Felix Giovanelli, who taught French and Spanish. There are letters to both in this collection.

McLuhan made a great impact on the English Department at Saint Louis, bringing a wholly fresh approach to the teaching there with his devotion to the

New Criticism, which he had absorbed at Cambridge. Innovatively treating both early and contemporary literatures, he revelled in breaking down barriers between cultures and disciplines, extending his purview to include art and, in time, popular culture. Father Walter J. Ong—who took courses from McLuhan in Renaissance literature and Rhetoric and Interpretation—has written that a good teacher encourages others to think. "A superb teacher can make the thinking an overpowering activity, delightful even when it is disturbing and exhausting. By these criteria, Marshall McLuhan was always a superb teacher. He could stir people's minds. Even those who found themselves baffled or exasperated generally find themselves changed."

Among the books McLuhan read in his first period at Saint Louis were Evelyn Waugh's *Decline and Fall*, Wyndham Lewis's *One-Way Song, Count Your Dead*, and *Apes of God* (he picked up Lewis's *Apes of God, Childermass*, and *The Doom of Youth* for $2.00—"Great luck"), André Siegfried's *Canada: An International Power* and Wilfred Bovey's *Canadien*, Djuna Barnes' *Nightwood*, Jacques Maritain's *L'Art et scholastique*, Proust's *Swann's Way*, Mortimer Adler's *Art and Prudence*, V.I. Pudovkin's *Film Technique and Film Acting*, Mencken's *In Defense of Women*, Fitzgerald's *The Great Gatsby* ("feel grateful for Fitzgerald"), Edmund Wilson's *The Triple Thinkers*, Lewis Mumford's *The Culture of Cities* ("Mumford simply splendid"), Edith Wharton's *The Custom of the Country*, Dostoevsky's *The Brothers Karamazov*, Keyserling's *Europe*, and T.S. Eliot's *The Family Reunion*. He also read Robert Frost and Dante. He saw films (*Mayerling, Emile Zola, Tovarich, Room Service, You Can't Take It With You, Pygmalion*) and plays (*Richard II* with Maurice Evans, *The Plough and the Stars, Show Boat, Heartbreak House, Shadow and Substance, Susan and God* with Gertrude Lawrence—"She's a bitch, but bright", the Lunts in *Amphytrion 38*, John Barrymore in *My Dear Children*); and *Cavalleria Rusticana* in the Hollywood Bowl.

In the summer of 1938 McLuhan began a relationship that altered his life. On June 20 he left for California to study Nashe at the Huntingdon Library in San Marino. His mother enrolled at the Pasadena Playhouse School of Theatre to be near him and introduced him to a fellow student, Corinne Lewis, of Fort Worth, Texas. ("Tea at Miss Walkups' in the p.m. Met Corinne Lewis there—worth knowing!") He saw much of her thereafter, until she left on August 17 ("Corinne phoned good-bye. Feel quite a gap. Don't know what to think yet.") They wrote, and Corinne began to occupy his thoughts. November 8: "Wrote briefly, practically proposing." November 9: "Corinne's letter came—quite blissful." November 14: "Corinne dismayed by my lack of romance." November 15: "See grim time ahead before Corinne and I are either wed, or through." He was invited to spend New Year's at Fort Worth and during this visit their feelings for each other deepened. Later Corinne—who was experiencing negative parental pressure—wrote to say that "nothing is possible for us this summer"; but on June 9 McLuhan went to see her in Austin, where she was working, and they became engaged. Corinne visited him in St Louis on July 17; they looked at rings on July

22; Corinne decided to go home on August 3—and on the same day changed her mind. A "hectic rush" ensued and they were married on August 4. McLuhan's letters cover their wedding, their honeymoon trip to Europe, and their happy sojourn in Cambridge, where McLuhan worked on his thesis.

The McLuhans returned to St Louis in June 1940. The letters, however, jump to 1943 and the beginning of a long correspondence with Wyndham Lewis, the English painter and author whose works McLuhan had begun to read in his first year at Cambridge and whose thought—particularly the attention he paid to popular culture—would influence McLuhan's own writing. Lewis was then living in Windsor, Ontario. The correspondence documents a relationship that was founded on McLuhan's profound admiration for Lewis's books, on Lewis's evident respect for McLuhan—and, initially, on McLuhan's enterprise in arranging for Lewis a money-making visit to St Louis as a literary celebrity and distinguished portrait painter. It lasted, with one long interruption, into Lewis's sad old age.

In 1943—the year he was granted a Ph.D. from Cambridge for his thesis on Nashe—McLuhan began producing a steady stream of articles for academic, literary, and other periodicals that continued for over thirty-five years. The essays he wrote between 1943 and 1946 include "Education of Free Men in Democracy: The Liberal Arts" and "Wyndham Lewis: Lemuel in Lilliput" (*St Louis University Studies in Honour of St. Thomas Aquinas*); "Herbert's Virtue", "Eliot's 'The Hippopotamus'", "Henley's Invictus" (all for *The Explicator*); "Edgar Poe's Tradition", "Poetic vs. Rhetorical Exegesis", "Kipling and Forster", "Another Aesthetic Peep-Show", "Footprints in the Sands of Crime" (all for *The Sewanee Review*); "Dagwood's America" (*Columbia*); "Aesthetic Patterns in Keats' Odes" (*University of Toronto Quarterly*), "Out of the Castle into the Counting House" (*Politics*), "The New York Wits" (*The Kenyon Review*); and "An Ancient Quarrel in Modern America" (*The Classical Journal*).

Wyndham Lewis had a part in McLuhan's being accepted in March 1944 for an appointment at Assumption College, Windsor, Ontario, where McLuhan and his family stayed until 1946. In the autumn of that year he joined the teaching staff of St Michael's College, University of Toronto.

1937

To Elsie McLuhan

Dear Mother,—

O, what a dusty smoky city you are coming to![1] However you may find it as pleasant as I do. You must not imagine that you will meet instant success. Dont come with any such notion.

But first, poor old Rags. I'm afraid he wouldn't get along here with Sandy. It is of course ever so much easier for me to vote "curtains" for him, not having seen him for so long. But prudence almost requires it. We would probably be forced to do it in another year at most, in mere kindness. But certainly if any other way presents itself he should continue.

Once you get around a bit here you will soon chuck producing for concerts. There are heaps of chances—more money less effort. So *dont* come without settling with the Immigration folks about the concert question. There is not the least chance of your concealing your nationality, and "Mrs Hall" would complicate matters. If you were to produce as Mrs Hall and entertain as Elsie McLuhan where would you be? Or if you were to entertain as "Mrs Hall" think of the confusion with your previous "stage" reputation.

Since St Louis U. has its own play producer you would have to consider Washington U. (T.S. Eliot's father[2] was once its president and they have long thought of doing "Murder [in the Cathedral]") You could get your caste [*sic*] through the Little Theatre group here for a non University production. There are at least 4 very important girls' schools near or in St Louis. You should swing them—3 are Catholic. Maude Adams[3] is play producer at Stevens which is the 4th and richest. But, at 1st, stay clear of St Louis U. You will be able to stay here on McPherson for a while at least.

Talking to Madame Gerardot about Rags—she wont refuse him.[4] So, if it seems utterly brutal to snuff him out I suppose we might try him here.

Lovingly
Marshall

N.B. You had best freight the books unless you have room for them in your trunk. If so tell Red to keep that customs bill anyway.

[1]Elsie McLuhan arrived in St Louis for a visit on December 7 and returned to Detroit on December 29.

[2]T.S. Eliot's grandfather, the Rev. William Greenleaf Eliot (1811–87), was the founder of Washington University, St Louis.

[3]Maude Adams (1872–1935), a popular star of the New York stage from 1897 to 1918 and the creator of the title role in J.M. Barrie's *Peter Pan* (1905). In 1937 she was made Professor of Drama at Stephens College, Columbia, Missouri.

[4]McLuhan was living as a boarder in the home of Mme Marie Josephine Gerardot at 4343 McPherson Avenue. Rags died on December 4.

1938

To Elsie McLuhan

Dear Mother—What a life for you! Perhaps not so dull as it might be tho . . .

Classes have been going very well. Registration is much larger than usual. How much more I am enjoying things! The summer seems to have been good for me.

Have decided to have a sherry party for the lay faculty and wives 2 weeks to-morrow. About 30–40 people I imagine. Why not? May cost $10 but will be thoroughly worth it—"a bachelor entertains." Madame says OK and has the glasses. Hors d'oeuvres will be a simple matter.

Madame had her hair much primped up to-day. Came home blushing like a schoolgirl (ought to blush).

Sandy is *so* itchy.

There will be no war in Europe. The real villains in the piece are not Hitler etc but the Comintern, the free masons and the international operators who have their headquarters in Prague. Hitler is being backed by Chamberlain and Roose-velt (appearances to the contrary).

Am feeling better than ever before—the vitamin capsules seem to be of real assistance. You *must* take them.

Have begun a little Italian and Spanish.

Corinne seems to be very devoted.[1] Writes of endless orgies of dashing madly about really, one asks, will she ever grow up?

Wonder whether to write Red?

Cleveland is probably a vast improvement on Detroit—Best luck there Mother.

Lovingly
Marshall

[1]While McLuhan did research for his Ph.D. thesis on Thomas Nashe (see page 103, note 4) over the summer at the Huntingdon Library in San Marino, California, his mother took a house in nearby Pasadena and enrolled in the Pasadena Playhouse School of Theatre. One of her young classmates was Corinne Lewis of Fort Worth, Texas, whom Mrs McLuhan introduced to her son, thus begin-ning a romance that led to their marriage the following year.

To Elsie McLuhan

Saint Louis
[October 10, 1938]

Dear Mother, What a surprise to hear from you yesterday![1] Thought it was some-body trying to find out my address. The weather was perfect, so there was no occasion for wraps etc. Nearly everybody found his way hither—about 40–45 I believe. In the evening things became much more hilarious with Addie [Adelaide Coleman] and some friends of Harold [Gerardot] in the saddle. The sherry (only $2 a gallon) was sufficient and much praised. (Everything together cost $15). After some food we moved out on the back lawn and simply sat in a big circle— Full moon immediately overhead and the weather quite warm—too warm to-day.

The flowers were grand—fine tall ones, quite sufficiently noticeable. Thanks so much.

Wednesday night is The Veiled Prophet Ball—big civic affair. Clem. wants me to take her—she can get ticket via her Dad—complimentary.[2] There are no tickets for sale. So it will be white tie and tails.

I find my lecture schedule noticeably heavier than last year, but nothing to kick about.

Enjoy a daily pipe now—after dinner.

Glad the party is over, and my lecture. Will settle down to steady life I hope. I do so want to get a real grasp of the things I teach.

Have a Milton class in an hour and am still preparing for it.

So, most lovingly,
Marshall

[1]McLuhan's mother had phoned him from Cleveland the morning before as he was preparing to give his sherry party, which lasted into the evening.

[2]Clementine has not been identified.

1939

Corinne Lewis invited McLuhan for New Year's (1938–9) in Fort Worth. He spent a happy week there (from December 28 to January 3, staying at a hotel), even though he was not warmly received by Corinne's parents. This stranger from the North was quite alien to their genteel Southern world and their plans for their daughter. McLuhan's religion was another obstacle in his courtship.

To Corinne Lewis

[No complimentary opening]

Another time you may relax, darling!

You *can* write such gratifying letters when in a weakened, fatigued state! Stay that way. However you are probably repenting the foible by now.

You ask by the way whether I go to daily mass. No. But, really, during vacation it does seem the least that one can *do*. You see, to hear mass and/or to receive communion, are spiritual *acts*. Not merely acts of worship but acts which have definite, specific merit. This merit can be applied to any other person either on earth or in purgatory. The merit of these acts does not, and this is crucial, proceed from the person performing the act. Since human merits, all of them in their entirety from the beginning of history, are not sufficient to compensate for the tiniest sin. For even the tiniest sin constitutes an act of spiritual rebellion against God. The tiniest imaginable sin is thus infinite in its enormity since it is a sin against an infinitely good, the only Absolute Being. Thus the merit, to return to the 1st point, of spiritual *acts* is derivative. It is derived from Christ. The infinite merit of His Incarnation, His infinitely humbling Himself, was alone sufficient to 'liquidate' all human sins for all time. But the subsequent acts of His life have a mysterious value (a mystery is, strictly, not something queer or hidden, but something unfathomably and inexhaustably rich in meanings) which *naturally* (in their very nature) dwarf every historical event and every philosophical or scientific truth.

So in going to Mass and assisting at that bloodless sacrifice, one is simply applying the merits of Christ either to oneself or, as the phrase goes, to one's "friends and benefactors", known or unknown. And nothing could be more natural when it is realized that the Church is strictly a society, tho supernatural in character.

Let me point out some immediately obvious conclusions or implications attaching even to the brief suggestions here. First, since all sin is infinitely horrible and insulting to God (we are dependent creatures, owing our entire being to Him) Catholics are *taught*, and generally recognize, that one man is quite as great a sinner as the next. Knowing himself to be *essentially* imperfect he readily conceives charity for the imperfections of others. But charity for the sinner is quite compatible with intense repulsion from the sin. Moreover, he realizes that any moral virtue which he or anybody may achieve is directly owing to the mercy of God and the merits of Christ. He knows that he can take no credit for any goodness he achieves. And in reverencing the saints, and relics associated with them, the Catholic is venerating the *signs* of God's *favor* toward a creature.

Another important Catholic attitude follows. There is no sense of strain such as arises in Calvinistic quarters where the *means* of grace are denied, and either a deliberate effort of "the will to believe" is insisted on or else mere predestination is taught.

More important than any other single difference between Catholic attitudes and others is perhaps that the Catholic does not "fear" God, but has every reason to love Him. The *first* thought which a Catholic has of God is that which a man has for a *real* friend. It is only his second thought which may suggest to him how little he deserves such friendship. Taking this fact, together with the social nature of the Church, it is easy to see why Catholics speak so freely and naturally of their prayers and devotions.

There is nothing proper to human nature which is not perfected and assisted by the Church. Every human faculty finds its true use and function only within the Church. That is hard for Protestants to realize, because religion with them is so commonly a matter of restrictions and prohibitions. The Church, on the other hand, is primarily concerned with *action*. Since *potency* can only become *real* through *act*. The Protestant has, or had, a half-truth. He starves on a half loaf, foregoing his rightful heritage, much as the paranoiac imagines his dinner to be poisoned.

This brings up a dozen other matters. One doesn't take the Protestant errors very seriously after one has looked into a dozen or so similar heresies which sprang up in the 3rd and 4th centuries—there were heresies before the 3rd as well as after. And to understand orthodoxy, some study of the history of the Church is necessary.

Orthodoxy is intellectual honesty as regards divine things. Heresy is intellectual and spiritual lying—lying to God himself. It is thus the most hateful of all sins, the one most bitterly punished by an orthodox state or polity. But there are no longer any orthodox states. This makes it difficult for us to sympathize with historical times when heresy was "persecuted".

Now, a man like Luther was a heretic. He lied to God. He knew the truth. But subsequent Lutherans etc were never told the truth, and they were denied the sacraments which lead to an 'inferior' awareness of the truth. Thus, it requires some considerable 'luck' or effort on the part of a Protestant to-day to rediscover orthodoxy. That is why most converts tend to be intellectuals, people with special knowledge of history and philosophy. It is true, for example, that a majority of Protestant Ministers (even non-Anglican) in America to-day are *intellectually* convinced of the claims of the Catholic Church. But one can readily appreciate their *practical* obstacles to becoming Catholics. Furthermore, it is possible to be intellectually convinced and yet to have no spiritual grace or *motive* to assist one. This latter, in such instances, is lacking simply because the person refuses to pray or to ask for it.

To return to the 'poisoned food' of the paranoiac—I refer, of course, to the Eucharist. Luther used to fall in a fit when celebrating Mass—he was terrified by the *actual* presence of God owing to his really terrible defection from God. But, perhaps oddly, heresy never begins by attacking dogma. At the time of the Reformation nobody ever denied the reality of God's Presence in the Mass, *at first*. The 'reformers' lied in their hearts, but they pretended to be concerned only with the correction of abuses *within* the Church. Gradually, by appealling to the cupidity of Kings and Princes, they produced schisms and schisms, such as the Anglican, were soon widened by heresy. But note, the heresies were *imposed from the top*. The *vast* majority of Englishmen were as horrified as they were helpless when the Mass was abolished. There were at least 5 serious but badly organized revolts. But meantime the aristocracy was bought off by the enormous bribe of monastic lands, and the English people were deprived of the sacraments. At first they thought it would be only for a few years. . . . Human weakness accomplished the rest. To-day England is returning to the Faith.

I just read a most interesting book by Clara Longworth, Countess de Chambrun, "Shakespeare Rediscovered".[1] She produces an enormous amount of evidence to show how *all* of Shakespeare's friends were Catholics, from Richard Field, his printer to the Earls of Southhampton and Essex, his patrons. Even his friend Whitgift, the Archbishop of Canterbury, was a profound Catholic sympathizer. Of course, it has long been known that his father and mother were staunch Catholics, and that his father was ruined, as were the rest of English Catholics, by the enormous fines imposed for non-attendance at Anglican services. Shakespeare himself had to pay about $2000, in our money, to the local Anglican bishop for the privilege of being married by a priest. He was finally driven to London by the persecutions of Sir Thos Lucy (of "humourous" fame).[2] Lucy was one of the most prominent harriers of Catholics of the day.

I merely mention this as an instance of the complete and sordid silence which official English history has imposed on all these long known facts.

You speak, Corinne, of the sufficiency for your present needs of your present beliefs. I fully understand that. As I mentioned, I felt no *need* of Catholic dogma or belief even after I was received into the Church. If ever there was a self-sufficient mind or person (and of course there never can be such, since we are *created* beings) it was I. But I came to know so much about orthodoxy that it was impossible to retain my intellectual integrity any longer except by acting. I saw quite clearly that my only alternative was atheism—active hatred of the Church. For, after a certain point one either moves rapidly towards the church or, equally rapidly, away from it.

I don't think it is unfair of me to talk about these things to you. But I must say, that I am anything but *eager* to do so. For I am more than a little afraid that you may become discouraged. And, since our free will is the most fundamental character we possess, (it being inseparable from the rational nature) I feel the utmost

---

[1] Clara Longworth, comtesse de Chambrun (1873–1954), *Shakespeare Rediscovered; By Means of Public Records, Secret Reports and Private Correspondence Newly Set Forth as Evidence of His Life and Work* (1938).

[2] There is a tradition that Sir Thomas Lucy (1532–1600), acting as Justice of the Peace at Stratford-on-Avon, prosecuted Shakespeare for deer-stealing in 1585 and that the poet wrote a ballad about it—an incident that is said to have precipitated his departure for London.

repugnance to influencing another person, except where readiness to inquire, examine, or consider, is obvious.

However, you should know that, in the event of a 'mixed marriage', the non-Catholic is obliged to receive a certain minimum of instruction about the Church, and to agree that the children, if any, should be reared as Catholics. In point of fact, *most* mixed marriages are not too successful. But neither are most marriages, people being what they are!

Having been a Protestant most of my life, the idea of marrying one seems much more natural to me than it does to a "cradle Catholic". And obviously, the ideal marriage for a convert is with a convert. But life-long Catholics look with intense repugnance on marriage with Protestants. And this I have discovered somewhat to my surprise.

You and I are faced with one of those situations (which fortunately are not very numerous in one life-time) which cannot possibly be *adequately* judged beforehand. It strikes me as a colossal gamble, or rather, a very great adventure. And personally I am considerably exhilirated by the risks! This exhiliration may compensate for the absence of "romance"! The greatness of the adventure perhaps consists partly in the fact that as a Catholic I can marry only once! But, as with being born, perhaps once is quite sufficient! In the Church, you know, there is a great heightening of every moment of experience, since every moment is played against a supernatural backdrop. Nothing can be humdrum in this scheme. Every least act of the mind has infinite significance. (Dostoevsky, by the way, is one of the few novelists who has succeeded in *realizing* this in art. In the world of Passos on the otherhand, *no* act has *any* significance. There are no standards beyond those of immediate sensation. Passos himself recognizes this, and, in consequence presents the situation not despairingly but satirically) And just as there is nothing good or true which is not Catholic, so there are a great many excellent things which can be had only by the Catholic. Needless to say, however, most Catholics are too lazy or too feeble to use what they possess. And particularly in America where the main currents of life are profoundly anti-Catholic, the average Catholic is too timid, too over-awed by the surrounding material "splendor", to feel able to be anything but an 'interior' Catholic. As the "splendor" rapidly becomes ludicrous and stupid the Church will press forward in America. This is happening even now.

You speak quite truly of my lack of "worldly" ambition. *Perhaps* this lack in me is simply a lack of competence for such success. But please dont imagine that I despise such competence. I am prepared to do all I can to achieve a reasonable "standard of living." My trouble, of course, is that I now enjoy such a high standard of *living* (most students can have pleasures which no money can ever command) that I am loath to sacrifice my intellectual standards to achieve a more popular success. The question then arises, can I reconcile the 2 things? Is it possible to achieve success through sheer excellence? Well, I know many who have done so. But many more, who are equally excellent, do not. And my unyielding, independent temperament is agin' me here. I simply can't bring myself to curry favor among men who I consider inferior in ability. But I can be utterly congenial with people who I know to be equal or superior—and with inferiors from whom I expect nothing, or on whom I depend for nothing. Really, Corinne, I'm not boasting about this. It is not, perhaps, entirely creditable to be this way.

Nor do I see how the most marvellous possible wife (do you recognize yourself!) could do much to alter this. But she could undoubtedly do a very great deal to assist a man along the road to excellence. I am very aggressive, very ardent in anything I do; but I need *drive*. There are any number of ways in which you could help me. But I hope you know that I would never ask or require it. It is quite obvious though, that if you were not to help me, but simply expected things to happen by magic, we would fail miserably.

So far as money is concerned, I have never been tempted to spend more than I have. My *personal* expenditures always have and always will be small (books perhaps a slight exception here!). I have never been able to understand why a man earning a fixed stipend should concern himself about money. My "instinct" is to turn *all* of it over to the other partner in the enterprise! This I have heard is the traditional European method. It strikes me as utterly natural. Isn't it queer, at first glance, that in America of all places, where women are ostensibly the *only* object of "money-making" that men should "budget" them? It is of course merely another evidence that the American male has an *essential* contempt for, as well as a fear of women.

Well, I've arranged my year's leave of absence with Father McCabe.[3] So its Cambridge now, without query. It will be ever so much more satisfactory to have the Phd.[4] And besides, it will give me a most refreshing year, and one in which to get a job of "scholarship" done, or at least on the way to completion. Most of my work is going to be critical, I can see. One *must* get things into print, you know, in order to command attention and salary. Good teaching goes for nothing in our universities to-day.

[3]Father William H. McCabe, S.J., was Chairman of the English Department at Saint Louis University. See also page 146.

[4]McLuhan's Ph.D. thesis, accepted by Cambridge in 1943, was "The Place of Thomas Nashe in the Learning of His Time". The pamphleteer Thomas Nashe (1567–1601)—who had been a student at St John's College, Cambridge—wrote several dramas and satires in the decade before his early death, along with the first picaresque romance in English, *The Unfortunate Traveller; or The Life of Jacke Wilton* (1594), a tale of adventure that includes much literary parody and pastiche. The thesis (as explained in McLuhan's abstract) focused on the conflict that existed in the world of sixteenth-century learning between those who were for or against the patristic method—based on grammar, dialectics, and rhetoric—in theology and formal expression, particularly on the quarrel between Gabriel Harvey (c. 1550–1631), who turned his back on classical rhetoric after leaving Cambridge, and Nashe, who became "a daring exponent of the traditional patristic program of learning and eloquence." The thesis also includes a history of the trivium, the medieval university course of grammar, rhetoric, and logic. McLuhan discusses his thesis in a letter to Tom Wolfe of October 25, 1965.

Incidentally, don't concern yourself over the "regrettable incident" cited in the last letter. There was nothing *scandalous* about it![5]

Thought you might enjoy 2 of my freshmen's exam papers. I didn't choose the topic, and think it a poor one. Their prepared themes are *much* better than this, naturally.

By the way, could you send back the Passos[6] as soon as you have done with it? Hate to stop this. *Do* some more letters like the last one! You are dear to me beyond thinking, Corinne—   Yours Marshall

[5]This might refer to the fact that Mrs Lewis had a party for McLuhan while he was visiting Corinne Lewis in Fort Worth to which she also invited several young men friends of Corinne's, including one who had hoped to marry her.

[6]The trilogy *U.S.A.* (1938) by John Dos Passos.

To Elsie McLuhan

[St Louis]
Thursday [January 25, 1939]

Dear Mother,

Well, skating with Clem last night. We have become quite proficient. That is to say that Clementine has improved very considerably, so that we are able to move quite speedily and also with a considerable degree of safety—a minimum of bumping into others etc. It is unquestionably an interesting and pleasant sport, greatly preferable to dancing to present day bands.

Your dream of *my* "wedding" garbage was scarcely exaggerated! Though the remark about the 55 berries [dollars] doesn't seem quite in character does it? Unless it was intended ironically! One thing, when I am married, (or if), I shall not wear any borrowed or rented stuff—that means no morning suit for me.

I have fully made up my mind that so far as Corinne and I are concerned we either get married in August or never. While leaving it entirely to her to decide, it is obvious that there are a 1000 ways in which I could break it off without even appearing to wish to do so. But the thought of becoming engaged while remote is unthinkable. I will not return to Fort Worth ever, until Corinne makes up her mind to get married. To return to see her there while she was still undecided is a harrowing thought. And she may not get to St. Louis till June. We haven't had much chance to know each other have we?

Cant keep track of all the irons you have in the fire these days! But its grim your having flu with it all. And I suppose 616 is utterly nightmarish?[1]

Have to read 3 Ben Jonson plays for this afternoons seminar in the Jacobean Drama

Most Lovingly
Marshall.

[1]616 Pallister was Elsie McLuhan's address in Detroit.

To Corinne Lewis

[St Louis]
Tuesday night [January 31, 1939]

'lo Goose-pimples!

Here is a cock-eyed picture of the very cultivated and charming lady who had charge of the Boys Choirs in which *I* sang! Isn't it queer that Dad should have sent me this picture almost at the very moment that I was recalling her, after so many years!

Imagine my astonishment on approaching the class-room (in which I was to give the first lecture on 'Rhetoric and Interpretation') to find a large group huddled promiscuously outside! I thought the door must be locked, but on reaching the door I could see standing room only inside! Graduate classes seldom consist of more than 12–15 people. There are at least 35 in this one. I'm glad the *first* lecture is over. I was quite moist before I had got well started!

When I got home at 5.30 Addie was dangling her feet over the arm of a chair— she is a friend of the family *now*![1], and had decided to come to dinner since a Bridge was in progress at her place. So I hauled out the remnant of a 1/5 of Cribari [?] brandy that I brought back from California, and Harold (who has begun to take a great interest in Addie) soon arrived to join us.[2] I really couldn't, after the 1st glass, hold back the news of your possible Easter visit. And Addie *insists* that you come by plane since it is such *great* fun to meet people at the air-port! Anyhow, we have planned a week-end in the country (on "The Hill") for you. And really, nothing could be more ideal, provided you can "manage" your Aunt here! Mr and Mrs (Harold's sister) Shaw would be our chaperones. This would be, to my mind, a very superior way of spending our time to dashing from one club to another in St. Louis. So put in your "old" shoes and leave your evening slippers behind. It should be very delightful in the country by Easter, tho it *is* early this year. But that is sheer speculation, since I wouldn't be "liable" to notice those nymphs fauna and flora if you were along.

Sinclair Lewis is coming with his play next week, and Cornelia Otis Skinner the next week—she is *in* a play for the first time.[3]

The envelopes I got recently are a bit too transparent—tell me if there are any complaints about their being tantalizing in this respect!

[1] Adelaide Coleman, who a few months later became engaged to Karl Strobach. The Strobachs and the McLuhans became friends and never lost touch.

[2] Harold Gerardot, the son of McLuhan's landlady.

[3] It is not clear which of Sinclair Lewis's plays—*Dodsworth* (1934), *Jaywalker* (1934), or *It Can't Happen Here* (1930)—toured to St Louis at this time. The American actress Cornelia Otis Skinner (1901–79) appeared in a selection of her monologues; she did not tour in a play until several years later.

To Corinne Lewis

[St Louis]
Wednesday [February 1, 1939]

[*No complimentary opening*]

I must apologize for the 'champagne' in my letters. At least, you *seem* to have been suffering from a sodden hangover when you sat down to write Sunday! I'm going to see to it that you have a day or 2 to sober up, Toots old thing! (pronounced with an aristocratic lilt, as Tŭhts). Its easy to see how little you appreciate *me*. Here I go to all the trouble of discovering a brand *new* vocable, a nice cosy ice-melting sound, and then you become nostalgic for 'adolescent adulation' —"Lady Astor" stuff! Incidentally, have you *seen* that awful old frump? Perhaps it is just as well!

Its a pity you didnt know me before I went to Cambridge, before I was "spoiled" as you say. *Then* you would have had at *least* one poem a day, celebrating your perfections, real, dubious, and imaginary! You would have been showered with gorgeous epithets, and it would have served you right! Fatal fare, my fairly faery fair!

If it is unfortunate that you didn't know me *then*, it seems to me a greater pity that you know me no better *now*! Really, Corinne, you will have a better chance here in St Louis than in Fort Worth.

Look here, how could "the philanderings of Juppiter!" (I like it this way!) be "a solid background" for anything![1] I never-look at 'Stage'—Should I?

You are wrong about the compensation motif being universal. Americans abroad spend much breath be-moaning the "dowdiness" of Old Country dress. And your reference to animal life is unfortunate in that the *female* of the sub-rational species is, apparently, without any compensation motive. At *that* level it is just as Milton would have it, "He for gaudiness, and she for gaud in him!

(He for God alone, and she for God in him)[2]

You ask about Harold [Gerardot], that spoiled 'ittle baby? Well his reading habits have been improving since I have had so much good fiction lying around. He got "a big boot" out of 'Brother Rat' the other night.[3] You never *did* condescend to tell me what the hell that show was about—now I know. Harold spent at least half an hour enthusing about it, in detail. As he said, "I guess I've had too many beers". I'm usually reading when he comes in so we have our nightcap bottle together. All of —

[Throws away next sheet and replaces with:]

(pinch-hitter for cancelled sheet!)

—his friends have been getting married to one another recently, and he is becoming restive, like Sandy in the mating season.

---

[1] An obscure reference, probably to something in *Stage* magazine.

[2] "He for God only, she for God in him", *Paradise Lost*, Bk IV, 1. 299.

[3] The comedy *Brother Rat* by John Monks Jr and Fred Finklehoffe ran on Broadway from 1936 to 1938 and was on tour.

Having seen only 'Snow-White' and 'Room Service' in the past 12 months I am almost vain of the fact.[4] I often wish the pictures *were* better, if only because that having seen them one has *much more* in common with freshmen, for example—they make (movies) useful handles in teaching I have found. I always spend at least 2 weeks introducing them to the writings of Pudovkin and Eisenstein on film technique, and make them adapt a novel to scenario form.[5] But movies as at present are the opium of the people, quite as much as 'opium', is in its turn, the religion of the people.

I cant find it in me to compete with your public on Feb. Fourteen! Instead, I shall pay you the greater compliment of sulking in my tent, foregoing all joysome pastime on that great day!

By the way, it strikes me that you have rather lost your nerve lately, or that you are thinking about a number of things (not *necessarily* concerning me) which you simply dont mention. My own candour usually leads me up to, and often beyond the point of rashness. But I dont expect other people to be that way, even though it might avoid difficulty in the long run.

Down here I had been saying that you can depend on Madame Gerardot to protect me from *my* 'public'. For despite her 67 years she is as jealous of my feminine acquaintances as could be *reasonably* expected. Since I seldom go out any more, I tend to see my friends 'at home', if at all. To my infinite amusement, I have 'caught' Madame saying the *meanest* things to them when she thought I was out of hearing! She wont deliver your letters to me when they arrive, and I would hesitate to ask her to post one to you! However you may be sure she will make a special effort to be polite to you when you meet! In fact you may depend on more than politeness (which is simply insulting when warmth is in order) for I shall impress upon her your remoteness from *home*!

As for Adelaide Coleman, you will like her a great deal. (She plans to become a nun in September—having given herself 9 years, to a day, in which to savour 'the world'.[6] Having had an Old Country education, even though brought up in St. Louis, and being a *very* able and independent sort of person, she simply cant take the Yankee momma boyes [*sic*] seriously.) But there aren't *many* people here that I should care for you to meet, on so brief a visit. And even if there were I simply wouldn't share the time with them.

By the way, Addie isn't just 9 years old! She is your age. But, 9 years ago on leaving high school, several of her best friends took Orders. She took some time instead. You will probably find it difficult to imagine Addie becoming a nun

[4]Walt Disney's *Snow White and the Seven Dwarfs* (1937) and the Marx Brothers' *Room Service* (1938) were two popular films of the time.

[5]V.I. Pudovkin (1893–1953) and Sergei Eisenstein (1898–1948), two great Russian film directors in the twenties, when they were rivals, and the thirties. Pudovkin's lectures to the Moscow Film Institute in 1926 were published in English in *Film Technique and Film Acting* (1929); Eisenstein's essays on film—written in an "ideogrammic" style that interested McLuhan, with short paragraphs interspersed with drawings and photographs—were published in several volumes, including *The Film Sense* (1942) and *Film Form* (1949).

[6]See page 105, note 1.

since she is a very *healthy* and attractive specimen indeed! Has a B.A. etc.

After, getting the picture of teacher and the apples, I'm moved to ask if this is your plight? For some reason I never think of myself as a teacher, but as a person! I'm simply unimpressed by all the stock responses associated with the occupation. Perhaps I'm prone to think of myself as "too big" for the job—if so, its too bad, and I can only shake my head sadly over my pejor [?] self. I know at least one prof. who is delighted to find apples on his desk—considers it a mark of genuine affection I believe. All I know is, that if ever I find such an object in such a place I shall heave it through the window and see that the culprit pays for the pane of glass.

I have finally decided to rip up the preceding sheet. Not that it contains anything more than ordinarily stupid but simply that it was laboriously written—my mind was on other things perhaps. But this, I think is the *first* time that I ever cancelled a page of writing. And I am impressed, that you should inspire me with such caution and reserve! What about you?

Am enclosing the Phd. thesis abstract of John Pick.[7] He was my best friend at Wisconsin. He is Catholic, one of the very few on the staff there, and was my sponsor when I was received into the Church. I shall always remember the occasion. I was to be received at 10.30 P.M. 2 days before Easter 1937 [March 24], and I spent the evening with Pick and some friends in a strenuous and heated discussion of the work of Aldous Huxley. It struck me, later, as quite appropriate that the work of this celebrated modern and nostalgic agnostic should have been the subject of conversation at *that* time. I have never given him a thought since. You have read him?

Have you tackled [Gerard Manley] Hopkins? Try such simple things as 'Pied Beauty', 'Hurrahing in Harvest' etc. to begin with. Read him aloud. He *insists* on it!

Big faculty round table to-night followed by beer and ham etc. I was cornered by Benny Bommarito afterwards and listened long and sympathetically (!) to his present pre-matrimonial difficulties. (It is late, and only as I turn this sheet I note that it is not of the same weight as the others!) Couldn't help smiling to myself as I contrasted his very simple obstacles with mine ours! His fiancé is an orphan and a Catholic, so what the hell!

I certainly don't fancy casting you *gratuitously* for a role in the sort of meller-drammer that you perceive I might write, so easily, in collaboration (*do* I need *any* help!) with Gorky! It 'gives one spuriously to think' n'est ce pas?!

Very amusingly, the letter box at the U. had 3 items for me this morning. They were from 3 people I seldom hear from, and the main matter in each was Catho-

---

[7]John Pick had been a Teaching Assistant with McLuhan at the University of Wisconsin, while working on his Ph.D., and acted as godfather when McLuhan was received into the Roman Catholic Church in 1937. He later became Professor of English at Marquette University, Milwaukee (1952–75). Author of the well-known *Gerard Manley Hopkins: Priest and Poet* (1942)—he and McLuhan often read Hopkins together—Pick was for a while editor of the magazine *Renascence*, in which McLuhan occasionally published. He died in 1981.

licism! One said I *must* not take holy orders and thus *waste* myself—this from a professor at home who admits he is a 'fanatic' on the subject of 'race and family'. "I feel it would be tragic if your fine qualities of intellect and spirit should voluntarily perish with you"!! What queer ideas people have about priests! Another wanted to know how much it *cost* to get a soul out of purgatory! And so on! However the letter bag seldom produces such offerings.

Incidentally, the professor had no notion that I *was* intending 'holy orders'. And indeed I have never *had* such a vocation.

Well your cute little pink sheet, prognostic of brief jottings(!), surprised me this morning (Wednesday). Thought you had quite outgrown letter-writing.

Anyhow it is now well into Thursday, so I'm for bed, et vous?

> Thursday sometime or other
> (Candelmas Day)

Dont trouble to return the Hardwicke interview.[8] Is he going to visit Ft. W.? I'm going Sat. night to see him. To-night is the 'Book and Quill' meeting (what a fatuous title!) We have been doing rather well this year. I haven't made the slightest effort to disturb their convictions about the 'literary' value of current best sellers. But they have begun to wake up all by themselves. And we have no outside talent brought in. At the beginning of the year the only girl left in the club from last year was the secretary. Hearing that I was pleased at the prospect of its becoming masculine, and serious (!), she dashed around and herded in 10–12 nurses! (As I have mentioned, no women may belong to St Louis U. proper. They get courses at the U. by belonging to the schools of Nursing, Education, or Social Service.) The nurses are all scholarship people, and for the most part exceptionally interesting, so the club hasn't suffered *too* badly. Of course *I* suffer!

I miss my own books a great deal. There are 1500–2000 volumes belonging to me up in Toronto. Here, I have only 200–300, and even they loom as a problem when I consider moving them. However, I can safely entrust *anything* with the Gerardots. But "life" would be much more complete if I could reach for any standard English writer whenever a passing reflection kindles a momentary curiosity.

Well this is the point at which I intend to *stop*.

> Lovingly
> Marshall

[8]Sir Cedric Hardwicke (1893–1964) was performing in St Louis with Sara Algood and Julie Haydon in Paul V. Carroll's *Shadow and Substance*, which McLuhan saw on February 4.

To Elsie McLuhan

[St Louis]
Sunday [February 12, 1939]

Some Valentine!

I didn't send anything to Corinne—simply told her I refused to compete with her "public". She will be swamped by Valentines. Of course I didn't sound too serious. But, on the other hand I was glad to have such an "excuse", for I'm a bit too proud to afford even the more harmless kinds of adolescent display—particularly with such an audience as her "family"! I really doubt whether anything will come of our affair. You see, I've left everything up to her. Until she makes up her mind my role is strictly passive. She writes 3 times a week, but simply dashes them off. Gives no thought to them. Regrets this, really. But won't go beyond regret, I imagine. No reproaches come from me, however. I have no desire to "change" her. Either she will decide such matters for herself or else I shall lose interest. Meantime, I lose no sleep! Much too busy. She is *such* a thorough-going sort of American that I really doubt my sanity at times. And, regarding her "adolescence" Hersey was *not* wrong.[1] There is obviously something haywire in the family situation. How else account for 2 very attractive girls remaining so very 'teenish and single till their ages?

But if Corinne did decide to marry me, I don't think I would know what to do! I would have a violent reaction probably! Lose my memory, and wander off to Asia! One thing, we would not be married in Fort Worth. Quite unthinkable. I think Corinne would agree. On the other hand, if her family suddenly became very "enlightened" about me, and friendly, then *she* would probably get cold feet. And her folks are not too dumb to recognize this ace of spades in the family sleeve!

After meeting a dozen or 2 of her Fort Worth "dates", I had no difficulty in understanding her interest in me! Really, she deserves something more even for an evening of dancing. They aren't too noticeably superior to "Joe" in Pasadena this summer. What has happened to American men! And what about my Mama-boy article?[2] Just waiting for a moment to complete it. My interest is still white-hot.

Have spent a perfectly quiet Sunday. Last night however I went to see Father Lord's review "Matrimonial Follies 1939".[3] It was quite good fun in spots. Friday evening I spent with Bernie Muller-Thym, Henshaw, and Crisafulli reading Provencal poetry[4]—Most lovingly   Marshall

[1]Hersey was the eurythmics and fencing teacher at the Pasadena Playhouse School of Theatre. Corinne and her sister had very protective parents who did not allow them to have any male friends whose families were not well known to them.

[2]See page 127, note 2.

[3]Father Daniel A. Lord, S.J. (1888–1965), who taught at Saint Louis from 1917 to 1920, became well known for his many books and pamphlets and for his work with young people in the Sodality of Our Lady (renamed Christian Life Communities), for which he wrote numerous musicals, etc.

[4]Bernard Muller-Thym (see next page, note 2), Millett Henshaw, a professor of English, and Alessandro Santi Crisafulli, an instructor in French, were colleagues.

To Elsie McLuhan

[St Louis]
Wednesday [June 21?, 1939]

Dearest Mother,

Wonder how Red is thriving? Must be on his [mission] field by now. Car or no car. Haven't heard from Dad either so they must have been much together.

Yes, the heat descended yesterday and one really waits for classes to end in this weather. Tho they are waking up a bit.

Corinne hopes to get here on June 17.[1] Cant say how long she may stay, but at least a week I imagine. Hope Harold will let us drive his car in the afternoons, since he leaves it at home these days.

Corinne and I dont want to *do* things so much as to get some matters talked over. After all we didn't get engaged until my last night in Austin [June 17], so we weren't quite in a position to talk point blank about many matters.

Have just had words with Wash. U. about the new School of the Theatre. Nobody who matters is in town at present. And no new appointments have been made, since Little Theatre people plus the present staff of Wash U. are to take it over. But new appointments are to be made (in all liklihood [sic]) in the fall. So you can look into it when you come down.

Now, whats up for the summer? What do you plan on? Is Cleveland a dead issue?

So good to hear about the success of your play. Was there a big crowd? You have no place to rest there. Why not come on down here soon?

You shall have the snaps of Corinne. She *is* a most lovely person, all the way.

The Muller-Thym's are[2] sending their children to Kansas City on July 17 for 6 weeks or so. It will be nice to visit them there!

Most lovingly yours
Marshall.

[1]McLuhan wrote "June 17" because earlier, before he decided to visit Corinne Lewis in Austin, where she was helping to revise the curriculum of the Fort Worth public schools at the University of Texas (he was there from June 10 to 18), she had planned to arrive in St Louis on that date for a visit. The new plan was for her to arrive on July 17, which she did.

[2]The brilliant polymath Bernard Muller-Thym (1909–74) was a friend and colleague. With a B.A. in English literature, an M.A. earned with a philosophy thesis written in Latin, and a Ph.D. (1938) from the Pontifical Institute of Mediaeval Studies, University of Toronto (his thesis, later published, was on the fourteenth-century mystic Meister Eckhart), he taught in the Philosophy Department of Saint Louis University, which he would leave in 1941 to join the U.S. Navy. After the war he became a renowned management consultant in New York. There are several letters to Muller-Thym later in this collection. See also page 262, note 1.

To Elsie McLuhan

[St Louis]
Wed. night [July 26, 1939]

Dearest Mother,

Pierre came by yesterday—no Monday—for a few minutes—a very pleasant chap indeed.[1] He took a picture of Corinne and I in the back yard here—said you didn't come because I hadn't urged you sufficiently! In fact, had you been here things *might* have been more difficult. As it is, C. and I are very little alone.

Last night we dined here, then went to the Municipal Opera with Harold [Gerardot], Bernie and Mary [Muller-Thym].[2] To-night we dined with B & M and spent the evening. You can imagine what sort of an education Corinne is getting over there! With Mary getting ready for her 5th baby?

Corinne and I have been downtown a bit. Have decided against an engagement ring. She spends some afternoons here with me—Haven't opened a book since she arrived.

Last lectures to-morrow!

She will probably stay a week yet. We are getting along very well indeed. But no definite determination about marriage date yet. Shall tell you that as soon as possible.

Probably shall hear from you to-morrow—All my love

Marshall.

[1]Pierre is unidentified.
[2]They saw Smetana's *The Bartered Bride*.

To Elsie McLuhan

[The New Hotel Jefferson, St Louis]
Saturday 4 P.M. [August 5, 1939]

Dearest Mother—

What a rush—the whole thing was quite at the last minute. Corinne decided to go home Thursday A.M. and decided to get married here on Friday [the 4th] on Thursday afternoon. You can imagine our frantic rushings around for license, ring, dispensation, steamship reservations, passport (for Corinne) to say nothing of the wedding itself.

Bernie [Muller-Thym] was best man, and Corinne's cousin was bridesmaid. It was at 11 A.M. in the Cathedral rectory. Mary Muller-Thym was the only other person present. We were married by Fr. Helmsing—a fine young priest.

Madame [Gerardot] had cake and wine for us afterwards, then we had to dash for the Federal Bldg. to arrange C.'s passport affadavits. Then home to her cousin's (Mrs. J. Strupper). Then off for no destination in Harold's car. (Corinne driving!) We had a grand evening and dinner at St Alban's Farm (where we had been before) and came back here to the Jefferson at 1 A.M. We shall stay here till Sunday at 5 when Corinne leaves for Ft. Worth alone. We have thought it all over. I shall go down to bring her back in a day or so. We will leave Ft. Worth for N. York (via St. Louis and Pittsburg [*sic*]) on Thursday afternoon—sailing on the Rex Saturday morning.

I shall get to Ft. W. on Wed. That gives me Monday to pack and arrange everything!! What a nightmare. Really it has been a terrible ordeal for Corinne. How she wishes you had been here—but what did we *know*? Nothing until the last moment. We shall [be] quite quite down by the time the Ft. Worth agony is over. We shall have an hour in St Louis between trains and an hour or so before sailing in N. York (if trains are on time)

The best way to see us would be to come to St. Louis before I go to Fort Worth—that is, to get here Monday morning if possible. I shall be terribly rushed but that won't matter.

Must write Dad a note now. He hasnt heard yet. Everything is really terribly confused. But all will straighten itself out before long—by sailing time anyhow. You can imagine how little able I am to compose letters at present![1]

Most lovingly
Marshall.

[*At the top of the first page:*]
How many wedding announcements do you want when they are priced.

[1]Corinne also wrote to Elsie McLuhan on this day, giving her own account of her sudden marriage:

"Dearest Mrs. 'Mac'—

"Well, it's all over, now, tho I do dread the several days necessary in Ft. Worth. How I've wished for you these past few days! We *needed* you so!! You know, I really didn't expect this to happen; I was planning to leave last Thursday for home—on the point of packing—and suddenly I just *couldn't* go. It was a huge bewildering sudden shock of realization of how much Marshall really meant to me; the next thing I knew we were married.

"We've experienced such stress and strain these last few days—and in anticipating these *next* few days. Cross your fingers for our survival! How I want to see you; you're my mother now, too, you know. Of course, my *foremost* thought will always be for Marshall's happiness, for we're going to build a significant life together.

"I hope to see you in a few days. With most *special*

Love,
Corinne"

To Elsie McLuhan

[St Louis]
Tuesday [August 8, 1939]

Dearest Mother,

It may easily happen that Corinne and I may be unable to make the Rex. [by] noon Saturday. We may get there to find necessary passports etc etc not at the pier for us. If so we might have to stay over for a week. Now that would be fabulously expensive in New York. So if we might find some of our relatives it would be all to the good. Send me some addresses by return air-mail and they will be brought to the train for me by Harold.

Have had a hectic day with income tax etc—all necessary before sailing. It cost me $160.

Havent quite packed yet and I leave in 5 hours.[1] Bernie was a big help packing the trunk last night.

Corinne says all is rather better at home than she hoped. Do send this crazy clipping back to us![2] What a mess of boners! Whose imagination was it?

Mother, why havent you phoned or sumpn'? No money? I haven't had nearly enough time to worry about you, but really shall be worried before long.

It would be fun for you to visit with the Lewis' in Ft Worth. They would like you I know.

Most most lovingly
Marshall

[*In margin*]

Send Mrs. C.W. Lewis (602 West Second St., Ft. Worth, Texas) a list of the people to whom you want wedding announcements sent. Corinne asked me to tell you this.

[*Top of first page:*]

Just got a telegram from Mrs and Mr Lewis "So looking forward to seeing you tomorrow.

Love Mr & Mrs"

So!!?

---

[1]Marshall and Corinne McLuhan were about to leave by train for Fort Worth to visit Corinne's parents. They arrived the next morning and stayed overnight, leaving for St Louis at 4 p.m. on Thursday the 10th.

[2]This refers to an article that appeared in the *Fort Worth Press* on August 7, 1939—headed "Couple Sail on S.S. Rex on Aug. 12: Corinne Lewis and St. Louis Man Wed in Missouri"—stating inaccurately that the newlyweds had met in St Louis and that after the honeymoon McLuhan would return to "Missouri State University".

To Herbert McLuhan

[En route to New York]
Friday night [August 11, 1939]

Dear Dad,

Corinne and I got your letters to us this A.M. when we got to St Louis. We had a 40 minute stop there and were met by several friends. We had had a terrific day of packing and farewells in Fort Worth yesterday. Everybody was very much astonished by our getting married but everybody was most kind to us.

We are quite exhausted Dad. But shall have a grand time from now on—until we begin to pull our belts in for economical reasons in Cambridge.

Say hello to my friends for me. And say some prayers for us. We shall write from the boat.[1]

[1]Appended to this letter was a note to Mr McLuhan from Corinne:

"Dearest Mr "Mac"—

"I do appreciate so very much your sweet letter which greeted us this morning in St. Louis. I regret more than I can say that I shan't be able to know you until we return. I'd been looking forward to our meeting for Marshall has said so many lovely things about you. I shall probably be writing you frantic S.O.S.'s for advice in managing this handsome husband I've just acquired.

"I shall drop you a line at our first stop.

Lovingly, Corinne"

After meeting Elsie McLuhan in New York, the bridal couple sailed at noon on the Rex *for Italy, disembarking at Naples on August 20. They visited Rome, Florence, Venice, and Paris, and then left for England, arriving in Cambridge on September 2. War was declared the next day.*

To Elsie McLuhan

(2nd day in Paris) Thursday August 31 [1939]

Don't know where to begin Mother!

Left off in Florence didn't I? While in Italy it didn't seem advisable to mention that we were being followed everywhere as spies! It began in Rome, but I think they gave us up for a couple of nuts after Florence. In Rome the poor chap who followed us really had to hustle and puff to keep us in sight! Our last act before train time was to dash to the Protestant cemetery just outside the walls to see the graves of Keats and Shelley. On leaving the place we caught a train so neatly as almost to leave the poor old detective in the rear. He simply galloped, throwing aside all air of detachment. (He wore a naval uniform.) In Italy every other man has on a splendid uniform. There are dozens of varieties of them, and all of them attractive.

Well, we had a grand time in Florence, tho it was very quiet. Its big season is in April and May. But Venice was in high season and hotel rates were away up in the air. We met a brisk and amusing little Parisien (Jean Dejieu) on the way to Venice. So when we got there we had decided to go to the same hotel. (You see I had bought special hotel coupons on the Rex which are valid anywhere in Italy) On coming out of the station, imagine our disappointment at not finding a bus, train or taxi in sight, but only a big canal full of gondolas and gondoliers!! It took us the best part of an hour to get to our place (right beside St. Marks Cathedral and the Doge's Palace). En route we came out onto the Grand Canal where all the buildings were floodlit with pinks and blues and where there were thousands of gondolas simply festooned with Japanese lanterns. We had hit on a fiesta night when the whole town stays up till dawn. There was a moon too. At length we left the main canal for some tiny twisty ones. Venice is simply honey-combed with them. There are no roads whatever—no land vehicles of any sort, but foot ways only. It surpassed every notion I had ever formed of the place. We had an entire evening (next night) together in a gondola, drifted out onto the Adriatic, and back through many canals. Our gondolier sang arias from the operas to us! Sunday A.M. we went to High Mass in St Marks. It was gorgeous. Monday we came on to Paris via Turin arriving Tuesday at 7 P.M. A long tiresome trip. We have a grand place here—quite central. Only a few steps to Notre Dame, the Louvre, the Luxemburg Gardens etc. We are next door to St Sulpice Church. Paris is enjoying a warm spell—the temperature is nearly 70 in the shade! So Corinne finds her grey coat suit quite useful. She wears socks when out walking, to save silk hose. Altogether I am quite fed up with travel and movement and plotting the next meal or the next move! But Corinne revels in it of course. As [Hermann] Keyserling says in defining the difference between the sexes "Women like to live in hotels"! Now, the Louvre is closed. So are all the libraries and galleries, owing to the war scare. (There will be no war of course) But all stained glass has been removed from the old churches etc. Art treasures have been sent to the provinces etc. It is the same in London.

We shall leave here on Sunday and spend the day with Kath and Ted staying on for awhile with them. Meantime we have much to do in Paris which we shall tell you about later on. Now is the time to see and not to write. We think about you frequently Mother—

Most lovingly Marshall and Corinne

To Elsie McLuhan

[Cambridge, September 5, 1939]

Hello! Hello! England calling. But no distress signals yet. We are writing an hour before the 11 P.M. Clipper Post on Tuesday night. Our present host and his wife are here with us in Rose Crescent (a little corner in Cambridge where Tennyson lived as an undergraduate). They are a cherubic old couple—straight out of Dickens. He is 78 and pink and hearty and active. This afternoon a government man knocked on the door and said the Lord Chancellor wanted the house. On Saturday 10 or 12 men will move in. They must be fed and attended to for the duration of the war for $5 a week. Cambridge being out of danger from air-raids is to receive a great many civil servants who will carry on clerical work here. The colleges will be jammed up with them. Meantime the town is full of children—26,000 from London in the past week—all taken and freely supported by voluntary hosts. It is only the greatest piece of good fortune which has enabled us to get a place at all. And such an ideal place! In the aristocratic part of town, immediately beside and behind the big new Cambridge Library where I shall work. Out our window one has on one side a view of the big garden attached to the house. Out the other side one sees the great green playing fields of Trinity College. The rooms are huge and have been newly redone. And my old supervisor—Mr Elvin—is giving up his house for the year. So instead of storing his furniture (which is very sumptuous indeed) we are to have all we can use, including crockery! There is a piano as well. Our bedroom is to be in 17th century style. The bed is 17th century as well as the other bedroom furniture. The living room furniture is very modern and ample—We are even to have books and bookcases— The dining room suite is Hepplewaite [Hepplewhite] done in mahogony. We shall have a very opulent apartment when we are all moved in in a day or two. More about it later.

About not coming home—We have quite sufficient assurances of safety here, and of the possibility of eating (and working at the library). As regards the matter of travel, bookings are impossible to make at present, and, until the submarine menace is removed even travel on American boats appears risky.

Do drop Father McCabe a line however, Mother, and say that I am writing immediately, but that he need not be worried about seeing me back in St Louis before the second semester, if then.

There are no signs of war fervor, or of fear in England. There is only grim, hard-eyed determination to end Hitler. I wish that we could be as certain of a wise peace at the end of this business as we can be certain of another German failure.

Shall write 602 West Second Street and 616 Pallister in more detail shortly.[1]

Had a grand visit with Mr and Mrs Leavis.[2] Cambridge is at its best now. The mere idea of war seems quite incredible.

Most Lovingly
Marshall

New address—50 Grange Road, Cambridge

---

[1] These were the addresses of Corinne McLuhan's parents in Fort Worth and of Elsie McLuhan in Detroit.

[2] The Leavises had received the McLuhans for tea the day before.

To Charles W. Lewis[1]

[Cambridge, September ? 1939]

Dear Mr Lewis,

There was once a Texan in Cambridge whose dismay at the frequent dullness of the sky finally led him to exclaim, "I wish I were in Texas on the hottest day, where I could sit on the hottest rock, until I panted like a turtle". Corinne will probably be echoing his eloquence before long. You see, it has been raining for 2 or 3 days.

Well I have finally got down to work. That means daily visits to the library. But the blessed place is open only from 9 A.M. till 1 PM and 2.15–4 P.M. (in the winter 3.30 PM). So one doesn't have time to get very tired.

I am now in statu pupillari, which translated is "a bloomin' student." In January I become a senior member of the University (as soon as I proceed to the M.A.) Meantime I must regard college regulations, wear a cap and gown after sunset, when out-of-doors. And be in by 12 P.M. Corinne is officially my landlady and must make an official report to the college of the nature of my behaviour, proper or improper. Do you think she would dare to tell the truth?! Time will tell.

Most Sincerely Yours
Marshall.

[1]Corinne's father.

To Elsie McLuhan

[Cambridge]
Thursday Oct 19/39

Dearest Mother,

How comfortable we are in our place! Really it is a dandy. Tuesday saw us giving our 1st dinner, although we had had others in before. Elvin and Prof [F.P.] Wilson of Be[d]ford College London [University] were our guests. Wilson is my new research supervisor, and is here in Cambridge in consequence of the removal of his college Thither, tho I'm not sure whether he will be teaching or not.[1] He is a man of 50 or so, stout, able, pleasant. He is not a critic but a scholar. And so I'm in for a dose of scholarship of the Oxford-London variety (he is an

[1]Frank Percy Wilson (1889–1963), a distinguished scholar of Elizabethan and Jacobean literature, was Professor of English Literature at Bedford College, University of London, while he supervised McLuhan's Ph.D. thesis on Thomas Nashe. (From 1947 to 1957 he was Merton Professor of English Literature at Oxford University.) During his wartime removal to Cambridge, the McLuhans saw much of him. In November 1943 he gave the Alexander Lectures at University College, University of Toronto. See also page 139, note 1.

Oxford grad) here in Cambridge! It will probably be a very good thing for me however.

Corinne now has a readers ticket for the year (cost only one pound). And has just finished up an article on evacuation for the Ft. Worth papers. She plans to perfect her skill on the typewriter and to get on with an MA Thesis for herself.

There are 2 plays in Cambridge this week. [Emlyn Williams'] "The Corn is Green" and [Henrik Ibsen's] "The Doll's House." We may see both.

How I enjoy my food these days! And how I hate dishes. We wash up the entire day's dishes each night after supper, and seldom take more than 15 minutes. You see, we save fuel by spending the day until 4 P.M. in the Library. Then we light our own fire at tea-time.

We are having 2 chaps to tea to-day and are going to give them hot muffins and honey! A dish for the gods surely!

Corinne and I have finished reading Sax Rohmer's "Dr Fu-munchu"[2] in French and are going to tackle something else. We have read Jane Austen's Sense and Sensibility and L H Myers [The] Root and the Flower [1935] and are now beginning Trollope's "[The] Warden". We read these aloud. When I read Corinne knits, when she reads I smoke.

Amusingly, the $500 bond which I had to have when here last I had to have again this time. But the previous one (signed by you in Toronto) is still valid. So everything is so much simpler this time. Hence I'm getting more done.

Corinne is really doing wonders here in spite of the natural difficulties and strangeness she encounters. The great difficulty is to get her to dress warmly. Well, on with my reading—

Of course, in writing you I am writing Dad and Red as well. Haven't heard directly from either of them yet.

Most Lovingly
Marshall.

[2]Perhaps a French translation of the 1913 Rohmer novel published in England as *The Mystery of Dr. Fu-Manchu.*

To Elsie McLuhan

Since reaching Cambridge we have spent £70=$350 £15 went for caution money.

Saturday Nov 4/39 (3 months married today)
50 Grange Rd. [Cambridge]

Dearest Mother,

Picked up your 2 air-mail letters at the general P.O. yesterday. Heaven knows they would have been welcome when they reached Cambridge. But I never thought that you would send mail anywhere else than Trinity Hall.

It is 9 A.M. and Corinne and I are in the Library! Yes, its quite feasible, we find, if I go to 7.45 Mass while Corinne makes breakfast and dresses. Since it is Saturday morning she is going to her 10 o'c lecture by Geo. Rylands on "Producing

Shakespeare".[1] She says that it is quite rudimentary. We go together to hear F.R. Leavis on "Appreciation and Analysis" at 11 A.M. on Wednesday. He is my man, and superb at his job. Sometimes we go to an evening lecture, as on Thursday to the St John's Historical Society where R.H. Tawney of London gave a fine paper on "the rise of the Squirearchy".[2] Ted Willison came with us. He arrived in Cambridge on Wednesday, to take up his new job as "assistant to the Master in Lunacy".!! The job consists not in the management of lunatics but in managing their property. So Ted will be here till the end of the war, and will bring Kath and the boys here as soon as he can find a place.

There is no lack of entertainment, for besides the college societies there is always The Festival—and the New Arts Theatre. The last is playing Shaw's new "Geneva" this week. But the house was sold out before we got ready to go. Next week there is the Vic Wells Ballet. Well, I suppose it was last Saturday that we went to a party of Elizabeth Munroe's. It was a dance. The main result was meeting Ronald Bottrall the poet.[3] He too has been sent up to Cambridge from London, by the Civil Service. He is a tall Cornishman. Looks like an English Huck Finn. Well, he can *talk*. So we had him to dinner Wednesday with Miss Bradbrook of Girton. (Ted had dropped in to tea and so had Mavis—quite unopportunely, since it made a great rush at the last). Elvin came in later to coffee. Elvin and Bottrall were undergraduates together here (Incidentally, I have always liked Bottrall's poetry, and own it all.)

Corinne and I finished reading the Root and the Flower aloud. We are now enjoying Wm Saroyan's "Daring Young Man [on the Flying Trapeze, 1934]" in the same way. I shall send you a copy in a few days.

My supervisor, Prof Wilson, came to me in the Library yesterday and took me to the lunch room for a cup of coffee. We talked over my thesis and he is going to be most helpful. I feel a 100 times more like working at it now. We go to tea to him Monday.

Tuesday last, Elvin phoned at tea and asked if we could come to his rooms for a glass of sherry before Hall. He wanted us to meet Powell of Trinity, an Ottawa boy who graduated from Toronto last year.

We are having him to tea to-day with Eliz. Munroe. More about him later—

All our love—Marshall and Corinne

---

[1]George Rylands (b. 1902) taught English literature at Cambridge and edited *Elizabethan Tragedy: Six Representative Plays (excluding Shakespeare)* (1933) and *The Ages of Man: Shakespeare's Image of Man and Nature* (1939). He was later director of the British Council's series of recordings, *The English Poets from Coleridge to Yeats*, most of which appeared in the 1960s.

[2]R.H. Tawney (1880–1962) was an English historian and a leading socialist and Labour Party economist.

[3]Ronald Bottrall (b. 1906) had published *The Loosening* (1931), *Festivals of Fire* (1934), and *The Turning Path* (1939). (The diary entry for November 1 reads: "Ted [Willison] arrived and stayed to dinner with Bradbrook and Bottrall—Elvin came in for coffee.") T.S. Eliot, in a *New York Times* interview in 1932, ranked Bottrall with Auden, Spender, and MacNiece as one of the most important young English poets of the day. His *Collected Poems* was published in 1961.

To Elsie McLuhan

Dearest Mother,

It was Ted's birthday yesterday and we had a little party for him at tea time, cake (with one large candle) and Benedictine (liquer [*sic*] salvaged from our French experience) afterwards. We then went on foot (Corinne is fond of walking) to the Festival to see [G.B. Shaw's] "The Devil's Disciple" very well done by William Devlin. Not having read the play it was quite amusing from the point of view of plot alone. We were somewhat surprised to note a large contingent of R.A.F. (airmen) in the audience, but soon understood that they had come to hear the Army debunked in Act III. They seemed quite happy about it all.

Last week was the premiere of Denis Johnston's "The Golden Cuckoo" which has G.K. Chesterton for its hero. Ted was with us, and we enjoyed the play a great deal. It is very witty and eloquent and deserves to be successful.

Corinne and I saw a French picture last week and hope to see one this week—last week,—Gens du Voyage, a story of circus life, this week—Quai des Brumes, about which we know nothing.[1]

Well Monday night I spoke to the Doughty Society of Downing College on American Universities. We were dined in college before the meeting, and since we had been entertaining Mr & Mrs Crawley (my tutor) and Prof Wilson at tea, Corinne was dressed and ready to go to dinner as well as I. We dined in the rooms of my friend Gordon Cox where the meeting was held at 8.30. There was a big turnout. And Dr. Leavis was there. Corinne, (other than Mrs Leavis, the only woman who had ever been present at the Society I believe), had been sworn to silence—a silence assisted by knitting but which became very hard for her to keep as my exposé proceeded! However, I was quite sure of the audience, and knew that they needed no prompting to point out the abuses of Oxford and Cambridge. They stayed and stayed, asking endless questions. After they had gone we had tea and a chat with Leavis and Cuttle (head tutor of Downing). Then Cox let us out the back gate of the College into Fitzwilliam Street and we proceeded by starlight (the new moon had set) to Grange Rd at 1.30 A.M. Where I drank some sherry and ate some muffins to relieve the general tension.

Bewley came around next day to tell us how successful he thought the evening had been.

To-night we go to Prof. Wilson's—(I to talk over my thesis). We have 2 Franciscan Friars coming to tea. Sunday we go to tea to Mrs Brown of the Victoria League, who plans some "social life" for us—for Corinne at any rate.

It has been deliciously warm this past week. But the days are still very short. Mail comes seldom and takes 15–19 days. But there should be a note from all of you quite soon. (No rationing till after Xmas—hooray!)

Most Lovingly
Marshall.

[1]*Les Gens du voyage* (1939), directed by Jacques Feyder, and *Quai des Brumes* (1938), a famous film directed by Marcel Carné and starring Jean Gabin and Michèle Morgan.

To Mr and Mrs E.H. Keller[1]

[Cambridge]
Monday, Dec. 4th, 1939

Dearest Pop and Muz,

Corinne and I have been observing our 4th "anniversary" (really, mensaversary!) with some mutual congratulation. We have a great deal to feel happy about, and when people are happy they wish that others may also be happy. So we particularly hope that everybody at 602[2] is as happy as we hope they are and know they deserve to be.

Well, I believe Corinne has been looking over some clippings from the press which may interest you. Did she mention the new book on Columbus by the great Spanish writer, Salvador de Madariaga [*Christopher Columbus*, 1939]? He has discovered that Columbus was a Jew! And that although born in Italy (his parents having been ejected from Spain) he never spoke anything but Spanish. Yet the Spanish King and Queen financed his voyage to the New World. And he wrote them an ironical letter pointing out that they were helping *him* to find a new country for his own people just when they were booting the Jews out of Spain. Which reminds me that we have some very good Jewish friends here—a married couple.[3] They are wealthy and cultured, and have several homes in France, England, and Italy. Mr. Morris wants us to look up a French friend of his who has gone to New York—he is the well known painter, Jacques Ozenfant.[4] So we shall have a first-rate contact for us in New York.

The planes have been over Cambridge ceaselessly for the past week—English planes. But that's all we know about a war. Hope we don't see any more.

Most lovingly
Marshall

[1] Corinne McLuhan's maternal grandparents in Fort Worth.
[2] 602 West Second Street, Fort Worth—the Lewis address.
[3] Ronny and Charlotte Morris.
[4] Amédée Ozenfant (1886–1966), French painter, author of *Foundations of Modern Art* (1931), who formed the Ozenfant School of Fine Arts in New York in 1938.

To Elsie McLuhan

[Cambridge]
Dec 27 [1939]

Dearest Mother,

a year ago to-day I left for Fort Worth![1] Well such a Xmas with cables from both you and Red—much too extravagant really and Red with you in Detroit. How on earth? We shall await your letter about it all. We sent 2 cables to Fort Worth but no presents.

Now, Xmas we delivered 4 pumpkin pies—2 down stairs, one to the Leavis'es and one to the Friars. We went to Sunday Mass at 7.30 A.M. and had breakfast afterwards with Bewley. Then Ted and Kath came to dinner (his parents had come so she was able to get away) and we had a 3lb. baked haddock with stuffing. Poor Corinne has had a very busy time cooking. Well at 12 we went off to a beautiful midnight Mass at the Dominican Priory, and got home at 2 A.M. and hung up our stockings and opened presents. Corinne got me a dandy Dunhill pipe and a Tobacco jar and match holder with the college arms on them and a pipe rack plus a big box of brownies which she made for me etc etc. I gave her gloves, the suit, diary etc. At 9 A.M. we were awakened by Carols outside our door, and mince pies with holly and mistletoe were brought in by the children. Later Mr Patton came up and brought us 3 books—good ones.

Well we had a grand dinner with Ted and Kath, visited the Allens, then had tea with Prof. Wilson and family and played games. Then we rode off in the full moonlight to the other side of town for Xmas supper with the [Ronnie and Charlotte] Morris'es. (Such perfect Xmas weather.) They produced a galaxy of marvellous wines and brandies and we had a grand time of it.

Next day (yesterday) we got up at 4.30 P.M. just in time to get to tea at the Capt. Holt-Hughes where there were more Xmas games.

Prof Wilson and his wife want us to call them David and Joanna but we are a bit bashful about it yet!

Really Mother it has been a glorious Xmas and our special prayers are with you as we send this hoping you may have it by Jan 10.[2]

Most lovingly Marshall
and Corinne.

[1] See page 98.
[2] Elsie McLuhan's birthday.

1940

To Maurice McLuhan

[London]
Jan 11/40

Dear Red,

Here am I squalled in the Reading Room of the British Museum waiting for some books to be brought to me. (Corinne and I, by the way, were most happily surprised by your Xmas greeting.) We came up to London yesterday about noon with Mr Patton who stays in Cambridge with the Vicar (our landlord) a good deal. Patton is a benevolent old batchelor [*sic*] from Nova Scotia—a mild grey old chap with a foxy eye, a rather more feminine version of the Henry Ford cast of countenance and figure. He doteth on Corinne, along with the Vicar and his sisters, to them I appear to be a big bad wolf who has captured Little Red Riding Hood. And so we are his guests in London, and a most princely host he is. Last night it was dinner at Simpsons where they push the joint or duck on wheels to your table, produce a vast blade with operatic flourish and flash it on a steel 2 or 3 times and then with critical ear await your orders. Corinne is still shivering with delight over this performance and thinks to open such a restaurant in good old U.S.A. Then we went to see Sybil Thorndike in [Emlyn Williams'] "The Corn is Green" (we had been to Noel Coward's "Design for Living" with Diana Wynyard in the afternoon) all about a reforming super-school-marm who comes to a frightful Welsh mining village, converts the Squire and finds a genius in a coal-pit. Coward's play, by the way, dates terribly even now. His mode of "love among the artists" in which prudish people simply tingle with horrified delight at the spectacle of their own lubricious vagaries and speak of sleeping together as "a roll in the hay", all this is as ridiculously old-fashioned and quaint as a melodrama of the nineties.

Patton is taking Corinne to see the sights and to all the best shops and I'm not one little bit sorry or jealous. However there are a few places we must see together. Patton is a bit deaf and devilishly and periphrastically loquacious. He explains everything from an English phrase to a tram-car or a historical event as though it was a fussy bit of trick mechanism. First he gives you the facts concisely, and then assuming that so brief an explanation is quite beyond any but miraculous apprehension launches on a long and thorough account, clinging tenaciously to you the while with fish-hook eye. Corinne is a marvel of enthusiastic patience, having obviously had to contend with elaborate bores all her life in Texas. Texas men are incredibly infantile, and, of course as tough outside as they are slushy inside.

Well, tonight we see Gielgud in the Impt. of Being Ernest [*sic*],[1] and may hap

---

[1]John Gielgud was playing in Oscar Wilde's *The Importance of Being Earnest*, which he had also directed. He was John Worthing, a role in which he had achieved a great success in 1930 and with which he became identified.

the Ballet Russe this afternoon. Then there will be something to-morrow as well.

London is a bit of a mess, littered with boarding and sandbags, but not quite ruined yet. The balloons (there are 1000's) are very picturesque—You heard about the old lady who came up to London and after a period of fright at these objects, recovered herself and said "If those Germans think they can frighten me theyre nuts." The balloons anchored to large cable ascend 10–000 feet or more and force planes to remain at that height.

And a story a little more apropos of the meenestry: about the missionary to the Eskimos who preached on the fiery torments awaiting the wicked. Afterwards his flock clamoured around him expressing deep interest. ["] Yes, yes, yes, we know. But you havent told us how to get there."

Have been reading a bit of Alfred Adler recently. See whether you can obtain his "Social Interest" "Understanding Human Nature" or "The Nervous Character."[2] Quite certainly, you would find these of great interest, and incidentally, you would find a patient account of all the kinds of neurosis which can grip a person whose life pattern or life-style is that of a second child. I'm not exaggerating when I say that you will be in a much better position to conquer your habits of procrastination, of systematic inefficiency in studies etc etc. Above all he will put you on your guard against reposing in facile explanations of "failure". He proves that all people who for various reasons have an acute and special *interest* in avoiding any *real* failure such as a partial achievement in initial attempts, such people invent an elaborate system of evasions and never permit themselves to come to any test which they would admit to be a test. His mode of explaining these things I have found extremely helpful to myself Red and so do have a go at him. Now here are the books—

With love
Marshall

PS. Do forward to mother papers and things we send you, after you have seen them.

[2]The Austrian psychiatrist Alfred Adler (1870–1937) was the author of *Social Interest* (1939), *Understanding Human Nature* (1928), and *The Neurotic Constitution* (1921).

126

To Elsie McLuhan

[Cambridge]
Jan 21 (Sunday) [1940]

Dearest Mother,

I dont suppose you much mind the above![1] Written before we went to London, but never finished. Well its been a busy time since and nevermore busy than yesterday when I got my M.A. The day before, I asked my tutor when it came off. He had forgotten about me. So there was a bit of racing around, and it cost me exactly £4 and 1 shilling. I managed to borrow hood and bands from a friend, Maurice Evans, a scholar here who began his Phd. here when I left—I knew him when I was here in 1934–6. He is coming to coffee Thursday night.

By the way we had tea with Lorraine Robertson, daughter of the physics prof. at Queens Univ. (Canada) on Friday. She is a poor 'lorn crittar. We had had her to tea previously—she is working fanatically at Shelley.

Thursday we went to see a movie and afterwards went over to Ted and Kath and suggested we mind the house Saturday night while they went off to the Festival to see "Major Barbara". So it was arranged. They are very good to us and Corinne enjoys being with them.

Well, I dined in the Senior Combination Room with the Fellows of Trinity Hall before going to gather up my M.A. Elvin is the praelector who presents candidates for degrees (a job he has assumed since I left) So at 2 we went to the Senate house and it was soon all over. He made a Latin speech to the Vice Chancellor assuring him of my moral and intellectual integrity and then kneeling with my hands clasped in the Vice-Chancellor's lap he admits them to the degree "in artibus magistris" in the name of the Father Son and Holy Ghost (he says this regardless of his own creed, and indeed it is a medieval form, formerly uttered by a priest[)]. Elvin says the great danger in his little speech is lest half-way through he wander off into the familiar latin grace (said daily in Hall.) Well, Corinne is telling you about the "bald-spot" so I'll mention that last Sunday we trundled 20 miles by bus and back again to a rather dismal tea with Elvin and his wife. She is now living in a village near Ely, and is not such a dandy genial sort as she might be. We are turning over the linens to her and buying sheets and pillow-cases for ourselves. (2 sets only)—but they didnt *ask* for them. Meantime I am afraid to look at our bank balance.

And now to bed with
dearest love for you—
Marshall

[1]Corinne McLuhan had begun a letter to Elsie McLuhan at the top of the sheet this letter was written on.

To Elsie McLuhan

[Cambridge]
May 1st [1940]

Dearest Mother

Its been too long since we have written, and what a lot has been going on. The ideally green, balmy, blossomy out-of-doors is at present a major distraction. But there have many people to tea dinner and coffee, and many efforts to work. This afternoon however we had a game of tennis with some friends and got gloriously warm—a rare experience in England. Recently the plumbers have been tearing up the whole house and blasting and belting away at pipes and bath-tubs till we are glad to stay away.

This evening we had the Ronny Morris's and the Harold Osbornes[1] to coffee and there was some good talk.

By the way, we saw Shaw's new play "In Good King Charles' Golden Days" which is quite up to his best standard we thought. And next week is Ben Jonson's *Volpone* and John Ford's (same period) *'Tis Pity She's a Whore*—2 plays which one has seldom an opportunity to see.

It doesn't appear that my thesis can be *written* before I return. But all that will be settled shortly. At any rate I shan't have to come back here unless I wish. Dont get alarmed about this matter please. For it has been a most profitable year scholastically. And the Phd. will be mine soon.

Later: Have got permission to submit the [Ph.D.] thesis from America without any oral exam. So all is OK.

To-morrow we are off with Jack and Elfriede Allen for a 2 day tour of Suffolk. If the weather is comparable to to-day's we shall be very happy. (Corinne is reading Dorothy Sayers' "Nine Tailors" [1934] just now. It is supposedly the best of all detective stories.) Quite interested in your notes from Bell's lecture on education. You may have noticed that I attack the same problem from a different point of view in my "Mama Boys."[1] I have masses of material for articles on a dozen subjects including education. But I feel that I must first make my mark as a "scholar" in Eng. Lit. before seriously embarking on any other careers. Because, once you are caught up in the hurly-burly of controversy and journalism there is small opportunity to cultivate the qualities of mind which can alone make such activity worthwhile. Now a space for Corinne to say hello.

Most Lovingly Marshall

[1]Harold Osborne (b. 1905), a Cambridge graduate, served in the Foreign Office and the Board of Trade, published many books on aesthetics and art, and in retirement edited several Oxford reference books, including *The Oxford Companion to Art* (1970).

[2]An article entitled "Fifty Million Mama's Boys", about the emasculated American male, was not published (it has not survived); it was probably the forerunner of "Dagwood's America", *Columbia*, vol. 23, January 1944. See page 138, note 3

To Elsie McLuhan

[On board the *Ascania*]
Tuesday June 11 [1940]

Dearest Mother

I shall be in Toronto to-morrow night.[1] I shall phone Dick Thompson who lives at 95 Seaforth Ave as soon as I get in. Depending on what I hear I shall stay over Thursday or come straight on. But it has occurred to me that there may be a few household effects of yours in Toronto that we might just as well have with us in St Louis during this year. Actually, I dont know exactly what we might find useful, since we shall certainly be taking a furnished place. And it would be absurd to transport anything bulky or heavy. The only thing I know of that would be decidedly handy, therefore, is cutlery. I would love to have my books with us, but, they are quite out of the picture.

As a matter of fact Mother, I feel like doing anything but waiting over. I want to see you for a few days before going to St Louis. The difficulty is that Corinne may already be in St. Louis. But I have her trunk with me owing to a slip up on the part of the U.S. Lines. She has the key. Now if she is in St. Louis already I can see nothing for her to do but to go on down to Ft. Worth before I see her. (This wretched boat has been 14 days out of Liverpool—and has 600 Jewish refugees on board: so you can imagine how much fun it has been.) Personally I shan't go to Ft. Worth, having neither money time nor inclination to do so. This has really been a maddening trip and I shall need a rest.

So this is your cue. If you think it is worth my staying over in Toronto to pick up a few articles please phone or wire Dick Thompson and then write an air-mail special to him telling me what to do. Or, if you prefer, tell them to have me phone you, giving your number. I shan't get to Toronto before the evening, so dont plan to have me phone you before 9 or 10 P.M. In order to have this letter go thru without bother I am not giving you any particulars about the boat or its present port.

Just a moment. Since it is 12 hours to Toronto, it may be that I shant get away before noon. That would mean Toronto Thursday morning. So plan on this as an alternative to Wed. night.

One irritating fact has been the complete lack of news of Corinne's boat.

All right Mother.   All my love—Marshall.

P.S. Have just heard that we may get on 10 A.M. train to-morrow.

---

[1]Because McLuhan was a citizen of Canada, which was at war, and his wife was an American, they had to leave England on separate boats: Marshall sailed from Liverpool to Montreal on the *Ascania* and Corinne sailed from Galway to New York on the *President Roosevelt*. Corinne went to Fort Worth for a brief stay before joining Marshall in St Louis.

1943

Below is the first of many letters McLuhan wrote to Wyndham Lewis (1882–1957), the distinguished British painter and much-published author who was then living in Windsor, Ontario, and teaching at Assumption College. McLuhan first encountered Lewis's books as a Cambridge undergraduate in 1936. His diary entries for that year record that between the end of February and the end of June he was reading Paleface *("very stirring"),* Time and Western Man *(he was "very much excited" by it.),* The Lion and the Fox, The Apes of God, *and* The Art of Being Ruled.*

Since December 1940 Lewis had been living in Toronto. Father J. Stanley Murphy (1904–83)—Associate Professor of English, and Registrar of Assumption College (now Assumption University), Windsor—met Lewis there in the summer of 1942 and invited him to give a lecture in the Christian Culture Series that Murphy had founded at Assumption. This lecture took place in January 1943; it was followed by another lecture across the (Detroit) river in Detroit. Elsie McLuhan heard him lecture and reported having done so to her son. After writing Father Murphy about his interest in meeting Lewis, McLuhan sent the following note to Lewis, who had by then accepted a teaching post at Assumption.

See McLuhan's tribute to Father Murphy, and his account of his first meeting with Lewis, in his letter of October 5, 1973, to D. Carlton Williams.

To Wyndham Lewis

Saint Louis University
Saturday July 24/43

Dear Mr Lewis,

Father Murphy said that he had mentioned me to you as one who was much interested in your work. When our summer-school winds up here in a few days I have to go to Detroit. If you are not too busy or too exhausted by our heat, there is nothing I should more enjoy than a chat with you.

Yours Sincerely
Marshall McLuhan

Cornell University Library

Shortly after the previous note was sent, McLuhan, accompanied by his colleague and friend Felix Giovanelli (see page 182, note 1), spent a happy evening with Lewis, his wife Anne, whom he called Froanna (a phonetic elision of the German form of addressing her, Frau Anna), and Father Murphy in the Lewis apartment in Windsor. McLuhan and Giovanelli enthusiastically proposed that they attempt to arrange speaking engagements and portrait commissions for Lewis in St Louis. Lewis—who was always in need of money, in England as well as in Canada—warmed to this plan. However, his high reputation in England as a portrait painter had not reached St Louis. As the following letters reveal, McLuhan's progress in arranging commissions was slow. (This Wyndham Lewis episode in McLuhan's life in St Louis is recalled more than thirty years later in a letter of May 7, 1976, to Robert Cowan: see page 519.)

To Wyndham and Froanna Lewis

Saint Louis University
Aug. 17/43

Dear Mr and Mrs Lewis,

My silence until now has been somewhat prompted by the hope of having eventually some good news for you. Of course, Giovanelli[1] keeps in touch with me, and only this morning we travelled out to see Nagel[2] at the Art Museum. The result, in a word, is that you will be asked to lecture there in February. N. has become an admirer of your work, but he is a soft, adolescent sort, easily intimidated by irrelevant considerations. He bears all the marks of being the cream-puff son of a multi-millionaire, and I know that Giovanelli has revised his opinion of him since writing to you. However, he is certainly worth cultivating, since many people ask him about painters to do portraits, and he has given us a few more leads to follow up. By the way, he is an architect.

As G. has told you, the press is lined up, and ready to give your visit real attention. By February we can certainly arrange for at least one more lecture, probably a big affair sponsored by the Junior League and one which should bring you at least 500 dollars. We have found one serious (!) sitter—that is one intelligent person of small means who would pay for a pencil drawing or study. We can probably find several such jobs, but it would be well if we knew your approximate fee for such work. Nagel says that St. Louis is a town of bargain-hunters; but if one person with a reputation for shrewdness can be persuaded to sit, then the rest flock along. For that reason we are trying to reach some of the prominent

---

[1]Felix Giovanelli (see page 182, note 1) was a colleague and friend at Saint Louis University, who taught French and Spanish.

[2]Charles Nagel (b. 1899) was Acting Director of the City Art Museum of St Louis from 1942 to 1946. On August 20, 1943 Lewis received an invitation from Nagel to give a lecture in February 1944 for a fee of $150.

people here. August is, however, a bad time since many are out of town. Incidentally, St. Louisans are rather fond of having their portraits done, and most of the "right people" have already had it done, and done badly. That we can arrange for at least one big portrait of a person who would wish a serious treatment, I think is fairly certain. Have you heard of Vladimir Golschmann,[3] the French Jewish conductor of the St Louis Symphony? There are some hopes of him.

It now seems unlikely that anything can be done in the lecture or portrait line before Sept 20. Christmas vacation is a bad time too. So the kindness of Fr. Murphy will have to show itself in February. As soon as possible dates will be sent to you. If, however, we can get a sitter for you before Sept. 20 we shall do so, if only because of the pleasure in seeing both of you here in St. Louis.

Recently I wrote to Stanford University (near San Francisco) about you, and I am writing to Prof. Nef of Chicago U. as well. Either of those would be admirable cities to be in or near.

Most Sincerely Yours
H.M. McLuhan

Cornell University Library

[3]Vladimir Golschmann (1893–1972) was the principal conductor of the St Louis Symphony Orchestra from 1931 to 1956.

The following letter contains the first reference to Sigfried (sometimes given as Siegfried) Giedion (1883–1968), whom McLuhan met in St Louis. He was a Swiss historian of architecture who taught at the Massachusetts Institute of Technology and Harvard University, where he became Chairman of the Graduate School of Design. In the Foreword to the First Edition of his Space, Time and Architecture: The Growth of a New Tradition, *published by the Harvard University Press in 1941, Giedion wrote: "I have attempted to establish, both by argument and by objective evidence, that in spite of the seeming confusion there is nevertheless a true, if hidden, unity, a secret synthesis, in our present civilization. To point out* why *this synthesis has* not *become* a conscious and active reality *has been one of my chief aims. My interest has been particularly concentrated on the growth of the new tradition of architecture, for the purpose of showing its interrelations with other human activities and the similarity of methods that are in use today in architecture, construction, painting, city planning, and science." McLuhan once said in an interview: "Giedion influenced me profoundly.* Space, Time and Architecture *was one of the great events of my lifetime. Giedion gave us a language for tackling the structural world of architecture and artifacts of many kinds in the ordinary environment. . . . " ("A Dialogue—Marshall McLuhan and Gerald Emanuel Stearn",* Encounter, *June 1967; included in Gerald E. Stearn, ed.,* McLuhan Hot & Cool, *1969.)*

To Wyndham Lewis

Saint Louis University
Wed. Aug 18. [1943]

Dear Mr Lewis,

Since writing you yesterday I received a copy of "The Vulgar Streak" which both my wife and I have just finished.[1] I was able to get at it while she was busy at other things! It is a fascinating and most satisfactory book. Without any reflection on the quite separate merits of your other novels, I should say that you show a remarkable dramatic sense in this book. One feels that it *must* develop its action from the first page, and the action which you contemplated could only have been conceived as one of complex and tragic irony. The pathos of the vision in this work is truly related to the basic conflicts of our time and constitutes a superb critique. Surely you have just begun to explore this area of your experience for us?

A matter which I forgot to mention yesterday concerning the immediate appetites of American publishers may interest you. Sigfried Giedion wrote me recently that the Oxford Press rep. in New York had besought him for a book on art which would interest the public.[2] S.G. is tied up with another publisher and simply passed on the news. Apparently the publishers are really looking for some books of this kind just now. Since you are lecturing at the level of the general public a good deal perhaps they would be glad to have some of these things of yours.

Apropos of S.G.'s book *Space Time and Architecture*, you might very well be interested in his fine sections on American architecture. Title, and some superficial aspects apart, I imagine you would find a good deal which is congenial in S.G. With him the analysis of social and building surfaces is closely allied.

With kind remembrances to Mrs Lewis,
H.M. McLuhan

Cornell University Library

[1]This melodramatic novel (1941) by Wyndham Lewis, attacking the British class structure, is about the clever young Vincent Penhale, from a poor background, who "tried to escape from my Class" by adopting the speech and mannerisms of the upper class. He passes counterfeit money, becomes an accessory to a murder—the disclosure of which, to his wife, is followed by her death in childbirth—and eventually hangs himself.

[2]In 1948 the Oxford University Press, New York, published Giedion's *Mechanization Takes Command*.

To Wyndham Lewis

Saint Louis University
Sept 2/43

Dear Lewis,

Giovanelli and I are still working at the outer defences of the big pocket-books [i.e. the wealthy citizens] of St. Louis. It has been instructive. The extreme timidity and shyness of these people astonishes me. Also their humility and professions of holy poverty whenever their own abilty to commission a portrait is broached. However they are rather eager to suggest other "victims" so that we have been getting around. Golschmann is only just back in town and hasn't heard from us yet. A few weeks ago Mayor Becker of St. Louis was killed in a plane crash. Via his best friend (it took some time to find out who he was) we have begun negotiations to have you do a job from photography. We haven't forgotten your comments on the subject, but this portrait would be for the City Hall, not a sentimental affair; and Becker was blonde, bald, round, and unwrinkled—plainly a cinch! Plans to have him painted by Chambers of New York are on foot, we learnt to-day from B's friend Leaky. But Leaky was much interested in you as a possible for the job. He is a hard-headed ignorant Irish lawyer, and wants some solid *American* opinion of you to go on. Since this kind of problem is likely to recur it is probably worth tackling immediately. To whom could we write? What about the people at the Museum of Modern Art in New York? The Carnegie Institute people who had planned the Oregon job for you? The President of Buffalo University?[1] Nagel of course will be of some help, as also the material you sent us. As a matter of fact we presented that when we met Leaky.

Best regards to you and Mrs Lewis,
Sincerely Yours,
Marshall McLuhan

Cornell University Library

[1] Shortly after arriving in Toronto from England in September 1939, Lewis and his wife spent three months in Buffalo, where Lewis had been commissioned to paint a portrait of Samuel Paul Capen (1878–1956), Chancellor of Buffalo University.

To Wyndham Lewis

St Louis U, St Louis, Mo.
Wednesday Sept 22 [1943]

Dear Lewis,

The Barr letter will be useful.[1] In the general press of work incidental to the opening of regular school (Giovanelli and I have heavy programs this year) we have had to slack off on the portrait work. A little lull will do no harm, since most people are too busy just now to be talked to.

I have been asked to give a book review to a fairly good club here, and I am going to give one of *The Vulgar Streak*. It may open up some portrait leads too. The comparison of your novel with Evan Harrington[2] suggests a reviewer who wished to seem widely read rather than illuminating. I know the book well. Its donnish stuff for the most part. However, Meredith did have a detachment from English society (not quite that of G.B.S.) which makes him refreshing at times. Not that this is *the* formula for good writing. But Meredith and Shaw are provincial minds, whereas your critique, it seems to me, has much wider bearings.

We shall take good care of Barr's letter.

Most aimiably yours
Marshall McLuhan

Cornell University Library

[1]In a letter to McLuhan of September 5, 1943 Lewis said he would write to Alfred Barr, Jr (1902–81), Director of the Museum of Modern Art, New York, "and ask him for a testimonial". Lewis had met Barr in London in 1927.

[2]A novel (1861) by George Meredith.

To Wyndham Lewis

Saint Louis University
Saturday night. Oct 9. 1943

Dear Lewis, What a wretched time to be shifting residence, with classes beginning, and the Broun lectures hanging over you.[1] I really wish I'd been on hand to help you. As for things here, nothing has been done worthy of report, but a few energies may soon be available to carry on the campaign to get you some good assignments. For one thing, I have been writing "learned" papers lately, since publication is the only way out of the morass of petty pay and inferior students. I really enjoy teaching as very few people do, but naturally wish to find the best possible sphere to work in. St Louis U. is the best Catholic school in the U.S.A.,

[1]The Heywood Broun Memorial Lectures: twelve lectures given in Windsor, connected with Father Murphy's Christian Culture Series, which Lewis delivered between November 7 and December 19, 1943.

so that means I'm done with Catholic schools. However I dont say these things carelessly, since my opinions are scarcely pleasing to my employers. Your promised letter will be eagerly awaited. Meantime, a bit of news which may not be news to you. There is a visiting exhibition of "20th century portraits" here at the Art Museum at present. It is to be here until Oct 25. One of your Eliot pictures is in this exhibition. Stupidly, I failed to note the name of the lender.[2] However it was not The Museum of Modern Art but a private owner. The picture is without the border motif of the "official" portrait—is simply plain. I had, of course, expected to see Barr's copy (?) of *the* rejected portrait.[3] I shall check the name of the lender for you, perhaps to-morrow. The person might prove a useful contact. What about getting the Pres. Capon (?) [Chancellor Capen] portrait into this exhibit. Might it not be good publicity, and, at the same time, a means of recovering the enthusiastic confidence of Capon? If only you could pop a portrait of some American big-wig into this show!

Most aimiably yours
Marshall McLuhan

Cornell University Library

[2]In a note to Lewis written a few days later (October 13, 1943), McLuhan told him that the lenders were Mr and Mrs Stanley Rogers Resor of Columbus, Georgia. The portrait of T.S. Eliot in the exhibition was therefore the oil-on-canvas sketch—bought in London for Mrs Resor by Alfred Barr, Jr—of the portrait that the Royal Academy rejected in 1938, causing an uproar in the press and the resignation from the Academy of Augustus John.

[3]It is this oil study of the rejected portrait that McLuhan did see.

To Wyndham Lewis

Saint Louis University
Tuesday Oct. 26/43

Dear Lewis, I am sending you a book which I have just read, and which I wish I had read long ago.[1] It seems never to have been reprinted and is hence rather scarce. Only library copies are available here, but this one is not due till Nov. 19. The esoteric appeal of this book has brought it to an obscurity which seems to rival that of your work in this country. Perhaps it may not be too late to provide you some ammunition for your work on American politics.

You asked some time ago about Siegfried Giedion. He comes to mind now because of his conscious exploitation of "Space-Time" metaphors in his exposi-

[1]This book was *The Rise and Growth of American Politics* (1898), by Henry Jones Ford, which Lewis acknowledged with thanks in a letter to McLuhan of November 9, 1943.

tion of architectural history. It is astonishing how helpful and how crippling a big unconscious metaphor can be in directing the thoughts of whole periods of history. I mean such things as "organism" in Rousseau. Yet how different a concept of organism from that of the sixteenth century when it was hierarchical, or of the 19th when it was animal. I sometimes feel that such a notion of organism got into the surging rhythm of [Tolstoy's] "War and Peace" in such a way as to create the psychological reality of cinema before the mechanical fact. Curiously, the Greeks invented "organic" as a metaphor from "mechanic". Your work shows a constant awareness of the nearness of these supposed opposites, I am fully aware.

Well, Siegfried Giedion is a wealthy Swiss architect who was isolated here on the outbreak of war. He had been giving the Chas. Eliot Norton lectures at Harvard. Beyond that fact, and his book, I know nothing. He seems to be a great "Friend of the Stars", however.

Concerning my enquiries at certain universities I must simply say that I have had no answers. I sent off my letters at a bad time—just at the lag-end of summer. Ordinary procrastination meant they should have been answered just about the time school was opening. But this fact provided a major opportunity for postponement. I have sent off 4 or 5 articles in the past 2 months and have had no word about them. American professors are commonly burdened by endless petty administrative jobs. They do very little real work, even when they want to.

The Vulgar Streak could easily be a best-seller in this country if Malcolm Cowley[2] were to tip off Clifton Fadiman[3] and Carl Van Doren[4] in advance. It is first-rate Hollywood scenario material—the natural sequel to *Pygmalion*.[5] In fact, it is in many respects that. Shaw quits where you begin. Basil Rathbone[6] might be directly approached as a good candidate for the role of Vin. Penhale. George Sanders[7] could do the job even better. The present political situation makes such a view of the English scene one which many are eager to obtain. Giovanelli and I had thought of writing to some people, but realized that you know a hundred times as much about how to manage such things.

We are preparing to open up a second-front here. A new offensive for lectures and pictures. Haven't talked to Nagel but have heard that owing to an 85,000

---

[2]The American literary critic Malcolm Cowley (b. 1898)—who had published the well-known *Exile's Return: A Narrative of Ideas* in 1934—was writing a book-review column for the *New Republic*.

[3]Clifton Fadiman (b. 1904) was Book Editor of *The New Yorker* (1933–43) and host of the popular radio program "Information Please" (1938–48). In 1944 he became a member of the editorial board of the Book-of-the-Month Club, a position he still holds.

[4]Carl Van Doren (1885–1950), professor of English at Columbia University from 1911 to 1934 and the author of several literary studies.

[5]The play by George Bernard Shaw.

[6]Basil Rathbone (1892–1967), educated in England, who specialized in playing suave villains in Hollywood films, though he was a notable Sherlock Holmes.

[7]George Sanders (1906–72), American film actor, who grew up in Britain and brought a smooth, supercilious manner to his roles.

dollar fake Holbein which has to be paid for this January, they don't know what money will be on hand for Feb. Had your lecture been *dropped* Nagel would certainly have written. It is rather a matter of waiting to look into the treasury after the dealers have cleaned out 85,000. We should have some definite things to report on soon. Golschman has yet to be approached. Further lecture possibilities are now ready to be explored.

Did you get to draw Fulton Sheen?[8] Or didn't he come to Windsor? Men like him could do you much good. How do you stand with Maritain?[9] Badly, I imagine. Unfortunately, he controls a large group—most of the literate Catholics of the U.S.A.

Giovanelli is having the Barr letter photo-stated. Will send it on to you to-morrow by special delivery.

We sincerely wish that you and Mrs Lewis are comfortably settled at last.

Sincerely Yours
H. Marshall McLuhan.

Cornell University Library

[8]Monsignor (later Bishop) Fulton J. Sheen opened the Christian Culture series annually in Detroit and Lewis did a black and coloured chalk drawing of him in Sheen's hotel room.

[9]Jacques Maritain (1882–1973), French philosopher who converted to Roman Catholicism in 1906 and was much influenced by the philosophy of Thomas Aquinas. (McLuhan became acquainted with his writings in his first year at Cambridge.) From 1932 to 1945 he lectured annually at the Pontifical Institute of Mediaeval Studies in Toronto. The recipient of the Annual Christian Culture Award Gold Medal of Assumption College, he was about to give a special lecture there—before which Lewis made a pencil sketch of him. From 1945 to 1948 he was French ambassador to the Holy See and from 1948 to 1952 he taught at Princeton University. There is a letter to him later in this collection (see page 369).

To Wyndham Lewis

St Louis U.
Sunday Nov 27/43

Dear Lewis,

The utterly gratuitous misery you have been subjected to these past weeks makes me very indignant.[1] That you should be trying to finish up important work in such conditions is simply the opposition of the fiend. It is good to know that Mrs. Lewis is better. Heaven send that there is still enough law in Canada to suppress the noxious human elements that surround you.

My name on the *Who IS WYNDHAM Lewis* card was very flattering, but it is sad

[1]In a letter to McLuhan of November 9, 1943 Lewis complained about having to move, about his unsatisfactory landlord who was not providing enough heat, and about how these concerns had interfered with the preparation of his Heywood Broun lectures.

that your prestige should have to stoop to such a green prop or crutch as mine is.[2] Perhaps my article on "Dagwood's America" coming out in *Columbia* may help you in this regard![3] (*Columbia* is the Kts of Columbus monthly mag. It has a big circulation—1/2 a million, and its level of writing is well above that of the Sat. Ev. Post.) I regret becoming entangled in Catholic journalism before having properly won my spurs in other fields. Could I do you any good by trying to place an article on your work with with some magazine in Canada or the U.S.A.? Do you have any special one in mind as best suited to you? I'm sure that I could get such an article published if I had the audience well-focussed beforehand—focussed in my mind.

Tuesday

Well, good news! I waited till to-day to continue this letter, feeling sure I'd have something to tell you. Another Feb. "lecture" has been arranged for you here—at the Wednesday Club, a snooty affair. However, I was so successful in presenting you to the president that she thought that your interests would be better served (portrait commissions more likely) by your appearing at the *Womens Club* of St Louis. It pays better too. Big homes would yawn to receive you, and you, no doubt, would yawn too. So she will keep the Wed. Club date open for you (it can be made to coincide with Nagel's) while she helps me explore better possibilities. She has developed a yen to promote you here. Having looked you up in the public library here, she has decided you are "really stuff", and quite "undiscovered" into the bargain. Somewhat nervously she asked: "What sort of a personal appearance does he make?" "Oh, a duke at least," I said. That really settled it. You can't be too Bond Streetish for these people.[4]

So things are really going ahead in the next few weeks for you here. Now, if it is possible at all to obtain a complete set of your drawings and designs from

---

[2]A small two-sided publicity card ("unexpectedly produced by Father Murphy", according to Lewis) bearing the heading "Who is Wyndham Lewis?", a photograph, and a blurb describing Lewis as a "world-renowned painter, novelist, critic, poet, philosopher", and founder of the "Vorticist genre of art. Cosmopolitan in outlook. Witty, profound, daring. One of the major modern prophets." It includes three encomiums—from the "Modern Museum of Art, N.Y.C." [Alfred Barr Jr.?], Fulton Sheen, and Marshall McLuhan, who describes Lewis as "One of the truly great men of our time". The reverse side announces and lists Lewis's Heywood Broun Lectures in November/December 1943. To McLuhan's remark about the use of his name, Lewis replied: "That 'green prop' you refer to is very valuable, however, for it is the young who assure one of 'time's revenge' . . . " (Letter of December 5, 1943, PAC.)

[3]Herbert Marshall McLuhan, "Dagwood's America", *Columbia*, vol. 23, no. 6, January 1944. The article discusses the comic strip "Blondie" by Chic Young in which Dagwood, who has lost his masculine ego and is ineffectual and helpless, and his wife Blondie, who is "efficiently masculine" and controlling in her family role, portray "a basic pattern or conflict in American life". McLuhan elaborated on the implications of this in his several drafts of the book that was eventually published as *The Mechanical Bride* (1951), in which the commentary entitled "Blondie" further examined the significance of the comic strip, whose title by then had been changed to "Dagwood".

[4]Lewis responded to this remark by ordering a dark blue suit—"it will be a lulu", he wrote in a letter to McLuhan of December 11, 1943.

England (or from any place here) it would be well to do so at once. These people would pay for such. But they want some sort of exhibit to put up a week or two before you come. It would really be a great advantage to you. Might it not even be possible to borrow Barr's copy of the Eliot portrait? What sort of reproductions of others of your works might be suitable to exhibit? What about that Capon [*sic*] job? Would it be a good one to show? The recent card publicity is helpful indeed, but I think a little 6–8 page booklet would be better. Giovanelli and I will see what we can work up.

At the moment I am waiting for G[iovanelli] to call me. He is trying to reach Nagel for a comment on the February date. As far as we can see now, however, Nagel or no Nagel there will be something worthwhile lined up by then. Golschmann has been snowed under. Can't get to him even yet.

No word from G. Since I want to put this in to-night's post I'll let him write to you about Nagel. Also a chap called Chaney has a book out recently on Modern Art.[5] You are mentioned four or five times, quite favorably.

With every kind wish for you both,
Marshall McLuhan.

Cornell University Library

[5]Sheldon Cheney, *A Primer of Modern Art*. First published in 1924, it was revised many times; McLuhan was perhaps referring to the 10th edition (1939).

To Wyndham Lewis

[St Louis]
Dec 2/43

Dear Lewis,

Giovanelli will be writing you soon. Nagel seemed to take the Feb. date quite for granted. However there is a board meeting to day. He said he would gladly accomodate [*sic*] his date to any others which we might "make" for you. Of course, we are not glibly assuming that you are obliged to take on a lecture just because it is offered to you.

I *have* to be in New York from Dec 19–21. A friend is sailing for England— Professor F.P. Wilson of London University.[1] Could he help you in any way in the matter of carrying something back there for you? He is a very competent and genial man. Could I do anything for you in New York? Simply let me know by Dec. 17.

The Henry Jones Ford is overdue here, and a mild clamor has begun for it. I could renew it and send it back to you.

Most aimiably yours
Marshall McLuhan

Cornell University Library

[1]Frank Percy Wilson (see page 118, note 1) had delivered the Alexander Lectures at University College, University of Toronto, in November. They were published in *Elizabethan and Jacobean* (1945).

To Wyndham Lewis

[St Louis]
Tuesday Dec. 28, 1943

Dear Lewis

May this [coming] year inaugrate [*sic*] a most auspicious season for you and Mrs Lewis. I have only a few moments in which to say that Giovanelli and I saw Vladimir Golschmann this afternoon. He proved surprisingly intelligent. He was eager to make suggestions and to use his influence—at least to a degree which is beyond what we have met with here. He is a good friend of our ex-mayor's wife. Mayor Becker killed in plane crash a few months ago was a popular figure. Golschmann urged this: without a name here, without an advance exhibition of your work, you can do little. However, short of painting a great millionaire you could do nothing so useful to yourself as to do a study (chalk, ink, oil) of Becker from photographs to be supplied to you in Windsor by Mrs Becker. Then the work to be sent here, reproduced with great eclat in the photogravure section of the Sunday papers, exhibited at the Museum (perhaps conferred on the Museum?). If this sort of thing seems at all feasible to you, give us the green light and Golschmann will go to work on Mrs. Becker. Becker's mug is a typical one. Nothing crotchety about it. He was 50 yrs. old. Bald, blond. Perhaps it might be worth having a look at the photos.

With most cordial wishes
Marshall McLuhan

Cornell University Library

To Wyndham Lewis

[St Louis]
Dec. 31/43

Dear Lewis

Mrs Knight of the Wednesday Club called to say that you had been booked for the night of Feb 19, Nagel acquiescing. You are to speak at the Museum Feb. 21. The Wed. Club will pay you $100, and I was to write you. As for topic at the W.C.—"Personalities in the world of modern art and letters." Yes, frankly, they want anecdotes about "Long-haired people I have known." You can please them completely, simply by making it a chat about familiar names—Yeats, Joyce, Eliot, Picasso, Augustus John, T E Lawrence etc. Let it embrace more than one field. A musician wouldn't be amiss. The more your own life is seen to be merged in all theirs the more thrilled they will be. However, if you feel rebellious about this sort of lecture you can revamp it pretty much as you please.

Depending on what arrangements you can make with Father Murphy and also having regard to the best moment for your presence here to become known, we can make hotel reservations. The Chase Hotel will be best. It is commonly the choice of visiting bigwigs, has the advantage of view, Zodiac bar (!), and location. It is reasonable too. If you were to do some painting here, would a western exposure do? Would you want bedroom and sitting room, or more? In present conditions it isn't too early to attend to these things.

By the way, Nagel has agreed to let the W.C. [Wednesday Club] have you first. The women were too much for him. The W.C. wants you for a little reception afterwards. My New York visit[1] proved a pleasant interlude between two attacks of flu, and I'm still groggy. Xmas festivities and visitors have dispersed my wits so that even writing a letter is a major task.

Most aimiably yours
Marshall McLuhan

Cornell University Library

[1]He had attended the annual conference of the Modern Language Association.

1944

The following letter contains the first of numerous references, in the letters to Lewis, to Edna (Mrs George) Gellhorn, the mother of Martha Gellhorn (b. 1908), who was married to Ernest Hemingway from 1940 to 1945. In his memoir "Wyndham Lewis" (Atlantic Monthly, *December 1969), McLuhan wrote that Mrs Gellhorn—in the interests of a committee that wanted to have a portrait painted of Dr Joseph Erlanger, recent winner of a Nobel Prize and Professor of Physics at Washington University, St Louis—sought the advice of her son-in-law about the appropriateness of Lewis for this commission. Hemingway urged her "to do anything she could for Lewis, speaking of him in the highest terms" (McLuhan's words). Lewis, when he heard of this, expressed surprise. He told McLuhan that Hemingway—after reading, in Sylvia Beach's Paris bookshop Shakespeare and Co., Lewis's essay "The Dumb Ox: A Study of Ernest Hemingway" (which combines devastating criticism and forthright praise) in the current (1934) issue of* Life and Letters *(it was reprinted in Lewis's* Men Without Art, *(1934)—threw an inkwell across the room and flipped over a table (other accounts say he merely smashed a vase of tulips on Beach's desk). On Lewis's visit to St Louis later in 1944, he did paint an oil portrait of Dr Erlanger and a study in black and coloured chalks, as well as a coloured-chalk portrait of Mrs Gellhorn.*

To Wyndham Lewis

[St Louis]
Sunday Jan 4/44

Dear Lewis,

Felix (its much easier to say and write than "Giovanelli", and "Mac" is easier than "McLuhan"[1]) will write you details about the matters you mention in your last letter. Also about recent developments—the landing of a token commission for a drawing or chalk of Mrs Gellhorn. She jumped at the forty dollar figure. I'm ashamed to report such a job for you except for the fact that she is the public lady number one of St. Louis and Hemingway's mother-in-law to boot. She has no money, but she was genuinely interested in getting you known here. She says she can get you heavy commissions (mentioned two names in particular) if Nagel will go to bat for you. She is the sort who will really pitch in when interested. If we could persuade (I think we can) Golschmann to put out a few bucks for a drawing, then you would have something to exhibit while here. Mrs Giovanelli's picture would then be a valuable item, when framed by such names. We have managed to interest everybody who counts here. They are eager to find the leverage whereby to swing the big money commissions (at least something between one and 5 thousand dollars) and as things stand at the moment anything can happen. A Becker drawing,—a study rather than verisimilitude would be safest—would have value and might turn the scale.

Of course Mrs Gellhorn understands that the 40 dollar figure is a secret and that her *name* alone explained such an offer. I think you can pick up a chalk or two here at a 200–500 dollar figure.

I remember your objections to the doing of jobs of the dear-departed, but thought that a study (definitely not oils) would free you from the dangers you spoke of. Now, to have your Becker sketch with you when you arrive would be like riding into St. Louis on a charger. The barrage of publicity of your previous feats would take instant effect. It would become a case of the Emperor's new clothes among the public here. Nobody would dare to expose himself by raising a skeptical note when such a signal compliment had been paid their king by a world-famous painter. It could be managed in the press that way. It would become a matter of local pride to boost the drawing. It would be talked of as much here as the Eliot was in London,[2] and would probably be reproduced in many other cities. This may be extremely naive of me. But, here, the atmosphere we have generated gives it great plausibility. Nagel, too, would *have* to praise the picture. And

---

[1]Lewis replied on January 13: "Mack is not too matey, but it is too generic. I have known so many 'Macks'—it blurs the image. Shall think up a less dignified abbreviation for my Feldherr." To the end of their correspondence Lewis usually opened his letters with "Dear McLuhan"—though once, in 1955, he used "Dear Mac".

[2]A reference to the controversy that surrounded the rejection of Lewis's painting of T.S. Eliot by the Royal Academy in 1938.

Golschmann would do so with gusto. Those two men alone would be asked to decide its merits. Thus the more "queer" the picture were the better.

As for the write-up of you when you come, the man to do that will be given much advance data on your work—*in writing*. He can study it. You can then polish it off with the needful personal matters which will enliven it. I mean, further details about your career. Unless something very untoward occurs you will get a much bigger spread than the enclosed Golschmann article would suggest. Various pictures of you and your paintings will appear. (Bring the volume *Wyndham Lewis The Artist* with a view to its plates being reproduced.[3] It is unavailable in this city and almost nowhere to be had in the country—certainly not for sale. We have tried to get it.)

I can very well understand your stark perception of taking the cash and letting the credit go. But don't run off with only a few dollars if a few extra days here in St. Louis would shake down a bushel basket of it. You can probably manage to return here, profitably, and you might even manage a triumphal march into Chicago supported by the fifth column recruited inside St. Louis. Had Felix and I been in Chicago we could have done things for you in an impressive style.

As it is, your European reputation may yet prove to be importable *in toto* even at this place. We have found that people get keenly interested *because* you aren't known here. They are flattered that *they* should be approached for the purpose of launching you here. (Here you will find no refugee artists to queer the pitch). Especially are they flattered after they learn that Nagel and the Wednesday Club have invited you. They feel safe, and can afford to be sy[m]pathetic.

Heaven knows what Felix has been writing about me, but be sure that I do less and he does more than he suggests. He *is* an generous person in every way. I know he has offered you his apartment. Do accept. Money apart it offers many advantages to you both and has the kind of location and elevator service which make it convenient for city notables popping in on you. We can put Felix and Margaret up easily. Sufficiently private and independent in the matter of having people coming and going. You will understand what I mean when you see the stupid way in which the space of our apt. has been squandered. But do take the Giovanelli's up and remember that you are conferring an honour on them in their eyes and ours.

Aimiably yours,
Mac.

[3]*Wyndham Lewis the Artist, from "Blast" to Burlington House* (1939), a collection of essays on art by Lewis.

To Elsie McLuhan

[St Louis]
Mon. Jan 10/44

Dearest Mother,

A birthday greeting with our blessings for you. Eric is shouting "Mudder".[1] "Mama" is too easy for him now. He still says "Nana on choo-choo." To-day he said when Corinne asked where I was: "Dada school." He can and does say a great many words now—new since you left.

Last night I landed Lewis a commission. Mrs Gellhorn, the no. 1 public lady of St. Louis. She will not only sit (for a drawing) but swears she will land something good for him here.

Really, with this sort of leverage we may be able to do something good for him yet.

Meantime, no word from draft board.

All our love on this your birthday
Marshall Corinne and Eric.

[1]The McLuhans' first child, Eric, was born in 1942.

To Wyndham Lewis

[St Louis]
Wed. Jan 13/44

Dear Lewis, relax! All that rhetoric about Becker and your riding in here on a charger can be checked. I saw Tom Sherman of the Post-Dispatch this morning.[1] He is the music and art critic, but also chief of the rotogravure division which would carry the Becker job if done. He told me that recent war priorities have forced them to reserve most space for advertisers—certainly all colored stuff. Thus he won't put in Becker *or* the Eliot. The Eliot is a natural for St Louis.[2] However, Sherman thinks Eliot a dope, as do all St. Louisans. The one concession Sherman would make was to send out photographers to seize you in the act of drawing or painting some local yokel. Then he shipped me along to the feature editor who assigned your interview on arrival here to a Miss Clanton—an intelligent but ignorant girl. She will be provided with data and books about you for the next month or so.

Oh yes, a word about dates. Mrs. Knight was in error. You are to be at the Wednesday Club on Friday Feb. 18, not 19. If, however, you have a few drawing commissions would it be best to come before that time to attend to them? Mrs Gellhorn saw me yesterday. She is most enthusiastic and may be induced to part

[1]Thomas B. Sherman died in 1968 at the age of 77, after more than 40 years on the *St. Louis Post-Dispatch*.

[2]The reference is to Lewis's portrait of T.S. Eliot, who was born in St Louis in 1888 and lived there until 1905, when he was sent to Milton Academy, a private school outside Boston.

with more than $40. I imagine, if you were to suggest some slightly more expensive mode of treating her. She was once painted by a man who simply made her look like a grim suffragette on the rostrum. So that's out. I'm not sure that she's really that sort anyhow. She wants to present this drawing to one of her sons. Then she is very keen to have her [daughter] Martha (Mrs Hemingway) painted. And Martha is no mean subject. However she is in England, war-correspondent for Colliers. Would she (Martha) regard you as a "bloody fascist"? She married Hemingway in Spain during the Civil War—both violent Loyalist at *that* time. Perhaps its a good thing that Martha ain't here now! Mrs. Gellhorn is having some wealthy and likely people to tea to-day and is going to start her campaign in your behalf. She will prove to be a Fifth Column by herself. If only Nagel weren't such a timid little squirt. She says that he could get you a dozen big commissions in a day. But Brockhurst is the gruel for Charlie.

With your visit imminent everybody seems more amenable to suggestion, so that it will be strange indeed if we don't have a few chalk jobs lined up for you, and perhaps a really big job or two. Couldn't you leave things in such a posture that urgent telegrams to Fr. Murphy from St. Louis would win you an extra week or so in which to finish up an oil for some wealthy person? Once you had one of those tucked away you could return for another at any time.

Mrs. Knight was rather eager to know that you had accepted the suggested subject.[3] Do you think you can manage to make it gossipy?[4] They would really love it and it would put them in grand humor for the reception for you afterwards. There may very well prove to be some commissions in that reception.

This is frightful paper, but I never seem to have anything around me fit to write on. I envy you your proficiency at the typewriter. Simply cant bring myself to sit down at one.

Some sort of exhibition of your books and pictures is being arranged by the Wednesday Club. There's not much Felix and I can do to help out beyond adding a book or so and a dust-jacket perhaps. Dare you part with a few more things? (Bring them with you if you come early, or send them a week in advance if you dont?) I mean drawings, dust jackets etc?

In view of your probably being here longer than you anticipate, the Giovanelli apartment becomes even more inevitable doesn't it? I hope it doesn't sound too forward of me to urge this, but they will be comfortable *chez nous*.

Golschmann is the next objective. Its most desirable he should part with $150 or so, so that he can be photographed sitting for you. You see, he is a recognized connoisseur and picture bargain-hunter.

Heartiest good wishes to you
Mac.

Cornell University Library

---

[3]That is, the subject mentioned in the letter of December 31, 1943: "Personalities in the World of Modern Art and Letters".

[4]In his reply of January 16, 1944, Lewis wrote: "You may reassure the Wednesday ladies that I will do nothing but *gossip*, and that the subject of my idle bavardage will be men and women celebrities. . . . In other words, I will earn my hundred bucks."

The second paragraph of the following letter requires some explanation. McLuhan's first department head at Saint Louis University in 1937 was Father William H. McCabe, S.J. (1893–1962), who had received a Ph.D. from Cambridge. He left the University in 1940 and was succeeded by Father Norman J. Dreyfus, S.J. (b. 1898), whose doctorate was from Johns Hopkins University, where the older German-rooted philological outlook was hardly compatible with that of the New Criticism of the Cambridge English School. However, investigation reveals that McLuhan's account, which follows, of the attitude towards him in the English Department was at least somewhat exaggerated. In fact Father Dreyfus, with the collaboration of one of McLuhan's doctoral students, Father Maurice B. McNamee, S.J.—later Dreyfus's successor as head of the Department—soon became a vigorous promoter of the New Criticism, although not exclusively so. While a few faculty members, Jesuit and lay, and a few graduate students were nonplussed or even (defensively) hostile to McLuhan, by far the greater number were inspired by him and enjoyed his outlook and manner. Many Jesuits from across the United States were at the time studying English at Saint Louis University and would later spread McLuhan's influence as a spokesman for the New Criticism (rather than as the media analyst that he became).

To Wyndham Lewis

[St Louis]
Jan 17/44

Dear Lewis, "McLuhan" suits me and is preferrable to "Mac", but I felt that in suggesting "Felix" in place of "Giovanelli" that I should do a bit of shamanizing myself. Perhaps I was misguided by sympathy for your typing probem when you had to tackle "Giovanelli" so often. However "Felix" does suit him admirably, and life here these past 3 years would have been wholly unfelicitous without him and Margaret. The données [facts] about my present position here are brief, and it is easier to mention such things in letters. Anyhow, when you are here there will be no opportunity or disposition to be lugubrious. You are like to be a busy man as artist, critic, and diner-out.

To mention the situation first. I came here in 1937. My dept. head, a Jesuit, was a Cambridge graduate too. We worked together perfectly and had begun to build things here on good lines. During 1939–40 I returned to Cambridge for a year, and he was made president of another school. My new head hated his predecessor and everything he stood for. That meant me too. Since then there has been a campaign of attrition against me. Shunting me into the K.P. duties of the dept. where others took on the jobs I had done and for which I was especially qualified. Sabotaging of my work among the students and general tabus invented to keep intelligent people away from my contact. This is a familiar tale to you I'm sure. Well, why didn't I get out? Many reasons exist. First, that's what the head wanted. He couldn't fire me because I had too much the respect of other Jesuits. Again, this is the best Catholic School in the country, and the next step must be up. Again, I hadn't my Ph.D. (until Dec./43) and was thus like a man presenting himself in a bathing suit at an embassy ball. There are other reasons. Now, looking back, I can see that I was right to stick. Of course, with the draft hanging over me the head was able to tighten the thumb-screws considerably.

Thus, you see, your coming visit, the sort of work I've done for you here (and heaven knows it could all crash easily enough even before you can get here to exploit it) has been a means not only of salvaging my self respect but of solving my own problems parabolically by tackling yours. I am already much in your debt intellectually, and now morally. During these past months I have had to contemplate your achievements in a new way. Presenting you in St Louis brought me into contact with all the people that American academic life was (not unwisely) created to exclude. I have found that these people aren't very hard to manage. That was quite a surprise. And, of course, I have *earned* a knowledge of what kind of matter [the general lack of interest and sympathy] you have had to work with all your life.

As for my aims and projects. Sensing, these past years, a kind of indeterminancy in my life and milieu, yet having a strong need to work towards making more and more of my studies, and the life around me, intelligible,—of raising the particulars to the level of intelligibility, I have cultivated a sort of "negative capability", trying to achieve a readiness to act in some unforeseeable way when that way should define itself. That is the present position. There is some sort of work in me. I shall impinge in some sort of way, but whether academic or not I am unable to see. But what complete isolation governs the maturing of any thought in this country! You have had a big taste of it.

Mrs Gellhorn is enthusiastically at work. She says that nobody will sign on the dotted line for any big job until they have met you. That's fair enough. Incidentally, that suggests that your Wednesday Club lecture may be crucial, unless you should come a few days early. What you say (or how they feel about what you say) wouldn't make much difference if you had already done some drawings of the right people. You can certainly afford to make the Wed. C[lub]. lecture a chatty, breezy sort of account of the bigwigs you know, letting them know that your wig is even bigger but without direct assertion. In other words the sort of anecdotal lecture they want could easily (and, from their point of view, most desirably) become a big puff for yourself. They want to feel: "Here is a big shot who we have been smart enough to snag before anybody else got him." Latest title suggested by Mrs Knight: "Famous people I have put in my books and on canvas." God help us! And forgive me for seeming to dictate your lecture to you. I'm simply playing the cards in such wise as may secure you the best commissions. It will be easy to be nice to these people once you have some of their money in your pocket and some of their whiskey where it will do the most good!

Mrs Gellhorn wants Mrs Golschmann to have a drawing of herself. That's still in the air. I shall report to you immediately on what happens. Papa G. is a notorious picture-dealer, a bargain-hunter. Music is a side-line with him. He is going to say: "My dear, I know a guy who will do it for less." If that happens ($200 is the only price we mention for a drawing now, though $150 had been cited to one or two earlier) it might be well to write Vladimir and in all secrecy offer to draw him on condition that it appear a commission to the town. If anybody were to think that he had *put out money* to be drawn you would have a mail order business on your hands, lines forming in all quarters where you might expect to be found. Perhaps he *will* put out money. Nagel goes in dread of Vladimir's knowledge of art-works. Nagel is an oaf, a bewildered puppy. He knows nothing of art. You will have to allay his dread of you by some means. Of course, his dread takes the superficial form of arrogance. But he is likely to bolt, to hide under the table at a moment's notice. Actually, Vladimir does have some knowledge and taste. He also owns some good things, including a few Picassos. He must be had!

Letting Mrs. G have it for $40 was a good thing. She knows that it was a bargain and wants to consolidate and enhance her bargain by having others pay the full price. She certainly has secured 3 or 4 commissions for you already. I'm not quite sure of her precise interest in all this. Somehow it all fits into her present plans. Incidentally, you will find her a very tolerable sort. No American Club Woman she. She despises that "Flossie culture" as she calls it, and has a more masculine taste than most men in matters of this kind.

From now on the problem is timing. Too much enthusiasm and interest mustn't be crested too far ahead of your arrival. It would be hard to make the beach on a receding wave! So it will be low-gear for 2 or 3 weeks, with Mrs Gellhorn mainly in control. Do you think it would be well to drop her a note? Confirming the commission and offering a bit of encouragement?

> Mrs George Gellhorn
> 4366 McPherson Ave.
> St Louis

More news soon.

Most aimiably yours
M. McLuhan

To Wyndham Lewis

[St Louis]
18? Jan. [1944]

Dear Lewis, No time for deflation yet.[1] I said "Relax" meaning that there was now no point in undertaking what I was sure would be for you a distasteful job.

---

[1]To McLuhan's suggestion, at the beginning of his letter of January 13, that Lewis relax, Lewis had replied "Right! I deflate myself." (January 16, 1944.)

As far as playing St Louis "big" is concerned, the prospects are steadily improving. The Becker job may still fall to you as a commission (they are still looking for a man to oil him for the city hall), but those interested in sitting for you are of sufficient magnitude to keep the St Louis situation both fluid and promising. At least one famous Jesuit will (I am fairly sure) have a drawing. In a vulgar way he is even better known than Sheen. I refer to Fr. Daniel Lord.[2] I have enlisted the enthusiasm of his friends at least to the extent of $200. For awhile I was playing for $5000, even writing his friend Cecil B DeMille to chip in with that sum.[3] No answer, of course. One or two more Jesuits may very possibly get staked to a portrait. One of them a beautiful lad. Just bethought me of our venerable Archbishop now 80 odd. Must go to work on him at once. If only Golschmann can be jockied around, then we can rope in the big game. Some may be had anyhow.

Felix has gotten up a fine account of you and your work which we are having mimeographed down at school. (No cost to us.) It runs to about 3000 words, and will prove very useful here in the next few weeks. Shall send you some copies as soon as they are ready. Father Murphy might know how to utilize them there. You may be inspired to augment and recast it, in which case your interests would be well served.

There is in this town a big reptile known as Queenie[4] of Monsanto Chemicals. He is possible game, having been mentioned to us frequently as amenable to the portrait idea. Fortunately we haven't spoiled things by rushing in too soon. As the wave of interest here mounts we shall watch for the moment to meet him.

I'm just a little upset that my "relax", intended to reassure you, should have acted as a disappointment.

I was saying to Felix last night that had I any good students here at St Louis, I would send them up to Windsor for the rest of the year to get your courses.

By the way, Nagel himself is *locum tenens* for [Perry T.] Rathbone. Rathbone is a frantic little esthete of the Dresden collecting type. Nagel somehow hopes to do nobler things in his absence. Nagel is nettled about the Wednesday Club getting priority over him, but is fatalistic in his dealings with women. He assumes that they can always out-slug him, so gives in right away. A good thing for us. We shall see that 200 or so are turned away from your Museum lecture (hall only holds 250) so that he will be happy.

Greetings to Mrs Lewis.
Yours
Marshall McLuhan.

P.S. Both lectures are in the evening. "Smoking" is formal evening wear here, but I'll check on tails.

Cornell University Library

[2]Father Daniel Lord, see page 110, note 3.

[3]Cecil B DeMille (1881–1959) was the famous director of Hollywood biblical epics.

[4]Edgar Monsanto (his mother's maiden name) Queeny, who has been credited with making the Monsanto Company of St Louis, founded by his father, the huge multinational chemical company it now is.

To Elsie McLuhan

[St Louis]
Sat. 1.30 P.M. [January 23, 1944]

Dearest Mother,

Haven't written you for some time. Have been working very hard for Lewis. And getting places. If a position in this town meant anything to me, or were even of indirect value as a job-getter I could have what I asked for. In the past few weeks I have met all the big-wigs—some of them decent, but none intelligent. It is easy to impress them and to manage them. They offer to invite me here and there but I slip out on the plea of being too busy—which I am. But it is reassuring to know that one can manage that sort of thing when necessary.

To-night Corinne and I shall get to see *The Lady Vanishes*—Hitchcock's best picture, made in England 1936 or so.

Do you want another copy of *Columbia*?[1]

Am feeling more like scholarly work again after recovery from a debauch of army themes. My schedule for next semester is fiendish in its composition. I shall have simply to ignore it.

Eric is in great fettle. Has a marvellous new toy. Mind, he doesn't need any more of the fit-together things. He has enough to last him a year.

He enjoys the new tailor-tot, and the weather lately enables him to go out in sweater alone.

This afternoon I intend to devote to an article on Dale Carnegie which will go to *Columbia*.[2] If only I had 2 free months to write things.

All our love
M and C.

[1] Containing McLuhan's article "Dagwood's America" in *Columbia* (January 1944).

[2] "Dale Carnegie: America's Machiavelli (Dale Carnegie's Moral Arithmetic)" was apparently never published; a manuscript is in the Public Archives of Canada. About the author (1885–1955) of the famous bestseller *How to Win Friends and Influence People* (1936), this essay begins: "Dale Carnegie is the American Machiavelli, the cheerful apostle of unprincipled action and duplicity."

To Elsie McLuhan

[St Louis]
Thursday Jan 27/[1944]

Dearest Mother,

The March issue of *Columbia* is to carry a reply to my Dagwood article. The editor sent me the galley sheets of the article to-day.[1] WOW! What an out burst of

[1] This article, "Dagwood—The People's Choice", by Joseph A. Breig (*Columbia*, March 1944)—a response to McLuhan's January article "Dagwood's America" (see page 138, note 3)—is a spirited defence of Dagwood. It ends: "I give you the greatest of American husbands and fathers; the happiest, most humorous and most human of the lot; I give you, Mr McLuhan, Dagwood Bumstead, that you may learn of him; for he is meek and humble of heart." McLuhan's reply, headed "Closing the Dagwood File", was inset in the first page of the article.

feminine rage—what clawing and screaming over my phrases. Then it shifts to deep, deep sentiment and private revelation. Of course the author is a male. He identifies himself with Dagwood. My reply is brief. I simply say that he doesn't refute but illustrates my points. Actually he has written an article which represents the response of the average guy. I will now write a book feeling sure that his article will ensure its being published.[2]

Last night I had locked Eric in the nursery and was preparing my retreat by saying "Daddy tired. Daddy lie down." He said: "Rug, rug." Got his dog-rug for me. Made me lie on it. Then got a blanket to put over me. Then he lay on it.

Warm day to-day. Too warm all at once. It has made us groggy. Corinne is too fagged for choir.

All our love
M and C.

[2]This book became *The Mechanical Bride* (1951), which treats the subject in the piece entitled "Blondie".

To Wyndham Lewis

4256 Maryland [St Louis]
Sunday night [January 23, 1944]

Dear Lewis, Giovanelli thinks he may have been confusing about your date of departure and arrival. He thinks your announced plan quite the thing—that is, arriving Sunday Feb 13 at 6.55. On what line by the way? Be sure to avoid any train which would involve a change from one to another at some smallish town. There is at least one such train. The one we got on!

Here is an item for you which may turn out very well indeed. Hutchins of Chicago U. is to be here Thurs. Feb. 17, to lecture.[1] His parents live here, so he may be around for a few days. We are writing him to arrange a lunch or dinner for you with him. We hope this affair will prove as pregnant as it appears!

Mrs Hutchins is the infamous painter and sculptor Maude Phelps. Shall get a brief on her for you in the event of her showing up with him. She could be a big help or just the reverse.

St. Louis can be delightfully bland in the matter of weather at this time of year. After the sort of winter you've had up there we pray something benign may occur here.

With every prosperous wish,
Yours,
Marshall McLuhan

Cornell University Library

[1]Robert Maynard Hutchins (1899–1977) was president of the University of Chicago from 1929 to 1945. See page 180, note 1.

To Wyndham Lewis

[St Louis, Mo.]
Tuesday Feb 1st. [1944]

Dear Lewis

I'm getting jumpy! Will this Bergsonian flux jell when you arrive?[1] Will all these eggs I've been sitting on these past weeks hatch the moment you appear in the papers? This morning a typical sort of temporary setback occurred. Mrs Sayman the Soap Queen who studied with Papa Haymann at Munich in 1934 was on the phone. Her attitude toward commissioning you she had determined would depend on the following fact: Her daughter had married young Smithers (English naval attaché at Washington) a few months ago. Of course he is a prodigy. An Oxford man. A trustee of Ox. U. A connoisseur. What he said about you would decide the matter. What the hell! Of course I knew the sort of man in advance, but I'm angry anyhow that a little snot of that type should travel so far to spoil good work here. He simply has never heard of you. So Mrs. Sayman concludes you are nobody.

However, there are dozens of people here whose pants have been impressed right off them. There are dozens of others sitting on the sidelines offering advice and assuring us that you have a sure-fire proposition in St. Louis. These people are unanimous in asserting that you must put up at the Park Plaza if you are to get any commissions. All agree that you can't fail of commissions, that many people want to be painted, and can easily be convinced that you are the man for them. But the Plaza "front" is necessary. They wont part with money if you wont.

Well the Plaza isn't too expensive at that. Moreover, you can be sure of sizing up the situation within 3 or 4 days in order to decide whether to stay on or not. I think you will be given a suite there—bedroom and sitting-room—for 10 dollars a day. Anyhow, I'll give you exact information soon.[2]

Since it is desirable that your publicity should precede the lectures by a day or two, what about the 16th? Mrs Gellhorn has offered to give a very exclusive reception for you on the night of the 16th—from 5–7 sort of thing. She plans to have the Golschmann's and those who can well afford to be painted. It would be well that the feature interview appear in the Post-Dispatch that same day. That would involve your arrival on the 15th—Tuesday. None of the time spent here before the lectures would be wasted, since there are two or three people who want to see you about paintings the moment you arrive. They aren't the ones who will provide bait for bigger game, but they can well afford to pay you for all that.

[1]The French philosopher Henri Bergson (1859–1941) believed that reality was a pure flow or "flux", which could be made to freeze (or "jell") by the intellect, or by the understanding. This idea is wittily applied here to McLuhan's hope that the complicated arrangements of Lewis's visit will fall into place when he arrives.

Apparently it is understood in St. Louis that anybody invited to a reception for an artist is a prospective client. There is no hypocrisy in the air at all. You will find that a relief.

The Wednesday Club chairman reports that tails are "out" for the duration. Dinner-jackets are the peak of formality, and not absolutely necessary. You could well afford to bring one however. (Afternoon dresses are now regarded as formal wear for women in St. Louis, but evening dresses are still being worn.)

We shall probably wangle a really large reception for you on Thursday the 17th which will be attended by all the new wealth of St Louis plus some of the old. There is one prospect here for you—Adrian Fraser—who made 6 million clear this past year. He has a wife and daughter who would like to get into society via a painting perhaps.

Everybody wants to see some of your work, so we are combing the libraries of the country for a set of *Thirty Personalities*.[3] They would make a suitable show by themselves.

More news soon from a panicky field marshal!

Sincerely
Marshall McLuhan.

Cornell University Library

[2]In his reply of February 9, Lewis wrote: "The Plaza *cannot* be considered. If it is not to be Gio's apartment, we must look round and somehow or other exist, without spending all our money, until 22nd (morning)."

[3]*Thirty Personalities and a Self-Portrait* (1932), a portfolio of drawings by Lewis that included portraits of J.B. Priestley, Augustus John, G.K. Chesterton, Edith Evans, Noel Coward, and Rebecca West.

To Wyndham Lewis

Friday Feb 3. [1944]
4256 Maryland [St Louis]

Dear Lewis, Gio[vanelli] is a bit embarrassed about the Plaza business. He has been pretty well convinced ever since Edna Gellhorn came over to our side that his apt. wouldn't quite do. But both he and Margaret were very keen that you and Mrs. Lewis should confer that honour on them. I mean that they regarded your possible occupancy of their apt. as a very great event—something having an unpurchasable quality. That's the way I look at it too. Thus in turning to the Plaza we were personally disappointed.

A recent event at the Plaza may change your view of the subject. You are to have a 10 dollar room for 5 dollars a day. Naturally this is not to be discussed here, in view of O.P.A. rulings. However, I had a chat with Mr Jones the asst. mgr. and asked him about studio apartments there. "Well, says he, Brockhurst always takes the North exposure apt. at 15 dollars a day. Its really our only studio apt." I then learnt that Brockhurst had been back recently for 2 weeks. Another 30,000 bucks for him. Jones despises Brockhurst and is now a 100% W. Lewis man! He said, "I know the people he paints, and I've seen his paintings, and I wouldn't have one of those sickly jobs." So, I told him that he might discreetly inform his millionaire clients that he had an "in" with Mr. W. Lewis and *might* be able to get a job done for them. Not much hope of course. But just a chance that Lewis might relent for 5000 dollars. (Jones to get 10%).

As regards expenses at the Plaza, the wealthy notoriously breakfast and lunch in the Plaza drugstore at the usual drug store rates. Not that you will be on your own so much that you will have to explore their larder. As for dinner it will be a tug of war between Gio and me. When you wish to be alone there are suitable spots within easy reach of the Plaza. (The Plaza is a suburban hotel, on the edge of the posh residential part of St Louis, and much more convenient and pleasant than any down town hotel. Moreover, it is only two blocks from us.

Now Gio doesn't want to write you about the Plaza because he feels that would smack of withdrawing the apt. offer. Such isn't the case. The apt. is there for you at any moment it seems advisable to move.

Now a big relief for you! This matter has never been broached for one moment with any of the bigwigs here. Only when seeking "professional" advice from people who know about these things, and seeking it in the capacity of your "manager" have we ever raised the hotel question. Then it has always been: "Which hotel do you think Lewis ought to put up at?" It was apropos of this particular question that the information was always volunteered: "If he wants to make any impression here he must put on a front." You can be quite sure that we are jealous of your integrity in our dealings here. After all, it is because of that integrity that we are determined that you should get a "break" here. There has been no high-pressure stuff, and we have studiously avoided personal contact with the people who are likely to put out big money for paintings. Mrs Gellhorn handles all that. She doesn't have to shout or push or nudge to get a hearing. Her reception for you is to be small but select indeed—about 15 people. Her house isn't large.

By the way, a simple means of getting your drawings down here without fuss is simply to consign them to the Art Museum as a "loan." You could claim them on arrival here. No set of *30 Personalities* has yet been tracked down in the U.S.A.

Your first press interview is to be with Miss Helen Clanton of the Post-Dispatch. She is married to an Irish doctor. On my way out to mail this I have to lend her some of your books.

The French painter Chevil (?) has done several things for the Gellhorns at 5000 a throw. Be prepared to see some of his delicate whimsies at her home! Mrs Gellhorn's husband was a famous and much-loved St Louis doctor.

Heaven send that you shan't be exhausted when you get here! My heart sank when I heard about another moving problem facing you.

Somehow, I think we are all going to manage to be rather gay during your visit—especially Mrs Lewis. And if that gaiety is touched off by cash on the line, so much the better!

> Happy hunting!
> Most aimiable regards,
> Marshall McLuhan.

To Wyndham Lewis

> 4256 Maryland [St Louis]
> Wednesday 2 P.M. [8 February 1944]

Dear Lewis, Plan to have dinner with us Sunday night. The Giovanellis will be here of course. Gio and I shall be at the train to meet you and Mrs Lewis, so keep an eye out for us. You are sure to be fagged by that trip, but a few drinks may put all that right. Then we can discuss things properly.

Big things are pending. There seems to be a remarkably good prospect that you *shall* paint or draw Archbishop Glennon, the 86 year old dean of the American hierarchy. Much depends on the sponsors knowing either nothing or much about your writings. It is that slight knowledge which is so damaging—the hearsay. Fulton Sheen could be a decisive factor. We may have him wire an O.K. to Glennon.

The "climbing clergy" here would like to ingratiate themselves with Glennon by some such means. The picture would be reproduced at once all over the country. (So would a Hutchins drawing.)

One potent lever I have found is the casual reference to your coming portfolio of "American Personalities".[1] This has brought immediate *tentative* offers of sitters from the Pres. of St. Louis U and of our medical school—for "the publicity." You will find that you can fill that portfolio in any American city with such bait to offer.

The "world-famous painter" estimate has every sign of being the present St. Louis estimate of you. It cannot be rubbed off by isolated acts of sabotage because it has been set up in too many quarters.

Don't talk to the press until you have talked to us!

> Bon Voyage! Yours Marshall McLuhan

[1] Nothing came of this project; but among the portraits executed by Lewis in St Louis were those of Dr Erlanger, Mrs Felix Giovanelli, Mrs Ernest William Stix (paintings), and Mrs Gellhorn (coloured chalk drawing).

To Elsie McLuhan

[St Louis]
Feb. 17--1944

Dearest Mother

Eric's handiwork on the other side.

Nothing to come of the Hutchins visit since he is arriving just before lecture and leaving right after.

Mrs. Gellhorn's show [reception] was superb. She spent a $100 and had everybody of note in St. Louis. There is nothing that can be done for Lewis that hasn't been done. Something is going to click soon. Something big for him. A little time is needed.

Mrs Gellhorn said that her sister pronounced Corinne "The most beautiful woman I have seen in many a day." She did look lovely indeed.

All our love
M and C

Lewis and his wife lived in St Louis from February to July 1944 at the Plaza and Coronada Hotels, and in the flat of the Giovanellis. Lewis had to return to Canada monthly (he had a Canadian passport) to renew his visitor's visa to the USA, and in March he carried with him the following letter of application to Assumption from McLuhan, which Lewis gave to Father Murphy with his endorsement. This led to McLuhan's appointment.

To J. Stanley Murphy, C.S.B.[1]

[St Louis]
March 9/44

Dear Father Murphy,

Lewis is bringing this to you directly since some of my intentions might not please my draft-board here if relayed to them by some censor at the U.S. border. At present I am in 1a and have been these 3 months. That means that I can be put in the army at a moment's notice. Loaded down with Army Courses here, however, I may look or appear unhappy enough to be passed by. However, the army may withdraw from St. Louis U. Ordinary prudence thus suggests that I canvass other possibilities.

As a Canadian who hasn't taken out first papers I can return to Canada without embarrassment. However, were I to be drafted here I could not return to Canada save to serve in the Canadian army—supposing, at least, I wish to be *persona grata* in the U.S.A. after the war.

Of course I know nothing of the situation at Assumption College. But, were I there would my position with regard to the draft be better than here? If not, nothing more need be said. If I would be better off there, then I can only ask that you look at the following data to see whether they might render me a useful and feasible addition to the set up at Assumption.

[1]See page 129.

(There may be other courses which occur to you—such as a nominal position at Assumption while I took some sort of defense job to support my family. My point in avoiding the army is partly, and primarily, to be able to support my family and to be with it. Also, my writing and research are at a point difficult to relinquish without permanent loss of momentum. Heaven knows how many years one would be kept in the army, combat duty apart.)

Since regular courses at Assumption are probably well taken care of I shall suggest only "feature" courses.

I Practical Criticism of prose and poetry. I have given this sort of work here for years. Although some other places have such work I believe I am the only man in the U.S.A. who had a thorough grounding in the techniques of Richards Empson and Leavis at Cambridge. I can do the sort of thing with a text which Adler and Hutchins are always talking about but never do. Enclosed are a couple of samples of the technique. However, the written critique lacks the flexibility and detail of the oral or class-room method.

II Culture and Environment. A course in the analysis of the present scene. Advertisements, newspapers, best-sellers [,] detective fiction [,] movies etc. Contrasted with a true pattern of homogeneous culture, rationally ordered. This contrast made in concrete detail by analysis say of a section of sixteenth century society—its architecture, literature, music, economics etc.

III The Dichotomy of European and American culture. An extension with detailed study of the sort of thing adumbrated in the Poe article which I enclose.[2]

There are many other possibilities. I write in great haste between classes.

One important paper I'm working on at the moment is "Culture and Neurosis: From Machiavelli to Marx."[3] An analysis of the entirely emotional and "neurotic" character of the political and literary cycles of development of "Renaissance Man." Upshot of paper is that to-day our "nervous breakdown" is a blessed opportunity to escape from the cycle back to reason. If this were to be given as a course I could work it up into a book.

Loaded down here these past 3 years with freshman English I have written articles instead of books. I have tried to condense books into articles so that, later on, they could be expanded.

Since many of the enclosed items represent my only copies, please send the batch to me again.

Yours in Xt.

Marshall.

[2]Herbert Marshall McLuhan, "Edgar Poe's Tradition", *Sewanee Review,* vol. 12, no. 1, January 1944.

[3]In the Public Archives of Canada is the manuscript of an unpublished essay entitled "Catharsis and Hallucination From Machiavelli to Marx" in which McLuhan states: ". . . the importance of a Machiavelli, a Hobbes, or a Marx is not primarily intellectual but cathartic. They don't offer conceptual systems so much as emotional strategies." In *The Mechanical Bride*, McLuhan says that "Machiavelli stands at the gate of the modern age, divorcing technique from social purpose" (p. 87).

To J. Stanley Murphy, C.S.B.

[St Louis]
Friday night [March 1944]

Dear Father Murphy,

Lewis, I believe, is as happy as we (Corinne and myself) are over your summer offer. Now comes your suggestion about extra-mural lectures. They would help a great deal. There are a great many projects for books in my mind at present, and they need development and clarification in just such an atmosphere as Assumption College. I need conversation with congenial minds—Catholic minds. Also time and leisure for reading and writing is indispensable.

Despite the specious attractiveness of such a course as "From Marx to Machiavelli" (a book I intend to do) I imagine that the course in Practical Criticism, stressing the reading and analysis of prose and poetry would be, initially, most helpful. Moreover, texts and corollory reading in such a course present no problem—a fact of importance for summer school students.

My ordinary schedule here in St. Louis has been 10 or 12 hours. What with army work it has gone up to 16 these past two years. That has been stultifying. Pressing on with my writing under these conditions has been a great drain on energy.

As for regular teaching, I have handled as upper division or graduate courses, most of the periods of English literature from the beginning of the 16th cent. to the present. I can easily manage Chaucer for undergraduates. I have a book ready on the history of English literature—written from a novel point of view—which I will show you.[1]

You probably knew from Lewis that my Cambridge doctorate was conferred last November? That makes an Assistant prof. here. I had my B.A. and M.A. from Manitoba before doing the Cambridge B.A. So that gives me 5 degrees (including the titular M.A. Cantab.). This, heaven help me, is only for your information should you need to use it!

Lewis is taking a new lease on life. Feels he is back in stride again. Wants to get to writing and serious painting now. His relative St. Louis success merely caps the good you have done him. He certainly has no yen to be done with Windsor! He likes all of you there too much for that.

Depending on what sort of library facilities turn up in or near Windsor, I should push on (without relinquishing other things) with the preparation of my thesis for the press. It has some quite new things in it about the 16th century.

As for your kind offer about keeping an eye out for a place for us to stay. We are tired of the crowded city. Would like space and safety for Eric to prowl about in. Also, we aren't afraid of a house—even a very big house, provided it isn't beyond reason in rent. We have an 8 room apartment here. That has spoiled us a bit. Anyhow, we have a good deal of furniture. Also it would be nice to have a big, old house for the sake of studious privacy and for the sake of guests. But we

[1]This may have been an anthology McLuhan had been compiling that was not published.

shall take what we can get, of course. If Lewis isn't back in Windsor when we arrive (late May?) we might stay in his apt. for a few days while I scout around. We have always had superlative fortune in the matter of housing!

Most gratefully and cordially yours in Xt.
Marshall.

Four of the letters that follow—May 26, June 1, June 2, and June 26—concern Lewis's having borrowed $100 from Giovanelli because of extra expenses incurred for having stayed, unwillingly, at the Plaza Hotel in St Louis. On May 25 Lewis told McLuhan in conversation that he wanted him to assume the debt—an arrangement that McLuhan did not object to—and to advise Giovanelli. On May 26 Lewis confirmed this request in writing, while outlining what to him seemed to be becoming "a messy situation". The note that follows immediately, which did not reach Lewis, was written on the same day in reply.

To Wyndham Lewis

[St Louis]
Friday 4 P.M.
May 26/44

Dear Lewis,

Your letter got put in our box this morning, instead of coming to the door. I called Giovanelli a few minutes ago, asking about his view of my becoming liable for the sum you owe him. He said that he preferred to cancel the debt, but should that be totally unacceptable to you he would regard the debt as transferred to me. He said also that he would write you a cancellation at once.

Most cordially yours
Mac.

Cornell University Library

To Wyndham Lewis

Thursday June [1, 1944] 9:30 A.M.
4256 Maryland [St Louis]

Dear Lewis

Much haste necessary. Enclosed is copy of letter sent you by me last Friday [i.e. the previous letter]. This morning you asked "Have you written me a letter?" I said "No." Naturally, I assumed you referred to a letter "written" yesterday but not yet received by you. That is, that you supposed I had written you recently. That you should not have gotten my Friday note is fiendish. I have phoned the post-office to have it traced. You may get it yet. Regret is a stupidly inadequate word for this sort of thing. Some hideous jinx presides over these matters.

Yours
Mac.

Cornell University Library

To Wyndham Lewis

37 Garrison
Battle Creek, Michigan[1]
Friday June 2/44

Dear Lewis,

The enclosure was in a note to me from Father Murphy which I picked up at school yesterday on the way to the station.

We are to stay here till Monday with some friends. By then, furniture will be in Windsor.

Humiliation and chagrin I had much time to taste during yesterday's train journey. That any carelessness of mine should have added anything to the distress you have had to endure these past years in America is a bitter thought for me.[2] You had been, for years before I met you, a major resource in my life. These past months have been a very great experience indeed. To recruit understanding students for your work will always be part of mine. One day I shall have some influence. To-day, when I could be of direct aid to you, I have none. But I shall do what I can in Detroit, and explore the San Francisco matter. Groton, I have been told, has a resident artist who turns back his salary to the school.

When I lecture on the Christian Culture Series why couldn't the subject be you? May I ask Fr. Murphy's permission?

My "No" to your query "Have you written me a letter" was quite natural. Had you only hinted that you meant the letter you had *asked* me to write! But my mind was full of thoughts of departure. I hadn't seen you to say adieu. So I thought you meant: "Have you written *a* letter of that sort?" not: "Have you written *the* letter." From the letter [May 28] I received from you Monday [May 29] I was aware that my Friday letter [May 26] had not reached you Saturday. I was sure it would reach you Monday. No doubt ever entered my head or I should have phoned you. I would have phoned in any case had I not felt that once the letter was in your hands you would call me *if you wished to do so*. You must feel that there was some inconsistency in my phoning you that Mother could manage to let me send you money at the same time that the non-arrival of my letter suggested that I was unwilling to assume the obligation of the Giovanelli debt? Naturally, had I *not* written the letter you asked I would never have told you of Mother's offer. I am not "insulted" at your lack of trust in me. You have no reason to trust me or anybody else. You have every reason to protect yourself

---

[1]McLuhan was visiting his mother here.

[2]This alludes both to the meeting recorded in the previous letter and to a testy letter from Lewis (May 28, 1944) blaming McLuhan for putting him in the position of "forcing upon you an arrangement which you obviously do not desire"—or else, Lewis said, McLuhan would have told Giovanelli that the $100 debt was not Lewis's but his. McLuhan had said as much to Giovanelli, but apparently Giovanelli, in his note to Lewis, expressed reservations about imposing the debt on McLuhan. This irritated Lewis who—being Lewis, and having invented a grievance—proceeded to hold his most loyal supporter responsible for his aggravation, though one cannot see how McLuhan could have acted more considerately.

against presumption and fraud, even when they are only potentially present, from people who instinctively detest and distrust great superiority of talent and achievement. This, of course, means a great diminution of creative activity. I was foolish enough to suppose that I might assist you to means to engage in such activity in St. Louis. You foresaw everything.

The day before I left St. Louis there arrived John Farrelly[3] who has been at sea for 6 months in the merchant marine. He has long known your work. He is a person of great acuteness and sensitivity. He belongs (on his Mother's side) to an influential St. Louis family. He is going to study in Cambridge after the war. If he is in St Louis for a month or so he could be helpful.

Yours

Mac.

Cornell University Library

[3]A former student of McLuhan's.

To Wyndham Lewis

Assumption College [Windsor, Ontario]

June 11/44

Dear Lewis,

Perhaps these meat coupons may come in handy. We are gradually getting unpacked. Not an easy job to move into a place smaller than you've moved out of.

I can conveniently manage to send you money should you need it.

Most cordially yours

Cornell University Library

Mac.

To Wyndham Lewis

Assumption College [Windsor, Ontario]

June 26/44

Dear Lewis,

The postmaster here in Windsor has just phoned me to advise me of a tracer which you filed in St. Louis about a letter which you addressed to me at Assumption Coll. He had spoken to Murphy first and had been told that no letter had arrived for me from you. Such is indeed the case. Meantime I hope that my tracer on the letter which I wrote you on May 26 has been more successful.

We are getting settled here. My first class is to-morrow morning at 10. When I met Fr. Lee he popped 3 of Auden's poems under my nose for interpretation. I'm glad that he won't be around this summer nor next year either. He has at least 2 more years of work at Chicago.

Most cordial regards

Cornell University Library

Marshall.

The letter that follows is the first of many letters to Walter J. Ong, S.J. (b. 1912),
who pursued his first studies at Saint Louis University in 1938–41, taking courses
with McLuhan in Practical Criticism and Renaissance Literature. McLuhan
directed his M.A. thesis, "Hopkins' Sprung Rhythm and the Life of English
Poetry". Ong wrote his Harvard Ph.D. dissertation on the French philosopher
Petrus Ramus (1515–72)—see page 188, note 4. A distinguished scholar and the
author of a great many books and articles, Father Ong is well known for his
work in Renaissance literary and intellectual history and contemporary culture,
and for his studies in the evolution of consciousness. He is University Professor
of Humanities, William E. Haren Professor of English, and Professor of Human-
ities in Psychiatry at Saint Louis University. His memoir of McLuhan at Saint
Louis, "McLuhan as Teacher: The Future Is a Thing of the Past", was first pub-
lished in the Journal of Communication, *vol. 31, no. 3, Summer 1981. In 1985*
Father Ong gave the Alexander Lectures at University College, University of
Toronto; they were published in Hopkins, the Self, and God *(1986).*

To Walter J. Ong, S.J.

Assump Coll. [Windsor, Ontario]
Tues Aug 19 [1944]

Dear Walter,

The next issue of the *Sewanee* [Review] comes out under [Allen] Tate's
direction. Perhaps he will make something of it. The Kenyon [Review] disgusts
me. The *Southern R.* was better. *Scrutiny* is done for. Leavis has nothing new to
say. *Partisan Rev.* is best in some respects.

The New York Times asked me to review El. Ruggles book.[1] I did so. They
haven't printed the review, but paid me for it. I suspect that my claims for
G.M.H[opkins] were too shockingly major. To my astonishment, I find he is
still regarded in U.S.A. as a curiosity. That's why *Time* turned out that long
non-committal review. With characteristic adolescent uncertainty *Time* wants
to be in on the new but to be safe with the old.

El. R's book is mediocre, but since it is the first non-Catholic tribute of any
note, I spoke very glowingly of it.

The final form of your Punctuation paper, I like.[2] Wasn't there any space for
illustration of your point?

From now on I get down to the business of writing. All the time, tho not all the
stimulus I need here. You too. Write, Walter.

Yours in Xt.

Walter J. Ong   Mac.

[1]Eleanor Ruggles, *Gerard Manley Hopkins: A Life* (1944). McLuhan's review appeared in the
New York Times on September 3, 1944.

[2]Walter J. Ong, S.J., "Historical Backgrounds of Elizabethan and Jacobean Punctuation Theory",
Publications of the Modern Language Association of America, vol. LIX, no. 2, June 1944.

To Wyndham Lewis[1]

Assumption College
Sept 24 1944

Dear Lewis,

It was a good thing I stopped by college for mail yesterday. Your letter had probably been there 48 hrs as it was. I have just put a note in the mail to my Mother at Battle Creek Michigan—street address: 37 Garrison. She will very probably be able to manage it without selling a war-bond. This fact is a little surprising to me since solvency is a sporadic trait in our family. When you have the cash please send it to her in Battle Creek.

A pox on Stix.[2]

If you should care to see more copies of the *New Leader* I'll gladly forward mine.

Most aimiably yours
Marshall McLuhan.

Cornell University Library

[1]Lewis taught a three week summer course on the visual arts at Assumption in July/August 1944, but went back to St Louis, where he remained from September to December in order to carry out portrait commissions. He then returned to Canada, where he stayed until August 1945, when he returned to England.

[2]On his return to St Louis, Lewis had expected to paint Mrs Stix, but she was in Cape Cod. (Mr Stix was the partner in a large department store in St Louis, later bought out.) Because of this, Lewis was desperately short of money and asked to borrow forty dollars—which McLuhan requested that his mother provide.

To Wyndham Lewis

Assumption College
Windsor Sept 27/44

Dear Lewis,

The Alphamet will be on its way to-day. Try the U.S.A. product "BAX".[1] It is superior.

This morning came a note from my Mother in which she said she had written you to say "a loan for two weeks as requested by my son." This is distressing. The fact is that she will be here in a week or two and can be reimbursed by me. In any event you must overlook the "two week" phrase. It is quite irrelevant and unfortunate.[2]

There is a chap here at the moment who will mail this for me in Windsor, so with haste

Yours
Mac.

Cornell University Library

[1]Vitamin preparations.

[2]In a letter of September 28 reporting that he had received a cheque from McLuhan's mother, Lewis wrote: "The phrase you refer to is unobjectionable. Please do not chide Battle Creek for that." He planned to reimburse Mrs McLuhan soon.

To Wyndham Lewis

RR #2 Tecumseh Ont
Oct 28/44

Dear Lewis,

The enclosed card contains a quote from the current *Commonweal*.[1] It seems to me to be an inaccurate statement which it may be to your advantage to correct.

Well the news is good from this end. For the present at least, I seem to have placated Garvey. Murphy is thriving. My lectures go well both here and as arranged hereabouts. At the alumni meeting this month I was asked to speak about you. They seem to have taken it well, and to have been quite pleased with the prospect of seeing the portraits soon. No word about the mural yet.

Sunday I stayed in Toronto en route to Ottawa. Tuesday also in Toronto where I gave a lecture on [Gerard Manley] Hopkins. F.O. Matthiessen[2] of Harvard was, with the entire Toronto English faculty, the guest of the President. I got in too. On my left was the Warden of Hart House, Bickersteth, back after 4 years in England.[3] His theme was "Women." His treatment was "Blast Them." He champed and chafed and swore one would never enter Hart House. This show I permitted myself to enjoy with spontaneous heartiness, knowing that I would be accorded a putative innocence. However, on all sides, I noted long faces, and chagrin that knew not how to express itself. Really, I shouldn't be surprised if Bickersteth were doing a bit of leg-pulling. His excessive canvassing of the table for assent to his propositions could scarcely have been guileless in view of his previously having been *en tapis* about these matters. Moreover, undergraduate women swim in the Hart House tank daily.

Toronto is truly a broncho corrall. There was much evidence of that even in my two day visit.

Most disconcerting. The Canadian govt removes 43 dollars a month income tax from my check. That amounts to more than 10 times the tax I paid in USA on the same income. Were it not for the lectures we would be destitute—almost.

We hope to hear that St Louis is proving more satisfactory.

Most cordially
Mac.

Cornell University Library

[1]*Commonweal* (1924-) is a weekly review of current events and the arts expressing mainly the point of view of Catholic laymen.

[2]F.O. Matthiessen (1902–50)—professor of history and literature at Harvard University from 1929 until his death—was a distinguished literary critic and the author of several important books, including *The Achievement of T.S. Eliot: An Essay on the Nature of Poetry* (1935), which McLuhan had read and been impressed by at Cambridge, and *Henry James: The Major Phase* (1944).

[3]Burgon Bickersteth (1887–1979) was Warden at Hart House from 1921 to 1947. Hart House was built (in 1911–19) to accommodate athletic, social, and dining facilities for the men of the University of Toronto (until 1972, when women were admitted). Lewis had been entertained by Bickersteth at Hart House on November 30, 1939, and portrayed this event—in a rather forced satirical style—in *America, I Presume* (1940), in the chapter called "I Dine with the Warden".

To Wyndham Lewis

Dec 13/44
RR #2
Tecumseh Ont.

Dear Lewis

With the help of books borrowed from Toronto and Ann Arbor I'm pushing my New York papers together.[1] Between that and travelling back and forth to classes and shops life seems to be sliding by rather quickly. A visit from Murphy, a lecture to the local librarians (which shocked the pants off them) on the book racket, devising barricades against the insolent ingenuity of Eric, bearing up against the lethargy of the student mind—such is the present area of effort.

Subsequent contacts with Joe O'Connor have much improved my opinion of him.[2] He is a *good* boy. Assumption is a little bay of silence—a little backwater in a stagnant stream. Oh the mental vacuum that is Canada. Bruce Hutchison has out a novel "The Hollow Men."[3] Not very good. But he does resist and protest. He struggles against this tepid bathos. There is terrible social cowardice, and all action here seems so furtive that one can only conclude that some unacknowledged guilt is behind it all. Canada needs about 2 million Jews to bring life to it.

Once in a while we see Pauline[4]—usually on Sunday evenings after the Culture Series events. Damn the filthy protracted war. It looks worse every day. How are you ever to get back to England at this rate?[5]

Most Cordially
Mac.

Cornell University Library

[1]That is, preparing papers to be read at the annual Modern Languages Association meetings in New York after Christmas.

[2]Joseph T. O'Connor (b. 1907) was employed at the Catholic Worker House of Hospitality in Windsor, and later assisted Father Stan Murphy in the Registrar's Office of Assumption College, where he became friendly with Wyndham Lewis and then McLuhan. (He was also a friend of Pauline Bondy; see note 4 below.) On returning home to Montreal he graduated from McGill University in social work and worked for the John Howard Society; he retired in 1977.

[3]The journalist Bruce Hutchison (b. 1901) had achieved national prominence with his book *The Unknown Country: Canada and Her People* (1943). In 1944 he published his novel *The Hollow Men* about a newspaper correspondent.

[4]Pauline Bondy (b. 1911) taught French at Kennedy Collegiate, Windsor. She met Wyndham Lewis in 1944 through Father Stan Murphy, and when Lewis needed samples of his portrait work to take to St Louis, he painted Miss Bondy in oil and did four chalk drawings of her. She became a friend of the McLuhans and was godmother to Corinne McLuhan when she became a Roman Catholic in 1946. Miss Bondy left Windsor in 1957 to teach at York Mills Collegiate, North York (Toronto), and retired in 1971.

[5]After this there was a long interruption in the McLuhan/Lewis correspondence. It can be attributed to a brief letter Lewis wrote to McLuhan—from the Prince Edward Hotel, Windsor, Ontario, on February 4, 1945—that suddenly, cruelly, and unfathomably (McLuhan did not know what prompted it) denounced McLuhan for no stated reason and rejected his friendship. However, the correspondence resumed in July 1953 as if this had not occurred.

166

To Walter J. Ong, S.J., and
Clement J. McNaspy, S.J.[1]

[Tecumseh, Ontario]
Dec 23/44

Dear Walter and Clem,

Being flat on my back with flu has become a regular Xmas gesture with me in recent years. It fills me with rage. Poor Corinne has 5 jobs to do. Out here in the country every job is much heavier since it must be done in addition to long bus rides. Well, I shall be up to leave for New York Tuesday. Two papers at the M.L.A. A glance at their program is a grim experience. It satisfies me that no form of Groucho Marx-like defiance or ridicule is undeserved there. My papers, if heard at all, will horrify. Confidence has given me the power to compromise a little with many things. But, fortunately, I'm not tempted to make serious concessions. Recent contact with the staff of Western Ont. University has shocked me into vigilance once more. Not merely mediocrity but tepidity of soul, timidity of mind and a horrible rebellion against anything real marks these people. The are the obverse of Babbitt,[2] not the antithesis. Smirking little automatons. L'infame.

I'm out of touch with most things here. The latest Scrutiny, however, is one of the best there has been. Of course the trouble with Leavis is that his passion for important work forbids him to look for the sun in the egg-tarnished spoons of the daily table. In other words, his failure to grasp current society in its intellectual modes (say in the style of [Lewis's] Time and Western Man or Giedion's Space Time and Architecture) cuts him off from the relevant pabulum.

Increasingly, I feel that Catholics must master C.G. Jung.[3] The little self-conscious (unearned) area in which we live to-day has nothing to do with the problems of our faith. Modern anthropology and psychology are more important for the Church than St. Thomas to-day.

You would like Peter Drucker's books.[4]

Sorry, but sitting up fags me quickly.

A blessed Xmas and new year
from us in Xt.
Yours   Mac and Corinne.

Walter J. Ong

[1]Father Clement J. McNaspy (b. 1915) was teaching at Saint Louis University at the time.

[2]The title character in Sinclair Lewis' *Babbitt* (1922); see page 232, note 7.

[3]Carl Gustuv Jung (1875–1961)—Swiss psychiatrist, founder of analytical psychology, and author of the revolutionary *Psychology of the Unconscious* (1916) among other books—postulated two dimensions in the unconscious: the repressed events in a person's life and the archetypes of the collective unconscious.

[4]For Peter Drucker, see page 259, note 1.

1945

To Elsie McLuhan

[Tecumseh, Ontario]
6 P.M. Sunday [December 2, 1945]

Dearest Mother

Just shooed Corinne off for a few hours. She's probably going to Pauline's whose mother is quite ill. So Pauline is immobilized. First time Corinne has been out of the house for a long time. I'll give twins their next bottle.[1]

Dad left last night. It was a very pleasant visit for all of us. He was *quite* bowled over by Eric's quickness and competence. And you can imagine that he was much delighted with Corinne. Also, he managed to be quite helpful. However, we talked so much that my time disappeared too fast for any work to get done. Now I've mountains above me.

Prof. Wilson sent me a copy of his latest book from London, in which I'm mentioned in a footnote.[2]

No word from [Allen] Tate, who, I hear indirectly, is getting a divorce.[3] Probably he's too miserable to attend to business.

Suppose we plan the baptism of Mary and Teresa for Dec 16—2 weeks from to-day? Unless they are—or one is—ill, we can't decently postpone it longer.

You can certainly be a big help with them young ladies. If only Eric had a play-mate, life would be simple.

Bought "Peter and the Wolf" for Eric last week.[4] He manages the new machine with considerable care. It's a great occupation for him.

All our love, Marshall
and Corinne.

[1]The McLuhan twins Mary and Teresa were born in October 1945.

[2]F.P. Wilson (see page 118, note 1), *Elizabethan and Jacobean* (1945), the Alexander Lectures, which Wilson delivered at University College, University of Toronto, in November 1943.

[3]Allen Tate (1899-1979), poet and literary critic, was editor of *The Sewanee Review* from 1944-1946. McLuhan published eight articles and reviews in this journal in 1944-7. Tate had been married to the novelist and short-story writer Caroline Gordon.

[4]A recording of the symphonic fairy tale by Sergei Prokofiev.

Elsie and Marshall McLuhan in Pasadena, California, summer of 1938.

Corinne and Marshall McLuhan immediately after their marriage, August 4, 1939.

Marshall and Corinne McLuhan leaving Fort Worth
after visiting Corinne's parents, August 10, 1939.

Corinne and Marshall McLuhan at the Hotel Chase, St Louis, c. 1941.

After the christening of Teresa and Mary McLuhan, November 1945.
Seated: Pauline Bondy (godmother) holding Teresa, and Miss Dunaway
holding Mary. Standing: Elsie McLuhan, Mr and Mrs McLean (family
friends), Corinne, Marshall, and Eric McLuhan, and Father Dwyer

Wyndham Lewis, 1951

Marshall McLuhan,
Windsor, *c*.1946. This
photograph was used
on the jacket of *The
Mechanical Bride*
(1951)

Introduction
1946–1979

In the autumn of 1946 McLuhan joined the staff of St Michael's College, University of Toronto, beginning an association that lasted until the end of his life. He taught Shakespeare (First Year); Modern Poetry and Drama (Fourth Year Honours), a course he never gave up; and, beginning in the early 1950s, English Poetry 1500–1660 (Second Year Honours), Contemporary Criticism, and an interdisciplinary seminar in communications. A co-operative member of the English Department, McLuhan also taught other courses and parts of courses. He became known as a generous teacher and a considerate examiner—always more interested in the student than in the curriculum, and in his students' fresh ideas and understanding than in their formal learning. Happily affiliated now with a large Canadian university in a city he liked, he set out on a path of discovery, applying his immense and ever-growing knowledge to an examination of society. From being an unconventional but sound literary scholar he became in his first book an unconventional critic of society and then a penetrating, non-judgemental interpreter, a self-proclaimed "student", of the electronic age. McLuhan's intellectual activities were conducted not only in the academic environment but in that of a large family of growing children. When Marshall and Corinne McLuhan moved to Toronto they had three children: Eric, and the twins Mary and Teresa. Stephanie, Elizabeth, and Michael followed between 1947 and 1952. Before 1968, when they settled in Wychwood Park, the McLuhans occupied three successive Toronto residences at 91 St Joseph Street, 81 St Mary's, and 29 Wells Hill Avenue.

Notable in McLuhan's first Toronto decade, and easily forgotten in the attention paid to the work of the later communications theorist, are the scholarly articles he published in the late forties and early fifties. Many of his essays in literary criticism—he wrote on Herbert, Keats, Coleridge, Tennyson, Hopkins, Yeats, Chesterton *et al.*—are of lasting interest. They include formal discussions of themes that are alluded to often in his letters and his books. "Landscape" is an important metaphor. In "The Aesthetic Moment in Landscape Poetry" (1951) McLuhan begins with Tennyson and his manipulation of "the external environment as a means of evoking art emotion", and then examines the manipulation of an *interior* landscape by Poe, Baudelaire, and Rimbaud, and the Symbolists' perception of the aesthetic experience as an "arrested moment"—which leads him to Joyce, Pound, and Eliot, who produced their own symbolist landscapes and aesthetic moments. In "Joyce, Mallarmé and the Press" (1953)—which states that in Mallarmé's late essays "he is probing the aesthetic consequences and possibilities of the popular arts of industrial man"—McLuhan enlarges on a theme that appears at the beginning of *The Mechanical Bride*, published two years before.

He discusses Mallarmé's essay "Le Livre, Instrument spirituel", which describes newspaper layout as a popular art form whose "impersonal juxtaposition" creates a symbolist landscape, one that illustrates daily a cross-section of human behaviour. For Joyce—whose *Ulysses* can be approached as a "newspaper landscape"—"the press was indeed a 'microchasm' of the world of man." Joyce is the subject of another important essay, "James Joyce: Trivial and Quadrivial" (1953); its sub-title refers to the medieval *trivium* (grammar, logic, rhetoric)—which Joyce studied under the Jesuits, and a history of which was part of McLuhan's thesis on Thomas Nashe—and the *quadrivium* (arithmetic, geometry, music, and astronomy). Joyce's central place in McLuhan's imagination is evident in the many references in his letters to *Finnegans Wake* and *Ulysses*. McLuhan also wrote essays on Wyndham Lewis and Ezra Pound, both of whom he corresponded with in the forties and fifties, and on T.S. Eliot. His letters of this period reveal his fascination with the literary world of London in 1908 (when Pound moved there) and after, and with the revolution in poetry and aesthetics these writers brought about. McLuhan visited Pound in June 1948 and a long correspondence ensued. This contact with Pound fired McLuhan intellectually. Having been greatly impressed by Pound's poetry while at Cambridge, he now read more of his prose; he was most receptive to Pound's esoteric knowledge of literature, while more or less disregarding his heated prejudices and recondite theories. McLuhan's letters to Pound soon echo the elliptical mode and anti-establishment tone of Pound's letters to McLuhan (which allude only infrequently, and cryptically, to subjects McLuhan discusses) —though not Pound's verbal eccentricities (seen in short quotations in the footnotes), nor the cantankerousness (what Hugh Kenner called, in a letter to McLuhan, Pound's "epigrammatic snarl"), which McLuhan ignores in his relatively conventional, and respectful, replies.

In an interview with Gerald Emanuel Stearn, published in *Encounter* in 1967, McLuhan described the origin of his examination of popular culture: "In 1936, when I arrived at Wisconsin, I confronted classes of freshmen and I suddenly realized that I was incapable of understanding them. I felt an urgent need to study their popular culture: advertising, games, movies. . . . To meet them on their grounds was my strategy in pedagogy: the world of pop culture. Advertising was a very convenient form of approach." (One thinks here of his diary entry of March 26, 1930 about the lecture he heard, as a student in Winnipeg, on modern advertising.) This interest impelled McLuhan to write two drafts of a book that was published in 1951 as *The Mechanical Bride: Folklore of Industrial Man*. By illustrating "typical visual imagery of our environment"—ads and other word-and-picture creations in popular culture—and "dislocating it into meaning by inspection" in allusive and trenchant commentaries, he reveals an insidious output of "sex and technology".

McLuhan's thinking about the media was guided into new channels in the late 1940s when he met, and became acquainted with the writings of, a colleague in the Department of Political Economy, Harold Adams Innis, who pioneered the study of various media of communications in history and their economic and social consequences. In a letter to Pound of July 16, 1952, McLuhan lists ideas for a book he is planning on "The End of the Gutenberg Era". They gave birth to *The Gutenberg Galaxy: The Making of Typographic Man*, published by the University of Toronto Press in 1962. Employing his now well-known technique of quoting extensively from, and discussing, works of literature, philosophy, and history in a discontinuous but suggestive way, he explores in this book the profound changes that took place in Western society with the invention of movable type and the printing press, and with the mass-production of books.

While McLuhan was studying media and technologies in Western history he was also addressing, in the 1950s, the changes imposed on the lineally oriented print-reader by electronic media, and their effect on the senses. Three events gave impetus to his studies. In the late 1940s he had met Edmund (Ted) Carpenter, who was teaching in the Department of Anthropology. With Carpenter as editor, and McLuhan as one of several associate editors, the first issue of *Explorations: Studies in Culture and Communication* was published in December 1953. In the six years of its influential life it published articles by David Riesman, Hans Selye, Gyorgy Kepes, Gershon Legman, Jacqueline Tyrwhitt, D. Carlton Williams, Walter J. Ong, Ashley Montagu, and John Wain (to all of whom McLuhan wrote letters that are in this collection). Other contributors included Robert Graves, Northrop Frye, Dorothy Lee, Roy Campbell, Kenneth Boulding, Jean Piaget, and Sigfried Giedion. *Explorations* was partly funded by the Ford Foundation. For 1953–5 McLuhan was appointed Chairman of the Ford Foundation Seminar on Culture and Communication: with five faculty members and some graduate students he considered the effects of the electronic media on society. His studies then became more formal and more detailed when the (American) National Association of Educational Broadcasters engaged him to lead a research project on the media. The information and insights he gained from this work, published in his *Report on Project in Understanding the New Media* (1960), contributed greatly to McLuhan's best-known book *Understanding Media: The Extensions of Man*, published in 1964 by McGraw-Hill, New York.

In the meantime Dr Claude Bissell, President of the University of Toronto, and Dr Ernest Sirluck, who was then Associate Dean of the School of Graduate Studies, had been instrumental in establishing in 1963 the Centre for Culture and Technology—one of several Centres in the University devoted to various disciplines—as an interdisciplinary adjunct of the Graduate School. This was done to strengthen McLuhan's attachment to the University and to provide a base for his studies and his writing and for the increasing demands that were being placed upon him as a speaker. While continuing to teach at St Michael's College, McLuhan was Director of the Centre, to which his secretary, Mrs Margaret Stewart, was transferred. In 1968 he was provided with a Coach House near the College that had office space and a large seminar room. McLuhan conducted Monday-night seminars, which often included celebrity guest-speakers, and were also a forum through which graduate students—with the permission of their Departments in the University—could do work that would contribute to a graduate degree. The Centre itself had no credit-granting privileges.

In 1964 the State of New York endowed five chairs in the humanities named for Albert Schweitzer, and one of them was awarded to Fordham University. Through John Culkin, then a priest who was Director of the Center for Communications at Fordham, McLuhan was appointed to the first Fordham chair. His twelve-month tenure, beginning at the end of August 1967, was seriously interrupted in November by a long operation for the removal of a brain tumour. (For some eight years before he had been afflicted with occasional blackouts and dizziness.) The subject of illness, at this time and later, is referred to in McLuhan's letters lightly and vaguely.

The popularity of *Understanding Media* could not have been foreseen. The paperback edition, published in 1965, sold some 100,000 copies. McLuhan's claim that electronic media had made books obsolescent; that while the phonetic alphabet had converted a pre-literate tribal culture into a manuscript culture, and print had created privacy, individualism, and nationalism, television had turned people back into a tribal culture because it enabled them to experience distant occurrences and other peoples with more senses and more involvement and had weakened the sense of privacy; that it was important to study the effects and implications for the future of new technology and media to avoid crises brought on by them; that any new technology permeates society and its institutions only until it is replaced by a new environment created by another technology; that people become aware of their environment only after they have actually moved on to another one created by a new technology; that television is an audile-tactile rather than a visual medium; that the change of scale or pattern introduced by a new technology into human affairs is more important than its content ("The medium is the message"); that the media are either "hot", extending a single sense and providing much detail (as in radio), or "cool", with little detail but inducing much involvement without exciting or otherwise arousing the viewer or user (as in television)—these and other insights, and the attention McLuhan paid to popular culture by examining familiar possessions and technologies ("extensions of man") as a kind of seer of the electronic age, captivated members of the media industries and heads of corporations. Young people of the sixties were impressed that he gave a stamp of academic respectability to pop culture. A slow surge of attention appeared in the press, until 1966 and after when articles on McLuhan, and interviews, appeared everywhere: in *Fortune, Newsweek, Life, Esquire, Time, The National Review, Partisan Review, Look, The New Yorker, The Nation, The Saturday Review, The New York Times Magazine, Encounter, Family Circle, Vogue, Mademoiselle*—the list goes on and on. In 1967 alone, the year he went to Fordham, 27 articles about McLuhan appeared in the *New York Times*. Between 1967 and 1971 eight books on McLuhan were published: *McLuhan Hot & Cool* (1967) edited by Gerald Emanuel Stearn; *McLuhan: Pro and Con* (1968) edited by Raymond Rosenthal; *The McLuhan Explosion* (1968) edited by Harry Crosby and George R. Bond; *Sense and Nonsense of McLuhan* (1968) by Sidney Finkelstein; *Marshall McLuhan* (1969) by Dennis Duffy; *McLuhan* (1971) by Jonathan Miller; *The Medium Is the Rear View Mirror: Understanding McLuhan* (1971) by Donald Theall; and, in French,

McLuhan (Paris, 1971) by Alain Bourdain. Translations of *The Gutenberg Galaxy* and *Understanding Media* made the name of McLuhan well known in over twenty languages.

Much of the discussion was critical, even adversarial. McLuhan was incorrectly seen to dismiss print technology and the book. His obvious dependence on, and respect for, printed literature was considered a paradox, a contradiction of his message. The "mosaic" approach in his books to building up his examination of "galaxies" or environments by means of a discontinuous and discursive presentation of quotations, explications of other people's works, aphorisms, metaphors, analogies, "headlines"—making connections between anthropology and psychology, literature and technology, history and philosophy, and combining brilliant insights with what some called nonsense—provoked irritation. As did the public image he conveyed to some of being a jester, uttering startling pronouncements, puns, and wisecracks in order to arouse interest and reaction, though not discussion. "O.K., throw the idea out. Don't explore my statements. Explore the situation. Statements are expendable. Don't keep on looking in the rear-view mirror and defending the status quo which is outmoded the moment it happens" (*Weekend Magazine*, March 18, 1967). To questions about his insights, McLuhan replied, "I explore, I don't explain"; or, "I'm making probes, I'm taking soundings." But the torrent of discussion and argument McLuhan unleashed simply confirmed that in attempting to illuminate transformations in the environment produced by technology, and the changes they bring about in social relations and perceptions of experience, he had uncovered new dimensions of an area of life that people knew was affecting them in ways they did not understand. He educated people about the fast-changing electronic age they lived in, and in the process gave them a new apprehension of it.

The books that followed *Understanding Media* included *The Medium is the Massage* (1967), *War and Peace in the Global Village* (1968), *Through the Vanishing Point: Space in Poetry and Painting* (with Harley Parker, 1968), *Counterblast* (1969), *Culture Is Our Business* (1970), *From Cliché to Archetype* (with Wilfred Watson, 1970), and *Take Today: The Executive as Dropout* (with Barrington Nevitt, 1972). As well as his own books, an abundance of articles, reviews, letters to editors, several textbooks, introductions to other people's books, and contributions to collections of readings issued from McLuhan well into 1979. It is difficult to imagine how all this was accomplished—with health problems hovering and sometimes laying him low—while he was also taking off on trips, often to distant places, giving speeches and interviews, receiving honorary degrees, teaching, leading his Monday-night seminars, participating in Ph.D. orals—and talking, thinking aloud, testing his ideas on anyone nearby, which he much preferred to writing them down. " . . . I do a lot of my work while I'm simply talking. I think a lot when I'm talking and perfect many ideas that way" (*Weekend Magazine*, March 18, 1967). "Conversation has more vitality than books, more fun, more drama," McLuhan said in a *Life* interview of February 26, 1966. His discourse often tended to silence people with its insights, pronouncements, analogies, wide-ranging references, quotations, abstractions, generalizations, puns, jokes—uttered in a low-keyed stream. For his friend Tom Easterbrook, "He churns up the atmosphere. I think he's aware of doing it, but he does it for shock effect. He goes at his adversaries until they become numb. But he has zest—he's full of fun. He conveys a marvellous feeling of being alive" (*Weekend Magazine*, January 4, 1964).

In the media hype of the late 1960s and the 1970s McLuhan was sometimes called an oracle, and indeed his ideas were steadily conveyed orally, not just in conversation and speeches but in widely disseminated interviews. "I simply have ideas that seem to intrigue people. Actually I'm a pattern watcher. That's it, a pattern watcher" (*Weekend Magazine*, January 4, 1967). Even towards the end of the seventies he never seemed to tire of amplifying ideas he had already presented in his books, applying them to yet more questions about television and advertising; to subjects of current concern, such as youth, violence, and pollution; and dwelling on a new subject of interest to him (which may have been aroused by his recent medical history)—the left and right hemispheres of the brain, and the dominance of one over the other. These topics are also discussed in his letters, but it is of interest to read how some of them were treated in his interviews.

"[With television] you are drawn into that tube, as an inner trip. You're totally involved. You have no objectivity, no distance. And it is acoustic. It resonates. But this is a hidden ground, because superficially people think they're looking at a visual program. And they're not. They're not looking at all—they're absorbed, involved in a resonating experience. And it is not objective, it is entirely subjective." Interview with Jerry Brown (*The CoEvolution Quarterly*, Winter 1977–8).

"The TV thing itself is very, very polluting. It goes right into the nervous system. The problem is how literate is your society, your family circle, your immediate circle. Your child is coming out in an intensely literate world, so he can take a fair amount of TV without too much harm. But to the ordinary kid without a lot of literacy, TV will just turn off any possibility of left hemisphere." (*Maclean's*, March 7, 1977.)

"[About advertising] . . . it's all aggression. The developers are aggression. All forms of program change tend to be aggression and of course the draft, the military draft is an extreme aggression. A force against people. But Madison Avenue is a very powerful aggression against private consciousness. A demand that you yield your private consciousness to public manipulation." (*op. cit.*)

"Well, when things change at very high speeds, a need for continuity develops. You see, you're in such a complete discontinuity at high speed. Everything you're looking at now is gone in a second and our demands are to hang on to older things. So the antique stores and the love of taking the varnish off of old tables, revealing their original state, and that sort of thing is a passion today. In order to think, you have to forget most of what you are experiencing in order to relate it to earlier things that you knew, otherwise you can't infer anything from what you are seeing. So, at the speed of light, which is now the normal speed of most information, on TV, radio, telephone and so on—at that speed the need to forget has become a form of nostalgia." (*op. cit.*)

"The kids are looking for some sort of stability. And the old comics have that kind of solid moral values—everything was right or wrong. And there are no moral values at the speed of light. Moral values just dissolve. That's why you have separatism all around the world. Legal structures will not hold up at the speed of light. Electric information takes the place of legal bonds. The separation of Quebec is based upon an upsurge of old acoustic memories, nostalgia for the past and the sudden desire to break the legal bonds with Canada. It ain't gonna happen. But that's the motivation." (Brown, *op. cit.*)

"Violence as a form of quest for identity is something the people who have been ripped off feel the need of. He's going to show who he is, what his credentials are, that he's tough. So anybody on a psychic frontier tends to get tougher or violent and it's happening to us on a mass scale today." (*Maclean's, loc. cit.*)

As examples of McLuhan's oral style, and of his method of viewing the significant background (and its effects) of any given subject, rather than immediate and familiar aspects of it (looking at the *ground*, as he would say, and not the *figure* that interplays with the *ground*), these few quotations from interviews lie somewhere between his talk—which people were instructed, surprised, puzzled, charmed, amused, sometimes dazzled by—and his letters. When, in 1959 and after, his letters were no longer handwritten but dictated, they too represented a medium of relaying his ideas orally. Frequent and sometimes long, the letters of the sixties and seventies (which form the greater part of this collection) satisfied McLuhan's constant need for conversation with scholars and other friends, many of them very well known, and with strangers who had attracted his attention. They often contain rehearsals or amplifications of ideas that appear in his books and articles, and offer a discursive and clarifying gloss on them. They were also a means of communicating discoveries McLuhan had made in his reading, and the ideas they generated. Or they radiate outwards, as in the many letters to Pierre Elliott Trudeau, which comment on subjects of moment that McLuhan thought might illuminate some of Trudeau's concerns as Prime Minister of Canada; and as in his comments on war, hijacking, abortion, Vatican II, the ordination of women, censorship, streaking, dyslexia. Or they address his critics—for example, his responses to Jonathan Miller's *McLuhan* (1971)—as well as published statements that conveyed to him a misunderstanding of his thought. Though the mass-media attention paid to McLuhan subsided (but by no means ended) in the early 1970s, occasional references in his letters to his peripatetic activities as the decade progressed reflect the demand in which he was held internationally.

Any collection of letters is enjoyed partly for what it conveys about the writer. The McLuhan letters of this period are devoted mainly to ideas—personal references are mostly to his family—and for all the richness and variety of their content they seem on the surface to convey only a partial portrait of the man, of the qualities and characteristics that those who knew him well have spoken of and most appreciated. Yet they reveal, sometimes indirectly, a great deal about McLuhan. The extraordinarily wide compass of his reading, his esoteric knowledge, and the astonishing reach of his mind are of course ever-present; and the stimulation of thought that contact with him induced can easily be imagined—he was known as an inspiring teacher. Less evident, but also present, are his kindness and generosity, his verbal wit and sense of fun, the laughter with which he greeted the ironies that confronted him, his dismissive attitude to physical problems (which masked endurance and courage), and his piety. There is also the humorous detachment with which McLuhan surveyed the world and handled his fame. "Temperamentally, I'm a stodgy conservative," he once said. "If there are going to be McLuhanites, you can be sure that I'm not going to be one of them." But he enjoyed his fame, and responded to it co-operatively, while treating it lightly and never giving second place to his ceaseless intellectual probings, or neglecting to present these informally to his friends in letters.

The letters reveal much about the sources of the thought, and about the life, of one of the influential men of our century whose vision illuminated some of its most profound changes. We are too close to McLuhan now to judge the depth of his influence. (A comment in *Time* on May 18, 1987, on the media's revelations about a former American senator—that they were "straight Marshall McLuhan; the medium is the message"—suggests the lasting usefulness of his famous aphorism.) But six-and-a-half years after his death we are still living in the midst of speed-up, unexpected turns of events, scientific discoveries, political turmoil, and are as bemused as ever by the uncertainties they bring with them. In the middle of 1987 we have been told about the evolution of another "extension of man"—superconductivity—and about unimaginable changes that could develop from its phenomenal savings of energy. One thinks, as with any announcement of this sort, "What would McLuhan say?"—while remembering his belief that we resist change, and that he wanted to study change so that some power could be gained over it. A radical new McLuhan insight about superconductivity is denied us. But in fact his writings—not least his letters—contain a message to heed: that any potentially crucial new technological development should be confronted squarely, and its hidden dimensions imagined so that we can foresee and prepare to master their likely effects rather than be surprised, decades hence, when they have carried us in unwanted directions.

1946

To Clement McNaspy, S.J.

Assumption College
Windsor Ont Can.
Dec 15/45 [January 15, 1946?]

Dear Mac,

Flu before and during Xmas together with a 2 week visit in New York has put me 'way behind in many things. But it would be a wretched way to begin the year by omitting to ask your blessing and prayers and not assuring you of mine.

I am conscious of a job to be done—one I can do, and, truly, I do not wish to take any step in it that is not consonant with the will of God. What an object lesson a Christian has to-day in seeing so much good produce so much ill. Not for a moment do I imagine that I can frame a course of action which will do good.

My increasing awareness has been of the ease with which Catholics can penetrate and dominate secular concerns—thanks to an emotional and spiritual economy denied to the confused secular mind. But this cannot be done by any Catholic group, nor by Catholic individuals trained in the vocabularies and attitudes which make our education the feeble simulacrum of the world which it is.

It seems obvious that we must confront the secular in its most confident manifestations, and, with its own terms and postulates, to shock it into awareness of its confusion, its illiteracy, and the terrifying drift of its logic. There is no need to mention Christianity. It is enough that it be known that the operator is a Christian. This job must be conducted on every front—every phase of the press, book-rackets, music, cinema, education, economics. Of course, points of reference must always be made. That is, the examples of real art and prudence must be seized, when available, as paradigms of future effort. In short, the methods of F.R. Leavis and Wyndham Lewis applied with all the energy and order denied them from faith and philosophy—These can serve to educate a huge public, both Catholic and non-Catholic, to resist that swift obliteration of the person which is going on. Hutchins and Adler have part of the solution.[1] But they are emotional illiterates. Dialectics and erudition are needed, but, without the sharp focussing of training in moral sensibility, futile.

How easy it would be to set up a school on these lines, utilizing the encyclopedic learning of our age. But whether that is desirable?

Affectionately in Christ
Mac.

[1]Robert Maynard Hutchins (1899–1977) was President (1929–45) and Chancellor (1945–51) of the University of Chicago. An enthusiastic supporter of adult education, he promoted the famous "Great Books" program. With Mortimer J. Adler (b. 1902), Professor of the Philosophy of Law there, he edited the 54-volume series *Great Books of the Western World*. This provided McLuhan with a subject to discuss in *The Mechanical Bride*: "The Great Books". With Cleanth Brooks, McLuhan visited Hutchins at the University of Chicago on June 20, 1946.

To Elsie McLuhan [Assumption College, Windsor, Ontario]
[April? 1946]

Dearest Mother

Wish I could take time to give you a full account of the trip [to Montreal and Toronto]. This [*sic*] snaps, taken entirely by Dunny, may serve instead.[1] But the lectures went well. Cleared only 70 dollars. Spent 55. Didn't pay a cent save for travel, berth and meals on train. Pauline's friends in Montreal were delightful. Montreal looked like paradise after Windsor. And Toronto is certainly inferior to it. Fieldhouse had me to lunch at McGill.[2] Utterly satisfactory 2 hours. Says that his 17 years in Wpg. were utterly wasted. Arthur Smith had me to dinner Sat. nite.[3] A grand time. He's the poet lad. With me on Xian Culture Series here. After my Sunday night lecture various people including our old pal Pyper[4] and Prof. Phelps[5] spoke to me.

Left Mon. nite. Hied me to St Mikes.[6] Phelan delightful to me. Asked much about you and Red. Hopes I'll come to Toronto. Father Shook, head of English at St. Mike's wants me very much.[7] Says final offer can't be made for a month. But he hopes it will be a full professorship at 5000 a year with lots of travelling expenses thrown in. The house problem will probably lick us. Its hopeless in Toronto. But, while I think we might do *very* well in Toronto, we are not set on it. Or on anything else. U. of Detroit has made an offer. No point in taking it.

Am eager to get back to work.

And to hear that you are in health again.

Lovingly
Marshall and Corinne

[1]Family snaps taken by Miss Amy Dunaway, an Englishwoman who stayed for a year with the McLuhans as an unpaid nanny.

[2]Professor H. Noel Fieldhouse (b. 1900), who was head of the Department of History, University of Manitoba (where he taught McLuhan), and later Chairman from 1930 to 1945, when he became Professor of History at McGill University.

[3]A.J.M. Smith (1902–80), whose first poetry collection, *News of the Phoenix* (winner of a Governor General's Award), and first anthology, *A Book of Canadian Poetry*, had both been published in 1943. He was Professor of English at Michigan State University. A graduate of McGill, he would have been staying in the home of his father-in-law on this visit to his native city. He apparently had been, or was about to be, a speaker on Father Murphy's Christian Culture Series in Windsor.

[4]Unidentified.

[5]Arthur Phelps (1887–1970) had a part-time appointment in the English Department of McGill University while he was general superintendent of the International Service of the Canadian Broadcasting Corporation (1945-7). From 1945 until his retirement in 1953 he taught English at McGill as a full professor.

[6]St Michael's College, University of Toronto. Its President at this time was Father L.J. Bondy (1894–1985), brother of Pauline Bondy and a Basilian, who became acquainted with, and was impressed by, McLuhan on his visits to Assumption and was instrumental in arranging for his appointment to St Michael's in the fall of 1946.

[7]Father Laurence K. Shook (b. 1909) later became Superior and President of St. Michael's College (1952-8). He was President of the Pontifical Institute of Mediaeval Studies from 1961 to 1973.

To Felix Giovanelli[1]

Tecumseh, Ont.
Sunday May 5/46

Dear Felix,

Hey, am I being rationed? Is all your correspondence going to the Black Market? Absit! Pour yourself out for us. I'm just back from an 8 day trip to Montreal and Toronto. A couple of lectures. One in Montreal one in Woodstock. In Montreal (which you would like at once and forever) I had delightful friends, unexpectedly. In Toronto I had some good visits with Frye[2] of the dept of English and with Phelan[3] and the rest. It *may* be that I shall go to Toronto this year. Mainly a housing problem. They want me there. Students are of good calibre. Its closer to N[ew] York than Windsor. I would be given a travelling allowance to get to N.Y. 4 times a year. My plan is to start a mag. Not for Canadians by Canadians. But something serious. Not an imitation of Sewanee Kenyon or P.R.[*Partisan Review*]. Something with a strongly practical bias in the direction of estimating and prescribing detailed procedures in school and college plus a department persistently focussed on the hatred being manifest everywhere at every level at present. Obviously not a mag to be begun at once without much luck. But one which might function well in Toronto by reason of the very hostility of the environment. It wouldn't be tempted to be complacent. It would, in Toronto, be free from the need to play ball with any existing U.S. cliques. No publishing or other rackets to sidestep. Must *talk* to you about it soon. *Feel* I shall have to be in N.Y. before summer. Nothing definite in mind though. Joe wrote at length.[4] Wants you to write him. Asks me are you sore at him. I should write him Felix. He is a bit cut off. Easy to brood about such a matter. Can't imagine why he was taken 18 mos. to drop me a line.

[1]Felix Giovanelli (1913–1962), who had taught French and Spanish at Saint Louis University, in 1944 accepted a temporary appointment teaching Spanish at New York University; he was a free-lance translator for several years and returned to N.Y.U., in the Division of General Education, in 1949. In the Public Archives of Canada are many letters from Giovanelli to McLuhan written between 1944 and 1949 (with one 1951 letter)—most of them long (many handwritten) letters filled with interesting, discriminating comments and chat about literature, writers, St Louis friends and former students, and mutual acquaintances in the world of literary magazines. They kept in touch, meeting on McLuhan's visits to New York, until Giovanelli's death; their later correspondence has not survived.

[2]Northrop Frye (b. 1912) was at this time Associate Professor of English at Victoria College, University of Toronto; the next year he would publish his famous work *Fearful Symmetry: A Study of William Blake* (1947).

[3]Father Gerald B. Phelan was President of the Pontifical Institute of Mediaeval Studies. See page 82, note 1.

[4]Joe Privatera taught Italian at Saint Louis University.

Expect to hear about Nash from you.[5] Or about *your* being as modified by Nash.

Eric has emerged into a more moderate phase of childhood. More self possessed. Less urgently personal towards us. The twins are hefties. We enjoy them. Corinne has had much help from our English friend Miss Dunaway. A great boon. A cliff, a rock, an oak. An abyss of good nature.

Let me be more discursive later. Just wanted to resume communication. Best of us to both of you.

[5]Eugene Nash was a student at Saint Louis University.

To Felix Giovanelli

[Tecumseh, Ontario]
May 10/46

Dear Felix

Corinne and I were at breakfast—2nd breakfast—when your letter came. So we dawdled over it. Enjoyed it. Were glad that you were getting on top of Sender's mss. etc.[1] We had been poking around through the dung-heap called *The Unquiet Grave*.[2] Found it in a local library. Send it on anyhow. I find it amusing, edifying. Bernie would enjoy it very much. Makes me sorry I haven't been taking *Horizon* these past years. Simply as means of keeping *au courant*. Shall get some back numbers at once.

Please add *Go Down Moses* (Faulkner) and Burke's *Permanence and Change* to list of books to buy for me.[3] Sooner the better.

I repeat Bernie must be given a copy of The Unquiet Grave—from me. Bill me for it. It is his dish.

Looking at Joyce recently. A bit startled to note last page of Finnegan is a rendering of the last part of the Mass. Remembered that opening of Ulysses is from 1st words of the Mass. The whole thing an intellectual Black Mass. The portion which Joyce read for recording concludes with an imitation of the damnation of Faust. As he reads it (I heard it in Toronto for 1st time) it is horrible. Casual, eerie. Speaking of Existenz and the hatred of language—what about Finnegan?

[1]Giovanelli was translating from the Spanish *Proverbio de la muerte*, a novel by Ramón José Sender, which was published in English as *The Sphere* (1949).

[2]*The Unquiet Grave: A Word Cycle* (1944) is a collection of aphorisms and reflections by Cyril Connolly (1903–74). Connolly was editor of the literary magazine *Horizon* (1940–50), to which McLuhan contributed "American Advertising", nos. 93–4, 1947.

[3]*Go Down, Moses* (1942) is a collection of stories and a famous novella, "The Bear", by William Faulkner. Kenneth Burke's *Permanence and Change: An Anatomy of Purpose* (1935) is a philosophic investigation of the evolution of ideas.

Yesterday I read H.D. Smyth's report on "Develop. of Methods of Using Atomic Energy for Military Purposes."[4] It reads like a Walpurgis Nacht transposed into the lingo of the newspaper. His account of the building of "the first self-sustaining chain-reacting pile" sounds like a parable of a robber baron: "The whole graphite sphere was supported by a timber framework resting on the floor of a squash court under the West Stands of Stagg Field." We have made our pile and now we can sit on it. That it should be situated symbolically in a football stadium is too perfect. American sport, the artistic imitation of American business. Our great emotional educator and indicator.

You see, American business, excluded from the lib. arts curriculum conquered the college for all that. The dialectically organized curriculum omits all emotional education. That is entirely in the hands of the symbolic stadium. You see how perfectly this ties up with the "real life" of the outside world—the alumni. Lethal nostalgia and revenge on the pedagogues. From outside the school the business man conquers the curriculum. What need to fool with actual courses?

I have all this stuff on slides. Show the entire interaction of all levels of our wake-a-day and dream lives. The areas of consciousness, though, are now pin points. Just a mind here and there struggling against freeze-sleep. Sent it as book to Reynall Hitchcock but haven't heard from them. Embraces the entire business of Existenz by anticipation.[5]

As I move through these correlations you can see why I crave the materials provided by Connolly and Existenz. I begin to see deeper into the consciousness of Poe and Faulkner. Their rage is relatively noble. Rooted in a community born in the decadence of the Greek revival they were peculiarly alive to the impact of technology. Invalid or Dying from their inception, they had the hyper-awareness of the sick-man for his enemies. Disgust with themselves was mounted on disgust with their external foes. Inner exhaustion was called on to fight an empty robot. A nightmare of nullity. And yet symbolically in such as [Allen] Tate and [Cleanth] Brooks, note a modest confidence in renewal of the human condition. Not the abstract assertion of such a possibility as in [Lewis] Mumford the urbanite,[6] but the quiet cultivation of a positive *grammatica*. Stirrings, however dim, of a genuine culture. Knowledge and supply of a real pabulum. That's where, I too, take my stand. The view is horrible, but the garden is there too.

More anon—Mac

[4]H.D. Smyth, *Atomic Energy for Military Purposes: The Official Report on the Development of the Atomic Bomb Under the Auspices of the United States Government* (1945).

[5]*Existenz* philosophy, associated with Karl Jaspers and Martin Heidegger, places man in the middle of a world where the only certainty is the existence of the individual.

[6]See page 208, note 1.

To Elsie McLuhan

[Tecumseh, Ontario]
Tues May 14/46

Dearest Mother

Back from Toronto this morn. after a very lucky 13th of May. Got in at 8 A.M. Went directly to breakfast at [St Michael's] college. Then to business. Father McLaughlin is President.[1] First we talked housing. Yes, possibilities on the campus there were. We settled on one. Went to look at it. Took it. As of Sept 1st. Better things may open up soon. But there are 3 bed-rooms. 2 fireplaces. Larger than our present house. And my study will [sic] and office will be elsewhere—a few yards away. That means an extra room. Rent 65, heat furnished at that figure. We are on the campus itself. 50 yards from Elmsley Place. It is on St Joseph St between Queens Park and Bay Street. So we are in the park land itself. Classes and colleages 50 yards away.

Salary only 4200 for 1st year. But that is exclusive of summer school. Can pick up extra during summer. Most of the difference between 4200 and 5000 would go to income tax anyhow.

Toronto is on same 25 cycle as here. So we shall try to get ice-box at once. College will pay moving costs to Toronto. Shall have to get washing machine too. Not sure about stove. Shall know soon.

But, obviously, without the car, we shall be better off at 4200 in Toronto than at 4000 here. Can get on with books the faster too.

More angles anon.

We stay here till end of Aug.

Wish you would get out of Pittsburg before it gets you down entirely. Your fatigue is owing to suppressed anger.

All love
Marshall and Corinne

[1]Father Terence P. McLaughlin, CSB (1903–70)

To Walter J. Ong, S.J.

Assumption College
Windsor Ont. May 18 [1946]

Dear Walter,

Your parcel of publications was here when I got back from Toronto recently. It seems fairly certain that I shall be at St. Michael's College there from September on. Even a house has been found. Right on the campus! And the campus is a vast park of great beauty. However, Church and classes are not a hundred yards from the house. And classes are in the same building as the Institute [of Mediaeval Studies]. Met Gilson there.[1] He looks like a football coach. He has just finished a great set of lectures on the history of Essence and Existence—They may appear this fall. Students at Toronto are of high quality. So, Walter, I must regard this move as a permanent one. I must pitch in and do, for the first time, an uncompromising and unremitting job. Keep us in your prayers, always. Corinne is teeter-tottering towards the Church. The metaphor scarcely implies movement, and it is hard to judge whether she *is* moving.[2] We have been blessed in our children. Eric would please you. He keeps us on the lam all the time with his snide propositions and concupiscent sophistries. He is precociously vocal and glib. The twins, Mary and Teresa, are nearly 7 months old, and are as little trouble as children can be. They are so unlike that they are really a great source of quite satisfactory small-talk with us. We have never regarded them as anything less than *blessed* events. (Which phrase recalls a harrowing item of last Xmas in the Cleveland Catholic Register: "Its a Boy in Bethlehem. Congratulations God! Congratulations Mary!"—That was a leadline.)

Now a word about your essays. The *America* papers were good but your analysis would have been better for a closer view of the typical items.[3] In fact, you yourself would have been shocked had you taken even the very best items and considered them closely. I mean with regard not only to their structure and texture but with a view to their assumptions about audience. The whole function of thought and entertainment embedded in that mag. can be a parabola of the most profound contemplation. (Have you seen the last 2 issues of *Partisan Review*?) But I am being tough with you here Walter only because its the only point at which I can be of help to you.

As for the Newman Essay on Dev.[4] That arouses my admiration. I found it most edifying and helpful. (Having kept up philosophical reading, especially these past 2 years). Clearly, the present-day Thomists have much to learn from Newman's procedure. They are painfully in the position of lacking that general culture, vitalized by a genuine community, which alone confers relevance. Gilson and Maritain[5] do belong to a community in which a general awareness of our age at all its points is cultivated. Yet both of these men have evaded (or for lack of time and faculty they have done nothing) the application of Thomistic principles

[1]The French philosopher and historian Etienne Gilson (1884–1978) founded in 1929 the Pontifical Institute of Mediaeval Studies, an independent research institute on the campus of St Michael's College, whose staff also teach in the School of Graduate Studies of the University of Toronto. He was Professor of Mediaeval Philosophy and Director of Studies until his retirement in 1971. The lectures referred to were published in French: *L'être et l'essence* (1948).

[2]Corinne McLuhan became a Roman Catholic in the autumn of 1946, after the McLuhans moved to Toronto.

[3]Walter J. Ong, S.J., "Mr. Barnum and the 'Reader's Digest'", *America*, April 6, 1944 and April 13, 1944.

[4]Walter J. Ong, S.J., "Newman's Essay on Development in Its Intellectual Milieu", *Theological Studies*, vol. VII, no. 1, March 1946—a discussion of *Essay on the Development of Christian Doctrine* by John Henry (later Cardinal) Newman (1801–90), written in 1845.

[5]For Jacques Maritain, see page 137, note 9.

to the area of Freud, Fraser and Malinowski—psychology and anthropology.[6] These are the areas of most intense contemporary awareness and they have not found their Newman. For example, in his discussions of poetic Maritain has never ventured into the question of taste. Yet this is the major nexus of educational discussion. Maritain's Education at the Crossroads [1943] is an irrelevant treatise. The question of training in sensibility, the education of the passions, the fluid interplay of thought and feeling in the development of value judgements apropos of particular works of art (inseparable from dev. of value judgements with reference to the entire social milieu)—the way in which the liberal arts should be focussed to re-create the total loss of human community in contemporary life—This question no Thomist has ever faced. I mention this to you Walter because you can do something about it. Perhaps Newman may offer an entrance into the matter. I'm sure he does. You can see how this faces the question of literature. Strictly, French, English, Latin etc are not subjects. They can't be taught. One can only *train* sensibility in these areas. Literature is not a subject but a function—a function inseparable from communal existence. That it should be taught—these 150 years   according to the modes of a debased scholasticism is the first fact to be exploded with the maximum amount of noise. I myself have some plans to make such a noise fairly soon, but many people are needed to co-operate in such matters.

With regards to Clem [McNaspy] and old friends when you may see them

Yours in Xt.

Mac

[6]Sigmund Freud (1856–1939), the famous Austrian psychologist and originator of psychoanalysis; Sir James Frazer (1845–1941), author of *The Golden Bough* (1890–1915), a 12-volume work on comparative religion and mythology that became a popular classic in its one-volume condensation; and Bronislaw Malinowski (1884–1942), Polish-born English anthropologist.

1947

To Walter J. Ong, S.J.

St Michael's College
Toronto 5
April 13/47

Dear Walter

A long time since I wrote. Term about over here. Exams a major terror for Toronto students. They take them once a year. Oddly, courses here are given in an extremely descriptive manner. Took me long to discover this. The genesis of that condition I have yet to discover however. But even more than elsewhere a practical critical approach is difficult. Largely because exams loom so large. Paralyzing independence of mind.

Have many irons in fire. Some ready to come out, at last. Book of exhibits with commentary on popular culture *may* appear from Dial Press.[1] They are very keen about it at the moment. In spring *View* you will find a paper of mine on Time Life and Fortune[2] and an essay on Death in America by [Marius] Bewley.

As for your query about *where* to get Ph.d. Cleanth Brooks goes to Yale as full professor this fall.[3] He would be interested in your project and an excellent chap to work with. Congenial in every way, and, of course a practising critic. So I can't imagine a better place for you to be. There you would be in direct contact with the New England mind. Also, I think that you ought to work on Ramus[4] and his influence in Ren[aissance] England. You are rarely qualified for the job. A job of great importance which I think will be a long long time in getting done unless somebody like you tackles it.

[1]This was eventually published by the Vanguard Press, New York, as *The Mechanical Bridge: Folklore of Industrial Man* (1951).

[2]"Time, Life and Fortune", *View Magazine* (Spring 1947).

[3]There is a letter to Cleanth Brooks (b. 1906) on pages 528–9.

[4]Ong went to Harvard for his Ph.D. and did indeed write his dissertation on the French philosopher Petrus Ramus (Latin form of Pierre de la Ramée, 1515–72; he was a Protestant who perished in the Massacre of St Bartholomew) and it was published in two volumes: *Ramus, Method, and the Decay of Dialogue: From the Art of Discourse to the Art of Reason* (1958), dedicated to Bernard and Mary Muller-Thym, and *Ramus and Talon Inventory* (1958), dedicated to Herbert Marshall McLuhan "who started all this". McLuhan introduced Ong to Ramus after he read Perry Miller's *The New England Mind: The Seventeenth Century* (1939). Ramus established a set of attitudes—concerned with language, rhetoric, logic, clarity, precision, and testing—that had a revolutionary effect on sixteenth-century thought and even affected the scientific enquiry of the age. The study of Ramism, Ong says in the Introduction to *Ramus, Method and the Decay of Dialogue*, reveals "connections between pedagogical developments and the rise of modern physics, between rhetoric and scientific method, or between dialectic and the invention of letterpress printing."

Interested to note recently that James Joyce's esthetic doctrine of the *epiphany* (cf. Sewanee Rev. Summer 1946[5]) is same as Hopkins' *inscape*. Scotus Erigena [c. 810–77] uses term epiphaneia in this sense. Plato implies it apropos of intuition which occurs *during* dialectical activity. And it is the *claritas* of St. Thomas [Aquinas]. But I haven't looked far into the matter.

Yours in Xt.
Mac.

Walter J. Ong

[5]Irene Hendry, "Joyce's Epiphanies", *The Sewanee Review*, vol. 54, no. 3.

To Elsie McLuhan

[Toronto]
Sept 12/47

Dearest Mother—A memorable day. Lunch at college with Malcolm Ross[1] and Prof. Gilson. Ross is from Fredericton N.B. Teaches at Manitoba. Great admirer of mine. Also of Maritain and Gilson! So I arranged lunch for him. Ross isn't a Catholic. Well, after lunch Fr. Bondy[2] suggested that I ask Gilson over sometime! So I asked him for cock-tails at 4 O'C to-day, and he came with Fr. Shook. He [Gilson] is an effervescent and also incisively witty man. His present membership in the French Chamber of Deputies gives him many inside angles on current affairs. So we had a political time of it. Eric met him. But Corinne decided to stand clear since it is a busy time of day for her. Peggy Warren and she are now out at a movie. Hugh Kenner[3] dropped by with Mary Jo [Kenner] at 5.30. So Ross's bliss was complete. Kenner he has heard much of.

Hot and sticky this past 2 weeks. A stinking time of it in that respect. Very hard on Corinne just now. She's eager to get to the hospital.[4]

[1]Dr Malcolm Ross (b. 1911) taught English literature at the University of Manitoba (1945–50), Queen's University, Kingston (1950–62), the University of Toronto (1962–8), and since 1968 at Dalhousie University, Halifax, where he was appointed Thomas McCullough Professor in 1973. As editor, critic, and teacher, he has been notably influential in the field of Canadian literature.

[2]Father L.J. Bondy was President of St Michael's College. See page 181, note 6.

[3]When Hugh Kenner (b. 1923) was a recent M.A. graduate of the University of Toronto, he met McLuhan in June 1946 in the office of Father Basil Sullivan, Registrar of St Michael's College, not long before McLuhan moved there from Assumption College. At McLuhan's suggestion Kenner applied for, and obtained, his teaching post at Assumption, where he remained for two years. He then went to Yale (1948–50; Ph.D. 1950) and taught at the University of California, Santa Barbara, and Johns Hopkins, beginning in 1973, where he is Andrew W. Mellon Professor of Humanities. Among Kenner's books are *The Poetry of Ezra Pound* (1951), *Wyndham Lewis* (1954), *Dublin's Joyce* (1956), *The Invisible Poet: T.S. Eliot* (1959), and *The Pound Era* (1971).

[4]Stephanie McLuhan was born on October 14.

Shall drop Red + Bryda a line.[5]

Have been made full Professor. A good thing to have been before leaving academic life. It is worth more to me than a 1000 dollar raise.

Eric is back at school. Is white and lean, but no sign of snuffle wheeze or cough. But what climates that poor lad has had to put up with. Heaven send us a salubrious spot this next move.

Am very serious about the college. Shall ask Dr. Wright about use of hay fever medicine. When he comes by.

All our love
Marshall and Corinne.

[5]Bryda-Rae King was Maurice McLuhan's first wife.

To Walter J. Ong, S.J.

St Michael's College
Toronto .5
[December 1947]

Dear Walter, a blessed Xmas to you.

Have just finished your Speculum essay with enormous satisfaction.[1] My Latin is steadily improving so that I have no trouble with ordinary problems in it. And that do give me a certain Pepysian glow.

But how well you have entered this problem of wit—writing in the middle ages. Are you not the very first to enter that world with comprehension in a century or more? Even [Etienne] Gilson doesn't comprehend it sympathetically because he has no developed sensibility in contemporary art. I heard him on the puns in St Aug's Confessions. He noted that they were inseparable from the multi-levels of simultaneous presentation without seeing that this is precisely our contemporary "cubist" sensibility. What is true of Gilson at only one level is the crippling condition of most present-day Thomists. Their isolation from the main currents of awareness starves even their philosophical and theological being. But, in view of the spectacular indiscretions of my introduction to Kenner's book on Chesterton[2] I may add that Gilson concluded his course on St. Aug. with the

[1]Walter J. Ong, S.J., "Wit and Mystery: A Revaluation in Mediaeval Latin Hymnody", *Speculum*, vol. XXIII, no. 8 (July 1947).

[2]McLuhan refers to his ten-page Introduction to Hugh Kenner's *Paradox in Chesterton* (1947). After acknowledging the contemporary relevance of Chesterton, and Kenner's presentation of him as a perceptive Roman Catholic thinker who gazed into "the heart of the chaos of our time" in his search for moral and political order, McLuhan embarks on a capsule history of Catholic thought, contrasting St Thomas Aquinas with modern Thomists and implicitly criticizing their failure to address problems in social and political ethics, leaving it to the artist "to discover order in man's psychological life".

proclamation of the present need for the fusion of the Thomistic synthesis with Augustinian psychological awareness. That is what I *meant* in my preface. I was simply unequipped to clarify a perception which has long bothered me. But it is plain enough to me that the abiding achievement of the past century has been in analytical psychology and as such the Catholic mind has yet to ingest let alone digest that achievement. But your essay shows one main road back from the central point of contemporary awareness through medieval culture to St Augustine. Notice that your own discussion on ''tension'' as the mode of Xian being is specifically psychological—the basic approach of present-day esthetic analysis.

What is now needed is a great revival of patristic study in light of these things. But current translations of the Fathers wont do for this purpose I fear. How grand if *you*, Walter, could do a series of selections from the fathers, Latin and English on opposite pages—English translation capturing all the effect of the figures of speech. Lyly[,] Donne and the rest would be a help.[3] Notes to clarify the matter of *relevance* to contemporary sensibility. Even 50 pages of this sort of thing done well would possibly start things moving.

The Fathers fathered French symbolical linguistic technique. There was a widespread revival in France of the Fathers from 1800 on. Owing to whom? What? Chateaubriand? What a state of affairs when one has to do everything oneself! No use to ask any colleague in any other department a single question bearing on a specifically contemporary development as it is related to the past. I am at work on a book on Eliot. Two books on popular culture are in process of circulation through editorial hands.[4] But one works alone here as anywhere else. Tiresome. But you know me Walter. Tireless!

[*Marginal note*]
He [Eric] is recovering rapidly. Our fourth child is Stephanie, born Oct. 4 [14]. Corinne is blooming but in spite of a trying job. No help of any kind is available at a salary less than my own. But we are far from grimly gay.

                      As ever in Christ, Mac. (What's the word from McNaspy?)
Walter J. Ong

---

[3]McLuhan perhaps meant that the translation of selections from the writings of the Greek and Latin Fathers (e.g. Athanasius, Augustine) would benefit from a knowledge of the diction of John Lyly (?1554–1606) and John Donne (1572–1631), whose writings are supreme expressions in English of the rhetorical tradition.

[4]*Guide to Chaos* and *Typhon in America*, early versions of *The Mechanical Bride*. Their manuscripts and typescripts, along with related notes and clippings, are in the Public Archives of Canada.

1948

The letter below—the first of many letters McLuhan wrote to the American poet Ezra Pound (1885–1972)—led to a visit by McLuhan and Hugh Kenner to Pound, from 2 to 4 p.m. on June 4, 1948, at St Elizabeths Hospital for the Criminally Insane outside Washington, D.C. For his wartime broadcasts of Fascist propaganda from Rome, beginning in 1940, Pound had been indicted for treason. He was returned from Italy to the United States in late November 1945, and on February 13, 1946 there was a public hearing to determine his sanity and fitness to stand trial. He was judged to be of "unsound mind" and mentally unfit to stand trial (a finding that was disagreed with by 40 psychologists who examined Pound over the ensuing twelve-and-a-half years [E. Fuller Torrey, Psychology Today, *November 1981]). Pound was confined in St Elizabeths from December 1945 to May 1958. During this long period he saw many visitors, carried on a large correspondence, and completed important works, including* The Pisan Cantos *(1948).*

To Ezra Pound

117 West 13th Street
New York City
May 31, 1948

Dear Mr. Pound

My friend Mr. Kenner and I are much looking forward to a visit and some talk with you about contemporary letters, and your work, in which we have long taken a serious interest. We live in Toronto and are visiting here in New York with John Farrelly.[1] We have written Dr. Overholser[2] to say that we will be in Washington Thursday or Friday of this week.

Cordially yours
H.M. McLuhan

Lilly Library, Indiana University

[1] One of McLuhan's students at Saint Louis University.

[2] Dr Winfred Overholser, Superintendent of St Elizabeths Hospital. He had been one of three psychiatrists appointed by the court to examine Pound and from the beginning insisted that Pound was "insane and mentally unfit for trial" (Torrey, *op. cit.*).

To Ezra Pound

St Michael's College
Toronto 5
June 16/48

Dear Mr. Pound

Otto Bird is in New York and a friend of mine who sees him often will ask him to send you his thesis.[1] Of course you could have it from the Toronto U. Library on inter-library loan but that would be less satisfactory. Meantime I shall check on how much of it is available in the *Mediaeval Studies* series.[2]

It would be of the utmost interest and value if you would make some recordings of your poems. An album of 5 or 6 discs is indicated. The machine for doing this is a light portable affair. Records initially on tape etc. An album would do more to get you a hearing than anything else. Laughlin[3] would surely be interested

The Pisan Cantos are truly wonderful, showing a range [of] experience that it would be mere impertinence for me to praise.[4] Are not your affinities (so far as English poetry goes) with Ben Jonson? The same plastic and sculptured world?

The prime difficulty of your poetry—The Cantos—so far as contemporary readers are concerned is surely the intensely masculine mode. This is an age of psychologism and womb-worship. Your clear resonance and etched contours are intolerable to twilight readers who repose only in implications.

Your Cantos, I now judge, to be the first and only serious use of the great technical possibilities of the cinematograph. Am I right in thinking of them as a montage of *personae* and sculptured images? Flash-backs providing perceptions of simultaneities?

Cinema as at present is womb-worship because of the conditions of projection

---

[1]Otto Bird (b. 1914) received a Ph.D. in Philosophy from the University of Toronto (Pontifical Institute of Mediaeval Studies) in 1940 with a thesis entitled *A Text and Commentary on the Canzoni d'Amori of Cavalcanti According to the Commentary of Dino del Garbo*. In the 1938 *Guide to Kulchur* ("5. Zweck or the AIM"), Pound wrote: "The eminent professor and historian G [Etienne Gilson, who taught at the Pontifical Institute] promised me light on Medieval philosophy. I sent him vainly my best set of photographs of del Garbo's commentary on Guido [Cavalcanti]. And there have ensued years of silence." A footnote to this passage states: "Professor Gilson has now set Otto Bird to a thesis on Dino del Garbo." In *The Letters of Ezra Pound (1907–1941)* (1950) there are two letters to Otto Bird: the first (1938) advising him in some detail about his thesis, and the second (1940) enquiring about it and giving further advice. Pound, who translated all the poems of Cavalcanti, had long been an advocate of his importance.

[2]An Annual published by the Pontifical Institute of Mediaeval Studies, University of Toronto, since 1939.

[3]James Laughlin (b. 1914), as a twenty-year-old Harvard student, visited Pound in Rapallo, Italy, in 1934–5 and formed a friendship with him. In 1936, at Pound's instigation, he started a publishing house in New York—New Directions, dedicated to avant-garde literature—and eventually became Pound's American publisher.

[4]*The Cantos* of Ezra Pound, representing the main body of his poetry, were published in sections, beginning in 1919. *The Pisan Cantos* (LXXIV–LXXXIV) were published on July 20, 1948. Pound gave McLuhan, on the occasion of his visit, an advance copy autographed.

in dark-room. No hope there. Didn't Joyce tend to develop his technique in that darkroom?

I've been pondering your remark that Cantos 1–40 are a detective story. Should be glad of further clues from you. But one thing about crime fiction that I have noted may or may not be apropos here. Poe in 1840 or so invented the cinema via Dupin.[5] Dupin deals with a corpse as *still life*. That is, by cinematic montage he reconstructs the crime, as all sleuths have since done. Are Cantos 1–40 such a reconstruction of a crime? Crime against man and civilization? Are the entire Cantos such a reconstruction at once of a continuing crime and of the collateral life that might have been and might still be?[6]

Cordially Yours
Marshall McLuhan

Lilly Library, Indiana University

[5]C. Auguste Dupin is the brilliant amateur detective in *Murders in the Rue Morgue* (1841) and other stories by Edgar Allan Poe, who is considered to be the inventor of the detective story.

[6]Pound replied to this letter, on June 18, saying that McLuhan should go on writing but not expect him to answer questions; on June 21 he asked: "What else hv. you got in print?"

To Ezra Pound

St. Michael's College
Toronto 5
June 30/48

Dear Mr. Pound

You ask what else I have in print. No books at the moment, but 20 or 30 essays. However one job on current ads, comics, gallup polls, press, radio, movies etc. etc. is to be brought out late this year by Vanguard Press. Popular icons as ideograms of complex implication. About 70 exhibits with comments of 2–4 pages.[1]

As I mentioned, having undertaken with Kenner a book on Eliot[2] in which we planned sections on yourself Joyce and Yeats, we began a study of your poems which is now in progress. So we now see that you must have a volume to yourself. Your poems—the Cantos—make heavier demands on the reader than anything else of our time. So time will work in your favor.

[1]*The Mechanical Bride: Folklore of Industrial Man* was not published by Vanguard Press, New York, until 1951. It presents 59 exhibits. See pages 216–17.

[2]In the Preface to his study *The Invisible Poet: T.S. Eliot* (1959) Kenner says: "Ten years ago Marshall McLuhan and I planned an 'Eliot book' and spent some weeks reading through the poems and essays, conversing and annotating as we went. Though this book is very different from the one we projected and abandoned, it owes more than I can unravel to those weeks of association" (pp. xii–xiv). The planned collaboration referred to in the letter above did not lead to a joint study of Eliot. In the next two years, however, McLuhan wrote two articles on Eliot for *Renascence: A Critical Journal of Letters*, published by the Catholic Renascence Society: "Mr. Eliot's Historical Decorum" (Autumn 1949) and "T.S. Eliot" (Autumn 1950).

Read closely, your prose yields the preparation necessary for the Cantos, and the kind of debt Eliot owes you becomes very plain. This debt is by no means clear to Eliot fans since his highly associative and psychological imagery is so very distinct in mode from your etched precision that they never imagine any possible influence.

Looked up John Reid whom I find pleasant enough.[3] Shall see more of him. Hope you will get out that album of readings of your poems. Regards to Mrs. Pound.[4]

Cordially Marshall McLuhan

Lilly Library, Indiana University

[3]John Reid (1915–85), who lived in Toronto, was a young aspiring writer when he went to Europe in the middle thirties and on shipboard met T.S. Eliot, who gave him some introductions. He got to know Wyndham Lewis, and he spent some nine months in Rapallo, Italy, to be near Pound, before returning home in 1939. After McLuhan's visit Mrs Pound included Reid's address in a letter to McLuhan (June 21, 1948). McLuhan and Reid maintained a friendship until 1954. Reid later wrote two novels, *Horses with Blindfolds* (1968) and *The Faceless Mirror* (1974), which he published himself in a limited edition.

[4]Dorothy Shakespear Pound left the Pound home in Rapallo in June 1946 and found a room near St Elizabeths to be near her husband. She visited him nearly every afternoon throughout his confinement and was present during McLuhan's and Kenner's visit.

To Dorothy Shakespear Pound

St Michael's College
Toronto 5   July 3/48

Dear Mrs Pound

We find John Reid a very agreeable sort of person. Very glad you put us on to him. Hope to see him often. Poor chap can't bear to read works of W. Lewis since the great and inexplicable goring.[1]

The *Mediaeval Studies* printed here at the Med. Institute (same premises as St Michael's College) has the Otto Bird thesis in vols 2 and 3. These you could borrow on inter-library loan from the Institute Library. But, of course, they are in the Library of Congress. It is disappointing that you haven't heard from Otto B. himself. But he is out of teaching and study now, and, I gather, has lost interest in such matters.

Looking through the 100 or more pages of the Bird stuff, I can say it is much too technical and detailed for any brief resumé. Should you not be able to get to see it any other way I think that Kenner, when next in Toronto, will photostat it for you. The *Studies* are $5 a volume or so. Bird has obviously got some fascinating

[1]In 1939, when Lewis decided to leave England, John Reid encouraged him to go to Toronto and helped him with introductions when Lewis settled there. In 1941 the deeply discouraged Lewis suddenly turned on Reid (a not untypical treatment of his friends), blaming him for his misfortunes, and some bitter letters were exchanged—though Lewis claimed in one that he never had anything against Reid.

material rounded up. But the job as a whole has, I hear, not escaped a blast or so from specialists.

So far as Gilson himself is concerned you may be sure his action was not motivated but that your not hearing from him was merely the typical effect of his getting along without files, without typewriter and without any sort of secretarial aid. Bird makes due acknowledgement to you in his preface.

Shall check li-bury[2] for your own copy of G[uido] C[avalcanti] since you mention it.

More later
Marshall McLuhan

Lilly Library, Indiana University

[2]In his letters to Pound McLuhan sometimes indulged in a friendly imitation of the "pun-ish" backwoods dialect Pound affected.

To Ezra Pound

St Michael's College
Toronto 5 July 7/48

Dear Mr Pound

Kenner was in town Tuesday and took the Otto Bird material to Peterborough where he will photograph it and send it to you soon.

Since he's well on the way with a Joyce book[1] and both of us are working on Eliot,[2] it is my intention to present your work to the lazier readers of our time. This sounds presumptuous. It is presumptuous. And I know how much work it involves. Reading your prose carefully, and reading the things you suggest should be read, will take time. But the time so spent will be much rewarded. Aware of the general disadvantages of books *about* poets, I shall not be in a hurry to decide on the pattern or the approach. I know that the rationale of any such job should be to direct attention always to the texts. To keep them before the reader. To insist on the sharpest focus. To let the texts speak for themselves. In practice, would you agree that this means arranging texts and expositions in an immediately contemporary focus? To give them their maximum of immediate impact? Rather than relying on historical perspectives?

You see I am thinking aloud, not asking for information. But should you disapprove of the project I shall desist.

In a merely historical perspective should not something be said of the fact that the job of getting English poetry into the central European current (the work you did in 1908–14 with Gaudier, Lewis and others) could not have been done by the

[1]*Dublin's Joyce* by Hugh Kenner was published in 1956.
[2]See page 194, note 2.

English?[3] That Yeats and Joyce,[4] Pound and Eliot, two Irishmen and two Americans, were obviously more aware and more receptive of what had fallen out of the English mind?

Cordially

Lilly Library, Indiana University

Marshall McLuhan

[3]This refers to the English art movement called Vorticism, named by Pound, which grew out of the Rebel Art Centre formed by Wyndham Lewis in 1913. Lewis edited its magazine *Blast: The Review of the Great English Vortex*, the first issue of which is dated June 20, 1914. (See also page 245, note 2.) The Vorticists included Pound and the French sculptor Henri Gaudier-Brzeska (1891-1915), about whom Pound wrote a memoir (1916). 1908 was the year Pound arrived in London, where he remained until 1920. He met T.S. Eliot there in 1914 and sent Eliot's "Prufrock" to Harriet Monroe, editor of *Poetry* (Chicago), where it was published the next year.

[4]In December 1913 W.B. Yeats introduced Pound to the writings of James Joyce. Pound immediately wrote Joyce and began a long correspondence in the course of which Pound, out of admiration for Joyce's work, took it upon himself to act as Joyce's unpaid literary agent. Pound first met Joyce in 1920 in Italy.

To Ezra Pound

St Michael's Coll.

July 15/48

Dear Pound,

The present abbot of the Benedictine abbey of Saint-André in Belgium is a Chinese: Dom. Pierre Lou Tseng-Tsiang former minister of foreign affairs for China about 1895–1906. In his *Souvenirs et Pensées* (Desclee Brouwer 1943) he speaks of the deep affinity between Confucianism and the Benedictine rule—sense of the family in that rule especially. The sense of work and studies. Also of close relation between Gregorian and Chinese music and language.

Characteristic of your generosity that you should suggest prior claims of W[yndham] Lewis to a book. I know Lewis's work in its full extent. Would be glad to do a book on him (for Jas. Laughlin?) after one on you. The work of the musqueteers in 1908–14.[1] That's the job to get into sharp focus. The vortex[2] you created then has become a kiddies' slide in the subsequent work of the Spenders Sitwells Audens and co. Thanks to Freud. Thanks to lack of sustained attention. Lack of energy even to contemplate what's been happening. To know what's going on. The devil of a job in isolation. Problem: How to achieve a milieu. How to get 10 competent people together in one city. And keep them there to talk. To think. To write. I haven't met anybody who even imagines the need for such a group. It can't be done *in* New York. No one university contains more than one or two such potential allies. So it can't be done at a university unless one had power to hire. The latter possibility is the one always in my mind.

Regards to Mrs Pound

Lilly Library, Indiana University

Marshall McLuhan

[1]Presumably the writers, including Pound, referred to in notes 3 and 4 above.

[2]In the *Fortnightly Review* of September 1, 1914 Pound published an article on Vorticism in which he called a vortex an image "from which, and through which, and into which, ideas are constantly rushing."

To Ezra Pound

Dear Pound,

I stand in less danger of professorial ruination than might be supposed. My temperament is sufficient to alienate the breed instantaneously. On the side of stimulating non-professorial contact with the young consider this. On this continent grade school and high school education together do not suffice to nourish two years of adolescent growth. Result, the level of college education is now that of grade school or early high school. By age 20 there are a tiny handful of men who are vaguely aware of having been starved and cheated. By 25 they have discovered a few good authors. By 30 they have begun to lay in the necessary stocks of Latin French Italian to enjoy these authors. How small is this group of self-taught swimmers? Not more than 200 on this continent. Probably 50. I mean of age 25–30. The Philadelphia of your day, the Dublin of Joyce's day were radiant with widely-diffused intelligence compared to the same places or to New York to-day. The current *literati* who begin to splash about in print at 25 to-day (when a man's powers should begin to amount to something) are, mentally, refugees from Buchenwald. Their only fare has been soup made from straw. *Show* me some of the vigorous non-professorial young of today. I've been prowling about looking for them everywhere.

For the prudence and timidities of the professorial mind I have no use whatever. But from the point of view of leisure to work and of possible contacts with those young enough to be furnished with some tools and directives, the university is increasingly important. It is a place of ambush only.

Personally I have no power to hire anybody. Reason is simply this. St Michaels College is run by the Basilian fathers. There are 3 laymen in the place. The college is federated with Victoria College
>Trinity College
>University College

These comprise [*sic*] The University of Toronto. Graduate courses are open to the students of all colleges. I offer graduate courses. The undergraduate work is useless routine to which I devote no more than 8 hours a week. 6 hours in class. But I do not lecture *about* poets. I produce the poems. The ABC of Reading method.[1]

No college and no business city or govt. is run by human persons anymore. I have yet to meet anybody who knew *what* he was doing let alone why he was doing it. Universal Abdication of the human motive is now plain. How to tackle that situation? Zombies. Sleep-walkers. Can't argue with such. They agree with

---

[1]In Section Two of the *ABC of Reading* (1934) Pound offers "exhibits"—a small anthology of poems and extracts; the reader is invited "not to look at my footnotes until they have at least tried to find out WHAT THE EXHIBIT IS, and to guess why I have printed it."

anything you say and go on. Mark that as the present feature. No more disagreement.

For example I am busy getting a Latin school started for the very young.[2] I see dozens of people every week about it. *Everybody* is in favor of it. Nobody will do a thing about it. This is a specific job which one man can handle. So I'll swing it. But if only somebody would disagree with me I would feel more hope.

Cordially yrs

Marshall McLuhan

Lilly Library, Indiana University

30 Jly 48

P.S. I am preparing a booklet for the young. A bibliography of necessary reading in all the arts and sciences with sufficient commentary on each item to provide a coherent picture of when and how to use one book to encounter another. About 100 pages with preface on the abeyance of all education to-day.

[2]Neither the Latin school, nor the ''booklet for the young'' mentioned in the PS., came to fruition.

To Ezra Pound

[St Michael's College]

Toronto 5

Aug 16/48

Dear Pound, reading Clement of Alexandria[1] recently I came across a statement which would sound well in Guide to Kulcher [*sic*]:[1]

> These 3 [three] things, therefore, our philosopher attaches himself to: first, speculation; second, the performance of the precepts; third, the forming of good men;—which, concurring, form the Gnostic. Whichever of these is wanting, the Elements of Knowledge limp.

In Guide to Kulcher I have found all the help with the Cantos that anybody needs,

[1]Clement of Alexandria was born about A.D. 150 in Athens and became associated with the church in Alexandria, where he taught in the catechetical school there. The work referred to was probably *The Writings of Clement of Alexandria* (vol. II, 1869), translated by the Rev. William Wilson. The quotation is from Chapter X, "To What the Philosopher Applies Himself" (p. 29).

[2]Pound's *Guide to Kulchur*—published in England by Faber in July 1938 and in the U.S. in November by New Directions under the title *Culture*—is a compendium of digressive and disconnected notes, pronouncements, explications, and quotations ranging widely and wildly in subject (literature, philosophy, music, history, government, the *Nichomachean Ethics*, the Vortex, usury), arcane references, and names (Aeschylus, Aristotle, Socrates, Plato, Homer, Confucius, Malatesta, Dante, Cavalcanti, Shakespeare, Bach, Vivaldi, Frobenius, Gaudier-Brzeska, Roosevelt, Eliot, et al.). It represented for Pound "one's ideogram of culture, or say one's road map intended to aid the next man to a few of the summits". (It is sprinkled with Chinese ideograms.) For a contemporary reviewer, Dudly Fitts, it was compounded of "profundities and balderdash" (*Saturday Review*, May 13, 1939).

including full light on your remark made to me in Washington that 1–40 are a sort of detective story.

The Penguin Books have recently issued Fordie's

> Some Do Not
> A man could stand up
> Last Post
> The Good Soldier.

So I've been through them for the first time. For some "reason" No More Parades was not issued. These books repay the reading certainly, and I'll get them read by others.[3]

One thing I've discovered about *all* contemporary readers. Each one has a single reading pace. The books each one likes (understands) are just those adapted to his particular pace. Nobody dreams that some pages should be read very slowly and very often. This is an unconscious effect of mechanism. People really do think of themselves as specialized machines nowadays. "That's just my speed" is a most revealing remark.

My eyes goggled at a statement of Edmund Wilson[4] in an essay on The Dream of H.C. Earwicker (p. 335 of the [Seon] Givens' edition of "Two Decades of Joyce Criticisms 1948):

> One had to think about the book, read chapters of it over, in order to see
> the pattern and to realize how deep the insight went.

This by way of an artistic indictment of Joyce: "The moments of critical importance were so run in with the rest that one was likely to miss them on first reading."

This is an unintentional revelation of intellectual slobbishness all the more valuable because Wilson assumes that one reading is all that a good mind need give any work.

Apropos of your valuable comment (in G. to K.) anent Francis Picabia[5] and the technique for getting rid of rubbish by transposition of terms, inversion of clichés etc., I have thought of *Finnegans Wake* as a gigantic experiment in that mode. "Ulysses lanced the boil on the mind of Europe".[6] F.W. was intended to wash it out. Hercules-Augean stable diverted river. Rivers in F.W. benefi-

---

[3]During their meeting in June, Pound had put McLuhan and Kenner on to the novels of Ford Madox Ford (1873–1939). The first three novels listed, and *No More Parades*—published between 1924 and 1928—comprise a tetralogy known as *Parade's End. The Good Soldier* (1915) is considered to be Ford's finest novel. Pound's friendship with Ford (whom he called by his nickname Fordie) began in 1909 when Ford, then known as Ford Madox Hueffer, published Pound for the first time in Britain in his *English Review*.

[4]Edmund Wilson (1895–1972), the American literary critic.

[5]In his *Guide to Kulchur* Pound says that the French painter Francis Picabia (1879–1953), whom he knew in Paris in the early 1920s, "got hold of an instrument which cleared out whole racks full of rubbish" ("10. Guide").

[6][With "The katharsis of 'Ulysses' . . .] The sticky, molasses-covered filth of current print, all the fuggs, all the foetors, the whole boil of the European mind, had been lanced." (*Guide to Kulchur*: "13. Monumental".)

cent, benign, purging the images of day. Is not this the rationale of that Rabelaisian drama?

Frobenius[7] not to be had in English in Toronto. Is he to be had in French? I must get my hands on him.

Most cordial regards to you and Mrs Pound
Marshall McLuhan.

Lilly Library, Indiana University

[7]Leo Frobenius (1873–1938), German archaeologist and anthropologist and the author of many books that illuminated African history and pre-history. His *Erlebte Erdteile* [Countries I Have Experienced] (7 vols, 1925–9), and also the section published separately as *Paideuma* (1921), made a great impression on Pound. In the *Guide to Kulchur* ("ZWECK or the AIM") Pound says that Frobenius used the term Paideuma "for the tangle or complex of the inrooted ideas of any period."

To Felix Giovanelli [*Undated*]

Dear Felix

Keep a look-out for Corbière and Gautier for me.[1] Also Laforgues Moral Tales in French or English.[2] Latter are wonderful things. Simply haven't reached English audience yet save in rather ponderous Eliot form. Al Capp[3] at his best is not unlike Laforgue.

Also try to get me Pound's prose (except for Make It New [1934] and Polite Essays [1937]) but as for

> ABC of Reading [1934]
> How to Read [1931]
> Pavannes and Divisions [1918]
> Spirit of Romance [1910]
> Instigations [1919]
> Guide to Kulcher [*sic*, 1938]

Grab any or all of them.

Pound's prose is precise. It has to be read *very* slowly. Everything he mentions has to be read. His method in prose and verse is the ideogram. That is the sculp[t]ed item, whether historical, excerpted or invented. These he sets side by

[1]In his long "Study in French Poets" (*The Little Review*, February 1918—reprinted in *Make It New*, 1934), Pound wrote: "After [Théophile] Gautier [1811–72], France produced, as nearly as I can understand, three chief and admirable poets: Tristan Corbière [1845–75], perhaps the most poignant writer since Villon; [Arthur] Rimbaud (1854–91), a vivid and indubitable genius; and [Jules] Laforgue—a slighter, but in some ways a finer 'artist', than either of the others."

[2]The French poet Jules Laforgue (1860–87) had a great influence on T.S. Eliot and on Pound (see Canto CXVI). The reference is to Laforgue's *Moralités légendaires* (1887), a prose work.

[3]Al Capp (1909–79), American satirical cartoonist, creator of the comic-strip "Lil Abner". McLuhan praised Capp in *The Mechanical Bride* as "the only robust satirical force in American life."

side in analogical ratios in accord. with Aristotelian principle of metaphor. He eschews the associational devices of ambivalent language which is Eliot's main stock in trade. He detests psychology and isn't interested in sensibility. His whole bent is intellectual,—aesthetics pushed to metaphysical intuition of being. Side by side with his passion for intellectual ratios or analogies is his insistence on melopoeia. Cantabile. Musical ratios. This cuts him off from rhetoric and the dramatic functions of language of the Elizabethan type—so much used by Eilot.

Tried Dorothy Richardson[4] for 20 minutes too. One big well of infantile loneliness. Unbelievable. Something ought to be done about it.

Souhaits

Margaret W. Giovanelli   Mac

[4]Dorothy Richardson (1873–1957), English novelist. Beginning in 1915 she published a series of autobiographical novels, employing the stream-of-consciousness technique, that ended with the posthumously published *March Moonlight* (1967). They are now respected for their feminist content.

To Felix Giovanelli

[St Michael's College]
Monday Sept 5/48

Dear Felix

Regards to Margaret [Giovanelli] of whom nothing said of late. I enclose letter from Mrs Pound. A charming lady. Let me say that you will get much pleasure and enlightenment from Ford Madox Fords Return to Yesterday. Light on Pound, Lewis et al.[1] (Please try to snag me copy of Blast and Bombadiering.[2] Natch I'm interested to know what Percy's latest book contains. Novel about Toronto?[3]

Ford deals with *res non verba*. His anecdotes always point to social, political, economic aesthetic axes and dynamisims within a situation. His March of Literature (1939) is the best book on comparative lit I've ever come across.[4] Please give me your opinion.

Many people bobbing in an out of here in recent weeks. Time much broken by it. Tom [Easterbrook] is back. Kenner is practically cleared for Yale. Did *very* well in grad. record exam. His recent successes in publication etc. have much swelled his dome. That's O.K. But it's a poor condition in which to enter a next [*sic*] of academic timidities and mediocrities. I've tried to dim him down with suggestions of self-effacement as a necessary strategy. [Cleanth] Brooks has very

[1]*Return to Yesterday* (1931), one of Ford's volumes of autobiography, is notable for its reminiscences of Joseph Conrad, Henry James, and Stephen Crane. However, towards the end of the book, in connection with the early days of his periodical *The English Review*, Ford describes his first meetings with, respectively, Ezra Pound and Wyndham Lewis (whom he calls "D.Z.").

[2]Wyndham Lewis, *Blasting and Bombardiering* (1937), an autobiography to 1926.

[3](Percy) Wyndham Lewis's "latest book" was *America and Cosmic Man* (1948), which grew out of his life in America and his lectures in Canada. The "novel about Toronto" (*Self-Condemned*) did not appear until 1954.

[4]Ford Madox Ford, *The March of Literature: From Confuscius to Modern Times* (1938, U.S.; 1939, U.K.), an idiosyncratic and impressionistic history of literature.

little production left in him and is scared to death of Kenner and me. Kenner has to get a bursary for his 2nd year. Give him some advice about keeping his mouth shut. He hasn't any social sense whatever. Partly result of deafness. Dont let on I've tipped you off on this theme. But he's going to Yale for one purpose only. To get his union card—carte eclatant. Not to impress anybody with his *present* crudition but rather to please his instructors by a show of his capacity to *learn from them*. And there is much he can learn from them. No point in his trying to teach them. What he can learn from them is not immediately connected with his own intellectual interests. What he can teach them is not at all connected with their interests. *Ergo*: His only strategy is to shut up. To receive and not to give *while at Yale*. I can see all these dangers clearly because I made these mistakes myself. But my excuse was that I was seeking intellectual guidance from the profs. Hugh is not. He's got his intellectual bearings. All he needs is facts and credit for knowing the same. His *views* he can afford to conceal. Their views he can afford to ignore. Right now I could enter a grad. school and do good course work because I would not be bothered with the intelligence or stupidity of the instructor. But it has taken mc a long time to take stupidity and indifference for granted as a universal and irremediable human condition. Pound has never reached that point. All his strategies depend on the prior condition of alertness and eager appetite for truth. W. Lewis: "I write from the standpoint of genius". E.P.: "I write for those who are top flight inventors and creators in the arts." T.S. Eliot: "I croon to those who are living and partly living a song of their remote but better selves." Therefore Lewis and Pound are ignored and Eliot is *widely* misunderstood. But *widely*. Old Possum [Eliot] was the shrewder man. And I dislike him for his virtues.

Say hello to Marius and John F for me.[5] I think of them much.

Margaret W. Giovanelli   Yrs   Mac.

[5]Marius Bewley and John Farrelly had been students of McLuhan (at Saint Louis University) whom he encouraged to continue their studies at Cambridge University; this they did.

To Felix Giovanelli   [St Michael's College, September 1948]

Dear Felix, a grand letter from you.[1] Much good feasting in it. Wish I could take time to reciprocate. Let me answer a few questions first. No I dont have a copy of Mach-Marx at all.[2] But think you haven't either. In current Kenyon there is an essay on Marx which gets at a tiny bit of my idea.[3] That piqued and annoyed me.

You are right about Bennett. Light weight. Morgan too.[4] I must have annoyed

[1]Giovanelli's letter of September 8.
[2]See page 157, note 3.
[3]Wylie Sypher, "Aesthetic of Revolution: The Marxist Melodrama", *The Kenyon Review*, vol. x, Summer 1948, no. 3.
[4]Joseph Bennett and Frederick Morgan were joint editors of *The Hudson Review*.

Morgan by my very off-hand dismissal of Winters.[5] Since then I've had to write about Winters because of his views on Eliot. Winters is a naive, unconscious Kantian who can place everybody but himself. I'm going to place him very hard. Kantian esthetics, as I'll explain in said essay are unconsciously behind all American critical activity.

Please canvas this fact Felix. Why have *none* of the expatriates or why has *no* American artist or man of letters ever written down his life and contacts with his own kind? A major stimulus to young talent is not only lacking thereby, but a major defect of American talent *and* society is thereby opened for observation. Radical flaw in our equipment yawns through the family horse-collar. The Case of the Missing Anecdote. We think to create by the *idea*, or to triumph by technique in the abstract. Can't save our skins by arranging such bones.[6]

Ford omits [from *The March of Literature*] Proust, Joyce, Eliot Lewis partly for artistic, partly for private reasons.[7] Mainly his intense loyalty to Pound. The March of Lit is *the* commentary on The *Cantos*.[8] Ford had big row with W. Lewis.[9] Lewis claimed he was center of conspiracy to boycott Lewis. All rot of course. But it left a very bad taste in the mouth of the very affectionate and obliging Fordie. All samee with John Reid here in Toronto. Ford and Pound talked and talked about everything from 1908–22 when Pound went to Italy. They agreed on everything except Cicero, and Mommsen.[10]

I am delighted with Pavannes and Diversions. A rare book to get. Still want: [Pound's] Make It New, Guide to Kulch[,] ABC of Reading, Spirit of Romance, ABC of Economics [1933], Jeff[erson] and/or Mussolini [1935]. Guide to Kulch above all. It is the Cantos in prose. And harder to read. Ford's memoirs are not mere chat. The chat is a series of epiphanies of carefully considered social and literary structures and their inter penetration.

Superb Fall weather. Wish you'd drop in. Our best to you and Margaret.

Margaret W. Giovanelli   As ever   Mac

---

[5]Yvor Winters (1900–68), poet and critic. The essay mentioned is "The Difficulties of Ivor Winters or Rymer Redivus", an unpublished manuscript (PAC).

[6]An unpublished essay enlarging on this theme, "The Case of the Missing Anecdote" (PAC), grew out of an article by Harold Rosenberg, "Herd of Independent Minds", in *Commentary*, September 1948. Giovanelli sent McLuhan's essay to *Commentary*, but it was rejected by Clement Greenberg (Giovanelli's letter of October 6).

[7]Ford Madox Ford's *The March of Literature* barely touches on the modern period for reasons that probably had to do with his ill health and lack of energy rather than with personal feeling.

[8]That is, because the discussions of literature are so wide-ranging and esoteric.

[9]In *Return to Yesterday* Ford recounts that Lewis suspected him of "conspiring with Academicians to suppress his activities" and of "willing his undoing", when he merely said to him: "I wish you would give up your other arts and concentrate on writing. The other arts can look after themselves but in England writers are desperately needed." Lewis—who was prone to blame friends and acquaintances for his lack of commercial success as a writer—may have told McLuhan his own version of the "row", but this has not been recorded.

[10]Marcus Tullius Cicero (106–43 B.C.), the Roman orator, letter-writer, and Stoic philosopher; Theodor Mommsen (1817–1903), German historian, author of *History of Rome* (1854–6, 1885), and winner of the 1902 Nobel Prize for literature.

To Dorothy Shakespear Pound

St Michael's College
Toronto 5
[Late September 1948]

Dear Mrs Pound,

Thanks for the offer of Frobenius. But I read only French. However I've been able to get The Voice of Africa, and the Childhood of Man.[1] No mean samples of his work I take it.

My immediate program is to get out a book on Eliot (since I'm committed to that job and have been at it for some time.)[2] But it will be a book which will do something useful in getting certain other matters in focus.

Next a Baedeker for the university frustrates. A list of books with specific indications of their *kind* of relevance.[3] A Guide to Kulch. for the kind of people who remain illiterate through the misfortunes of current educational misguidance. (I should much like to see EP's Guide to Kulch. in a Penguin. I should like to see it on every Walgreen counter. It is, in fact, very hard to get at all.

Next job, a book on E.P.[4] If I can summon the courage. Because the more I read him the less competent I feel to do a good job. W. Lewis can wait till after that. Though something will have to be said about him in the Eliot book, the Baedeker and also the E.P. books. It is the reading habits of the current high-brows, their unbelievable slackness and inattention which makes the work of E.P. and W. Lewis inaccessible. Also the four or five catch-all concepts, Freudian, socialist, etc. These satisfy the avant garde gentry who receive grace from the Holy Zeitgeist which renders effort on their part quite needless. A long habit of diagnosis on my part has forced me to observe the very tiny measure of autonomous existence which these influential folk choose to exercise. It is the abeyance, wilful or compulsive, of all faculties of mind which has occurred. To the extent, therefore, that these people are no longer viable at all, some preliminary therapy is indicated. They cant be set at tasks of average civilized intensity without collapsing, or reacting sadistically, at least.

The appeal must be to the young. But the young have been robbed of their energies by association with these mental sad-sacks. Worse, they have been systematically deprived of all the linguistic tools by which they could nourish their own perceptions at first hand at the usual traditional sources. In the name of the

---

[1]Leo Frobenius, *The Voice of Africa: Being an Account of the Travels of the German Inner African Exploration Expedition in the Years 1910–12* (2 vols, 1913), translated by Rudolf Blind; *The Childhood of Man: A Popular Account of the Lives, Customs and Thoughts of the Primitive Races* (1909), translated by A.H. Keane. In her reply (September 17, 1948) to this letter, Mrs Pound commented that *The Childhood of Man* was "hardly Frobenius at all, sort of summary of what things were when he started".

[2]See page 194, note 2.

[3]This project, which is mentioned in later letters, was never completed.

[4]McLuhan did not write a book on Pound. However, his "Pound's Critical Prose", a short but cogent appreciation, was included in *Examination of Ezra Pound: A Collection of Essays* (1950), edited by Peter Russell.

sacred and unimpeded unfolding of their little egos the old have withheld all linguistic training from the young on this continent for the past 40 years. The young are tired. They are easily discouraged when they see what ground they have to make up. In the name of what, they ask, should we bother to rack ourselves to repair that damage?

Personally I'm not tired or discouraged. So I am a cause of much annoyance and discomfort wherever I happen to be. But isolation is a poor stategy [*sic*] except for the mystic.

Most cordial regards
Marshall McLuhan

Lilly Library, Indiana University

To Ezra Pound

Sunday Nov 7/48
St Michael's College
Toronto 5

Dear Pound

My epistolarly [*sic*] socks have sagged lately. You know, going through Ford, and trying to read all that he says I must, has given me quite a feeling of inadequacy and irrelevance. That will pass by the time I have finished the next 200 volumes. But the sense of only now reading the things I should have known all along has sapped me. And to write to yourself, who have for forty-five years taken for granted all this learning, perception and art, well it seemed sheer impertinence.

Curious isn't it how almost the only qualification for those twirps associated with literary mags in our century is complete ignorance. And yet, perversely, the public regards them as ever so knowing. Result, current views about you and others totally unrealistic. Hard to account for the huge discrepancy between the equipment of yourself, Joyce, Yeats, Eliot and the totally inferior equipment of those engaged in promoting or discussing you.

Of course the public will not believe that an artist can be a scholar, or a serious intelligence. The artist is simply a goose who lays (unwittingly) golden eggs for others. Any signs of wit or erudition in the artist-goose are a scandal which must be hushed up so that the egg may be stolen with clear conscience.

Can you or Mrs. Pound tell me why T.S. Eliot carefully suppresses any reference to Ford or his writings? There must be some explanation. My interest in the matter is not at the gossip level. It seems to me to be necessary for an understanding of 20th cent. letters.

Douglas Goldring (who writes like a sap) in *South Lodge*[1] and Joseph Hone in his *WB Yeats*[2] both attribute definite influence to you in the matter of assisting at

---

[1]Douglas Goldring, *South Lodge: Reminiscences of Violet Hunt, Ford Madox Ford and the English Review Circle* (1943).
[2]Joseph Hone, *W.B. Yeats, 1865–1939* (1943).

the birth of the "later" Yeats. That is a theme I should like to publish on at once. Also the kind of thing Joyce picked up from you. Can you suggest any persons or reading which would be relevant?

Regards to Mrs Pound

Lilly Library, Indiana University

Marshall McLuhan.

To Ezra Pound

St Michael's College
Toronto 5
Dec 21 /48

Dear Pound,

Much delighted with the Trieste newspapers. The job on Hemingway most amusing. And the Joyce item a gem. Very significant too the Ciaro review. My Italian not too adequate even for newspapers though.

The post has just brought The Great Trade Route.[1] So I now have the only copy in Toronto. Am keen to get at it. Giovanelli and I are talking Ford up into a small boom. The time is ripe. And it is the best strategy for preparing the ground for a more adequate approach to your own achievement. Intellectually at least, the obfuscators via Marx are pulling rocks over themselves.

Seon Givens of Vanguard Press, the editor in charge of my book on Industrial Folklore [*The Mechanical Bride*], is a Mary Butts collector.[2] Has everything. She [Seon Givens] plans to visit you soon.

As Giovanelli and I work up the W. Lewis cause we discover any number of Lewis fans who have warmed themselves secretly at his fires these 25 years!

The American mind is not even close to being amenable to the ideogram principle as yet. The reason is simply this. America is 100% 18th century. The 18th century had chucked out the principle of metaphor and analogy—the basic fact that as A is to B so is C to D. AB:CD. It can see AB relations. But relations in four terms are still verboten. This amounts to deep occultation of nearly all human thought for the U.S.A.

I am trying to devise a way of stating this difficulty *as it exists*. Until stated and publicly recognized for what it is, poetry and the arts can't exist in America. Mere exposure to the arts does nothing for a mentality which is incorrigibly dialectical. The vital tensions and nutritive action of ideogram remain inaccessible to this state of mind.

With most cordial seasonable wishes for you and Mrs Pound

Lilly Library, Indiana University

Marshall McLuhan

[1]*The Great Trade Route* (1932) is an extended essay by Ford Madox Ford. In the course of travelling in the Deep South of the U.S., across the Atlantic to Madeira, Gibraltar, and the Mediterranean, he reflects on the salvation of mankind.

[2]Mary Butts (1893–1937) was an English writer admired by Ford, who published her in his *Transatlantic Review*. She was the author of ten books, including three short-story collections and three novels. There is a verbal portrait of her in Douglas Goldring's *South Lodge* (see previous letter).

To Lewis Mumford[1]

St Michaels College
Tor. 5 Dec 28/48

Dear Mr Mumford

At lunch with H.A. Innes [*sic*],[2] Karl Helleiner, and W T Easterbrook[3] recently I was congratulating them on the way in which they had pulled into a unity their Economic, Sociology and Political Science departments.[4] I was illustrating further possibilities of a genuine encyclopedic synthesis from your work and suggesting how English, Modern Languages, History and the Fine Arts departments might be got to work together. At this point, Innes, who is head of the graduate school of Toronto University asked me to write and ask you to visit us—A commission which bestows much honor on me and which I hasten to carry out.

Your visit would not involve more than a day or two of informal chats with small faculty groups. Toronto is overnight by train from New York (12 hours), or two and a half hours by plane. And something more than your expenses would be paid. $150 is the standard Toronto fee. I wish it were much more.

Naturally the mere possibility of a visit from you raises most pleasurable hopes here.

With greetings of the season.

Very Sincerely Yours
Marshall McLuhan.

[1]Lewis Mumford (b. 1895) wrote many books exploring the relation of people to their created environment, and by this time had written three volumes of a four-volume series called *The Research of Life:* these were *Technics and Civilization* (1934), *The Culture of Cities* (1938), and *The Condition of Man* (1944). He graciously declined the invitation that follows because of other obligations, among which was finishing the fourth volume, *The Conduct of Life* (1951). In Mumford's later writings, scattered references to McLuhan reveal a strong negative bias.

[2]Harold Adams Innis (1894–1952)—Professor of Political Economy and, as McLuhan says, Dean of the Graduate School, University of Toronto—was the author of two seminal economic histories, *The Fur Trade in Canada* (1930) and *The Cod Fisheries* (1940). By the time of this letter his interests had moved into examining communications field systems as the economic foundations of society, and in May of this year he had delivered the first of six Beit lectures at All Souls College, Oxford, out of which grew his famous book *Empire and Communications* (1950). See also pages 219–20.

[3]The Viennese-born Karl Helleiner (b. 1902) and W.T. (Tom) Easterbrook (1907–85), McLuhan's old friend, both taught in the Department of Political Economy and would eventually become full professors.

[4]This refers to the conversation rather than to actuality. In the University of Toronto, Economics and Political Science were then one department known as Political Economy; but all three departments mentioned became separate.

1949

To Felix Giovanelli

Dear Felix,

Well, I think the breath is getting hotter on some of the cultural rubber necks.

Legman would surely be worth an evening's chat.[1] His piece on the Comics in Neurotica 3 was dandy. Written, however, in *Typhon* tone. Tell him how to let up on moral earnestness without loss of intellectual point. Change of tone required only to get his stuff printed. I haven't told him about Vanguard doing my folklore because [Seon] Givens[2] turned down his book. Perhaps you could break the news tactfully without loss of an ally. He sounds like a good sort of gent.

Good news about Eliot letter. Very good.[3] A book on Ford just the thing for New Directions series don't you think? But Eliot must be done first. Shall do the Ford piece for Hudson. Just 2 days work. But shall read more of the novels. And *do* send the *Provence*.[4] Not to be had here. I think we'd better buy up some Ford before the rush begins. Especially *Thus to Revisit*.[5] Key book. Haven't even got at the Great Trade Route yet. You do realize I think that Ford had much to do with the shape of the Cantos via *Provence*?[6]

A book to grab whensoever: Pound's Gaudier-Brezska.[7] Worth $7 anytime. I'll pay gladly.

---

[1]Gershon Legman (b. 1917), whom Giovanelli had met in New York, was the second editor of *Neurotica*—a magazine that was published nine times between 1948 and 1951 and emphasized the popular arts in observing that neurotic people were simply responding logically to an abnormal society. His article in *Neurotica* 3 was "The Psychopathology of the Comics". (McLuhan contributed "The Psychopathology of *Time* and *Life* to *Neurotica* 5, 1949.) Legman's *Love & Death: A Study in Censorship* (1949), an analysis of sex and violence in popular culture, is cited more than once in *The Mechanical Bride*. The U.S. Post Office labelled this book "obscene" and refused to deliver mail to Legman's home in the Bronx; as a result Legman left the United States to live in France. Among his other books is the influential *The Horn Book: Studies in Erotic Folklore and Bibliography* (1964). See also page 382, notes 1 and 2.

[2]See page 214, note 1.

[3]In a letter to McLuhan of January 7, 1949 Giovanelli quotes from a letter to him from T.S. Eliot (December 28, 1948) encouraging Giovanelli in his attempt to interest an American magazine in doing a special issue on Wyndham Lewis.

[4]Ford Madox Ford, *Provence* (1938), an impressionistic cultural history. Apparently McLuhan did not write the piece on Ford.

[5]Ford Madox Ford, *Thus to Revisit: Some Reminiscences* (1921).

[6]About this notion Giovanelli sounded out Pound, who said that Ford had nothing to do with the Cantos and Provence, and that Provence was "strongly IN" the Cantos long before Pound went to London.

[7]Ezra Pound, *Gaudier-Brezska: A Memoir* (1916).

I now have an extra copy of The Spirit of Romance (rare book) which is for you. Friend picked it up in England. Guide to Kulch—try to get even via Gotham Bk Mkt. Also Make It New.[8] Tho I have most of latter in other forms.

Apropos of Amer. Vortex, have sent to Sewanee.[9] Sense of "changed" (Maritain-Giedion) same as Eliot uses word in Trad. and Ind. Talent: new work modifies old willy-nilly.[10]

Catholic U. still bearing down on me. I've heard at 1st hand that students there are pitiable. Wot to doo? Give me your thoughts.

Marius [Beweley] wrote me at length this week. Feeling aggrieved about my manners towards him (but not saying it in so many words). Reassure him of my regard. I must write oftener.

Haven't heard from Morgan yet. It wouldn't take me long to do a rip-roaring bit on W. Lewis. Not in mere discipular vein either.

More very soon

Margaret W. Giovanelli
Mac

[8]Ezra Pound's *The Spirit of Romance* (1910) and *Make It New* (1934) are both collections of essays.

[9]"The New American Vortex"—in which some American writers are discussed in the context of the "London vortex of 1908–1921, as represented by Ford, Pound, Lewis, and Eliot"—was not published. The manuscript is in the Public Archives of Canada.

[10]"Tradition and the Individual Talent" is a chapter in T.S. Eliot's *The Sacred Wood* (1920), in which Eliot states that when a new work of art is created in literature, the past is "altered by the present as much as the present is directed by the past."

[11]The Catholic University of America, Washington, D.C., had made an offer of an appointment to McLuhan. In not accepting it he may have been influenced by what Giovanelli, in a letter of January 14, saw as a disadvantage: having to identify his future authorship as "By Marshall McLuhan, Catholic University".

To Ezra Pound

St. Michael's College
Toronto 5
Feb 22 /49

Dear Pound

We shall be as curious to note the results of the prize for the Pisan Cantos as we are glad you have it.[1]

Have just this minute been bracing myself with the pages on prosody in your

[1]On February 20, 1949 it was announced that *The Pisan Cantos* had won the first annual Bollingen Prize for poetry, which carried with it $1,000. The award—made by the Fellows in American Letters of the Library of Congress (who included Conrad Aiken, W.H. Auden, Louise Bogan, T.S. Eliot, Robert Lowell, Katherine Anne Porter, Karl Shapiro, Allen Tate, and Robert Penn Warren) —elicited much criticism, in both daily papers and journals, that continued for over a year. (Objections have been voiced off and on ever since.)

ABC of Reading.[2] May my pate become a glue-pot if I dont try to get that book reprinted.

Am gradually getting pushed out of the current Quarterlies myself as result of not hewing to current party-lines. Has the advantage of turning one's attention to basic issues. Kenner and I plan to work together again this summer and hope to get something *out*. Most cordial regards to you and Mrs Pound.

Marshall McLuhan

Lilly Library, Indiana University

[2]Pound's "Treatise on Metre" at the end of his *ABC of Reading*.

To Felix Giovanelli
[St Michael's College]
March 4/49

Dear Felix

Well, you must be up to your neck! Let me say you should look at Frank Budgen's Making of Ulysses at once and buy me a 2nd hand *or* new copy *any* time you can find one.[1] Budgen was an impressionist painter. His strong plastic sense endeared him to Joyce. His [Joyce's] feeling for factual and plastic aspects of words is unusual in our very literary Anglo-Saxon tradition. Think of Dante dividing words into "shaggy" and "buttered" ![2] Budgen is full of help. Equivalent of 3 readings of Ulysses.

Have been making many basic and useful discoveries lately. Pass a few on to Hugh [Kenner] from time to time. He wants that I should appear in New Haven this Spring to consolidate certain matters he has broached there with [Cleanth] Brooks, [Maynard] Mack and others. I can see that Brooks is already having a divel of a time trying to hold his arse up to Hugh's level. As you can see from note in enclosed Letter about his class for Joyce beginners. It's plain too that Hugh is pursuing his lonely way unattended by any easy social life with the folks who matter. That being, in less degree, my own state, how easily I can diagnose the human weakness that brings it about. Hope I can persuade Seon[3] to buy me a ticket to N.Y. instead of her coming here. Really a waste of hers and my time if

[1]Frank Budgen, *James Joyce and the Making of Ulysses* (1934). Budgen, a painter, met Joyce in Zurich in 1918 and they became good friends. Joyce often talked at length to him about *Ulysses* while he was midway in its composition. *The Making of Ulysses* intersperses illuminating and agreeably unpretentious expositions of the text with accounts (also illuminating) of these conversations. In 1960 the book was reissued in paperback by the Indiana University Press, with an Introduction by Hugh Kenner.

[2]McLuhan picked this up from Pound's *ABC of Reading*: ". . . Dante called words 'buttered' and 'shaggy' because of the different NOISES they make" (p. 37). Dante Alighieri (1265–1321), in his uncompleted treatise *De Vulgari Eloquentia* (On Vernacular Speech), ascribes tactile qualities to words used in the Italian vernacular, applying such adjectives to them as *yrsuta* (hairy), *pexa* (combed), and *lubrica* (glossy, smooth, or slippery).

[3]Seon Givens, McLuhan's editor at The Vanguard Press. See page 214, note 1.

she does come. A waste of my time in so far as what social life here I'd dig up for her would be useless to her and a bore to me. A waste of my time in that I'd be more profitably engaged socially for the same period in N.Y.

Legman sent me his piece on Love and Death. It's queerly static. He doesn't seem to grasp the dialectic of the sado-masochist relations. But by hammering away at one point he may succeed. More in a day or so

Mac.

Margaret W. Giovanelli

[*Written in the left margin:*] Get copy of *Poetry* (Chicago) current issue for essay "Ezra Pound in the Pisa Stockade."[4]

[4]On May 24, 1945 Pound was taken to the American Disciplinary Training Centre outside Pisa—a barbed-wire stockade—and held there as a military prisoner for nearly six months. He was kept for some weeks in an enclosure of heavy grillwork (the "gorilla cage") with a tarpaper roof; at night he slept in a pup-tent he rigged up. This reference is to "The Background of the Pisan Cantos", *Poetry* (Chicago), January 1949, by David Park Williams, who was a guard at the DTC from May through October 1945.

To Felix Giovanelli

[St Michael's College]
April 30/49

Dear Felix, Most of my time lately seems to have gone into just such activities as are indicated on the other side of this sheet. Have had a week of bronchitis. But OK now.

Horrified at bilge in Hudson.[1] Vernon Young on Conrad! And Frank on Mann! It is Mann who is to tell us at this time of day that the arts are decadent! [2] He's [Frank's] got hold of the same sausage role as Van Wyck Brooks.[3] I have actually read his [Mann's] Dr. Faustus. Amazing! (remember Albert Scholz's epithet.[4]) *There* is a book for the psychoanalyst rather than the literary critic. The German in search of human relations is like the roots of a tree "feeling out the ground." Every facet of his friend produces a corresponding knobby protuberance in his own soul. So, all his human activity being vegetable his intellectual activity is bound to be angelic. Such childish dialectics. Mann engaged in thought is zomzing terrific. Morgan *would* go for that stuff. This is not too coherent about Mann but

[1]*The Hudson Review*, vol. 2, no. 1, Spring 1949, includes among its articles Vernon Young, "Joseph Conrad: Outline for a Reconsideration"; Joseph Frank, "Reaction as Progress; or, The Devil's Domain"; and Yvor Winters, "The Poetry of Gerard Manley Hopkins (II)".

[2]Thomas Mann (1875-1955). His *Doktor Faustus* (1947), which had recently been published in translation (1948), treats the demonic nature of the imagination.

[3]Van Wyck Brooks (1886-1963) wrote a five-volume history of American literature, the fourth volume of which, *The Times of Melville and Whitman*, was published in 1947.

[4] Albert Scholz taught in the German Department of Saint Louis University; he was the godfather of Teri McLuhan.

like EM Forster he remains the bourgeois as esthete.[5] Nostalgic about the dullness he has dared to half-repudiate. That neither bourgeois nor esthete is of the slightest interest as category for a perceptive intelligence has never occurred either to Mann or Forster.

Tell me has our *Neurotica* friend [Legman] read W. Lewis on the Homo as child of the Suffragette?[6] That section remains for me a high-point. It ruined Lewis.[7] But there's not even a hint of such awareness in Freud or Horney.[8] Freud on the causes of homosexuality is just a bloody comic—Penis envy for girls, castration terror for men.

Reviewed Freud's last 2 books for Morgan recently.[9] Shall now try to do Ford for him. Kenyon bit on Ford, I was glad to see, extremely poor.

Wrote a bit of reply to [Yvor] Winters.[10] Wot a guy. How he has bulldozed and four-flushed on just exactly nix in his mit. Good luck with Pound venture—public, relations. If Pound is willing to make statements of strongly pro-Semitic bent—plugging work of *specific* Jews, why he'll have a dozen medals in 6 months.[11]

[5]E.M. Forster (1879-1970), British novelist and essayist and honorary Fellow of King's College, Cambridge.

[6]In Lewis's *The Art of Being Ruled* (1926) there are two very short "chapters" entitled "The Role of Inversion in the War on the Intellect" and "The 'Homo' the Child of the 'Suffragette' ", in the second of which Lewis states: "To come, then, to the heart of the reason why it is worth while to spend so much time in analysing this fashion [i.e. 'male inversion, the latest child of feminism']: it is because in the contemporary world it is a part of the feminist revolution. It is as an integral part of feminism proper that it should be considered a gigantic phase of the sex war. The 'homo' is the legitimate child of the 'suffragette' " (p. 244). In his essay "Wyndham Lewis: Lemuel in Lilliput" (*St. Louis University Studies in Honor of St. Thomas Aquinas*, vol. 2, 1944), McLuhan says in a footnote that Lewis's *The Doom of Youth* (1932) "is an elaborately documented analysis of all aspects of 'feminism', and of its twin—homosexuality." *The Doom of Youth*—in which the latter part of the above passage is quoted (p. 206) but not discussed at length—is mainly an attack on the cult of youth.

[7]Lewis's comments on homosexuality did not ruin him. The allusion may be to what took place after the publication in 1932 of *The Doom of Youth*. (The title is a parody of Alec Waugh's 1917 bestseller *The Loom of Youth*.) Godfrey Winn and Alec Waugh were incensed by remarks made about them in two chapters called "Winn and Waugh" and "Three Score and Ten" (the title of a book by Waugh) and applied for an injunction against further sale. Though a judge found the book not to be libellous, it was withdrawn from circulation, after a small sale, and remaining copies were pulped.

[8]Karen Horney (1885-1952), German-born American psychiatrist—the founder in 1941 of the American Institute of Psychoanalysis, and author of *The Neurotic Personality of Our Time* (1937)—deviated from orthodox Freudian analysis in ascribing the origins of neuroses to environmental and cultural, rather than biological, factors.

[9]There is no record—in the *Hudson Review* or elsewhere—of this review.

[10]"The Difficulties of Ivor [*sic*] Winters or Rymer Redivus" (PAC, unpublished).

[11]In a letter of March 8, 1949 Giovanelli told McLuhan of a Jewish acquaintance who had phoned him at Pound's suggestion. He had written Pound begging for assurances of his "non-anti-Semitism" and Giovanelli showed him a letter he had from Pound about the "pro-Semitic" things he had done but warned him that Pound's anti-Semitism could not be easily disposed of. Giovanelli said he would like to see Pound defended by a Jew but feared the reaction of this acquaintance when he read the transcripts of Pound's wartime broadcasts from Rome.

What happened with Hugh [Kenner] and [James] Laughlin and you? Hugh has said nothing.

Looks like I'll go East for 3rd and 4th weeks of May. Spend some time with [Cleanth] Brooks I hope. And you *two too* but don't worry about my bedding there. By gum there *are* some things to talk over. Let's get together with Morgan *once*!

Supper coming up.

Corinne *very* tired yet.

Children getting to be more manageable and interesting.

As ever
Mac.

Margaret W. Giovanelli

To Felix Giovanelli

[St Michael's College]
Friday Nov 11/49

Dear Felix

Saw Bernie [Muller-Thym] off to N.Y. last night from Malton airport. What a wonderful thing an airport is *visually*. Especially with enough twilight left to provide a sky. Well Bernie is in *good* spirits. Able to communicate and enjoy himself and others a bit. And it was a great week. *You* my dear Felix would be much the better for a week here. Bernie has taken home some speaker equipment which should do wonders for his records. Be sure to see him soon.

Apropos of Vanguard, I dare not *write* Seon. But I'm beginning to feel that only hope lies in pestering Evelyn and Jim until they will yield to suggestion to let Seon do the whole thing.[1]

---

[1]The Vanguard Press, New York—whose editorial staff Giovanelli knew in his capacity as a translator—accepted *Typhon in America* (Typhon is a hundred-headed monster in Greek mythology) but sat on it; then they exasperated McLuhan with signs of editorial uncertainty. James Henle, the former president of Vanguard, was at this time a consultant, and Evelyn Shrifte, a line editor, was a colleague of Seon Givens in the editorial department. The anguish expressed in what follows reflects McLuhan's impatience with the editors' apparent unwillingness to come to terms with his commentaries, and his resistance to their efforts to convert the original deliberately outrageous satirical text into the more "linear" and restrained shorter version that was published in *Typhon's* reincarnation as *The Mechanical Bride*. Two weeks later, in a letter to Giovanelli of November 27, McLuhan complained: "They [the editors] are obsessed with the old monoplane, monolinear narrative and exposition, and conceive of intelligibility as the imposition of a single concept on diverse materials. To see it otherwise is for them to revise all they know and feel about most topics. And that is the crux. WHY they should suppose that they must see and agree with everything I say I do not know." Because the illustrations discussed in the text had to be reproduced from clippings, there was also uncertainty about design matters and permissions. Ernst Reichl was finally commissioned to design the book.

This business is beginning to affect my health. Sheer rage and frustration 1st declared itself physically at your apt. when I arrived with that "headache." A kind of "heart" condition associated with that same rage and "headache" occurs whenever I think about Evelyn. This can't go on. But they mustn't know. I really depends on you Felix to break up this log jam.

They would be delighted to think they were affecting my health. I mean that. Say nothing of that to Seon either. But ask Seon whether the strong suggestion from you or me to Jim to put the entire job in her hands would be good tactics.

Their plan is to tire me out. to drop the whole job. They hate the book. Its saleability or otherwise doesn't enter into the question any longer. (Apparently it's unheard of for author to get his own permissions.)

Please let's act fast.

I've asked Jim to send Evelyn here *at once* for final check over. I cant go to N.Y. until much too late for Spring publication.)

As ever
Mac.

Margaret W. Giovanelli

1950

To Walter J. Ong, S.J.

81 St Mary St
Toronto 5
Sept 23/50

Dear Walter

You may be seeing Mariana Thompson before Paris.[1] She expects to be in Oxford and London during October and has your address. She is working on a wonderful subject.

Hope you will keep me up to date with your off-prints Walter. They interest and help me much.

If you should ever encounter a copy of Christopher Hussey's *The Picturesque* (1927 Putnam London and N.Y.) snag same for me. Probably expensive. Also I'm in the market for McKerrow's *Nashe* and expect to have to pay 30–40–50 dollars for same.[2] Have asked my former supervisor F.P. Wilson of Oxford to explore market for mc. Be sure to look him up when you are at Oxford.

---

[1] Mariana Thompson was doing research in Paris for a Ph.D. thesis on Mallarmé and the Symbolists, which McLuhan was directing.

[2] Ronald B. McKerrow, ed., *The Works of Thomas Nashe* (1904–10).

Our Elizabeth arrived [was born] Aug. 2. John Peter 2 wks later![3] We had him for 10 days during the rail strike. So I'm *au courant* with Cambridge gossip now.

Grand visit here with John Pick in Aug. too. I'm doing a few jobs for him.

Hope to go to work on Thesis re-write during term this year. It has rewritten itself via my work on Eliot Joyce Pound Valéry etc. So I can now write it in double simultaneous perspective from Cratylus[4] to Joyce and from Valéry to the *Timaeus* [of Plato]. I can now say more in much less space while being more comprehensible. Much thanx for plug with Woodhouse.[5] [Cleanth] Brooks is dickering with Yale Press too. Hope to have final word from Brooks before talking with Woodhouse. It will probably be Tor. U. Press.[6] Doesn't much matter I think.

Eric is now in grade 5 at Cathedral Choir School where he learns music at least. No school teaches anything . . . in the grades any more . . . [*words lost in slitting air-letter open*] much to do at the moment. More soon Walter.

As ever in Christ

Walter J. Ong   Mac.

---

[3]The novelist and teacher John Peter, who was born in South Africa, received his Ph.D. from Cambridge around this time and then taught English at the University of Manitoba and the University of Victoria, British Columbia. He died in Victoria.

[4]The *Cratylus* dialogue of Plato. Cratylus was a contemporary of Socrates and teacher of Plato.

[5]A.S.P. Woodhouse (1895–1964) was head of the English Department of University College, University of Toronto, and of the School of Graduate Studies. He had taught at the University of Manitoba from 1923 to 1929.

[6]See note 2 (bottom), page 497.

1951

The following letter refers to the completion of McLuhan's The Mechanical Bride: Folklore of Industrial Man *(1951), his first book and the first widely published presentation of his many insights into the sources and meanings of popular culture. It contains 59 concise, illuminating, and subtle articles—in which irony and criticism are elegantly subdued—on comic strips, advertisements, and other promotional imagery of the American press, all with playfully chosen illustrations, through which "many thousands of the best-trained individual minds have made it a full-time business to get inside the collective public mind", bringing about a "condition of public helplessness". His preface continues: "Why not assist the public to observe consciously the drama which is intended to operate upon it unconsciously? . . . Poe's sailor [in "A Descent into the Maelström"] saved himself by studying the action of the whirlpool and by co-operating with it. The present book likewise makes few attempts to attack the very considerable currents and pressures set up around us today by the mechanical agencies of the press, radio, movies, and advertising. It does attempt to set the reader at the centre of the revolving picture created by these affairs where he may observe the action that is in progress and in which everybody is involved." In an undated letter to his mother, probably written in the fall of 1952, McLuhan says he has decided that* The Mechanical Bride *"is really a new form of science fiction, with ads and comics cast as characters. Since my object is to show the community in action rather than* prove *anything, it can indeed be regarded as a new kind of novel."*

To Ezra Pound

81 St. Mary St.
Toronto 5
Jan 5/51

Dear Pound

Yrs to hnd as a very great letter writer has been known to begin his communiqués.[1] Now that Harcourt Brace has come across with that volume yrs will I hope be to hand for many readers.[2] I rather think this vol. will do much to get your poetry read. Kenner's book will do something too.[3]

This year I have a very 1st rate group of grad students who are really latching on to contemp. poetry, and some of whom are stunned at contact with yours. They can't get over the way they've been kept away from it by pedagogic devices and pretexts.

Vanguard Press have now been 6 years mucking about with my book on industrial folklore (a sottisier[4] among other things) castrating and textbookizing a job which originally was sprightly and not unworthy of Wyndham Lewis to whom it owes much.[5] Publishers offices now are crammed with homosexuals who have a horror of any writing with balls to it.

Well, Kenner did forward your letter with suggestion we launch at least a mimeographed weekly sheet.[6] As matter of fact I had already taken steps to arrange internatl. copyright for same, before he wrote. Now I have replied to him with detailed queries and suggestions.

I don't know whether you have heard about the present crowd at Mass. Inst.

---

[1] "Yrs to h[a]nd": McLuhan's father often began his letters with this phrase
[2] *The Selected Letters of Ezra Pound 1907–1941* (1950) edited by D.D. Paige.
[3] Hugh Kenner, *The Poetry of Ezra Pound* (1951), which did indeed stimulate Pound studies. The dedication reads: "To Marshall McLuhan, A catalogue, his jewels of conversation".
[4] *sottisier* (Fr.), a collection of foolish sayings.
[5] Part III of Lewis's *The Doom of Youth* (1932) contains "A Gallery of Exhibits" made up of newspaper headlines and extracts, with comments by Lewis—illustrating what Lewis saw as the "class-war of 'Young and Old' "—that prefigures McLuhan's treatment of advertisements and other examples of popular culture in *The Mechanical Bride*. Lewis discusses advertising—"The spirit of advertisement and boost lives and has its feverish being in a world of hyperbolic suggestion"—in Book I, Chapter II of *Time and Western Man* (1928).
[6] This plan was not carried out, though it anticipates the "Media Logs" McLuhan occasionally sent out to friends and acquaintances beginning in the late fifites.

of Tech.? They show more promise than all the literary blokes on this continent. They are what you and Lewis used to refer to as "serious characters". At any rate my idea is to by-pass the literary cliques and characters altogether. To send sheets to 30–40 serious characters personally known to me, and to let them retype and pass on sheet to anybody they know and/or to feed back comments, idiograms etc.

Object of sheet to open up intercommunication between several fields. To open eyes and ears of people in physics, anthropology, history, etc. etc. to relevant developments in the arts which concern them so that they in turn can contribute their newest insights to the arts.

Another procedure, to ideogram important new books in such wise as to indicate precise bearings of techniques involved on other fields. To ideogram single issues of *Life*, *Vogue*, *Satevepost* occasionally in order to indicate interrelations between popular and serious culture.

As for tone, to assume good will and right appetite. There is more of these now than a decade ago, because even the bastards are aware of nearness of ultimate breakdown.

S[ergei] Eisenstein's *Film Form*[: *Essays in Film Theory*] (Harcourt Brace 1949) excellent on importance of Jap NOH for cinema and of ideogram as basic grammer of *montage*.

Scholastic *article* form as used by Aquinas [e.g. in his *Summa Theologica*] is ideogrammic. Each article a short intellectual drama. Only Aquinas ever got it into that form.

My object is to learn the grammar and general language of 20 major fields in order to help on an orchestra among the arts. cf. S.Giedion's Mechanization Takes Command [1948] as sample of how I should like to set up a school of literary studies. Basic modes of cognition on this continent not linguistic but technological. Artistic experience comes to the young only via that channel. Must work with that *at first*. Present procedure is to slap an alien culture *over* the actual one. The real one is killed and the alien one is worn as a party mask. You and Eisenstein have shown me how to make use of Chinese ideogram to elicit the natural modes of American sensibility. But I've just begun. Feeling my way.

Have discovered the meaning and value of landscape in this connection. *Paysage intérieur* à la Rimbaud Pound Joyce as means of unifying and digesting any kind of experience. Should have got to it 20 yrs ago if I hadn't had the rotten luck to bog down in English lit at university.

Students *get* your Cantos at once when alerted to landscape mode. Am publishing on this soon.[7]

Blessings to you and Mrs Pound in this New Year Marshall McLuhan.

Lilly Library, Indiana University

---

[7]Marshall McLuhan, "The Aesthetic Moment in Landscape Poetry" in *English Literature Essays, 1951* (1952), edited by Alan Downe. It was included in *The Interior Landscape: The Literary Cricitism of Marshall McLuhan* (1969) edited by Eugene McNamara. See also page 224, note 3.

To Ezra Pound

81 St Mary St
Toronto 5
[January] 51

Dear Pound

McLuhan has corn-sidered usury and noted certain obsessions of his contemporaries which make it endemic.[1] Always struck by Aquinas's definition of incest as "avarice of the emotions". That sets usury in universal perspective of fear and hatred. Incest the impulse of the threatened patriarch. Usury the impulse of the fearful citizen.

Current illusion is that science has abolished all natural laws. Nature now pays 5 million %. Applied science now the master usurer. To hell with our top soil. We can grow potatoes on the moon tomorrow. How you goan to expose that while there is still human "life" on the planet?

2nd war produced great discovery of war as new way of life. Financial pages simply chortling these days over a prosperity rooted in 3rd war. Ordinary guy eats this up. Total war = total security he figures. THAT is the scale of imbecility now current.

Life Jan 1/51 War assets issue. Pin-up girls featured as major asset. I have *tried*, in forthcoming (March) *Mechanical Bride* to devise a technique for elucidating this scene. It can't be satirized. Trouble with duffers like Geo. Orwell[2] is that they satirize something that happened 50 yrs ago as a threat of the *future*! Effect is narcotic. Regards.

Lilly Library, Indiana University

[1] The economic theories of H.C. Douglas, the inventor of social credit, of Silvio Gesell (1862–1930), a German monetary reformer, and others produced in Pound a long-lasting obsession, beginning in the 1920s, with monetary reform, and accounted for repeated denunciations in his writings of usury (credit capitalism)—notably in *Canto XLV* ("With *Usura . . .*").

[2] George Orwell (1903–50), English essayist and political satirist, whose most famous books are *Animal Farm* (1945) and the anti-Utopian novel *Nineteen Eighty-four* (1949). In a 1977 interview in *Maclean's* (March 7), McLuhan said that *1984* "was not a prediction at all. It's nostalgia from 1934. All Utopias are rear-view mirrors. . . . 'New Speak', for heavens sake, was *Time* magazine. He [Orwell] made all those things push up a bit into a tension and called it the future."

The following letter—the only letter extant that McLuhan wrote to Harold Adams Innis (see page 208, note 2), his colleague at the University of Toronto—is of particular interest as a response to Innis's recently published Empire and Communications *(1950), which influenced McLuhan greatly. (For example, McLuhan's famous aphorism "the medium is the message"—by which he means that the medium through which information is presented, with its power of altering (exaggerating, reducing, distorting, etc.) content, and its subliminal effect on the user, are as important as, or more important than, the information itself—was perhaps anticipated by the germ of the following concept in Innis's Introduction: "The significance of a basic medium to its civilization is difficult to appraise since the means of appraisal are influenced by the media, and indeed the fact of appraisal appears to be peculiar to certain types of media. A change in the type of medium implies a change in the type of appraisal and hence makes it difficult for one civilization to understand another.") In attempting to suggest "the roles of different media with reference to civilizations and to contrast the civilizations",* Empire and Communications *ranges through those of Egypt, Sumer, Greece, Rome, and Europe; it discusses the effects on them of the oral tradition, parchment, papyrus, paper, and the printing press in disseminating informa-tion, and the impetus these media provided for cultural change. McLuhan, in* The Gutenberg Galaxy *(1962)—which he refers to as a "footnote" to Innis's work (page 50)—extends the subject matter of* Empire and Communications *and of Innis's* The Bias of Communication *(1951), concentrating on the effect of the media on the senses rather than on social organization.* The Gutenberg Galaxy *also reflects the influence of Innis's condensed, elliptical style, which leans heavily on long quotations and darting references.*

To Harold Adams Innis

St. Michaels College
March 14/51[1]

Dear Innis

Thanks for the lecture re-print. This makes an opportunity for me to mention my interest in the work you are doing in communication study in general. I think there are lines appearing in *Empire and Communications* [1950], for example, which suggest the possibility of organizing an entire school of studies. Many of the ancient language theories of the Logos type which you cite in [*Empire and Communications*[2]] for their bearings on government and society have recurred and amalgamated themselves today under the auspices of anthropology and social psychology. Working concepts of "collective consciousness" in advertizing agen-cies have in turn given salience and practical effectiveness to these "magical" notions of language.

But it was most of all the esthetic discoveries of the symbolists since Rimbaud and Mallarmé (developed in English by Joyce, Eliot, Pound, Lewis and Yeats) which have served to recreate in contemporary consciousness an awareness of the *potencies* of language such as the Western world has not experienced in 1800 years.

---

[1]The manuscript of this letter is headed in the upper-left corner: "Rewrite of letter for mimeo-graph HMM". The original letter was written some weeks previously because it was acknowledged by Innis on February 26 (with apologies for not doing so earlier). Innis said he had been "very much interested" in McLuhan's letter and that he would like to have it typed and circulated to "one or two of our mutual friends", adding that he wished to receive the "mimeographed sheet" referred to. Innis wrote over the body of the letter: "Memorandum on humanities".

[2]Added by Innis.

Mallarmé saw the modern press as a magical institution born of technology.[3] The discontinuous juxtaposition of unrelated items made necessary by the influx of news stories from every quarter of the world, created, he saw, a symbolic landscape of great power and importance. (He used the word "symbol" in the strict Greek sense sym-ballein, to pitch together, physically and musically). He saw at once that the modern press was not a rational form but a magical one so far as communication was concerned. Its very technological form was bound to be *efficacious* far beyond any informative purpose. Politics were becoming musical, jazzy, magical.

The same symbolist perception applied to cinema showed that the *montage* of images was basically a return via technology to age-old picture language. S. Eisenstein's *Film Form* and *Film Technique* explore the relations between modern developments in the arts and Chinese ideogram, pointing to the common basis of ideogram in modern art[,] science and technology.

One major discovery of the symbolists which had the greatest importance for subsequent investigation was their notion of the learning process as a labyrinth of the senses and faculties whose retracing provided the *key* to all arts and sciences (basis of myth of Daedalus, basic for the dreams and schemes of Francis Bacon, and, when transferred by [Giovanni Battista] Vico[4] to philology and history of culture, it also forms the basis of modern historiography, archaeology, psychology and artistic procedures alike.[)] Retracing becomes in modern historical scholarship the technique of reconstruction. The technique which Edgar Poe first put to work in his detective stories.[5] In the arts this discovery has had all those astonishing results which have seemed to separate the ordinary public from what it regards as esoteric magic. From the point of view of the artist however the business of art is no longer the communication of thoughts or feelings which are to be conceptually ordered, but a direct participation in an experience. The whole tendency of modern communication whether in the press, in advertizing or in the high arts is towards participation in a process, rather than apprehension of concepts. And this major revolution, intimately linked to technology, is one whose consequences have not begun to be studied although they have begun to be felt.

One immediate consequence, it seems to me, has been the decline of literature. The hypertrophy of letter-press, at once the cause and effect of universal literacy, has produced a spectacular decline of attention to the printed or written word.

[3]McLuhan read Stéphane Mallarmé—who saw an art form in the daily newspaper—in the *Oeuvres Complètes* (Gallimard, 1945), in which the press is discussed in "Etalages" (pp. 375-6), "Le Livre, Instrument spirituel" (p. 378 ff.), and "Deuil" (pp. 523-4). See the first article in *The Mechanical Bride*: "Front Page", opposite a reproduction of the April 20, 1950 front page of *The New York Times*. Here McLuhan says that "any paper today is a collective work of art, a daily 'book' of industrial man, an Arabian night's entertainment. . . . Notoriously it is the visual technique of a Picasso, the literary technique of James Joyce." See also McLuhan's essay "Joyce, Mallarmé and the Press" (which first appeared in *The Sewanee Review*, vol. 62, no. 1, Winter 1954) in Eugene McNamara, ed., *The Interior Landscape: The Literary Criticism of Marshall McLuhan* (1969).

[4]For Vico, see page 339, note 3.

[5]See page 271, note 4.

As you have shown in *Empire and Communications*, ages of literature have been few and brief in human history. The present literary epoch has been of exceptional duration—400 years. There are many symptoms that it is at an end. The comic book for example has been seen as a degenerate literary form instead of as a nascent pictorial and dramatic form which has sprung from the new stress on visual-auditory communication in the magazines, the radio and television. The young today cannot follow narrative but they are alert to drama. They cannot bear description but they love landscape and action.

If literature is to survive as a scholastic discipline except for a very few people, it must be by a transfer of its techniques of perception and judgement to these new media. The new media, which are already much more constitutive educationally than those of the class-room, must be inspected and discussed in the class-room if the class-room is to continue at all except as a place of detention. As a teacher of literature it has long seemed to me that the *functions* of literature cannot be maintained in present circumstances without radical alteration of the procedures of teaching. Failure in this respect relegated Latin and Greek to the specialist; and English literature has already become a category rather than an interest in school and college.

As mechanical media have popularized and enforced the presence of the arts on all people it becomes more and more necessary to make studies of the function and effect of communication on society. Present ideas of such effects are almost entirely in terms of mounting or sagging sales curves resulting from special campaigns of commercial education. Neither the agencies nor the consumers know anything about the social or cultural effects of this education.

Deutch's [*sic*] interesting pamphlet on communication is thoroughly divorced from any sense of the social functions performed by communication.[6] He is typical of a school likewise in his failure to study the matter in the *particular*. He is the technician interested in power but uncritical and unconcerned with social effect. The diagnosis of his type is best found, so far as I know, in Wyndham Lewis's *The Art of Being Ruled*. That pamphlet [*sic*] is probably the most radical political document since Machiavelli's *Prince*. But whereas Machiavelli was concerned with the use of society as raw material for the arts of power, Lewis reverses the perspective and tries to discern the human shape once more in a vast technological landscape which has been ordered on Machiavellian lines.

The fallacy in the Deutsch-Wiener[7] approach is its failure to understand the techniques and functions of the traditional arts as the essential type of all human communication. It is instead a dialectical approach born of technology and quite unable of itself to see beyond or around technology. The Medieval schoolmen ultimately ended up on the same dialectical reef.

[6]Karl Deutsch's paper (written for a 1951 conference), "Communication in Self-governing Organizations: Notes on Autonomy, Freedom and Authority in the Growth of Social Groups", was published in Lyman Bryson, ed., *Conference on Science, Philosophy and Religion in Their Relation to the Democratic Way of Life. 12 Session. Freedom and Authority in Our Time* (1953).

[7]Norbert Weiner, *The Human Use of Human Beings: Cybernetics and Society* (1950).

As Easterbrook may have told you I have been considering an experiment in communication which is to follow the lines of this letter in suggesting means of linking a variety of specialized fields by what might be called a method of esthetic analysis of their common features. This method has been used by my friend Siegfried Giedion in *Space, Time and Architecture* and in *Mechanization Takes Command*. What I have been considering is a single mimeographed sheet to be sent out weekly or fortnightly to a few dozen people in different fields, at first illustrating the underlying unities of form which exist where diversity is all that meets the eye. Then, it is hoped there will be a feedback of related perception from various readers which will establish a continuous flow.

It seems obvious to me that Bloor St.[8] is the one point in this University where one might establish a focus of the arts and sciences. And the organizing concept would naturally be "Communication Theory and practice". A simultaneous focus of current and historical forms. Relevance to be given to selection of areas of study by dominant artistic and scientific modes of the particular period. Arts here used as providing criteria, techniques of observation, and bodies of recorded, *achieved*, experience. Points of departure but also return.

For example the actual techniques of economic study today seem to me to be of genuine relevance to anybody who wishes to grasp the best in current poetry and music. And vice versa. There is a real, living unity in our time, as in any other, but it lies submerged under a superficial hubbub of sensation. Using Frequency Modulation techniques one can slice accurately through such interference, whereas Amplitude Modulation leaves you bouncing on all the currents.

University of Toronto Archives   Marshall McLuhan

[8]The Economics Building at 273 Bloor Street West, Toronto. It originally housed McMaster University and is now occupied by the Royal Conservatory of Music.

To Ezra Pound

81 St Mary St
Toronto 5
June 12/51

Dear Pound

In Harvard's Poetry room 2 weeks ago I heard your readings from Seafarer, Altaforte, H.S. Maub, Canto 56 etc.[1] Seafarer and Altaforte would make a superb disc which should be made available at once. It would sell and it would promote the right kind of interest in your poetry.

Listening to Canto 56 I heard many rhythms which Eliot picked up for his later poetry.

[1]"The Seafarer" (*Ripostes*, 1912), "Sestina: Altaforte", and *Hugh Selwyn Mauberley* (1920) were included in *Personae: The Collected Poems of Ezra Pound* (1926). Canto 56 was published in *Cantos LII–LXXI* in the US in 1940. The recording was made on May 17, 1939 in Sever Hall, Harvard University, for the Harvard Vocarium Series.

I am not at all aware of your own views about recorded readings, but can speak for several beside myself in saying that adequacy of rendering is of much less account than the authoritative stress or intonation which the poet's voice provides. The poet's own voice provides an entry to his world which is otherwise hard to discover.

Myself, I have the knack of reproducing other peoples' voices. So I've been reading Seafarer etc in your style to friends here since my return. They have found it an exciting and altogether unexpected kind of experience.

Also, I doubt whether there are half a dozen people in U.S.A. who have the faintest idea of how to manage the polyphonyic and other effects of your Cantos. Your reading of Canto 56 opened my ears.

Professional readers are useless because untrained in poetry.

Your reading of H.S. Maub. and Propertius disappointed me a little.[2] I had myself always heard in those verses the airiest lyric irony which your reading denied to them somewhat.

The effect of your *Letters* has been considerable in extending your public and in awakening a serious interest in your work.

I've been doing some work on the development of landscape technique (exterior and interior landscape) before and since Rimbaud.[3] Also I'm interested in such analogies with modern poetry as that provided by the vacuum tube. The latter can tap a huge reservoir of electric energy, picking it up as a very weak impulse. Then it can shape it and amplify it to major intensity. Technique of allusion as you use it (situational analogies) seems comparable to this type of circuit. Allusion not as ornament but as precise means of making available total energy of any previous situation or culture. Shaping and amplifying it for current use.

Most cordial regards to you and Mrs Pound.

Lilly Library, Indiana University

[2]*Homage to Sextus Propertius* (1917) was also included in *Personae*.

[3]McLuhan had previously mentioned this article-in-progress to Pound in his letter of January 5, 1951 (see page 218, note 7). In a letter to Pound of August 2, 1951 (not included), McLuhan wrote: "Work done in last 3 years on techniques of Flaubert, Rimbaud, Laforgue has opened my eyes for first time to the ways in which you, Joyce, Eliot have used 'landscapes' to achieve many of your effects. . . ."

To Ezra Pound

81 St. Mary St
Toronto 5
June 18/51

Dear Pound

Great news indeed! And well timed.[1] Because Huntington Cairns is still here.[2] So I told him and he will go into action at once with Conrad Aiken who is in charge of the records at Lib. of Cong.[3] Aiken is in the Maine woods at present. But the master discs were sent to Lib. of Congress from Harvard some years since.[4]

One of the Pisan Cantos ought to join Canto 56. The complexity and precision of orchestration in the Pisan Cantos would be revealed at once by your reading.

No, a professional reader would be pointless. *After* your reading had educated a public to the range and variety of the rhythms I can imagine a professional reader latching on and doing an interesting job. But the pedagogic value of a poet's own rendering is far in excess of any of the casual amenities provided by the professional voice. Especially in the present state of affairs where professionals are quite unable to understand the most ordinary word arrangements.

Had a most agreeable chat with Cairns Sunday. Told him of a group of Chinese priests who would like to establish a college of some kind in Canada or U.S.A.

They are a French trained community. Most of them have studied for several years in Rome and Paris. They speak English, French, Italian, Latin and know Greek. One of them has just finished his work here at the Medieval Institute. They are well aware of their responsibilities in bringing East to West at the present time. But I fear they lack political savvy, and that I lack competence to suggest exactly how they should proceed. Cairns is interested and will help, but how much he can do I don't know.

There is no chair of Chinese Studies at U. of Toronto. But there was until 2 years ago. So I'll try to find some local people to talk it over with. Toronto has a large Chinese community. Used to have a full time Chinese Theatre.

Excited to hear from Cairns about your new translations from Chinese.

Most cordial regards to you and Mrs Pound.

McLuhan

Lilly Library, Indiana University

[1] Pound had written (June 1951): "I will permit making of disc for sale of CANTO 56, Seafarer, Mauberley . . ."

[2] Huntingdon Cairns (1904–85), American lawyer and author who was at this time secretary-treasurer of, and general counsel for, The National Gallery of Art, Washington (1943–65). In the letter referred to in note 4 below, Pound said: "Cairns is perfectly useless re/ any real progress." See also the next letter.

[3] Conrad Aiken (1889–1973), American poet and novelist, had been elected in 1947 a Fellow on American Letters of the Library of Congress and in 1950 accepted the Chair of Poetry at the Library, with the title of Poetry Consultant.

[4] Pound's reply (June 20, 1951) was: "Don't be a NASS 'go into action with Aiken'/go into Aches with inaction. and why the HELL did Haaavud send discs to Kungruss? NOTHING doing with the Lib of Cong / call that OFF."

To Ezra Pound

Dear Pound

Cairns did strike me as a rather tepid dish of tea, but he came straight from you to me. That put the OK on his credentials for me.

I had been told a year ago that the master discs of your readings had gone from Harvard to Congress. A student of mine at Harvard sent that word to me. It may not be true. I'll check at once.

Cairns said he had organized the poet's record division in the Lib. of Cong.[1] So he seemed a suitable man for arranging the next move. Especially since he was personally KEEN on getting your records published. (This he discussed with me before your letter came).

Cairns said he had dined with Lewis recently and was getting him 3000 bucks to finish the Childermass.[2] Do you think a dictaphone will alter L's style for good or ill?[3]

I agree with your analysis of Foundation administrators and the beaneries.[4] As for the first, the Foundations, they are tax-evasion devices. Those who administer them are stooges chosen by public relations bureaus whose idea it was to set up the Rock-Gugg-Ros-Boll [Rockefeller-Guggenheim-Ros?-Bollingen]. Naturally the Pub. Relations counsellors hire flunkey brains.

I have *tried* to get an exposé of this situation published.

The beaneries are on their knees to these gents. They regard them as Santa Claus. They will do "research" on anything that Santa Claus approves. They will think his thoughts as long as he will pay the bill for getting them before the public signed by the professorry-rat. "Publish or Perish" is the beanery motto. To get published they must be dull, and stupid and harmless.

Hook that situation to the split between teacher and administrator *within* the beaneries. The very character of bureaucratic administration automatically screens out all those who are capable of doing any other sort of work. The teachers are hated by the administrators, and despised as deluded suckers cut off from the

---

[1]The Library of Congress has never had a "poet's record division". However, Huntingdon Cairns, as an officer of the Bollingen Foundation, had proposed in 1946 a contribution of $10,500 to the Library for a project to make phonograph recordings of contemporary American and British poets reading their poetry.

[2]Lewis planned to "continue" his novel *The Childermass* (1928) with two more novels to form a trilogy called *The Human Age* (see page 238, note 1). There is no record of Cairns' having obtained money for him to do this. However, in 1951 Lewis signed a profitable contract with the BBC for the dramatization of *The Human Age; The Childermass*, adapted by D.G. Bridson, was broadcast on June 18, 1951.

[3]Lewis became blind in April 1951. That month the Royal Literary Fund gave him £100 for a dictaphone, but he could not use it. He wrote in longhand—on a board with a wire across it to keep the lines straight—about thirty widely spaced words to a page.

[4]"beaneries": Pound's epithet for universities.

central pap of our culture. An administrator in a bureaucratic world is a man who can feel big by merging his non-entity in an abstraction. A real person in touch with real things inspires terror in him.

Now, the teachers. They are people of lowly origins and no cultural background or tradition. They take a dim view of themselves as persons out of touch with the extrovert drives of their own world. They have no tradition which would enable them to be critics of their own world. They have a temperament which prefers a quiet simple life, but no insights into anything at all. They distrust any of their number who has ideas.

45 years ago things were like this, but *less* so.

Nowadays there is no conversation at all. Teachers distrust talk as much as business men. It is a mirror in which they too readily see their own vacuous plight. So they won't have it. The 1st element is mud.

As for the fifth, it is space. How are the Kenners and McLuhans going to co-operate 3500 miles apart on salaries that won't pay postage?

This is not set down in pique, nor extenuation. I am an intellectual thug who has been slowly accumulating a private arsenal with every intention of using it. In a mindless age every insight takes on the character of a lethal weapon. Every man of good will is the enemy of society. Lewis saw that years ago. His "America and Cosmic Man" was an H-bomb let off in the desert. Impact nil. We resent or ignore such intellectual bombs. We prefer to compose human beings into bombs and explode political and social entities. Much more fun. Lewis clears the air of fug. We want to get rid of people entirely. And it is necessary to admire the skill and thoroughness with which we have made our preparations to do this. I am not of the "we" party. I should prefer to de-fuse this gigantic human bomb by starting a dialogue somewhere on the side-lines to distract the trigger-men, or to needle the somnambulists. In London 1910 you faced various undesirable states of mind. Since then the word has been used to effect a universal hypnosis. How are words to be used to unweave the spell of print? Of radio commercials and "news"-casts? I'm working on *that* problem. The word is now the cheapest and most universal drug.

Consider the effect of modern machinery in imposing rhythm on human thought and feeling. Archaic man got inside the thing that terrified him—tiger, bear, wolf—and made it his totem god. To-day we get inside the machine. It is inside us. We in it. Fusion. Oblivion. Safety. Now the human machines are geared to smash one another. You can't shout warnings or encouragement to these machines. First there has to be a retracing process. A reduction of the machine to human form. Circe only turned men into swine. Our problem is tougher.

Ever hear modern radio quiz program. The quiz-master sez every 3 seconds: "Are you ready for the next question?" The 2 dollar, the 4 dollar, the 64 dollar question? Only machines get *ready* for questions. The knobs have to be turned. Then comes the slug for the slot. Check on the contemporary pollster-geisters. Check on the stench from the collective ad noise. Little Bo-peep wants to lose her B.O. She isn't interested in her academic sheep no more no more. New deodorants fix you so'se your dog won't ever recognize you again. The cube root of fug-all.

Cordially
McLuhan

Lilly Library, Indiana University

To Ezra Pound

81 St Mary St
Toronto 5
July 24/51

Dear Pound

Library of Congress does not have master discs of *Seafarer* etc. readings. Never has had 'em. Harvard has them. Always has. Rumor I had received was false. Harvard is eager to proceed to actuation. And it is certainly time that the lugubrious notes of the Rev. Mr. Eliot[1] were dislodged by your renderings of these wonderful poems. It will do as much as your recently published *Letters* to awaken perception about the *source* of so much that has occurred in poetry in this century.

As I mentioned before, it was only hearing your rendering that made Eliot's debt to you unmistakable. Yet I had long been aware of that debt, in theory. Eliot's own way of alluding to his debt to you is maddeningly capable of killing any further curiosity in the matter. He never cites a passage or a line. The affair is left vague and general.[2] Your reading will end that state of numbness.

Interested in *Vigils*[3] which you sent me. Shall pass them on to others unless you indicate wish to have copies back.

Haven't read Frobenius German work but am curious in view of some recent books to know whether he illuminates the question of the Cumaean Gates, the ring wall cities, and Peripolesis-periplum, the Troy game etc. W.F. Jackson Knight[4] and R.W. Cruttwell[5] have been putting out comments on Virgil and these matters. They don't mention Frobenius.

From Joyce's *Stephen Hero*[6] I gather that he had with the combined aid of Aristotle, Dante and Rimbaud decided that the poetic process was nothing else

---

[1]An ironic reference to T.S. Eliot: see note 2 below.

[2]Though perhaps "vague and general", Eliot's debt to Pound was recognized as fully as was appropriate in the context of T.S. Eliot, "Ezra Pound", *Poetry*, LXVIII (September 1946). Acknowledging "one's greatest personal debt at once", Eliot cited Pound's efforts in making possible the publication of his first volume, *Prufrock and Other Observations* (1917), and later "Pound's critical genius" that acted upon "the manuscript of a sprawling, chaotic poem called *The Waste Land*, which left his hands, reduced to about half its size, in the form in which it appears in print."

[3]In a letter of June 27, 1951, Pound had written: "also 'Vigil', in Delhi might print McL's analysis of so called civilization (sending sample copy)".

[4]W.F. Jackson Knight, *Accentual Symmetry in Vergil* (1939).

[5]R.W. Cruttwell, *Virgil's Mind at Work: An Analysis of the Symbolism of the Aeneid* (1946).

[6]Part of a first draft of James Joyce's *Portrait of the Artist as a Young Man* (1916), *Stephen Hero* was published in 1944.

than the process of cognition. That sensation itself was *imitation* since the *forms* of things in our sensations are already in a new *matter*. Namely a human organ. So that the first stage of apprehension is already poetic. *Dolce stil nuovo*[7] based on this learning process as poetic process? Suggests that the impressionists were the first since Dante to slough off rationalized and rhetorical incrustations which did service in lieu of perception. Of course you have said this before.

Your revocation of recording OK concerned Library of Congress. Now that only Harvard is involved how do you see the matter? Most cordial regards to you and Mrs Pound

McLuhan

24 July 51

Apropos of a Canadian *Vers Demain*.[8] Quite interested. Where's the verse?

As for publication difficulties. Looks like Vanguard Press will finally let my Folklore of Industrial Man out of five year cold storage this Fall. Shall see about further essays in that direction after that. It is a book which would do well in France or Italy. Neurotica magazine has published some of it.[9]

Glad to have had a letter from La Drière.[10] Shall see him in N.Y. at end of August I hope.

Bread and butter assignments have me tied this summer

McLuhan

Lilly Library, Indiana Univ.

[7]"The sweet new style" (a phrase of Dante's) in Italian lyric poetry. A reaction against the conventions of the Provençal troubadors and the tradition of courtly love in the thirteenth century, it favoured simplicity and sincerity in expressing love and sorrow. The leading exponents of this "new style" were Cavalcanti and Dante.

[8]In a letter of June 27, 1951 Pound wrote: "I take it Mc is too high a brow fer the kenuk "Vers Demain".

[9]Marshall McLuhan, "Folklore of Industrial Man", *Neurotica* 8, Spring 1951. This is an abstract by Gershon Legman of the then forthcoming *Mechanical Bride*.

[10]Professor James Craig LaDrière of the Catholic University of America, Washington, had previously taught at Saint Louis University. (He, Otto Bird, McLuhan, and others were nominal members of a committee advising on the Square Dollar Series, which set out to publish little-known works considered by Pound to be essential for students.) In November 1956 the Washington *Star* published a letter from LaDrière in defence of Pound.

1952

To Elsie McLuhan

[81 St Mary St, Toronto
January 22, 1952]
Tuesday night

Dearest Mother

Cera just left.[1] He brought one of his best pictures to us. Had made the frame himself specially. Painted frame beautifully for the picture. Betty Trott, his friend who introduced us, came to supper. She has just left too. The children love her. So does Corinne.

Cera came at 8 before kids were in bed. He is a lot of fun. Very very lively and facetiously egotistical in his talk. A walking mass of contradictions, paradoxes and condundrums [*sic*] which he likes to tumble out for everybody's amusement.

Eric's birthday party came off yesterday after school.[2] Whew! They had fun. And today they had a set of quizzes.

Went to college for lunch today. Father Bondy tells me that [Prime Minister Louis] St. Laurent will be speaker at Arts banquet here March 16. This is centenary year for St Mike's.

Am enclosing D. L. Coles note to me. He is a chap much like myself at his years, panting to get to Cambridge. And it appears that he will make it.

Apropos of getting Gilson to write a plug for *The Bride*, he said to Fr. Shook, you write it, I'll sign it. So I wrote:

"An important and entertaining analysis of the effects of technology on daily life."

Point is to get his name into an ad. Should sell 2000 copies if put in Catholic papers. Copp Clark here express amazement at sales in Canada. They were sure from the 1st it would not sell. Wish I could get out a school edition. Money is in that quarter.

Your valentine gift is en route!

All our love
Marshall and Corinne

[1]René Cera (b. 1895) was born in Nice, France, where he was trained in architecture and painting until he was called to the French Army (1914–18). In 1925 he participated as an exhibitor in the International Exhibition of Modern Architecture held in Paris. In 1928 he went to Toronto as architectural designer for the T. Eaton Company and designed the detail and fittings for the main floor of the Eaton's College Street store (1928–30), an architecturally distinguished building that was notable for its Art Deco design elements. Cera remained with Eaton's as chief architect until his retirement to Lenox, Mass., in 1960. After becoming a widower for the second time, he married his Toronto friend Betty Trott in 1966. In March 1969 he painted a striking mural, "Pied Pipers All"—having as its theme TV in action—for the seminar room in McLuhan's Centre for Culture and Technology.

[2]Though Eric's birthday was on Saturday, January 19, the party was held on Monday after school.

To Ezra Pound

81 St Mary St
Toronto 5
July 16/52

Dear Pound

Reading your Calling Card pamphlet recently very grateful for your brief note on the Sanscrit mentors of T.S.E. and your own studies in Layamon's Brut, Catullus etc.[1] I know exactly what you mean. But I found out the hard way. Too late. Your own tips are always exact. But they are of little help to the unitiated. Once a man has got onto technique as the key in communications it's different. But somehow the bugbear of *content* forbids that anybody be interested in *technique as content*. For example you, Eliot and Joyce use as central guide in all matters of letters, sounds, phrases situations the whole traditional lore on the diverse labyrinths of the Cumaean Gates. Rock labyrinth. Water labyrinth and so on. It's taken me a long time to get wised up. Why couldn't one of you have given some tips on *this* matter 30 years ago? I can see of course how Yeats never did develop the mastery of these labyrinths that you Joyce and Eliot have done. Is there some secret cult knowledge in these matters. Masonic? Something no critic should know?

I'm writing a book on "The End of the Gutenberg Era"[2] Main sections: The Inventions of Writing-Alphabet. Transfer of auditory to visual.

	Arrest for contemplation of thought and cognitive process.
	Permits overthrow of sophist— rhetoric-oral tradition
Invention of printing.	Mechanization of writing.
	Study becomes solitary.
	Decline of painting music etc in book countries.
	Cult of book and house and study.
	Cult of vernacular because of commercial possibilities
	Republicanism via association of simple folk on equal terms with "mighty dead".

---

[1] *A Visiting Card* (1952)—a translation of Pound's *Carta da Visita* (Rome, 1942)—is a booklet published by Peter Russell in England as Number Four in a series called *Money Pamphlets by £*. In it Pound writes: "Eliot would recognize, I imagine, a greater influence of Lanman and Woods, his professors of Sansk[r]it, than the superficial influence of the French poets. And I consider the hours spent with Layamon's *Brut*, or copying a prose translation of Catullus by W. MacDaniel; Ibbotson's instruction in Anglo-Saxon, or W.P. Shepard's on Dante and the troubadours of Provence—more important than any contemporary influence." *Brut*, by the Middle English poet Layamon (*fl.c.* 1200), is a chronicle of the history of Britain through the arrival of Brutus and after.

[2] This is an early outline of *The Gutenberg Galaxy: The Making of Typographic Man* (1962).

Telegraph ultimate stage of mechanization of writing
>   Creates newspaper *form*.
>   Simultaneity of many *spaces* =
>   simultaneity of many different eras =
>   "abolition" of history by dumping
>   whole of past into the present.
>   Rimbaud

Radio-telephone   —mechanization of speed.
>   Cinema-TV   —mechanization of total human gesture.
>   Last 2 stages too steep for
>   present day adjustment

Since Rimbaud the newspaper as *landscape* enters all the arts? With landscape comes necessary musical adjustment of all parts of poetic composition. Juxtaposition of forces in field rather than continuous statement.

With mechanization of speech and gesture and swamping with visual-auditory matter after print-created drought we come to age of semi-literacy, at best.[3]

You could say this in 100 words. But are there some big facts I've missed? Of course I'm interested in a serious mag.[4]

Mencken discovered only real audience in America on American campus.[5] The undergraduate. He's still there. But nobody since Mencken has reached him.[6]

You have to have a program for the undergrad. *Some* icon smashing, plus a real bogeyman. For latter, in place of Babbitt,[7] I suggest the bureaucrat both inside govt and big business. He is the new Babbitt. His ways are worth study. E.g. *Fortune* Oct. and Nov 1951 "Wives in Management".[8] A honey.

Will get back to other points in your letter when I get a chance in a day or so.

> McLuhan.

[3]Two comments by Pound, in two successive letters, perhaps allude to this outline: "suggest that Mc L procedure is arcyFarcy / whether poisoned by Thos d' Aquin or some other /" (July 20, 1952) and " yr/ crit/ writing will become a lot livlier when yu start looking for credits rather than debts // not matter much where a man GOT what, but what he did with it (or without it) AFTER he got it" (July 21).

[4]In a letter of July 5, Pound had written: "McL/ ALSO invited to state what USE he cd/ be to a review IF an intelligent one were organized/ . . ."

[5]H.L. Mencken (1880–1956), American journalist and critic, was famous for his vitriolic attacks on Puritanism, conservatism, religion, and other subjects—though in old age he became very conservative himself. He studied the vigour of colloquial American usage in *The American Language* (1st ed, 1919), which McLuhan read while he was at Wisconsin.

[6]Pound's response: "thot I discovered the undergrad/ or at least started thinking : TEXT book in 1906 /" (July 20).

[7]A reference to the title character, George Babbitt—a prosperous real-estate broker who comes to doubt the virtues of middle-class values—of Sinclair Lewis's novel *Babbitt* (1922).

[8]W.H. Whyte, Jr., "Wives of Management", *Fortune*, October 1951, and "Corporation and the Wife", *Fortune*, November 1951.

To Elsie McLuhan

[81 St Mary St, Toronto]
Sunday [November 1952]

Dearest Mother

Enthusiastic letters [about *The Mechanical Bride*] continue to arrive from various quarters, some new some old. No denunciatory letters yet.[1]

Santa Claus parade much enjoyed here. Tom and Dorothy joined us for coffee in the kitchen while kids took it in. Eric made 8.50 Mike 4 bucks parking cars.

Tonight we are having in Jacqueline Tyrwhitt[2] visiting professor of Town Planning in the School of Architecture. Siegfried Giedion wrote me about her when thanking me for the book. Haven't had a single word from 6 copies sent to England. Must be customs hold up.

Much love

Twins report cards enclosed.   Marshall and Corinne

[1]In another (undated) letter written to his mother around this time, McLuhan reported: "Yesterday at Cocktails *chez* Ken MacLean [Chairman of the English Department, Victoria College, University of Toronto] for visiting Prof Richardson of Western Reserve University, the latter greeted me noisily: 'Ha, *McLuhan*! Your book is the rage of the campus in Cleveland. Copies getting stolen from library.' and so on."

[2]See page 277.

To Ezra Pound

81 St Mary St
Toronto 5
Dec 3 '52

Dear Pound

How right you are! But McLuhan is banned. No mag will publish me.[1] Unaware of the liturgical wars between the Secret Societies I did and said all the wrong things in my early appearances in the little mags. I had no party line. I was objective. I was a Fool. Now that I have found out all about the umpteen liturgies as revealed in all the "schools" of art, I'm just a wee bit disgusted with many things. I can't take the arts very seriously for the time being.

Kenner, however, rejoiced me with word that you were getting along with some more Cantos.

I liked Lewis's last book.

[The] Writer and [the] Absolute [1952].

Lewis used to say to me:

"The secret of success is secrecy."

I used to think that very funny.[2]

Best regards

Lilly Library, Indiana University   McLuhan

[1]What gave rise to this hyperbole is not known. (For "Secret Societies", see page 235, note 1. McLuhan sometimes attributed magazine rejections and other publishing difficulties to them.) In response Pound wrote: "As fer being banned, both he [Wyndham Lewis] and yr / anon / corrsp / know a bit re/ that. BUT that is no reason for passivity / yu refuse to USE means at hand/" (December 6).

[2]Pound commented: "No. wot W.L. sez is seldom funny/" (December 6).

1953

To Walter J. Ong, S.J.

81 St Mary St
Toronto 5
Jan 23/53

Dear Walter

Thanks much for off-prints. And for tip on Victor White O.P.[1]

I found M D Chénu O.P. on Pattern of [Aquinas's] *Summa* (emanation and return) verra inturresting, not to say arresting.[2] Since that figure of exitus and reditus [return] is the "standing" cyclic pattern of human cognition and therefore of the art process.

After 5 years of miserable health I am suddenly recovered and full of energy again. It was a gall bladder condition. Not serious. Just debilitating.

What are you up to just now. The Ramus project, I hope.

"God is dead" (Nietzsche) equals: God has abandoned the work of grace in creation? Prelude to incarnation as understood in pagan cults? At least so I hear from the inside boys. Catholic view of Neech would seem to be a bit off the beam there.

Am working on a book whose theme is The End of the Gutenberg Era. Tracing impact of print, and now, the switch to media which rep. not the mechanization of writing but of word and gesture. (radio movies TV) Necessarily a much greater change than from script to print. Your review of the Bride literally the *only* review that made any sense.[3] You were generous, but you saw what was up. The absence of serious study of these matters is total. i.e. universal emotional and intellectual illiteracy. And so unnecessary. Please mention items, books etc for my Gutenberg job. We are all well. Michael, our sixth arrived Oct 19. As ever in Xt.   Mac.

Walter J. Ong

[1]*God and the Unconscious* (1952) by Victor White, O.P. (Order of Preachers [Dominican]).

[2]M.D. Chénu, *Introduction à l'étude de saint Thomas d'Aquin*, Université de Montréal, 1950.

[3]Ong wrote a review article on *The Mechanical Bride* for *Social Order*, vol. II, no. 2, February 1952.

To Ezra Pound

81 St Mary St
Toronto 5
Feb 28/53

Dear Pound

Last year has been spent in going through rituals of secret societies with fine comb. As I said before I'm in a bloody rage at the discovery that the arts and sciences are in the pockets of these societies. It doesn't make me any happier to know that Joyce, Lewis, Eliot, yourself have used these rituals as a basis for art activity.[1]

Monopolies of knowledge are intolerable

The use of the arts for sectarian warfare! ugh.

The use of the arts as a technique of salvation!

     as a channel of supernatural grace!

 The validity of the rituals is entirely in the cognitive order.

 Art is imitation of the process of apprehension.

  clarification of   ,, ,, ,,.

Now that I know the nature of the sectarian strife among the Societies I have no intention of participating in it any further, until I know a good deal more. To hell with East and West.

           McLuhan

Lilly Library, Indiana University

[1] In the early 1950s McLuhan's interest in Renaissance and Neo-Augustan literatures (e.g. Pope and Swift, who were interested in Rosicrucianism and Masonry), as well as in modern literature, led him to undertake research into the effects of esoteric thought on the arts. Tracing the symbolism and rituals that were a means of transmitting gnostic and pagan religious thought in the Middle Ages and the Renaissance, he became fascinated with the role of Rosicrucianism and Masonry in the transition from the Renaissance to the Age of Reason, and with the continued presence of these themes and associated liturgies and symbols in modern art and literature—as reflected in such works as Eliot's *The Waste Land* and Joyce's *Ulysses*. As a Roman Catholic, McLuhan suspected that "secret societies", and "secret doctrines"—associated with gnosticism, Rosicrucianism, and Masonry—persisted among élites in the twentieth century. Following Wyndham Lewis's condemnation of the "freemasonry of the arts" in *Time and Western Man*, McLuhan protested—here and in other letters of the 1950s—what he felt was this continuing influence.

To Wyndham Lewis

81 St Mary's St
Toronto 5
April 15/53

Dear Lewis,

Good to hear from you. Got great pleasure from *Rude Assignment* and *Rotting Hill* stories. Also, *Writer and the Absolute* seemed to me at the top of your form.[1]

For Shenandoah magazine Lewis number I've attempted to present your Theory of Art and Communication.[2] Mainly in your own words.

Only in the past year have I become fully aware of the reality of the secret societies in the arts, philosophy and politics. Your own work has consequently taken on a much different significance for me.

Cordially yours
Marshall McLuhan.

P.S. There are now 6 children—4 girls and two boys.[3] We have a large house and 2 acres of ground right on the campus.

McLuhan

Cornell University Library

[1]Wyndham Lewis, *Rude Assignment: A Narrative of My Career Up-to-Date* (1950); *Rotting Hill* (1951), a collection of stories; *The Writer and the Absolute* (1952), essays.

[2]Herbert Marshall McLuhan, "Wyndham Lewis: His Theory of Art and Communication", *Shenandoah* (Summer-Autumn 1953).

[3]Eric (b. 1942), Mary and Teresa (b. 1945), Stephanie (b. 1947), Elizabeth (b. 1950), and Michael (b. 1952).

To Walter J. Ong, S.J.

81 St Mary's St
Toronto 5   May 31/53

Dear Walter

Have sent on a dozen off-prints to you. Living up here in Canada I have got so out of touch with people that I have even lost the desire to communicate. I can't think of a single person to whom I wish to send an off-print. Funny thing is I've just been given 43,000 dollars by Ford Foundation to run a 2 year Communication project here at Toronto University [see page 242, note 3]. We have 10 scholarships to offer at present 750 bucks a year for 2 years to anybody who wants to do a Ph.d. dissertation related to some aspect of communication study. Preferably people who have completed graduate courses. Begins this Fall. So pass the word along to likely candidates. Might be a way of your getting 2 years to write a book? We have in the project an architect-town planner, an economist, an anthropologist, and a psychologist. No holds barred. We need somebody to do a Thomist Theory of Communication.

Reading St. Thos De Trinitate Q VI a 2 objection one and reply thereto, a very Ramistic text, whether in spec. on divine things imagination must be altogether relinquished: ["]It may be answered: sacred Scripture does not propose to us divine truths under the figure of sensible things in order that our intellect should remain there, but that from these things it should mount up to such as are invisible":[1] "Wherefore use is made of things most common, that these may be even less occasion for remaining at their level," as says Dionysius (coel. Hier. ch. 2)".[2] My eyes bugged out! And Thomas is not quite 1/3 right on this point I think.

For the past year I've been exploring the relations between the Secret Societies and the arts.[3] A grisly business. I don't know what you know, but I know there isn't a living artist or critic of *repute* who isn't playing their game. I mean their rituals and doctrines as basis of artistic organization.

Eric Voegelein's recent *The New Science of Politics* [*:An Introduction*, 1952] (Chic. U. Press) is a denunciation of the Gnostic sects from Joachim of Flora[4] [*sic*] to Marx. Sees "Reformation" as re-emergence of these sects into the open. Relevant to Ramus of course. Odd how Dominicans seem to have yen for gnostic techniques of *gnosis* via passions. Bruno, Savonarola, Campanella.[5] Comes out very noticeably in Maritain's recent *Creative Intuition in Art* [*and Poetry*, 1953]. And [the Dominican] Victor White [*God and the Unconscious*] whom I have only read in part. H.N. Frye's *Blake* is best exposition of contemporary gnosticism I know.[6] That plus Thomson's *Melville*.[7]

Your off-prints much appreciated. Send more. Shall be watching for Jinni in [Cleanth Brooks'] The Well-Wrought Urn.[8] Hadn't heard of Allen Tate's Conversations.[9]

---

[1]Thomas Aquinas (1225–74), *Commentary on the "De Trinitate" of Boethius*, "Question VI, Article 2, Objection one, and reply thereto". See Armand Maurer, *St. Thomas Aquinas: The Division and Methods of the Sciences. Questions V and VI of his Commentary on the "De Trinitate of Boethius"* (1953), page 65.

[2]Pseudo-Dionysius (c. 500), *De Caelesti Hierarchia* (see the critical edition of *Celestial Harmony* edited by G. Heil, 1958).

[3]See page 235, note 1.

[4]Joachim of Floris (c. 1132–1202) was an Italian Cistercian monk who wrote scriptural commentaries.

[5]Giordano Bruno (1548–1600) was an Italian philosopher who entered the Dominican order in his youth but was accused of heresy and fled; he wrote several metaphysical works, expressing prophetic and poetic insights about the nature of the universe; he was eventually imprisoned for heresy and burned at the stake. His name appears repeatedly in *Finnegans Wake*. Girolamo Savonarola (1452–98) joined the Dominicans in Florence and became a popular preacher in that city, scathingly attacking laxity of all kinds. Tommaso Campanella (1568–1639), who entered the Dominican order at 15, was the author of *Civitas solis* (1632; tr. *The City of the Sun*), which describes a utopian society.

[6]Northrop Frye, *Fearful Symmetry: A Study of William Blake* (1947).

[7]Lawrence Thompson, *Melville's Quarrel with God* (1952).

[8]Walter J. Ong, S.J., "The Jinnes in the Well-Wrought Urn", *Essays in Criticism* (Oxford), vol. iv, no. 3, July 1954.

[9]Unidentified.

Yes, our six children make a complex life for us, in a way which 25 years ago they would not. The disappearance of servants and large house (not unplanned) is linked to the Manichean hatred of the family, and the Church has been most culpable in allowing this concerted campaign to be met only by sporadic individual initiative and resistance.

Certainly I look forward to some chat with you when you get back. I find few I can talk to among Catholics. Fewer and fewer too. Educationally we have made a great blunder in dispersing talent instead of concentrating it. By dispersal we insure that a few able men are placed where they *must* be an irritation to a crowd of inert souls, and where they can't function themselves. Extremely able chap here finishing Ph.d. on Communication Theory in Joyce, Yeats, Lewis, Pound Eliot. Catholic. Yale BA. He will teach at St. Mike's and work in our Culture and Communications project.[10]

As ever in Xt.

Mac.

Walter J. Ong

[10]Donald Theall, who was then working under McLuhan on his Ph.D., which he received in 1954; taught at the University of Toronto until 1965; he is now President of Trent University, Peterborough, Ontario. He wrote *The Medium is the Rear View Mirror: Understanding McLuhan* (1971), a critique that displeased McLuhan.

To Wyndham Lewis

81 St Mary's St.
Toronto 5
July 14/53

Dear Lewis, Most interested that you have got on so far with *The Childermass*.[1] That is a work which I have only begun to appreciate. You ask about the *Shenandoah* W. Lewis issue. I must say that I know nothing about Carter, or Washington and Lee University.[2] Kenner I know very well. He did an M.A. here at Toronto and then succeeded me at Assumption College, though he is not a Catholic. After 2 years he went to Yale, got a Ph.d. with a Thesis on James Joyce, then took a job at Santa Barbara College, an extension of U. of California in Santa Barbara.

Ran into Ruthven Todd[3] in New York recently. He told me of your eyes. Your

[1]In a letter of May 12, 1953 Lewis told McLuhan that he was working on two novels: *Monstre Gai* and *Malign Fiesta* (they were published in one volume in 1955). With *The Childermass* (1928) they were to form a trilogy called *The Human Age*. A fourth novel was planned but not begun.

[2]The Wyndham Lewis issue of *Shenandoah* (Summer-Autumn 1953)—published by Washington and Lee University, Lexington, Virginia—was edited by Thomas H. Carter. It included a story by Lewis ("The Rebellious Patient"); a miscellany of comments on Lewis by Ezra Pound; an essay, "The War With Time", and a Lewis bibliography by Hugh Kenner; and "Wyndham Lewis: His Theory of Art and Communication" by Herbert Marshall McLuhan.

[3]The British writer Ruthven Todd (1914–78) had met Lewis in London in the 1930s.

getting on with important work in spite of the darkness is most impressive. I can only pray that the condition will improve.

Todd has married a young American girl and has a house in the village supplied by his father-in-law. He plays host to the visiting poets from England. When I mentioned that Roy Campbell[4] would be over here this Fall he looked very unhappy and said: "He will take a poke at me." Todd's work I do not know but suppose he must be in the precieuse camp. However he makes part of his living in New York by writing continuity for a comic strip of his invention. It is called *Space Cats*, and is an interplanetary affair.

Re-reading *Snooty*[5] recently I realized my own situation is not unlike his after reading *Moby Dick*. The range and character of the "cultic twalette" has just dawned on me in the past year. Like Snooty I'm trying to get my bearings.

Best Wishes
Marshall McLuhan.

[4]The South African poet and translator Roy Campbell (1901–57) lived in England for some six years after the First World War, becoming a disciple of Lewis and well known in London for his belligerence, his reactionary views, and for his long poem *That Flaming Terrapin* (1924). He gave a lecture at Brennan Hall, St Michael's College, on the evening of November 4, 1953 (he was introduced by E.J. Pratt) and stayed with the McLuhans, to whom he wrote a number of affectionate letters thereafter.

[5]*Snooty Baronet* (1932) by Wyndham Lewis. This comic novel was based on Lewis's stay with Roy Campbell in the south of France in March 1932.

To Wyndham Lewis

81 St Mary St
Toronto
Sept 1st/53

Dear Lewis

Very gratifying your praise of my essay.[1] I should much enjoy doing a proper study of your work. Kenner, however, has some such intention, and perhaps an arrangement with New Directions. A student of mine who got his introduction to your work *via* myself, he is likely to do much the sort of job I would do, so far as content goes.[2] If you would prefer me to do the job, that deal might be worked

[1]See previous letter, note 2.

[2]Hugh Kenner did write a study of Lewis, and finished it around this time. The typescript was sent by his London publisher, Methuen, to Lewis, who read and acknowledged it appreciatively to Kenner in October; Lewis commented on the text in a letter to Kenner of November 23. The book was published in London in June 1954, and in New York (by New Directions) the next year, under the title *Wyndham Lewis*, and McLuhan reviewed it in *Renascence* (vol. 7, no. 2, Winter 1955). Kenner was never a formal student of McLuhan's.

out with Regnery or with Jas Laughlin.[3] After all Kenner has to have your permission for quotes. Perhaps you may have a suggestion to offer? Kenner lives in California and we have mainly lost touch these past 4 years.

Here we are broiling in St. Louis[-like] summer weather. Wish you could have *some* of it to moderate the summer you describe.

Incidentally, I do know Laughlin of New Directions for whom I am to do a volume of Remy de Gourmont selections sometime.[4]

Best regards
Marshall McLuhan.

Cornell University Library

[3]The publishing firm of Henry Regnery Co., Chicago, and New Directions Inc., New York, of which James Laughlin was the head. Regnery became Lewis's American publisher with *Rotting Hill* (1952).

[4]Rémy de Gourmont (1858–1915), French critic, essayist, and novelist (whose work was very much admired by Pound). This anthology never materialized.

To Wyndham Lewis

81 St Mary St
Toronto 5
Oct 16/53

Dear Lewis

Shenandoah has arrived and I hasten to withdraw what I said about Kenner seeing eye to eye with me.[1] His Joyce enthusiasm has carried him a long way toward the time-cult. But apart from that there is the appalling manner and writing.

Your own piece was a perfect bit of high-comedy.[2] Your classical quality becomes more marked in your work of the past ten years.

No word of or from Eric Newton and his wife.[3] We should be most pleased to meet them of course. If he makes periodic visits here it would be easy to arrange a lecture for him before a Catholic audience. Is he himself a Catholic?

We expect Roy Campbell for a lecture here at St. Michael's College November 4.

Very best regards
Marshall McLuhan.

Cornell University Library

[1]See page 238, note 2.

[2]Lewis's story "The Rebellious Patient".

[3]In a letter to McLuhan of September 9, 1953, Lewis told him that the English art critic Eric Newton (1893–1965), a close friend, was making a lecture tour of Canada and would be in Toronto in early October. Lewis hoped that McLuhan would see the Newtons and "do them any little service you can. By this I mean, should the Catholics like being lectured to inform them of the presence of Eric."

To Wyndham Lewis

81 St Mary St
Toronto 5
Dec. 9/53

Dear Lewis

No word yet from Vanguard Press.[1] It's a bad time of year for that disorganized outfit. I also wrote Jas. Laughlin. No word from him. And put out several tentacles elsewhere. It's the time of year that paralyzes these people. The big Xmas push.

Ashley Brown[2] wrote to say he was trying to look out for a publisher for *The Vulgar Streak*. So I mentioned the new one to him as well. I thought your précis of the new one most promising. And I assume that the novel will be as rich in observations of N. America as Rotting Hill is of Socialist England. With Kenner's book coming out with Laughlin it seemed to me obvious that Laughlin would be eager to get something of yours on his list at the same time.

As you realize, Toronto is not a point from which one can exert much influence in the publishing or any other sphere. However I think we can bring something off.

As for my book. It owes much to you of course.[3] But it was so long in the publishing (6 years) that I had lost interest in its approach before it appeared. Now I see that I was trying to prop up the standards of book culture when we have passed out of the Gutenberg era.

Xmas greeting from us to you and Mrs Lewis.

Marshall McLuhan

Cornell University Library

---

[1]In a letter to McLuhan of November 12, 1953 Lewis told him he was reading page proofs of his new (unnamed) novel—*Self-Condemned* (1954)—and asked if he could help sell it in New York, suggesting Vanguard, the publisher of *The Mechanical Bride*. McLuhan also approached New Directions (James Laughlin). However, Henry Regnery published it in the U.S. in 1955.

[2]Ashley Brown was a member of the Advisory Board of *Shenandoah* and later became an Editorial Advisor.

[3]See page 217, note 5.

1954

To Wyndham Lewis

81 St Mary St
Toronto 5
Feb 7/54

Dear Lewis

Your sending *Encounter* with Doppelganger story much appreciated.[1] I have not enjoyed anything so much in a great while. It is masterly. Also uproarious. And leads me to hope you might be induced to handle Joyce and Eliot in story form. I have ordered *Self-Condemned* from Peter Russell and look forward to it very much. Toronto has been alerted and has begun to tremble.[2]

This year and next year I am Chairman of a Ford Foundation project here at the University.[3] We have a group of 5 faculty and a dozen graduate students to consider the impact of the new media of communication on any aspect of life and society which we choose. Your books are indispensable to us. Of course our group is split over time and space. We have both the vertical and horizontal doctrinaires to contend with.[4] Only a year ago did I find out the religious basis of these, to me, almost meaningless quarrels. *The Mechanical Bride* was written in all innocence of such knowledge. The world of the arts and of science has taken on a much more intelligible character for me since this self-initiation. For the present, at any rate, it has simplified but not ennobled the scene.

Best regards
Marshall McLuhan

Cornell University Library

---

[1]Lewis's story "The Döppelganger" in *Encounter* (February 1954) gently satirized Ezra Pound's urge to inform and instruct.

[2]Lewis's *Self-Condemned* (1954)—considered to be one of his important novels—includes a scathing portrayal of life for a British exile in Toronto in the early 1940s. In a letter to McLuhan of December 5, 1943, Lewis wrote: "We were nearly three years in that disgusting spot."

[3]McLuhan was leading a group of five faculty members and a dozen graduate students in a study of the effects of the electronic media on life and society. He had received a Ford Foundation grant for this purpose and was named Chairman of the Ford Foundation Seminar on Culture and Communication (1953–5).

[4]Vertical and horizontal were among the couplings—like hot and cool, environment and anti-environment—McLuhan used to express dualities or antitheses in characterizing phenomena. In this lexicon, horizontal could refer to a Joycean avant-garde perspective (and to cliché, to the audio tactile, to TV), while vertical could refer to the Miltonic, Frye-oriented aesthetic and criticism (and to archetype, to the visual world, to print).

To Wyndham Lewis

81 St Mary St
Toronto 5
May 9/54

Dear Lewis

A great thrill getting your novel [*Self-Condemned*] at the scene of the crime! I've circulated it so rapidly that I've not had a second trip through. I think it is a very important piece of work. The first time that anything Canadian has been given serious treatment.

The discourse on History is as timely now as *Count Your Dead* in 1938.[1] I'll see that the book is read, and I'll write a piece on it at once. But in view of the current plan to bring the world to an end, are there any courses of reasonable action open to isolated individuals? Can the Catholic Church do anything in the way of exposé or pronouncement? Is the hierarchy informed?

Toronto waits humped in silence for the book to hit the stalls.

Cordial regards
Marshall McLuhan

[1] "Rotter", a chapter in *Self-Condemned*, presents a view of history in which the novel's main character, René Harding, a historian, is said to believe that "the past can be visualized and written about only as a crime story. The criminals . . . [are] the heads of States." Lewis's *Count Your Dead: They are Alive! or A New War in the Making* (1937) was written as a "peace pamphlet" (though it is a cloth-bound book) during the political events that led up to the Second World War. It is a prolonged dialogue between "Ned", the proponent of common sense, and "Launcelot Nidwit", a "consummate imbecile" who nevertheless provided an "infallible index of British public opinion". He dies after confronting the truth, which was that "all these 'Communists', and 'Democrats' and 'Fascists', these Popular-fronters and Baldwinians I have been worrying my head about, are so many armed rackets, all equally having for guiding principle the philosophy of Force."

To Walter J. Ong, S.J.

81 St Mary St
Toronto 5
Oct 14/54

Dear Walter

Please explicate sentence on p 21 of your System Space and Intellect in Ren[aissance] Symbolism essay: "Out of it has come modern science, with the possibility it offers for increasing the subjection of matter and impregnation of matter by spiritual forces . . ."[1]

[1] This is a quotation from the brief of a paper by Walter J. Ong, "Space and Intellect in Renaissance Symbolism", delivered at the Catholic Renascence Society Symposium in Philadelphia in April 1954. It was published in full in *Explorations* 4, February 1955.

I've read a lot of Rosicrucian stuff lately and you make me wonder whether you have their thoughts in mind.

On p. 396 of Madame Blavatskys *Isis Unveiled* (vol I N.York 1889)[2] she cites the traditional Pythagorean distinction between Fancy and Imagination, citing Wordsworth as obvious recent exemplar: "Imagination Pythagoras maintained to be the remembrance of precedent spiritual, mental and physical states, while fancy is the disorderly production of the material brain." In context this means that imagination is contact with the Anima Mundi (e.g. Yeats) whereas Fancy is merely a portion of the Anima Hominis. That is Imagination concerns direct contact with divine archetypes whereas fancy is merely human and cognitive. As fallen spirits or devils men have their intellect which is of the earth earthy, presided over by the Earth mother, the White Goddess of Robt Graves etc.[3] The intellect is the dark principle. But the imagination is mode of divine union for the *uncreated* divine spark hidden in our corrupt clay etc. You are familiar with this aspect of the Old Religion, Gnosis, neo-platonism theosophy et al?

I dont see how it is possible to teach English literature, or any European lit. without full knowledge of the "secret doctrine" for which the arts are the sole means of grace.[4] I realize now that my own rejection of philosophy as a study in my pre-Catholic days was owing to the sense that it was a meaningless truncation. Not that my present interest is due to any conviction of truth in the secret doctrine. Quite the contrary. It is rather to a sense of it as the fecund source of lies and misconceptions. e.g. Puritan Inner Light.

Can you think of any reason why Catholic students of philosophy and lit. today should not be given the facts about these "secrets"? I can find nobody here who can or will discuss the question.

Turrible busy! Keep in touch.

As ever in Christ

Mac.

Walter J. Ong

[2]The major book of Helena Petrovna Blavatsky (1831–91), Russian occultist and co-founder in New York, in 1875, of the Theosophical Society.

[3]Among the many works of poet, novelist, and essayist Robert Graves (1895–1985) was *The White Goddess: A Historical Grammar of Poetic Myth* (1948), which argues that the primitive Moon Goddess, the female principle, was the Muse of poetry.

[4]See page 235, note 1.

To Wyndham Lewis

81 St. Mary's St.
Toronto 5
Dec 18/54

Dear Lewis

Much pleased with your Xmas letter, and with news about Monstre Gai and Malign Fiesta.[1]

As for your new book on *The Demon of Progress in The Arts* [1954] I've had it on order for weeks with Peter Russell.

If word of mouth goes for anything *Self-Condemned* should make its way here in Canada. I have coming out a new version of BLAST which takes Self-Condemned (1914–1954) as a focal point.[2] As theme for Blast forty years later I have taken in place of abstract art and industrial culture, the new media of communication and their power of metamorphosis.

A group of us here have been studying the new media and have been looking into the Character of Acoustic Space as reconstituted by the mechanization of sound.

Acoustic Space is spherical. It is without bounds or vanishing points.[3] It is structured by pitch separation and kinesthesia.[4] It is not a container. It is not hollowed out. It is the space in which men live before the invention of writing— that translation of the acoustic into the visual. With writing men began to trust their eyes and to structure space visually. Pre-literate man does not trust his eyes very much. The magic is in sound for him, with its power to evoke the absent.

I, at any rate, am not looking into these matters with any doctrinaire bias; but in our group the doctrinaires are much disturbed by Acoustic or non-Euclidean

---

[1]In a letter to McLuhan of December 3, 1954 Lewis wrote that he had at last finished "The continuations of Childermass—two volumes (1) Monstre Gai, and (2) Malign Fiesta." They were published in one volume in October 1955; together with *The Childermass* (1928) they formed a trilogy, *The Human Age*. Lewis also refers to "a slim book of mine, The Demon of Progress in the Arts . . . . It is, however, all about painting, therefore I shall refrain from sending it you."

[2]*Counterblast* (1954), a seventeen-page pamphlet (8-¾" × 11½") published by the University of Toronto Press inspired by Wyndham Lewis's magazine *Blast: The Review of the Great English Vortex* (1914) in which Lewis blasts the "enemies" of art. The first half of *Counterblast*—"BLAST/ england ancient GHOST of culture / POACHING the EYES of the / Canadian HAMLETS / U S A / COLOSSUS of the South, horizontal / HEAVYWEIGHT flattening the / canadian imagination" —was originally written as a review of the Massey Commission *Report* (1951) and in its elliptical style and expressive but eccentric typography echoes the letters McLuhan had been receiving from Ezra Pound as well as *Blast*. Most of the second section, "Media Log", is included in McLuhan's book *Counterblast* (1969)—a typographically playful collection (designed by Harley Parker) of insights and brief expositions about how innovations in technology have altered our lives and our perceptions of the world.

[3]See page 368, note 2.

[4]Kinesthesia: the sensation of movement, bodily position etc. resulting from the stimulation of sensory nerve endings.

space. It gives too complete and simple a physiological account of their meta
physics.

So far as I can see, the visual items in poetry are not arranged in formal visual
space until the later 17th century.

We are all well and Corinne joins with me in sending you and Mrs Lewis
wishes for a blessed Christmas and New Year.

Marshall McLuhan.

To Ezra Pound

81 St Mary's St
Toronto 5
Dec 18/54

Dear Pound

Your portrait by Lewis adorns our mantle.[1]

Lewis wrote recently about finishing the *Childermass* and about his *Demon of
Progress*.

A group of us here are working on the character of acoustic space — the space
of pre-literate man. Non-euclidean, non-container.

In a month or so I'll send you our magazine[2] which broaches these questions
in relation to the new media.[3]

Most cordially
Marshall McLuhan.

[1]From a reproduction in a book McLuhan had made a photostat of one of Lewis's charcoal
sketches of Ezra Pound, mounted it, and put it over the mantle.

[2]*Explorations: Studies in Culture and Communication* (1953–9) was designed "as a publication
that explores and searches and questions. We envisage a series that will cut across the humanities
and social sciences by treating them as a continuum." It was founded by Edmund Carpenter who
edited the first six issues, which were subsidized by the Ford Foundation and personal funds;
associate editors were W.T. Easterbrook, H.M. McLuhan, J. Tyrwhitt, and D.C. Williams. Issues 7
to 9 were funded by the Toronto *Telegram* (John Bassett): Carpenter edited 7, though he and
McLuhan were listed as co-editors; Harley Parker and McLuhan edited 8; and for 9 Carpenter got
backing to produce his book *Eskimo. Explorations in Communication* (1960), edited by Edmund
Carpenter and Marshall McLuhan, contains articles from the magazine. For Edmund Carpenter,
see page 250, note 1.

[3]At the bottom of this letter Pound scrawled "NUTS".

1955

To Wyndham Lewis

81 St Mary St
Toronto 5
March 7/55

Dear Lewis

Latest Hudson Review hard to get, so I havent read your selection from the new novel.[1] Demon of Progress in the Arts I did enjoy. Kept asking myself how your present position would have reshaped your earlier lines of development.

As for *Counterblast*, that is entirely my own work. Shall run a series of them perhaps. They sell off quite quickly here and cost almost nothing to print.

The local group to which I referred is simply four other university professors plus a few graduate students. We are spending some Ford Foundation funds by way of studying the new media of communication. My own approach finds neither favor nor comprehension among my colleagues.

Shall be reviewing *Self-Condemned* on C.B.C. coast to coast network early in May.

Cordially
McLuhan.

[1] An extract from *Monstre Gai* (1955), followed by "A Note on *Monstre Gai*" (pp. 522–6) by T.S. Eliot, appeared in *The Hudson Review*, Winter 1954[–5], vol. VII, no. 4.

To Wyndham Lewis

81 St Mary St
Toronto 5
July 11/55

Dear Lewis

Reviews of the 3rd program productions of Childermass successors most gratifying.[1] I am trying to get C.B.C. to produce them again here.

Am spending summer on a book on The Gutenberg Era—an attempt to assess the pre-literate, the pre-print, and post-print eras of culture.

We have a small sailboat in the bay here and get out a good deal.

Kegan Paul, or Mr Colin Franklin at Kegan Paul, have written to ask if they might look over a collection of my essays with a view to selecting some for publication.

I find myself somewhat lacking in pride of authorship. I prefer conversation. But I can scarcely afford to pass up such opportunities.

There is an able young painter here (Harley Parker)[2] who has got very interested in your writings.

Most cordial regards
Marshall McLuhan

Cornell University Library

[1] The BBC broadcast dramatizations of *Monstre Gai* and *Malign Fiesta* in May 1955. A dramatization of *The Childermass* had been broadcast in June 1951.

[2] See page 321, note 3.

To Wyndham Lewis

29 Wells Hill Ave
Toronto 10
[December 1955]

By gosh Lewis this college [Trinity Hall] stationery of 25 [*sic*] years ago got dredged up when we moved house last month!

Roy Campbell was with us for a week just before the move. It will be a few decades before the likes of you or him appear again. What a puny crowd there is moping about nowadays.

But Hegelian History is sure working overtime in putting a poet like Pound in a mental home. How far can allegory be tolerated?

Much looking forward to my copy of the latest section of Childermass. Blessings on you and Froanna

Marshall and
Corinne McLuhan

Cornell University Library

1956

To Wyndham Lewis

29 Wells Hill Ave.
Toronto 10
Aug 12/56

Dear Lewis

A friend returned from England this week after having been to the Tate Gallery exhibition of your work.[1] She brought a catalogue for us which we are very glad to have. It was a joy to hear and to read of the current reception of these paintings.

Perhaps I have not already written to you about the excitement and pleasure I got from reading *The Human Age*. It seems to me your finest work. And I flatter myself that many such subtleties as the relation of Third City to Third Program and the infernal relations of Hollywood superhumanism to the Satanic reform program, were not lost on me. Further readings will reveal a great deal I know. Meanwhile I pray you will be able to complete part Four.

Our family is growing up quickly now. Eric is 14. His interests are slightly musical, a bit more theatrical, and intensely electronic. He is very much the radio and electrical fanatic just now. The twin girls are 10. Stephanie and Elizabeth are 8 and 5. Michael is 3.

We keep you in our prayers

Most cordial good wishes to you and to Mrs Lewis
Marshall McLuhan.

[1]The Tate Gallery held an exhibition, called "Wyndham Lewis and Vorticism", of 155 paintings and drawings from July 6 to August 19, 1956. Lewis, very ill and blind, attended in a wheel chair. He died on March 7, 1957, at the age of 74.

1957

To Ezra Pound

29 Wells Hill Ave
Toronto 10
Jan 22/57

Dear Pound

I had mentioned to Carpenter that you were the one man of our time who had seen the typewriter as a new art form and had used it imaginatively.[1] But I didn't want him to bother you. He is now bothering Uncle Tom Eliot about the same question.

As a form of publication the typewriter has obviously had much to do with habits of verbal arrangement both written and oral. Anything you have to say on this subject will have interest for the student of your work.

Naturally I keep up with the new Cantos and find them exhilirating as they manifest more and more the unity of their predecessors.[2]

Most cordially
Marshall McLuhan

[1] Edmund S. (Ted) Carpenter (b. 1922) was an assistant professor in the Department of Anthropology at the University of Toronto from 1948 to 1958. He founded, and was editor of, the magazine *Explorations* (1953-9), of which McLuhan was an associate editor—the final issue of which took the form of Carpenter's book *Eskimo* (1959). From Toronto, Carpenter went to California State University, Northridge, as Professor of Anthropology and Chairman of the department. He joined McLuhan at Fordham University, New York, while McLuhan was there in 1967-8 and then returned to California as a professor at the University of California, Santa Cruz. He is now Vice President of the Rock Foundation, New York. Carpenter (who was acquainted with Pound) was at this time collecting quotations about the typewriter—including some from Henry James on dictation, from Pound, and various French poets—and he wrote T.S. Eliot on this subject.

[2] Ezra Pound, *Section: Rock-Drill* (Cantos 85-95), published in 1955.

To Walter J. Ong, S.J.

29 Wells Hill Ave
Toronto 10
Sept 21 [1957]

Dear Walter

Blessings and Greetings in our Lord.

Halfway through Denis De Rougemont's Man's Western Quest.[1] I want to hurry you to it if you haven't read it already. 1st book on the Person in the West. Problem no 1 in my mind for 5 years.

Next Dubarle's Scientific Humanism very useful for media approach, though he doesn't realize it.[2] Key book.

No 8 [of *Explorations*] will be in your hands 1st week of Oct. More and more I am baffled at my inability to get serious attention for psychodynamics of media since invention of *phonetic* alphabet. *Content* obsession is itself legacy of *print*. Leaves us helpless before all the hylomorphic action of all media including print. I have yet to discover one sentence in any student or author since 1500 that hinted at any awareness of the inherent psycho and social dynamics of any medium. (Are we to exclude the iconoclasts?!)

Must get your book on Catholicism.[3] Only heard of it recently.

The media issue concerns every minute of every teacher's day—

Every problem of every catechist and liturgist.

Am giving a private course this Fall to 30 secondary school teachers on the Grammars of the Media. Should be on the air for PTA etc.

But how does one talk about these things in a society which hasn't got a clue about print after 500 years?

The Church has more at stake than anybody. Should set up an institute of Perennial Contemporaryness!

Am doing new *Bride* for Beacon Press.[4]

Keep us in your prayers
Mac.

Find much sense in Bern. Lonergan's *Insight*[5]

Walter J. Ong

---

[1] Denis de Rougemont, *Man's Western Quest: The Principles of Civilization* (1957).

[2] Dominique Dubarle, O.P., *Scientific Humanism* (1956), a translation by Reginald Trevett of *Humanisme scientifique et raison chrétienne* (1953).

[3] Walter J. Ong, S.J., *Frontiers in American Catholicism: Essays on Ideology and Culture* (1957).

[4] An unchanged paperback edition of *The Mechanical Bride* was published by the Beacon Press in 1967.

[5] Bernard Lonergan, *Insight: A Study of Human Understanding* [1957].

1959

To Edward S. Morgan[1]

St. Michael's College
May 16, 1959

Dear Mr. Morgan,

I got your letter just as I was ready to leave town. Let me quickly put down a few notes about the topic, "New Business Rules In Our Electronic Age", a speech which I have already given at the Winnipeg Ad and Sales Club on May 11.

My theme was simply that the Electronic Age is one in which information comes to everybody in any job, in any social or personal activity, information comes from all directions at the same time. This creates a very peculiar field, as it were, "field" in the sense that the physicists use the word, or the psychologists. A field of instantaneous interrelationships—which causes decision makers to play it by ear, as we say. In the Jet Age, for example, an airplane pilot can no longer navigate by the old method of intersecting bearings or lines because the speed of the plane takes him past the point so established too fast. In the same way, he has to rely on a continuously picked-up electronic beam on which to fly. He has to have a continuous and instantaneous flow of information in order to navigate.

Now this, in terms of business, means, for example, as Peter Drucker[2] puts it, that for the first time in human history, production depends upon higher education. Drucker's theme, in *Landmarks of Tomorrow* [1959], is that education, higher education, is no longer an affair of prestige, status or mere amenity (a luxury product). Higher education is an absolute necessity of production. This has had as revolutionary an effect in business as it is now having in education. Both areas are upset by the pressure to intermingle their overall purposes. The change in information flow, which is created by the moving of information at the speed of light, means that the decision-maker lives in a kind of overall field of fact and data which alters the scope and character of the decisions he has to make.

For example, in the Electronic Age, the producer becomes consumer, the consumer becomes producer; simply because, before production begins in any line whatever, the producer has to know so much about the attitudes and needs of the potential market that the very inner life of the consumer is consulted before production begins, and in this way, the consumer is made the one who makes the

---

[1]Edward S. Morgan was assistant editor of *Marketing*, a Maclean-Hunter publication in Toronto. This letter—the first in this collection to have been originally typed—introduces some basic ideas that later became associated with McLuhan and that he enunciated and elaborated on many times.

[2]See page 259, note 1.

decision about what shall be produced, and when. In the same way, the producer, by becoming so sensitive to the motivations of his consuming public by
constantly projecting himself into the points of view and attitudes of his clients,
is more and more participating in the attitudes of the consumer.

The reason he has to know the consumer attitude thoroughly, better than the
consumer himself, really, is not simple; but is partly tied to the fact that with
such large budgets involved, the producer can no more afford to make a mistake
than a jet pilot can in approaching a landing strip. In the electronic age, there
[then], the role of the producer and the role of the consumer will tend to fuse,
just as higher education is tending to invade every aspect of industry and marketing.

Another aspect of the same kind of patterning in the Electronic Age which results
from instantaneous flow of information from every part of a situation, from every
quarter, is that we develop a new attitude to space, a new attitude to time. The
globe becomes a very small village-like affair,[3] under electronic conditions, in
which, whatever happens to anybody, happens to everybody; and living in this
very small new space, as it were, causes us paradoxically to take very long views,
in matter of time. For example, in industry today, the largest capital expenditure
is on research. This research is not in order to ensure a lot of change and innovation; it is rather to ensure that the producers will be so far ahead of the changes
that are being made that they'll be able to control change. Change will become
institutionalized in the Electronic Age. Change, as Margaret Mead[4] and others
have pointed out, is the only constant in our present world. The one thing of
which we're absolutely sure is high speed change—this has become itself a sort
of constant.

The long-term, the long-run point-of-view of the Institution will increasingly
characterize the Business of the Electronic Age. This is another way of saying
that we are returning to the old tribal patterns, abandoning the highly individ-
ualistic ways of the Western World, as we have know them for so long. This
individualism was, of course, achieved by the use of writing and printing, and

---

[3]An early statement of McLuhan's famous concept, later expressed in *The Gutenberg Galaxy*
(1962) as: "The new electronic independence recreates the world in the image of a global village."
McLuhan states in his 1960 *Report on Project in Understanding the New Media* (see page 255):
"When man lives globally to the notes of a tribal drum [radio] on a planet that is no more than a
village in scope and extent, he cannot avoid the all-at-onceness of pattern which is the auditory and
tribal type of structure." It is interesting that Wyndham Lewis, in *America and Cosmic Man* (1948),
which McLuhan owned, says on page 16: ". . . And since plural sovereignty anyway—now that the
earth has become one big village, with telephones laid on from one end to the other, and air
transport, both speedy and safe—must be a little farcical, the plurality implied in that title [United
States] could be removed as a good example to the rest of the world, and the U.S.A. become the
American Union."

[4]Margaret Mead (1901–78), American anthropologist and author, two of whose books—*And Keep
Your Powder Dry: An Anthropologist Looks at America* (1942) and *Male and Female: A Study of the
Sexes in a Changing World* (1949)—are discussed several times in *The Mechanical Bride*. McLuhan
met Professor Mead at the first annual Delos Symposium in July 1963. There is a letter to her on
page 463.

the formation of individual habits of self-reliance and self-initiative, from long accustomation to the solitary habit of reading and writing. We still use the technology of the phonetic alphabet as our principal means of detribalizing backward countries, but we have not sufficiently noticed that Electronic Technology can retribalize ourselves.

The tribe is a unit, which, extending the bounds of the family to include the whole society, becomes the only way of organizing society when it exists in a kind of Global Village pattern. It is important to understand that the Global Village pattern is caused by the instantaneous movement of information from every quarter to every point at the same time. Tribal man, or family man, is characterized by certain basic outlooks and strategies, of which perhaps the most obvious is a deep sense of togetherness, a strong resistance to change. It certainly sounds paradoxical to say that the Electronic Age, in which change is itself the only constant, will be the age which will be the most resistant to change, but the reason for this is perhaps obvious to us in our daily lives now.

If a plane is shot down in Pakistan, it disturbs the existence of everybody in North America, or Europe, or the Near East. Incidents of this type become intolerable in the long run because of their deeply disturbing effect upon our ordinary lives. Tribal Man, or Family Man, seeks avidly for ways of reducing all incidents to zero. He works for a world in which nothing happens, because the consequences of events are too extreme to be endured. That is why Tribal Man always works out a kind of static, unchanging pattern in his life. Another very obvious aspect of Tribal Man is that in a tribal society, there are no consumers: everybody is a producer, everybody is an artist. Most people are engaged in production, artistic or otherwise, and the patterns under those conditions are unchanging: the art styles, the food patterns, the living style of Tribal Man are typically fixed over long periods of time.

So that whereas in North America we have by process of rapid change managed to standardize our lives, to the extent that most of us lead the same kind of existence whether in Memphis or St. Louis, New York or San Francisco, Toronto, Vancouver or Montreal—it would now appear that the same dynamic logic is being extended to time, and that what we have standardized spatially, we may well come to standardize over long stretches of time. The Volkswagen is perhaps an illustration of a motor car which is named as a tribal object of the folk; it is curious that its pattern has changed scarcely at all; and in the same way with the new small cars, the design tends to be much more stable than the older cars, larger cars. The citizen of the Electronic Age is a do-it-yourself man, like the citizens of tribal societies. He prefers a car over which he feels a complete control, and which does not enclose him in a kind of boudoir, or living-room space.

In our Arts, we have seen this pattern shaping up for a long time. A hundred years ago, the painters abandoned pictorial space, the space of perspective, enclosed space as painters call it, in favor of what they call, "automorphic" space; a space in which each person, each thing, makes it own world. This is the kind of world that the Beatniks are struggling towards; they spurn consumer goods, they crave the do-it-yourself world, even though it is a shabby, and, from a consumer point of view, fourth-rate kind of world—because they insist on assuming the producer role in all matters, and at all costs. This trend is behind the change in the attitude toward the motor car, and the attitude toward housing; and it will invade many other sides of our economy, and social life. For example, everybody has noticed how work has taken on an increasingly creative and playful aspect; people are encouraged to be creative at work today. Contrariwise, people take their play very seriously, much more seriously than they used to. Leisure time activities have taken on a sternly business air; large investment capital [is] tied up in them, more and more skills [are] required for leisure today.

I would sum this up by simply saying that when you have a new kind of information pattern surrounding all individuals and all groups, their basic attitudes towards one another, toward work and play, toward production and consumption, these attitudes are all changed too. And the overall change is that the consumer insists on a larger role, creatively, and wants to become more and more a producer, at all levels. This means that we are, increasingly, insisting upon a do-it-yourself world, whether in decision-making, or in consumer goods; and that on the overall pattern of social life, we are retribalizing, after centuries of detribalizing; and that whereas we accomplished detribalization by literacy and segmental analysis of all thought, action and production, we are accomplishing our retribalization by the simultaneous, by the electronic, which tends to put us in a kind of auditory world, or field, of simultaneous sound in which the Intuitive Man takes precedence over the Analytic Man.

In 1959–60 McLuhan was commissioned by the National Association of Educational Broadcasters, an American organization, to provide an approach and a syllabus for teaching the nature and effects of the media in secondary schools. Called Project 69, or the Understanding Media Project, this study was assisted by a grant from the United States Office of Education and was based partly on interviews with (among others) Dr Harry J. Skornia, who helped McLuhan with the overall plan, Peter F. Drucker, and Bernard Muller-Thym, and on a program of media-testing conducted with the help of staff members of the Ryerson Institute of Technology, Toronto. The ensuing Report on Project in Understanding New Media, *"prepared for and published by the National Association of Educational Broadcasters for the Department of Education, Washington, D.C.", was completed on June 30, 1960. Drafts and a final version are among the McLuhan Papers in the Public Archives of Canada.* Understanding Media *(1964) grew out of McLuhan's work for the* Report.

The following extracts from the Report *include early statements of ideas McLuhan developed in his books and discusses in his later letters. The first three are from the General Introduction:*

"Early in 1960 it dawned on me that the sensory impression *proffered by a medium like movie or radio, was not the sensory* effect *obtained. Radio, for*

example, has an intense visual effect on listeners. But then there is the telephone which also proffers an auditory impression, but has no visual effect. In the same way television is watched *but has a very different effect from movies. These observations led to a series of studies of the media, and to the discovery of basic laws concerning the sensory effects of various media."*

"Today it is axiomatic that we live in a global space fed by information from every point on the sphere at the same time. What possible relevance to the student of media could a point of view be in such circumstances? He must adopt the mosaic approach. He must deal with all media at once in their daily interaction, or else pay the price of irrelevance and unreality. He must deal with each medium as it affects all of our senses, not as it makes an impression on one sense."

"Any medium necessarily is constituted by some ratio of proportion among the human senses. All media are necessarily extensions in technological form of one or more of our senses. The electronic media together add up to an externalization of our sensorium. No change in technology can touch us save by altering the existing ratio among our senses. The nature of sensation being itself comprised of a ratio among our various senses, any increase or decrease of intensity in any sense area immediately affects our awareness of the other senses."

"The so-called 'content' of any medium is another medium. So that the concept of 'content' naturally begins with writing, whose 'content' is the medium of speech."

"For the past century, the artist has been our only navigator in social and political terms."

"All of my recommendations . . . can be reduced to this one: study the modes of the media, in order to hoick all assumptions out of the subliminal, non-verbal realm for scrutiny and for prediction and control of human purposes."

To Wilfred Watson[1]

Understanding Media Project,
96 St. Joseph St.,
Toronto 5, Ont.,
October 8th, 1959.

Dear Wilfred:

As Sheila [Watson][2] has told you, I have been wanting to reply to your letter for sometime, and found it very useful.

[1]Dr Wilfred Watson (b. 1911)—author of *Friday's Child* (1955), a collection of poems that won a Governor General's Award—was Professor of English at the University of Alberta until his retirement in 1976. He collaborated with McLuhan on *From Cliché to Archetype* (1970). Wilfred Watson and his wife Sheila Watson (see note 2 below) were Research Associates at McLuhan's Centre for Culture and Technology, University of Toronto, in 1968-9.

[2]Dr Sheila Watson (b. 1909)—who in 1959 published her well-known poetic novel *The Double Hook*—had entered doctoral studies at the University of Toronto in 1957. She completed a thesis on Wyndham Lewis, under McLuhan's direction, in 1965. She joined the English Department of the University of Alberta in 1961 and retired as a full professor in 1975.

One point that occurs to me in relation to the code-language axis is simply that Lewis Carroll and Edward Lear may well represent the moment of culture when language began to shift back toward code. *Finnegans Wake* would, from this point of view, indicate a similar shift in the entire culture. It may be that the tell-tale feature of such shift is the emergence of the game or play attitude as, for example, when children began to play with numbers instead of doing their arithmetic straightforwardly. Would this not be the moment of saturation of learning? Is not the artist one who lives perpetually on this borderland between the code and language worlds, between technology and experience, between mechanical and organic form? And when a time or a culture is similarly poised between the new technology and traditional experience is not that the moment of maximal creativity for that culture? And are not we to-day, in every field, so poised? And understanding such principles would it not be possible to perpetuate that moment of poise by educational arrangement? In this respect, one might say that [Northrop] Frye's world is simply the slapping down of the poised balance on the visual side of the scale?[3] It occurs, as I write, to ask also whether [Laurence] Sterne had not made this discovery in the course of liberating himself from the lopsided tyranny of the printed word? To which one might add perhaps that the romantics who followed him bogged down in Miltonic solemnity losing the spirit of play which is necessary to maintain the poise between worlds of sensibility?

I am delighted with *pseudomorph* and *collotype*.[4] Did I mention somewhere the term *automorph* which perfectly describes the driver of the small car, but also defines any entity that imposes its own assumptions such as a melody or a poem?

Hoping to have some more chat before long.

Cordially,

[3]That is, in Frye's examination of imagery and symbols, drawn from all cultures, to increase our understanding of literature. For a note on Northrop Frye, see page 182, note 2.

[4]Wilfred Watson's letter of October 8, 1959 proposed "two terms of rhetoric (practical) which we [i.e. Wilfred and Sheila] devised this summer—*pseudomorph* and *collotype*. By his own definition, Frye's archetypes are collotypes, that is pictorial clichés. Pseudomorph I find very useful."

To David Riesman[1]

96 St. Joseph St.,
Toronto 5, Ont.,
October 14th, 1959.

Dear David:

I hasten to abandon the manuscript form of communication in order to get clear the meaning of my previous letter.

I had intended to speak of the subliminal message of print as "repeatability" not respectability![2] Repeatability as subliminal message of print has permeated every area of thought and culture in the Western world since Gutenberg. To the political ruler repeatability has meant the means of achieving a uniform regime within the patterns of a singular vernacular. In Canada, of course, there is no such uniform regime. We have two legal systems, one for the French and one for the English. For the reader of print, the consumer, repeatability confers non-conformity as a basic human right and makes of the print point of view a title to dignity and maturity. Repeatability makes possible the mobilization of man and resources within a uniform visual order which we call nationalism and which is unthinkable under pre-print conditions. Repeatability became the basis of scientific method in a print culture just as it made possible price systems and market organization. The minute fragmentation of continuous movements, whether of mind or hand, conferred upon the Western world the means of industrial organization and assembly-line method in commerce and education. With the advent of electronic tapes in production, the assembly-line has become obsolete and our educational establishment is in all areas characterized by similar aspect of obsolescence. This, David, is a far cry from respectability and I must apologize for having allowed my scribbling hand to have created this misunderstanding.

I expect to be in Cambridge [, Mass.] sometime this year and very much look forward to some leisurely talk with you.

Cordially,

---

[1]David Riesman (b. 1909)—who was a professor in the Department of Social Relations at Harvard University—wrote *The Lonely Crowd: A Study of the Changing American Character* (1965) in collaboration with Reuel Denney and Nathan Glazer, and other books.

[2]Misreading McLuhan's handwriting, Riesman had queried on October 9 whether there was any message of respectability in print for someone who read "so-called trash" and many other kinds of books.

To Peter F. Drucker[1]

Dear Peter:

David Riesman just told me of a book *Metamorphosis*, by Ernest Schachtel, which he indicated was closely related in its interests to the structural changes brought about by media impact.[2]

Print, for example, tended to obliterate awareness of formal causality and change (see Walter Ong's book on *Ramus Method and the Decay of Dialogue*, Harvard University Press). Ong's study traces the rise and the eventual dominance of visual statics in the late Middle Ages and renaissance, explicitly tying these changes to the consequences of printing. Print gave great stress and access to all phases of efficient causality. Electric circuits tend to re-establish sensitivity to formal cause. But I refer to formal cause not in the sense of classification of forms, but to their operation upon us and upon one another.

Kant salvaged formal causality by tucking it away within the mind. But the 17th and 18th century had already deprived the external world of any but efficient causes.

Had a fascinating evening with Bernie Muller-Thym, last week, discussing these matters. He agreed with the entire order of existence and change, because unintelligible if formal causality is banished from the center of study and awareness.

At any rate, my media studies have gravitated toward the center of formal causality, forcing me to re-invent it.

Two years ago I began to query the local Schoolmen[3] about formal causality, only to discover that they had no use for it whatever. As one of them said the other day, "The danger of formal causality is relativism. We prefer platonism with its static universals as less dangerous".

As Joyce would have said, "How cudious an epiphany".

Have just been talking to Claude Bissell, President of the University. He wants you to come, and suggests the following basis in terms of dates to guide your preferences: as for January, somewhere in the middle; as for February, anytime—

---

[1]Peter Drucker (b. 1909) is a Viennese-born American management consultant, teacher, and author. From 1950 to 1972 he was Professor of Management in the Graduate School of Business Administration, New York University, and maintained his own management consultancy firm. In 1971 he became Clarke Professor of Social Science, Claremont Graduate School, Claremont California. Among his many books are *The End of Economic Man* (1939), *The Future of Industrial Man* (1942), *The New Society* (1950), *The Practice of Management* (1954), *Landmarks of Tomorrow* (1959), *Managing for Results* (1964), and *The Effective Executive* (1966).

[2]Ernest G. Schachtel, *Metamorphosis: On the Development of Affect, Perception, Attention and Memory* (1959). McLuhan was exploring these "structural changes" in his *Report on Project in Understanding the New Media* (1960; see pages 255–6).

[3]"Schoolmen" originally referred to teachers of philosophy and theology at the medieval European universities; here it refers to McLuhan's colleagues at St Michael's College.

say the 10th to the 18th. Perhaps March would be best. If so, anytime in March. Of course, other commitments might occur fairly soon for Bissell. I said nothing about amount of fee. But your regular fee would be paid without demur.

As for aspects of the local developments which you might have in mind, a new University is currently in the state of formation.[4] It will be in the city itself, as is Toronto University. It is to accommodate the same students who are now beginning to crowd Toronto University. I do not think it is intended to do any less than Toronto University, but no policy has been established which would suggest that it is to be an inferior model. Only 7% of Ontario High School students enter university. Of these, 30% fail in their first year. This situation is the more ridiculous in that the Upper School Certificate for entering the university requires Grade XIII which is, in some ways, more difficult here than any year within the university. I have given no consideration to this problem myself, but it seems that Grade XIII carries numerous factual and informational stress. The University, on the other hand, is British in favoring the agile journalist mind.

When I asked Bissell about briefing you, I told him of your interest in Medical Schools. He said that he, above all, wanted you to meet his Committee of Counsellors (about seven men) for an evening of general discussion about educational concerns as they arise in your *Landmarks of Tomorrow*. He wants it to be an evening of dialogue, and he expects no specific presentation from you. He is a Prof. of English himself, and an enthusiastic student of your work.

With Cordial Christmas and New Year greetings,

---

[4]York University—at Downsview, on the northwest outskirts of Toronto—was founded in 1959 as an affiliate of the University of Toronto and became independent in 1965.

1960

To David Riesman

Dear Dave:

Have just written a note to Oscar Handlin thanking him for the specially help-ful insights on pages 22–23 of his *John Dewey*.[1] There he points out how even Vocational Training in the later 19th century was oriented to the past, but the same is true of our arts and science courses. History need never be oriented to the past. But to-day when we are again trying to make the new media do the old jobs we also have an orientation to the past which ensures the destruction of all achieved values, like recording on recorded tape.

Much enjoyed Friedenberg's *Vanishing Adolescent*.[2] As you know, my diag-nosis of the change is electronic. When the globe becomes a single electronic computer, with all its languages and cultures recorded on the single tribal drum, the fixed point of view of print culture becomes irrelevant and impossible, no matter how precious. But no, there is a chance of retaining such values, after due appraisal of both old and new media. But the old values cannot be achieved by the old methods. And I do not mean that we should attempt to achieve the values of print culture by teaching print by film or television. The latter course is totally destructive of print values.

A propos of the Oscar Handlin passage I referred to, I have always been inter-ested in the way in which we have tended to train our writers in the newspaper office rather than in the academy. This, of course, is not true in Europe or England. At least the newspaper world focuses attention upon the effect of the print medium. It is this non-concern with effect and with previously packaged content which may be the root cause of non-production in the academies.

Hope of have a chat with Handlin in Cambridge around the April 11 time.[3]

Cordially,

---

[1]Pages 22–3 of Oscar Handlin's *John Dewey's Challenge to Education: Historical Perspectives on the Cultural Context* (1959) discuss the historical concepts of vocational education and the training of good citizens through public education.

[2]Edgar Z. Friedenberg, *The Vanishing Adolescent* (1959).

[3]On this date McLuhan was the guest at a freshman seminar at Harvard University.

To Bernard Muller-Thym[1]

March 7th, 1960.

Dear Bernie:

Glad to see that you are going to be at Arden House Sunday night.[2] I am to perform before the same group, Monday. It would be nice to travel out there with you on Sunday, if that is feasible. I hope to see Wells Foshay in New York on Saturday, so may get to see you Saturday evening.

Since making the enclosed charts, a good deal has clarified and I can see the whole thing moving fast toward a systems development pattern. What strongly suggests this to me, Bernie, is that any intensity in the S-I input (ie. High Definition) completely alters the over-all structure as compared with Low definition.[3] So that, for example, manuscript is Low Definition for the visual part of writing and the speech within the visual code, as it were, is in relatively High Definition. So that a manuscript is read aloud and in depth. The same materials put in print have the visual code in High Definition and the speech goes into very Low Definition and print is read silently and on a single plane.

A road is at first in Low Definition, coming into existence to fetch rural produce to town areas (before road, of course, the pedestrian and the mounted man).[4] As it goes into High Definition, it fetch's the town to the country. It next becomes a substitute for the country and then destroys the country. As it continues to improve, or be more of a road, it destroys the city and is at that stage metamorphosed into a new kind of city. The current town planners talk of cities 3,000 miles long and of hundreds of millions of people. I have omitted the vehicle component in this dynamic, but obviously a road consists of two media simultaneously with constant interaction between them. So that as highway becomes city, it also becomes airway. And the airway is for travel and the highway for living. A similar sort of reversal

---

[1] After the war Bernard Muller-Thym (see page 111, note 2) moved with his large family to New York where, in the early fifties, he became a freelance management consultant renowned for his imaginative approach to problem-solving, and also a teacher and lecturer. There is an essay on Muller-Thym (and on McLuhan) in Richard Kostelanetz, *Master Minds: Portraits of Contemporary American Artists and Intellectuals* (1969).

[2] Arden House—the former home of the Harriman family—in Harriman, New York, is a seminar centre owned by Columbia University.

[3] The Understanding Media Project (see pages 255-6) examined the "language and grammars of the media" by exploring the character of speech, writing, prints, the press, photography, the telegraph, telephone, phonograph, film, radio, and television. The "dynamic symmetries" of the media's operation on man and society are illustrated with charts that lay out the sense factors involved, using the concepts SI (Structural Impact) and SC (Subjective Completion), LD (Low Definition, providing little visual information), and HD (High Definition, filled with data). McLuhan explains that SI refers to sensory impressions as they affect the beholder or audience, SC to the effect of these impressions as they are processed by the audience. These initials were also given the meaning Sensory Impact and Sensory Closure.

[4] This and what follows paraphrases a short section (pp. 15-16) of McLuhan's *Report* (see page 255) entitled "Poly-Antics of the Highway", which is supplemented by a chart.

occurs in the vehicle itself which gives the experience of travel up to a certain speed and then there is the reversal into stasis. So that in jet travel there is hardly any experience of movement at all and whether you are over Rome or Tokyo the experience is the same.

It just happens, Bernie, that having selected High Definition and Low Definition for my S-I corner, I discovered that the major bi-products of S-C shifted to the conscious or unconscious corners of the square also. For example, in radio—a High Definition medium—the conscious effects are private (H-D) and the L-D effects are group dynamics—Fascism, tribalism, teenager, etc.

One consequence of the over-all shift in educational budgeting, that is the relatively small expenditure of public education as compared with business, armed services and entertainment, implies a completion of a great cycle and a return to the apprentice system. The unrest of the teenager is really indicative. Our technology insists that he have an adult role, if only because it gives him a very large portion of the adult world on the installment plan via entertainment. We have only to leave the public school system for children up to the age of 10 or 12 and to abandon compulsory education. If the rest of the young population is employed from the age of 12 on it can escape the older segmentation imposed by a print education system, and instead of living under puerile teachers in a peer group milieu, it can join the adult world directly, just as it does by entertainment from the age of one. Since the commercial expenditure on education is so greatly in excess of public expenditure, a relatively small increase would admit the absorption of the young into the adult classroom in return for which the young would be employed and self-supporting. Under such conditions, the pluralistic variety of educational procedures would stand in striking contrast to the present regimented procedures. In a word, the pluralism of the electronic would get expression and the audio-visual aids would no longer have to skulk about in the old educational spaces and curricula.

Below is the first of many letters in this collection written to Dr Claude Bissell (b. 1916), who was President of the University of Toronto from 1958 to 1971. The Bissell and McLuhan families became friendly shortly after McLuhan joined the staff of St Michael's College in 1946, when Bissell was Lecturer in English at University College. He was Vice-President of the University from 1952 to 1956, and from 1956 to 1958 President of Carlton University, Ottawa. After he returned to Toronto as President—when his life became circumscribed by administrative duties and speaking engagements—McLuhan communicated with him mainly by letter and telephone. The letters to Bissell that follow were written to inform the President, who was one of McLuhan's supporters, of McLuhan's activities and ideas. They were not inspired by questions Bissell raised, and did not seem to demand (though they received) a reply.

In his Halfway Up Parnassus: A Personal Account of the University of Toronto, *1932-1971 (1974), Bissell says that he was first made aware of McLuhan's rep-*

utation in 1959 when he was invited to speak at the graduation exercises of Wayne State University in Detroit. At an informal luncheon with members of the faculty, they were invited to ask Bissell questions about Canada. After a prolonged silence, one person spoke up: "Could you give a brief summary of the ideas of Marshall McLuhan?"

To Claude Bissell

March 8th, 1960.

Dear Claude:

Enclosed are some sheets that may fill you in a bit more on current media gropings. I think you will find the Oscar Handlin points tie in very well with all we have been talking about.[1] The backspin on every pitch, as it were, in American education, culture and entertainment is inherent in the print technology which began as a new mechanical way of doing the old manuscript job. For more than a century the printed book was regarded as merely a cheap manuscript. It was more than a century before pagination began.

A basic item concerning writing and printing is that they are not one, but two media. Speech presented by visual code. Any shift in either affects both. Thus writing is a Low Definition visual code which gave speech the High Definition role, so that people read manuscripts aloud for 3000 years. Print gave the visual code the High Definition or ascendancy enabling people to read at much higher speed and silently. You are aware of the fact that we perform the muscular movements of speech while reading silently. The balance between the media of speech and visual code is precarious, and speech is always trying to break out of the charmed circle as the history of poetry in the past 500 years attests.

I wanted to draw your attention to the strange dynamic whereby the overall structure of any medium reverses many of its characteristics depending on whether the SI is of High or Low Definition. See the enclosed note on the Poly-antics of the Highway.[2] The same principle applies to this matter which we have discussed concerning the enormous educational expansion within industry and the defense services. These, taken in relation to the entertainment industries—which are also educational in the sense of attitude-shaping—represent an expenditure in education which may be 50 times more than all public expenditure in education. It has only dawned on me these last few days that the meaning of all this is that compulsory education in its present segmental and uniform patterns for the training of the nation's manpower as they say, not only is, but has been for a long time obsolete. In his *Vanishing Adolescent*, Friedenberg makes many points that fit perfectly into these discussions of ours. His first major point is that there is a new

[1]See page 261, note 1.
[2]See page 262, note 4.

kind of adult for which adolescence is not a phase of development, so the teenager has simply abandoned the role of adolescence. His second point is the teenager is an "aristocratic" being whose code involves basically courage, loyalty and confidence, i.e. tribal men. His third point, child and teenager alike can easily buy a large portion of the adult world on the installment plan. It is this third point that brings me to my issue; namely, that the teenager is impatiently awaiting his return to the adult world in a multiplicity of serious roles. And this will be done sooner or later by the simple means of employing the youngsters over 10 or 12, and educating them on company time. This would not involve an increase of more than 20% of the present educational budget of industry. The question of controls, policies, would be no more serious than now, and there would be no lag whatever in the use of new media for new educational goals. And the existing educational establishment could be left intact for pre-school and elementary-school effort on traditional lines, instead of dissolving it by the effort to incorporate old media to do the new work. Instead of uniformity and regimentation of education across the country, industry would automatically decentralize and pluralize its aims just as it has had to do with its own operations. I am not discussing this as an ideal, but as the obviously indicated development of the current dynamic factors in the situation. That is to say, Claude, that just as the improvement in the technology of highways precipitates a series of somersaults and reversals, so in all other aspects of our society. It is easy to see why tribal man chooses to freeze himself into a single attitude, and that of course is where we are heading. Accelerated change invokes the gyroscopic or vortex principles of rigidity. Also, to high-speed change no adjustment is possible. We become spectators only, and must escape into understanding. This may be why the conservative has an advantage in such an age of speedy change and is frequently more radical in his suggestions and insights than the progressive who is trying to adjust. The practical progressive trying to make realistic adjustments to change exhausts himself in minor matters and has no energy to contemplate the overall.

The supplement to my work paper on the new media and the new education produced quite an amazing result at the recent Cincinnati conference of DAVI (Department of Audio-Visual Instruction) of the NEA [National Education Association]. Thanks to the charts, which always have a paralyzing effect, a gap in attention was created through which my points actually moved. Apparently, Claude, a merely oral presentation rallies the resources and postures of the fencer, determined at all costs to protect himself from whatever is being said.

Cordially,

Below is the first of several letters in this collection to the English poet, novelist, and critic John Wain (b. 1925), who achieved literary fame with his first novel, Hurry on Down (1953), which placed him among the "angry young men" of the 1950s. (Since then he has published numerous novels, collections of poetry, and works of biography and criticism; he was Oxford Professor of Poetry from 1973 to 1978.) In a long and frank, but appreciative, memoir of his friendship with McLuhan, published in Encounter *in June 1985 ("The Incidental Thoughts of Marshall McLuhan"), Wain recalls his first experience, when he was an Oxford student, of reading McLuhan in* Horizon *("American Advertising", nos. 93–4, 1947) and in* Essays in Criticism *("Tennyson and Picturesque Poetry", July 1951), and also reading a copy of* The Mechanical Bride *lent to him by F.P. Wilson (see page 118, note 1), who was then Merton Professor of English Literature at Oxford. Perhaps through Wilson, McLuhan heard of Wain's interest in his work and wrote him, asking him to contribute to* Explorations. *(A short piece by Wain on the English social revolution since 1945 appeared in* Explorations 7, *March 1957.) McLuhan and Wain first met in Brooklyn in December 1958 and last met in London in 1971; afterwards the correspondence continued "fitfully" (Wain's word). They spent time together not only in Brooklyn and London, but in Washington, Oxford, and Toronto (twice, in 1962 and 1969). Wain's* Encounter *recollections of McLuhan are included in his* Dear Shadows: Portraits from Memory *(1986).*

To John Wain

29 Wells Hills Ave.
Toronto 10, Ont.
March 11th, 1960

Dear John:

Great news, indeed, about your marriage. I do hope my congratulations reach you before you leave for the continent.

Indeed, you have not neglected me at all, and your London Observer review was a doughty stroke, and no botch.[1] I only hope I can do things worthy of praise like yours.

As far as the [*Gutenberg*] project goes, rather large developments and discoveries have occurred in the last few weeks which will enable me to complete it in a very satisfactory manner while, at the same time, opening a new phase of media study which can link it to current electrical studies. I shall send you Media Log

---

[1]This reference has not been identified by Professor Wain, his bibliographer, Mr David Gerard, or by search (which is not to say that a commentary on McLuhan did not appear in the *Observer* some time before this letter).

III, shortly, explaining these matters.[2] Since you are going to Europe and the Soviet Union, let me ask you to notice the differing roles of press and radio and television in shaping their basic attitudes.

For example, I have been studying lately the ways in which all electric media promote the globe to the status of a tribal drum. I began to ask myself, what was the most obvious and massive change which occurred in the 20's and 30's upon the advent of the radio. The answer is fascism or tribalism. Even in Scotland, Wales and Ireland, not nationalism, but tribalism has become evident, but one has only to look at those parts of the world which have never been detribalized or defeudalized in order to see the meaning of radio. This may include Russia. It certainly includes China, India and Africa, where terrible new tribal intensity overlayers futile efforts of detribalization by means of literacy. In this respect the newspaper is national, not tribal, attempting a visual unity of all those who speak a common tongue. But the tribe is constituted via the ear, and even the all-at-onceness of the telegraph fosters this pattern. Hence the teenager. A new tribal man suddenly within a highly mechanical and literate culture.

Television is a tranquil and relatively individual medium, fostering many book values, indirectly. I wish I had time to go into it in detail, but as an example, the TV image unlike the film image constitutes you not the camera, but the screen. It is of low visual definition, and the image effected by luminous spots has a high tactual impact; like contour in prints and engravings giving the T.V. image a strong sculptural quality, which is also to say a strong auditory quality. (You know [André] Malraux, *The Voices of Silence* [1951].) Sculpture is perched on the frontiers of sight and sound, and is a necessary phase prior to the development of writing in any society. Our own re-conquest of the tactual, the kinesthetic and the sculpural in the past century is in a deep sense our retracking our way in the primeval forest.

I hope you don't mind my encouraging you to become media observers and political analysts in these terms. Shall take the whole of this summer off to do the Gutenberg book and shall continue to drop you notes to 25 Florida [Reading, Eng.], and may you and Eirian have a regular Marco Polo time of it.

Warm regards

[2]Beginning in 1959 McLuhan occasionally sent out "Media Logs", a mimeographed collection of insights, probes, statements, and questions—many of which appear in different forms in his books and letters. Typical examples: "Movie, radio, telephone, television, have now reshaped the modes of human sensibility to the point where the merely pictorial ordering of experience, with heavy stress on the visual kinds of enclosure, connection, sequence and control, are obsolete." "This 'content' approach to the media has real meaning for the newspaper as a medium. Its relevance outside the newspaper, for radio or movie or t.v., is very small." "Why must television elections be devoid of issues? Why must all points-of-view be excluded, or included (the result is the same) in t.v. elections?"

To Peter Drucker   April 18th, 1960.

Dear Peter:

Am much looking forward to seeing you later this week, even if it is only in a group.[1]

Claude Bissell has probably sent you the mimeo sheets that I here enclose. Due to my being away so much this year these matters came to my attention only a week ago. If Claude Bissell has read you aright he will be as opposed to this Woodside plan, which in effect seeks to achieve integration by centralization and the wiping out of all college autonomies.[2] The exactly opposite course would seem to be indicated as a means of achieving the ends proposed. The obstacles to introducing a tutorial system of instruction, instead of instruction by centralized lecturing, are much fewer here at Toronto than anywhere else on the continent. What is not understood here at Toronto is that the tutorial system does not depend upon having a group of superior students. Quite the contrary, it is for mediocrity. But because the British aim for a high-level mediocrity as a basis for a governing class, outsiders have supposed that governing-class airs, confidence and prestige belonged to the student as such. I shall always remember my shock on arrival at Cambridge to discover the ordinary mediocrity of the ordinary Cambridge undergaduate.

The Oxford Cambridge ratio of teacher to student is one to 19 or 20. Whereas here it is one to 13. Moreover most of the Oxford Cambridge tutorial work is handled by what we would call graduate students. It is the much dialogue, the weekly essay, and the direct processing of problems especially assigned to meet the needs of an individual student which constitutes the superiority to the lecture system.

To be asked to consult specific standard works on Demosthenes and at the same time to sample the most recent learned journals on the same subject, while preparing a weekly essay, develops a habit of speedy processing of information which fosters a journalistic mentality, which is what Oxford and Cambridge have always stressed.

Here at Toronto the University got away to a start guided by the patterns of London University with its antecedents in the lecturing techniques of the Scottish University with their roots in European methods. Paradoxically, Toronto University filled with Oxford and Cambridge men has had nothing to do with Oxford

---

[1] On April 22 Drucker held a seminar at the University of Toronto with the advisory committee to the President on principles of institutional administration and long-range planning and development.

[2] The Woodside plan was presented in a report by Professor Moffatt Woodside (1906–70) in the 1950s, when he was Dean of Arts and Sciences, University of Toronto. It proposed the adoption of the Oxford pattern of relationships between the constituent colleges and universities of the University of Toronto, with teaching appointments being made and financed by the University. The plan was substantially adopted over the years. The oppressive centralization McLuhan feared was not created, and the colleges were relieved of considerable financial responsibilities.

and Cambridge methods. And this is partly owing to the colonial antipathy to British governing-class attitudes.

Today you can see how Newman's idea of a University has strange new relevance in the electronic age of decentralism.[3] The College set-up at Toronto initially fostered by sectarianism can never meet present needs by pressing toward a centralism based on a 19th-century vision. Integration of the student mind, and the interplay of many subjects which can be achieved by decentralized tutorial could never be achieved by centralized lecturing. It would of course be a triumphal irony if Irish Catholic St. Mikes should become the insistent voice for Oxford Cambridge ideals of gentlemanly liberal education. But Newman does happen to be compatible with 1960 problems and patterns of teaching and learning and decision-making.

So far as I have heard, all the Colleges are violently opposed to the Woodside plan. It may therefore be an extremely propitious time to indicate a solution to all their difficulties by much strengthening rather than much weakening of their autonomies. To what extent this type of solution is applicable to the professional schools I cannot say. In practice, medicine and engineering and the sciences get an enormous amount of tutorial dialogue work in their labs and related assignments. It is paradoxically the humanities that have been most starved of dialogue in recent decades. Incidentally, should you choose to raise any of these issues when you are here, I am sure that it would be not only unnecessary, but more effective to omit any reference to me, or even to any of these arguments. Your enormous experience in related problems in many other fields would have more authority than any direct allusion to educational patterns as such. Some large breakthroughs have occurred in communication study and I am now working with the Electrical Engineering Dept pushing media towards Systems Development. I hope it may be possible for us to have a quiet drink together while you are here.

Most cordial good wishes,

[3]In *The Idea of a University Defined and Illustrated* (1873), John Henry (later Cardinal) Newman (1801–90) maintained that a university should train the mind and instruct rather than encourage research and the diffusion of knowledge, and he defended the tutorial system.

To Peter Drucker

April 26th, 1960.

Dear Peter:

What a superb show you did give us.[1] You can be sure it was a very fruitful visit from our point of view. Shall be seeing Bissell to-morrow night at a party and hope to hear of some of the highlight effects in several of the Departments represented there.

[1]See note 1 of the previous letter.

My friend Tom Easterbrook, from Political Economy, has been engaged these past years in historical studies of the relationship between bureaucracy and enterprise and of the ways in which they interchange roles. As with me in media study he has reached the structuralist stage where content is indifferent. He has isolated the dynamics of the inter-relation between power centers and marginal areas, and momentarily we have a bond in the matter of media as staples.

The effect of a new staple or natural resource upon an economy is much the same as the effect of a new medium. But the sense in which a new medium is a staple depends upon recognizing that media are the technological externalization of our senses. Such was phonetic writing. Such is radio. When electronics makes possible access to the human senses as natural resource, the whole nature of commodity and of services undergoes transformation.

The current impasse in information theory results from unawareness that so-called "information" is a second or sometimes a third medium, as in writing.

Please tell me what sources you had in mind when referring to the scholarly failure to understand the meaning of print in its first decades. Am sure I've missed quite a lot here.

Your visit was a real thrill, and personal gratification to me. Very warm regards.

To Bernard Muller-Thym

May 5th, 1960

Dear Bernie:

Very many thanks, Bernie, for your effort in the Merle Jones direction.

Am enclosing the *Teenager* script which was videoed here a couple of weeks ago, and which will be broadcast May 18th.[1]

TV is a cool medium, because Low Definition, as is telephone. But press, movie and radio are hot media, because High Definition. But TV is also an introvert medium; because people are the screen they are driven inward. And there is a vast difference between an inward togetherness and an extrovert togetherness.

I haven't studied your notes to Jones sufficiently to comment now. I want to mention some aspects of the Richard Meier script which came to mind yesterday.[2] A propos of his theme of substitutability, notice that when information

---

[1] *The Teenager* was a thirty-minute documentary on CBC-TV's program "Explorations" (producer Daryl Duke, program organizer Eric Koch), in which McLuhan took part.

[2] Richard L. Meier (b. 1920), who received a Ph.D. degree in organic chemistry, was at this time associate professor of conservation in the School of Natural Resources, University of Michigan. The subjects of his writings include the impact of science and new technology on society—he wrote *Science and Economic Development* (1956)—and organization theory. The paper referred to was "Information, Resource Use, and Economic Growth", read at Ann Arbor, Michigan, in April 1960.

flow reaches a sufficient level almost any resource material can be substituted for any other, then the situation closely resembles the activity of the sensus communis[3] in translating one sense into another. I wish you would meditate on this theme. I am trying to get the systems-development people to work out flow charts which would enable us to chart and predict the effects of input through any one sense, as it affects the ratio of intensities in the other senses. Recent perception theory strongly suggests that there are means of training the eye by means of the ear, and so with all the other senses. This is only to say that anything which affects one sense has a due effect on the others. Sam Renshaw, at Ohio State, told me yesterday, that as any one sense approaches virtuosity it requires less and less impression stimulus in order to perform great feats. Because the inner effectors take up an expression role which minimizes the impression role. What he referred to as inner effectors we did not get into. But I do have the relevant readings, and shall get at them right away. I see no reason to neglect the notion that with each of our senses becoming externalized electronically, we encounter the sensus communis in a collective form for the first time, and can and need to know very much more about the operations of the private sensus communis.

Renshaw urged me to contact Bell Telephone Labs where he said I would find teams of researchers happy to tackle my hypotheses, so I am writing them to-day and shall also write in the same connection to: Mr. J.M. Allen of AT&T.

Notice, Bernie, in the matter of substitutability that the principle manifests itself as the substitution of process for product as in the Edgar Poe theory of composition. With the symbolists in general, poem becomes the process by which poem is made.[4] This is, of course, closely related to organized ignorance. But à la Meier the increasing volume of information flow substitutes for products in the sense of becoming the major product. In terms of the university as an area of subjects, the tendency of awareness of process is certainly to make one subject substitutable for another. And so by a commodious vicus of recirculation (note

---

[3] *sensus communis* a term used several times in these letters, is the Latin translation of Aristotle's *aisthesis koine*, which in his usage has more than one meaning: "perception of movement, rest, number, shape, and size is shared by several senses" (*De Anima*, 418a) and "Since we can perceive that we see and hear it must be either by sight itself, or by some other sense" (425b)—the "common sense" which enables us to perceive *that* we perceive. See also page 281, note 4.

[4] In his essay "The Philosophy of Composition" (1846) Poe writes, "I prefer commencing with the consideration of an *effect*", and goes on to analyse the construction of "The Raven", showing "that the work proceeded, step by step, to its completion with the precision and rigid consequence of a mathematical problem." On pages 266–7 of *The Gutenberg Galaxy*, McLuhan says that it was Poe "who first worked out the rationale of this ultimate awareness of the poetic process ["of examining the *effect* of art and literature before producing anything at all"] and who saw that instead of directing the work to the reader, it was necessary to incorporate the reader in the work." Citing Poe's invention of the detective story, he writes: "Not only is the detective story the great popular instance of working backwards from effect to cause, it is also the form in which the reader is involved as co-author. Such is also the case in symbolist poetry whose completion of effect from moment to moment requires the reader to participate in the poetic process itself."

the chiasmic [chiastic] form here) we come back to Bernard, Eckhart, and the University of Being.[5]

I am exceedingly grateful to Richard Meier, but I understand what he is saying so much better than he does that I am really in some doubt as to what sort of credit to hand him when these things come to publication. It is very odd I find, Bernie, that as one moves into a faster and richer dialogue all desire for publication ceases. Which remark reminds me that I may not yet have sent to you the Domenico Farias essay. If you already have a copy, please return as I am already shy of copies. This essay was translated for me by our local seminarians.

Am going to Houston in a week. If I get favourable reactions from AT&T and Bell Telephone, I should be seeing you in New York fairly soon.

[5]The phrase "by a commodious vicus of recirculation" appears in the opening sentence of *Finnegans Wake*; "chiastic": from *chiasmus*, the rhetorical inversion of the order in the second of two parallel pharases; St Bernard (1090–1153), abbott of the Cistercian foundation of Clairvaux, exerted a powerful influence in Europe, developing the Augustinian contemplative tradition with its emphasis on faith rather than reason; Johannes Eckhart (c. 1260–1327), known as "Meister Eckhart" (or Eckhard), was a Dominican who was the founder of German mysticism (and the subject of Muller-Thym's Ph.D. thesis, which was published in 1939 as *The Establishment of the University of Being in Meister Eckhart of Ockham*).

To Claude Bissell

May 6th, 1960.

Dear Claude:

Your gesture in respect to summer aid is princely. It will take a considerable strain off us in the summer months ahead.[1]

Regarding the Canadian Manufacturers' Association address,[2] I am having a paper typed for you which was given last month by Richard Meier at a Conference on Natural Resources and Economic Growth.[3] He is an Economist who is also an Information Theorist, so he made the experiment in this paper of translating the basic economic concepts into information theory. The result is astounding, or as Joyce would say astoneaging. He discovered (a) that economic growth and information movement are the same thing; (b) at high levels of information movement, commodities or resources become substitutable. That is, there is no indispensable raw material or commodity; (c) process tends to absorb product; (d) staples and resources are media, and media are staples. I have taken the

[1]This refers to support for a seminar, originally financed by the Ford Foundation, to study culture and communications that led to experiments concerning the relative effectiveness of radio, television, and lectures in university instruction. McLuhan was chairman and the other members included Professors T.G. Easterbrook (Economics) and D. Carlton Williams (Psychology).

[2]Bissell had been invited to address the Annual General Meeting of the Association in Toronto on Monday morning, June 6.

[3]See previous letter, note 2.

liberty of translating some of his language into mine. But, as you well know, the world some decades ago reached the point where information became by far the largest product and/or commodity in the world. For example, AT&T is several times greater than General Motors, although it moves only information.

Now, from your point of view, it seems to me that some of these points directly concern the university. The principle that at very high levels of information movement substitutability occurs (this by the way applies also to our own sense lives in which each sense typically translates itself into each of the other five senses) applies to the studies of the university. When stress moves from product to process, all of the subjects in the university also become substitutable for one another. At the very high level of information movement in which to-day we are involved, we find ourselves less in a university of subjects than in what Meister Eckhart called the university of being. For in each subject concerned with method and creative insight tends to bring each subject directly into the mode of contemplation of its relation to Being. For example, Ken Boulding in *The Organizational Revolution*, on p. 66, mentions that "the idea that a theory of organization is possible is one of the important ideas of our time".[4] Notice that if information moves so fast that the causes and effects of any action are felt almost together—then it becomes indispensable to have a theory of organization, but it also becomes possible. It is the telescoping of actions and consequences which makes understanding of principles easier. Another way of putting this, Claude, is to say that control is only possible through acceleration of change. A ship that is moving at the same speed as the current has no steerageway. What is ordinarily called planning is, in effect, acceleration.

In the same way, the greatly increased speed of action and reaction, because of electronic information movement, compels organizations to assume an ethical character in the sense of having inclusive rather than exclusive purposes. Specialized lines of development are intolerable, when every line crosses every line.

That is to say, that the dialogue now characterizes the interplay of things themselves, and any effort to understand or control such situations by any means less inclusive than the dialogue will scarcely work.

Should be able to get the Meier paper to you late on Monday. Between him and Boulding, you should be able to manage very well indeed with the Manufacturers' Association.

By the way, Ken Boulding's book, *The Image*, 1959, is small and richly nourished.[5] It has lots of economic tie-ins.

I am going out of town to-morrow to work on a video production in Detroit. Please indicate any further elaboration of these things which you would wish me to provide.

---

[4]Ken Boulding, *The Organizational Revolution: A Study in the Ethics of Economic Organization* (1953).

[5]Ken Boulding, *The Image: Knowledge in Life and Society* (1956).

To Claude Bissell

St. Michael's College
December 14, 1960

Dear Claude,

Current recession seems to have had a bad effect on the flow of jokes, but there is one inexhaustible source, namely Father Sheridan,[1] who toils not and never ceases to spin a very good yarn. You are probably familiar with his designation of the various traffic arrangements of our colleges in terms of their theology. Before Trinity had its stoplight, there used to be a cop, and he pointed out the natural tie-in of the Established Church with the police force. Victoria with its push-button stoplight referred of course to the habit of private judgment. And St. Michael's of course, which has neither policeman nor stoplight, "but we have extreme unction."

A story he told recently is about an occasion when he was babysitting for some relatives of his. A little seven-year-old girl showed him over the house, mentioning the members of the family who occupied various rooms. When they came to the room of her oldest sister, a seventeen-year-old girl, she said with a somewhat gloomy note, "I had hoped to have this room for myself, but she *never* married."

Speaking of funny stories, I've been made an offer by Harvard's new Center for Visual Arts to join their staff.[2] This directly connected with last year's work on media.

And now just a note about Grade XIII and high school: it seems awfully hard to pop up with even the most obvious matters among those grave administrators, but again, they would seem to need reminding that even in the business world today major attention is given not only to the present mode of operation, but to the precise modes that will prevail within ten years.

Our present high-school system will not exist in ten years in any recognizable form. The pressures toward decentralism, from several levels at once: first the move toward decentralized pluralism felt throughout the community as a result of the speeded-up movement of information; faster-moving information coincides with rising levels of information generally. Rising levels of information exert specific changes on *any* situation, namely, they have the effect of making one component substitutable for other components. In the humblest material sense, as information levels rise, no raw material or natural resource is indispensable any longer. The same is true of subject matters. The more that is known about any one, say math or biology, the more readily they interrelate with and substitute for poetry or history.

[1] Father James J. Sheridan (1914–87)—Professor Emeritus, Department of Classics, St Michael's College, University of Toronto.

[2] On November 29, 1960 Jacqueline Tyrwhitt (see page 277) wrote to McLuhan from Harvard University suggesting that he go to Harvard "for a period". On December 16 she asked: "Wouldn't a term of research, with a minor teaching job on the side, be worth considering . . .?" The inquiry (by Tyrwhitt's admission) was unofficial.

In the personnel area, rising levels of information impose a multiplicity of roles where formerly there had been specialism. The top executive becomes a coordinator of other people's roles, somewhat in the style of a symphony conductor, rather than a decision-maker in the ordinary sense. The rising pressures which are already beginning to be felt from educational broadcasting and the teaching machine alike are both in the direction of private tutorial and person-to-person dialogue. It is understandable why the misconception persists that these teaching resources are centralizing in character. We naturally assume that any new pressure will drive things further in the direction they have already been following.

As information levels rise in the over-all global community, it is not only the boundaries between subject matters but age groupings that disappear. We are paralysed by an image in this matter, as in the current problem of the timetable. It is easy to escape from the bondage of this image at the center by paying some attention to the marginal developments in which new lines of force and new patterns of association in learning are already apparent.

I've been asked to answer a series of questions, one of which is this: "In your opinion will the television school broadcasts ever replace the teacher in the classroom?" Suppose in 1500 AD we had been asked whether we thought that the new portable teaching machine, the printed book, would ever replace oral scholastic debate in the training of the human mind. Why do people assume that there's an absolute, static fixed value inherent in some pre-existing situation, while they spend all their time and energy creating new situations which will surely liquidate the pre-existing one?

The patterns which will characterize the future high school, as contrasted with the present one, will include that team or syndicate approach to learning which is the heart of dialogue. This pattern which has already declared itself at the highest levels of research, of management and political discussion, has also appeared most emphatically in the study habits of high school students, who now say in the evening, "I'm going out to do my homework."

The lay-out of grades, subjects and timetable will assume an altogether more flexible character as the dialogue between learner and teacher, and learner and learner, develops under the increasing electronic impact. That is to say that the electronic movement of information simply imposes its own assumptions on any situation, and those assumptions consist in a field of decentralized nuclei quite unlike any visual hierarchy of time or space arrangements such as we're accustomed to in the Euclidean and Newtonian world.

The electronic patterns and pressures are already mounting and modifying the pre-existing patterns. The question arises how much resistance is in the old patterns, and how much we care to reinforce that resistance. But it is quite unnecessary to deliberate about the present situation, as if our job were to hold it like a Maginot line, thus allowing the Panzer forces to move round us on all sides. Is it not likely that the control of change consists in the anticipation of change, that it is necessary to go a little bit faster than the actual changes themselves in order to be in control? A boat that is moving at the same speed as the current has no steerageway. Merely to yield to the immediate pressures is to be out of control.

These kinds of questions are of the sort that I felt were improper to raise in the committee. If I have been mistaken in this, please tell me.

Most cordially,

To Corinne McLuhan's family in Fort Worth

[29 Wells Hill Ave]
Sunday [December 25] 1960

Dearest "Moms" and "Muz" and *Everybody*!

I am really *delighted* with the swell-elegant glass tray (which arrived in perfect order and without duty to be paid). Since we serve a great deal of wine it will get shown off very often. I am very proud of it. We do have some very fine china and glass—more than most people ever have—and it's all from 602 West Second St!

Doing a good deal of entertaining now as always. We certainly get the use out of these things. And since we do our own washing up, etc., nothing has been broken to date.

You would have heard from me sooner except that I've been so keyed up over this book job [*The Gutenberg Galaxy*] that until Sunday comes I'm useless for anything else. However, the end is in sight. Proof-reading of typescript and chaptering is in progress. So I've written a 400-page book in less than one month.[1] Moreover, the very day it goes into the mail (Tuesday) I go to work on another book which will be done before school begins in late September. I've been reading and reading and reading for 20 years and now it's time to put out some things of my own. It's going to mean some extra cash eventually.

Corinne is the greatest help, not only in typing but in discussing the work in progress.

All our love to all of you
Marshall

[1]This refers to the typescript, since the total length of *The Gutenberg Galaxy* is 300 pages.

Below is the first of many letters to Jacqueline (or Jackie, as she signed herself to friends) Tyrwhitt (1905–83), who was born in Pretoria, South Africa, and trained at the Architectural Association, London, specializing in town planning. She became a dynamic presence at the University of Toronto when, on July 1, 1951, she was appointed to the Graduate School, and on May 31, 1954 to the staff of the planning department of the School of Architecture. In this period she spent a good deal of time with McLuhan and his friends and colleagues Tom Easterbrook, Carlton Williams, and Edmund Carpenter—she was an associate editor of Explorations—*and was always part of the group that welcomed and talked with such like-minded visitors to Toronto as Eric Havelock, Sigfried Giedion, and Ashley Montagu. Typically interesting herself in the city's good and bad features and its planning developments, she offended powerful interests after her class project on the development of Toronto Island was televised on the CBC. When Tyrwhitt left Toronto in 1955 she became Professor of Town Planning at the Graduate School of Design, Harvard University, of which her friend Sigfried Giedion was the head. She met C.A. Doxiadis in India in the 1950s and through him was enabled to build a house in Greece, at Speroza—where she lived for part of the year (she suffered from asthma) -and obtained the editorship of the magazine published by Doxiadis Associates,* Ekistics: Review on the Problems of Human Settlements. *The McLuhans visited her in Greece on several occasions.*

To Jacqueline Tyrwhitt

Toronto
Dec. 23, 1960

Dear Jackie,

In hopes that this will reach you before your trip overseas. After having written six single-spaced pages to Chermayeff, I think I can put them all in a couple of sentences, as follows.[1]

Now that by electricity we have externalized *all* of our senses, we are in the desperate position of not having any *sensus communis.*[2] Prior to electricity, the city was the sensus communis for such specialized and externalized senses as technology had developed. From Aristotle onward, the traditional function of the sensus communis is to translate each sense into the other senses, so that a unified, integral image is offered at all times to the mind. The city performs that function for the scattered and distracted senses, and spaces and times, of agrar-

[1]Serge Chermayeff (b. 1900)—a Russian-born architect and planning consultant, who had been a professor in the Graduate School of Design, Harvard University (1953–62), and was then teaching at Yale University (1962–72)—had asked McLuhan to comment on the typescript of *Community and Privacy: Toward a New Architecture of Humanism* (1963), which Chermayeff wrote with Christopher Alexander. McLuhan replied with a long critique dated December 19, 1960.

[2]For *sensus communis*, see page 271, note 3.

ian cultures. Today with electronics we have discovered that we live in a global village, and the job is to create a global *city*, as center for the village margins. The parameters of this task are by no means positional. With electronics any marginal area can become center, and marginal experiences can be had at any center. Perhaps the city needed to coordinate and concert the distracted sense programs of our global village will have to be built by computers in the way in which a big airport has to coordinate multiple flights.

Chermayeff made it plain to me that the problems are not just locational, nor to be approached merely by present planning concepts. As always when a serious problem emerges, the answer will be found to have been discovered somewhat earlier in an unexpected area. The problem of urban planning today in the field of nuclei that *is* the global village is assuming more and more the character of language itself, in which all words at all times comprise *all* the senses, but in evershifting ratios which permit ever new light to come through them. Is not this the problem that we have now to face in the management of inner and outer space, not fixed but ever new-made ratios, shifting always to maintain a maximal focal point of consciousness. Thus the human community would assume the same integral freedom and awareness as the private person? By electricity, Jackie, we have not been driven out of our senses so much that our senses have been driven out of *us*. Before we can return to one another, a good deal of clarification is needed for the purposes of reconciliation. I was put in mind of much of this by the problem of *noise* as it appears in Chermayeff's book. Noise is of course just any kind of irrelevance, and yet irrelevance is a needed margin for any kind of attention or center. In the field of attention, a center without a margin is the formula for hypnosis, stasis and paralysis. Again, when our senses are external to us, it becomes natural to regard a perpetual flow of programs through all media as indispensable to the community, just as much as the private individual considers that all of his senses should be receiving impressions all the time, even in sleep. In a word, that which is normal and desirable in a print culture with regard to the titillation of the senses may become quite nonviable under electronic conditions, even for the welfare of the private individual. Whatever we may wish in the matter, we can no longer live in Euclidean space under electronic conditions, and this means that the divisions between inner and outer, private and communal, whatever they may have been for a literate culture, are simply *not there* for an electric one. But the space-time of a preliterate society is not the space-time of our electric one.

It would seem, Jackie, that your prompting me to consider a role for myself at the Center [the Center for Visual Arts at Harvard] has inspired me with the conviction that you simply can't do without me![3] The thought of having daily access to and dialogue with all the departments of Harvard and MIT begins to assume in my mind the character of an absolute need! And so once more, a Blessed Christmas, and love from us all,

[3]See page 274, note 2.

1961

To Claude Bissell

Dear Claude,

You fill me with trepidation by the prospect of presenting patterns of educational change to your very formidable group.[1] But I'm not going to balk. It would be a very great help if I could make an initial presentation to *you*. Some matters have come up recently which clarify some of the issues. For example, what our technology has done electrically, and will do with ever-increasing intensity, is to increase the flow of information in all directions and at all levels. What is needed therefore is an understanding of what happens to existing center-margin relationships as the interplay between center and margin is affected by ever-higher levels of information. Classroom and curriculum as centers for community margins can undergo some strange reversals of roles, as well as considerable subdivision of roles, when the same levels of information are equally available at margin and center. It is this in a word which has caused the restructuring of management. But there is nothing in any management structure, so far as the response to such information change is concerned, which differs from an educational structure, a biological structure or an art structure. Any field of perception is a structure of center-marginal interplay, and when the center usurps margin, the patient is in an hypnotic trance; or alternatively, mad.

The same problems are faced now by town planners, for whom changes in center-margin roles and interplay have become sheer nightmare. We at least in education have available possible structures of moving transparencies, or montage patterns of multi-level kind, in which by means of dialogue centers and margins can change positions at high speed.

The immediate crisis of the modern world is this, and it may throw light upon educational problems as well: we have driven our senses out of ourselves, by externalizing all of them by technology, creating a new global envelope of sense which demands perpetual nutrition or titillation; but we have no con-sensus. In our individual organisms, there are powers which translate each sense into each other sense, as long as the impressions occur. It is now mandatory that we achieve similar consensus for our collectively externalized senses; hence the frantic calls to order, in our time. So long as the externalizations of sense were rudimentary in the form of writing and architecture, the pressures for consensus could be met by *urban* order. The traditional role of *city* is that of center or consensus for rustic margin. Now that our technologies are no longer positional but interplan-

---

[1]McLuhan spoke to an advisory group of senior academics, chiefly heads of divisions in the University of Toronto, that Bissell set up to discuss major educational problems.

etary, an urban consensus will not serve. The *university itself* would seem to become the only possible model of such consensus, inviting the concept of a university of being and experience, rather than of subjects. Such a concept of university could supersede the concept of urban center in an age of electronic information movement, and need not be locational, or geographic.

I enclose on a separate sheet a few gags and stories as gathered on a recent trip. In so doing I have no thought of your reciprocating, but merely the numerous occasions on which you might have occasion or need for an ever-renewed stock. I had a most delightful afternoon and evening with Peter Drucker and his family recently, and he is most interested in all that goes on here.

Regards as ever,

To Walter J. Ong, S.J.

29 Wells Hill Ave.
Toronto 4
Nov 18 [1961]

Our dear Walter

Such a joy to have had you here! Such a pity it was so brief. It would really take a few days to fill you in on my current interests.

You know Ed Hall's *The Silent Language*?[1] Do get same if not. He provides not my kind of thing, but a helpful approach to same. The media as extensions of the sense organs alter sensibility and mental process at once. All the *other* senses are altered in themselves, and in their ratios among themselves, by any technology that extends or externalizes any *one* of them. The history of art provides a massive check on this. Marx's idea of change was based on the idea of industrial production and consumption as extensions of our organic life. He got no further than that. But he could say that we are different when our organic life is extended beyond our sensory envelope. Probably if he had had a more adequate theory he would never have got acceptance.

My theory is only acceptable to Thomists for whom consciousness as analogical proportion among the senses from moment to moment, is quite easy to grasp. But print technology actually smashes that analogical awareness in society and

---

[1] The title of Edward T. Hall's *The Silent Language* (1959), a book that McLuhan often refers to, alludes to "the non-verbal language which exists in every country of the world and among the various groups within each country . . . . In addition to what we say with our verbal language we are constantly communicating our real feelings in our silent language—the language of behaviour." On page 79 Hall says: "Today man has developed extensions for practically everything he used to do with his body", and he cites the evolution of weapons, clothes, houses, furniture, power tools, TV, telephones, books, money, and our transportation network as extensions of "what man once did with his body or some part of his body." For Edward T. Hall, see page 383, note 1; see also page 515, note 1.

the individual. Mss. technology put it under great strain.[2] But an event like radio or even telegraph has the deepest consequences for the momentary sense ratios of the ordinary person. To understand these it is necessary to know the prior state of sense ratios. i.e. Radio has quite different effects in Germany or Russia than in France or England. And so with film or TV. But radio in Africa or China is worse than the plague.

I can now explain these matters very much better than I did in *Understanding Media*.[3] But no more evidence is needed of the hypnotic aspect of *all* media in human history than the absence of awareness among those who underwent them. Each is invested with a cloak of invisibility.

I am naturally eager to attract many people to such study as this and see in it the hope of some rational *consensus* for our externalized senses. A sensus communis for external senses is what I'm trying to build.[4] Does that make sense to you Walter?

Many blessings from us
Marshall

Walter J. Ong

[2]The analogy of proportion, an Aristotelian/Thomist concept, is exemplified in the differences perceived by each of the senses in the quality of one thing (e.g. motion); these differences are analogs of one another. But with the printed word, one sense cannot be used to check up on another—print technology creates a unified imaginative understanding. As the whole imagination is activated by the eye through the medium of print, the perception that there are many differences in, or ideas of, motion (for example) is lost. This analogical awareness was first put under strain with the advent of writing—"Mss. technology"—which initiated the development of other technologies.

[3]Not the book of 1964 but the *Report* of 1960; see pages 255–6.

[4]Further to the note on the *sensus communis* on page 271, Thomas Aquinas, in his *Summa Theologica* (Part I, Q. 78, Art. 4), discusses the *sensus communis* as a device for putting things together in an *internal* sense, McLuhan is concerned with the media's tampering with the input to our *external* senses, in such a way that a new reality is created, and would like to explain this by means of an externalized *sensus communis*.

1962

The Gutenberg Galaxy: The Making of Typographic Man, mentioned in the next letter as being in page proof, was published in Canada in June 1962 by the University of Toronto Press. (It was not published in the U.S. until 1965.) Employing what he called the "mosaic" approach—basing his discussion on, and drawing his insights from, quotations from some 200 authors and their works— McLuhan fashioned a complex and rich commentary on the causes of change in society (and, psychologically, in people themselves) when environments were transformed as the pre-literate, oral culture was altered by the phonetic alphabet and manuscript technology, and when the invention of printing and the book produced a radically new environment created by the resulting dominance of a visual orientation, by lineality and mass-production, changing people's sense of themselves (communion with books created a sense of privacy and individuality) and their relationship with their surroundings and with each other. Printing from movable type, McLuhan says, created the "public" and caused the formation of "nations". The era of print-domination was in turn the prelude to the present electronic age, beginning with the invention of the telegraph.

To Walter J. Ong, S.J.

29 Wells Hill Ave
Toronto 4
Jan 24/62

Dear Walter

Am pushing the Gutenberg Galaxy through the U of Tor. press now. Hope to get some page proofs in 2 weeks. Since I use you much *in* the book I can scarcely expect you to appear on the jacket also! One ideal bloke for a jacket phrase would be C.P. Snow.[1] Would you guess he could be induced? Me, admirer of *The Masters* etc and the 2 cultures of course! My book aims to make them *one*.

Hope you will get something from it after all I've got from you.

Warm regards
Mac.

Walter J. Ong

[1]See the two letters following. *The Masters* (1951) by C.P. (Sir Charles) Snow (1905–80) is the best known of his many novels, which have academic (Cambridge) and scientific settings. Snow coined the phrase "the two cultures" in his Rede Lecture delivered at Cambridge in 1959 and published as *The Two Cultures and the Scientific Revolution* (1959), in which the respective cultures of "literary intellectuals" and "physical scientists" are contrasted and the lack of communication between them is described.

To Walter J. Ong, S.J.

29 Wells Hill Avenue
Toronto 4, Ontario, Canada
February 1, 1962

Dear Walter,

It was good of you to reply so quickly. I enclose the letter [to C.P. Snow] you suggested.[1] Don't hesitate to send them back if you think of desirable improvements.

The Snow suggestion for the jacket came from a young Scot [R.I.K. Davidson] who is my editor at the Press. It does seem to be the ideal suggestion. I really do imagine that Snow will approve of the book, even though it gives a totally different meaning to his idea of the two cultures. The real animus against the book will be felt in gnostic and masonic quarters, who will rightly find the rug pulled out from their matter-spirit bias.

That review you sent of the Gilbert book is most timely and helpful.[2] Many thanks. Do keep in touch.

Apropos *Understanding Media*, which I am now turning to re-write completely (and at once),[3] I would so much welcome data and reading suggestions on any point whatever. I expect to add to the present form of *Understanding Media* several media like money, railways, ships and 'planes and cars—in fact, all of those externalizations of our bodily functions and perceptions which cause all human technology to exist in the ablative case.

Warm regards
Mac

Walter J. Ong

[1] This letter follows.

[2] Neal W. Gilbert, *Renaissance Concepts of Method* (1960).

[3] That is, he was rewriting the *Report on Project in Understanding the New Media* (1960); see page 255. *Understanding Media: The Extensions of Man* (1964) would result from this.

To C.P. Snow[1]

St. Michael's College
University of Toronto
Toronto 5, Ontario, Canada
February 1, 1962

Dear Sir Charles:

When Walter Ong was lecturing here a few weeks back, he spoke of the great satisfaction he had had in conversations with you and Lady Snow at Wesleyan University. I, too, was delighted to talk with one who had become acquainted

[1] See previous page, note 1.

with the author of *The Masters* and *The Two Cultures*. Perhaps it is as a Cambridge man, myself, that these books mean so much to me.

Thinking you were still at Wesleyan University, I wrote Father Ong a few days ago, asking him to mention to you a book of mine which is now in the University of Toronto Press, *The Gutenberg Galaxy: the Making of Typographic Man*. This book undertakes, almost as a sequel to your *Two Cultures*, to explain the historical divergence of these two cultures, both before and since Gutenberg. I dreamed, therefore, of seeing a phrase of yours on the jacket of *The Galaxy*, and I hoped that Father Ong could act as *liaison* in this matter.

May I [*word unclear*], therefore, to send to you page proofs of this book in a fortnight or so? Indeed, I would not have entertained this thought at all, were I not reasonably sure that you would find this book entirely relevant to your own concern with our Western culture.

With much gratitude for the pleasure I have had in your work.[2]

Sincerely
Marshall McLuhan

[2]Father Ong, to whom McLuhan sent this letter to send to Snow, typed a message in the lower left-hand corner. There was apparently no reply from Snow.

To Walter J. Ong, S.J.

29 Wells Hill Ave,
[February ? 1962]

Dear Walter
The piece on Eliot in St Louis was excellent.[1] On Mcpherson St I lived across from Corinne Lucas who went to dancing school with Eliot when he was a wee lad. She used to say to him: "Tom, you would be a real fine boy if you would give up that poetry stuff."

There is a good deal of St. Louis imagery in [Eliot's poem The] Dry Salvages by the way.

Muriel Bradbrook at Girton [College, Cambridge] is an old friend of ours.[2] Say hello for us.

Everything happening at once here at this time—much exam committee

much meeting of planning
and advisory groups. Such
the penalty of federation.

Blessings

Walter J. Ong

Mac and Corinne.

[1]Walter J. Ong, S.J., "'Burnt Norton' in St. Louis", *American Literature*, vol. XXXIII, no. 4, January 1962.
[2]Professor Muriel C. Bradbrook is the author of *T.S. Eliot* (1950). See page 462, note 1.

To Walter J. Ong, S.J.

29 Wells Hill Ave.
Toronto 4
Feb 8/62

Our dear Walter

Ever so many thanks for getting note off to Snow. Page proofs [of *The Gutenberg Galaxy*] won't be available for a month but I could send the carbon copy if you have time to look at it and talk it up. The press men here say that pre-publication talk among those who see advance copies has become a more effective way of building a book than reviews. However, it would be nice to get it a good spot in the N.Y. Times. How does one wangle such things?

Mind you Walter, I'm not concerned to get any kudos out of this book. It seems to me a book that somebody should have written a century ago. I wish somebody else *had* written it. It will be a useful prelude to the rewrite of Understanding Media that I'm doing now.

Look at page 79 of Ed. Hall's *The Silent Language*. Is not our approach to media the one indicated there? i.e. all technologies as ablations of sense and faculty—all in the ablative case? And all acting as separate closed systems that re-enter our sensibilities with metamorphic power? All my media work has assumed this. But who else assumes this approach? The orientals only? Is it not the approach from *formal* cause?

Warm regards in Our Lord

Mac.

Walter J. Ong

To Walter J. Ong, S.J.

29 Wells Hill Ave
Toronto 4
Feb 20 [1962]

Dear Walter

In Cambridge (England) don't neglect Donald Davie fellow of St Catharine's. He was at Santa Barbara for a year.[1] Do you know John Wain? Good friend of mine. You would like him. Lives at "The Keep" Hampstead or some such. Check him out in the phone book. He lectures at the Stratford Festival here this year.

David Riesman writes that he was never able to get the Lonely Crowd reviewed in the New York Times. Sunt lacrima verum.

---

[1]The English poet and critic Donald Davie (b. 1922). To the series *Patterns of Literary Criticism* (1965-74), of which McLuhan was a co-editor (see page 470, note 1), Davie contributed *Russian Literature and Modern English Fiction: A Collection of Essays* (1965).

Did you get the point of "closure" from my charts? SI–SC.[2] Chair for example is ablation of squat posture. Chair itself is an ablative absolute, that is. But its existence effects a "closure" or rearrangement of other gestures. Closure of chair is table, of wheel is road, of radio is intense visualisation etc.

Walter you have been a big help, and will be. Our work is complementary. We greatly assist each other.

Many many thanks and blessings

Mac.

Walter J. Ong

[2]These abbreviations, which formerly stood for Structural Impact and Subjective Completion, now refer to Sensory Impact and Sensory Closure. (See also page 262, note 3.)

The following is a sample of the many "sheets" McLuhan sent periodically to a small mailing-list of people who shared his interests. While it is not strictly a letter, an interesting (handwritten) note to Father Ong is appended to this one.

A "Sheet"

29 Wells Hill Ave

Toronto 4

Feb 27/62

The TV Image: One of our Conquerors

When we hear that *Life* magazine is in trouble, or that the motor-car industry is running scared, or that the text-book industry, like the school system, is in the process of total restructuring, few people are inclined to suspect that all of these changes and a very great many more are directly due to the impact of the TV image on the American senses. The TV image is not the first to have reshaped the outlook, the preferences, and the desires of a society. There have been earlier outerings of the human senses in technological form. Externalizations of our senses, such as the wheel, and the phonetic alphabet, of radio and photography, also constituted closed systems which invaded the open system of our senses with tremendous transforming power. But the TV image is the first technology by which man has outered his haptic, or tactile, powers. Its effects, therefore, on the balance or ratio among our senses. Since at all times consciousness involves a ratio among the senses, any alteration of intensity in any of our senses causes an immediate "closure" or completion of pattern. Such new "closure" or completion is, in fact, a new posture of mind charged with new preferences and desires, as well as with new patterns of perception.

The elementary and basic fact about the TV image is that it is a mosaic or a mesh, continuously in a state of formation by the "scanning finger". Such mosaic involves the viewer in a perpetual act of participation and completion. The intensely dramatic character of this image is shared in no way by the photograph or by the movie image. The TV image is not a shot, now [*sic*] a view of anything, so much as an experience. Its primarily tactile, rather than visual, character is a quality familiar to art historians in connection with mosaic work and with abstract art. These also, like the TV image, foster an intense experience of structure and inter-relation of form for which the visual experience of Western man since the Renaissance has prepared us not at all. For the tactile image involves not so much the touch of skin as the interplay or contact of sense with sense, of touch with sight, with sound, with movement. As this image invades our lives, we suddenly discover new cravings for new kinds of order in our immediate environment and in our daily lives. Our sense of taste and texture is altered at once in food and in clothing. What becomes satisfying or acceptable in spatial arrangement, or in the organization of time, or in our involvement in the learning process suddenly takes on new contours and new rhythms. After centuries of packaged learning and visually organized curricula, men suddenly rediscover the primacy of dialogue and interplay of mind as indispensable to insight. Insight, itself, is a revolutionary demand, the typical "closure" of man experiencing the TV image. So shaped in the new participational mode, the entire population suddenly develops a distaste for the older consumer values, and insists on new design in which the consumer is an integral part of the making process. With the TV image, our age-old separation of senses and functions terminates.

Walter, its about time that we did something for philosophy in regard to "touch," that "interface" transforming moment when the sensus communis translates one mode into another. Our media now do this *outside* us and thus calls urgently for an outer consensus of media proportioned to the proportional ratios of consciousness.

Have you encountered the work of Ed T Hall? He says he got the idea of our technologies as outerings of sense and function from Buckminster Fuller. I got it from nobody.[1] But now I find it the core of Wm Blake. Blake saw that when outered (uttered)[,] any sense of faculty becomes a *closed* system.[2] You know, Walter, the Schoolmen [academics] will never help us with these problems. They will never come to grips with anything at all. Why wait for them?

In Xt. Mac

[1] On the subject of attributions, see the notes to letters to Buckminster Fuller (September 17, 1964) and to Edward T. Hall (December 8, 1975) on pages 308 and 515 respectively.

[2] In *The Gutenberg Galaxy* McLuhan stated that "*Jerusalem*, like so much of his [William Blake's] other poetry, is concerned with the changing patterns of human perception. Book II, chapter 34 [Chapter II, Plate 34, ll. 55–6] of the poem contains the pervasive theme:

> If Perceptive organs vary, Objects of Perception seem to vary:
> If the Perceptive Organs close, their Objects seem to close also."

1963

To Harry J. Skornia[1]

29 Wells Hill Avenue
Toronto 4
March 3, 1963

Dear Harry

How goes your new work? Do let me see some of the mimeos you are using for projects. There are a couple of items I want to catch you up with. First, I've been given job of building a new Center here for the study of Media and Society.[2] Entirely graduate. To work by cross appointments at first. Full-time staff later. This fall we will mount a very good inter-dept. seminar as starter.

General basis of study will be of *all* technology as extensions of man's body, and of electric technology as the extension of the central nervous system. Seen as extensions of ourselves all technology manifestly is inter-related in its origin and effects. The only remaining act of extension is for consciousness itself.

The new job gives me direct access to all the talent and knowledge in the university. Shall organize teams, projects grants as soon as possible. Do wish we could talk.

Second point, the *Galaxy* has had most benign influence in England. (Got me the Governor General's award for non-fiction in Canada). Institute of Contemporary Arts in England plans 1965 Show on the Extensions of Man. So I expect to visit England this summer to discuss and to learn.

Let's hear Harry!

Salud,
Marshall

---

[1]Dr Harry J. Skornia (b. 1910)—who has been called "the father of public broadcasting in the US"—was Professor of Radio and TV at the University of Illinois, Urbana, and President of the National Association of Educational Broadcasters. He met McLuhan at a Modern Language Association meeting and had him give the keynote address at the 1958 convention of the NAEB in Omaha. He also helped McLuhan plan the study that resulted in the 1960 *Report on Project in Understanding New Media* (see pages 255–6).

[2]McLuhan had been made the founding director of the Centre for Culture and Technology (1963–81), which was established for him as an inter-disciplinary graduate seminar in the University of Toronto.

To Stewart Bates[1]

29 Wells Hill Avenue
Toronto 4, Ontario
June 17, 1963

Dear Dr. Bates:

Perhaps the best way to explain this rather sudden approach to you is to quote directly from Doxiadis' invitation to the Delos Meeting:[2]

> I realize of course that this is a rather belated time to invite someone on such short notice but I want to say frankly that I have just finished reading your wonderful book 'Gutenberg Galaxy', in which I found so many of the things that we also believe in and so many of the ideas which I think are relevant and essential to human settlements and their problems.

My concern with the crisis in the evolution of human settlements stems from years of study of the effects of media of communication and transportation on changing patterns of human association and living. In fact, I am engaged in completing a book on the extensions of man, which includes matters of immediate concern in housing and town-planning. In the electric age it is the extension of the central nervous system itself (not just the extensions of the body) that so much confuses the problems of living-space. The extension of the nervous system by electric media has no precedent in human culture. The Meeting comes most opportunely for my studies, which would be greatly deepened and nourished by the wisdom and knowledge of the famous participants in the Meeting. On the other hand, I have been led to believe that I can make some contribution to the conference, myself.

My report of the work and related insights developed during this Meeting could be of very real importance to the study of changing problems of our national housing. It is this feeling that leads me to apply for financial aid such furtherance of these studies.

There is also the matter of national prestige. Since all of the other major countries of the world will have representatives present, it seems to me most desirable that Canada also should share in the work and achievements of this highly significant gathering.

Since my studies of these problems would be greatly advanced by participa-

[1]Dr Stewart Bates was President of Central Mortgage and Housing, Ottawa, and one of the participants at the 1963 Delos symposion.

[2]On May 20, 1963 McLuhan was invited by the Athens Technological Institute and C.A. Doxiadis, President (see page 392, note 1), to take part in a week-long (July 6–13) seminar of experts, to be held on board the *New Hellas*, sailing in the Aegean, to discuss the evolution of human settlements. This was the first annual Delos "symposion" named after the Greek island of Delos, where the last day of discussion took place and the Declaration of Delos was drafted. Among the 34 participants— besides Dr Bates and McLuhan from Canada, and Doxiadis—were Buckminster Fuller (USA), Sigfried Giedion (Switzerland), Barbara Ward Jackson (Britain), Margaret Mead (USA), and Sir Robert Watson Watt (Britain). Corinne McLuhan accompanied her husband.

tion in their Meeting, I hope that it will be possible for you to allocate some grant-in-aid towards this end.[3]

Sincerely yours
Marshall McLuhan

[3]This request for funds to pay McLuhan's transportation costs to and from Athens was not granted.

To John I. Snyder, Jr[1]

August 4, 1963

Dear Mr. Snyder:

Some quite basic points about automation and the new pattern of Learning a Living for mankind were omitted from your very interesting discussion in *Life* magazine.[2]

First off, by far the largest commercial commodity in every part of the world today is packaged information. For some decades, the packaging and moving and consuming of information have outranked all the combined forms of heavy commodities, hardware and services. The wheel is an obsolescent form, as is indicated by its hypertrophy. AT & T is very much larger than General Motors, and moves only information. The point of all of this is that with electro-magnetism we extended the central nervous system itself in a global embrace so that the next immediate step technologically is the extension of consciousness. We are very close to this event, and yet no inkling of its imminence or its implications has dawned upon us. The Aldous Huxleys and all that crowd are not twentieth-century minds. On the eve of the Industrial Revolution—in fact, in 1810—the only reaction that the English could muster to that tremendous change was a panic about scarcity. Are we not behaving very much in this same way concerning jobs in automation?

Automation means involvement in depth, as opposed to the old specialist fragmentation by which all forms of mechanization were accomplished. The extension of the central nervous system automatically evokes involvement in depth. That is another name for leisure. When man is involved, he is at leisure. When he is fragmented, performing a specialist acrobatic feat, he is working. It is the involvement aspect of the electric age that creates joblessness. It is only in terms of nineteenth-century mechanical specialism that involvement in leisure means joblessness.

[1]John I. Snyder Jr (1909–65) was chairman of the board of U.S. Industries, Inc., a manufacturer of industrial automation equipment.

[2]Snyder was quoted at length in an article by Keith Wheeler, "Big Labor Hunts for Hard Answers", in *Life* (July 19, 1963), dealing with the process of automation and its possible effect on labour unions, management, and the individual.

We are already deep into a revolution in human learning in which the creation of wealth is a mere incident in knowing and learning. The whole of mankind is already engaged in a full-scale course of learning, which we call the Cold War. The war of icons and images is a war of depth involvement, in which one culture permeates another. So while we talk about joblessness we are already moving in depth into a situation in which learning becomes a total process, with or without benefit of subjects, from infancy to old-age. The pattern by which one learns one's mother tongue is now being extended to all learning whatever. The human dialogue itself becomes not only the economic, but the political and social, fact.

This Fall I became the Director of a new Center at the University of Toronto for the Study of the Extensions of Man. All our culture and technology are immediate extensions of our own bodies and senses and nervous systems. But each extension has quite distinct psychic and social consequences. We hope to study them all. I began with the study of the extension of the sense of sight *via* Gutenberg technology in a book called *The Gutenberg Galaxy* (University of Toronto Press, 1962). Some indication of its drift you can gather from the enclosed leader in the *Times Literary Supplement*, which I wrote recently.[3] McGraw-Hill is bringing out a sequel to this, in which I deal with two dozen extensions, from speech and clothing to computer.[4] For three thousand years, all human technologies have been fragmentary extensions of the human body. The electric extension of the central nervous system has never occurred before, and, therefore, we are without any navigational chart whatever. Mechanical systems are not closed in the way that electric ones are. As we push our electric technology it will flip open in the form of corporate consciousness. The present interim is baffling because it has a closed character, with which we know not how to deal. An electric system is very much like a small tribal society—that is, ecological and homeostatic. After centuries of a literate open system, additive and fragmentary, our sudden confrontation with closed electric systems renders us quite helpless.

Since I have a very big job on my hands with the new Center, I feel that people like yourself will know how to help me to avoid many blind alleys, and will be able to provide insights and personal contacts in handling what are, after all, problems common to us all.

Sincerely yours
Marshall McLuhan

[3]Marshall McLuhan, "Printing and the Mind", *The Times Literary Supplement*, July 19, 1963.
[4]*Understanding Media: The Extensions of Man* (1964). See pages 317–18.

To John I. Snyder

29 Wells Hill Avenue
Toronto 4, Ontario, Canada
August 14, 1963

Dear Mr. Snyder,

I am very eager to be of all the help I can.[1] Not an electric engineer myself, although closely associated with them here, I had assumed that all people in automation were engineers. That electro-magnetism as such is an extension of the central nervous system is a persistent theme of Teilhard de Chardin in his *Phenomenon of Man*. It is a concept familiar to biologists and psychologists alike. It has very much to do with the instant speed of electric structures and of the brain. Such speed makes inevitable the handling of vast quantities of information in a highly structured and, indeed, "mythic" way. Under electric technology today man lives mythically, as it were, simply by virtue of the speed with which he is confronted by consequences of every kind of action. This factor is completely altering our forms of government at this moment: No less, it is altering the forms of our educational establishment and our legal structure. As you know, electric systems, unlike literacy and mechanism, are not open, but closed, systems. Electric or instant circuits, by the same token, are not centralist, but de-centralist, in form. Our entire Western world has been structured by centralist forces, and is very much confused by electric technology.

In my prevous note to you I had merely wished to make the link between information movement, as the dominant quantitative fact of our age, and automation. Automation is information movement. It reduces hardware to information. It withdraws the work force from industry because fragmented, specialist activities are incompatible with electric involvement. Electricity as such is joblessness, just as it spells a future program of total learning as the future human occupation. When a man is deeply involved in any kind of activity whatever, when all his faculties are in use, he is at leisure. That is why the electric age is the age of leisure, of involvement in depth, and of joblessness.

Since I am in New York often, perhaps it would be possible to have a little chat about these things sometime this month.

Sincerely yours,
Marshall McLuhan

[1] Snyder replied to the previous letter (August 4) on August 7: "We apparently use different kinds of vocabularies because I really don't know what you are talking about. If you could express your ideas in terms that might be more acceptable to a non-academic person like myself I would appreciate it."

To Ernest Sirluck[1]

December 2nd, 1963

Dear Ernest:

I enclose a copy of Madeleine Doran's letter. In replying to her, I invited her suggestions for suitable substitutes for herself in the Shakespeare division.[2]

One item that has come much into focus here at the Centre concerns graduate studies. It can be put very briefly this way: whereas for centuries the Universities have been the main processing plants for young minds, they have become in the electric age, the principal organs of perception for the entire community. The undergraduate division still carries all the marks of the older University, being mainly verbal in its approach to the training of perception and judgment. In the electric age the instruments of perception are mainly concerned with seeking data that are beyond the reach of our unaided senses. The sheer bulk of this new data, in addition to the speed with which it is made accessible, has created entirely new problems of decision-making at every level of action and of policy. With increased speed of obtaining and handling data comes the need for integral awareness on a corporate scale. Whereas formerly we could classify data visually, we are now pressured into structural analysis. At the new speeds, a predictability becomes as necessary and as natural as the older methods of "rule of thumb" and "wait and see". Graduate studies could thus become more and more related to the corporate life of communal action and less and less oriented towards the preparing of young minds. When fully discerned, this large cultural change that stems from the new electric technology can be moderated and controlled. Unrestricted and unacknowledged, the electric pressures will tend to by-pass verbalized training that has for so many centuries been the core of Western culture.

Sincerely,

[1]Dr Ernest Sirluck (b. 1918), a Milton scholar, was at this time Professor of English and Associate Dean, School of Graduate Studies, University of Toronto; he became Dean in 1964. He was instrumental in getting the Council of the School of Graduate Studies to approve the creation of McLuhan's Centre for Culture and Technology and as Dean he administered its budget. He was President of the University of Manitoba from 1970 to 1976.

[2]The Elizabethan scholar Madeleine Doran (b. 1905)—who taught from 1935 to 1975 at the University of Wisconsin, where she met McLuhan—wrote *Endeavours of Art: A Study of Form in Elizabethan Drama* (1954) and *Shakespeare's Dramatic Language* (1976). The letter referred to here had to do with Professor Doran's editing one of three projected volumes on Elizabethan literature, which were not developed, for the series *Patterns of Literary Criticism*, of which Sirluck, McLuhan, and Richard J. Schoek were general editors (see page 470, note 1).

To Maurice Stein[1]

December 9th, 1963

Dear Maurice:

That was the week, *that* was! I mean that Friday at Brandeis. It was a grand time and I enjoyed your very lively students, as I enjoyed getting acquainted with you. I am assuming that this is the beginning of our association and that we shall manage a good deal more dialogue before too long.[2]

It was good to be with Jack Seeley, though I have not really had much acquaintance with him in the past.[3] This has been a mistake, but also a natural result of academic proximity. When we are on campus we are "walled-off" from many people, far more than when we are off campus. Maybe somebody has done a study on this? There seems to be a law here not unrelated to our not visiting famous buildings and institutions that are quite near by our daily work. A visitor to Oxford or Cambridge, for example, does all the colleges. Those who live and study there seldom get to see more than four or five. We live here in Toronto quite close to Casa Loma, the only landmark in the city. One of our girls is a guide there in the summertime. I have never been inside the place.

Had a delightful visit with Jerome Bruner, *chez* [Morton] Bloomfield.[4] I hope that I get to do some work with him before long.

Enclosed is a travel voucher and list of incidental expenses. Many thanks again for a most delightful visit.

Sincerely yours,
H.M. McLuhan

[1]Maurice R. Stein was Associate Professor (later Chairman) of the Department of Sociology at Brandeis University, Waltham, Massachusetts.

[2]On December 19, Stein replied: "*That* was the colloquium, *that* was! We really are going to be hard put to save any later colloquia that we may have from being strictly anticlimactic after your performance. The students are still talking about it and so are the faculty."

[3]Professor John R. Seeley (b. 1913) had taught at the University of Toronto in the Department of Psychology from 1948 to 1953 and at York University, Toronto, from 1960 to 1963. From 1963 to 1964 he was visiting Professor of Sociology at Brandeis University.

[4]Jerome Bruner (b. 1915) was at this time Professor of Psychology and Director of Cognitive Studies at Harvard University. Morton Bloomfield, a friend from McLuhan's Wisconsin days (see page 473, note 1), was also a Harvard professor, in the Department of English and American Literature and Language.

1964

To John Bassett[1]

Dear Mr. Bassett:

Not unmindful of favours received from you in the past,[2] I pass along this item which may serve you well. It concerns the need for a column to be written in such a way that parents can be of some use to their children in their homework. At present subjects have changed so much since parents were in school that they can be of little use to their children during homework. Such a column could easily be made to appeal to the general reader as well.

Our new Centre here is currently engaged in designing experiments to measure changing sensory preferences in the population at large. These experiments concern changes resulting from new media. Such changes affect our attitudes to the older media quite independently of the content of media. Changing attitudes to typography as a form of experience concern us very much. We have graduate students who need subsidies to carry on this kind of work. The overwhelming change in our electrified works is that electric technology extends the central nervous system itself. Among other major changes, the electric extension of the central nervous sytem revolutionizes the role of the University. The Universities become the organs of perception of the entire society. Without graduate students, production and development in the community at large ceases. Formerly the University had merely been a Centre for processing young minds. This changeover confuses all levels of education as much as automation confuses patterns of work.

Cordial regards,
H.M. McLuhan

[1]John Bassett (b. 1915) was then Chairman and Publisher of the Toronto *Telegram*.
[2]Mr Bassett had provided a subsidy of $7,000 that went towards the production of *Explorations* 7 and 8.

To Louis Rubin[1]

Dear Professor Rubin:

I am much indebted to you for your loan of *The Virginia Railroads*.[2] It is

[1]Professor Louis Rubin was a member of the Department of English, Hollins College, Virginia, U.S.A.
[2]Angus James Johnston, *Virginia Railroads in the Civil War* (1961).

exactly what I wanted. I wonder whether any further work has been done in studying the effects of the railroads in reshaping the Southern economy? You see, one of the consequences of railways is the concentration of power in urban centers. Electric systems and even airways have a quite contrary effect.

I am interested in learning how much the Old South was threatened by the rise of the railways insofar as they syphoned off agrarian power in the metropolitan direction.[3] This matter would have been operative well before the Civil War. Since radio and television, even since movies and electric power in general, it is plain that the South has recovered a great deal of power and influence which was lost to it during the railway phase. Most significantly this recovery is at the level of art and literature. New electric technology favours the old southern cohesion of awareness. Mechanical fragmentation and specialism more characteristic of the North, does not serve the arts at all well.

Sincerely yours,

[3]This reflects McLuhan's continuing interest in historical aspects of the society and culture of the American South, which he had written about in two significant articles of the 1940s: "An Ancient Quarrel in Modern America" (*The Classical Journal*, January 1946) and "The Southern Quality" (*The Sewanee Review*, July 1947).

To Jacqueline Tyrwhitt March 24, 1964

Dear Jacky:

You are right. March and April are hopelessly filled in. One of the few dates in May that is taken up is May 26th, but I could manage the 25th, or 27th or 28th.

You surely don't consider that my permission is needed to use your own talk for the student journal! If you feel inclined to mention that you had given it here, it would be a nice prestige bit for our Centre! Many thanks for the action on photos and Ekistics.[1] Edward A. Hall, 1218 Astor Street, Chicago (he is at the Illinois Institute of Technology now) is very interested in Doxiadis.[2] Plans to visit Greece this summer. Would be a tremendous man for the Delos Seminar this summer. He is worth a half-dozen Margaret Meads. Is a linguistics man, an Anthropologist and Psychologist and many other things.

Love from us all,

[1]*Ekistics: Reviews on the Problems and Science of Human Settlements*, a monthly periodical published by Doxiadis Associates, of which Jacqueline Tyrwhitt was editor.

[2]For Edward T. Hall, see page 383, note 1.

P.S. Have a look at once at a most exciting book—"Preface to Plato" by E.A. Havelock. It would be of the utmost interest to Doxiadis. It is the first study of the oral tradition in Greek culture as that which Plato is attacking in his entire work.[3]

[3]Eric A. Havelock's *Preface to Plato* (1963) is frequently mentioned in the letters that follow. (There is a letter to Havelock and a note on page 406.) In his Foreword, Havelock states that this book is the beginning of his study of the growth of "the early Greek mind". Its context is that in Homer's day "the Greek cultural 'book' had been stored in the oral memory. . . . Between Homer and Plato, the method of storage began to alter, as the information became alphabetised, and correspondingly the eye supplanted the ear as the chief organ employed for this purpose." He discusses poetry in Plato's day as "a kind of reference library" of ethics, politics, and warfare—fulfilling "its immemorial function in an oral culture", but existing as an effective educational instrument only as it is performed—which the community must conspire to keep alive in order to reinforce its collective memory; this is described as a "total technology of the preserved word". The attack in McLuhan's statement refers to Plato's denunciation of the oral poetic tradition when, in performance, it became a kind of drama that was an obstacle to the objective, rational examination of an object by "reliving experience in memory instead of analysing and understanding it".

To Wilfred Watson

March 31, 1964

Dear Wilfred:

I haven't had time to work through your suggestions properly. They look utterly fascinating.

An hour ago I was looking at [Andy] Warhol's Pop Art show. He uses the technique of redundancy and repetition to transform the pictorial into the iconic. i.e. any high definition image can be made environmental and involving by repetition. The reverse of this would seem to be pushing up in part of the environment into high definition as a means of dismissing it from attention. As soon as one has paid special attention to any part of one's environment it tends to be ignored or dismissed.

The icon combines the environmental and the anti-environmental much in the manner of the pun. The pun by means of low definition permits interplay between itself as environment and itself as anti-environment.[1]

Tonight we tackle the problem of tape recording poems in varied modes. In this way the poem can alternate between environment and anti-environment.

Fondly
Marshall

[1]i.e. the interplay between the pun and its context, or the language itself.

To Ernest Sirluck April 20, 1964

Dear Ernest:

Was fascinated by your article on Milton's Prose.[1] One aspect that loomed very large was the use of Hendiadys.[2] It is perhaps the most important posture of the 17th-century mind, though to my knowledge, it has had no study at all. On opening *Paradise Lost* I counted 19 instances in the first 100 lines. You know, "Death and Woe, Restore and regain, Raise and support" and so on. This figure begins in Shakespeare with *As You Like It* and dominates *Hamlet* and the plays thereafter. It has multiple functions as a figure or posture and they naturally concern a habit of ambivalent vision that can well afford some careful study. Would like to talk to you about this.

[1] Ernest Sirluck, "Milton's Political Thought: The First Cycle", *Modern Philosophy*, LXI, no. 3, February 1964.

[2] *Hendiadys*, the expression of a single complex idea by two words connected with *and* (from the Greek words meaning "one by means of two"). See page 399.

To Jacqueline Tyrwhitt May 11, 1964

Dear Jackie:

The old plate is piled very high indeed. I must forego any thought of a visit to Harvard this Spring. Work here at the Centre has become more and more demanding.

Last night I was reading Finnegans Wake pages 492 to 505. I thought at once of writing to Giedion about it. In these pages Joyce runs through the letters of the alphabet from A to Z as a social cycle. When he gets to Z, the cycle begins again. He explicitly indicates the return to primal undiscriminated auditory space, then begins again the discovery of the vertical plane and enclosed space and numbers and measurement. Joyce is quite explicit that (page 501) as the alphabet ends its cycle we move out of visual space into discontinuous auditory space again. This he mentions as the return to "Lewd's Carol", that is, through the looking glass into the world of non-Euclidean space once more, lewd, ignorant, tribal, involved totally as in group singing. In his "Beginnings of Architecture" Giedion cites the evidence several times that there is no architectural enclosing of space before script.[1] Giedion does not know why this should be. Visual space alone of all the space discriminated by our various senses is continuous, uniform and connected. Any technology that extends the visual power imposes these visual

[1] Sigfried Giedion's *The Beginnings of Architecture* (1964) is Volume II of *The Eternal Present: A Contribution in Continuity and Change*. Volume I is *The Beginning of Art* (1962). The two volumes were published by the Bollingen Foundation.

properties upon all other spaces. Our own return in the electric age to a non-visual world has confronted us suddenly with this tyrannical and usurping power of the visual over the other senses. Kevin Lynch doesn't understand this matter at all.[2] My own phrase for city planning is that the city has become a teaching machine.[3] The planner's job is to program the entire environment by an artistic modulation of sensory usage. Art is a CARE package dispatched to undernourished areas of the human sensorium. What the artist has formerly done on a private entrepreneurial basis the planner now must do on a corporate or group basis. This is equally true of education and government. Instead of worrying about program content, the job is now to program the total sensorium.

Understanding Media will be published May 26th by McGraw-Hill. You should be receiving a copy soon.

Had lunch with a Greek chap who is in the research division of McCann-Erickson. He is greatly interested in my proposal about a pre-TV study of the Greek population. We have our sensory typology experiments ready to go. I enclose a description of one of them for you. Our friend, Philip Deane, has left the U.N. to become Secretary-General to the King of Greece.[4] He will be a great help in any matter that we undertake.

Please tell me your dates of departure and where I can reach you.

[2]Kevin Lynch wrote *The Image of the City* (1960; paperback edition 1964).

[3]Years later McLuhan, with Kathy Hutchon and Eric McLuhan, edited a textbook called *The City as Classroom: Understanding Language and Media* (1977).

[4]See page 348, note 1.

To Maurice Stein

May 15, 1964

Dear Maurice:

The Eclipse of Community arrived most timely.[1] I was in the process of going through the work of Robert Park preparatory to doing a preface to *The Bias of Communication* by Harold Innis.[2] Innis was studying at Chicago in the 20's, so your chapter on the Chicago school was a great help. The rest of the book I have barely skimmed over so far. It looks very entrancing.

I must ask McGraw-Hill to send you a copy of *Understanding Media* as soon as it is published, which should be very soon.[3] Father Culkin says he is to review it

[1]Maurice Stein (see page 294, note 1), *The Eclipse of Community: An Interpretation of American Studies* (1960).

[2]In McLuhan's Introduction to the 1964 edition of Harold Innis's *The Bias of Communication* (first published in 1951) he discussed the influence on Innis of Robert Ezra Park—who was teaching at the University of Chicago when Innis was working on his Ph.D. there in the early 1920s—citing particularly an article by Park entitled "Physics and Society", reprinted in Park's *Society* (1955).

[3]*Understanding Media: The Extensions of Man* (1964), McLuhan's most widely read book, discusses (in very general terms) how life and culture are being influenced and shaped by the new electronic communications technologies.

for the Saturday Evening [*sic*] Review of Literature.[4]

One overwhelming bias of the North American makeup is its commitment to visual space and organization. This is owing to our unequalled acceptance of literacy as an art form and as a model of perception. Europeans never accepted literacy in this way. Visual space is the only one of our senses that provides the experience of uniformity, continuity and connectedness. That is why in the increasingly non-visual orientation of the electric age North America is in real trouble. I find it almost impossible to discuss the peculiar parameters of the visual modality with Americans. They insist that the visual and the real are one. To question this is to undermine the American way of life. By contrast even English people have little difficulty in accepting a proprioception[5] and the other senses as constitutive of the real.

Very best wishes for the success of your book.

Cordially,

[4]John Culkin (see page 309, note 1) did not review *Understanding Media* for *The Saturday Review of Literature*; but for that magazine he later wrote a cover story (portrait by Karsh) on McLuhan, "A Schoolman's Guide to Marshall McLuhan" (March 18, 1967) that reportedly became the most reprinted article in the history of the magazine.

[5]That is, a proprioceptor—a sensory receptor (in muscles etc.) that responds to stimuli within the organism.

To Robert Fulford[1]   June 1st, 1964

Dear Bob:

It's amazing that you got anything out of my writing at all, since you misconceive my entire procedure.[2] I do not move along lines. I use points like the dots in a wire-photo. That is why I must repeat and repeat my points. Again, insights are not points of view. I do not have a point of view on anything. I am interested only in modalities and processes. You assume that I have a point of view. No wonder I sound "arrogant." My main theme is the extension of the nervous system in the electric age and thus the complete break with 5000 years of mechanical technology. This I state over and over again. I do not say whether it is a good or bad thing. To do so would be meaningless and arrogant.

I do value your friendly approach.

Cordially,

[1]The Toronto cultural journalist Robert Fulford (b. 1932) was at this time an editor on the staff of *Maclean's* magazine; in 1968 he became editor of *Saturday Night*. This letter was a respone to Fulford's full-page review of *Understanding Media* in *Maclean's* (June 20, 1964).

[2]Fulford was not unfaithful to McLuhan's beliefs. He described the person with a "linear mind", who values solely the printed word, as "an intellectual sleepwalker, stumbling through the twentieth century", and referred favourably to McLuhan's insight that "television unconsciously restructures the character of the viewer". But he also stated that *Understanding Media* was "arrogant, sloppy, repetitious and brilliant". He concluded by saying that McLuhan dealt with "the crucial issues of this period. I'm as aware as his enemies are that his work is disorganized and erratic, but he has taught me more about his subject than any six well-organized, consistent writers."

To David Riesman

June 4, 1964

Dear Dave:

Thanks for your generous note about *Understanding Media*. One fact which you may misjudge about my style is this, I do not have a point of view. My seemingly stark statements are flat and iconic forms that I learned from symbolist writing. An insight is not a point of view. It is concerned with process, not product.

Les Dewart[1] was showing me some copies of *The Correspondent* this morning.[2] Please put me down for a subscription at once.

Your mimeo format would seem in many ways to have advantages over the magazine format. By the way, *Explorations* has begun again in a small way. You will find its first installment in the pages of the Toronto University Varsity Grad, which I have sent on to you.

Kindest regards to you and Evey,

[1]Leslie Dewart (b. 1922) is a theologian who teaches at St Michael's College, University of Toronto.

[2]This was a periodical (1961–5), with a liberal political slant, edited by Riesman.

To Glenn Gould[1]

June 4, 1964

Dear Dr. Gould:

It was delightful to hear you last night on "Festival."[2]

I look forward very much to that dinner we promised ourselves when we had lunch some weeks ago.

It was splendid that the University [of Toronto] had the perception and spirit to give you a Degree [LLD]. It makes me proud of them.

I shall be out of town until June 10th. Let's get in touch after that.

Cordially,

[1]Glenn Gould (1932–82), the internationally famous Toronto-born concert pianist who, in 1962, decided to confine his performances to recording studios and occasionally to television.

[2]A popular live TV cultural series of the 1960s, produced by the CBC (Canadian Broadcasting Corporation). On the evening of June 3, Gould played, and talked about, the music of Sweelinck, Bach, Webern, and Beethoven.

To Robert Russel[1]

June 15, 1964

Dear Mr. Russel:

As you might have suspected, I found your review most agreeable! Not that I am an anti-book person, or an anti-lineal thinker. If I have any normal and natural preferences, they are for the values of the literate world. In so far as print bias renders us helpless and ineffectual in the new electronic age, I am strongly inclined to cultivate the kinds of perception that are relevant to our state. If I had the world's ten best books on a desert island, I should be strongly tempted to spend my time in shipbuilding rather than browsing the printed page.

I do appreciate your sending me your review.

Very best wishes,

[1]Robert Russel, of Montreal, had sent McLuhan a copy of his review of *Understanding Media* delivered on the CBC radio program "Sights and Sounds" (June 11, 1964).

To Bascom St John[1]

June 15, 1964

Dear Mr. St. John:

Congratulations on your article on "Test of Memory." I hope you can follow it up. It seems to me you have highlighted in effect a breakdown in communications within our school system. It seems to be a common assumption that we all manage to communicate most of the time. Much of the significant work of our time, whether it be that of Freud or I.A. Richards in criticism, or countless social and political analysts, has indicated a very wide breakdown of communication between individuals and between societies. It is just this breakdown that calls for close study of the processes of media of communication. The enormous speed-up in information movement is quite sufficient to account for breakdown and for the irrelevance of older arrangements. "Improvements" can also be disasters. However one of my themes in Understanding Media is that great speed-up also makes the patterns of change discernible for the first time in human history.

Understanding of the modalities of change while these changes are still in process is now possible. Such understanding creates the possibility of human social autonomy in place of near historical retrospects.

In terms of schooling, the substitution of autonomy for retrospect holds out

[1]Bascom St John (1906–83) wrote a daily column on education, called "The World of Learning", for the *Globe and Mail*, Toronto, from 1958 to 1964.

the possibility of programming education for discovery rather than for mechanization of classified data. Student and teacher can now share in the actual learning processes as they concern personal development and social change.

Please count on me for any help you may need in handling *Understanding Media*.

Sincerely yours,

To Ashley Montagu[1]

June 26, 1964

Dear Ashley:

What a wonderful surprise getting your books on the Dolphin and the Anthropology.[2] Have read both of them already with great profit to myself indeed. Your books are always of the greatest use to me in writing my books. At present am doing one called *From Cliché to Archetype* which is proving a lot of fun in doing.[3] Another one that I have nearly finished with a collaborator who is a painter, is *Space in Poetry and in Painting*.[4] Nobody seems to have considered the physical spaces in language and in verbal art.

Very much looking forward to having a chat with you one of these days. Would that we had you here at our Centre! Please do pass along your insights into the relationships between culture and technology. I am sure you have articles on these subjects which I should have known long ago.

With sincere regards, and admiration,

[1]Ashley Montagu (b. 1905)—the anthropologist, social biologist, and prolific author—was at this time teaching at Princeton.

[2]Ashley Montagu, *The Dolphin in History* (1963), written with John Lilly, and (possibly) the recently published *The Science of Man* (1964).

[3]Marshall McLuhan, *From Cliché to Archetype*, written in collaboration with Wilfred Watson. Though it was not published until 1970, McLuhan and Watson began discussing it (i.e. the question "What is a cliché?") in 1963; a contract was signed with Viking Press in September 1965. See page 416, note 2.

[4]McLuhan was also working with Harley Parker on *Through the Vanishing Point: Space in Poetry and Painting* (1968).

To Michael Wolff[1]

July 3, 1964

Dear Professor Wolff:

Many thanks for your invitation to visit the School of Letters. Naturally, I would have enjoyed such a visit a great deal, and certainly an opportunity to chat with George Steiner[2] would be a highlight in my day.

Last summer was partly spent at the Delos Conference, and in England, and Europe. The result was a great falling behind in publication schedules. That has to be remedied this summer. For years I have been working on a book called [*Through the Vanishing Point*:] *Space in Poetry and in Painting*. It is being done in collaboration with a painter and designer [Harley Parker] and is quite a new kind of approach to language and literature and painting. A book I really look forward to finishing is my Cambridge Dissertation on Thomas Nashe. I have not wandered as far from literature as might appear. In so far as literature is the study and training of perception, the electric age has complicated the literary lot a good deal. However the new extensions of our senses have greatly enhanced the role of language as training for coping with the total environment. As the total environment becomes a technologically prepared environment, language assumes new roles over and beyond the confrontation of the printed page. Yet the literary man is potentially in control of the strategies needed in the new sensory environment. Language alone includes all the senses and interplay at all times. Perhaps the weakness of literacy as such is its tendency to play up the visual aspects of language at the expense of all the other senses. Hopkins would seem to have begun the strategy of playing down the visual in order to play up the other senses in speech. Frank Budgen points out [in *James Joyce and the Making of "Ulysses"*, 1934] that the Gerty McDowell episode in *Ulysses* is the only visual one in the book. Gerty is a "pastiche" of visual cliché, verbal and pictorial, and is, like Madame Bovary, a victim of mechanized culture.

Tell George Steiner that there is a book by Eric Havelock (*Preface to Plato*, Harvard, 1963) that I would dearly have loved to have had available to me both for the "Galaxy" and the new [*Understanding Media*:] "Extensions of Man." It is a study of the clash of oral and written traditions in 5th century Athens. I have, of course, made many discoveries about the various media since the book went to press. For example, the electric circuit is the successor to the mechanical wheel. More intensive study of any medium whatever reveals these metamorphoses in great plenty. James Joyce, by the way, refers to the electric circuit as "where the hand of man never set foot." Mechanical wheels are extensions of either the hands or the feet.

The new topless matter is perhaps an excessively obvious documentation of my claim that there has been a considerable drop in the visual component of

[1]Professor of English, Indiana University, Bloomington, Indiana.
[2]See page 361, note 1.

perception since TV. It may seem paradoxical that a highly visual culture insists on much covering up of the body. This is partly owing to the need for channelling physical energies to the eyes. An easy tolerance of nudity is natural to people for whom the visual component in experience is secondary. The 19th-century painterly interest in the nude goes together with the rediscoveries of sculptural values. Even the English are more inclined to accept the nude as sculptural than are Americans. Our visual orientation is more acute by far than the English. This sort of statement, by the way, I do not consider to be a value judgment any more than it is an expression of a personal point of view, or preference. I always assume that anything I say can be checked by anybody. If I thought it were merely private perception or point of view, I would not bother to say it.

By the way, we have begun to publish *Explorations* again, though in a somewhat restricted form.[3] Shall send you a couple of copies at once. Again, my real regrets for not being able to be on your campus this summer.

Sincerely yours,

[3] *Explorations* was appearing as an insertion in the (University of Toronto) *Varsity Graduate*.

To Harry J. Skornia

July 6, 1964

Dear Harry:

Many congratulations on your *TV in the Court Room* piece![1] Would that it had been available when I was writing the *Understanding Media*. Please send me a dozen copies if possible. Glad to pay for them. I want to send them around to people like Ted Carpenter and Father John Culkin.

I only realized today that we cannot transcend our "flat-earth" view of media as long as we rely upon private impressions at a particular time and place. The meaning and effect of a medium is the *sum total* of all its impact upon pysche and society. Such a vision requires the historical dimension as the laboratory in which to observe change. Your piece offers a model of this historical approach. It is contemporary history, of course, but history for all that. By showing the effect of a medium upon a diversity of institutions, you gain the historical dimension in the present.

[1] "Television in the Courtroom: A Danger to Civil Rights" is the title of an address Dr Skornia gave on May 17, 1964 to the Illinois News Broadcasters Association, a copy of which he sent to McLuhan. It is a commentary on Canon 35 of the Canons of Judicial Ethics of the American Bar Association forbidding the taking of photographs in the courtroom and the broadcasting or televising of court proceedings. Noting that "Whereas television may come only to report, it usually seems to end up running the show", Skornia gave cogent reasons for supporting this ban—which network executives and others opposed—though he also gave specific recommendations for conditions that would make cameras in the courtroom acceptable.

Am finishing up the successor to the *Mechanical Bride*.[2] If you have any summer students, I would appreciate your asking them to collect some samples of what they consider to be new techniques in advertising, new ways of handling the visual, new ways of relating the verbal and the visual, new kinds of verbalizing, punning, etc.

I enclose a letter I have just written to *Time*, since I am not sure they will get around to publishing it.

Warm regards to all,

[2]*Culture Is Our Business* (1970)—on electronic man (McLuhan had previously studied industrial man in *The Mechanical Bride* and typographic man in *The Gutenberg Galaxy*—is a graphically arresting anthology of advertisements, paired with a series of statements and quotations that they evoked for McLuhan.

To Bascom St John

July 10th, 1964

Dear Mr. St. John:

I feel a personal satisfaction in your appointment and hope that we shall not lose touch.[1] In fact, I hope very much to translate *Understanding Media* into a text book for school use. You see, the world of media is one in which the young are deeply versed. It is one that not only shapes their earliest perceptions, but which nourishes them as well, far beyond any nutriment received in the classroom. This area of experience, therefore, is one that cries out for clarification. The fact that literate adults in our world have very simple-minded ideas about media does not prevent these media from having very complex results on psyche and society. It occurred to me a few days ago that until our time men have regarded all media and technologies in a pre-Copernican spirit. Copernicus was, and is, anti-common sense.[2] The only people to have any experience of a round earth are the astronauts. In the same way, private encounters with the various media afford no evidence of their actual powers or dimensions. Such evidence can only be acquired by distancing in time, just as the character of the earth can only be perceived by distancing in space. The fact that the psychic and social consequences of the various extensions of man are just as complex as the dynamic interplay of our own nervous systems seems to appal many people.

Wolfgang Kohler in his *Gestalt Psychology* (which approaches the human senses the way I approach media) writes: "What was so shocking in Galileo's astronomical discoveries? That he found so much going on in the sky, and that as

[1]St John was about to leave the *Globe and Mail* to serve in the Ontario Department of Education as Chairman of the Policy and Development Council, a position he held until his retirement in 1973.

[2]The Polish astronomer Nicholas Copernicus (1473–1543) advanced the theory that the earth and all other planets revolved around the sun while spinning on their axes, refuting the Ptolemaic system that placed the earth at the centre of the universe.

a consequence the astronomical order was so much less rigid than people had been able happily to believe before."[3]

It was a great relief when Newton reduced the chaos of the Heavens to a simple formula.[4] But the new physics has scrambled the Newtonian universe again. I enclose a letter from my friend, and old colleague, Ted Carpenter, since it concerns these matters. I thought you would be especially interested in his last paragraph concerning the Natural Science Foundation group who propose to discover media biases in order to improve education. Needless to say, they have no such intention. But in your new role you will no doubt encounter such people frequently. Their natural instinct is to avoid all discovery in the interest of strengthening conventional procedures. Personally, I have no objections whatever to conventional procedures in any area of human action, if these procedures do not endanger the whole enterprise of survival. Many people seem to assume that survival is synonymous with the continuance of conventional procedures even though new technology may have undermined the whole basis of such procedures. It will be well for us if this strategy of identifying the conventional with the means of survival should prove to be well founded because we are not likely to be provided with any other kind of strategy. A tour through Toynbee[5] will reveal that all the civilizations of the past have gone down through failure to devise cultural strategies suited to their new technologies. They failed to see the new pattern because they looked at it through the old spectacles. Today, however, electric speed-up offers the possibility of pattern recognition amidst the force of change. The speed-up offers this possibility on a scale that may break through our acquired habits of perception in time to prompt the formulation of viable new strategies of culture.

Again, most cordial good wishes in your new role.

Sincerely yours,

[3]Wolfgang Kohler's *Gestalt Psychology* (1929) was published in a revised edition as *Gestalt Psychology: An Introduction to New Concepts in Modern Psychology* in 1947. The Italian astronomer, mathematician, and physicist Galileo (1564–1642) constructed the first astronomical telescope and published in 1632 his *Dialogue Concerning the Two Chief World Systems*, a work that upheld the Copernican theory.

[4]Among the discoveries of the English mathematician and physicist Sir Isaac Newton (1642–1727) was the principle of universal gravitation, which explained the movement of heavenly bodies and the falling of bodies on earth.

[5]*A Study of History* by Arnold Toynbee (1889–1975) was published in 10 volumes between 1914 and 1954 and in a bestselling one-volume abridgement in 1960. McLuhan met Toynbee at the 1972 Delos Symposion.

To Ashley Montagu

August 10, 1964

Dear Ashley:

Good of you to ask me to contribute to your volume.[1] Perhaps if you had a look at my *Understanding Media: The Extensions of Man* (McGraw-Hill) you would have some ideas of what you would like me to do.

One thing that comes to mind that is not in that volume concerns the habit of new media in swallowing older media, transforming them strangely. Perhaps the latest example is the swallowing of film by TV. The press had swallowed the book, and film had swallowed the press earlier. This had gone on since the origin of script, as is magnificently illustrated by Eric Havelock in his *Preface to Plato*. When swallowed, the older media tend to become high-class *art* forms. The new medium is never considered an art form, but only a degradation of the older form. This piece could be called "Inside the Whale."[2]

Regards,

[1]McLuhan wrote "The Relation of Environment to Anti-Environment", which was included in *The Human Dialogue: Perspectives on Communication* (1967) edited by Floyd W. Matson and Ashley Montagu.

[2]See page 322, note 1.

To Buckminster Fuller[1]

September 17, 1964

Dear Bucky:

I was not at all happy about missing the [Delos] seminar this summer. There was too much on the plate here.

Have had a good deal of luck in analysing various problems lately. I enclose a note on one of these. If one says that any new technology creates a new environ-

[1]Buckminster Fuller (1895–1983), American architect and engineer noted for his revolutionary technological designs based on the Dymaxion principle—that of gaining maximum results from minimum material and energy. McLuhan had met Fuller at the 1962 Delos symposion.

In a letter (PAC) of November 7, 1966 to Mr John Ragsdale, editor of the *Biophilist*, Denver, Colorado, Fuller wrote: "Regarding McLuhan, I have known him for five years. He acknowledges use of my concept and phrasing of the "Mechanical" and other "Extensions of Man" which was first published in the "predictions" in my preface to *Nine Chains to the Moon*, Lippincott—1938, and also in my charts in 1938 and republished in my book *The Epic of Industrialization*, written in 1940. I speak about such phenomena as a scientist, McLuhan speaks as a Professor of Literature. He is well read and has good insights . . . [and] he is skilled in verbal duelling. . . . I greatly enjoy his foot and rapier work. I have been present when hostile audiences thought they had him on the run only to discover themselves chasing themselves up dead-end alleys as he himself reappeared far down another highway. I like him, personally, respect him and appreciate the respect and friendliness he shows toward my own work."

ment, that is better than saying the medium is the message. The content of the new environment is always the old one. The content is greatly transformed by the new technology.

Supersonic flight will create a new environment which makes our present cities somewhat useless. In fact, if they are to be approached within any convenient distance at all, they will have to be "roofed over." Supersonic take-off and landing alike blow the glass out of a city, so your Dymaxion Dome becomes a necessity, just as much as the road is a necessity for the wheel. One environment creates another.

Would appreciate your suggestions about readings in the matter of technology as creator of environment. Today the environment itself becomes the artefact. The consequences for learning are quite extraordinary. The prepared environment for learning separates the old curriculum.

Warm regards,

To John Culkin[1]

September 17, 1964

Dear Father John:[2]

Have been out of town and so am not clear whether I sent you the enclosed item before, or not.[3] I think it represents a very useful new development. To say that any technology or extension of man creates a new environment is a much better way of saying the medium is the message. Moreover, this environment is always "invisible" and its content is always the old technology. The old technology is altered considerably by the enveloping action of the new technology.

Now about this in relation to sleep, and consciousness and the unconscious? If the unconscious is an environment for consciousness, is not consciousness in some sense an environment for the unconscious? Is sleep a means of merging these two environments so that one can reprocess the other? An excessive activ-

[1]John Culkin (b. 1928), who was a Jesuit priest until 1969, first met McLuhan at a seminar at Brandeis University in 1963, while he was working on his doctorate at Harvard, where one of his projects was to write a clear explication of McLuhan's ideas. (He found this difficult until he was directed to McLuhan's fourteen-chapter *Report on Project in Understanding New Media* (1960): see pages 255-6). In 1965 Culkin was appointed Director of the Center for Communication at Fordham University and was instrumental in arranging for McLuhan's appointment to the Albert Schweitzer Chair in the Humanities at Fordham in 1967-8. Culkin later founded in New York City the Center for Understanding Media, and a graduate-school program in media studies at the New School for Social Reasearch, both of which are explicitly based on McLuhan's work.

[2]McLuhan wrote the same letter as the one below to David Reisman, Harry Skornia, Maurice Stein, Jacqueline Tyrwhitt, and to Father G. F. McGuigan, Department of Economics and Political Science, University of British Columbia. This practice—writing identical letters, spaced several days apart, containing his latest ideas that would be of particular interest to more than one friend—was often followed by McLuhan.

[3]Marshall McLuhan, "New Media and the Arts", *Arts in Society*, vol. 3, no. 2, September 1964.

ity in either consciousness or the unconscious would result in insomnia?

Technologies would seem to be the pushing of the archetypal forms of the unconscious out into social consciousness. May this not help to explain why technology as environment is typically unconscious? The interplay between environmental and content factors, between old and new technologies, seems to obtain in all fields whatever. "In politics, the new conservatism has as its content the old liberalism," says Richard Hofstadter in his *Age of Reform*.[4] In fact, his entire volume illustrates this theme of environment and content in political history.

In the age of information the University becomes itself environmental, whereas in the mechanical age it had been merely the content of a machine technology. One of the most illuminating applications of this principle is the light it throws on the origins of Romanticism. As the mechanical and industrial environment shaped up, its prey or content became the old environment. That is, Nature and the traditional crafts. Under these conditions, Nature itself became an art form, just as film is now becoming an art form as the content of TV. Telstar creates a totally new kind of environment of which the planet itself is the content. The planet will become an art form. An art form implies cliché and convention. Most of these observations stem from work being done on a book called *From Cliché to Archetype*.

It seems to me that the direction in which the basic changes of our time lead us is towards confronting the environment as artefact. In a non-literate society there is no art in our sense, but the whole environment is experienced as unitary. Neolithic specialism ended that. What we call art would seem to be specialist artefacts for enhancing human perception. Since the Renaissance the arts have become privileged means of perception for the few, rather than means of participation in a common life, or environment. This phase now seems to be ending, except that we are extending the privileged artefact principally to the environment itself.

Is not this acceptance of the environment as artefact part of our drive to improve the learning process, instead of concern with the right content for learning, the right environment for maximizing learning?

Thinking about the Hawthorne experiment the other day, it struck me that instead of concluding negatively, they could have concluded positively.[5] Instead of saying that testing falsifies the content or distorts the perceptions of those being tested, might they not have said that testing itself is an ideal environment for the learning process? Testing represents a set of controlled conditions which in effect accelerate and improve learning and work.

In the age of information, man the food-gatherer returns as man the fact-finder. Our ecological approach is Paleolithic, is it not? It assumes total involvement in process rather than fragmentation and detachment.

I am sure you will have some very useful observations on the following theme.

[4]Richard Hofstadter, *The Age of Reform: From Bryan to FDR* (1955).

[5]This refers to a study published in Henry A. Landsberger, *Hawthorne Revisited*. The "Hawthorne experiment" investigated the monotonous working conditions of factory personnel at Western Electric's Hawthorne plant in Cicero, Illinois, in the late 1920s. For a fuller description, see page 459 note 3.

An I.B.M. friend said to me the other day: "My children have lived several lifetimes by the time they enter Grade One, just as they have travelled farther by the age of seven than their grandparents ever travelled." He mentioned this by way of his own determination to return to Grad school in order to make possible several new careers for himself in his remaining years. Acceleration of information movement can have as one of its consequences a multiplicity of jobs for everybody. In fact, joblessness as the consequence of automation may well mean the end of the single job for the single lifetime, and the switchover to a multiplicity of jobs for every lifetime. Please comment on whatever aspects of these matters strike you. I have a selfish reason as well as an intellectual wish to hear from you on these themes. I have to do a chapter in a book on Automation shortly.

To Harry J. Skornia

29 Wells Hill Avenue
Oct 3, 1964

Harry me boy, it works.

Over and over I've talked to groups and individuals about new techology as new environment.[1] Content of new environment is old environment. The new environment is always invisible. Only the content *shows*, and yet only the environment is really *active* as shaping force. As Drucker shows in his *Management (sic) for Results*,[2] in every situation 10% of the events cause 90% of the events. The 10% area is the sector of opportunity, the 90% area is the area of problems. The opportunity or environmental and innovational area is ignored. All sensible people deal first with problems—that is, the dead issues.

To deal with the environment directly is my strategy Harry. To attack the new environment as if it were an artefact capable of being molded. Today Telstar is about to create a new environment.[3] Its content will be not only TV and computer but the planet itself. TV will become an art form just as movie has done since TV. But in order to have autonomy we must push the unconscious and environmental parameters right up into consciousness.

All that I've said about the medium is the message is sound. But it becomes acceptable when put as "new technology is new environment". Everybody knows that environment is a force.

---

[1] McLuhan saw an environment as being composed of various elements that are so accepted as part of the fabric of everyday life that they are virtually invisible, and he considered that any new technology tends to create a new environment. This is discussed in "The Relation of Environment to Anti-Environment" in *Communication: The Human Dialogue* (1965) edited by Floyd Matson and Ashley Montagu.

[2] Peter Drucker, *Managing for Results* (1964).

[3] Telstar was one of two privately financed low-altitude communication satellites launched by the U.S. in 1962 and 1963 for commercial use to transmit television pictures and telephone messages.

The principle works in many ways e.g. at what point does the supply of any item become environmental? Answer: "when it creates demand". It works also for all modes of perception. Can now put the entire *Gutenberg Galaxy* on a single page.

I do want some copies of the TV and the courtroom ["Television in the Courtroom"]. Thanks for checking. Regards to Mary, Lee, Lorene

Fondly
Marshall

To Wilfred Watson   November 11, 1964

Dear Wilfred:

The Nation has asked me to do an essay on William Burroughs.[1] Looking at his *Naked Lunch* [Paris, 1959; N.Y. 1962] and *Nova Express* [1964] I discover right off that they are anti-Utopias. He is very much aware of media as environment and regards drugs as anti-environmental. He insists upon the hard drugs and despises the hallucinatory drugs like L.S.D. It would seem that the latter belonged to the old technology of the movies and "dreams that money can buy," whereas the hard drugs are totally paralyzing. That is, when we put our nerves outside, and bodies inside, the hard drugs are mandatory. By "Naked Lunch" he means that total human involvement is cannibalism. He is not a very bright person. He is reacting rather than acting.

What would be your nomination for the world's great anti-Utopian items? In a degree, I suppose [Cervantes'] *Don Quixote* as well as Swift and [Pope's] *The Dunciad*? Would you agree that the Utopia provides an environment for a new gimmick whereas an anti-Utopia records the psychic consequences of the new gimmick? Burroughs opens up a whole new range of possibilities for our cliché and archetype. What about [Wyndham Lewis's] *Apes of God* as anti-Utopia?

Warm regards,

[1]This appeared as "Notes on Burroughs" in *The Nation*, December 1964.

To Les Wedman[1]   December 3, 1964

Dear Les:

I received a copy of your column on [Barry] Goldwater and me from Ted Carpenter in California! I enclose $1.00 for as many copies of that particular column as it will get me. I thought you did a very interesting job. Incidentally, I believe the date was November 3rd.

[1]Les Wedman was a columnist for the *Vancouver Sun*.

Recently Dennis Braithwaite[2] was glorifying the Charlie McCarthy program as a cultural event of the highest calibre. If you come across striking examples of this tendency to raise old media to art forms, I would much appreciate your making a note of this for me. Better still, why not do a column on this very subject? I think we had discussed the basic principle involved: that when a new medium creates a new environment, the older media become the content of the new environment. The new environment is regarded as corrupt and degrading. The old environment, or content of the new, gets hoisted up to art level. This is now happening to both radio and movies as content of TV, but it is a principle behind the entire illusion of "the good old days." It worked for new art fads, including pop art. Every time a new environment forms, a new art fad is created. The new fad is simply the old environment in a new setting. When Telstar finally creates for us a new environment, we shall have this principle in operation on an epic scale.

Best wishes,

[2]Dennis Braithwaite was the television columnist for the *Toronto Star*.

To Harold Rosenberg[1]

December 11, 1964

Dear Harold:

It was really quite splendid being with you on that panel. I greatly enjoyed my chat with Mrs. Rosenberg at dinner.

I would like to do the piece for *Location* right away. Please, in light of our renewed acquaintance and conversation, indicate the sort of theme that you would prefer that I work at. There is such a range of possible topics and themes that I wish you would help me out in making a choice.[2]

Maurice Stein[3] assures me that the *New Yorker* review that you have done is a noble piece indeed that will be of great benefit to me and of aid to the reader.

I look forward to seeing you in New York before too long.

[1]McLuhan addressed this letter to Harold Rosenberg (see pages 317–18) to the Longview Foundation, New York, publishers of *location*, which Rosenberg was editing.

[2]Rosenberg replied on December 18 that he had suggested the subject for McLuhan's article in his letter of October 16: in the light of statements made in *Understanding Media* (a review of which Rosenberg had written for a forthcoming issue of *The New Yorker*, see pages 317–18), "Can the artist ignore existing social conflicts as things that his work is helping to resolve on a more fundamental plane?" The article McLuhan wrote was entitled "Art and Anti-Environment", which was published not in *location* but in *Art News Annual*, XXXI, February 1965— a "change in plan" that was mentioned by the secretary in a letter of November 16, 1965 to McLuhan's secretary, Mrs Stewart, but remains unexplained.

[3]See page 294, note 1.

To Sheila Watson

December 16, 1964

Dear Sheila:

The thesis looks superb.[1] [Malcolm] Ross and [Milton] Wilson wish you could provide a list of illustrations to go with the table of contents. This would entail numbering illustrations and indicating page of thesis text to which they correspond. The notation could go on the back of the illustrations in order to avoid disfiguring them.

Have got saddled with too many out-of-town assignments again. This includes a week in England in January.

Is there any possibility of getting a copy of your thesis to Mrs. Lewis now that it has been re-typed?[2] I am sure it would mean a great deal to her.

With love to you both.

[1]Sheila Watson's Ph.D. thesis was entitled *Wyndham Lewis and Expressionism*. Professors Ross and Wilson were among the examiners.

[2]A copy was not sent.

The letter below contains the first of numerous subsequent references to McLuhan's elder son Eric (b. 1942) as an adult. He developed a precocious interest in, and knowledge of, James Joyce that gave rise, while he was in his early twenties, to an unpublished work What the Thunder Said at Finnegans Wake. *Receiving his early education in the 1950s at De La Salle College, Toronto, he was in the United States Air Force for four years, spent two years at the University of Toronto, worked for his father at the Centre for Culture and Technology (1966–9), received a B.Sc. from Wisconsin State University in 1972, taught at Fanshawe College, London, Ont (1972–3), and did his course work at the University of Dallas (1975–7) for a Ph.D., which he received in 1982 for a thesis on* Finnegans Wake. *He is now President of McLuhan and Davies Communications, a company that trains businessmen and professionals in writing and editing techniques.*

To Froanna Lewis

December 21, 1964

Dear Mrs. Lewis:

I think I mentioned that Sheila Watson's Dissertation had now been completed. Perhaps she will be able to send you a copy before long. Her oral exam has not yet taken place, but it won't be very long in being arranged. It means a trip from Edmonton to here, however.

There has been a very nice exhibition of Lewis' drawings and paintings and books at York University. York University is a new one here in Toronto itself.

Mr. Clark at York is a Lewis fan, and he was able to get together a quite extensive exhibition by drawing almost entirely on local sources.

Eric is home from the American Air Force, and is going to University. It is grand to have him at home again. He has begun to read Lewis and finds *Time and Western Man* of great aid in his Philosophy course. It is wonderful to have him around for conversation of that sort.

I have begun to get some quite new insights into Lewis' work, especially in the matter of the environmental as it is affected by new technology. New environments encompass old ones, turning the older ones into pseudo-art forms. This Lewis finds out in *The Diabolical Principle* [1931] apropos the fox-hunter.

We think of you much and pray that you will have a blessed Christmas.

Marshall

1965

To Jonathan Miller[1]

January 8, 1965

Dear Jonathan:

Since sending you my note on technology as new environment I have been meditating on anti-environments. Technologies tend to be unconscious as much in their origin as in their effects. A new technology enjoys a brief reign as an anti-environment. Then in becomes environmental in turn. The need for the anti-environmental seems to be deeply grounded, as with dream and sleep. Dream seems to be anti-environmental control over the physiological sleep. In waking life the unconscious is environmental even as the environment is unconscious. That is, technologies not only emerge from the unconscious but accumulate a sort of collective unconscious as corporate social fact. With regard to them, the arts and sciences provide anti-environments that represent efforts at environmental control, as it were. It may be that as these anti-environments prove inadequate we resort in desperation to technological innovation and change as an attempt to control the environmental effects of earlier technologies. Or, it may be that as art fails to cope with new environments we try to substitute environmental novelty for genuine artistic controls.

Art as anti-environment awakens perception of the environment. Conventional

---

[1]Jonathan Miller (b. 1934) qualified as a medical doctor at Cambridge; co-authored and appeared in *Beyond the Fringe* (1961–4); and became a distinguished director of plays, operas, and TV films (including the famous BBC series "The Body in Question", 1978). McLuhan met him shortly before this letter was written when he appeared on a BBC Third Programme of which Miller was chairman. Miller also contributed to the discussion in another BBC radio program on May 24, 1966 entitled "The World and Marshall McLuhan". There are no letters from Miller, but he entertained the McLuhans in his home in 1969. Miller's study of *McLuhan* appeared in 1971; see page 425.

art would then seem to be a mere repetition of the environmental by way of a soothing hypnosis.

This anti-environmental approach works very well in the history of the arts themselves. Whether it is Ovid with his plots and subplots, or Japanese haiku, or just plain cosmetics, as consider Baudelaire "sur le maquillage."[2] Whether it is perfume or whiskers, these extensions create anti-environments that alert us to the meaning of the environment.

In a more primitive sense speech and clothing alike are anti-environments that beat time and clime alike. Speech and then writing beat time. Clothing beats clime. In commerce and perhaps in all institutional activities including the party system in politics, the anti-environmental control seems necessary. The market and prices are anti-environments for production. Humour as an institution can be seen as anti-environment for grievances, whether it is Hamlet's "antic disposition" or Steve Allen's theory "the funny man is a man with a grievance." What a light that sheds on the institution of the medieval clown, and King Lear!

[2]Charles Baudelaire (1821–67), in his *Figaro* article "Eloge du maquillage" [In Praise of Make-up] (in "Le Peintre de la vie moderne", *Oeuvres complètes*, vol. 2) wrote: "To confine ourselves to what today is vulgarly called 'maquillage', anyone can see that the use of rice-powder . . . is successfully designed to rid the complexion of those blemishes that Nature has outrageously strewn there, and thus to create an abstract unity in the colour and texture of the skin . . . ."

To Glenn Gould

January 11, 1965

Dear Glenn:

The tape was absolutely fascinating for me, simply crammed with insights and valuable observations.[1] I hope there will be a typed script of it eventually.

Would it be possible to use some of it in *Explorations*? You know, the little portion of *Varsity Grad* that I now edit under that heading? Alternately would you consent to do a piece on music for film and its relation to the photographic image and the audience? About 1500 words would do very well.[2]

I hope that Ted Carpenter will have an article on the film in the coming issue of *Explorations*. Film has changed a great deal since TV, even as it changed a great deal after the addition of sound track.

Again, heartiest congratulations on that fine program. I hope to see you as soon as I am back from England.

Cordially,

[1]The tape was of a radio broadcast on "CBC Sunday Night", January 10, 1965, entitled *Dialogues on the Prospects of Recording*, in which Gould talked with various people, including McLuhan, and provided music examples.

[2]Gould did publish in *Explorations* (within the *Varsity Graduate*, University of Toronto, April 1965) "Dialogues on the Prospects of Recordings", which was drawn from the program's conversations.

To Sheila and Wilfred Watson

January 28, 1965

Dear Sheila and Wilfred:

Just back from England where I discovered that Mrs. Lewis no longer resides. I think the caretaker tried to say that she lived in Las Palmas.[1] You should probably try to establish contact with her before forwarding thesis.

Everybody was very nice in England. I stayed with the Wains in Oxford for several days and lunched with Christopher Ricks, the little man who wrote the *New Statesman* review.[2] He is that combination of pedant and aesthete that Oxford produces in large numbers. He is very much like Endicott.[3] He put me in mind that the Aesthetic Movement itself in the later nineteenth century may be a corollary of the Romantic Movement, just as the worship of nature had to wait for the industrial environment, so with the worship of art.

Please plan to stay with us two weeks hence. Come early if that suits you. It would be nice to have a party after the exam.[4] Perhaps you would rather make it Saturday than Friday.

John Wain[5] has written a new, long poem called *Wild Track* [1965] which I heard on tape and found quite impressive. He is going to do a two-months' lecture tour mid-March. He will be in Seattle as well as Toronto. It was very pleasant having dinner with him and Cleanth Brooks at the Mitre. I heard Brooks talk on the New Criticism at the Oxford Critical Society the same evening.

Frank Kermode[6] turned out to be very pleasant and seemed to find everything I said very much more acceptable than what I had written.

Please remind me of anything I should do and tell Wilfred we hope he can come along with you.

[1]Mrs Lewis (who now called herself Anne Wyndham Lewis) was living temporarily in the Canary Islands.

[2]Christopher Ricks (b. 1933), Fellow of Worcester College, Oxford, had reviewed *Understanding Media* in a long article entitled "Electronic Man" (*New Statesman*, December 11, 1964). He also wrote "McLuhanism" for *The Listener* (September 28, 1967). These pieces were included in, respectively, Gerald B. Stearn, ed., *McLuhan Hot & Cool* (1967), and Raymond Rosenthal, ed., *McLuhan: Pro & Con* (1968).

[3]See page 320, note 2.

[4]Sheila Watson was about to travel to Toronto to defend her Ph.D. thesis (on February 12) on Wyndham Lewis.

[5]See page 323, note 2.

[6]See page 375, note 1.

*The following letter to Harold Rosenberg (1906–78)—distinguished art critic and author (*The Tradition of the New, *1969, etc.), art critic for* The New Yorker *from 1967 until his death, and a friend of McLuhan's—refers to Rosenberg's long review of* Understanding Media, *headlined "Philosophy in a Pop Key", which occupied the entire book-review section of* The New Yorker *for February 27,*

1965. A perceptive appreciation and critique of McLuhan's thought and vision, beginning with a lucid exposition of The Mechanical Bride *and* The Gutenberg Galaxy, *it describes McLuhan variously as a crisis philosopher, as an idealogue whose account of the effects of the media on people "lies between fact and metaphor", and as "an artist working in a mixed medium of direct experience and historical analogy", giving "a much needed twist to the great debate on what is happening to man in this age of technological speedup." Rosenberg concludes that "*Understanding Media *is a concrete testimonial (illuminating, as modern art illuminates, through dissociation and regrouping) to the belief that man is certain to find his footing in the new world he is in the process of creating." (The review was included in Gerald E. Stearn, ed.,* McLuhan Hot & Cool, *1967.) When he wrote this letter to Rosenberg, McLuhan—who was averse to reading reviews and discussions of his work—had not read his review. He had still not read it on March 9, when he wrote to Harry Skornia (see page 321).*

To Harold Rosenberg

March 1, 1965

Dear Harold:

I wish I were nearby so that we could have a proper celebration over your *New Yorker* review. Of course it comes at a time when the book is out of print, though a paperback is due any day from McGraw.

One theme that you raise, as well as some other reviewers, is that of my repetitiveness. This has always puzzled me since I am sure that I don't repeat. But it suddenly dawned on me that my basic method has always been that of drilling, as it were. My method is vertical rather than horizontal, so the scenery does not change but the texture does. For what it is worth, when I was being introduced by Jonathan Miller of the B.B.C. program last month, he said: "McLuhan is doing for visual space what Freud did for sex". Flattery apart, that does make sense to me. Freud revealed the pervasiveness of sex as structure in experience and environment and in situations that seem to have just nothing at all to do with sex. As soon as you begin to deal with the sensory modalities, you quickly discover that the visual mode may occur in situations that are quite unvisualizable. For example, central heating structures the thermal space of a room visually. That is, a centrally heated room has a thermal space that is uniform, and continuous, and connected. That is visuality as such.

In the same way the structure of acoustic space is characteristic of electric circuitry, no matter what that circuitry is designed for. Acoustic space is a simultaneous field of relations containing nothing and contained in nothing, having neither centre nor boundary. Mass audiences, for example, are acoustic spaces regardless of their makeup or content. So with all the senses. Each has its unique mode modality.

Cordial regards to both of you.

To Claude Bissell

March 4, 1965

Dear Claude:

Many thanks for you enthusiasm about the [*New Yorker*] review. I am equally gratified by Peter Drucker's generous comments. Chatting with him, he seemed quite ready to go along with a new idea of mine on which I have just begun to work. It is this, that the U.S.A. is socially and informationally the environment of Canada. Canada is, by way of being anti-environment, a prepared situation that permits perception of the environment. Such indeed is the role of the arts and sciences. Each is engaged in creating a special environment by means of which to perceive and control an environment. Environments, as such, are imperceptible (this is the theme of *The Silent Language* by Edward T. Hall). But environments are not mere containers. They are active and pervasive processes.

Canada as anti-environment to the U.S.A. is able to perceive many of the ground rules and operational effects of the American environment that are quite imperceptible to the U.S.A. If the U.S.A. has built its distant-early-warning system in Canada for military use, let us observe that we can be of far greater use to the U.S.A. as an early-warning system in the social and political spheres generally. Thus it is no accident that Canada produced Harold Innis with his uniquely structuring perception of large environments. He was a product of the Canadian anti-environment. The function of the anti-environment, whether in the arts or sciences or society, is that of perception and control.

The research program that we have in mind for the Centre is very much in accord with the above observation.[1] The plan is to establish the sensory typology or preferences of entire populations, starting with our own population. This means to discover the hierarchy of preference that we unconsciously accord to our sensory lives. i.e. how much sight and sound and movement, etc. do we consider natural and agreeable. Naturally these levels differ with age groups within any population. They certainly alter with the advent of new technologies that create new social environments. Our concern therefore is to quantify the level of preference in sensory life before and after new technologies. We would like very much to be able to run sensory levels for a country like Greece which as yet has no television, and then to run levels after it begins to acquire TV in a year or two. Sensory levels are really quite useless without knowledge of sensory modalities. At the Centre we began with the study of the sensory modalities. You may remember the wonderful work that Professor Bott did on the auditory and acoustic modalities of space.[2] We have done a good deal of work on the visual modality. It is the mode that dominates our Western world and which is rapidly dissolving under the impact of electric technology.

---

[1]Bissell was to speak to the University of Toronto Alumni in New York on March 18 and had asked McLuhan for a paragraph on the research he was supervising.
[2]See page 364, note 3.

In a word, if one knows the physical and spatial modalities of the various senses, and understands the ways in which human attention and awareness is shaped by each of these modalities, then knowledge of the sensory levels of a particular population enables one to read its cultural outlook and future with high accuracy.

Will be glad to elucidate these matters further at any time. It would seem very desirable to initiate an extensive series of sensory readings for many parts of the world as a natural function of our Department of External Affairs.

Cordially,

To Sheila Watson

March 9, 1965

Dear Sheila:

Many thanks for the help with Mr. Ower's thesis.[1] He would do well to follow your advice exclusively. Anything that you arrange for him to do about it will be acceptable to me. I am sure it would also make his chances as good as they can be with Endicott[2] and Co.

Have been out of town some more. Did have an unexpected and pleasant meeting with Robert Graves in Buffalo.[3] The University is having a Festival of the Arts and Graves came to substitute for Randall Jarrell—a most satisfactory substitution, you may say. Graves' theme was: "You can't write poetry unless you're in love." That seems to fit the Edwardian outlook quite well.

Have a most interesting Joyce item which I am sending shortly.

[1]John Ower, who had been a student of McLuhan's at the University of Toronto, completed his MA thesis, "Thematic Imagery in the Poetry of Edith Sitwell", under the supervision of Sheila Watson at the University of Alberta.

[2]Professor Norman J. Endicott (1902–76) of the Department of English, University of Toronto.

[3]Robert Graves (1895–1986)—English poet, novelist, essayist, and critic—who lived in Majorca, was at this time Professor of Poetry at the University of Oxford (1961–6). McLuhan refers to his book *The White Goddess: A Historical Grammar of Poetic Myth* (1948) on page 244.

To Harry J. Skornia

March 9, 1965

Dear Harry:

Congratulations on your *Television and Society*.[1] Have just sent a note on it to Fisher of McGraw-Hill at his request.

Have just got back in town, Harry, and haven't had a chance to open my mail let alone meditate on your criticism of the experimental design. In addition to the

[1]Harry J. Skornia, *Television and Society: An Inquest and Agenda for Improvement* (1965).

five senses we are including the visceral, the kinesthetic and the proprioceptive.[2] This approach is that of contemporary neurology. A totally different approach to the experiment could be followed. It would be possible to make up kits of images and materials to accommodate the various senses. There could be score sheets on which the preferential responses of individuals to each of the kits could be recorded for punch card purposes. Such kits, being mobile, could even be devised to cross language barriers. The difficulty with the Dan Cappon design is its unwieldiness on one hand and the slowness with which it would have to be pursued on the other.

The Harley Parker whom I mentioned is my old friend and colleague who is the display chief at the Royal Ontario Museum. He is a painter and art historian. You would find him a very exciting person to have visit your campus.[3]

Yes, I have heard about the Rosenberg review in the *New Yorker*. In fact I *like* hearing about it, but I have not read it.

Mr. Efron I saw recently at the University of Buffalo.[4] I don't think he knows what I'm talking about.

Have lots of new developments to report to you when I can get my breath.

[2]The visceral (intensely emotional feelings), the kinesthetic (relating to the sense of motion), and the proprioceptive (relating to stimuli produced and perceived within an organism).

[3]Harley Parker (b. 1915)—who first met McLuhan in 1947—is a painter who taught at the Ontario College of Art and later became head of the display department of the Royal Ontario Museum, Toronto, in the division of Art and Archaeology. He joined McLuhan in 1967–8 at Fordham University and returned to Toronto to become part of the Centre for Culture and Technology as a Research Associate until 1975—during which time he collaborated with McLuhan on *Through the Vanishing Point: Space in Poetry and Painting* (1968). He also designed McLuhan's *Counterblast* (1969).

[4]Arthur Efron is editor of a small circulation magazine of book reviews, *Paunch*, published in Buffalo.

To Peter Drucker

March 11, 1965

Dear Peter:

You left this town in a state of considerable flutter.[1] It was a real experience for them all. Your exceedingly generous remarks about me seem to have had quite a magical effect.

Keep in mind the theme of Canada as an anti-environment or early-warning system for the U.S.A. European countries perhaps have not tended to be environmental to whole groups of other countries. Have they not rather tended to be anti-environments to one another, heightening perception thereby? Now that the U.S.A. is becoming environmental to Europe and, indeed, to the world, the anti-environmental function takes on new meaning as distant-early-warning system.

[1]Drucker had given a formal lecture, sponsored by the School of Business of the University of Toronto, to a large and enthusiastic audience in Convocation Hall.

To Ashley Montagu

April 13, 1965

Dear Ashley:

I enclose a short piece on environment which could perhaps qualify for the *Inside the Whale* item.[1] I had written this in another connection. It might not be suitable, and it is probably too late, also.

It only occurred to me today how helpful this environmental approach is to the Negro question. The agrarian self has long tended to regard the Negro as environmental. As such, the Negro is a challenge, a threat, a burden. The very phrase "white supremacy" quite as much as the phrase "white trash" registers this environmental attitude. The environment is the enemy that must be subdued. To the rural man the conquest of Nature is an unceasing challenge. It is the Southerner who contributed the cowboy to the frontier. The Virginian, the archetypal cowboy as it were, confronts the environment as a hostile, natural force. To man on the frontier, other men are environmental and hostile. By contrast, men appear not as environmental but as content of the urban environment to the townsman.

The American North tended to confront Nature less directly than did the South. For the Northern men tended to be the content of technological environment. To the urban man integration seems fairly natural because black and white alike live in a city environment that contains them both. Physically, at least, city men do not think of themselves as environmental. But to the rural man the human figure and the human being are elemental. They create the environment.

Parallel to the Negro question is the French Canada problem. The English Canadians have been the environment of French Canada since the railway and Confederation. However, since the telegraph and radio and television, French Canada and English Canada alike have become the content of this new technology. Electric technology is totally environmental for all human communities today. Hence the great confusion arising from the transformation of environments into anti-environments, as it were. All the earlier groupings that had constituted separate environments before electricity, these now have become anti-environments or content of the new technology. As such, the old unconscious environments tend to become increasingly centres of acute awareness. The content of any new environment or technology is necessarily the old environment. The new environment is just as unconscious as the old one had been initially. As a merely automatic sequence, the succession of environments and of the dramatics thereto apertaining tend to be rather tiresome, if only because the audience is very prone to participate in the dramatics with an enthusiasm proportioned to their unawareness.

[1]A typescript of McLuhan's "The Relation of Environment to Anti-Environment", which was published in *Communication: The Human Dialogue* (1965) edited by Floyd Matson and Ashley Montagu. The discussion that follows in this letter appears at the end of the above article—some of it word for word. The "Inside the Whale" image from McLuhan is elucidated in his letter to Montagu of August 10, 1964, in which he agrees to contribute to the above book. It brings to mind George Orwell's 1940 essay "Inside the Whale", in which Orwell counsels novelists to "Get inside the whale . . . . Give yourself over to the world-process, stop fighting against it or pretending that you control it; simply accept it, endure it, record it."

To John Wain

July 21, 1965

Dear John:

This is my birthday and *Wild Track* just arrived most opportunely.[1] All of us are going through it with much fun and excitement. We look forward to the tape of it. By the way, apropos the taping of poetry, we finally made a breakthrough here. After much experimentation we discovered that the most effective means of involvement for students is to proceed as follows: a group of three or four students, text in hand, select any poem. Read it over casually. Then, clockwise, take it one sentence for each person and record and play back at once. Discuss poem, its effects, the effects of the various readers. Then record again at once and play back. Up to this point no more than fifteen minutes should elapse. Then tackle another poem in the same way at once. Then another. By the time three poems have been done, the group is cohesive and enthralled in a quite magical way. The young people who have shown no interest in poetry until that moment are suddenly most interested in poetry and want to go on and on and on. The ages of the group can range from ten upwards. This process seems to have some of the character of progressive jazz, or, as Eric puts it: 'it creates a group awareness of structures rather than semantics'.

Please try it out quite uncritically and tell us what happens. The effects are quite beyond anything that can be achieved by the individual voice. The whole stress shifts from consumer outlook to dissipation.

Again, deep thanks for *Wild Track*, and heartiest congratulations on a very moving poem.

Our love to all of you.

[1]*Wild Track: A Poem by John Wain* (1965) includes comic song, prose dialogue, and quotation in creating "a meditation on the theme of human interdependence".

To John Wain

September 1, 1965

Dear John:

So much to tell you. Must wait, however, until I get back with Eric [McLuhan] from New York. Viking has taken my book on *Cliché to Archetype*, which I am doing with Wilfred Watson. Shall also show them Eric's book on *What the Thunder Said at Finnegans Wake*.

Has Pop Art begun to catch on in England? It really consists in noticing the current environment as art form instead of the usual procedure of noticing the preceding environment as art form. This is really an interesting procedure and might have some large consequences.

Am using crutches as of today because of a badly sprained foot. First time in my life I ever used crutches, or a cane. It is really like discovering one's body in a completely new way.

Shall tell you what comes of our Viking visit.

Fondly,

To Sheila Watson

September 20, 1965

Dear Sheila:

The pages on clothes are wonderful indeed.[1] Shall send them along to the press. By the way, ask Alison White[2] if she has made a study of the textual changes which Carroll made when printing the hand-made version of Alice. There are a lot of them and they seem to go in one direction, namely, accommodation of the colloquial to the more formal character of printed and pictorial form. Eric is thrilled to have the note on Dido and Finnegan.[3]

In Leonard Woolf's *Beginning Again* [1964], pages 48–49, there is a passage that I include for Wilfred. There is a weird quality of naive complacence in Leonard Woolf. The whole [Bloomsbury] circle seems to have taken the child cult totally to heart. They were simply not grown up, and they knew it, and were proud of it. In his chapter on Alice, in *Some Versions of Pastoral* [1935], Wm. Empson points to the strange union of child, artist, aristocrat, and snob indicating it as the formula for Oscar Wilde. Perhaps the real power in the child cult is the freedom to play and to probe. This formula is dear to the learning process.

[1]This refers to an essay by Sheila Watson, "Power: Nude or Naked", which was published in the "Explorations" supplement to the *Varsity Graduate*, December 1965; it was republished in the periodical *Open Letter*, Third Series, no. 1 (1975), an issue devoted to Watson's uncollected prose.

[2]Dr White was then a professor in the English Department of the University of Alberta, where she established the first course for the study of children's literature in the late fifties. She is now retired.

[3]Sheila Watson had written up some observations concerning an echo from Purcell's opera *Dido and Aeneas* in the final pages of Joyce's *Finnegans Wake* and, at McLuhan's request, sent these to Eric McLuhan, who was working on the *Wake*.

To Harry J. Skornia

September 27, 1965

Dear Harry:

Delighted to see your piece in *TV Guide*.[1] I perceive that you are creeping up on the important truth that "the medium is the message", but you are doing it from a surprise angle.

Have just reviewed a book by Jacques Ellul, *Propaganda*.[2] His theme is that propaganda is never the content, is never the ideology. It is rather the pattern of all the media themselves. What he is really saying is that under electronic conditions all cultures whatever become propaganda.

Cordially,

[1]Harry J. Skornia, "Don't Give the Public What it Wants", *TV Guide*, September 18–24, 1965.

[2]Jacques Ellul, *Propaganda: The Formation of Man's Attitudes* (trans. by Konrad Kellen and Jean Lerner, 1965). McLuhan reviewed this book in the *New York Herald Tribune: Book Week* (October 1965).

To Wilfred Watson

October 6, 1965

Dear Wilfred:

Apropos the invisible environment and the habit of looking at the present through the immediate past, how about calling this human bias the "rear view mirror approach to experience?"

Bill Blissett of the Toronto Quarterly tells me that they can't do anything about Pound after all, because of the timing of the issue.[1] However, he urges me to push on with Milton Wilson and the *Canadian Forum* as outlet for anniversary Pound material.[2]

Some of the notes that I am going to append here seem to me to be appropriate to the Pound era and as perhaps indicating an outline for Chapter 4 of C/A.[3]

If one looks at romantic landscape art as the use of the landscape to snapshot or arrest a state of mind, it is possible to say that the Symbolists deliberately fragmented these large pictorial structures in order to turn them into probes. It was a sort of chiasmus or reversal whereby what had become a wrap around aesthetic became instead a means of exploration "to lose beauty and terror [,] and terror in inquisition".[4] Eliot seems to have had this reversal very much in mind all through his work. The first two lines of Prufrock announce this reversal. The first line—landscape, the 2nd—probe.[5] In this same regard is not the entire Aesthetic Movement from Pater and Hopkins forward the reversal of the sensory life from impressionism to probe? Pater's "To burn always with a hard gem-like flame" is explicitly an image of probe and exploration.[6] "Art for art's sake" takes on a completely different meaning if art is probe.[7] In the same way 'le mot juste' is a probe rather than a kind of matching of one thing against another. Has there not been a great confusion in regarding the aesthetes as consumer oriented? The very terms "symbolism" and "imagism" really indicate this breaking up of the large landscape into new tools and probes. If art is probe then "make it new" is a simple conclusion. If a work of art is to explore new environments, it is not to be regarded as a blueprint, but is rather a form of action-painting. Apropos probe and Pater, Pound's last Cantos were titled 'Rock and Drill' [sic]. His *ABC of Reading* uses past literature as probe, not package.

---

[1]William Blissett (b. 1921)—Professor of English, University College, University of Toronto—was editor of *The University of Toronto Quarterly*. McLuhan had written an article on Pound that was apparently not published.

[2]Milton Wilson—Professor of English, Trinity College, University of Toronto—was editor of *The Canadian Forum*, Toronto.

[3]From *Cliché to Archetype* (see page 416, note 1), on which McLuhan and Watson were both working.

[4]From Eliot's "Gerontion", line 56, in *Poems* (1920).

[5]The first three lines of "The Love Song of J. Alfred Prufrock" are: "Let us go then, you and I,/ When the evening is spread out against the sky/Like a patient etherized upon a table."

[6]"To burn always with this hard, gemlike flame, to maintain this ecstasy, is success in life." Walter Pater, in the Conclusion to *Studies in the History of the Renaissance* (1873).

[7]"Art for art's sake" ("L'art pour l'art et sans but"), Benjamin Constant, *Journal intime* (1804).

And here we have the same drama as that between plot and sub-plot. The sub-plot is used as a heuristic probe of the main plot. In the same way, new media serve as environments, as hidden actions, as probes and processors of the older culture. How about Yeats' poem that begins: "We were the last romantics"?[8] Is not Yeats announcing his role as that of content or the old culture undergoing the processing of the new media? Ireland was a country that had not had a 19th century, had indeed not had a Renaissance. It pushed into the 20th century straight out of the middle ages. It could use its unique culture as a probe or control for the 20th century. Is Eliot's etherized patient the audience?

I am looking forward to your comments on Ellul.

[8]"We were the last romantics" begins the last stanza of William Butler Yeats's poem "Coole Park and Ballylee".

To Tom Wolfe[1]

October 25, 1965

Dear Tom:

Just a note about the Thomas Nashe dissertation.[2] Studying Nashe's style led me to look at the rhetorical education of his day. I soon got on to the history of this form of symbolic action. Having tracked it back to 5th century Athens, I moved forward, relating the rhetorical program to the dialectical studies, and especially, to the grammatical studies. Plato's *Cratylus* presents a theory of language as the key to an inclusive consciousness of human culture much in the style of *Finnegans Wake*.

Philologists since the Renaissance have pooh-poohed this inclusive approach, but it lasted until the time of Bishop Sprat and got going again with the Symbol-

[1]Tom Wolfe (b. 1931), the American author of brilliant essays on contemporary American culture, written in what has been described as a "baroque pop style", attracted attention with his first collection of articles, *The Kandy-Kolored Tangerine-Flake Streamline Baby* (1965). He corresponded with McLuhan—and saw him several times in New York, Toronto, and San Francisco between 1965 and 1978. (The letters to McLuhan from Wolfe—who is also a graphic artist—were handwritten, in rust-coloured ink, in a freewheeling italic script with occasional graphic ornamentation that expressed his wit and warmth.) In 1965 Wolfe wrote a memorable portrait of McLuhan, "What If He Is Right?" (see page 330, note 1). McLuhan refers to this in a double-page spread (pp. 212-3), entitled "Sheep in Wolfe's Clothing", in his *Culture Is Our Business* (1970).

[2]For a description of McLuhan's Ph.D. dissertation on Thomas Nashe, see page 103, note 4.

ists.[3] In the age of Kenneth Burke and William Empson it is once more totally acceptable.[4]

Cicero and Varro[5] in the Roman world kept alive and flourishing the idea of language as an inclusive traditional consciousness. They taught it as a key to the mysteries of being and of power. Their program was taken over by St. Augustine as the charter of medieval education. Both the exegesis and the stylistics of the Church Fathers enhanced the whole tradition. Christian humanism in the 16th century gave the Patristic program [i.e. that of the Church Fathers] a mighty boost. Peter Ramus thought he had devised an instrument for cutting it down to manageable size. Francis Bacon thought that the linguistic program could be extended to the entire book of Nature. Thomas Nashe used all aspects of the Patristic program for polemic and satire. Hence I called my dissertation "The Place of Thomas Nashe in the Learning of His Time". Nashe is a Patristic humanist using all the latest journalistic techniques of Aretino[6] to prompt the traditional program. This brought him into head-on conflict with the Puritan left-wing of the English Church.

I have learned so much about the entire problem since writing the thesis that I have hesitated to go ahead with publication without complete re-writing. In terms of your own interests in American studies, you can see how the American South remained faithful to the humanist and Ciceronian tradition whereas the Puritan and technological North followed the course of Peter Ramus in schematizing language and stripping words of their traditional attributes. Paradoxically, it is the North that continues the tradition of the abstract Schoolman.[7] Equally paradoxically, it was the Puritanical Pound and Eliot who steered American culture back into the traditional fold of linguistic awareness.

I hope that these notes may have some use for you, Tom. Call on me for any help that you think I can provide.

Cordially,

---

[3]Thomas Sprat (1635–1713), Bishop of Rochester, wrote the *History of the Royal Society of London* (1667), in which he defended a "close, naked, natural" writing style. The Symbolists, a group of late-nineteenth-century French poets (Mallarmé, Verlaine, Rimbaud, Laforgue), reacted against realism, direct expression, precise description, and explicit analogy by advocating the importance of suggestion and evocation and the power of symbol and metaphor to convey subjective emotion and the element of mystery in human existence.

[4]Kenneth Burke (b. 1897), American literary critic, philosopher, and poet, among whose books are several works of linguistic analysis and *The Philosophy of Literary Form: Studies in Symbolic Action* (1941). For (Sir) William Empson (1906–84), see page 462, note 2.

[5]Marcus Terentius Varro (116–27 B.C.) was a Roman scholar of the Latin language, the author of *De Lingua Latina*.

[6]Pietro Aretino (1492–1556), of Arezzo, Italy, was the author of five comedies and a tragedy and other satirical works, and was mentioned by Nashe ("one of the wittiest knaves God ever made", in *The Unfortunate Traveller*) and by Milton (in the *Areopagitica*).

[7]This was discussed by McLuhan in his 1944 essay "Edgar Poe's Tradition", *Sewanee Review*, vol. 12, no. 1, January 1944.

To William Jovanovich[1]

November 10th, 1965

Dear Bill:

You may be acquainted with *The Paper Economy* [1963; 1965] by David Bazelon. I think it concerns our project on the future of publishing.[2] Bazelon is vividly aware of paper as money, and credit, and contract. That is, he is aware of the Emperor's old clothes. He cannot see the Emperor's new clothes. These consist of information and electric circuitry in general. Since, however, the world of books is very much a paper world, the new electric environment concerns publishing as much as it does banking. It may be the soundest strategy to stress the positive new factors for publishing in the world of electric technology rather than the backlash of these new factors upon the old circumstances of publishing. After all, the new factors constitute a world of enormously more effective services and enormously increased wealth.

The Secular City [*: Secularization and Urbanization in Theological Perspective*] by Harvey Cox (MacMillan paperback, 1965) has a theme that may also be relevant. He begins by doing a historical job on Judaism and Christianity as the creators of the secular city. Without these revealed features, he argues, there is neither human person nor human city. All is part and parcel of the cosmos as a divine animal. When one is looking for ground rules and boundary lines in the electric age, facets like these may prove helpful.

It would seem that this year I shall have to file an income tax return in the U.S. as well as in Canada. I am delaying the return of our contract to you until I have checked out a few items relating to income tax. It won't take long. Tell me if the delay creates any problems.

Regards,

[1]William Jovanovich (b. 1920), president of Harcourt, Brace & World, Inc. (later chairman of Harcourt Brace Jovanovich, Inc.), met McLuhan in September 1965 and maintained an extensive correspondence with him until the early 1970s. (Jovanovich's article "The Universal Xerox Life Compiler Machine" appeared in the "Explorations" section of the University of Toronto *Graduate*, Winter 1970.) His firm published *Counterblast* in 1969 and *Take Today: The Executive as Dropout* in 1972.

[2]Jovanovich had asked McLuhan to consider writing a short book on authorship and publishing, and their future. A contract was signed for *Concepts of Authorship and Publishing*, of which Jovanovich and McLuhan were to be co-authors. This proposed work was transformed into *The Future of the Book*, which (at Jovanovich's suggestion) was to take the form of letters between them. At least one long letter was written by McLuhan; but on July 2, 1969 Jovanovich asked to be released from the project owing to his inability to combine his end of the collaboration with other obligations.

To Graham Spry[1]

Dear Mr. Spry:

Many thanks for *The Listener* pages. Mr. Steiner gives a very adequate rendering of the role he gratuitously assigns to me while commenting on myself. He is a very good example of the literary type of person who feels the need to express a point of view, at all costs. This point of view they associate with precision and responsibility. What they invariably fail to notice is the structural form of situations. Such form is quite independent of point of view. This is a precise, structural statement of fact which any merely literary person would regard as egotistical, wild, and imprecise.[2]

Again, thanks for sending me Mr. Steiner's thoughts.

Sincerely yours,

[1]Graham Spry (1900–83)—Canadian journalist, international business executive, and pioneer advocate of public broadcasting in Canada—was at this time agent general for Saskatchewan in the UK, Europe, and the Near East.

[2]In the second of a two-part enquiry into the teaching of English in *The Listener* (October 28, 1965), George Steiner (see page 360, note 1) wrote: "*The Gutenberg Galaxy* is an irritating book, full of wildness and imprecision, full of unnecessary gesture, egotistical, almost at certain points megalomaniac; but so of course is Coleridge's *Biographia Literaria* or Blake's *Descriptive Catalogue*." These are the negative comments to which McLuhan did not take kindly. However, Steiner went on to say: "And like Blake, who has greatly influenced his thought, McLuhan has the gift of radical illumination. His analysis of the manner in which print has shaped our literature between the time of Gutenberg and that of Joyce; his work on the nature of poetics and communications in an oral, non-poetic culture; his conjectures about the changes which the new electronic media of instantaneous visual statement and limitless recall, the memory of the computer, will bring to art and language are compelling. Even when we cannot follow his leap of argument, we are made to re-think our basic concepts of what literature is, what a book is, and how we read it. Together with Sartre's *Qu'est-que ce la littérature?* the *Gutenberg Galaxy* should stand on the shelf of anyone who calls himself a student or teacher of literature."

To Tom Wolfe

November 22, 1965

Dear Tom:

I am very happy about your portrait of me.[1] Sitters are not supposed to enjoy their portraits. So when I say I am pleased with your portrait of me, I mean that I can recognize its power and fidelity, but like hearing one's own voice for the first time, or seeing one's self for the first time on video, or film, there is a considerable mood of disillusionment that is both deserved and salutary.

Corinne, by the way, is convinced that we should send you a sample of my neckties. It was a clip-tie that I was wearing in San Francisco.[2] She feels that you implied that there was some mysterious plastic band that went all the way around the neck! Rhetorically, I understand full well the usefulness of that ploy. Your success in elucidating my approaches to various problems is really considerable. The only serious disadvantage of your article may develop in the internal revenue quarter. They may begin to demand a bank statement!

Corinne is only now getting into your Tangerine book.[3] She is finding it quite exhilarating.

Please advise the circulation department to send a dozen copies of your article, and to bill me for the same. I am sure we will need more copies than that before long. It is sure to prove a major asset to McLuhan Inc.

Lots of new developments here. When our sensory threshold study is completed, it may be possible for you to do a story on it. It is really quite a unique and exciting study that is developing.

[1]Wolfe's profile of McLuhan, "What If He Is Right?", had recently appeared in *New York*, the Sunday magazine section of the New York *World Journal Tribune*. It was later included in Wolfe's book *The Pump House Gang* (1968).

[2]At the beginning of his article Wolfe says that McLuhan was wearing, at their first meeting, "some kind of a trick snap-on necktie with hidden plastic cheaters on it."

[3]Tom Wolfe, *The Kandy-Kolored Tangerine-Flake Streamline Baby* (1965).

To William Jovanovich

December 28, 1965

Dear Bill:

The Life of Montaigne paid off splendidly.[1] Assuming that you can get access to a copy of Mr. Frame's book, which you so generously sent to me, let me draw your attention to the following pages. Pages 81–83 explain how the essays were in a deep sense a substitute for conversation and dialogue with his friend, La Boétie.[2] Had his friend lived, he would probably have settled for letters rather than essays. Dialogue had been the basic form of the scholastic disputation of the preceding age. This is a good, but not a rare example of how the environmental actions of one time become the artistic, archetypal forms of the succeeding age.

On page 82 Montaigne says: "Many things that I would not want to tell anyone, I tell the public; and for my most secret knowledge and thoughts, I sent my most faithful friends to the bookseller's shop." The concept of the public gets further elaboration on pages 144, 253, and 291, where he says (at the bottom): "I owe a complete portrait of myself to the public." The man of letters as engaged in self expression is meaningless without his public. He can, as it were, carry on an inner dialogue between himself and his public.

I will look into the matter of the man of letters in ancient Rome. Publication for Horace, as well as for Chaucer, tended to take the form of oral recitation. This was presumably due to manuscript conditions. Yet, compared to the Greeks, the Romans had a book trade.

It is my own suggestion that what print made possible for Montaigne and others was the technique of snapshotting the motions of the mind, the possibility of isolating single instants. A point of view tends, in the same way, to be the isolation of a particular moment in a situation. This is a point that Parker and I work on a good deal in our *Space in Poetry and Painting* book.[3]

I think that we should certainly keep Erasmus in mind as a prototypical man of letters. There is a new book on him called *The Adages of Erasmus* by Miss Phillips.[4]

---

[1]Donald M. Frame, *Montaigne: A Biography* (1965), published by Jovanovich's firm Harcourt, Brace & World. McLuhan had asked Jovanovich to send him this book in a letter of December 14.

[2]Montaigne's famous essay "On Friendship"—in the first two books of the *Essais* of Montaigne (1533–92), which appeared in 1580—commemorated his friendship with the young French judge and writer Étienne de La Boétie (1530–63).

[3]Marshall McLuhan and Harley Parker, *Through the Vanishing Point: Space in Poetry and Painting* (1968). See page 358, note 2.

[4]Margaret Mann Philips, *The "Adages" of Erasmus: A Study with Translations* (1964).

1966

To Saul Steinberg[1]

January 7, 1966

Dear Mr. Steinberg:

I was most gratified to receive a copy of *The New World*. It is indeed new! "A model [mighty] maze, but not without a plan," to use the words of Alexander Pope's *Essay on Man*. In fact, it could be sub-titled "An Essay on Man."

Your imagery is splendidly suited to probing the new world of TV. I mean the new sensory world, not the TV programs, but the structure of the TV image.

It was a delight to encounter you at the Anshens.[2]

Very best wishes for the New Year.

[1]The drawings of the graphic satirist Saul Steinberg (b. 1914), which frequently appear in *The New Yorker*, have been published in several collections, including *The New World* (1965). McLuhan had met Steinberg in New York.

[2]Ruth Nanda Anshen planned and edited the World Perspectives series for Harper & Row, in which *Through the Vanishing Point* was published in 1968.

To Tom Wolfe

January 13, 1966

Dear Tom:

A very happy New Year to you.

Much enjoyed your chat with Pierre Berton last night on our Channel 9.[1] You handled him very deftly and amusingly.

Are you familiar with *The Art of Being Ruled* by Wyndham Lewis? Another man you might glance at is Julien Benda. His *Trahison des Clercs* was translated as *The Great Betrayal*.[2] The treason of the intellectuals that he attacked was precisely the selling-out to politics. Quite unconsciously, the habit of perspective, or a fixed stance from which to observe a slice or facet of any situation, tends to breed intense emotional responses. When you try to find out "what's going on", a point of view is not very useful. Within any organization, each individual tends to have a point of view. The consultant who is called in to diagnose has the advantage of not having a point of view. In an environment of electric information, a total field approach is natural, since all types of data are simultaneously accessible.

Looking forward to seeing you next month sometime.

[1]This was "The Pierre Berton Show", hosted by the well-known Canadian journalist and historian.

[2]Julien Benda (1867–1956), French philosopher and essayist, was the author of *Treason of the Intellectuals (La Trahison des clercs)*, 1927—also translated as *The Great Betrayal*—which criticizes intellectuals who engage in politics instead of defending the abstract principles of truth and justice.

To Claude Bissell

January 28, 1966

Dear Claude:

I thought your remarks about the U.S. well timed and valuable.[1] Canada as a cultural DEW line, or distant early warning system, has a large untouched potential in relation to the U.S. The U.S.A. as our environment, tends to be an area of unconsciousness. We, as an anti-environment of the U.S. should, naturally, tend to push it up into archetypal form. As the only country that shares the continental milieu of the U.S.A., there is probably a sense in which this gives us a connatural knowledge of the U.S.A. that is not shared by any other country. As the U.S.A. becomes a world environment, our status as anti-environment to the U.S.A. becomes an invaluable asset. We are best situated to create and to provide awareness of the process of being and making Americans. Yet we have no ultimate commitment to be American, or even to be Canadian. It is this detachment *in* action that would seem to give us our opportunity to share the creative process of the culture without any mere merging in it. This is what the jazz musicians mean by "real cool."

I enclose a few notes on the strange relation of environment and anti-environment. I have found that to consider art as an anti-environment or as a means of perceiving the hidden dimension of the environment, is exceedingly useful. Instead of explaining to people that art is something to be taken seriously because of some inherent superior quality, it makes more sense to point out that art has an indispensable function in cognition, and that men without art strongly tend to be automata, or somnambulists, imprisoned in a dream.

By the way, if you feel that there are any statements whatever in *The Gutenberg Galaxy* that are vague, inaccurate, or exaggerated, I would like an opportunity to scrutinize some of them with you.[2]

It would be easy to mount a DEW line Seminar at the Centre for Culture and Technology. When you point out the Canadian "ignorance" of the U.S.A., you may also be pointing to a primary asset, but one that has not yet been brought

---

[1] This refers to a speech Bissell made to The Canadian Society of Los Angeles on January 26, 1966. He hinted at the concept of Canada as a cultural DEW line, but did not make use of the McLuhan phrase.

[2] Bissell had been one of ten people asked to write about the best or most important books they had read over the past year for the *Globe Magazine* (supplement to the *Globe and Mail*, Toronto, December 25, 1965). He wrote in part: "It is more fashionable these days to talk about McLuhan than to read him. The assumption is that he is deliberately difficult, mired in verbiage and non-sequiturs. Certainly a book like *The Gutenberg Galaxy* supports this, for it is a pastiche of quotations and bold, unsupported generalizations. *Understanding Media* is quite a different book . . . witty and eloquent, with passages of lucid exposition, moving exhortation and, occasionally, delphic grandiloquence. It is certainly one of the most important books published in this country." In his reply to McLuhan of February 1, Bissell said that *The Gutenberg Galaxy* was difficult "by reason of the techniques of extended quotation and symbolic juxtaposition" and that he had been referring to "techniques of presentation".

into play. You know how, in operations research, the basic procedure consists in "organized ignorance." The experts can never get off the ground with a problem because they know that everything has been tried before.

Have you heard the story of the big-hearted surgeon who, when his patients could not afford surgery, would offer to touch up the x-ray for free?

Cordial regards,

P.S. Wednesday, Stephen Spender's talk on the 1930's brought in *Ends and Means* [1937] by Aldous Huxley. I suddenly realized that the entire discussion of how means shape and twist ends can be a massive comment on the "medium is the message." Is this not an odd example of how a mere phrase can conceal a world of relevance?

To the Editor of Life[1]

March 1st, 1966

Dear Sir:

Not "obsolete", but "obsolescent" is the term that applies to my analysis of the present status of the printed book. Obsolescence often precedes an extraordinary development in technology. The arrival of electric xerography certainly does not mean the end of the book, but rather a great enlargement of its scope and function. Earlier, photo-engraving and also photography had transformed the world of typography and of book production.

The consequences for literature that stem from major changes in technology are only inevitable to the extent that they are unforeseen. Determinism is the result of the behaviour of those who are determined to ignore what is happening around them. Recognition of the psychic and social consequences of technological change makes it possible to neutralize the effects of innovation. If we maintain lively dialogue with, and among, the technologies, we can enlist them on the side of traditional values instead of watching those values disappear while we play the helpless bystanders.

Sincerely yours,

[1]Part of this letter was published in *Life* in the issue of March 18, 1966. It was a comment on "Oracle of the Electric Age", a close-up of McLuhan by Jane Howard in *Life*, February 25, 1966.

To William Jovanovich

Dear Bill:

The Goldschmidt volume is in stock here and will be on its way to you very soon.[1]

I am reading *The Rise of English Literary History* by René Wellek. It is a McGraw-Hill paperback, 1966. It has a good deal of material that we can use because it traces the changing relations between the author and his time and his audience. For example, on page 25 he notes:

> . . . A comprehension of the uniqueness of a work of art increased with the new demands on "originality" or "invention." The old communism of subject-matter broke down, and "imitation" became slowly a term of reproach. A book like Langbaine's lists of "thefts" and "plagiaries" shows how sharply the so-called unoriginality of an older period was suddenly felt. The individuality of the poet was also stressed more and more; anonymity and community of authorship decline, at least in the higher ranges of literature; and the "genius" and "inspiration" of the writer comes more and more to be regarded as the essential factor in the creation of literature.

Shall bring Corinne along with me to the Book Awards dinner, and to the St. David's panel.[2] Hope you and Martha get to meet her.

One way of looking at the future of the book might be as follows: as print ceases to be the ordinary and pervasive environment, the book can be prescribed as a specific therapy for cultures where there is little or no "alpha-thinking" and a great excess of "beta-thinking." That is, to use the language of Owen Barfield in his *Saving the Appearances*,[3] we can approach the book as a cultural therapy, an indispensable ingredient in communal diet, necessary for the maintenance of civilized values as opposed to tribal values. In a word, as we move towards the programming of environments rather than the mere programming of curricu-

---

[1]This was probably the recently published second edition of E. P. Goldschmidt's *The Printed Book of the Renaissance: Three Lectures on Type, Illustration, Ornament* (1966). Goldschmidt's *Medieval Texts and Their First Appearance in Print* (1943) is discussed at some length in *The Gutenberg Galaxy*.

[2]Marshall and Corinne McLuhan attended the National Book Awards dinner at Lincoln Centre (Philharmonic Hall) on March 15.

[3]McLuhan mentions several times in his letters Owen Barfield's *Saving the Appearances: A Study in Idolatry* (1965?). It is a difficult and densely written argument for a new apprehension of the physics of phenomena (having to do with the nature of the universe and the history of mankind) as revealed by science in the nineteenth and twentieth centuries; and their relation to the current unconscious "figuration" of them that enters the realms of physiology, psychology, and philosophy, where they have become "idols". Barfield argues for a new awareness that will make our collective unconscious about these things become conscious. The title is taken from Simplicius's commentary on Aristotle's *De Caelo:* all hypotheses were devised to "save" the "appearances" of phenomena by accounting for them without infringing fundamental principles.

lum, we can keep our eye on the effects of the book, not just the content of the book. It occurs to me that Parkinson's law can be translated to say that in facing any given task, the whole environment goes into action.[4] His phrase that any task automatically tends to absorb all available time and all available personnel, may really point to the peculiar action of the human and technical environment as a unified force. Has this not been the great dawning awareness of the present age? That all things cohere and inhere as a single process? The example of the "safety-car" will serve. The car, as isolated engineered object, is suddenly seen as having a whole set of effects. Is it not typical that this awareness should emerge with regard to an older technology rather than a new one?

Looking forward to next week.

[4]The opening words of *Parkinson's Law* (1958), by C. Northcote Parkinson, are: "Work expands so as to fill the time available for its completion."

To Mother St Michael[1]   August 10, 1966

Dear Mother St. Michael:

You have been prancing to some purpose in your Harvard stall![2]

Apropos "knowing is making", I think it concerns the process of recognition and *re*cognition. Somewhere Aquinas says "What does the agent intellect make?" and he adds: "It makes sense."

The human translation of all phenomena into sense via the sensus communis is extraordinary work. It is data processing. Now that we are putting our sensus communis outside in technology, the amount of information to be processed increases hugely. We live in an environment that is made of information. The natural habitat is now enclosed by a man-made environment, even the planet itself.

Am scrambling to complete the *Space in Poetry and Painting* book. Pardon haste.

[1]Mother St Michael (Winnifred Guinan, b. 1904), OSU, was educated at the University of Western Ontario, London, and Assumption College, Windsor, Ont. She received her Ph.D. in Philosophy and Psychology from Laval University and pursued post-doctoral studies at the Universities of Ottawa, Notre Dame, Harvard—at which time McLuhan wrote the letter that follows—and Toronto. Her brother, the Reverend Vincent Guinan, CSB, was President of Assumption College when McLuhan taught there. Mother St Michael was teaching then at Brescia College, University of Western Ontario. She and five of her students took a summer course at Assumption from McLuhan that in her words was "one of the most brilliant courses on humanism from the Greeks to the present that I could ever imagine." She was asked to leave university teaching by the Ontario government to be their first officer on aging and became a much-published authority on gerontology; in 1975 she founded the Canadian Institute of Religion and Gerontology, an ecumenical body. She was made Professor Emeritus of the University of Western Ontario in 1983.

[2]Mother St Michael was doing research at Harvard's Widenar Library. Study cubicles at Harvard are called stalls.

To William Jovanovich

October 18, 1966

Dear Bill:

You will find relevance in *The Step to Man* [1966] by John R. Platt[1] for our *Future of the Book*. I am committed to six series of *Look* Magazine issues on the Future of Education, the City, the Book, etc. The editor with whom I am working for the Future of Education is George Leonard who is most knowledgeable and able.[2] He was looking at Eric's recently completed *James Joyce's Guide to the Media*.[3] He became quite excited about it and took part of it with him. I am sure you will find it of the greatest help in considering the Future of the Book, so I am asking Ralph Baldwin to let you have a copy that is now in his hands. Don't think about it from the point of view of publication, but simply as preparation for our effort. Also keep in mind that Eric is taking the year off to write *A Young Peoples' Guide to the Media*.[4] Currently he is planning it as a series for elementary and secondary schools. You will see when you read *James Joyce's Guide to the Media* why he turned to the school text as a natural sequel. *James Joyce's Guide to the Media* would be the third in the series, i.e. for college use. It is quite an extraordinary thing to read.

Perhaps it would be possible for you to meet George Leonard sometime. I think you would find him very refreshing.

Shall keep in touch.

P.S. Publisher of *The Step to Man* is John Wiley & Sons Inc.

[1] A collection of essays on the evolving nature of man in a technological age.

[2] McLuhan wrote "The Future of Education. The Class of 1989", *Look*, vol. 31, no. 4 (February 21, 1967) and "The Future of Sex", *Look*, vol. 31, no. 15 (July 25, 1967). George Leonard was at this time West Coast Editorial Manager for *Look* in San Francisco.

[3] This was Eric McLuhan's *What the Thunder Said at Finnegan's Wake*, which in some twelve chapters discusses the thunders (the 100-letter words) and the themes of technology they represent.

[4] This became *The City as Classroom: Understanding Language and Media* (1977), edited by McLuhan, Kathy Hutchon, and Eric McLuhan.

To Peter Drucker

October 24, 1966

Dear Peter:

It is quite wonderful to think of you writing a preface for *Understanding Media*.[1] That gives me a real lift. What you say about current developments in Germany

[1] Peter Drucker wrote a Preface to the German edition of *Understanding Media*, which was published by Econ Verlag under the title *Die Magischen Kanäle* (1968)—"The Magical Channel".

is very apropos that business of new environments making the old ones very visible while themselves remaining invisible.

Your letter comes just as I am enroute to the airport, so I will merely mention a few of the matters you raise. The title might well retain the idea of technologies as extensions of our bodies. Whenever we make a new technology, that creates a new environment which we automatically assume as our cultural mask. We do this via our senses, not our concepts. Each new environment creates a new body percept, new outlook and new inlook. As the East goes West, we can switch the processes from afar since it does not alter our body percept. Electric technology is sending the West eastward faster than the East is going westward. The orientalizing of our world by inner involvement in depth occurs via circuit or feedback along with speed-up of data. An all-at-once world is structurally like the subconscious. It tends to be mythical and archetypal. Consciousness becomes incidental rather than structural. It is the old environment, not the new one. The individual yields to the tribal man. Electronic man is the first since neolithic times to live in a man-made environment. Preliterate man naturally regarded his world as man-made. An information environment like ours is man-made. Media are, as it were, cultural or corporate masks.

I am sure you will think of some phrase that will have much meaning for a German reader. I have a very able young man in Zurich who has translated the *Gutenberg Galaxy* into German.[2] I shall appeal to him for suggestions and will keep in touch with you.

[2]The German edition of *The Gutenberg Galaxy* was translated by Dr Max Nänny and published as *Die Gutenberg-Galaxis: Das Ende des Buchzeitalters* (1968) by Econ Verlag.

To William Jovanovich

December 1, 1966

Dear Bill:

The Beacon-Vanguard matter is indeed an unedifying one.[1] Looking back on the beginnings of the whole affair, I can only say that had the entire matter been handled properly there would have been no book.[2] A considerable amount of destructive anarchy is indispensable to production. Premature tidying up kills

[1]This refers to the confusion McLuhan created when, in 1956, he signed a contract with Beacon Press for the paperback rights to *The Mechanical Bride*—a contract that was inoperable (as Jovanovich explained to McLuhan in his letter of June 24, 1966) because the rights were held by The Vanguard Press, the original publisher. A colleague of Jovanovich's, on McLuhan's behalf, had agreed to a settlement of the "Beacon-Vanguard matter" and this is indicated by the publication in 1967 both of the Vanguard reissue of *The Mechanical Bride* in hardback and of the Beacon Press paperback edition.

[2]i.e., no paperback edition of *The Mechanical Bride*.

creativity. All children are geniuses until they go to school and learn to read and write, or so many people feel. The artist has to live in messy circumstances in order to keep his senses in play. Tidiness belongs to only one sense, the sense of sight.

I had hoped that you would be able to attend the December 8th meeting of the James Joyce Society. Eric will present a tentative sample of his book. The side of Joyce that he is opening up is larger than the Joyceans have ever looked at, so Eric will expect a fairly rough time.

There is a marvellous new book by Frances A. Yates called *The Art of Memory* (Routledge and Kegan Paul [1966]). It may not be on sale. I have a review copy. It reopened some missing vistas in the history of Western culture and is a book that you and I can make much use of in writing our book. Memoria was the fourth branch of rhetoric and was developed by architectural and imagistic means simultaneously. Dante's *Commedia* was recognized as a "memory theatre" in its time and later, as were the Summas of the philosophers. Vico[3] was the first to spot language itself as a memory theatre. *Finnegans Wake* is such a memory theatre for the entire contents of human consciousness and unconsciousness. These theatres were non-literary simply because they were based on *topics* or places that were given an architectural form for the convenience of the rhetorician or orator. With the arrival of the printed word, the whole fabric of these theatres collapsed quickly. The medieval cathedrals were memory theatres. *The Golden Bough* is a memory theatre of the corporate rather than the private consciousness and marks a major transition toward the retribalizing of human consciousness.

Had Frank Taylor[4] on the phone yesterday in great excitement and distress about the Bantam and Random House issue of *The Medium is the Massage*.[5] I didn't write anything for that book. It is excerpts with pictures. I think I reassured him that it would be a boost for the other books.

---

[3]There are several references in this collection to Giovanni Battista (Giambattista) Vico (1688–1744), who was a grammarian, a professor of rhetoric at the University of Naples, and a philosopher of history. His *La Scienza Nuova* (New Science), published in 1725, and *La Scienza Nuova Seconda* (1730, 1744)—which discuss history in terms of a natural cycle of growth, decay, and regrowth and reflect a concern with words and the poetics of words—had a great influence on thinkers in the nineteenth and twentieth centuries. McLuhan's interest in Vico relates to his influence on James Joyce, who said of Vico, "my imagination grows when I read Vico as it doesn't when I read Freud or Jung." While Joyce's interest in Vico is seen in his uses of Homer and in several references—such as the Vico Road, Dalkey, in the "Nestor" episode—it is most apparent in *Finnegans Wake*, which was influenced by Vico's treatment of language, by his elaborate theory of cyclic recurrence (used by Joyce as a "trellis") drawn primarily from Vico's three ages—of gods, heroes, and men—and by such imaginative images in Vico as the divine thunderclap, represented in the *Wake* by a 100-letter word.

[4]Editor-in-Chief of the Trade Book Division of McGraw-Hill, New York, publisher of *Understanding Media*.

[5]*The Medium is the Massage* (1967) by Marshall McLuhan and the graphic designer Quentin Fiore was co-ordinated by Jerome Agel. In a letter to McLuhan of September 14, 1965 from New York, Agel had discussed creating with Quentin Fiore an illustrated book "based on your published works", with McLuhan acting as "adviser and approver". Agel, as agent for the book, arranged

To Peter Drucker

December 6, 1966

Dear Peter:

The Syracuse lecture notes made much sense to me. They are in what I call "iconic prose," that is, prose used as probe rather than as package. This leaves the reader the task of manipulating the probe instead of merely adopting a pro or con view of what is being said. Perhaps the best accompaniment for iconic prose is the anecdote. It is this that gives appropriateness to the human interest story in the newspaper, for the anecdote is also a kind of probe. Have been doing a good deal of work lately on the future of the services industries as they relate to electronic circuits and feedback. Most of this goes into a book for McGraw-Hill called *Culture Is Our Business* [1970].

Canada as a somewhat backward country enjoys many advantages. These become more evident as I encounter more advanced territories in the U.S.A. You could do a great deal of good for us all by making an inventory of particular advantages enjoyed by backward territories in the appraisal of advanced situations (by the way, a German friend here suggests "Vorposten" as the best translation for "The Extensions of Man"—there are some nice puns, including four-poster, and the Colonial idea of outpost). For example, California and the west coast leap-frogging from the 18th to the 20th century. Never had a 19th century. That's why they could have Hollywood. A 19th-century area like Chicago was too highly structured to accommodate a free-wheeling enterprise like Hollywood. Canada can accept some very advanced things in the arts and in a municipal government simply because we have no vested interests in any of the procedures that preceded these things elsewhere. Quebec is leap-frogging out of the 17th century into the 20th century. English Canada, relatively, is of 19th century origin and can only creep out of the 19th century into the 20th. A geographic inventory on these lines but of European and even global scope could throw floods of light on many developments past and present. This is the kind of inventory that calls for very iconic prose such as you devote to the matters in your Syracuse lectures. For example, your simple observation of years ago that the motorized work-truck had much to do with racial integration in the South. That is a nice example of how the iconic probe can also contain a human interest story. Had you heard about the Negro who went to the local Cadillac dealer to inquire what sorts of models he had? The dealer replied that he had a variety of

publication by Bantam Books and Random House in the U.S. and by The Penguin Press in Great Britain. It is described on the jacket flap as "an inventory of effects, an exposition of McLuhan's prophecies of the electronic age. . . . " In an hour-long NBC-TV program on McLuhan in March 1967 he said that the title of this book was intended to suggest that "a medium in not something neutral—it does something to people. It takes hold of them. It rubs them off, it massages them, it bumps them around."

colours, red, green, and, of course, "flesh colour." The customer said: "Oh, what do you mean by 'flesh colour'?" Answer: "Black, of course."

Regards to all of you

To William Jovanovich

December 14, 1966

Dear Bill:

Fordham University has offered me a Schweitzer Professorship for the coming year.[1] No lecturing.[2] It looks as though our books are going to get written after all. Perhaps it would be best not to say anything about the Schweitzer deal until it is firmed up. It also means that Eric will do a year of studies at Fordham and that he can get on with *The Young Peoples' Guide*. Indeed, he is working on that right now.

Eric discovered at the Joyce Society that he was the only person who had read *Finnegan* at all.[3] Personally I would be at a loss to mention a single Joyce student who could read Eric's book except on the basis of doing his study of *Finnegan* as he read the book. Hugh Kenner, for example, is an old student of mine from my pre-media days. He hasn't a clue about media and James Joyce. The same is true of his books on Yeats, Pound and Eliot. The literary Brahmins were able to cling to Joyce as far as *Ulysses*. Then they lost him. Meantime, Joyce had not lost touch with media developments. It was his sudden breakthrough into the electronic world that gave him access to language on a new basis.

I do hope you will be able to read Eric's book as providing a basis for our own efforts concerning *The Future of the Book*.

A Blessed Christmas to Martha and you and the family.

[1] Fordham University, New York, had been awarded by the State of New York an Albert Schweitzer Chair in the Humanities, which carried with it a stipend of $100,000 to pay a visiting scholar and staff for a one-year contract. Shortly before this letter was written John Culkin (see page 309, note 1), Director of the Center for Communications at Fordham, visited McLuhan in Toronto to offer him the Chair, and he accepted for the academic year 1967–8. Included with this appointment was the use of a large, elegantly furnished house in Bronxville, New York. (The Fordham campus was then in the Bronx.) It was later arranged for Harley Parker (see page 321, note 3) and Professor Edmund Carpenter (see page 250, note 1) to accompany McLuhan.

[2] There *were* lecturing duties, which McLuhan, Carpenter, and Parker shared.

[3] Eric McLuhan had recently addressed the Joyce Society, New York, at the Gotham Book Mart.

1967

To Hubert Humphrey[1]

February 9th, 1967

Dear Mr. Vice-President:

I did much appreciate your sending me that splendid photograph of us both.

When seated with you I had jokingly explained the advantages of living in a backward country like Canada. Now I am to have an opportunity to expand that theme in a series of lectures here that are given annually on a Foundation basis.

One other theme that had risen at that same dinner concerned the difficulty of covering a hot war like Viet on a cool medium like television. Viet is our first TV war. TV creates an audience involvement in depth that automatically creates alienation of the public. The same news covered by the old hot media like press has a very different effect.

While we are Westernizing the East by our old technology, we are Easternizing ourselves by the new technology. TV is an orientalizing force, taking us all on an "inner trip" that blurs the old idea of private identity altogether.

Again, thanks, and very best wishes.

Sincerely yours,

[1]McLuhan sat next to Hubert Humphrey (1911–78)—Vice-President of the United States from 1965 to 1969— at a dinner in Washington to which he had been invited to meet government officials.

To Tom Easterbrook

February 22, 1967

Dear Tom:

This morning's *Globe* carried a nice background piece on Nyerere.[1] It reminded me that I am to give the [University of Toronto] Marfleet lectures on March 16th and 17th. The first, "Canada the Borderline Case", and the second, "Towards an Inclusive Consciousness." The overall theme is "Canada in the Electronic Age."

What effect does electric technology have on Tanzania as compared to the older mechanical technologies? Wish you would send me anything available on radio in Africa, etc. Apropos the Marfleet, who are the people I should talk to here?

Mel Watkins presented me with a copy of your new *Approaches to Canadian*

[1]Professor and Mrs Easterbrook were in Dar Es Salaam, Tanzania, where he was economic adviser to the Minister of Economic Affairs and Development Planning. Julius Kambarage Nyerere was the first President of Tanzania.

Economic History.[2] Shall go through it for the Marfleet, of course. Should I venture to suggest that the entire issue of American ownership of Canadian resources is a considerable red herring? If the United States is the Canadian environment in the electric information age, does not the property issue become irrelevant? Is not property, as such, the old environment upon which we focus in the rear-view mirror? The real environment of electric information remains like all new environments, invisible? Have recently been working on that formulation that new technologies create new environments which mirror everything but the present, because they *are* the present. Is this not characteristic of the entire human past? Has not every age and every culture failed to see its own present while being fixated by the image of the preceding phase or situation?

Please speed suggestions about Marfleet. The more, the better.

[2]*Approaches to Canadian Economic History* (1968) was co-authored by T.G. Easterbrook and Mel Watkins.

To John Wain

March 23, 1967

Dear John:

My current crop of modern poetry students have been getting great use and yardage from your anthology of modern poetry.[1] They were thrilled to hear that you were working on the "Anthology of Modern Poetry"—somebody back from England recently had mentioned your turning to this job.[2]

My only complaint at present is the excess of adulation and attention that has been blizzarding my life. When you go into the public domain by the media route everybody develops the illusion that they own you. They resent even slight efforts at privacy.

Warm regards to all of you.

[1]John Wain, ed., *Anthology of Modern Poetry* (1963).
[2]To *The Twentieth-Century Mind* (3 vols, 1972), edited by C.B. Cox and A.E. Dyson, Wain contributed two essays, both called "Poetry", one each in Volume 1 and Volume 2.

To Claude Bissell

March 29, 1967

Dear Claude:

Thanks for the Marfleet honorarium.[1] It reminded me of the need to clarify the status of my sabbatical next year.[2] It is just seven years since my previous

[1]McLuhan had just delivered the annual Marfleet Lectures at the University of Toronto. See the letter of February 22, 1967, to Tom Easterbrook.
[2]In 1967–8 McLuhan held the Schweitzer Chair at Fordham University.

sabbatical when I used the grant from the U.S. Office of Education. I have assumed that the payment of half my salary, both from the College and from the University, is a matter of course.

Had a phone call from Harold Town[3] this morning advising me not to *read* lectures. He didn't call merely to make that gloomy observation.

A "Morning Smile" of a few days ago [in the Toronto *Globe and Mail*] you may have seen. Son: "Dad, what's a beat?" Dad: "Son, a beat is a cat that chickened out of the rat race."

Had you noticed that the word "escapism" has almost disappeared from the language? "Involvement" has taken its place. Under electric conditions there can be no escape.

Cordially,

[3]Harold Town (b. 1924), the distinguished Canadian painter and printer-maker.

To George Woodcock[1]

March 30, 1967

Dear Mr. Woodcock:

It would be nice to be able to get around to putting together my memories of Lewis, but it would take time that is impossible to find at the moment.

Father Murphy is still at the University of Windsor to my knowledge, and is very much alive. It was through him that I first heard of Lewis's presence in Windsor. It might be possible for him to make a tape of his recollections of Lewis. This would include Lewis standing on a street corner in Windsor for days asking passers-by where he might find an apartment. It would also include Lewis's classroom habits, the donning and removing of large, heavy sweaters and his manifestations of terror when anyone sneezed: "The room is filling up with viruses!"

Lewis was deeply offended when the [Assumption] College presentation of *Murder in the Cathedral* took place without his being invited to attend.

Best wishes,

[1]The well-known Canadian man of letters, author of many books of non-fiction and poetry, George Woodcock (b. 1912) was at this time editor of the quarterly *Canadian Literature* and was commissioning articles on Wyndham Lewis for a special issue of the magazine (No. 35, Winter 1968) that was published separately in book form as *Wyndham Lewis in America* (1971). He wrote to McLuhan on March 18, 1967.

To William Jovanovich

April 24, 1967

Dear Bill:

"America Revisited" is quite splendid.[1] Corinne read it last night and was

[1]"America Revisited: Radicalism and Alienation" was delivered by William Jovanovich as a lecture at Berkeley in March 1967. It was published in J.G. Kirk, ed., *America Now* (1968).

enthralled. You have got very close to some big issues that remain quite opaque for most people.

I think electric technology is Orientalizing the entire Western world even while we are trying to Westernize the Orient by old technology.

Eric has just come back from giving some talks at a television conference on the west coast. He goes to Harvard in a few days to talk to the architects about changing spaces in our world. Joyce has been of the utmost help in motivating all his studies now. He has just finished a course in speed-reading. If for no other reason I am grateful to have discovered that speed means depth. It is a kind of X-ray of the page that reveals the author's thought form directly. In the same way a newspaper page is not so much a picture as an X-ray of the world at a given time. Mosaic forms like *The Waste Land* or *Finnegans Wake* are X-rays of entire cultures in depth. The future of reading and of literature may well depend upon the cultivation of this approach. One effect of speed-reading is a vast increase in the motivation of the reader. Motivation literally seems to result from getting a move on.

I have to give a talk in New York on May 15th and look forward to being in touch with you at that time.

To William Jovanovich

August 9, 1967

Dear Bill:

Sorry about delay in talking about *The Fourth Dimension* by Wallis. I found it most interesting. Am not sure that I should undertake to write any preface.[1]

To me the disconcerting thing about scientists is their very large and unacknowledged backlog of literate assumptions. As they become more aware of these, it will become much easier for them to talk to the layman, as well as for the layman to talk to them. C.P. Snow's idea of *The Two Cultures* [*and the Scientific Revolution*, 1959] is mostly an illusion.

Have been doing a course in speed reading at the Evelyn Wood Institute. My plan was to get some ideas about *The Future of the Book*. It worked.

Our plan is to leave here by the end of the month. There's lots to do before then.[2]

Cordially,

---

[1]Jovanovich had sent McLuhan the proofs of a forthcoming book—*Time, the Fourth Dimension of the Mind* (1968) by Robert Wallis—to be published by his firm Harcourt, Brace & World, asking him if he would write a Preface, and McLuhan said he would (July 28, 1967). In his August 15 reply to this letter, Jovanovich was understandably taken aback by McLuhan's reluctance, saying that he would be "rather in a bind" if McLuhan didn't write the Preface, and reminding him of his promise to do so. McLuhan duly sent the Preface on August 30 and it was included in the book.

[2]McLuhan was preparing to take up his appointment at Fordham University.

To Wilfred Watson

[Bronxville, N.Y.]
November 10, 1967

Dear Wilfred:

I, too, must be clairvoyant, because I have kept all the time in December from the 9th onward absolutely clear, save for an occasional luncheon here at Fordham. Six weeks ago I made the resolution to avoid all out-of-town trips. I am beginning to reap the benefits thereof.

Corinne and I do very much hope that Sheila will be able to come along with you.[1] We have ample space. In fact, I think that Corinne is very eager to show it off to you. Bronxville is a "beauty" spot and has lovely trees and grass. We have fireplaces and shall enjoy them, too. The kids are now at a stage very much more interesting than when you last saw them. Michael has been commissioned by Tom Wolfe [sic] to write an article on the hippies for *Esquire*.[2] This has mostly been completed already. When I came into the house a few days ago, Michael was interviewing some teen-aged lads, and I heard him ask, "What do you think of the arts?" I kept moving. Terry is in her senior year here at Fordham, loving it. Elizabeth is a freshette, wildly enthusiastic. Mike is at Roosevelt High School, concerning which he has much to say.

Many, many breakthroughs on the C/A front. Am sure we can complete that book in ten days. Have bundles of memos, each of which could become a chapter. We are going to find ourselves embarking on half a dozen more books while writing this one.

Have no doubts about our accommodating both of you.

[1]Wilfred and Sheila Watson were not able to visit the McLuhans in Bronxville, N.Y., but Wilfred Watson stayed with them there the following May. This letter was written a little over two weeks before McLuhan's brain-tumour operation: see the next letter.

[2]The *Esquire* editor Tom Hedley commissioned sixteen-year-old Michael McLuhan to write an article on youth. Michael did this and was paid for it, but it was not published.

To Wilfred and Sheila Watson

[Bronxville, N.Y.]
December 15, 1967

Dear Wilfred and Sheila:

It is glorious to be home. The operation took place three weeks tomorrow.[1] I

[1]In a letter of the day before to Harry J. Skornia, McLuhan explained this more fully: "Our Toronto doctor referred us to the great neurological institute (at Columbia Presbyterian Hosp.). Three weeks ago I had a massive but benign brain tumor completely removed. It was not connected to the brain at all—a work of pure symbolic juxtaposition. However, I was on the operating table 22 hrs. Just as phenomenal has been my recovery. Came home two days ago. Friends have been wonderful."

came home on the 12th, refusing to come on the 13th. To start a new life on the 13th seemed a bit much. I rejoice that Cardinal Léger also started out on his new life in the leper colonies of Japan on December 12th.[2] I may meet him over there. The Japs have gone wild for McLuhan. There is a book called *McLuhan's World* in Japanese that came out in August. It sold a quarter million in two months and now they're translating everything I've written.

I am sending you a copy of a letter I've written to Philip Deane,[3] since it may have some relevance to *Cliché to Archetype*, which I now refer to as *CA*.[4] Have made huge yardage on that book. It began with reflection on the nature of ricourso as a purgative. Remember the washers at ford in *Finnegans Wake*? Endless repetition by the flowing river. The first Adam was cliché, environmental. His job was classifying plants and animals. The second Adam was archetype. Redoing old things. Remember the phrase in the mass?

Mirabiliter condidisti

Mirabilous reformasti[5]

It is the difference between matching and making, between spectatorship and total dramatic participation. Through the drama of the mouth, we participate daily in the total re-creation of the world as a process.

As I recall Eliade, he had little to say about the Return as a process of purification.[6] Remember [W.B.] Yeats: "the unpurged images of day recede."?[7] In dreams we purge the images by repeating them and transforming them. The technique of the sub-plot or the anti-environment yields the same result in art.

I have a huge bundle of materials accumulated for *CA*. I see the form of the book as exemplary with many illustrations from art and literature and many from all the arts and sciences. This way we can help people in many fields to develop interests in many other fields. I know that when we get together (and I can see many advantages if Sheila will join us) that we can assemble the mosaic of the book very rapidly. Since you are getting the word about Eric's McGraw Hill contract in Philip's letter I will merely say that Eric is quite prepared to rewrite the book at once.

Christmas joy and blessings to yez both.

[2]Paul-Emile Léger, who had been consecrated Archbishop of Montreal in 1950 and was created a Cardinal in 1953, gave up that position in 1967 to become a missionary priest with lepers in Africa.
[3]This letter follows.
[4]McLuhan was co-authoring with Wilfred Watson *From Cliché to Archetype*, which would be published in 1970. See page 416, note 1.
[5]"Miraculously founded,/ Still more miraculously re-formed."
[6]In Mircea Eliade's *The Myth of the Eternal Return* (1954). Professor Eliade (b. 1907), Romanian-born historian and author, taught the history of religion at the University of Chicago.
[7]The first line of Yeats's "Byzantium".

To Philip and Molly Deane[1]

[Bronxville, N.Y.]
December 15, 1967

Dear Philip and Molly:

Got home the 12th. A day at home is worth a week in the hospital. One fruit of the hospital experience is an article to be called, "The Future of Convalescence." Perhaps my biggest thrill in the hospital came on the night of December 9th when Eric brought me his McGraw Hill contract to witness. They have accepted his Joyce book. He is teaching a Joyce course at Fordham and having a great year. Same with Terry and Liz.

Have a new book just about ready called *War and Peace in the Global Village*.[2] The sub-plot is the effect of the computer. The main plot is simply that every new technology creates a new environment that alters the perceptual life of the entire population. Since violence is the inevitable means of quest for identity when the old image, private or corporate, is smudged by the new technology, war is automatic as a means of recovering identity. Remember the yellow peril in the twenties? That was one effect of the age of radio. When the radio generation reached the job plateau and decision making, they were quite incapable of pursuing the old goals and objectives. They had left the age of mechanism with its specialists and fragmentary patterns and found themselves quite incapable of playing anything less than the total field. That is formula for SLUMP. The attempt to recover the old image and to return to the old specialist ways gave us our second war. (The first world war had been the effect of the industrial peak reached by the railways. The German encirclement, etc.) We are now in the middle of our third world war, our first TV war. Like *Bonanza* and the Westerns generally, it helps us to recover our image of the frontier when the red man was the peril. It enables us to resume the Indian wars by bringing civilization to the tribal world. Economically, we are now in the midst of the greatest depression ever, since we have lost all goals and all objectives of the 19th-century variety. When the present TV generation, aged 15 and downward, reaches the job plateau, the Prayer Mat will succeed the Cadillac. Their need is total involvement.

[1]Greek-born Philippe Deane Gigantes (b. 1923)—then known as the journalist and author Philip Deane—received his early education in England. He met McLuhan in 1956 in Washington, where he was a correspondent for *The Observer* and later for the Toronto *Globe and Mail*. He lived in Toronto from 1965, when he was employed by the CBC, until 1970, having earned his B.A., M.A., and Ph.D. in Classics from the University of Toronto in three years from 1967 to 1970. He became Director General of the Language Bureau, Ottawa, in 1972 and was later made special assistant to the Prime Minister. He was appointed a Senator in 1984. This letter was sent to several friends.

[2]*War and Peace in the Global Village* (1968) by Marshall McLuhan and Quentin Fiore, co-ordinated by Jerome Agel, is a collection of "probes", photographs, and extensive marginalia—many of them quotations from *Finnegans Wake*—that explore "the pain" caused by new media and new technologies and the pain inflicted, in illuminating them, by artists who at the same time bring about an adjustment to them: peace in the global village will come about through this adjustment, which is also implicit in the action of technology.

Our Mike, aged 15, burns incense in front of his Buddha and reads Herman Hesse. He has nothing in common with his older brother and sisters. He just barely made the TV generation. The younger ones will be much more extreme. I had opportunities to check this out in the hospital with doctors and patients who had ten-year-old children. TV is the end of the western world. We have gone Oriental while the Orient tries to go West.

Another major theme of my book is that war is the great educational agency. To contend is to acquire the knowledge of one's enemies with the utmost speed. On the other hand, education is war conducted against the sense life, and we now do this by new media.

It is glorious to be home. All I need is a bit more hemoglobin. I was twenty hours on the operating table, and that was three weeks tomorrow.

Bless you for all your care of Stephanie.[3]

[3]Stephanie McLuhan lived for a while with the Deanes while her parents were living in Bronxville, New York, during McLuhan's appointment to Fordham University.

To Hubert Humphrey

[Bronxville, N.Y.]
December 28, 1967

Dear Mr. Vice President:

It was a little less than a year ago that you introduced me to a Washington dinner. You were hosting for President Johnson who was away. After my talk you remarked that my jokes had restored your faith in the academic community. I will place a couple of recent ones at the end of this letter in case they can be of use to you.

I want to be as brief as possible. My theme is War and Peace in our Global Village. Speaking as a person who has spent a good many years studying the political effects of new media, it is plain that this is our first TV war, just as World War II was a radio war and World War I a railway war. We are now in the midst of World War III, and it no more resembles World War II than World War II did World War I. The big change now is that there is no more division between soldiers and civilians. In the TV age the entire public is participant in the war.

The Kaiser in 1914 protested that Germany had been encircled. He saw the Slav countries and Russia as terrible threats to German security. They were backward countries just beginning to industrialize. Today in our global village created by instant communications, all backward countries are "threats" to all developed countries. Like the Negro and the teen-ager in our own country, they get "turned on" by the new electric age. They never had an industrial age or a 19th century. They start with the latest, electric information. The electric environment is totally involving. It is not an environment of consumers. That is why

World War III is also a depression, whereas World War II had been a struggle to get out of a depression. All backward countries are "communist." They have never known social or political individualism. The Orient is entirely tribal and family oriented. Russian communism was similarly oriented for the benefit of a tribal people. They are still tribal.

To regard the global encirclement of the USA by backward tribal communities presenting a "communist" threat to the USA is a very confusing affair. It represents a state of mind at least as confused as the Kaiser in 1914. It also ignores the fact that electric technology is totally tribalizing the USA.

> The Hippie hath said in his heart
> The prayer-mat shall replace the Cadillac.

Indeed it will, if we allow our information environment to banish all our hardware.

And now for a couple of the gags I promised you:

> When all is said and done, more will have been said than done.

> When the dust settles, then you'll know whether you've been riding on a horse or an ass.

> Teacher to class: "What does this century owe to Thomas Edison?" Student: "If is weren't for Edison, we would have to watch TV by candlelight."[1]

Most cordial regards,
Marshall McLuhan

[1]Vice-President Humphrey replied on January 19, 1968:

"Dear Marshall

"Thank you for your keen and perceptive analysis of our current world dilemma. As usual, through a few well chosen words, you have presented concisely what is ailing our global village.

"I see that your humor and wit still maintain my faith in the academic community.

"Sincerely
"Hubert H. Humphrey"

The following was the first of many letters addressed to The Honourable Pierre Elliott Trudeau (b. 1919). At this time he was Minister of Justice, a post to which he had been appointed the year before. On April 6, 1968, however, he was elected leader of the Liberal Party of Canada to replace the retiring Prime Minister Lester Pearson. Trudeau was sworn in as Prime Minister of Canada four days after this letter was written, on April 20. It was the beginning of a friendly correspondence that continued (on Trudeau's part) until 1980. Trudeau soon made it clear that he welcomed McLuhan's letters and his insights. He almost always replied to McLuhan's letters personally—in the Public Archives of Canada there are 42 letters from McLuhan to Trudeau and 44 short letters from Trudeau to McLuhan—and they spent time together on several occasions.

1968

To Pierre Elliott Trudeau

[Bronxville, N.Y.]
April 16, 1968

Dear Pierre Trudeau:

It was a piece in the Toronto *Telegram* by Douglas Fisher and Harry Crowe that emboldened me to drop you a note. The piece was entitled "Good Will for Trudeau, for a time".

The men of the press can work only with people who have fixed points of view and definite goals, policies and objectives. Such fixed positions and attitudes are, of course, irrelevant to the electronic age. Our world substitutes mosaics for points of view and probes for targets. Knowing of your acquaintance with De Tocqueville, I can understand why you have such an easy understanding of the North American predicament in the new electronic age. The U.S.A., in particular, began with the latest technology, namely, printing from movable types. The dynamics of that process inspired and permeated the entire industrial and social establishment that grew so rapidly and consistently between 1776 and the present. Any "backward" country tends to enjoy the advantage of starting with the latest technology, so that in the electric age, all the countries that missed the 19th century and its mechanical orientation can now speedily adapt to electric technology without endangering any literate and mechanistic backlog of achievement, e.g. Russia, Japan, etc.

French Canada never had a 19th century. May this not be increasingly a basis for its great advantage over English Canada? Never having had the intense specialism of a mechanized consumer economy, French Canada retains its bonds with oral cultures and their total field approach. The all-at-onceness of electric data is not only organic and inclusive but reshapes the entire imaginative lives of highly literate communities. The TV generation, for example, is almost oriental in its involvement in the inner rather than the outer life. This means, naturally, a total loss of goal orientation in the old sense. The outer space programs thus in many ways represent 18th-century rather than 20th-century orientations.

I have always felt that one of Canada's greatest assets was its being a kind of "backwater". Never having been totally involved in current trends it has been able to enjoy a flexibility that is now rare. The rigidity of commitments of all powers that were great in the 19th century confronts them with anarchy as they attempt to readjust to the total field awareness demanded by the speed of electric information. The de-Romanization of the Catholic Church is only one instance of the decentralizing effects of electric information on older bureaucracies. By the same token the liturgical revival is that kind of involvement and participation that goes with the simultaneity and coexistence of electronic experience.

At present I am studying the American political developments, noting the utter conflict between Policies and Images as it concerns the candidates. May not the same thing happen here as in Canada recently? The old political professionals simply exhaust and liquidate themselves by going through the old motions, making room for quite unexpected candidates at the last moment.

Like most Canadians, I am delighted that it happened that way for us and that you are to enter into this complex new role.

With most cordial wishes and prayers,
Marshall McLuhan

To Pierre Elliott Trudeau

[Bronxville, N.Y.]
June 3, 1968

Dear Pierre Trudeau:

After seeing the Kennedy-McCarthy "debate",[1] I wish that you were not going to be on TV at all.[2] It is not a debating medium.

Trying to formulate the chances of the American candidates for publication, I can find only one word: "somnambulism."

It was Professor Broughton of McGill who recently explained that somnambulism is a highly motivated state.

The real drama of our age, the shift from hardware service environments of the 19th century to the software (electric information) service environments of the 20th century, is as big a leap as that from primitive tribalism to literate individualism. For our Western world, this is a shift from outer orientation to an inner, oriental trip. It renders all of our institutions obsolete, as the young TV generation fully recognizes. (The TV generation is now 12 to 14 years of age and hasn't reached the college plateau yet.)

In these circumstances "political" action takes on the appearance of a paraplegic soccer match. It is not evident that any responsible figure in the Eastern or Western worlds has a clue to the erosion of human identity that follows upon the "software" environment. There is a corresponding release of violence to recover identity after technological innovation. The TV kids cannot accept the identity of their parents' generation so they will simply destroy any institutional or legal attempt to impose it upon them. The liquidation of the feudal system with the

---

[1]The TV debate between Senators Robert Kennedy and Eugene McCarthy, who were seeking the US Democratic presidential nomination, took place on June 1, 1968, before the California primary on June 4, which Kennedy won. Kennedy was mortally wounded by a gunman three days after this letter was written, on June 6.

[2]Trudeau was engaged in the campaign for the national election, held on June 25, that would give his Liberal Party a substantial majority.

advent of printing and gunpowder represented a very slow change from corporate to private identity, compared to the reverse of that process that we are now undergoing.

Radio created Hitler as a delinquent Peter Pan, charged with cosmic emanation.

Would not a high degree of awareness of these media effects (e.g. radio in Nigeria or in any tribal territory) enable us to set up social therapies and immunizing programs exactly comparable to medical action in the face of an endemic disease?

Pardon me for feeling very uncomfortable in the presence of what is called "political" discussion in circumstances such as these.

Cordial good wishes for June 9.
Marshall McLuhan

To Sheila Watson

[Bronxville, N.Y.]
June 12, 1968

Dear Sheila:

Thanks for *Canadian Literature*. They didn't send me a copy, nor did they ask me to contribute.[1] I think it is a useful issue.

The new space for the Centre is grand.[2] Shall defer decoration until you are on hand to choose suitable color schemes.

Shall simply send Mrs. Lewis a check for $50, hoping she will accept same.[3]

Obtain cover of *TV Guide* for June 8–14. It is a Dali explanation of the tactile nature of the TV image.[4] Wonderful interview inside, too.

If you can't round up a copy, tell me.

Yours,

[1]See page 237, note 1.

[2]The "new space" for the Centre for Culture and Technology was a coach house—owned by St Michael's College but leased to the University of Toronto—at 39A Queen's Park Crescent, containing a large seminar room, a reception area, and three offices.

[3]McLuhan, who was always concerned for Mrs Lewis's welfare (he had been given to understand that he would be her literary executor), sent her fifty dollars as a fee for the inclusion in the Wyndham Lewis issue of *Canadian Literature* (no. 35, Winter 1968) of a reproduction of the pastel and pencil drawing by Wyndham Lewis, *Mother and Infant with Male*, 1943, which McLuhan owned.

[4]The cover, painted by Salvador Dali, depicted two thumbnails as TV screens. "This is pure poetry, acute new perception. Dali immediately presents the fact that TV is a tactile mode of perception"—McLuhan in the Foreword to *The Interior Landscape: The Literary Criticism of Marshall McLuhan* (1969).

To Pierre Elliott Trudeau

[Bronxville, N.Y.]
June 12, 1968

Dear Pierre Trudeau:

I was shown the video tape of the great debate in Toronto on Monday and taped a comment to be used later by CFTO.

The witness box cum lectern cum pulpit spaces for the candidates was totally non-TV. I had not seen you or Stanfield before.[1] Stanfield's image is that of the Yankee horsetrader, as shrewd as sabbatical or hebdomadal. I gather he is a distant relative of mine. My mother's people came from the same territory. Nova Scotia is one of the most Yankee parts of North America. Boston is the cultural capital still. The other side of Stanfield is "Honest Abe"—the vote splitter.

Your own image is a corporate mask, inclusive, requiring no private nuance whatever. This is your "cool" TV power. Iconic, sculptural. A mask "puts on" an audience. At a masquerade we are not private persons.

Your book on *Federalism* is at the Edmund Burke level.[2] My favorite quote from him is:

> The first right of every man in civilized society is the right to be protected against the consequences of his own stupidity.[3]

The cover of the June 8–14 *TV Guide* is a Dali masterpiece.[4] It manifests in detail the tactile quality of the TV image. The extension of the central nervous system via electricity is environmentally indicated in the upper right corner by a segment of brain tissue. The two thumbs with the TV images on the nails are carefully separated to indicate the "gap" or interval constituted by touch. The age of tactility via television and radio is one of innumerable interfaces or "gaps" that replace the old connections, legal, literate and visual.

Very best wishes,
Marshall McLuhan

[1]Robert L. Stanfield (b. 1914), formerly Premier of Nova Scotia, was elected leader of the Progressive Conservative Party of Canada on September 9, 1967 and was therefore leader of the Opposition and Trudeau's opponent in the election campaign that was taking place.

[2]Pierre Elliott Trudeau, *Federalism and the French Canadians* (1968). McLuhan reviewed this in *The New York Times Book Review*, October 28, 1968.

[3]Unidentified.

[4]See previous letter, note 4.

To I.A. Richards[1]

[Bronxville, N.Y.]
July 12, 1968

Dear Dr. Richards:

I want to mention at once my gratification at your kindly reference to me on page 63 of *So Much Nearer*.[2] Naturally, I owe you an enormous debt since Cambridge days. I also owe a great deal to S[amuel] T[aylor] C[oleridge].

You may know that Dwight Culler in *The Imperial Intellect*[3] discusses how Newman's *Idea of a University* derives from Coleridge's idea of an encyclopedia.

Bartlett's *Remembering*, long out of print, makes such a natural introduction to your own work that I wish you could encourage somebody to reissue it with an introduction by yourself.[4]

Using Coleridge's principle that the most effective approach to anyone's knowledge is via his ignorance, would you agree that Plato was quite unaware of the imperceptible environment of "visual space" created for the first time in human history by the phonetic alphabet? This concerns your Plato citation on page three. Do you think it indicates that Plato regarded phonetic letters as giving the eye dominance over the other senses for the first time, thus creating a new environment?

As the evolutionary process has shifted from biology to technology in the electric age, I am fascinated by your suggestion (on page three) of the possibility of a non-verbal language of macroscopic gesticulation, an interface of entire cultures.

Is it your impression that Red China expects to attain the effects of Western literacy by the universalizing of Chinese literacy in their educational program? Naturally, the iconic and tactile quality of the Chinese written character keeps the Chinese entirely unacquainted with visual and continuous or connected space.

Your wonderful word, "feedforward", suggests to me the principle of the probe, the technique of the "suspended judgement", which has been called the greatest discovery of the 20th century.

Sincerely yours,
Marshall McLuhan

[1]McLuhan studied under Richards at Cambridge. See page 50, note 2.

[2]I.A. Richards, *So Much Nearer: Essays Toward a World English* (1968). A note reads: "This immensely important topic [the principle of complementarity]—publicized recently by Marshall McLuhan—is discussed at length in my 'Toward a More Synoptic View' in *Speculative Instruments*."

[3]Dwight Culler, *The Imperial Intellect: A Study of Newman's Educational Ideal* (1955).

[4]Sir Frederick Charles Bartlett, *Remembering: A Study in Experimental and Social Psychology* (1961, 1964).

To Pierre Elliott Trudeau

October 17, 1968

Dear Mr. Prime Minister:

Bill Lee happens to be here at present and is enroute to Ottawa and I take this opportunity to have him bring this letter to you directly in order to expedite matters.

Naturally, I hope you were pleased with last night's affair. This letter concerns it immediately. After you and your colleagues had left, Dick Stanbury, Bob McCormack and myself were chatting.[1] It occurred to us that a strategy that might emcompass the entire program of "participational democracy" might be mounted as follows: the student-power groups in high schools and colleges are available as a Canadian mosaic. If you could chat with the leaders of such groups on TV (four or five at a time) it would itself be participation in the highest levels of government, since these people represent one of the principal problems of government today.

The answer to their problems, as we discussed it last night, does not consist in plugging them into some existing bureaucracy, whether of high school or of college. They are not looking for "feed-back" but "feed-forward." It would be inevitable that as soon as they began to discuss their problems there would begin a resonance with many problems of your own. It would be perfectly natural for you to illustrate and to discuss their problems while briefing them on yours. They in turn could comment on yours, setting up a natural interface between areas of community life on one hand, and government on the other. Such an encounter via TV has never occurred before.

During such discussions (and let me suggest that there be no studio audience whatever) your own natural, easy, flexible way would relax them and alert them to many features of the world in which they live, in a totally new way.

Just as the gap between culture and business has closed by virtue of an electric information environment, so the gap between politics and youth has closed. Teenagers are no longer young persons mentally or emotionally. Indeed, part of their dilemma consists in being *categorized* as teenagers or as youngsters. The immediate consequence of such a political education strategy would be to remove an enormous burden from the backs of educational administrators and parents alike. They, too, could enjoy the immediate sensation of participating in problems at the highest level. The merely parochial aspects of their dilemmas would vanish.

The time is long overdue for you to be back in circulation and to be in the Canadian living room as a "gap-bridger", the unifying image of our society that

[1]Senator Richard J. Stanbury (b. 1923), who was then President of the Liberal Party of Canada, had organized a discussion of "participatory democracy" between Prime Minister Trudeau and McLuhan. Bob McCormack (1923–72), Program Organizer for Talks and Public Affairs for CBC Radio, was present as an observer. This was a private evening of discussions that contributed to the Liberal Party's well-known efforts, over the next few years, to develop techniques of participatory democracy, and perhaps encouraged Trudeau's occasional sympathetic engagements with students.

you became during the election. It is impossible to exaggerate the advantages in political education that would result. "Government of the air" would by-pass all bureaucracy yet make it possible to consider the problems of bureaucracies of all kinds. Data from government departments could be brought to bear in follow-up sessions. Perhaps it might be more effective to canvass various features of this kind of program by telephone.

I am prepared to contact the leaders of the student activists on this campus to invite you at once to appear with them on such a program. No preliminary briefing or scripting of any kind would be necessary or desirable. All protocol could be tossed aside. I feel confident that the obvious obstacles to this innovation can be by-passed. This kind of political mountain-climbing could be done in spite of all the obvious road-blocks. The program would not only be a political one but an educational one so far as the C.B.C. is concerned.

Medium-mystically yours,
Marshall McLuhan

To Pierre Elliott Trudeau

November 13, 1968

Dear Mr. Prime Minister:

Just a note about media strategy. In your discussion with students from the floor, shown on "The Way It Is" last Sunday, November 10th [on CBC-TV] you could not have been in a more dangerous position media-wise.

An auditorium violates the very nature of TV, hence the disaster of the political conventions in the U.S.A. Television demands close, casual, intimate discussions. Also no notes, no script, and no debating. The discernment and conception of process prompts total avoidance of debating. The process by which the business community is switched from private goals to conglomerate inter-marriage is identical with the process of decentralism and participation which all students demand of their institutions today. The same process has deprived students of their identity. The loss of identity and goals in the political and business spheres causes the same indiscriminate resort to violent struggle.

Paradoxically, the business community demands a "double standard." While making rapid adjustments to changing technologies, it expects the educational and political establishments to remain rigidly fixed in the old patterns. This is the result of visual classification which avoids the awareness of function and process.

In my *War and Peace* book I explain how technological change deprives individuals and societies of their identity images, with resulting struggle for new images.[1] In *Through the Vanishing Point* (which I am taking the liberty of send-

---

[1] *War and Peace in the Global Village* (1968) by Marshall McLuhan and Quentin Fiore, co-ordinated by Jerome Agel. See page 348, note 2.

ing you), Harley Parker and I explain how many new kinds of space, psychic and social, result from technological change.[2]

Most cordial good wishes,

[2]Marshall McLuhan and Harley Parker, *Through the Vanishing Point: Space in Poetry and Painting* (1968), Volume 37 in the World Perspectives series of Harper & Row. Most of this book is devoted to double-page presentations of a painting or a poem, with aphoristic statements or quotations opposite that offer comments on, or counterpoints to, the work reproduced. It concludes with an essay, "The Emperor's New Clothes", that discusses many of the ideas—including environment and anti-environment—that are put forward in the preceding letters.

To Jacqueline Tyrwhitt   November 18, 1968

Dear Jacky:

Apropos space observations of *Through the Vanishing Point* I should wish to add now *The Chemical Bond* by Linus Pauling. Since Heisenberg the structural bond of all material forms has been regarded as "resonance."[1] This is the world of the interface and the interval, which Parker and I designate as tactile space. This would seem to be the space inaccessible to the planners since Ebenezer Howard.[2] Perhaps you know of some planners who do not use visual space whether vertical or horizontal? All scientists are trapped in visual space as much as museum curators. The reason is simply that they don't know there is such a thing as visual space as contrasted with the multiple other spaces familiar to non-literate man.

Jane Jacobs is in Toronto to live with her family.[3] Her famous book on the city shows the same inability to disengage from visual space. She is quite aware that all "live" spaces are created by diversity of interface—diversity of occupations, age groups and schedules.

[1]Linus Pauling (b. 1901), who was awarded the 1954 Nobel Prize in chemistry, wrote the classic study *The Nature of the Chemical Bond and the Structure of Molecules and Crystals: An Introduction to Modern Structural Chemistry* (1959). In his later *The Chemical Bond: A Brief Introduction to Modern Structural Chemistry* (1967), in a section entitled "Resonance and the Chemical Bond: The Concept of Resonance", Pauling explains that "The concept of resonance was introduced into quantum mechanics by Heisenberg in connection with the discussion of the quantum states of the helium action." The German physicist Werner Heisenberg (1901–76), a founder of the quantum theory, was awarded the Nobel Prize in physics in 1932; he wrote *The Physicist's Conception of Nature* (1958), a long quotation from which is discussed in *The Gutenberg Galaxy*.

[2]Sir Ebenezer Howard (1850–1928) was an English town planner and the principal founder of the English garden-city movement.

[3]The urban theorist Jane Jacobs (b. 1916), who moved with her family to Toronto from New York City, is the author of several books, including the well-known *The Life and Death of Great American Cities* (1961).

359

To Pierre Elliot Trudeau   December 2, 1968

Dear Mr. Prime Minister:

Miss McDermott of your new Information Task Force has contacted me. She will be coming to participate in our media seminar at the Centre tonight (we meet every Monday evening from 8 to 10).

I wish I had much more time to be of help. I still have a full academic program and I am still convalescing from the brain surgery of one year ago. It is this latter fact that restricts my travels.

My forte is structural analysis of new problems and environments that, unawares to us, re-program our sensory lives. In effect I am saying that it is now possible to by-pass what used to be called "fate" by anticipating the effects of new man-made environments.

Naturally this concerns every level of our personal and political lives. I am therefore very eager to be of help to you. Perhaps we can invent a way of making this possible within the severe limits imposed upon your time. Do you think the telephone a practical possibility? Would a personal representative of yourself, visiting me here, be another possibility?

Your Grey Cup kick-off was, of course, a media triumph.[1] This is audience participation and image-making at its best. Fire-side dialogues with small groups of students would be even more potent.

One theme that may have some immediate relevance: Canada is the only country in the world that has never had a national identity. In an age when all homogeneous nations are losing their identity images through rapid technological change, Canada alone can "keep its cool." We have never been committed to a single course or goal. This is now our greatest asset. The parallel is to be found in the recent need of the business world to switch from private enterprise to tribal conglomerates on the pattern of medieval dynastic marriages, another massive example of decentralism foisted upon us by electric speeds.

With cordial good wishes and prayers for your welfare,

[1]The Grey Cup is the trophy (donated by Lord Grey in 1909) presented after the annual Grey Cup Game in the late fall to the best professional football team in eastern or western Canada. (In 1968 it was won by the Ottawa Rough Riders.)

To Jacqueline Tyrwhitt   [December 1?, 1968]

Dear Jackie:

The enclosures may help you to follow my work more easily. For thirty years, at least, I have been using the two hemisphere approach under the names of the *written* and the *oral*, the *visual* and the *acoustic*, the *hot* and the *cool*, the *medium* and the *message, figure* and *ground*, and so on. Now it turns out that medicine has been building a great beach-head for this approach with its new understanding of the two hemispheres of the brain. If you look at the traits of the left hemisphere, you will discover the lineaments of the First world—the literate and industrial world—and, on the other hand, in the right hemisphere you will perceive the characteristics of the Third World—the world without the phonetic alphabet.[1]

During the past century, while the knowledge of the two hemispheres has been growing, there has also been a new electronic milieu or environment which automatically pushes the right hemisphere into a more dominant position than it has held in the Western world since the invention of the phonetic alphabet. The two hemispheres naturally respond to the milieu or total surround in which people live and work. My work has been a dialogue between the two hemispheres in which the characteristics of the right hemisphere are given so much recognition that I have been unintelligible to the left-hemisphere people. It happens that the left-hemisphere people are completely out of touch with the results and the formal characteristics of their own new electric technologies.

Tomorrow Corinne and I leave for Paris for a week at a UNESCO Conference on "The Place of the Artist in Society." Corinne's hearing is still a great worry. Will catch you up on some of the goings on of the rest of the family, when I get back.

[1]This subject held much interest for McLuhan from this point on. The characteristics of the hemispheres of the brain have been formally divided into the following hierarchies. *Left hemisphere*: Verbal; Sequential, temporal, digital; Logical, analytical; Rational; Western thought. *Right hemisphere*: Nonverbal, visuo-spatial; Simultaneous, spatial, analogical; Gestalt, synthetic; Intuitive; Eastern thought.

To J.G. Keogh[1]

December 12, 1968

Dear Joe:

A fourth-year student recently reported that Sweeney, in Celtic folklore, was punished for insulting the gods by being stuck in a tree and being compelled to learn the language of the birds. Starting with [T.S. Eliot's] 'Sweeney among the nightingales' it makes a lot of additional sense.

Would love to use your 'City as Mock Pastoral' in the *Varsity Graduate*. Shall check with Sheila and Wilfred Watson on the feasibility of this.[2]

Would very much appreciate your reactions to my *Through the Vanishing Point: Space in Poetry and Painting* (Harper & Row, 1968). Of course I owe much of

[1]J.G. Keogh (b. 1937) met McLuhan in his second year at St Michael's College, University of Toronto (1955-6), where he was studying English and philosophy. In the course of four stints as McLuhan's research assistant, an enduring friendship developed. Keogh became a teacher of English and Communications in the U.S. and Canada. He is now teaching English at Niagara University, Niagara Falls, N.Y.

[2]Sheila and Wilfred Watson were Research Associates at the Centre for Culture and Technology (on leave from the University of Alberta) in 1968-9.

this work to Harley Parker. You are one of the few people who could benefit from it at present. It has sold well, but as yet has not been reviewed at all. It is a large breakthrough in English studies, among other things.

Please note Linus Pauling's resonance as chemical bond. Scientists themselves do not recognize acoustic space or its properties. They are visual *naifs*. Hence they are hung up today in all the new non-visual properties they confront.

Keep your eye open for the monthly McLuhan *Dew-Line Newsletter*.[3] Insist that your library subscribe. The publisher is The Human Development Corporation, 119 Fifth Avenue, New York, N.Y. 10003. Naturally I am putting all of my latest material in here. "The book arrives too late."

Blessings to you and Ann Marie.

Cordially,
Marshall McLuhan

[3]Twenty *Dew-Line Newsletters* were published from July 1968 to September–October 1970 by McLuhan and the Human Development Corporation, New York City.

To George Steiner[1]

December 19, 1968

Dear George:

Through the Vanishing Point (*Space in Poetry and Painting*—Harper & Row) is another stage in the "new criticism." Whereas the new criticism had discovered multi-semantic levels, Parker and I deal with the multi-levels of sensory space in poetry and painting. In fact, it is concerned with the training of the whole sensorium, i.e. with the different kinds of space created by each of our senses. Psychologists have never recognized anything but the inputs, i.e. they are "flat earthers."

Parker and I use poetry and painting as areas in which to illustrate the different modes of space, e.g. tactility, the space of the interval; sight, the space of the connection; hearing, the space of the total sphere, etc. etc. We stress the changes in spatial preference and sensory dominance from cave art to color TV.

The book is selling well, but nobody has reviewed it. Do you think you could tackle it?[2] Or do you know some ideal person who would?

Cordial regards,
Marshall McLuhan

[1]Dr George Steiner (b. 1929)—scholar, author of *Language and Silence* (1963), among other books, and occasional book reviewer for *The New Yorker*—was at this time Professor of English at New York University. The next year he was appointed Extraordinary Fellow of Churchill College, Cambridge University. He discussed *The Gutenberg Galaxy* in *The Listener* (October 28, 1965). See page 329, note 2.

[2]Steiner did not review *Through the Vanishing Point*.

1969

To James Taylor[1]

January 15, 1969.

Dear Mr. Taylor:

I find myself unable to fill in the questionnaire simply because it calls for much more meditation than I can provide at present. I can say that I do not think of God as a concept, but as an immediate and ever-present fact—an occasion for continuous dialogue.

Yours in Xto,

[1] James Taylor, Assistant Editor of the *United Church Observer*, Toronto, had sent McLuhan, and nineteen others "most influential in shaping the opinions of people in their area", a questionnaire about their beliefs and philosophy.

To Pierre Elliott Trudeau

January 24, 1969.

Dear Mr. Prime Minister:

Your very cool dealings with our very hot medium, the press, naturally produces intense interface or friction. The press has to have hot quotes and sharp points of view. Real news is bad news. Since the press lives on advertising, and all advertising is good news, it takes a lot of bad news to sell all this good news. Even the good news of the gospel can only be sold by hellfire. Vatican II made a very big mistake in this matter, as in other matters.

The very cool corporate mask that is your major political asset goes naturally with processing of problems in dialogue rather than in the production of packaged answers. That is why I urge you to go on the air with small groups and to trade problems with them rather than seeking answers or stating mere points of view.

In his new book *The Age of Discontinuity* (Harper & Row, 1969), my friend Peter Drucker presents a magnificent inventory of problems in current decision-making. He hasn't a clue as to why these problems have arisen but he cries out for a new theory of organization. He indicates that every organization in the world, whether in the home or the school, the business or the political or the religious, has broken down today regardless of ideology or geography. On page 223 he focuses these problems onto the concept of the new "ministate". Every centralist organization large or small is now broken up into mini-states; even the Catholic individual, as he relates to the Mystical Body, regards himself as a mini-state.

This is the exact antithesis of 16th-century individualism based on a private interpretation of scripture. Superficially, doctrinal anarchy today and 16th-century schismaticism look alike. Strict regard to structural character enables one to avoid confusion.

The change in all organization today is the result of putting fast electric information services around slow ones. Jet City transforms the globe into a single metropolis, but it also destroys all existing metropolitan areas based on slow transport. In the same way, the telephone destroys the bureaucracy based on the memo or the letter.

Paradoxically, the slow system is "open" and the fast one is "closed". Electric telecommunications create multitudes of tribally structured mini-states. These now begin to appear inside all the older maxi-states, whether of business or politics. The unions and universities are mini-states; so are the police, the armed services, all media and all branches of business and government bureaucracies. The hierarchy of the organization chart is finished. Job specialism leads to role-playing in the global theatre.

You are the only political image of our time able to use the T.V. medium without being forced to become a tribal buffoon or cartoon like De Gaulle. All the other political figures of the Western world are merely faded photographs on the T.V. medium.

F.D.R[oosevelt] had the press against him and this was his major asset as long as he relied on radio. But radio is a hot medium and fostered the lecture.

T.V. permits audience participation in problem sharing. T.V. is a mini-state that has created various other ones such as the teeney-boppers and the hippies, to say nothing of innumerable separatist tribes around the globe.[1]

Most cordial good wishes,

[1] In his reply of February 13, thanking McLuhan for this letter, the Prime Minister said that he had not had time to read it until that day because of preparations for the recently ended Constitutional Conference. He invited McLuhan to convey his views on the impact of television on such conferences, of which there would be more, because he would like to see "how we could use such occasions to help Canadians to better appreciate their country and the problems of its government."

To William Wimsatt[1]

March 7, 1969

Dear Bill:

I have a copy of *Thesaurus Linguae Romanae et Brittannicae*, Thomas Cooperi, Magalenensis hexastichon Richardi Stephani, Impressum Londoni, 1584. This

[1] William Wimsatt (1907–75), Professor of English at Yale University, was a noted scholar of eighteenth-century literature whose books included *The Prose Style of Samuel Johnson* (1954); (with Cleanth Brooks) *Literary Criticism: A Short History* (1957); and *The Portraits of Alexander Pope* (1965).

is a Latin-English lexicon of large dimensions, loaded with Latin phrases and corresponding English idioms. Shakespeare was twenty years old when it appeared. Just for fun, check any of Shakespeare's Latinisms against Cooper. It is quite fascinating.

I have no idea whether any comparable lexicon predated Cooperi in Europe or postdated him in England. Would like to have your impressions.

Had you heard of the College president's remark: "This institution is a store-house of learning. Freshmen bring new knowledge every year, and the graduates take away very little!"

Cordially
Marshall McLuhan

To D. Carlton Williams[1]

April 2, 1969

Dear Carl:

Great to hear about Arthur Porter's "invasion"![2]

Just very briefly, could you do a couple of pages on Papa Bott for *Explorations*?[3] You know how important his idea of auditory space has been for me. Linus Pauling, in *The Nature of the Chemical Bond*, devotes the whole book to *resonance*. There isn't a scientist in the world who knows anything about auditory space *or* resonance. No wonder thay are "mucking up" our lives.

I enclose Eliot's observations on auditory space which are perhaps relevant.[4] But I think it would be great to give Bott a mighty boost in order to shake those NASA [National Aeronautics and Space Administration] idiots down to their open-toed sandals. Outer space is for the birds. They should have spent their lives on inner space and produced anti-gravitational transport fifty years ago. Let us recall that Newton did not discover gravity, but levity!

Regards to all of you,

[1]Dr. D. Carlton Williams (b. 1912) was President of the University of Western Ontario from 1967 to 1977. He had been Professor of Psychology at the University of Toronto (1949–58). While Director of the Division of University Extension there (1958–65), he was a member of the original group, led by McLuhan, that studied culture and communications under a Ford Foundation grant.

[2]Professor Arthur Porter (b. 1910) was the Chairman of the Department of Industrial Engineering, University of Toronto, from 1961 to 1976; he was also acting Director of the Centre for Culture and Technology in 1967–8, while McLuhan was at Fordham. From 1969 to 1971 he was Academic Commissioner of the University of Western Ontario.

[3]E.A. Bott (1887–1974), whom McLuhan never met, had been Professor of Psychology at the University of Toronto for many years, and Director of the Psychology Lab there. He was in retirement and had suffered memory loss. Williams never wrote this article. See also page 372, note 2.

[4]T.S. Eliot's description of the "auditory imagination" in *The Use of Poetry and the Use of Criticism* (1933), included in the Penguin edition of Eliot's *Selected Prose* (1953), p. 94.

To Robert Manning[1]

April 11, 1969

Dear Mr. Manning:

One of the many anecdotes that I had forgotten to include in my Lewis memoir[2] is as follows: Lewis told me of being present at the first reading of *The Waste Land* to a small intimate group which included friends of Eliot and the first Mrs. Eliot. After the reading, a young chap with red splotches on his face spoke to Lewis aside, asking: "Do you think that these marks on my face might be called 'carbuncular'?" He seemed to think that he might be identified with the young man, "Carbuncular" in the typist episode of *The Waste Land*.

This has rather startling implications for Eliot students. The young man with splotches on his face was apparently one of the first Mrs. Eliot's boyfriends. She spent most of her later life in a mental home. Eliot refused to marry until she died.

Sincerely yours,

[1]Robert Manning was Editor-in-Chief of *The Atlantic Monthly*.

[2]"Wyndham Lewis", a memoir by McLuhan, appeared in the December 1969 issue of *The Atlantic Monthly*. See page 374, note 1.

To Pierre Elliott Trudeau

April 14, 1969

Dear Mr. Prime Minister:

Thank you for sending Mr. Jim Davey.[1] We had a very pleasant chat. Please let me clarify at once that matter of consulting fees. Naturally it would not concern any personal conversation between us, whether in private or by phone.

As for "remuneration" for consulting with your colleagues on a variety of problems, it might be possible to arrange fellowships for people of your own choice to study at the Centre for a few weeks. This, in turn, may call for some resource material to assist them.

For example, Paul Hellyer's report is entirely a 19th-century study of "hardware" that omits all awareness of the new dominance of the knowledge industries.[2] As electronic "software", or information, creates the main environment or garb-age of the planet and cities, the meanings and role of buildings and industries are completely altered. In the knowledge industries a man can work at home, or beside his home, as readily as "downtown." Business itself has become a

[1]J.M. Davey (d. 1975) was Program Secretary in the Office of the Prime Minister. The letters to him that follow were intended for the Prime Minister, Pierre Elliott Trudeau.

[2]Paul Hellyer (b. 1923) was a Member of Parliament at this time and the Minister responsible for the Central Mortgage & Housing Corporation; he was Chairman of the Task Force on Housing and Urban Development (1968–9). He resigned from the Cabinet in 1969.

dozen times more involved in education than schools and colleges. The educational budgets of personnel on company time (not even mentioning the armed services) is twenty times that of the communal budget for schools and colleges. This new dominance of information and the knowledge industries completely alters what has been called "zoning." Nineteenth-century hardware industry is now receding into insignificance. This means the end of the old division between work and residence.

Jet city is a circulating city. People now circulate in the same way that books used to, one hundred years ago. This means that it is pure folly to spend money on classrooms for schools and colleges. It is much cheaper and more effective to send the young to the areas of the world in which they have need to immerse for their studies. This is "crash-programming" instead of the assembly-line package job they now get. But Dr. [Claude] Bissell has asked, "What will I do with all these buildings?" The answer is simple. They will now serve for continued education of the elders of the tribe.

As knowledge replaces experience in human affairs, senior businessmen feel a deep urge to go back to the campus. Having circulated around the world, and having immersed themselves in many problems, they now feel the need to specialize. That is, they are eager to do what the young detest, and the young are eager to do what the elders are fed up with. These inversions, or reversals, result from the exhaustion of the potential of any form, as Aristotle points out in the *Physics*. It is a pattern of growth: as the caterpillar said as he scornfully watched the flutterings of a butterfly: "You'll never catch me up in one of those danged things!" It is also known as the Hertz law: the consequences of the images will be the images of the consequences.[3]

The big TV networks, including the C.B.C. [Canadian Broadcasting Corporation], are collapsing by attempting packaged programming, 19th-century style, For the same reasons the same fate is overtaking the bureaucracies and governments of the world. It is the attempt to pursue goals and policies in an instantaneous world of total public involvement.

Last Sunday, after the Smothers' Brothers [TV] show, the C.B.C. did a study on "violence." It consisted in simply asking a diverse group in age and occupation what they thought violence was. They did not ask about any *cures* for violence. There was instant and total participation. Let me take the opportunity of this instance to urge you to experiment in problem inventories with small diversified groups. It is important to avoid all attempt at solutions. The "solution" is always the mark of the 19th-century packaging mind. The real solution is in the problem itself, as in any detective story.

Jacques Ellul has written a new book entitled *Political Illusions*.[4] Under exist-

---

[3]Heinrich Hertz: "The images which we may form of things are not determined without ambiguity by the requirement that the consequents of the images must be the images of the consequents." From the Introduction (p.2) to *The Principles of Mechanics* (1956), translated by D.E. Jones and J.T. Walley.

[4]*The Political Illusion* (1967). The author, Jacques Ellul (b. 1912), taught in the Law Faculty of the University of Bordeaux. His books of social criticism—which were translated from the French,

ing political forms, he says, the first illusion is participation. The second illusion is that there are solutions, e.g. there is no ignorance where there is no learning. There is no poverty where there is no affluence. There is no privacy where there is no public. These, and many forms, are complementary. The white man creates the coloured man, as affluence creates poverty. A convict has no privacy. He has solitude. A tribal man has no privacy. Under electric conditions there can be no privacy. The privacy invaders are the bulwark of the new knowledge industries, from the pollsters, to the insurance companies, and the credit ratings, "the eye in the sky", the age of the "snoop."

I collect funny stories since they are infallible indexes of public grievance. You cannot only predict, but pin-point areas of grievance by the jokes that circulate. There are now floods of bilingual jokes, as well as Newfie jokes. Perhaps you have heard of the big Newfie breakthrough: the first hernia transplant, . . . etc. The reason for the flood of Newfie jokes is quite simply the shift of the Newfoundland population from rural to urban areas. There is a new interface, creating much irritation. East Berliners express their grievances by pointing to the great Russian breakthrough: the crossing of glow-worms with body lice now permits the entire population of Russia to read *Pravda* in bed at night!

Our own grievances concerning drugs and cops may break out in many forms, e.g. the reporter checking the man-in-the-street opinions on LSD, is told: "I think he is a great President, even if he has many enemies. History will vindicate him!" He then asks, "What about marijuana?" He is told, "Well, my wife and I spent a week there last year and found it absolutely delightful!" In a quite different category, Lord Birkenhead asked, jocularly, to render a legal opinion on whiskey and water, observed: "Making water in public is a misdemeanor; making whiskey in private is a felony." Woodrow Wilson, asked how many times he thought it permissible to use the same speech, replied: "I can't answer that question, I'm still using mine!"

I hope you find some of this useful.

Sincere good wishes,

and which McLuhan frequently mentions—have been criticized for their overly pessimistic view of the technological society. A layman in the French Reformed Church, Ellul once declared his intention of bringing "a new interpretation" to modern society and of determining "whether the Christian faith has power in this society".

To P.F. Strawson[1]

April 17, 1969

Dear Professor Strawson:

On getting *Individuals* in hand, I turned at once to your section on "sound." You indicate that: "Sounds, of course, have temporal relations to each other, . . . but they have no intrinsic spatial characters." Professer E.A. Bott of Toronto,

[1] This letter was addressed to Professor Strawson c/o the Toronto office of the English publisher, Methuen, of Strawson's *Individuals: An Essay in Descriptive Metaphysics* (1959).

now retired, is a psychologist who has devoted his life to the study of acoustic and auditory spaces. His experiments reveal that acoustic space is a perfect sphere whose centre is everywhere and whose margins are nowhere.[2] This, of course, is the character of a pun. The word is derived from *punctum*. The point about pun is that there is no point or fixed semantic position. The point is everywhere and its resonance extends to the verbal universe. Acoustic space as defined by E.A. Bott happens to be the definition of God by many ancient writers, especially the neo-Platonics. Many medieval writers continued this concept of acoustic space as the divine Logos. The Catholic church was founded on a pun, very naturally.[3] Each of our senses creates a unique physical space. Sight is the only sense that provides a continuum in space. Neither osmic, kinetic, proprioceptive nor haptic spaces present any continuum. They are entirely discontinuous.

The quantum physicists are quite innocent in these matters when they talk of resonance as the chemical bond (Heisenberg, Linus Pauling, etc.). They attempt to visualize it in their models, as all literate people inevitably do. Each culture is a dominant sensory mode. For the Japanese it is the tactile MA, or interval. Touch is the space of the gap, not the connection.

I have a book on these matters which I did with a painter, Harley Parker— *Through the Vanishing Point: Space in Poetry and Painting* (Harper & Row, N.Y. 1968). I hope you find it as interesting as I found *Individuals*.

Sincerely yours,

[2]Compare: "This intellectual sphere, the centre of which is at all points and the circumference at none, which we call God"—François Rabelais (c. 1494–c. 1533), *Pantagruel*, V. 47, and "It [Nature] is an infinite sphere, the centre of which is everywhere, the circumference nowhere"—Blaise Pascal (1623–62), *Pensées*.

[3]Matthew 16:18: "Thou art Peter, and upon this rock I will build by church." (Peter = rock.)

To John W. Mole, O.M.I[1]   April 18, 1969

Dear Father John

Thanks for the issue of *Christian Communication[s]*.

Am currently finishing off a book which I have to take to New York.[2]

Your piece on me[3] brings to mind that I am a Thomist for whom the sensory order[4] resonates with the divine Logos. I don't think concepts have any rele-

[1]John W. Mole (b. 1911 in Durham Eng.) was ordained a priest in 1947 of the Oblate Order (Missionary Oblates of Mary Immaculate, O.M.I.). In 1960 he founded the Canadian Institute of Communications and edited its quarterly *Canadian Communications* (1960–2). He also founded and edited *Christian Communications* (1962–75), and in 1969 founded the Institute of Social Communications, Saint Paul University, Ottawa, where he lectured on the Philosophy of Communications.

[2]This could refer to the proofs of *Counterblast* (1969) or to the typescript of *Culture Is Our Business* (1970).

[3]"John W. Mole, "From Heraclitus to McLuhan", *Christian Communications*, no. 28, April 1969.

[4]i.e. the sensible world.

vance in religion. Analogy is not concept. It is community. It is resonance. It is inclusive. It is the cognitive process itself. That is the analogy of the divine Logos. I think of Jasper, Bergson and Buber as very inferior conceptualist types, quite out of touch with the immediate analogical awareness that begins in the senses and is derailed by concepts or ideas.[5]

Best wishes with your work.

Yours in XTO,

P.S. Have just read Maritain's *The Peasant of the Garonne*.[6] 100% right as far as he goes. He is totally ignorant of the new electric environment as creating the world before which misguided Christians kneel. This strictly Luciferan product is ethereal and a highly plausible mock-up of the mystical body.

[5]Discussed in Mole's article were Karl Jaspers (1883-1969), the German philosopher; Henri Bergson (1859–1941), the French philosopher; and Martin Buber (1878–1965), the Austrian-born Jewish religious thinker and philosopher.

[6]Jacques Maritain, *Le Paysan de la Garonne* (1966), translated as *The Peasant of the Garonne* (1968), a synthesis of Maritain's views on life.

To Jacques Maritain

May 6, 1969

Dear Monsieur Maritain:

Having read your *Paysan* [*The Peasant of the Garonne*, 1968] with much reward and approval, may I venture a few additional observations? The Gutenberg technology retrieved antiquity and junked the Middle Ages. The tensors of our electric technology (the environmental extension of our own nervous system) retrieves all the impoverished areas of the world, dumping them into the Western lap and simultaneously junking the nineteenth-century industrial hardware and its numerous descendants. Every new technology is an evolutionary extension of our own bodies. The evolutionary process has shifted from biology to technology in an eminent degree since electricity. Each extension of ourselves creates a new human environment and an entirely new set of interpersonal relationships. The service or disservice environments (they are complementary) created by these extensions of our bodies saturate our sensoria and are thus invisible. Every new technology thus alters the human sensory bias creating new areas of perception and new areas of blandness. This is as true of clothing as of the alphabet, or the radio.

James Joyce put the matter very simply in *Finnegans Wake* (page 81, line 1): "As for the viability of vicinals, when invisible they are invincible."[1] By "vicinals" Joyce alludes to [Giovanni Battista] Vico whose *Scienza Nuova* asserts the principle of the sensory and perceptual change resulting from new technologies

[1]This line in *Finnegans Wake* reads: "Yes, the viability of vincinals if invisible is invincible."

throughout human history.[2] Hence the ancients attributed god-like status to all inventors since they alter human perception and self-awareness. Heinrich Hertz stated the same principle of complementarity and metamorphosis of our identity image in relation to technologies in his famous dictum: "The consequences of the images will be the image of the consequences."[3]

It was Aquinas who alerted me (I delighted in the phrase "Should old Aquinas be forgot", with its allusion to the Scottish song "Should Old Acquaintance Be Forgot and Never Brought to Mind") to the principle of complementarity inherent in all created forms. (In the *Summa*, I–11, Q.113, a.7, ad quintum).*

The same principle is stated in the *I Ching* that when any form reaches the end of its potential, it reverses its characteristics.[4] The matter is neatly illustrated in the joke about the caterpillar sceptically observing the flittings of a butterfly and saying: "You'll never catch me up in one of those darned things!"

When the Gutenberg technology hit the human sensibility silent reading at high speed became possible for the first time. Semantic uniformity set in as well as "correct" spelling. The reader had the illusion of separate and private individuality and of "inner light" resulting from his exposure to seas of ink. The chiasmus of the process is given epic treatment in Alexander Pope's *The Dunciad*, whose closing lines sum up the liquidation of trivium and the quadrivium: "Art after art goes out and all is night."[5]

The speed-up of print permitted a very high development of bureaucratic centralism in church and state, just as the much greater speed-up of electricity dissolves the echelons of the organization chart and creates utter decentralism— mini-art and mini-state. Whereas the Renaissance print-oriented individual thought of himself as a fragmented entity, the electric-oriented person thinks of himself as tribally inclusive of all mankind. Electric information environments being utterly ethereal fosters the illusion of the world as spiritual substance. It is now a reasonable facsimile of the mystical body, a blatant manifestation of the Anti-Christ. After all, the Prince of this World is a very great electric engineer.

May I suggest that just as the Roman clergy defected in the Gutenberg era on the illusion of the inner light, even greater numbers may be expected to defect under the mystical attractions of the electric light. Since our reason has been given us to understand natural processes, why have men never considered the consequences of their own artefacts upon their modes of self awareness? I have devoted several books to this subject. There is a deep-seated repugnance in the human breast against understanding the processes in which we are involved. Such understanding involves far too much responsibility for our actions.

I know of no philosopher who has ever studied the effects of technology on philosophical concepts, though the ascendancy of the eye provided by the pho-

---

[2]For Vico, see page 339, note 3.

[3]See page 366, note 3.

[4]The *I-Ching* (Book of Changes) was one of the *Five Classics*, the basis of Chinese education, which contains mystical speculations. McLuhan used a reprint of the James Legge translation of 1874. See also page 419, note 10.

[5]This is line 640, Book IV, of *The Dunciad*, which ends with line 656.

netic alphabet obviously made Euclid and Plato possible. It is equally obvious that the degradation of the eye by the visceral extension electrically of our proprioceptive lives creates the attitudes of "involvement" and "participation" and the world of Existentiality. The nineteenth-century bureaucrats in charge of implementing Vatican II are quite helpless in the face of a world of instantaneous information. Since we are doing these things to ourselves, there is no earthly reason for submitting to them unconsciously or irrationally. Perhaps now, when things happen at very high speeds, a formal causality or pattern recognition may appear for the first time in human history. Analogy of proper proportionality, for example, is a mode of awareness destroyed by literacy, since the literate man insists on visual connections where being insists upon resonance.

Let me speak to you of an occasion when you talked at the Royal Ontario Museum in Toronto on "The Longing for God". Throughout your address you pronounced "longing" "lungeing." It had a very mysterious resonance. On consulting the big Oxford Dictionary I discovered that "lunge" means "a length of rope on which a horse is exercised in a circle". "Lunge" is the root and origin of "longing". Is not this a nice example of the reverberations of the Logos reaching across language barriers?

My first encounter with your work was at Cambridge University in 1934. Your *Art and Scholasticism* was on the reading list of the English School. It was a revelation to me. I became a Catholic in 1937.[6]

Yours, with many prayers,
Marshall McLuhan

P.S. *Summa—*
   *Et ideo in toto tempore praecedenti,
        quo aliquid movetur ad unam
     formam, subest formae oppositae; et
   in ultimo instanti illius temporis, quod
           est primum instans . . .* [7]

[6]Maritain replied with a long letter (May 15, 1969), written in French, agreeing with several of McLuhan's statements; expressing concern over the rapidity of change that did not allow time for adaptation and over the grave "troubles" the technological revolution was producing for some Catholics; but taking comfort in his belief that the endurance of certain doctrinal perspectives was surely a sign that they were superior to the times and founded on truth.

[7]"And therefore in the preceding time, by which anything is moved towards a form, it is supported by the opposite form; and in the final instant of its time, which is the first instant . . . " (St Thomas Aquinas, *Summa Theologica*).

To D. Carlton Williams   May 6, 1969

Dear Carl:

Wish we had managed to see more of you and Peggy last Thursday.
Glad to enclose copies of your essay from *Explorations #4*, February, 1955.[1]

[1]The title of Williams' essay, which he had called "Auditory Space", was changed to "Acoustic

We really must devote an issue of the U of T *Graduate* (32 pages) to Bott. The quantum physics boys talk about resonance as the chemical and material bond, but don't know anything about acoustic space. Why not really rally some dialogue from scientific quarters on Bott's hypothesis as it relates to their problems?[2] Milic Capek makes plain in *The Philosophical Impact of Modern* [*sic*] *Physics* the unconscious visual bias of scientists.[3] Even psychologists have not studied the physical characteristics of visual space as contrasted with the visual mechanisms.

Warm regards,

Space" and the article was otherwise altered and extended, without permission, by Edmund Carpenter, with some additions by McLuhan, for *Explorations* 4. In the anthology *Explorations in Communication* (1960), edited by Carpenter and McLuhan, it was included under their names.

[2]The "hypothesis" of Dr. E.A. Bott (see page 364, note 3)—which Williams, who had served briefly as Bott's class assistant, once described to McLuhan—was that in auditory space a person is at the centre of an n-dimensional sphere and can therefore detect sound waves along any radius of that sphere. However, the article in *Explorations in Communication* mentioned in note 1 states, "auditory space lacks the precision of visual orientation." When blindfolded one can determine whether the sound of a buzzer on the end of a long moving boom comes from left or right. "But it is impossible, while blindfolded, to judge accurately whether a neutral buzzer, at a constant distance, is directly before or behind one and, similarly, whether directly overhead or underfoot."

[3]Milic Capek, *The Philosophical Impact of Contemporary Physics* (1961). "Unconscious visual bias" refers to our general tendency (including that of scientists) to conceive space in visual terms. We "see" distance, perspective, depth, height, etc., and therefore equate visual experience with reality, ignoring auditory and tactile space.

To Prince Bernhard of The Netherlands[1]

May 14, 1969

Your Royal Highness:

It was good to be there. It is good to be back. As you know, I was a rather bad boy at Bilderberg.[2] Frankly, I was staggered at the very low level of awareness of the contemporary world exhibited by all the guests present. As my friend Wyndham Lewis, the painter, put it: "The artist is engaged in writing a detailed history of the future because he is the only person who lives in the present". Ordinary people live thirty years back in a state of motivated somnambulism. Such was the state of the delegates at Bilderberg. Association with poets and painters of many lands have accustomed me to dealing with people of trained perceptions and contemporary awareness. Without a knowledge of all the poets and painters and artists from Baudelaire to Joyce, it is futile to attempt any appraisal of the *formal* or *efficient* causes initiated by the evolutionary extensions of our bodies which we call technology.

[1]Prince Bernhard sponsored the Bilderberg Conference on international themes held at Elsinore, Denmark, on May 9-11, 1969. McLuhan attended with Dr Claude Bissell.

[2]See page 531, note 1 (above).

The paper readers as well as the bankers and statesmen and educators present at Bilderberg had undergone no perceptual training. They were men of a few simple old-fashioned concepts. As a colonial, I had nourished the illusion that Europeans, at least, were aware of the contemporary arts as necessary guides to change. My disillusion was total! The delegates at Bilderberg were embalmers (embombers) of a dead past. They live in a rear-view mirror, blowing both horns of their dilemmas!

The great advantage in participating in Bilderberg is that it gives one a means of estimating the level to which the incompetence of the participants has enabled them to attain. Every man has a right to protect his own ignorance. However, these men are responsible for coping with a changing world which has sent them scurrying for cover in the opposite direction of the changes that we have released. I asked them to instance a single example in human history of any community that had been able to foresee the consequences of any innovation. The group was unable to comply. When I explained that in terms of services available to the ordinary man in 1830, England at least had achieved Communism, they were unable to demur. That observation concerned the old-fashioned industrial hardware only. When travel and information and education services are available to the ordinary person, the services that the greatest private wealth could not possibly provide for itself, that is Communism. It happened long before Karl Marx. Such service environments are invisible to accountants and actuaries and bankers who deal in entries of double entries and political arithmetic which conceal technological and environmental realities completely. Today, with the multi-billion dollar service environments available to everybody, almost for free, (these include the massive educational and information world of advertising) it means that we have plunged very deep into tribal Communism on a scale unknown in human history. I asked the group: "What are we fighting Communism for? We are the most Communist people in world history." There was not a single demur.

One fringe benefit of the conference for me was the sudden realization of what is meant by "class war". It means people deprived of identity. It is only accidentally the result of poverty. Today the entire TV generation has been deprived of its identity by the new image (cf. Hertz law), "The consequence of the images will be the image of the consequences." It is the affluent young today who are the deprived proletariat of our world. It is *they* who are fighting the new class war. Marxism is quite unable to cope with any 20th-century problem. The so-called "Communist" countries are merely trying to have a 19th century of consumer goods. Witness the cargo cults of the backward lands.

I hope you will correct the unfortunate space arrangements which the participants at the conference had to endure, with a consequent loss of dialogue. If I appear to be rude, it is because I am not addressing myself to persons, but to issues of great urgency. Naturally I appreciate the splendid urbanity with which you conducted the proceedings. I am honoured to have been a participant, Your Royal Highness. Most cordial thanks for your hospitality at Bilderberg.

Marshall McLuhan

To Robert Manning

Dear Mr. Manning:

I enclose a wee essay I wrote on Lewis years ago when he was visiting us in St. Louis ["Wyndham Lewis: Lemuel in Lilliput"]. This appeared in the St. Louis University *Studies in Honour of St. Thomas Aquinas*, Vol. 2, 1944. Feel free to use any excerpts whatever to augment my mosaic of anecdotes. I have several essays on Lewis that I can't find.

It would be possible to lead off the essay by saying: the main reason for the sudden revival of interest in the iconic art of Wyndham Lewis is TV. Like [Georges] Seurat and Paul Klee and others, his art and writing anticipated the rear-projection and strong bounding lines of the iconoscope form of the TV image. His own work validates his maxim: "The artist is engaged in writing a detailed history of the future because he is the only person who lives in the present."[1]

Lewis was an ecological observer and analyst. He was never caught in the booby-trap of the "Peter Principle."[2] He never stopped needling those who had attained the level of their own incompetence in the vast bureaucracies, political and professional, that environed him. In *The Caliph's Design* he revealed the total incompetence of the architects and town planners of his day.[3] In *The Apes of God* he pilloried the literary mandarins of Bloomsbury. In *The Art of Being Ruled* he revealed the vast new *lumpen proletariat* of the affluent who have since become so painfully obvious as the successors to the Marxist proletariat. In *The Doom of Youth* he explained the idiocy of the child-cult long before the Dr. Spock undertook to sponsor permissiveness. In *The Human Age*, his last work, he presents the dehumanizing forces of the magnetic city. He starts with the telegraph press and its power to generate cosmic political disturbances as a means of selling advertising copy. He concludes with TV and its power to alter the images of self-identity on a world-wide scale. Lewis was a "giant in Lilliput", and was avoided as such. We can now read him as a remote literary classic and begin to admire and understand the carapace of his art forms.

Sincerely yours,
Marshall McLuhan

[1]Written to the editor of *The Atlantic Monthly*, this quotation and the next paragraph (minus the last sentence) were incorporated in the second and final paragraphs of McLuhan's "Wyndham Lewis", *Atlantic Monthly*, December 1969. The final sentence of the memoir reads: "Is it any wonder that his analysis of the political, domestic, and social effects of the new technological environments had a great deal to do with directing my attention to these events?"

[2]The Peter Principle: in every business or institutional hierarchy, an employee tends to rise to his or her level of incompetence.

[3]*The Caliph's Design: Architects! Where Is Your Vortex?* (1919) is a 71-page hardbound "pamphlet" of brief, rather negative, polemical articles on art, a few of them touching also on architecture and town planning.

To Frank Kermode[1]

Dear Frank:

Much interested in the possibility of a book for your series. Also enormously flattered that Jonathan Miller should take the trouble to even look at my stuff. He should know that *Counterblast* will be out from Harcourt Brace in a few weeks, and *Culture Is Our Business* from McGraw-Hill, also *From Cliché to Archetype* from Viking.[2] The latter may be a bit of a block-buster.

Let me tentatively suggest for your series a wee book called *Walden III*. Our house is No. 3 and is the only house on a lovely pond in the heart of Toronto. This pond is fed by an artesian spring and constitutes the head waters of Taddle Creek (cf. Tattle creek and gossipacious Anna Livia Plurabelle) which runs across the city (now underground, of course). The pond ripples outward into a heavily treed neighbourhood of twenty-two acres and fifty-four houses. The Park has no "roads" or sidewalks, but simply these "Viconcan" circles of homes and people in a most unusual, dramatic relationship.[3]

Naturally, I could tie these patterns into many features of cities past and present. Waldon III is a theme that may suggest many further possibilities to you, and I will be glad to hear of them from you.[4]

Cordially,

[1]The distinguished Shakespeare scholar Frank Kermode (b. 1919)—then teaching at University College, London, and later to become a Fellow of King's College, Cambridge—was Editor of Collins' Fontana Modern Masters Series, in which Jonathan Miller's *McLuhan* was published in 1971. (Kermode first asked John Wain to write a study.) Kermode had reviewed *The Gutenberg Galaxy* in *Encounter* ("Between Two Galaxies", February 1963), and in January 1967 he had interviewed McLuhan on a BBC television program (produced for *Monitor* by Jonathan Miller) that was never transmitted.

[2]For *Counterblast*, see page 245, note 2; for *Culture Is Our Business*, see page 306, note 2; for *From Cliché to Archetype*, see page 416, note 1.

[3]In 1873 the English-born landscape painter Marmaduke Matthews (1837–1913) purchased a ten-acre estate on Davenport Road, Toronto, west of Bathurst, and built his large house called "Wychwood". In 1888 he and Alexander Jardine subdivided their estates, with the plan of forming an artist's colony, into seventeen large lots grouped around an eighteenth ravine lot reserved as park land; a revision in 1891 produced 38 large and small lots. The area, known as Wychwood Park, developed after 1907 with Cottage Style houses, and artists and academics moved there; it has retained its pleasant rural atmosphere within the city. The McLuhans moved to Wychwood Park in 1968. "Anna Livia Plurabelle": a character in Joyce's *Finnegans Wake*. "Viconean": the reference is to Giovanni Battista Vico and the Vico Road in Dublin in James Joyce's *Ulysses* (see page 339, note 3).

[4]Nothing came of this proposal.

Ezra Pound in detention,
before leaving Italy for the
United States, *c.*November
1945.

Felix Giovanelli

John Culkin and McLuhan at the Fordham Media Conference,
New York, summer of 1966.

McLuhan and Hubert Humphrey at a Washington dinner,
1967.

McLuhan and Buckminster Fuller, Bahamas, January 1970.
(Photo: Robert J. Fleming & Associates)

McLuhan in front of the coach house where the Centre
for Culture and Technology was located, April 1973.
(Photo: Robert Lansdale)

McLuhan in the Seminar Room of the Centre, April 1973.
(Photo: Robert Lansdale)

Marshall McLuhan in the early 1970s.
(Photo: Horst Ehricht)

McLuhan and Pierre Elliott Trudeau leaving The Three Small Rooms, Toronto,
December 1977.
(Photo: Toronto Star Syndicate)

To Gershon Legman[1]

July 16, 1969

Dear Gersin [*sic*]:

Heaven knows how many times I have described that amazing supplement to the O.E.D. that I saw years ago in your apartment in New York. It was the pornographic supplement edited by C.T. Onions, etc.[2] Until a few days ago I had never met another mortal who had even heard of it. However, Ernest Sirluck, now Dean of the Graduate School here, told me that *he* knew that it certainly was to be seen at the Bibliothèque Nationale in Paris. They have an *Enfer* division where it is housed. Sirluck also mentioned to me that the only word in the regular O.E.D. for which any value judgment is indicated is the word "transpire", as related to events. This use they designate is *erroneous.*[3]

Naturally I am eager to hear from you concerning the pornographic supplement to the O.E.D. Is it accessible in any American institution, or in a British museum? Is it for sale from any private owner? Do you still have your copy? Are you in a mood to sell same? Would you write a brief bibliographic note on its origin and subsequent uses, surreptitious or otherwise?

I edit a little section of the *Varsity Graduate*. The section is called *Explorations*. I can manage short articles. It would be a glorious coup to have a few words from you about the great hidden dimension of Mr. Onions' endeavours. Failing such a bibliographic note, can you think of someone who might be able to provide one?

Probably in the entire history of scholarship and publishing there is no item as obscure and secret as that O.E.D. Supplement!

Hopefully,

---

[1]Gershon Legman (see page 209, note 1) was at this time living in Paris (he still lives in France).

[2]In a letter of May 14, 1950 to McLuhan, Legman referred to *Slang and Its Analogues Past and Present* (7 vols. 1890–1904), edited by John Stephen Farmer and W.E. Henley—calling it, metaphorically, the "slang supplement" to the OED. Mr Legman has explained that what he showed McLuhan was Henry Cary, *The Slang of Venery and Its Analogues* (2 vols, Chicago, 1916, privately printed), which had been given to him by H.L. Mencken. He reports that the sexual terms and definitions in Cary's compilation were "plagiarized" from the Farmer and Henley work, which he understood to have been based partly on quotation slips that had been rejected from, and had been given to Farmer by an editor of, the *Oxford English Dictionary*—thus the OED connection McLuhan remembered. It has since been learned that in the Preface to Volume I (A–BYZ) of *Slang and Its Analogues* (1890), Farmer states that he received "about 12,000 quotations" from G.L. Apperson, of Wimbledon, who had "sub-edited certain sections of the *New English Dictionary* [the original title of the OED]" in the A–B volume (1888) of which Apperson's assistance as a sub-editor is indeed acknowledged by the Editor, James Murray.

[3]Definition 4b of the 1933 edition reads: "Misused for: To occur, happen, take place." 4c reads: "Of time: *To elapse, Obs. rare, erron*". Dr Sirluck, in pointing out to a colleague that the OED was not purely descriptive but gave the normative status of words, had looked up "transpire", but he did not claim that this was the only example of a "value judgement".

To Edward T. Hall[1]

July 23, 1969

Dear Ned:

The *Time* bit on June 6, page 51, apropos Kinzel prompts me to drop you a note.[2] Glad to have the excuse anyhow. I am working on a book on management structures with Barry Nevitt.[3] While so engaged this morning I had a call from a political machine man associated with Tony Schwartz, the sound wizard.[4] His queries prompted me to note the desperate efforts made by people today to defend their ignorance of media and other matters. The old gag, "Every man has a right to defend his own ignorance" is directly related to the problem of identity. I think the space approach to identity and security is basic. Recall War I and the Kaiser's panic about "encirclement" and War II and Hitler's panic about Lebensraum. Identity and "self image" are much the same, I assume. His image can be changed or obliterated by many kinds of events, private or cultural. Kinzel seems to ignore about 99% of all factors affecting identity, private or corporate. This, of course, is called "science." The scientist rigorously defends his right to be ignorant of almost everything except his specialty. The NASA Mafia are a splendid current example. As you know, in *War and Peace* [*in the Global Village*] I explored some of the major changes of identity brought on by new environmental factors created by new technologies. Specialism in any sphere, private or corporate, is surely a principal means of achieving identity. The complement to such identity is, of course, vast ignorance which must be defended at all costs, e.g., currently color TV is upgrading the Negro identity image via its iconic power. The WASP image then is speedily dissolving in co-relation with the same. The inevitable effect will be within three or four years a genocidal blood bath, i.e., the WASP will turn on the Negro and eliminate him totally. Tribalist people have very tender and fragile identities. The literate individual with his callous carapace of visual enclosure is the toughest type of identity ever devised by man. Naturally he is wilting in front of the electronic barrage.

UNESCO is currently distributing free transistor radios to native populations. To an ear-oriented population, radio is worse than "fire water." However, even if every member of UNESCO knew of this, no policy change would occur. If

---

[1]The anthropologist and author Edward T. Hall (b. 1914) first met McLuhan in 1963, when McLuhan spoke at the Insitute for International Development at Johns Hopkins University, Washington, where Hall was Professor of Political Theory and Cultural Relations. At the time of this letter he was Professor of Anthropology at Northwestern University, Evanston, Illinois, and had written *The Silent Language* (1959)—see page 280, note 1—and *The Hidden Dimension* (1966).

[2]Hall and others had advanced the theory that people unconsciously project a sphere of personal space around themselves. The psychiatrist Augustus F. Kinzel tested the theory of "personal space" on convicts at the U.S. Medical Center for Federal Prisoners in Springfield, Missouri, and a report on this appeared in *Time* in the issue of June 6, 1969.

[3]*Take Today: The Executive as Dropout* (1972), written with Barrington Nevitt (see page 397, note 6).

[4]See page 480, note 1.

every politician in the United States *knew* that color TV will produce the slaughter of millions of whites and blacks within three or four years, exactly nothing would be done. I am, of course, interested in understanding why this motivated ignorance and somnambulism is so necessary a part of our human makeup. I don't think it is new or eradicable. I am sure that it is closely related to the identity image-making needs and limitations. I would not hesitate to add personally to you that only supernatural means are proportioned to the needs of the case. I deliberately keep my Christianity out of all these discussions lest perception be diverted from structural processes by doctrinal sectarian passions. My own attitude to Christianity is, itself, awareness of process. As John Culkin says, "I don't believe in *shoulding* on people."

I have decided to phone you this afternoon during the composition of this note. I am sure I will be told you "will be back in two weeks."

This fortnight syndrome has begun to fascinate me as a mythic and ritualistic thing that has nothing whatever to do with dates or times. Surely it has to do with the fortnightly power to defend ourselves through vacation joy "Kraft durch Freude."[5] If I miss you on the telephone, my theme is this: The peculiar attitudes of wild animals to enclosed spaces, i.e., their power to identify with the space as if it were an extension of themselves in the style of "clothing." This seems to apply even to their keepers. It was a form of behaviour that is reported by Frankel of the Jews in the death camps. Why will caged lions refuse to leave these spaces when the gates are left open? Jack Parr tells me that he could not even induce them to leave by putting food outside the cage. (Jack Parr was a neighbour of mine in Bronxville, last year.) Would enjoy a chat or visit with you. Have given up nearly all travel in order to keep up with local tasks and assignments. Any chance of luring you hither to chat with our group in the fall or at any time? We always have a group in conversational action at any time of the week or year.

---

[5]"Strength Through Joy" was a Nazi slogan coined by Robert Ley, Minister of Labour in the Third Reich. It expressed the belief that people would work harder and produce more if they were entertained through sport, government-sponsored holidays, theatre, etc. KDF was adopted as the official name of the Nazi labour union.

To Robert J. Leuver[1]

July 30, 1969

Dear Fr. Leuver:

I would like to clarify some of Mr. James Parker's observations on war.[2] He was kind enough to draw attention to some of my notes of the subject.

There seems to be a general unwillingness to consider the impact of techno-

---

[1]This letter was addressed to Father Robert J. Leuver, C.M.F., Editor, *U.S. Catholic*, Chicago.
[2]James Parker, "The Joys of War", *U.S. Catholic*, August 1969.

logical innovation on the human sensibility. The reason that Joyce considered Vico's new science so important for his own linguistic probes, was that Vico was the first to point out that a total history of human culture and sensibility is embedded in the changing structural forms of language.[3] Today we are very conscious of slang as a frontier of linguistic change and response to the new service environments created for our senses by electronic information. Even old forms like "dig", "gutsy", "groovy", indicate a large shift from the "cat's pyjamas", and "hot mammas", and "I'll tell da world" of the 1920's. The twenties were going corporate and tribal fast enough under the huge speed-up of information movement by radio. But their slang is still visual and square (i.e. Euclidean) compared to the tactile, haptic, proprioceptive, and acoustic spaces and involvement of the slang of the TV age.

Because total new environments are always hidden from perception (e.g. the satellite environment of the earth which for the first time makes the earth the content of a man-made container), people not only ignore them but assume that they have no effect upon them.

Plato and Aristotle were quite unaware of the ways in which the phonetic alphabet had created a new primacy of visual or Euclidean space. They imagined that their sudden preference for connectedness of analytic reasoning and clarification had arisen from their own conceptual activities merely. Eric Havelock's *Preface to Plato* records the sudden revulsion against the bardic modes of education with the coming of phonetic literacy. Today we have returned to the bardic tradition through the universal use of the sum word both in ads and entertainment. In fact, the poets had fervently moved in this direction from Blake, Wordsworth, and Coleridge, forward. The poets merely preferred the bardic to the more ludicrous extremes of mechanism that had been perceived by Swift and Pope. *The Dunciad* is a dismissal of the crushing impact of an excess of printed matter on the human intellect.

With Gutenberg the first mechanization of a handicraft was by segmentation of the scribal processes, demonstrating the powers of rapid repetition to create mass production. Gutenberg wiped out scholasticism and scribal culture almost overnight. In the same manner that TV uses movies, Gutenberg used the old medieval content as his programming. Soon his technology created a new environment that altered the human sensorium drastically, providing the presses with individual authors eager to express fragmented opinions, or what we later began to call "private points of view." Just as there was nobody in the ancient classical world to notice the effects of the phonetic alphabet and papyrus on the human psyche and social organization, so there was nobody at the council of Trent who noted that it was the *form* of printing that imposed a totally new formal causality on human consciousness. In the 16th century and after, many God-fearing readers were sure that the "inner light" emanated from the black ink of the printed page. It was the same speedy form of repetitive print that not only revolutionized

[3]For Giovanni Battista Vico, see page 339, note 3.

education in the Renaissance, but created the "Romanization of the Catholic church" which is now being de-Romanized by an even greater speed-up of the electric information environment.

Nobody at Vatican I or II paid any attention to the *causes* of the new "needs" for the church of our time. The "need" of any period is always the puppet-like response to a new hidden service environment that shapes the awareness of all occupants of the same environment, whether they are directly involved in it or not. The motor car, for example, changes all the spaces in housing and urban arrangement. Using a motor car has nothing to do with the effects of the new spaces upon human perception.

Going along with the total and, perhaps, motivated ignorance of man-made environments, is the failure of philosophers and psychologists in general to notice that our senses are not passive receptors of experience. Each of our several senses creates unique modalities of space which have been ignored by psychologists in all periods. They prefer to study the mechanisms of the senses rather than the worlds created by them. The work of Edward T. Hall (*The Silent Language* and *The Hidden Dimension*) has directed attention to the amazing variety of social spaces created by different cultures of the world. He does not try to relate the diversity of these spatial forms to technological impact on our sensibilities.

Back to war and Mr. Parker. Every human being is incessantly engaged in creating an image of identity for himself. This image differs with the stages of youth and age, but even more it differs with the technological service environments within which this image-making activity proceeds. The tribal and more Oriental mores of the TV generation is rooted in a response both to the iconic TV image and also to the new satellite environment of the earth. The latter has transformed the earth into a global theatre in which jobs and dress become an anathema, and each seeks to "do his thing", to achieve a unique role with a unique costume. That the entire planet should become show business on a twenty-four hour basis is not only inevitable now, but it creates "challenges" for all levels of the establishment on a scale that will gradually obliterate consciousness.

When a new problem becomes greater than the human scale can cope with, the mind instinctively shrinks and sleeps. Today, for the first time, things happening at the speed of light also illuminate even the inveterate human somnambulism, forcing pattern recognition and intelligibility on the most reluctant. It is not brains or intelligence that is needed to cope with the problems which Plato and Aristotle and all of their successors to the present have failed to confront. What is needed is a readiness to undervalue the world altogether. This is only possible for a Christian. Willingness to laugh at the pompous hyperboles and banalities of moon-shots may need to be cultivated by some. The "scientific mind" is far too specialized to grasp very large jokes. For example, Newton did not discover gravity, but levity, not earth-pull, but moon-pull. To this day no scientist has a single clue as to what "gravity" is. In the eighteenth century it was defined as: "a mysterious carriage of the body to conceal the defects of the mind." The comedy of science as presented by Swift in the third book of *Gulliver's Travels*

(Leputa, the floating island) employed the principle of levity to enlarge the gaiety of nations.

In Christian terms, the components of Mars, or the rest of the systems of the cosmos, can reveal nothing comparable to the dimensions of experience available to the most grovelling Christian. Christians, however, have a peculiar war to fight which concerns their identity. The Christian feels the downward mania of the earth and its treasures, and is just as inclined to conform his sensibilities to man-made environments as anyone else. He also knows that he has constantly to create another identity that does not conform to the gravity and solemn masks of time and space. When the secular man senses a new technology is offering a threat to his hard-won human image of self identity, he struggles to escape from this new pressure. When a community is threatened in its image of itself by rivals or neighbours, it goes to war. Any technology that weakens a conventional identity image, creates a response of panic and rage which we call "war". Heinrich Hertz, the inventor of radio, put the matter very briefly: "The consequence of the image will be the image of the consequences."[4]

When the identity image which we enjoy is shattered by new technological environments or by invaders of our lives who possess new weaponry, we lash back first by acquiring their weaponry and then by using it. What we ignore is that in acquiring the enemy's weaponry, we also destroy our former identity. That is, we create new sensory environments which "scrub" our old images of ourselves. Thus war is not only education but a means of accelerated social evolution. It is these changes that only the Christian can afford to laugh at. People who take them seriously are prepared to wipe out one another in order to impose them as ideals. Today there is no past. All technologies, and all cultures, ancient and modern, are part of our immediate expanse. There is hope in this diversity since it creates vast new possibilties of detachment and amusement at human gullibility and self-deception.

There is no harm in reminding ourselves from time to time that the "Prince of this World" is a great P.R. man, a great salesman of new hardware and software, a great electric engineer, and a great master of the media. It is His master stroke to be not only environmental but invisible, for the environmental is invincibly persuasive when ignored.

War has become the environment of our time if only because it is an accelerated form of innovation and education. If war, according to the Hertzean principle of complementarity, is the natural result of shifting loyalties and identity images, we can use the same Hertzean principle to understand other conundrums. e.g., Affluence creates poverty, just as the public creates privacy, i.e., where there is no affluence there may be hardship, but no poverty, and where there is no public, there may be solitude, but no privacy. These are matters that I have discussed in the *Dew-Line Newsletters* at length.[5] The principle of complemen-

---

[4]See page 366, note 3. Hertz (1857–94) was a German physicist who produced and studied electromagnetic waves (radio waves).

[5]See page 361, note 3.

tarity is indispensable to understanding the unconscious effects of technologies on human sensibility since the response is never the same as the input. This is the theme of *The Gutenberg Galaxy* where it is explained that the visually oriented person stresses matching rather than making in all experience. It is this matching that is often mistaken for truth in general.

The hallucinogenic world, in environmental terms, can be considered as a forlorn effort of man to match the speed of power of his extended nervous system (which we call the "electronic world") by intensifying the activity of his inner nervous system. This is somewhat like the use of the fast motor car as a way of fighting back at the over-powering scale of high-rise and metropolitan buildings.

Please don't regard this as anything more than a few random responses to Mr. Parker.

Sincerely yours,

To J.A. Bailey[1]

September 25, 1969

Dear Mr. Bailey:

Your letter was much delayed in reaching me. I am interested in your suggestion about a seminar. For years I have studied many aspects of space unknown to scientists or psychologists. These studies concern your type of operation directly and would rationalize it.

We no longer live in a visual world. Quantum mechanics began to call it the world of "resonance" in 1927. Physicists, then and since, do not understand either the peculiar properties of visual space, or tactile space, or kinetic, proprioceptive, or osmic space. All of these spaces enter into the most ordinary compositions that we still call "pictorial". Our studies here have taught us that the TV child has lost the habit of visual convergence and has become monocular, or Cyclopean in his adjustment to the outer world. Cyclopean vision is that of the hunter. The hunter has no point of view, no goals, no perspective. These changes are the result of electric technologies and are causing the collapse of all existing bureaucracies with their visually programmed structures.

I mention these matters briefly to indicate that what I have to say to your group concerns your very existence. Naturally, therefore, I don't think of a casual chat as a very adequate mode of presentation. I propose that my associate, Harley Parker with whom I co-authored *Through the Vanishing Point: Space in Poetry and Painting* (Harper & Row, 1968) come with me and that we present some images by slide as a basis for discussion. Our fee for the first session would be $5,000. My own fee for ordinary talks out of town is $2,000. I accept these very seldom. Your proposal interests me not at all for the money, but because I con-

[1]This letter was addressed to Mr J.A. Bailey of the Marketing Education Center, Eastman Kodak Company, Rochester, N.Y. McLuhan, with Harley Parker, attended the seminar that is referred to.

sider it a significant opportunity to alert your best talents to areas greatly in need of research. I am turning increasingly to E.T.V. since my primary interests are in education and the training of sensory perception. E.T.V. is probably an area in which your operation is also interested.

I can be of enormous aid to you in your area. What time I take for such ventures as you suggest, I have to make, since I don't *have* it. Every minute is taken here. Therefore the possibility of a series of presentations is not great. What you would probably discover as desirable would be to send some of your top men here for subsequent work.

At present I am completing a book with an electrical engineer on *The Executive as Drop-out Or The Future of Management.*

Sincerely yours,

To William Carey[1]

October 8, 1969

Dear Mr. Carey:

Apropos proposed title "News Media and College Unrest", it tells all, i.e. would the unrest be less if the news coverage were less? The answer is *Yes.* If wars were never even mentioned in any media whatever, there wouldn't be any. By the same token, if the slaughter houses were on all media every day, meat would disappear from our diet at once. Photographic news coverage killed public hangings. TV coverage makes the Viet business difficult to get on with.

May I suggest therefore that we add another dimension to the topic by saying "Old and New Media and Student Unrest"? The interface between print culture and electric culture not only creates student unrest, it creates a collapse of all existing organizations in business and other establishments of the world. This has nothing to do with ideology or concepts.

Happy to be very flexible about the title. Even the old one. If you retain it, we can correct it in discussion.

I will arrive in Baltimore on Friday, November 7th, at 1:10 p.m. I understand that you will arrange my accommodations for that night. I will leave for New York on Saturday morning at 9:25 a.m.

I look forward to meeting you on November 7th.

Sincerely yours,
Marshall McLuhan

[1]Carey was Director of College Relations, Towson State College, Baltimore, Maryland.

To Jack Paar[1]

October 13, 1969

Dear Jack:

The great expert on Eskimo mechanical skills, as far as I know, is E.S. Carpenter, the anthropologist. You will find some of the story in his book *Eskimo*, the last issue of *Explorations*, which came out from the University of Toronto press in 1959.

Carpenter is in Borneo but may be back soon, for all I know. Shall be writing him at once and will mention your interest in a film.

As for the American Indian adaptability in high steel, there is the Edmund Wilson book on the Iroquois.[2] Wilson hasn't a clue. The answer is quite simple. As with all preliterates, the world presents itself visually to them, close up to their faces. There is no perspective or seeing at a distance in our film way, i.e. they do not use convergence but Cyclopean or monocular scanning, such as is now becoming current among the TV generation. My optician friend, Arthur Hurst,[3] has studied this subject. He reports the disappearance of convergence as a major tendency in the youngsters today. The well-adapted ones simply suppress the use of one eye.

I don't know of anybody who has done any study on changing sensory patterns resulting from technological innovation. It is a universal assumption among psychologists that all people are given the same sensory equipment and therefore use it in the same way. This homogeneous assumption is a normal part of the equipment of Gutenberg man.

You are quite right. I am in one heck of a bind about a dozen unfinished things. Very best wishes with your project.

Cordially,

dictated by Professor McLuhan
and signed in his absence

[1]The American TV personality Jack Parr (b. 1923), who succeeded Steve Allen as host of the "Tonight" show from 1957 to 1962 (and was in turn succeeded by Johnny Carson), had been a neighbour in Bronxville, N.Y., during McLuhan's tenure at Fordham University.

[2]Edmund Wilson, *Apologies to the Iroquois* (1960). A double-page spread (pp. 242–3) in McLuhan's *Culture Is Our Business* bears this title and alludes to Wilson's book.

[3]The optometrist W.A. Hurst, O.D., of Gravenhurst, Ontario.

To Edward T. Hall

Dear Ned:

I think I made my most exciting discovery while reading *Nil* by Robert Martin Adams.[1] His inventory of discontinuities and negations in the 19th century revealed to me that the cultures of the world have often been engaged in trying to restrict the continuum of visual space by various strategies of negation, nihilism, discontinuity, etc. Not knowing the properties of visual space, or the spatial properties of any of the other senses, has thus resulted in a huge waste of time and energy.

As a result of my brain operation (I am still on sedatives two years later), several years of reading got rubbed out and I am now re-reading many books, including [Hall's] *The Silent Language*. It is a ball! On page 45 of the paperback (about four pages into Chapter 3) you raise the question of the specific properties of a culture. You would probably tackle it differently today, but you simply omit the approach of indicating the preferred stress on each of the senses as a means of defining cultural patterns. For example, the whole of Adams' *Nil* can be stated simply as the efforts of 19th-century art and poetry to break out of the dominant forms of visual space: uniformity, connectedness, and continuity. The position of auditory space in visual culture is often absurdly high, as in the importance attached to "music" as a separate package deal.

Since writing *Through the Vanishing Point* with [Harley] Parker, I have hit upon one means of identifying the cultural bias of any society by its special phrase or phrases for "knowing something thoroughly and totally." e.g. the American phrase: "I know it inside out" is a puzzler to Englishmen and Europeans. It betokens the supremacy of manipulative and kinesthetic savvy in the Yankee world at least. It would probably mean nothing in the South. The Greek word for this is *despotein*, a sort of aerial perspective. The Englishman says: "I know it like the back of my hand." The Russian says: "I know it like the palm of my hand," the one indicating a visual, the other a tactile or iconic bias. The German says: "I know it like the inside of my pocket" (tactile and proprioceptive), whereas the Frenchman knows it *au fond* (i.e. auditory bias, resonance). The Spaniard says: "I know it as if I had given birth to it". The Jap says: "I know it from top of head to end of toes." (i.e. the interval of the MA, or touch and interface.) The Hindu says: "I know it nerve by nerve", and the Thailander says: "I know it like a snake swimming through water", and so on.

Such phrases indicate not a single isolated sense, of course, but a mix of senses, with fairly adequate marks of which dominates. They can be used as touchstones, which can be checked out against the rest of the culture very readily. Would it be possible to get a kind of symposium of such observations concerning

[1]Robert Martin Adams, *Nil: Episodes in the Literary Conquest of Void in the Nineteenth Century* (1966).

these phrases, as is attempted by a very large number of languages? Would you be willing to contribute a few yourself? Would not a mere inventory of such phrases be useful? Even without full discussion of them as marks of a cultural bias in the sensory life?

Now that the satellites have enclosed the planet in a man-made environment, "Nature" is no more. Only programming and understanding of the ecological field remains as a human task. Ecology and Echoland are close. Linus Pauling's *The Nature of the Chemical Bond* stresses the acceptance by physicists and chemists of *resonance* as the physical bond of the universe, i.e. interfaces but no connections, as in wheel and axle. Yet, scientists remain heavily biased on the visual side as a result of the unconscious effect of our Western culture. That bias has ceased with the young since TV, because the TV image is not visual so much as tactile, not convergent or bifocal so much as Cyclopean. Optometrist friends report a mental separation of the activity of one eye in the young today—especially in the well-adjusted or viable young. This separation appears to be the result of TV viewing on one hand, and near-point reading distances on the other.

Greetings to Mildy and warm regards.

To C.A. Doxiadis[1]   December 17, 1969

Dear Dinos:

"The medium is the message" presently applies to every form of transaction, including housing and road traffic. The expressway becomes a parking lot, simply by putting a faster spin on the hardware of the motor car than it can accommodate. The satellite environment of the planet has put a new spin on the earth, transforming our vision of it. The satellites "scrapped" Nature, turning the planet into an art form as decisively as TV turned the movie into an art form. As soon as the planet became an art form we became aware of the universality of pollution. The rim spin of "inflation" creates not economic but psychic depression. At high speeds the satisfactions disappear from previous human arrangements and arrangements [*sic*]. It's like eating a good meal in five minutes. The food may get better and better, but the rim spin of the transaction makes it inedible.

Any system, or any configuration of any components whatever, collapse when subjected to new speed-up. Ordinary speed-up simply creates obsolescence. More intense forms create war itself. Pardon me for jotting aloud.

I want you to know that I think of your cruise much, but the speed-up in my life has made such orbiting as it suggests very difficult.

Seasonal good wishes,

[1]Constantine A. Doxiadis (1913–75) was a Greek architect, engineer, teacher, town planner, author, and proponent of Ekistics, a word he coined, meaning the science of human settlement. He was President of Doxiadis Associates, Athens—Consultants on Development and Ekistics—and Chairman of the Board of Directors of the Athens Technological Institute. The organizer of the famous Delos Symposion (see page 289, note 2), he met McLuhan at the first one in 1963 and at the last in 1972.

To Ann Landers[1]

December 17, 1969

Dear Ann:

Are you familiar with the *McLuhan Dew Line Newsletter*? The last issue carried as a bonus a new deck of playing cards called the "Dew Line Deck." It is for the playing of management games as well as the conventional games. On each card there is an outrageous aphorism, such as "Thanks for the mammaries." If any-body deals a card or two to a group of associates or subordinates, or if a single card is picked by the Chairman, the request is: "Relate this aphorism to your top hang-up." For example, a high school principal friend of mine said to his staff: "Our problem is to get more films into this school. Relate that problem to the aphorism on the card." He was amazed at the variety of solutions that immediately appeared. In a word, the deck has turned out to be a superior form of operations research, although intended merely for fun.

I took at random a card on which was the sentence: "You have no proof of sanity unless you have been released from a mental institution." This was at home, and I said: "Just for fun, let's relate this remark to the question of "twins." What occurred to us at once is that twins have a peculiar identity problem. They live the life of an artistic transparency with one of their images superimposed on the other. Having twins, I noticed how from earliest infancy they necessarily watched each other incessantly. It was impossible to do otherwise. One was always getting attention of which the other was being deprived. As they grew up I encouraged them to make notes in anecdote form about the experience of being a twin. This, of course, they refused to do. Then I began to look around in literature for anything at all on the subject of twins, and I was quite amazed to discover that there was nothing at all except "The Bobbsey Twins." Since one in eighty births consists of twins, the population of such people is vast. Add to that group their parents, and brothers and sisters and husbands and wives, and you have one of the largest reading publics whatever.

At present, when the problem of identity has become a major hang-up in the cultures of the world as a result of technological and environmental changes (with corresponding loss of identity images, both private and corporate), the twin gestalt offers a major beach-head into the identity crisis which psychologists need desperately. The merely individualist psychology of Freud has flunked out in the new age of tribal and corporate identities. You may have noticed that psychiatrists have almost dropped out of sight.

I suggest that you are in a privileged position to make a creative contribution in this troubled area of identity image. It is a matter that concerns everybody, but one for which the question of twins offers a kind of "open sesame" previously unthought of.

The idea of eliciting anecdotes from twins via your column may not be a practical

[1]Ann Landers (b. 1918), who lives in Chicago (and is a twin), began her advice column in 1955 and it became syndicated in newspapers throughout North America. She had met McLuhan in Puerto Rico at a conference of the Young Presidents' Organization.

approach that it had appeared to me to be. At first glance it seemed that a column that reached many people could tap the untouched resources of observation of many twins. What is needed is a great collection of anecdotes, minus any point of view whatever. The anecdote can yield multitudes of diverse insights unsuspected by the narrator of the anecdote.

The "Dew Liners" are having a seminar on The Future of Management at West End, Grand Bahama Island from January 7 to 9. Just one hundred or so people, and lots of Bucky Fullers and such sitting around and chatting. It would be grand if you could come. Data is available from The Human Development Corporation, 200 Madison Avenue, New York, N.Y. 10006.[2]

Seasonal Greetings,

[2]Landers replied that she would be lecturing in Salt Lake City at the time of the Bahamas meeting (at which Buckminster Fuller was a guest speaker).

1970

To William Glenesk[1]

January 5, 1970

Dear Bill:

Snowed under here with delayed mail. Very pleased at the recent coverage you got in the press here. I actually did see you do the Tiny Tim "knot".[2] It was *yare*. Really found it a quite touching and beautiful wedding. I pray that there will be happiness and endurance in all of it.

Have a look at Luke 8–18: "Heed *how* you hear". Note the importance of the *how* in the figure-ground relationship of the seed and ground in the verses above it. Those who conceptualize the seed without perceptualizing are those who are not with it and therefore cannot keep it. After all, the church is a thing, and not a theory. That is why the poor and the children of the world can grasp it, whereas the wise and the learned have serious conceptual problems blocking their perceptual lives. The Jews had many concepts about the Messiah which defeated their confrontation with Him.

A Blessed Decade! Note how with speed-up the year unit yields to the decade.

Cordially,

[1]The Rev. William Glenesk (b. 1927) graduated from Victoria College and Emmanuel College, University of Toronto—where he took a course with McLuhan on Eliot, Joyce, and the Symbolists—and was ordained a United Church minister in 1952. In 1955 he moved to the United States and became a Presbyterian, presiding over Spencer Memorial Church in New York. In 1975 he returned to Toronto and became a teacher.

[2]Tiny Tim (Herbert Khoury, b. 1922) had a short but publicized career as an eccentric entertainer who sang sentimental songs in a high-pitched voice to his own ukelele accompaniment. His (brief) marriage to Vicki Budinger was solemnized on television in a non-denominational ceremony, conducted by Glenesk, on the "Tonight" show on December 17, 1969. A double-page spread (pp. 244–5) in McLuhan's *Culture Is Our Business* is devoted to Tiny Tim.

To Claude Bissell

January 14, 1970

Dear Claude:

This is a delayed congratulation on your lucid observations in the current *Varsity Graduate*.[1] My piece in *Esquire* about the University of Toronto really avoids all mention of what has happened since the student subsidies began.[2] The colleges have really been swept away in the resulting bureaucratization and centralism. However, the piece may well have some use as a testimonial. Naturally I wish to recall our understanding that in return for this essay published in a major national magazine of the U.S.A., you would rally to the cause of the Centre with a substantial sum.

We are broke. This past year I promoted $7,500 from which I provided my secretary, Mrs. Stewart, with a raise. The rest of the money went into minor equipment and materials, and further secretarial aid. The daily mail is vast, mainly because of my publications and the feedback, all of which directly concerns the work of the Centre.

In addition to the $7,500 I obtained the services of John Culkin, the film Jesuit, who is known throughout the world among film makers and teachers. Culkin's patron simply paid St. Michael's College the necessary sum to install Culkin as a full Professor of English. This permitted him to be cross-appointed to the Centre as a film expert. He has already begun to contact the film people across the campus and in the satellite universities.[3]

We need about $5,000 to complete the present fiscal year. The budget for the Centre that had been approved by the Centre Committee was cut back from $41,856.00 to $38,856.00 for 1969–70. The Centre has begun to assume a considerable role in the eyes of the world. This may or may not be desirable.

I look forward to the luncheon meeting of the heads of the Centres which takes place on January 26th.

Cordially,

---

[1] Claude Bissell, "The University Presidency and the Academic Revolution", *Varsity Graduate*, Winter (December) 1969.

[2] This article written for *Esquire* was not published. The subsidies were federal grants to Canadian universities that saved them from bankruptcy; in the case of the University of Toronto, the colleges were not "swept away" as a result.

[3] John Culkin (see page 309, note 1) had received a grant from a patron to continue McLuhan's work both at Fordham University in New York and in Toronto, and he visited Toronto several times to speak at the Centre for Culture and Technology on film studies, his particular interest at the time.

To Ashley Montagu

January 20, 1970

Dear Ashley:

Many thanks for the copy of *Midway*. Your essay on "The New Ideology of Race" is packed with useful materials for me.[1] I have an essay somewhere entitled "Black Is Not a Colour." The "coloured peoples" are literally created by the white man. If there were no whites, there would be only people. Black is not in the colour spectrum at all, but is the interval between colours. White is all the colours at once, of course. One might say that the "white" peoples represent a maximum of miscegenations and that the coloured peoples are more "pure" and less mixed.

In TV terms, by the way, the small degree of chiaroscuro in the Negro face, as compared with the white countenance, gives the Negro image great power, i.e. the power of the bounding line and sculptural, plastic form. In contrast, the white man looks quite sick on TV, especially colour TV. The merely private and merely visual quality of the white face as compared with the iconic character of the coloured image results in an automatic downgrading of the white and up-grading of the coloured person. This result will not be of any benefit to anybody. The natural backlash will be a blood-bath.

[1]Ashley Montagu, "The New Ideology of 'Race' ", *Midway*, Autumn 1969 (vol. 10, no. 2).

To Barry Day[1]

February 4, 1970

Dear Barry:

You didn't include Jonathan Miller's address so I ask you to be so good as to pass along my suggestions for relating to books as yet unprinted. First of all, thanks for your generous offer to help for Kumar.[2]

As for forthcoming books, *Culture Is Our Business* has been rewritten three times to update it since it is built around fifty or more full-page ads that quickly lose their tang. The theme is the obvious one that we live in vast new information environments that are in effect universities without walls. Ads are a large part of

[1]Barry Day (b. 1934) was working for the London-based advertising agency Lintas in 1966 when he read *Understanding Media* and thereupon became a McLuhan enthusiast, writing several articles on his ideas that were published by Lintas under the title *I'm the Only One Who Knows What the Hell Is Going On* (1967)—a quotation that McLuhan later disclaimed. Day first met McLuhan in Bronxville, New York, in August 1968. In 1969—the year before he became Creative Director of the London office of McCann-Erickson—Day videotaped an interview with McLuhan in the CBC studios in Toronto and it was used in a London conference on advertising in September 1969. Day did not know Jonathan Miller but duly forwarded to him McLuhan's comments in the following letter (and other comments in letters to Day) that were intended for Miller—as well as McLuhan's letters addressed to Miller. Day is now Vice-Chairman of McCann-Erickson Worldwide, New York.

[2]Jitendra Kumar had been a Ph.D. student of McLuhan's.

this new curriculum of studies. However, in this total field the audience becomes hunter rather than consumer and needs perceptual training rather than doctrination. The percept takes priority of the concept. This book will be published by McGraw-Hill this Spring. *Cliché to Archetype* will be put out by Viking Press this Spring. The theme is more crucial than *Culture Is Our Business*, namely every new technology is a cliché environment that scraps the preceding one, turning it into an art form. It also retrieves in every instance a much older form. Thus, Gutenberg scrapped medieval manuscripts but retrieved antiquity, and mechanical industry scrapped agrarian life but retrieved medieval art and perception and craftsmanship. Electric technology scrapped mechanical industry and retrieved the most primal and occult forms of awareness, dumping all the primitive societies of the world into the Western lap. Electricity has retrieved many of the most forgotten modes of awareness in the Orient itself, e.g. medical therapies more than 4000 years old in Japan, and I Ching in China, etc.

The cliché, in other words, or the daily phrase, stores vast quantities of perception and experience which can be released by interface with other forms including other clichés. This is the secret of the interval in quantum physics. It is a world of interface and resonance and metamorphosis. The figure of hendiadys[3] with all its forms of metaphor, collage and double-plots, are modes of interval between clichés that release new forms.

Another book of mine which is due out in the Summer or Fall is my doctoral dissertation (Cambridge) which I am planning to title "Cicero to Joyce".[4] It is the study of the tradition of eloquence achieved by encyclopedism, which I refer to in the essay "James Joyce Trivial and Quadrivial".[5]

Another book which I am finishing with an electrical engineer, Barrington Nevitt, entitled *The Executive as a Drop-out: The Future of Management*,[6] is concerned with the total difference of human organization between the specialist or fragmented bureaucratic structures and the new decentralized, integral kinds of structure which demand role-playing and discovery.

One new sidelight on "the medium is the message" is perhaps relevant. When a new service environment such as that of Gutenberg typography begins to come into play, all existing forms are processed through that new form. All inputs, old and new, thus acquire the same final form. The Gutenberg environment processed every type of human awareness and activity from Machiavelli to Ben Franklin. Every kind of knowledge becomes applied knowledge by this process. By the

---

[3]See page 399, note 1.

[4]McLuhan's doctoral dissertation has not been published.

[5]Marshall McLuhan, "James Joyce: Trivial and Quadrivial", *Thought*, vol. 28, no. 108, Spring 1953. It was included in Eugene McNamara ed., *The Interior Landscape: The Literary Criticism of Marshall McLuhan* (1969).

[6]This became *Take Today: The Executive as Dropout* (1972); see page 433. McLuhan's collaborator, Barrington Nevitt (b. 1908), practised as an electrical and industrial engineer; he had worked on long-distance communications systems and had also taught the history and philosophy of science at McGill University.

same token, when the satellites go around the planet, Nature is scrapped and the planet becomes an art form. Nature itself appears as a mess. Pollution becomes universal awareness so that everything now must be programmed. The second atom [Adam?] is thus saddled with the job of restructuring the garden of Eden on much more august lines than His original garden.

Hoping that some of this may be of some value to you and Jonathan,

Very best wishes,

To Frank Sheed[1]

February 20, 1970

Dear Frank:

Here's one to play on Sheed's own trumpet! A guy who turns in a fire alarm is not necessarily an arsonist! Marshall McLuhan has never said that the printed page has come to an end. McLuhan has said that the book is obsolescent. So is handwriting. But there is more handwriting done today than there was before Gutenberg. Obsolescence never meant the end of anything—it's just the beginning. Take the motor car as an example. There is an old saying in the business world: "If it works, it's obsolete." This is literally true, since until a process has penetrated the sensibilities of an entire community, it hasn't begun to do its job.

As a full-time Professor of Literature my days are spent interpreting the printed page and in devising new ways for increasing our powers of perceiving and penetrating its mysteries. *Through the Vanishing Point: Space in Poetry and Painting* (Harper & Row, 1968) which I did with the painter, Harley Parker, offers an entirely new bridge to the printed word by comparing and contrasting the spaces created by its art form and neighbour art forms. I have spent a good many years in studying the cultural effects of print and in proclaiming the alphabet in its printed form as the sole basis of civilization. The electro-technical forms do not foster civilization but tribal culture.

Literacy in Traditional Societies edited by Jack Goody (Cambridge University Press, 1968) makes a few timid steps in the direction of recognizing the effects of Western literacy on preliterate societies. It shows not the slightest awareness that the many non-phonetic forms of literacy have no civilizing effects whatever. Civilization is a technical event. There is no other alphabet that has the effect of upgrading the visual powers at the expense of all the other senses. It is the dominance of the visual faculty that creates civilized values. Eric Havelock in his *Preface to Plato* explains the origins of Greek individualist civilization and Plato's war on the tribal poets as an immediate consequence of the phonetic alphabet.

[1] Francis Joseph Sheed (1897–1981), who was born in Australia, married Masie Ward in 1926 and together they established in England the firm of Sheed & Ward to publish English Catholic authors; the New York branch was founded in 1933.

As for the electro-technical development, its effect on our sensibilities and our human society has never aroused the slightest enthusiasm in Marshall McLuhan. I have never endorsed the events I have described, nor have I ever condemned any of the things I analysed. I am interested in understanding processes. Such are the opaquities and obliquities of "value" judgments that they have always stood in the way of human understanding. This applies as much to the revealed truth of the Catholic faith as [to] the artefacts of human ingenuity. The fact of the church is quite independent of human concepts or preferences. As for media and the church, it is obvious that there was not anybody at the Council of Trent who had any interest in the shaping power of the Gutenberg technology in creating private judgment on one hand, and of massive centralist bureaucracy on the other hand. There was nobody at Vatican I or II who showed any understanding of the electro-technical thing in reshaping the psyche and culture of mankind. The policies adopted at these Councils manifested the spirit of Don Quixote who donned the latest print technology as his armour and motive and rode off valiantly into the Middle Ages. Since Vatican I and II the Catholic bureaucracy has moved resolutely into the 19th century, supported by plain-clothed priests and nuns. If a few people could only stop asking whether this is "a good thing or a bad thing" and spend some time in studying what is really happening, there might be some possibility of achieving relevance.

Sincerely yours,
Marshall McLuhan

To the University of Buffalo Lockwood Library, James Joyce Division

February 23, 1970

Dear Sirs:

I have heard of a book by an Emily Hahn entitled *Hendiadys, What Is It?* (1923).[1] As Joyce students know, both the hen (Belinda) and hendiadys are pervasive modes of the *Wake*. I have been unable to get any clues about the whereabouts of this book. The big libraries don't list it.

There is an Emily Hahn living in England to whom I have just written for help.

Perhaps you might have some suggestions.

Hopefully.

[1]This is the first of seven letters, back and forth, concerning McLuhan's search for this work. He was eventually directed to the well-known American author Emily Hahn and addressed his letter to *The New Yorker*; she replied from Yale University, where she was teaching, saying that she could not help him. McLuhan describes the outcome of his search to Miss Hahn on page 403. *Hendyiadys:* the expression of a single complex idea by two words connected with *and*. "Hendyiadys: Cliché as Double Probe" is the title of one of the chapters in *From Cliché to Archetype* (1970) by McLuhan and Wilfred Watson.

To Brian Stock[1]

February 26, 1970

Dear Brian:

Hoggart is an utter sap![2]

Thanks for Cornford's "Marshalling the Clues."[3] He is lacking all clues about my sensory approach. We can talk about that when you come back.

Am ordering copies of *Counterblast, Through the Vanishing Point* and *Literary Essays* for you. They will be sent to the Paris address.

Things have been exceedingly filled in here and also filled out! There is nobody in the Institute with whom I can communicate. Their total lack of contemporary awareness is somewhat inhibited. Had a chat with Gilson and a group of the Institute men. It was not a waste of time. It revealed Gilson's total unawareness of the cultural reasons for the relevance of medieval studies a hundred years ago. He knew nothing about Blake or the pre-Raphaelites for example. Now that the kids have gone completely medieval, he is quite at a loss to conceive of any contemporary relevance for medieval studies. The historical approach has lost all significance to the degree that the Middle Ages have come back to us instead of our going back to them. This was a point on which he and Pegis had antithetic ideas.[4]

I missed your article on Canadian culture in TLS.[5] I shall xerox a copy from our local library.

[1]Professor Brian Stock (b. 1939), then a Junior Fellow of the Pontifical Institute of Mediaeval Studies, was on a sabbatical in Paris doing research at the Ecole des Hautes Etudes en Sciences Sociales. He is now a Senior Fellow of the Institute.

[2]This remark was elicited by McLuhan's reading Stock's (unsigned) front-page review in *The Times Literary Supplement* (March 5, 1970)—entitled "The Social Conscience of the English Critic"—of Richard Hoggart's *Speaking to Each Other: Vol. 1, About Society; Vol. 2, About Literature* (1970), in which Stock noted that Hoggart presented television as "an agency for reinforcing the 'classlessness' which he sees emerging in the 1960s."

[3]In 1968 Christopher Cornford (b. 1917), who was then Dean of the Royal College of Art, gave a talk to the British Society of Aesthetics entitled "Marshalling the Clues", setting forth McLuhan's ideas as Cornford understood them and stressing their implications for aesthetics. In 1969, at the University of California, Santa Cruz, Cornford met Edmund Carpenter, to whom he gave a copy of his paper. Carpenter sent it to McLuhan, who wrote Cornford appreciatively.

[4]Professor Anton C. Pegis (1905–78) taught the History of Philosophy in the Pontifical Institute of Mediaeval Studies, Toronto, and was President of the Institute from 1946 to 1954.

[5]Brian Stock, "Canadian Culture in the 1960s", *Times Literary Supplement*, August 28, 1969.

To J.M. Davey
Office of the Prime Minister

March 2, 1970

Dear Jim:

A couple of basic principles apropos administrative dynamics popped into mind while watching the movie "Z".[1] In a word, any conventional bureaucracy becomes a police state when speeded up by a new technology such as telephone or telex. Just as Machiavelli could regard the state as a work of art as soon as the medieval order had been scrapped by the new speed-up of Gutenberg technology, so our political structures become "works of art" as they are scrapped by new technology. The movie has become a work of art since TV. The planet has become a work of art since the satellite, i.e. the planet in the sense of "Nature" has been scrapped and we now confront it as an art problem in the name of "pollution." Once surrounded by human artefacts, Nature is a mess. A good example of new technology turning bureaucracy into a police state is the traffic question. As the motor car becomes obsolete and traffic is aided by helicopters and computers, etc. you have the extreme instance of police state resulting from the speed-up of obsolete technology.

The second theme. Drugs. The clue is in prohibition of the 20's. Booze was not new. It was the panic that was new. So with drugs today. It is the panic that is new. The new radio environment of the 20's created a new primitivism and tribalism which we associate with the jazz age. Tribal people cannot abide booze. It sends them berserk. They are already excessively involved in each other without stimulants. The Wasp, on the other hand, needs gallons of booze in order to be sociable. In the 20's the Wasp had gone tribal and booze began to terrify him.

The key to the drug panic is TV. TV intensifies the already numerous forms of inner-tripping. Colour TV is psychedelic input. The kids are simply putting jam on jam when they take to drugs. They seem to imagine that it helps them to relate to an electric speed world, whereas they are quite unable to relate to the fractured and fragmented specialties of a pre-electric school and goal and job system.

In the 20's booze created a huge police state as we tried to prop up the old form of social arrangements. Drugs likewise provide a field-day for the Mafia as we try to maintain the patterns of the pre-electric age while the kids are miming electric speeds and the externalization of their nervous systems created by electric circuitry.

The third matter concerns the need for a program on "learned ignorance". What has often been called "trained incapacity" flourishes as never before in our bureaucratic society. Computer speeds actually are making practical the return to the "cottage economy". It may soon be fashionable to run a factory from the kitchen. The Middle Ages have returned to us long ago by electric means as you can see in the kids' costumes and in their avid pursuit of role-playing. With the

---

[1] Z (1968), the film directed by Costa-Gavras and starring Yves Montand, about the murdered Greek left-wing deputy Lambrakis.

satellite surround the planet becomes a global theatre with the audience as actor. Hence the new politics of "unrest". The public has no intention of remaining in the spectator role. Hence a program in which all of the hang-ups of the learned in the arts and sciences and in all areas of our Establishment would be one means of getting the audience directly into the administrative act. Again, the pattern of the program should be inventory of hang-ups, not solutions. If the audience makes instant breakthroughs on previously insoluble matters, fine. This would happen, but it needn't be the main purpose of the program.

Cordial regards,

To the Editor, New Society[1]   March 10, 1970

Dear Sir:

Why did you leave Karl Marx out of your inventory of hot gospellers?[2] Are you trying to duck the pattern of finding categories for all? Do you think of him as an untalented scientist or also as an untalented quack like me?

Nobody has ever questioned my assertion that *all* media are extensions of man. Nobody has ever questioned my evidence for these extensions as creating new service/disservice environments which alter modes of private and corporate perception.

The Marxist hang-up has always resulted from accepting the products of human toil and knowledge as products that do not alter the total environment. Marxists have chosen to ignore the "invisible" or *total* information environment created by industrial hardware. Marx ignored the "flip" or reversal that occurred in his own time. That is, when public services, available to the ordinary worker, exceeded all power of private wealth to provide these same services for the wealthiest persons in the world. Such services abounded in publication, in postal systems, transportation and in information services.

Bookkeepers had no means of estimating the scope or value of such new environmental services. Today these service/disservices are so vast as to render personal wealth a parody.

Rationality includes the means of "making sense" of the processes which we initiate and experience as new corporate education. Understanding is not a point-of-view. Social scientists imagine that rational explanations involve not only a

[1]*New Society*, a New Science Publication, was published in London, England.

[2]McLuhan is alluding to an article by Michael Wood, "The Four Gospels (Laing, Levi-Strauss, Lorenz and McLuhan)", *New Society*, December 18, 1969. Wood's four authors "can be seen as focusing on several of our current and related worries. How sane are we (Laing)? How civilized (Levi-Strauss)? How human (Lorenz)? Are we the masters of our own machinery (McLuhan)?" For Wood these authors underestimated or ignored the power of reason in ordering human affairs, and imply that people have been bullied by instincts or technology into a blind alley. This he regards as an "abdication", since our problems are connected with "our relation with the world we live in, things and people. It is the *relation* we have to get straight."

point-of-view but a connected chain of events between the viewer and "actions at a distance". If they can find no visualizable links they consider that there is no rational explanation of the effects. Scientists used to be hung-up on the "space-time continuum". When they encountered the non-visual or resonating interval in matter they tried to translate it into the visual terms of "continuum". Our Western culture was commited to abstract concepts and classifications from the time of Euclid and the phonetic alphabet. Here, as Eric Havelock has shown at length in his *Preface to Plato* (Harvard University Press, 1963) was the origin of the private individual self which cannot bear up against the integral and instant information environments of our time. Even Xerox dims the fragmentary and movable types of Gutenberg, turning print into an "art form", as TV turned the movie into an "art form", and satellites create space-ship earth as a new art form for total programming.

Nobody can *see* how new technologies metamorphose earlier ones into art forms. There is certainly no *connection* between these events. If there were any connection *there could be no change. The action is where the gap is.* It has always been thus. Change requires the resonant and abrasive interval, whether in the tragic flaw of character in the tragic hero of Aristotle, or in the chemical bond of Linas Pauling. The gap created by the complementary forms of white and coloured, of affluence and poverty, of publicity and privacy, of war and peace, of ignorance and knowledge, all engender the processes of change.

Today the acceleration of these processes not only alienate[s] man from himself and others, but they provide the rational means of understanding and antici-pating effects with causes.

Value judgments of processes such as these create huge smoke screens. Even the most irrelevant and fatuous categories can muster the appearance of plausi-bility. Rigidity of stance or point-of-view creates a habit of moral valuation devoid of all the intellectual satisfactions of comprehension. The "play" of intellect is as necessary as the interval between wheel and axle to avoid seizures.

The "huge abdication" of which you speak relates directly to your inability to play and probe the problems of our time as the heart of all solutions. Your classifications are a visual system of avoiding the dynamics of pattern recognition in the actions of our time. The solutions of all problems are inherent in the struc-tures of the problems themselves.

Sincerely yours,

To Emily Hahn[1]

March 17, 1970

Dear Professor Hahn:

Many thanks for your note. Since I wrote you I have found "Hendiadys: Is

---

[1]The American author Emily Hahn (b. 1905)—who has written some 50 books and has been a frequent contributor to *The New Yorker* (as recently as November 24, 1986)—was at this time teaching at Yale University. See also page 399, note 1.

There Such a Thing?" in *The Classical Weekly*, Monday, May 8, 1922, Vol. 15, #25, pages 193–197. The author signs herself E. Adelaide Hahn, Hunter College. Her study of hendiadys had the utmost interest and relevance for James Joyce since it was based on Virgil's *Aeneid*. She takes the simple visual approach that the world of the metamorphic interval, which is hendiadys, is a mere illusion "which produces an illogical effect." The visually oriented person is always looking for connections rather than intervals. The gap or interval is where the action is. The connection is a hang-up.

By the way, the "Russian tart in Harbin" may have been the one who made it to Hunter![2] Apropos the name "Hahn", it gets a huge role in *Finnegans Wake* since it means "hen" and hence "The One" in Greek. Belinda, the hen, scratching around on her midden-heap, roots out the letter to posterity whose exegesis occupies the main bulk of the *Wake*. I hope you get a chance to discuss some of these things with Professor Ellman.[3]

Sincerely yours,
Marshall McLuhan

Hahn MSS, Lilly Library, Indiana University

[2]In a reply (March 12, 1970) to a previous letter from McLuhan, Miss Hahn had written that she once heard of another Emily Hahn, "but she was a Russian tart in Harbin, and I can't believe that she ever wrote a book."

[3]Richard Ellman (1918–87) was the author of the definitive biography of James Joyce (1959, rev. 1982). He was teaching at Yale, his Alma Mater; but this year (1970) he was made Goldsmiths' Professor of English literature at Oxford University.

To Jonathan Miller

April 22, 1970

Dear Jonathan:

I hope you can understand my satisfaction in hearing that you are about to query the observation that "the medium is the message." I had to get out of the U.S. when people began to accept this without understanding it. It is much safer to have it rejected by people who don't understand it.

What I am saying is what Wordsworth said in his phrase: "the child is the father of the man." This seemed like a wild statement at the time. All he meant was that youthful environments shape adult attitudes. All I am saying is that any product or innovation creates both service and disservice environments which reshape human attitudes. These service and disservice environments are always invisible until they have been superseded by new environments.

When we last met, you seemed to concur as a neurologist with the fact that inputs are never what we experience, since any input is always modified by the entire sensorium as well as by the cultural bias of the individual.

You have probably read the classic *Preface to Plato* by Eric Havelock (Harvard [University] Press, 1962). He is head of Classics there [*sic*]. It is a study of the collapse of the poetic educational establishment under the impact of the phonetic alphabet. He also explains the emergence of the rational individual from the matrix of the same alphabet. It is that individual which is now submerging in its Yellow Submarine of sound-light effects.[1]

I take it that you understand that I have never expressed any preferences or values since *The Mechanical Bride*. Value judgments create smog in our culture and distract attention from processes. My personal bias is entirely pro-print and all of its effects.

By the way, all the classical economists, including Marx and Keynes, ignored the new environments created by the "products" of the new mechanical industry. They studied labour, markets, products, rent, and prices, but never took one look at the service environments created by the new products. Hence all of their calculations have been wide of the mark.

As you know, my detractors work night and day to advance my reputation. It is impossible to buy so invaluable a service!

Your humble and obedient servant,

[1]An allusion to *The Yellow Submarine* (1968), the striking animated film fantasy, directed by George Dunning, that presents a series of surreal episodes inspired by Beatles songs. For Eric Havelock, see page 406, note 1.

To Maisie Hewlett[1]   April 30, 1970

Dear Mrs. Hewlett:

I am really grateful to Elizabeth (Trott) Cera for suggesting that you send your quite memorable memoir to me. The scenes and the events coincide with the life of my parents in the West before [World] War I. After homesteading, they went to Edmonton. My father was in a real estate firm until he joined the army in 1914. I left Edmonton when I was four, but remember much of it very vividly.

I think your record has great value and beauty. It is also very rarely that any-one of your generation has the time or capacity to put down any of those experiences.

Currently I am trying to organize a program of oral history of our country. It seems natural that elderly people should be given the opportunity to record their early experience. Small and convenient tape recorders are quite cheap and are constantly being improved. Since elderly people seldom have any community or social life today, it is my hope that the recording enterprise will create new forms of inter-communication among both young and old. The elderly love to recall and the children love to hear about the "olden times". Perhaps the whole thing will blossom out into a large educational enterprise.

Again thanking you most cordially for your beautifully written and fascinating story.

[1]Mrs A.E.M. Hewlett (née Annie Elizabeth May Brown, 1887–1974), a friend of Elizabeth Trott Cera (see page 230, note 1), was an English-born Saskatchewan pioneer—and a journalist and watercolourist—who wrote a memoir of her life in Saskatchewan, *A Too Short Yesterday*, which she published privately in 1974.

To Eric Havelock[1]

May 22, 1970

Dear Professor Havelock:

In June, Professor Wilfred Watson and I are publishing a book entitled *From Cliché to Archetype* [1970]. The meaning of the title is simply that every technology scraps the preceding service environment and retrieves a remote one. Two obvious examples would be Gutenberg's scrapping of the scribe and the schoolmen, and his retrieval of antiquity which had been mainly inaccessible to the reading public. Today, electric technology scraps mechanical industry while retrieving the most primal modes of human consciousness.

Your own unique study, *Preface to Plato*, prompts me to write this note. Is it possible that the phonetic alphabet, by upgrading the visual powers of man after many centuries of the dominance of aural culture, may have scrapped the poetic arts of tribal man and also retrieved the autonomous human entity? This would seem to have been the only time and only circumstances in which the metaphysical and independent human being had been able to manifest himself amidst the vast amorphous resonance of the tribal culture. Today, as we step up the tribal resonance again by electric technology, the importance of those fifth-century events seems to take on increasing significance.

My own studies of the effects of technology on human psyche and society have inclined people to regard me as the enemy of the things I describe. I feel a bit like the man who turns in a fire alarm only to be charged with arson. I have tried to avoid making personal value judgments about these processes since they seem far too important and too large in scope to deserve a merely private opinion.

I can assure you that each time I return to *Preface to Plato* I am very grateful for its existence.

Sincerely yours,

[*Postscript*:]
Dear Prof. Havelock:

Professor McLuhan is presently in the hospital and he dictated this letter to me over the phone, and asked me to sign it for him. He will be going home tomorrow— good news indeed![2]
Mrs. M. Stewart
Secretary

---

[1]This letter was (incorrectly) addressed to Professor Havelock (b. 1903) at Harvard University, where he taught from 1947 to 1960, latterly as head of the Classics Department; he then moved to Yale University. Havelock had previously taught Classics at Acadia University, Wolfville, Nova Scotia (1926–9), and at Victoria College, University of Toronto (1929–47). His *Preface to Plato* (1963), which is mentioned often in these letters, is described briefly on page 297, note 3.

[2]McLuhan describes his illness in the next letter. On September 23, 1970, Havelock wrote to McLuhan: "Please look after yourself. I still carry with me the feeling that you are a man who works always near the bone, pushing his nerves to the limit."

To John and Eirian Wain

May 25, 1970

Dear John & Eirian:

Am feeling very foolish about the long delay in telling you about having the poems and the novel.[1] The fact is, I have been ill again. This time with a bit of high blood pressure and some kind of arterial clotting. It resulted in many tests and much discomfort and disability. This has not prevented Corinne and me and Liz from having a great deal of pleasure with the books.

I want to get down to specifics as soon as possible—that is, as soon as I get back to the office. This note is going over the telephone to Margaret Stewart. God bless the telephone and Margaret Stewart—and also the Wains, all of them, and may they flourish!

Tell the boys about a little quip I heard recently: "Catch it. Keep it. See what it eats!"

Love to all,
Marshall and Corinne

[1]See next letter.

To John Wain

June 2, 1970

Dear John:

Now that I am up again for a while at least, I want to get down a few words about why I found *The Winter in the Hills* a great delight. I have opened at page 127 at random, and the paragraph beginning: "A few days later . . ." seems to me to possess many of the qualities that make this your best prose. I love the way you manage the light and the spaces, the intervals between your figures. It is done with all the care and richness of my favourite 17th-century painters. As with *The Smaller Sky*, it seems to me that you have taken infinite pains to provide a superb shooting script for a colour film or video.[1]

I am just at the office for a brief spell, trying to catch up on some urgent items. Corinne is going to pick me up shortly and I shall go home for an afternoon in the sun.

I think that you have here, in this new novel, made an ideal double plot, as between the mechanical culture and the old agrarian world. The interplay between these two complementary forms gives an ever growing richness to the narrative. Shall return to this more when a spot of leisure presents itself.

Cordially,
Marshall McLuhan

[1]Wain's novel *A Winter in the Hills* was published in 1970; his collection of poems *The Smaller Sky* was published in 1967.

To Jonathan Miller

June 4, 1970

Dear Jonathan:

I enclose a short essay on the figure-ground relationship[1] of the university and the city.[2] It is another way of approaching the hidden service/disservice environments created by media. This approach may afford you some aid in clarifying the "message" problem. The "message" is, of course, the totality of changes in psyche and society created by any new medium or service environment.

[1]The figure-ground concept, referred to many times in the following letters, is described by McLuhan in his unpublished *The Laws of the Media* (see page 475, note 2) as having been borrowed from gestalt psychology and the Danish psychologist Edgar Rubin, who used it in discussing aspects of visual perception. McLuhan broadens it to embrace all of perception and of consciousness. "All situations are composed of an area of attention (*figure*) and a very much larger [subliminal] area of inattention (*ground*) . . . *Figu*res rise out of, and recede back into, *ground* . . . ; for example, at a lecture the attention will shift from the speaker's words to his gestures, to the hum of the lighting or street sounds, or to the feel of the chair or a memory or association or smell, each new *figure* alternately displaces the others into *ground*. . . . The *ground* of any technology is both the situation that gives rise to it as well as the whole environment (medium) of services and disservices that the technology brings with it. These are side-effects and impose themselves willy-nilly as a new form of culture. 'The medium is the message.'"

[2]Marshall McLuhan, "The University and the City", University of Toronto *Graduate*, vol. III, no. 2 (April 1970).

To Mary Muller-Thym

June 5, 1970

Our Very Dear Mary:

Grand of you to drop me a note. The old blood pressure shot up and a gasket blew! Am now recovering from hospital tests—the cure that kills. They did all the same tests that they had done for the brain operation—pointlessly, needlessly, but devastatingly! All I really needed was an extra day of lying down.

Wish you could find some way of sneaking up here to stay with us for a while.

Cordially,

To Hugo McPherson[1]

June 12, 1970

Dear Hugo:

I want to tell you how very useful your *Hawthorne* has been for me in many ways. Living by a pond in Wychwood Park has led me to take a closer look at

[1]Dr Hugo McPherson (b. 1921), Professor of English at McGill University, had recently published *Hawthorne as Mythmaker* (1969).

[Henry David] Thoreau's *Walden* [1854]. Have in mind to write a *Walden III*.

Have been quite struck by the numerous Harold Innis qualities of David Thoreau. Thoreau had the same ecological concerns as Innis. As with Innis, his ecological vision has been classified as picturesque, or romantic, etc. As you know, perhaps from my study of "An Ancient Quarrel in Modern America", New England inherited a large component of the medieval scholastic concern with metaphysical processes.[2] It would be fun to really probe this matter properly sometime. Meanwhile I am getting my old doctoral dissertation ready for McGraw-Hill publication. It gives me a chance to tie everything together from Cicero to Joyce.

Have just had a very gratifying package from General Electric in New York. They have done a number of "brain waves" studies of media differences which, to their amazement, confirmed what they considered to be my hypothesis, that the medium is the message, e.g. "That is, the basic electrical response of the brain is clearly to the media and not to content differences within the TV commercials, or to what *we* in our pre-McLuhan days would ordinarily have called the commercial message. It seems also clear, as suggested by the earlier studies of involvement of eye-movement, that the response to print may be fairly described as active, and composed primarily of fast brain waves while the response to television might be fairly described as passive and composed primarily of slow brain waves."[3]

My contention, via endless illustration, that media transform people is quite consistent with the various meanings of *transport* people.

Have just made my first film. It is in colour. It is 12½ minutes long. It is called "A Burning Would" and concerns the city.[4] I managed to contrive a new kind of sound effect for the visual images, which proved quite effective.

Hope you will give me a shout sometime when you are in town.

---

[2]McLuhan's "An Ancient Quarrel in Modern America" appeared in *The Classical Journal*, vol. 41, no. 4 (January 1946).

[3]From a paper entitled "Electroencephalographic Aspects of Low Involvement: Implications for the McLuhan Hypothesis", delivered to the annual conference of the American Association for Public Opinion Research (at the Hotel Sagamore, Lake George, May 21-3, 1970) by Dr Herbert E. Krugman, manager of corporate public opinion research at the General Electric Company, New York. It was published (under the title "Brain Wave Measurements of Media Involvement") in the *Journal of Advertising Research*, vol. 11, no. 1, February 1971. See also page 411, note 3.

[4]This film, *The Burning Would*—conceived by Marshall McLuhan and Jane Jacobs, who appeared in it, financed by Sam Sorbata, and shot by Christopher Chapman, as a denunciation of the proposed Spadina Expressway, Toronto (see page 432, note 2)—was shown many times. The title comes from a parody of the witches' prophecy in *Macbeth* in James Joyce's *Finnegans Wake*: "For a burning would is come to dance inane."

To the Globe and Mail[1]

June 17, 1970

Dear Sir:

On Tuesday, June 16th, under the heading: "McLuhan Terms Press Obsolete", you printed Nicholas Cotter's report from Montreal. I want to supply a few facts missed by Mr. Cotter.[2] I did not refer to the press, or any other medium, as obsolete, either at the Association of Industrial Advertisers' luncheon or at the press conference afterwards. Apart from that fact, it is well to note that obsolescence never means the end of anything, but the beginning. Handwriting has been obsolescent since printing and typewriter, but there is a great deal more handwriting done daily now than was ever done before printing, or the typewriter. I spent most of my time at the luncheon describing the General Electric report on its series of media experiments, "Implications for the McLuhan Hypothesis."

Mr. Cotter does not refer to the General Electric experiments but he does attribute to me personally one of the conclusions of the General Electric experimenters in New York "that the viewer and not the message is being transported by the media." Experiments show (employing head-cameras and brain-wave profiles) that: ". . . the basic electrical response of the brain is clearly to the media and not to content differences within the TV commercials, or to what *we* in our pre-McLuhan days would ordinarily have called the commercial message."

It is not easy to convince people that if one describes a process, one is not taking a stand, pro or con. As a Professor of Literature, I am entirely on the side of print. As a person living in an electrical environment of information, I naturally study the effects of this new form on all of us. I do not endorse either electrical technology, or its effects. TV, for example, is a far more virulent pollutant than anything identified so far by the anti-pollution ecologists. The polluting powers of TV have nothing to do with the program content. The massive media effects of a language, Russian, Chinese, English, German, etc. on our entire ways of seeing and feeling are transformed—these effects have nothing to do with anything in particular that is said by a speaker of one of those tongues. The corporate language medium is itself the overwhelming "message". So it is with radio or telephone or TV or any extension of our bodies that will be invented in the future.

Mr. Cotter failed to grasp my exploration of why the advent of colour in advertising and journalism is bringing about the decline of the great magazines of yesteryear. The copy in story lines provided for the new colour medium by people trained in the print medium, simply won't work with colour.

---

[1]This letter was addressed to the Editor, Business Section, *Globe and Mail*, Toronto.
[2]The headlines of this story were "McLuhan terms press obsolete/Color tied to new communications medium".

To Hans Selye[1]

June 17, 1970

Dear Dr. Selye:

What a pity we were so rushed on Monday![2] I enclose my student Thompson's paper on the Japanese MA, or the tactile space of the interval in Japanese culture. Linus Pauling, Heisenberg and company, in speaking of the interval as the chemical bond, are not, I think, aware that the resonant gap or interface that is the chemical bond in quantum mechanics is familiar in many cultures as gap, or discontinuity, as in symbolism.

It occurred to me apropos the General Electric report about the non-impact of "content" that this situation may account for the enormous impediments in teaching and learning processes. For example, the child learns his mother tongue by age three. This is the medium, and its acquisition in so brief a time is a super-human feat when compared to the rest of our learning processes in this life. Language as medium is learned by immersion rather than by packaging, classification or content. And so with all other environmental forms of experience created by human means, from alphabet to satellite. It is the media which *inform* our nervous system, according to the General Electric report, and not their content.[3]

[1]Dr Hans Selye (1907–82), Austrian-born pioneer in the study of "biological stress" in individuals and groups, was Director of the Institute of Experimental Medicine and Surgery, Université de Montréal. In addition to his scientific publications, Selye popularized his concept of stress in several books, including *The Stress of Life* (1956) and *Stress Without Distress* (1974).

[2]McLuhan had visited, and spoken at, Selye's Institute at the Université de Montréal.

[3]In a letter written on the same day as this one, referring to the General Electric experiment—in which a subject's responses to television (described in the Report as presenting reality "minus the feelings") were monitored by means of a tiny electrode at the back of the head—Selye speculated that the EEG (electroencephalographic) responses would have been "vastly different" if, instead of bland TV messages, Krugman had used a series with distinctly different meanings: such as a bland commercial, plus a patient's being told of a three-month life expectancy for cancer, and a person's being told he had won the Irish Sweepstakes. See page 409, note 3; page 422, note 4.

To J.M. Davey, Office of the Prime Minister

June 18, 1970

Dear Jim:

This came like an electric bolt from the blue for a nut—the nut being me! If you start with the last few lines on pages 17 and 18[1], then look at the bottom of page 13, you will know what you are in for. Krugman has validated quantitatively everything I have been saying, even though he doesn't understand very

[1]See page 422, note 4.

much about it. The evidence that *all* media communicate themselves by transforming the participant but fail to convey very much of their supposed "content" applies as much to English or Russian as to print or telephone or TV. It throws a flash of awareness into the mystery of the blocks in the so-called teaching and learning processes.

People have always been able to absorb the media, whether linguistic or material. Their performance in this area is super-human compared to their power to absorb "content". The ability of a child to learn a complex mother tongue by three is a fantastic feat never duplicated again by any other activity of the individual human life. Suzuki's discovery of "learning by immersion" is really the transfer of the learning effort to the media rather than to their content.[2] The implications in politics are as weird as for education and commerce. When I gave a talk in Montreal yesterday to the Association of Industrial Advertisers, the General Electric report findings created a considerable hush and were duly omitted from the press reports.

Just wanted you to have an early look at this for the benefit of your department as well.

[2]The Japanese violinist Shinichi Suzuki believed musical talent could be acquired through immersion from infancy; Suzuki's method of teaching became highly popular in Japan, and in the US in the 1960s. See Shinichi Suzuki, *Nurtured by Love: A New Approach to Education* (1969), translated by Waltraud Suzuki; and Elizabeth Mills, ed., *The Suzuki Concept: An Introduction to a Successful Method of Early Music Education* (1973).

To J.G. Keogh

July 6, 1970

Dear Joe:

Thanks for the review and your concern about my state.[1] In fact, I am rather improved, but there is a good deal of yardage to gain yet.

Want to mention a few things about your review.[2] Am enclosing Fr. Johnstone's piece. He's the first to notice that my approach to media is metaphysical rather than sociological or dialectical. What your review seems to assume is that I *do* have a personal feeling about these things and about my public. (By the way, I only met Pound once for two or three hours at St. Elizabeths Hospital. Pound has a horror of popular culture,[3] which was the occasion of his blue-pencilling a good deal of *The Waste Land*. Much of what he threw out of *The Waste Land* was from the music hall world that Eliot loved. Pound took culture very seri-

[1]See letter to the Wains of May 25, 1970, page 407.

[2]Keogh's review of *Culture Is Our Business* appeared in the September 1970 issue of *Media & Methods*.

[3]This alludes to Keogh's reference, in his review, to Pound's alleged disapproval of *The Mechanical Bride*: Keogh quotes the conclusion to one of Pound's letters to McLuhan (not extant): "Cordially as if descending thru the shades to visit with McL."

ously and phonetically and moralistically. My metaphysical approach is not moral. That is why I get such very great joy from contemplating these forms of culture. Your review overlooks this side of my work and teaching. The language of forms is a source of perpetual joy and discovery that is quite inexhaustible. By the way, the quote on your page 3: "dislocates language into meaning" is from Eliot.

Joe, there is a simply amazing book *And There Was Light* by Jacques Lusseyran published by Heineman (in English), London, 1964. It is a super-sensitive sensory report on the effects of blindness on the total sensorium of this man. He confirms in many, many new ways how the medium is the message. As you know, the theme of *From Cliché to Archetype* (which should be out fairly soon from Viking) is that every new technology scraps the environment created by the preceding one, but at the same time retrieves a very much older mode of experience. Gutenberg scrapped the scribe but retrieved antiquity. Electricity scrapped industrialism and retrieved the occult. [Eric] Havelock's *Preface to Plato* shows how the phonetic alphabet scrapped tribal man but retrieved the primordial role of individual and pre-tribal awareness. Lusseyran reveals how the accident of blindness scrapped one world of sensation only to retrieve a much greater one. He is the pure case of Tiresias, the blind seer.

Your review proceeds in the most conventional mode of classification as a means of attaining knowledge. You cannot speak of the pursuit of the knowledge of forms and of the modalities of sensory space as a passing literary fashion. What had preceded the Symbolist quest for forms was by comparison a mere arrangement of experience according to concept classification. Bogging down in concepts seems to be a perpetual hazard to human life. It has befallen the "new theology" in large measure. To say, therefore, that *Through the Vanishing Point* is "the last of the modern movement that began with Eliot and Joyce" is meaningless, unless we are to think of abandoning the quest for forms altogether. Kenner is merely a commentator and classifier. He is not seeking any new insights into the experience of our time at all. He is happy to limit himself to a parasitic life on those who *do* seek such insights. In other words, he is an academic. I am not a "culture critic" because I am not in any way interested in classifying cultural forms. I am a metaphysician, interested in the life of the forms and their surprising modalities. That is why I have no interest at all in the academic world and its attempts at tidying up experience. I hope you will not get sidetracked into this academic pattern by trying to play their game.

By the way, it is not flattering to say "his observations on the current political scene seems straight out of George Orwell." I have always regarded Orwell as a complete ass, lacking in all perception and understanding. The political scene on which he comments is something that was going on 100 years ago. Apropos my "outrageous puns", have you never considered that the pun is itself a metaphysical technique for "swarming over" the diversity of perception that is in any part of language?

Looking forward to seeing you when you get to Toronto,

Yrs Mac

To O.M. Solandt[1]

July 10, 1970

Dear Omond:

It was good of you to write congratulations, which I now belatedly say to you also![2]

I hadn't thought about the Cambridge aspect. Thanks for sending on word from Lionel Elvin.[3] When I was in Cambridge last year there was nobody around at all.

Looking forward to the get-together when the honours are conferred.

Cordially,

[1]The distinguished Canadian research director Omond McKillop Solandt (b. 1909) received his undergraduate and first graduate degrees (M.D., 1936) from the University of Toronto. He then attended Cambridge University (McLuhan met him there in 1939), becoming a Fellow of Trinity Hall in 1945. During the war he was a leading adviser to the British army on scientific methods and superintendent of the British Army Operational Research Group. Among his appointments when he returned to Canada was that of Chancellor of the University of Toronto, 1965–71. From 1966 to 1972 he was chairman of the Science Council of Canada.

[2]McLuhan and Solandt had recently been appointed Companions of the Order of Canada.

[3]Solandt had just returned from Cambridge, where he had dinner with Lionel Elvin.

To Hans Selye

August 7, 1970

Dear Dr. Selye:

New developments here have immobilized me for the time.[1] Moreover I have been feeling quite a bit better. I was deeply reassured by your telephone comment that I was on the right course of treatment. As for the "stress" that besets my ordinary existence, there is probably little to be done about that short of a withdrawal from the world.

It appears, therefore, that I will not descend upon you this month, but I do look forward to more leisurely chat with you before too long.

At your convenience, would you be so good as to return my medical dossier to Dr. Joseph Moratta?[2]

I hear you have a new book that is to appear shortly.[3] Naturally I look forward to this very much indeed.

[1]McLuhan had received tests and x-rays in Toronto, and in London, Ont., that indicated a narrowing of the carotid artery. A blood-thinner was prescribed to postpone an operation until the following spring—when further x-rays in London showed that collateral circulation had developed. McLuhan describes this in his letter to Dr Selye of July 15, 1971 (see page 433).

[2]Dr J.T. Moratta of St Michael's Hospital, Toronto.

[3]Hans Selye's *Experimental Cardiovascular Diseases* (1970) had just been published. McLuhan had been invited to a *lancement* for it on July 29.

To Richard Kostelanetz[1]

Dear Richard:

I hasten to thank you for your *Possibilities of Poetry*.[2]

How do you tackle the problem of relating Rock and Bob Dylan to the poetic function? The *ground* for all song and dance is language. The *figures* which we experiment with against this *ground* are for the purpose of evoking new perception. Is it possible to discuss Bob Dylan in the context of the English language as *ground*? Since song is inseparable from the same ground, what sort of functions are served by Rock? What sort of awareness is evoked by the work of Bob Dylan, or any of the Rock bands? What sort of effects do these experiments have on the sinews of English? What new relations do they establish towards traditional poetry and prose? Is such dialogue finished? or is it about to begin afresh?

[1]Richard Kostelanetz (b. 1940)—American critic, poet, and editor, the author of many works of non-fiction—wrote *Master Minds: Portraits of Contemporary American Artists and Intellectuals* (1969), which contains chapters on McLuhan, "High Priest of the Electronic Village", and Muller-Thym. He also wrote "A Hot Apostle in a Cool Culture" for *Twentieth Century Magazine*, reprinted in *McLuhan Pro & Con* (1968), edited by Raymond Rosenthal. To *Beyond Left and Right* (1968), edited by Richard Kostelanetz, McLuhan contributed a chapter entitled "Guaranteed Income in the Electric Age".

[2]Richard Kostelanetz ed., *The Possibilities of Poetry: An Anthology of American Contemporaries* (1970).

To Pierre Elliott Trudeau

Dear Mr. Trudeau:

Since the dinner on Friday, November 27th, much of the time I have been down with flu. My first act since recovery is to thank you for the wonderful evening and the incomparable honour which you conferred upon me and my family.[1] Teri and Corinne insist that their lives have an entirely new dimension as a result of that event! Part of the satisfaction, however, was in the assured feeling that each of us was in fact being entirely 'himself'. The events of the next day—the unveiling of the dramatic hat and cloak, the kick-off, and the Alouette triumph[2]—all seemed to be an extended part of the same euphoric experience of our dinner meeting.

Your comments on the political developments in Canada have been recurring in my thoughts. I know some good fruit will come of this, and I shall report to you before too long.

In friendship and esteem,

[1]Prime Minister Trudeau had entertained Marshall, Corinne, and Teri McLuhan, and Mr and Mrs J.M. Davey, for dinner at Le Provençal restaurant in Toronto.
[2]The next day Trudeau performed the kick-off for the Grey Cup Game in Toronto (see page 359, note 1).

To J.G. Keogh

December 9, 1970

Dear Joe:

Thanks for your notes of December 1st. In passing, you mention that the moment of judgment would be a judgment by one's peers. This is indeed a terrifying thought and I am curious to know how you may have come by it.

The *Cliché to Archetype* process (C/A) is Ovid, is Dante, is Joyce (technique of epiphany). I could explain it to you in person in five minutes, but it would take quite a while to write it. It is only just become clear to me. It is the technique of arresting any process momentarily—the double-take, an instant replay—it can be as brief as Pound's "Mauberley". "Not, not surely the mendacities of para-phrase,"[1] or ["] just hint a fault, and haste dislike."[2] This phrase of Pope concerning Atticus is a perfect example of instant metamorphosis.

Thanks for sending the Ellul page. It reminds me to remind you to look at page 19 of Kenner's Joyce—the section on the central Joyce technique of parody.[3] Yeats' essay on the "Emotion of Multitude" in *Essays and Introductions* [1961] is all about this same technique of play-back by means of sub-plot.[4]

Lynn White here Dec 14-19[5]

Yrs Mac

[1]"Not, not certainly, the obscure reveries/Of the inward gaze;/Better mendacities/Than the classics in paraphrase!" From Pound's "Hugh Selwyn Mauberley II".

[2]In the "Epistle to Dr. Arbuthnot" Pope satirizes Joseph Addison (Atticus) as the worst type of critic, who will "Damn with faint praise, assent with civil Leer,/And without sneering, teach the rest to sneer;/Or pleas'd to wound, and yet afraid to strike,/Just hint. a fault, and hesitate Dislike."

[3]Hugh Kenner, *Dublin's Joyce* (1956).

[4]"Emotion of Multitude" is simply a long one-paragraph reflection about plays, in which Yeats writes: "The Shakespearian drama gets the emotion of multitude out of the sub-plot which copies the main plot, much as a shadow upon the wall copies one's body in the firelight. We think of *King Lear* less as the history of one man and his sorrows than as the history of a whole evil time . . . ."

[5]Lynn White, Jr,—who taught in the Department of History, University of California, Los Angeles, and had written *Machina ex Deo: Essays in the Dynamism of Western Culture* (1968)—gave a lecture at the University of Toronto and was a guest at the Centre for Culture and Technology.

To D. Carlton Williams

December 15, 1970

Dear Carl:

Having had word that you are to review *From Cliché to Archetype*, I thought I would venture to mention a few points that came into much clearer focus after the book disappeared from our hands.[1] You know the great gap between stopping writing and the appearance of the book. Very frustrating.

[1]*From Cliché to Archetype* (1970), which McLuhan wrote with Wilfred Watson, examines clichés (figures) and archetypes (grounds) in the context of a wide range of literary examples, and reveals ancient clichés turning into archetypes in our technological age, and the reverse, archetypes turning into clichés. Williams reviewed it in the *University of Toronto Quarterly*, 41, Summer 1972, p. 413.

Cliché appears in many modes. All media whatever are environmental cli-chés. The effect of such surrounds is narcosis or numbing. This is a kind of *arrest* which, mysteriously, results in metamorphosis. Even anaesthesia has this effect. I was told after my long operation that many recent memories would disappear and many older ones would re-appear. This indeed happened. It also happens with the environmental clichés that are media. They scrub, or erase, recent forms and retrieve ancient ones. Print scrapped scribe and schoolmen and retrieved pagan antiquity and primitive Christianity. The electric circuits of recent decades have "scrapped" the old industrial hardware and retrieved the occult. The same electric clichés or environments have tended to diminish private con-sciousness and to restore collective primal forms.

PS. I enclose a sheet of phrases sent to Viking in New York to prompt a panel show discussion.

To Eric McLuhan[1]

December 28, 1970

Dear Eric:

A Blessed New Year, and wish you could be with us right now.

Have been doing a certain amount of work in Ovid apropos *Dubliners*. It is a bit mortifying to discover at this time of day that the technique of metamorphosis is quite simply that of the *arrest*, the interval, whether of space or time or rhythm. It is this that causes the change or metamorphosis. So, even a replay in football acts as a metamorphosis. Wordsworth's famous phrase "poetry is emotion recollected in tranquility" has a very full formula for metamorphosis, and in effect, states the principle as such. Horace Gregory has a paperback on Ovid, Mentor books.[2] His preface has some very useful points when you read very carefully. Page xi mentions "dramatic moments of [their] indecision" as charac-teristic. Page xii "Ovid frequently remarks, 'so it is believed' or presents a story within a story at second-hand." Ovid is the re-teller of tales. It is the re-telling that is the metamorphosis. In *Prufrock* there is a metamorphosis almost every two or three lines. Eliot had just discovered the gimmick and was going flat out. The technique of the arrest is to give not the thing, but the *effect* of the thing. This is the fascination of child behaviour and child art. The child experiences the world in very low definition. SI [sensory input] in LD [low definition], but his SC [sensory closure] is in HD [high definition]. This is the formula for poetic experience and activity. The ordinary person has experience. The poet reports the consequences of the experience rather than the experience itself.

Eliot's essay on Dante explains this technique from Ovid as it is used by Dante

---

[1] At this time Eric McLuhan (see page 314) was an undergraduate at Wisconsin State University.

[2] *Ovid: The Metamorphoses: A Complete New Version by Horace Gregory* (1958) was published as a paperback in 1960. *The Metamorphoses* or *Transformations*—fifteen books, in hexameters, of stories involving changes of shape—was completed by the Roman poet Ovid (43 B.C.–A.D. 17?) in A.D. 8.

(I don't think that Eliot mentions Ovid, but it is pure Ovid).[3] The whole Crump book is now more intelligible.[4] So is symbolism. Symbolism by definition is interruption, arrest, in order to encounter experience in ever new ways. Ovid's first book of *Metamorphoses* is loaded with Finnegan material, including the quarreling brothers, the Prank Queen, and the effects of technologies in the ages of gold, silver, brass, and iron. I was angry at line 125 to see the word for brass, aenea, and it is followed at once by arma. In other words, Virgil's epic about *arma virumque cano*[5] is an epic of the age of brass and of the technical consequences of the age of brass = the Roman empire. What I want to know is why no classical scholar ever points this out. It is too obvious to be ignored, except deliberately. Virgil, by taking off from Ovid, is doing a satire on Rome which must have been enjoyed as a joke from the beginning. The P.Q. item in Ovid 1 is at line 131. It is in the age of iron "men now spread sails to the winds . . . men lived on plunder . . . Guest was not safe from host . . ." At line 180 or so you have the image of media as environments given in the form of the giants with the hundred hands able to clutch everything at once.[6] Ovid is a history of technology. When Lynn White was here I asked him if he had ever thought of Ovid in this way. He said he had not, but volunteered that this would explain why Ovid was so important in the Middle Ages. White's visit was quite pleasant. He is a large, jovial, blustery politician cum scholar. He gave good talks for everybody, including us.[7]

There is a book by Charles Reich called *The Greening of America* (Random House).[8] It is a left-wing job which does a quick tour of intellectual changes. His "Consciousness III" is really just the effects of the electric age, especially the TV age. On page 167 he has a prize misinterpretation of "the medium is the message" where he assumes that I simply mean that the medium has no content, as with the electric light. It will serve as a useful quote in the revision, which I am gradually working at. The electric light as a medium and message combined is clearly an environment that includes the viewer as content. The same however is true of all other media, as with fish in water—all media which surrounds or environments that use not only everybody but all earlier media as their content. Hence the metamorphosis.

The *Cliché to Archetype* thing could have been so much better if I had been able to do it alone and to have used the rhetorical figures as ideal examples of C/A. We really will have to get down to text and creases in order to cinch the full implications of frustration and hang-up and arrest as the metamorphic moment

---

[3]Part of T.S. Eliot's short book *Dante* (1929) discusses Dante's imagery and allegorical method. There is no mention made of Ovid.

[4]Marjorie Crump, *The Epyllion from Theocritus to Ovid* (1931).

[5]The opening words of the *Aeneid*: "I sing of arms and the man."

[6]These references are to the Loeb Classical Library edition of Ovid's *Metamorphoses* (1916; 2nd edn 1921), translated by Frank Justus Miller.

[7]See page 416, note 5.

[8]For a description of Reich's *The Greening of America* (1970), see page 422, note 3.

of epiphany. It helps to explain why illness is metamorphic. Insofar as an illness halts any given pattern of action, it ensures a replay, resulting in new kinds of action. An anaesthetic is a metamorphic arrest. By stopping action and pain, it ensures that the pent-up or arrested pains and experience will be spread out over a long period to come in a series of metamorphoses. Eliot was fascinated by anaesthetics as types of the metamorphic moment.[9]

One of the things that White mentioned apropos papyrus was that there seems to have been a blight or disease that destroyed the papyrus plant except in Ethiopia where papyrus has continued. Perhaps the pollution of the lower Nile by city life ended papyrus. White was quite interested in the possibilities of relating papyrus and the Roman road. Apropos the eunuch in scripture (Acts of the Apostles) who was being read to as he rode in his chariot, White mentioned that the Roman roads developed a marble-like surface which required extreme expense and skill to maintain. Also they ended iron-shod horses for such roads. In short, as the road went into HD, it put too much strain on surrounding LD technologies and skills and became impossible. This is a fascinating approach which suggests all sorts of new means of study. White pointed to the Roman road as "horizontal masonry walls" much as we talk about elevators as vertical streets.

White mentions pictures on the walls of Pompeii. No, he referred to the ruins of Pompeii, where the streets still have the stone tracks for chariot wheels. These tracks were made deep enough not only to guide the wheels, but to serve as water drains.

We had tried to reach you by telephone from time to time. On Sunday the wires were all jammed—no calls would go through. I have dictated the above by telephone, with Mrs. Stewart taking it down.

I have looked at the preface to the I Ching translation by James Legge (Dover paperback, page xvx). Legge writes that the key to the book "which I had unconsciously acted on in all my translations of other classics, namely, that the written characters of the Chinese are not representations of words, but symbols of ideas, and that the combination of them in composition is not a representation of what the writer would say, but of what he thinks."[10] That is to say, that the Chinese characters are presented not as SI, but as SC. The characters are not the thing but the *effect* of the thing. This explains in one sentence the entire interest of Fenollosa for Pound.[11] It also explains in one sentence the entire nature of Haiku.

Love,
Dad

[9]See page 326, note 8.

[10]James Legge's 1874 translation of *I-Ching* (*Book of Changes*), the standard one, was reissued in a Dover paperback edition in 1963. The quotation is from the "Translator's Preface".

[11]Ernest Fenollosa (1853–1908) was an American Orientalist whose essay "The Chinese Written Character as a Medium for Poetry", with its discussion of the ideogram, made a deep impression on Pound. In 1913 and after, Fenollosa's widow entrusted Pound with her husband's notebooks, from which the influential *Cathay* (1915) was developed—described as "Translations by Ezra Pound, for the most part from the Chinese of Rihaku (Japanese for Li Po), from the notes of the late Ernest Fenollosa . . ."

1971

To Peter C. Newman[1]

January 7, 1971

Dear Peter:

It was a most gratifying surprise to read the *Star* editorial of December 30th, "McLuhan, hurrah". The writer made some points that would be valid for any writer. James Joyce discovered that it was possible to be a "promising" young man in Dublin. Anybody could have a real career as a "promising" person. The moment, however, that any signs of accomplishment occurred, the honeymoon was over. Bitterness set in. He had to leave. Exile, physical or psychic, seems to be a necessary feature of the writer's existence. In my own case, my interest in popular culture as art form arouses uneasiness in many quarters. Manipulators of these arts seem to panic when their efforts are regarded seriously.

By the way, I thought the John Sewell "Diary" piece in yesterday's *Globe & Mail* [Toronto] a most remarkable example of analysis of the pathos of the executive or the politician in our world.[2] The mere act of assuming office isolates the occupant and alienates him from the people he desires to help. At the same time there is a growing demand on the part of the publics so alienated to share the decision-making process. Would it not be possible to have a series of such pieces from many quarters of the community?

Best wishes for 1971.   (dictated by telephone)

P.S. Thank you for your letter of December 30th which arrived today after the above letter had been written. Now that I know you wrote the article as well, I can thank you directly. Let's have lunch before too long.

---

[1]Peter C. Newman (b. 1929), the well-known newspaper and magazine columnist, historian, and author of numerous bestselling books, was at this time Editor-in-Chief of the *Toronto Star*.

[2]John Sewell (b. 1940)—who was first elected Alderman for the City of Toronto in 1969 and was Mayor from 1978 to 1980—was at this time writing a column, called "City Hall Diary", for the Toronto *Globe and Mail*; the one referred to was headed "A new alderman discovers flaws in the power game" (January 6, 1971).

To Etienne Gilson[1]

January 19, 1971

Dear Professor Gilson:

My interest in Symbolist poetry from Poe to Valéry inspired my interest in the study of media. Symbolism starts with effects and goes sleuthing after causes. With the media we have massive effects and little study of causes since the user

---

[1]See page 186, note 1.

of the media, whether a language or the electric light, is the "content" of the media. As content, we have almost no awareness of our surround. As somebody said: "We do not know who discovered water, but we are fairly sure that it was not a fish."

Ovid [i.e., the Ovidian tradition] made a great comeback with the symbolist techniques in poetry since he too was concerned with understanding changes that could be programmed. Joyce, Pound, and Eliot use Ovid pervasively and technically. It was my study of these men that made me aware that the tracking backward from effects to hidden causes, to the reconstruction of mental states and motives, was a basic pattern of culture from Poe to Valéry. That is why I mentioned the fifteen books of Ovid in relation to Darwin. Is it not the case that Darwin is dealing with effects for which the causes are hidden and remote? Does this not put him somewhat in the position of the Symbolist for whom effects minus causes constitute the challenge to pattern recognition?

I leave the volume of Harold Innis with you since he too began the study of media as makers of new species of behaviour and organization.[2] His initiating this program in economic history baffled and alienated his colleagues and his readers. In my own attempts at understanding media I have discovered a uniform distaste in even my friendly readers and critics for the attempt to discover causality of any kind in the environmental action of media on man or society. I have found that scientists and students regard causes as mere concepts or categories to be described and classified. I would much welcome light on the causes for the non-interest in causes.

[2]Harold Innis, *The Bias of Communication* (1951; reprinted with an Introduction by Marshall McLuhan, 1964).

To Edward T. Hall January 21, 1971

Dear Ned:

Happy New Year to yez and your family!

We had a very delightful visit from Lynn White here at the Centre recently. Among the many themes that arose was the whole question of the wide assimilation of optimism concerning technical innovation. In his book *Machina Ex Deo* his theme is that it was the medieval Christian optimism about human nature that released the flood of technical innovation that we think of as modern.[1] The only person I know of who discusses this question for North America is Leo Marx in *The Machine in the Garden.*[2] Apropos the response to my own writing, I am always baffled by the assumption that "if it happens it ought to happen", and further "if it can happen, it should happen." My own avoidance of value judgments about the effects of technologies is based on practical experience. Such opinions simply derail all further discussion of the nature of technology.

[1]Lynn White Jr., *Machina ex Deo: Essays in the Dynamism of Western Culture* (1968).
[2]Leo Marx, *The Machine in the Garden: Technology and the Pastoral Ideal in America* (1964).

On page 167 of *The Greening of America* Charles Reich notes that "the medium is the message means that there is no content in any medium."[3] This statement is actually one of the few useful remarks that has ever come to my attention about anything I have written. It enables me to see that the user of the electric light, or a hammer, or a language, or a book, is the content. As such, there is a total metamorphosis of the user by the interface. It is the metamorphosis that I consider the message.

I enclose a copy of Herbert Krugman's testing of my hypothesis, as he understands it. He too revealed an unexpected feature of the media to me on pages 17-18.[4] Electric media literally translated us into angels. On the phone "we are there" and "they are here", and so with radio and TV. Angelism[5] and the occult alike are the by-products of electronics. Ecology is incidental to that.

I have been trying to penetrate the causes for the lack of interest in causation in modern science and culture (at least prior to Sputnik and ecology). I enclose a note on the strange way in which the Symbolist period made a clean break between effects and causes in order to study the effects as containing all the causes. This is the basis of the aesthetic of T.S. Eliot, and James Joyce, and everybody from Poe to Valéry. I suppose that Darwin as much as Sherlock Holmes was in the same situation so far as causation is concerned. He had a lot of effects and no conceivable causes save those exceedingly remote and inaccessible. So he settled for natural selection and serendipity.

Etienne Gilson is currently giving a series of lectures here on Darwin's total lack of interest in evolution. Typically, Gilson offers no cause for everybody interpreting Darwin as an evolutionist. As a historian he is content to explain in detail why Darwin shunned the entire issue. Personally I have noted that Darwin's divisions of his *Origins* correspond to the divisions of Ovid's *Metamorphoses*. Without detailed study I can say that it is only natural that an English gentleman of his period would have thought constantly of Ovid when thinking of

[3]In *The Greening of America* (1970), to illustrate an example of "Marshall McLuhan's thinking", Reich offers two descriptions of a Father's Day. In the first the Father describes his struggles with traffic, his hurried lunch, his endless conversations with strangers; in the second he states his official function, "lawyer". Reich asks why the second description is more often accepted as "truth", while the first is repressed. "McLuhan's answer is that a medium itself tends to be overlooked because it has no content. A light bulb, he says, has no content. The content of the father's day is being a lawyer, the purpose of his activity. The medium, however, is the father's actual activities during the day. And, as McLuhan says, the medium is the message, although we don't know it."

[4]On pages 17-18 of his paper (see page 409, note 3) Krugman stated: "In short, *television man*, the *passive media audience*, is *an active but clumsy participant in life*, while *print man*, the *active media audience, is a selective, less active and more mature participant in life* . . . McLuhan was aware of the difference while none of our mass communication theory was relevant. . . . the *old* [communication] *theory* was concerned with the fact that the *message was transported*. The new theory must be concerned with the fact that *the viewer is transported, taken on a trip*, an *instant trip*—even to the moon and beyond."

[5]"Angelism" and "Discarnate Man" (separation from flesh) appear frequently in McLuhan's writings in this period to convey the disembodied aspect imposed on humans by electronic communication.

mutations. Another topic that I wanted to raise concerns the current dispute between public transit and private motorist. My suggestion is that the real hangup concerns the very special sense of space (Yellow Submarine style) which the car provides for the American psyche. I don't think that the issue is really one of convenience or practicality so much as psychic security for a troubled ego.

Would love to have your meditations on this one. The car is perhaps even more related to the iconic image of the lonely cowboy which seems to have been transformed also to the motorbike and the "easy rider."

To Ernest Sirluck   February 3, 1971

Dear Ernest:

I had thought that you had indicated a preference that we use the Shaarey Zedek talk rather than the Inaugural Address, since the Inaugural address has already appeared in the *Manitoba Alumni Journal*. Does this present any complications at this stage if we use only the Shaarey Zedek piece? Certainly, you will have as many off-prints as you wish. Proofs will be sent to you before publication.[1]

Apropos the joke file—alas! My stories exist as one-line reminders, on backs of various sheets and envelopes and are not in narrative form. It would take a long time to make them available.[2] However, I have written a letter to McGraw-Hill, asking them to send you a copy of their *Handbook of Modern Humour*, which should be useful. Right now, the best I can do is to send you the last joke I heard concerning the Scot out walking. When he came to an intersection, there had just been a motor crash, and bleeding and groaning and dying victims lay scattered about. He poked one of them with his cane, and asked: "Has the insurance adjuster been here yet?" The victim moaned: "No—" The Scot asked: "Do ye mind if I lie down beside ye?"

If you tell two or three stories of somewhat different character and then add the remark, in serious tone: "Of course, all funny stories are based on grievances of groups and individuals", there follows a deep silence during which everyone tries to think of a story that disproves this statement. Then you can tell two or three bi-lingual or Newfie jokes to illustrate ethnic and minority grievances that are always embodied in funny stories. This permits you to switch into any topic whatever as your main address.

I enclose a footnote to the medium is the message

Yrs Marshall

[1]The two addresses referred to are those Sirluck gave at Shaarey Zadek Synagogue, Winnipeg, on November 21, 1970, and his inaugural address as President of the University of Manitoba. The Shaarey Zadek address, "Speech to Canadian Friends of the Hebrew University", was published in the *Explorations* supplement to the *Varsity Graduate*, Spring 1971.

[2]Sirluck had asked McLuhan for some jokes to use in the many speeches he was having to give as a university president.

To Sheila Watson

February 17, 1971

Dear Sheila:

Liz has told us about the publication of her poems.[1] She, of course, is ecstatic, and we are very grateful to you for your pains and thoughtfulness. Moreover, we are looking forward to seeing the poems! Liz reports that she has been appointed as an instructor in Art History at Fordham for this coming year. She seems somewhat awed by this herself. Am unable to say how Eric is making out at Wisconsin except that he is toiling. He reports that his second-term students seem apathetic. Do you think that the role-playing of the "hippie" world may suddenly prove too exhausting to sustain? Or perhaps, they may decide to do an impersonation of the "squares" they might have been? Currently there is an act going on Toronto streets with nuns and Greek Orthodox priests being impersonated in order to promote begging. The Mendicants are back!

We did a video tape here of Ann Yeats and Walter Starkie, talking about Synge and the Abbey and many things Irish. They had been attending the Irish "Seminar" that also brought Buckminster Fuller and W.H. Auden here recently. It has been a wild Irish time indeed . . . a regular Donnybrook![2] I had to go off to lecture in Syracuse amidst the snow-drifts, in the very middle of it.

Apropos the French request for a note on Wyndham Lewis, I was wondering about doing a short piece on his mis-naming of "the eye" and its world. When Lewis opts for eye values and rationality and civilization, he was at the same time creating and sponsoring, graphically and verbally, art forms that are audile-tactile. Do you think that he really understood that icons and bounding lines are not visual but audile-tactile? Did he understand that "touch" is the acoustic interval? The other point I had in mind is the characters of *The Human Age* as *angels*. Electrically, it is the sender who is sent, whether on the telephone, or on radio, or TV. We are transported electrically and bodily. Thus the people of the Magnetic City are angels, literally. Good or bad, disembodied intelligences. Lewis seems to have grasped this, perhaps as early as *The Enemy of the Stars?*[3]

---

[1]Fifteen poems by Elizabeth McLuhan were published in the first issue of *white pelican* (Winter 1971), which Sheila Watson edited. They were included in Elizabeth McLuhan's *Routes/Roots* (1974).

[2]This was a centenary celebration of John Millington Synge (1871–1909) and Jack. B. Yeats (1871–1957)—the brother of William Butler Yeats—at St Michael's College from February 11 to 14, 1971, organized by Robert O'Driscoll. It was attended by Ann Yeats (b. 1919), the daughter of W.B. Yeats; the critic Walter Starkie (b. 1894); Buckminster Fuller (see page 308, note 1); the actor Jack MacGowran (1918–73); and W.H. Auden (1907–73). MacGowran and Auden, with McLuhan, took part in a panel on "Theatre and the Visual Arts". (O'Driscoll described this in the *Canadian Forum*, May 1981).

[3]*The Enemy of Stars* is a play by Wyndham Lewis that appeared in *Blast*, 1914, and was reprinted in 1932.

Jonathan Miller's McLuhan, *which was published in January 1971, was surprisingly hostile. Miller adopted this tone, he explains in his Introduction, "partly I must admit because I am in almost complete disagreement with the main body of McLuhan's ideas, but partly too in order to lend a certain rhetorical vigour to the discussion." The first half of the book is an extended critique of what Miller saw as the "cultural nostalgia" of the "conservative Agrarianism" expressed in McLuhan's articles of the 1940s, such as "An Ancient Quarrel in Modern America"* (The Classical Journal, *vol. 41, no. 4, January 1946) and "The Southern Quality"* (Sewanee Review, *vol. 55, no. 1, July 1947). The other half sets out to demolish McLuhan's insights into mass culture and the media—while relating them to works that had influenced him—by examining and refuting individual assertions. Miller dismisses McLuhan's "mosaic approach" as offering "no fixed point from which the reader can take his critical bearings." He concludes by acknowledging McLuhan's "important place in the history of cultural criticism" on the strength of* The Mechanical Bride, *and the value of* Explorations *in leading many critics to become aware of the fact "that they had never before intelligently used their physical senses." He also recalls "the intense excitement with which I first read McLuhan in 1960" and how this changed his understanding of print, the telephone, photographs, radio, and TV. "And yet I can rehabilitate no actual truth from what I read. Perhaps McLuhan has accomplished the greatest paradox of all, creating the possibility of truth by shocking us with a gigantic system of lies." See page 440, note 2, for Martin Esslin's comment on this final sentence, and note 1 for his own critique of Miller's book.*

To Frank Kermode[1]

March 4, 1971

Dear Kermode:

My colleague, Barry Nevitt, concurs with me in wishing that the enclosed letter get to somebody who has reviewed Miller's *McLuhan*.[2] Perhaps it should be the editor of *The Listener*,[3] or the *Times Literary Supplement*. Please feel free to copy this for trial distribution. I don't know what your attitude toward my work is, nor do I know what your thought about Miller's book is. Miller is debating

[1] Frank Kermode (see page 425, note 1) was Editor of the Fontana Modern Masters Series in which Jonathan Miller's *McLuhan* appeared.

[2] The "enclosed letter"—entitled "McLuhan Critics of the World Unite"—was published over McLuhan's name in the *Toronto Star* on March 16, 1971, and in a shortened form, over Barrington Nevitt's name, in *The Listener* on May 6.

[3] A review by Alan Ryan of *McLuhan* ("McLuhan's Something") had appeared in *The Listener* on January 14. On the whole, Ryan sided with Miller, saying that "True to his contempt for linear thinking and for the techniques of logical inference, McLuhan's recent writings amount to a series of frantic gestures. He doesn't describe, analyse and explain: he simply points—and he points to a quite extraordinary range of phenomena. . . . If there are connections, it's up to the reader to make them. . . ." Seven letters to the editor of *The Listener* followed this review, including the one by McLuhan cited in the note above, two others by McLuhan (August 11, see page 435; and October 8, see page 442), and one by Miller (September 9). In addition, an article on McLuhan by Miller appeared in the column "Views" on July 15, 1971.

at a juvenile level. He is not inquiring nor discussing along the lines I have opened up. He assumes that our sensory order is not violatable by new technologies. This is a universal assumption of our entire Establishments, humanist and scientific alike. Merely to challenge it creates panic, for it means that we have polluted not just the physical but the psychic and perceptual order of our societies without questioning our procedures. To argue whether there is any quantitative proof of this, is part of the panic. Nobody *wants* any proof. Most people desperately don't want it.

Herbert Krugman, of General Electric Research Laboratories, recently provided ample proof of the validity of the hypothesis, using encephalographic and head camera means of testing the responses to various media. Being an ordinary run-of-the-mill psychologist, he was flabbergasted to discover that there was no brain-wave response to the content of these media, but a very large and diversified response to the diverse media themselves. The last thing in the world that anybody wants is proof of anything I am saying. The evidence is plentiful for those who are interested. The poetry of the Symbolists, from Baudelaire until now, is massive and explicit testimony to sensory change.

As you know from many sources (e.g. Linus Pauling's *The Nature of the Chemical Bond*), there are no connections in matter, only resonant intervals. Such is the nature of *touch*. It is like the space between the wheel and the axle. The very scientists who hold to this quantum theory of matter refuse to admit its relevance in the handling of evidence. In discussing these things, they are themselves completely non-tactile people. The scientific establishment is literate in the sense of being unconsious of the effects of a visual culture in imposing visual standards of evidence—Othello's "ocular" proof. Having established the resonant discontinuity of the material world, they still cling to the old pattern of continuous and connected or logical processing.

Speaking of *processing*, it is impossible to have a point of view while following or discerning a process. It would be like trying to have a point of view while swimming. Yet, most people still try to achieve static positions and concept patterns as a basis for study. Naturally, this method dictates what shall be studied. If I have a point of view about the human condition as a result of investigating the effects of media, it is simply that people are somnambulist. They seem to be happily hypnotized by their own extensions of themselves. I suppose the traditional word for this is idolatry: "They became what they beheld and bowed the knee to themselves."[4]

Sincerely yours,
Marshall McLuhan

P.S. I might add that a copy of the Krugman report was sent to Jonathan Miller on June 10, 1970.

[4]The quoted sentence has not been identified. However, it combines William Blake (". . . they become what they beheld", a phrase that recurs in *Jerusalem*, Chapter 2, Plate 36) and Byron ("I have not loved the world, nor the world me;/I have not flatter'd its rank breath, nor bow'd/To its idolatries a patient knee", *Childe Harold's Pilgrimage*, III, stanza 113). Kermode wrote a friendly and sympathetic reply to McLuhan (May 12), saying that Miller "underwent a sort of conversion in the process of reading for the book, and the outcome was something that neither he nor I expected. Why he doesn't want to tell you about this himself I can't say."

To J.M. Davey
Office of the Prime Minister

March 8, 1971

Dear Jim:

We have naturally been delighted by the great Pierre and Margaret wedding event.[1] Surely there is nothing in the history of democratic politics to match the *mise en scène* of this event. It was not only a personal but a political triumph, putting both the opposition and the media in Pierre's pocket, as it were. The media people have to be grateful for being duped, since their unpreparedness was very much part of the show.

In this very connection I have a new essay, a copy of which I am enclosing, explaining that, why, and how the user is the content of any medium or environment.[2] I am still working on the many features of this situation, and am quite at a loss to explain why I had been unable to see so obvious a fact before. When Trudeau "uses" the media, as in the current nuptial drama, *he* is their content. When they use him, *they* are the content. It is sort of reciprocal hi-jacking. Only yesterday I was reading a chapter on "Judgment and Truth in Aquinas" by my friend, Fr. Owens, here at the Medieval Institute.[3] He concludes: "They involve the traditional Aristotelian view that the cognitive agent itself becomes and is the thing known. . . . Its structure comes from the thing known, and not from any apriori in the intellect."

It turns out then, that my communication theory is Thomistic to the core. It has the further advantage of being able to explain Aquinas and Aristotle in modern terms. We are the content of anything we use, if only because these things are extensions of ourselves. The meaning of the pencil, or the chair I use is the interplay between me and these things. Again, the *message* of these things is the sum of the changes that result from their social use. Thus, I have added two features to "the medium is the message", namely the content and the meaning. Perhaps Pierre Juneau or somebody at C.R.T.C. would like to have this essay apropos the problem of "Canadian content"?[4] The consequence for the discussion of the problem of Canadian content for the media is drastically simplified by noticing that the user is the content. If Canadians use or watch American programs or drive American cars, it is the Canadians who are the content of these things. The *meaning* is in the resulting interplay or dialogue between Canadians and these things, but there can be no question that the Canadian user of American things is the content of these things. The meaning and the message are

---

[1]Pierre Trudeau and Margaret Sinclair were married on March 5, 1971.

[2]Marshall McLuhan, "Putting on the Media: The User is the Content" (PAC). Apparently this was never published.

[3]Joseph Owens, "Judgement and Truth in Aquinas", *Medieval Studies* 33 (1970).

[4]Pierre Juneau (b. 1922) was chairman of the Canadian Radio-Television Commission, which required that private broadcasters increase the Canadian content of their programs, especially in the area of music.

something else. It is unfortunate that the C.R.T.C. ever involved itself in the question of content, especially since it does not understand the nature of media at all, except as hardware.

A note on hi-jacking apropos media and politics: in our book [*Take Today*] *The Executive as Dropout*, which is close to being sent to the publisher, we have a section on the nature of hi-jacking in business and in politics. Realizing that the very nature of hi-jacking is related to new services and environments, I asked a New York tycoon whether there were any parallels to hi-jacking in business. He replied at once that the bigger the business, the easier it is to hi-jack it. He said the biggest banks in the world today are being sued by their own share-holders for misallocation of funds. The Penn Central discovered that its entire funds had been appropriated for non-transportation uses. This is done in the bookkeeping division of the firm, unbeknown to the rest of the operation. It is almost impossible to check. Hence the larger the operation, the less it knows about whether it is going "to land." Cities are hi-jacked every day by developers who simply pressure the bureaucracy into "landing" in areas favourable to the developers. Countries can be hi-jacked as readily as a big business.

It is a useful metaphor since it really concerns the problems of the new service environments as created by jet planes at high speed. The question arises whether the passengers could agree to be hi-jacked by democratic process. Could everybody on the plane agree to go to Cuba instead of Miami? This raises the problem of swinging blocks of votes as a form of hi-jacking. Historically, the creation of the C.P.R. could be considered under the aspect of hi-jacking the country. Pollution is another form of taking over of an entire service environment, whether of land, water, or air and perverting its uses. If some private enterprise in fact *uses* land, water, or air, it is that enterprise that becomes the *content* of the environment in question, just as the hold-up man on the plane, by assuming the use of the plane to himself, becomes the content of the plane by usurping the role of all the other passengers.

Since the user as *content* is not a figure of speech but a basic dynamic and cognitative relationship, I think you will find that it can be pushed all the way as a means of orientation in media, economics and politics. I suggest that it can be the basis for a complete restatement of political and economic realities in the information age of the wired planet.

[*Indecipherable handwritten closing*]

To Claude Bissell

March 23, 1971

Dear Claude:

On Sunday I made the biggest discovery of my life. It happened while I was working on the preface for Innis's *Empire and Communications* which the University of Toronto Press is bringing out.[1] Put in a word, the discovery is this: for 2500 years the philosophers of the Western world have excluded all technology from the matter-form in entelechy treatment.[2] Innis spent much of his life trying to explain how Greek culture had been destroyed by writing and its effects on their oral tradition. Innis also spent much of his life trying to draw attention to the psychic and social consequences of technologies. It did not occur to him that our philosophy systematically excludes *techne* from its meditations.[3] Only natural and living forms are classified as hylo-morphic.[4]

Entelechy or energeia is the recognition of the new actuation of power brought about by any arrangement of components whether in the atom or the plant or the intellect. Pens and swords and ships and sealing wax which actuate human potential, creating specific new patterns of energy and form of action—these, along with all technologies whatever, have for 2500 years been excluded from philosophical study. They were *written off*. That is, the Greeks and their followers to the present time have never seen fit to study the entelechies generated by human arts. It is quite otherwise in the Orient, as you know. In the electric age when the actuation of human energies has gone all the way into the organic structure of life and society, we have no choice but to recognize the entelechies of technology. This is called *ecology*. Meantime we have the entire Western establishment against the recognition of the entelechies of technology. The entire academic establishment will fight it for centuries to come simply because it has a stake in the old ignorance.

I hope you will get around to commenting on my suggestion for a non-stop university seminar where everybody could table his ignorance rather than his knowledge. This, again, is the main hang-up of the academic person. He is proud of his knowledge and eager to hide his ignorance. This foible forbids discoveries. The biggest grants from the biggest Foundations are given on the understanding that they will lead to nothing. If anyone were to discover anything on a grant, chaos would ensue.

Naturally, I was interested in Warren Gerard's report on his interview with

---

[1]McLuhan wrote an eight-page Foreword to the revised edition (1972) of Harold A. Innis's *Empire and Communications*, which was first published in 1950.

[2]In a letter to J.M. Davey written the day before, McLuhan explained this discovery as "the fact that Western philosophers have never considered artefacts or technologies as entelechies." Entelechies are potentialities that become actual.

[3]*techne* (Gk.), art.

[4]Hylomorphic: pertaining to hylomorphism, the doctrine that primordial matter is the first cause of the universe and combines with forms to produce bodies.

you in the Monday *Globe & Mail*.[5] I was curious about why he was so eager to stress that "McLuhan was at the peak of his fame" before my brain operation. A great many people have taken up this ploy of suggesting that "McLuhan has passed the peak of his fame." Three years ago the ploy was "McLuhan was a late starter." Now the ploy is "he is an early finisher."[6]

I think you managed to scramble some of the facts about our chat at Cambridge [Mass.].[7] My motive in returning to Canada was then, as now, my fear of acceptance. I knew there was no danger of this in Canada. It is very salutary to have a daily charade of human malice and stupidity mingled with warmth and insight. In the U.S., surrounded with an atmosphere of success and acceptance, I could have lost my bearings very quickly.

I am invited every week to accept academic appointments in the U.S.A., and assailed with requests to travel to every corner of the globe. Shall probably accept the invitation to open the Salzburg Music Festival in August,[8] also the request for a series of Japanese appearances on TV in July.

Do you foresee any difficulties about the continuance of the Centre for Culture and Technology after your retirement? Perhaps we might have a word about this sometime.

Best wishes with the new house.

Yrs Marshall

[5]Warren Gerard, "The Troubled Years: Claude Bissell Looks Back", *Globe & Mail*, Toronto, March 23, 1971. This interview took place three months before Bissell's already announced retirement as President of the University of Toronto.

[6]McLuhan was reacting to a passage in the article that carried no such implication. Explaining that, while Bissell was at Harvard University in 1967–8 as Visiting Professor of Canadian Studies, McLuhan was also on a sabbatical at Fordham University, Gerard wrote: "It had been a difficult year for Prof. McLuhan. He had undergone major surgery for a brain tumor. He was also at a peak of his fame, and he could name his price at any university in the United States. Instead, he went to Cambridge to see Dr. Bissell."

[7]Bissell's meeting with McLuhan in Cambridge, Mass., was primarily to discuss, and negotiate, McLuhan's return to the University of Toronto. Bissell considered "the retention of Marshall McLuhan for his university and indeed for Canada as a major administrative obligation." After "good conditions" were established, and McLuhan agreed to return, Bissell suddenly realized that "negotiations were so easy in a sense because Marshall was deeply committed to Toronto and to Canada."

[8]In a letter of July 19, 1971 to John Wain, McLuhan says he is attending a radio and TV conference in Salzburg on music in the twentieth century.

To John Wain

April 2, 1971

Dear John:

It's been quite a while since I've heard from you. What's afoot with you? Have you begun to get down to the Samuel Johnson project?[1] Here, as usual, I

[1]Wain's biography, *Samuel Johnson*, was published in 1974.

have far too many irons in the fire, but there is never a dull moment. For example, this morning apropos the Nixon cancellation of the Calley life sentence, I suddenly realized that the electric media create audience participation on such a scale that in any public trial the audience is the criminal.[2]

For the last few weeks I have been exploring the fact that in all communication the user of whatever medium is the content. This turns out to be merely an ancient Aristotelian observation that the cognitive agent itself becomes and is the thing known. While noticing the enormous hiatus of media study in the Western world, I began to back-track a bit. Discussion with philosophers here revealed the obvious. The Greeks had provided entelechies or had studied the patterns of energy relating to natural forms, but had ignored the same where art and technology were in play. This gave me the main clue. The Greeks and their successors regarded Nature (*phusis* or physics) as an artefact. Having entelechized this massive product of their own literate technology, they never turned to the subsidiary technologies that were the extensions of man. However, they would have admitted at once, if asked, that any actuation of human potential generates an entelechy or pattern of energy that is new. It was not until Poe and Baudelaire that these patterns began to be studied. This was after industrialism had already abolished most of the Greek and Roman *Natura*. With the coming of electric technology whatever remained of Greek Nature was scrapped so that today we are back where they started with primitive Existence. They had reared the figure of Nature on the ground of Existence. They had done it by classification. The new ecology will use other means.

I enclose an item that began in the *London Times*.[3] It baffles me. I never was *in*—why am I out with such a group as is cited? Can you make any sense of this kind of ploy? Since I am entirely cut off from oral means of communication either with England or with the U.S.A., I would appreciate your thoughts or discoveries regarding this type of item. Is the Jonathan Miller book out of the same camp?

[2]On March 18, 1968, American soldiers led by Lt. William L. Calley invaded the South Vietnamese hamlet of My Lai, an alleged Viet Cong stronghold, and shot 347 unarmed civilians. When the affair was discovered in 1969 there were prosecutions, and on March 29, 1971, Calley was sentenced to life imprisonment, though the conviction was appealed. In September 1974 it was overturned by a federal court and Calley was released.

[3]McLuhan had read a reprint in the Toronto *Globe and Mail* (April 2, 1971) of a London *Times* article by Tim Devlin (headed, presumably by the *Globe*, "McLuhan Out?"), saying that "the vogue for Marshall McLuhan [along with that for Chairman Mao, Che Guevara, Herbert Marcuse, and other revolutionary heroes] appears to be over." (This finding was based on a reported decline in university-bookshop sales of books by these writers. Students were turning to fantasy and poetry.) To this letter from McLuhan, Wain replied that fashion affects 20% of the consuming public—that the other 80% "go for what they like". He added, "I think you are wrong to say you were never an "in" name with this swayable 20%", and that his reputation was stable with the rest.

To William Davis[1]

April 26, 1971

Dear Mr. Davis:

As a man aware of the seventies you know that we live in an information environment. Many of your colleagues, on the other hand, are still locked into the old hardware environment of the nineteenth century. As a man who has a vision of education and dialogue for the seventies, you see it frustrated by the "hardware" merchants. As a man able to meet the local political needs of the wired planet, you deal with men for whom the old specialist "goals" of *moreness* still conceal the scope of the present needs and opportunities of the seventies.

Instead of catching up by *matching* up with the nineteenth century of American cities, Canada has a unique opportunity to *make* cities for the seventies. Making, not matching, is an Ontario possibility lost to the U.S.A. by old hardware rivalry.

The Spadina Expressway is an old hardware American dream of now dead cities and blighted communities.[2] As a man of the seventies you know we need not *match* the American disasters. We can *make our own way.* Your vision of the seventies cannot survive a cement kimono for Toronto.

As a man of the seventies you know that monopolies of knowledge have ceased. Result: Every executive or leader is expendable the moment he turns from announcing the new challenge to performing the old job. By the time he has learned the old job, the new one has fallen into other hands. Under conditions of electric speed, key decisions are made far below the executive level. The *merely* efficient executive eliminates himself at once. Mere concern with efficient traffic flow is a cloacal obsession that sends the city down the drain.

Sincerely yours,
Marchall McLuhan

c.c. to each member of the
Executive Council of Ontario

[1]The Honourable William G. Davis (b. 1929) was Premier of Ontario (1971–1984).

[2]The Spadina Expressway was originally planned as a multi-lane highway to connect Toronto's northern ringroad with the downtown core, thus destroying several inner-city neighbourhoods and ravines (one of them close to McLuhan's house in Wychwood Park). In June 1971 it was stopped at the northern edge of the city; partially completed sections were then redesigned to include an extension of Toronto's subway system.

To William Jovanovich

June 9, 1971

Dear Bill:

I enclose the Russian piece on me from the magazine *Voprosy Literatury* (Problems in Literature). It could possibly be the means of some effective promotion.[1] Flat-out attack on McLuhan by the U.S.S.R. could be of interest to both left and right sympathizers. It is my analysis of the nature of visual culture (Western, civilized and absent-minded, ABCED-minded) as opposed to oral, auditory, acoustic, electronic (pre-literate, tribal, inward, intuitive, Oriental)—my studies of the differences between these two forms—[that] enrages the Marxist world since it explains why they are nineteenth-century people who cannot make it into the twentieth century. Worse, they have never had a nineteenth century and are determined to have one in order to achieve all the consumer advantages.

There have been several books written against me by leftists. All of them scream against my sensory analysis. Personally, I have no theory about these matters, no hypothesis. I simply start backward from the effects to discover the patterns.

It was grand having a tour of your new and very handsome accommmodations and offices, also wish we'd had time for a proper discussion of the communication series.[2] I assume that you are not interested in it and shall shop around a bit.

Expect to keep in touch with Ethel Cunningham, naturally.[3]

Warm regards,

[1]For *Take Today: The Executive as Dropout*, by McLuhan and Barrington Nevitt, which would be published 1972: it was in production at Harcourt Brace Jovanovich. Discussed in *Take Today* are many of the books, concepts (*sensus communis*, figure/ground), and observations that are rehearsed in the previous letters. It is an extensive collection of short and long probes or "Laws", each one with a heading. "It is not a book to be read through," McLuhan wrote in a letter of January 9, 1974 to Gerard Piel, 'but to be sampled and meditated [on] from time to time. . . . Our main concern was to illustrate the numerous flips and reversals which occur when man moves from hardware to software, from the industrial to the electronic age." At a time when the old natural order has been made obsolete by electric communications, "orchestrated programming", and satellites, the executive is advised to drop out of his old organizational structures.

[2]This project never got off the ground.

[3]Ethel Cunningham was McLuhan's and Nevitt's editor.

To Hans Selye

July 15, 1971

Dear Dr. Selye:

You may recall having seen my X-rays concerning the stenosis of the carotid artery.[1] When I went down to London [Ontario] to see Dr. Barnett about it in May, they took some more pictures. The pictures revealed that a large new artery extending over the brain, had formed. Though I am not sure what was meant, I was told that I now had a kind of arterial set-up which was characteristic of tigers. A picture was given to me, a copy of which I enclose. Barnett seemed to regard the arterial development as phenomenal, saying: "You go straight into the medical text books from now on." I am very grateful, regarding it as an answer to prayer.

With every good wish for your work,

[1]See page 414, note 1.

To John Wain

Dear John:

It was naturally a disappointment to learn that you will be in Wales while we are in England. Since the pattern is the same here in Toronto, I am quite able to adjust. Very few stay put here during the summer. That's what makes it the perfect time to be here. Especially on the weekends it is almost pastoral and the car population declines very noticeably. I think it would be utterly unreasonable that you would come to London in the midst of your vacation with your family.[1] Corinne and I will visit with Teresa and her friends, taking in a couple of shows, and relaxing generally. After all, we are enroute to Salzburg and Athens primarily. The Salzburg thing is a radio and TV conference relating to music in the 20th century. I am expected to open it and to close it. Since there's a week between these two events, we expect to visit Doxiadis and others in Athens. We fly directly to Toronto from Athens.

Just had a note from Christopher Tookey, President of the Oxford Union, asking me to speak in November on any of a number of dates and topics. I also had an invitation from the President of the Newman Society a few weeks ago. I might phone these chaps from London and go down for a chat if they happen to be there. I had thought of going to Stratford to do a taping of some old chaps in touch with an oral tradition of Shakespeare. However my enthusiasm has cooled off since learning of the difficulties of getting to and from Stratford at this time. Overnight space seems to be rather a problem also. So I shall probably skip Stratford. Actually, there are far too many exciting things going on right here to make travel of very much appeal. The Park happens to be very beautiful and satisfying, so much so that when I am away from it I feel quite unhappy. The period of its glory is brief, and absence correspondingly poignant. Should you get to London while we're there (August 17 through to 20), certainly we shall have a spot for you to stay. Teri reports that she has a large apartment. We do understand that it is quite unthinkable for Eirian to come to London at this time, and I do hope you will realize that we think it quite beyond reason that you should come either.

This summer I have begun to make some films relating to media and to books that I worked on. It will be possible to rent them out to people who are eager to get me to leave home. Eric has just appeared on the scene and perhaps it will be possible for him and me to do a half-hour on the Thunders in the *Wake*.

Shall keep you in touch with our movements,

Affectionate
greetings to all
Marshall

---

[1]Wain did indeed travel by train from Wales to see McLuhan during his London visit; they had a dinner and a lunch together—the latter just before Wain returned to Wales.

To The Listener[1]

August 11, 1971

Sir:

For those interested in exploration and discovery rather than in debating and classifying, the study of media technologies begins with their *effects*. Jonathan Miller charges me (*Listener*, July 15, 1971) with "the peculiar notion that television, in spite of its name is not a visual medium at all but what he calls an audio-tactile medium." Miller's confusion begins with his assumption that I have "notions" and theories, concepts rather than percepts. His difficulties with media study are entirely conventional hang-ups of the average person imbued with a nineteenth century outlook and attitude. It is not possible to modify such a huge cultural back-log by the mere introduction of new percepts arising from new environmental structures. However, in the interest of those who may be less burdened and overlaid by the middenheap of our immediate sensory past, I recently undertook to read Miller's *McLuhan* in which he peers at me uneasily as an undercover agent for Rome. At the very beginning of his squib he reads me backwards: "McLuhan also claims that the channel of hearing itself is intrinsically richer, or as he puts it 'hotter', than that of sight, say." Not a very promising or helpful start.

Let me apologise for Miller's obtuseness at once. If he does not dig "hot" and "cool", there is an historical excuse for Miller in that the first age of radio regarded itself as "hot". The 20's were the period of hot jazz, hot mommas, hot lips and hot tips. The "cool" age came with TV. But that which was called "hot" in the 20's was called "cool" in the fifties. Today "hot pants" are real cool and "far out". "Hot" meant involved in the 20's as "cool" did in the fifties. What had been called a "cool head" before radio, meant detached and disinterested and uninvolved. That is, in 1900 "cool" meant what would now be regarded "hot", in the sense of permitting specialized and fragmentary awareness to the individual. When one is "with it" one is "cool", sharing a corporate awareness. The private point of view is "hot" because it is detached and non-corporate. The great variety of paradoxical patterns of "hot" and "cool" point to a complex new *process* that resists mere classification. Understanding is not a point of view.

Any of our senses can be projected in modes that are either "hot" or "cool", involving or non-involving. Since "hot" and "cool" are not classifications but processes, not concepts but percepts, it may be possible to explore the matter of media a bit further by noting the *effect* of the deprivation of sight on the other senses. Alec Leighton observes "to the blind all things are sudden." There is not the same degree of continuity or connectedness in touch or hearing as in sight. Jacques Lusseyran's classic, *And There Was Light*, records the alteration of his *total* sensibility resulting from his sudden blindness. He confronts the prevalent

---

[1]This letter to *The Listener* was published on August 26, 1971. Miller's long reply was published on September 9—McLuhan's reply to which was published on October 28 (see page 442).

Miller attitudes to sense and experience, and laughs at those locked into the conventional attitudes of the bureaucratic Establishment:

> When I came upon the myth of objectivity in certain modern thinkers, it made me angry. So there was only one world for these people, the same for everyone. And all the other worlds were to be counted as illusions left over from the past. Or why not call them by their name—hallucinations? I had learned to my cost how wrong they were.
>
> From my own experience I knew very well that it was enough to take from a man a memory here, an association there, to deprive him of hearing or sight, for the world to undergo immediate transformation, and for another world, entirely different but entirely coherent, to be born. Another world? Not really. The same world rather, but seen from another angle, and counted in entirely new measures. When this happened, all the hierarchies they called objective were turned upside down, scattered to the four winds, not even theories but like whims. (p. 112)

What Lusseyran ascribes to the physical fate of sudden blindness, has in the electric age of instant information and new man-made environments, become a universal experience of sudden re-orientations and lost goals and identities.

In effect it matters little whether Miller gets with "hot" or "cool", since he cannot but project me through his nineteenth century mechanism of sensibility. If the medium is the message, the user is the content. That is the sense of Baudelaire's "Hypocrite lecteur."[2] The reader puts on the mask of the poem, the book, the language, the medium, and imbues them with the "sobsconscious inklings" of his own inadequacies. Media piggy-back on other media, so that when TV *uses* the film, the content is TV, not film. When Miller puts on or uses McLuhan, the content is the user, i.e. pure Miller. Projected through his bureaucratic categories, McLuhan is transmogrified into a nineteenth century bundle of exploded pretensions. Naturally, the electric surround exasperates Miller's sensibilities. Grievance is the ever-fruitful matrix of the comic which is one of Miller's more successful manifestations.

Apropos Mr. Miller's hang-up on the properties of the TV image, he has the conventional stereo-typical problem of the 19th century sensibility. The avant garde of the 19th century arts were the pre-Raphaelites with their stress on synaesthesia, and Pater's "the arts aspire to the condition of music." The pre-Raphaelite concern with medieval crafts and total human involvement in work sustained the ideals of Carlyle, and Ruskin, and William Morris, carrying over into the Omega workshops of Roger Fry. As with the work of Maria Montessori, the pre-Raphaelite stress on the multi-sensuous was opposed to the merely visual culture of the bureaucracies, whether in education or politics or commerce. In 1893 Adolf Hildebrand's *Problem of Form in Painting and Sculpture* summed up the pre-Raphaelite enterprise, as it were. As a sculptor, Hildebrand was very conscious of the "two functions of the eye":

[2]The epithet "Hypocrite lecteur" appears in the last line of the opening poem of Baudelaire's *Les Fleurs du Mal*.

The artist's activity consists, then, in further developing such of his faculties as provide him with spatial perception, namely his faculties of sight and touch. These two different means of perceiving the same phenomenon not only have separate existence in our faculties for sight and touch, but are united in the eye. (p. 14)

The TV image, with its light *through*, in the manner of a stained glass window, or a Rouault painting, were adumbrated by Seurat in the technique of pointillisme. It is a technique which Stockhausen later claimed as descriptive of his own work in music. Quantum mechanics has shown us in this century that touch, like the chemical bond itself, is characterized by the resonant *interval*. Hildebrand's insistence upon touch as essential in visual life anticipated the spatial character of quantum mechanics and of electric phenomena. The TV image is not a photograph nor does it, any more than Seurat, offer a visually *connected* space. Linus Pauling's *Nature of the Chemical Bond* provides a sufficient introduction to the problem of discontinuity in physical structures for those less interested in debating than in elucidation.

In the same way that Lusseyran observed the effect of loss of sight on the transformation of his other senses, the media student will study the effects of media on one another, as well as on the changing patterns of our sensory preferences. That is why the changes in *all* the arts and sciences can illuminate the effects of new media. To specialize attention in any one medium or sensory mode is to fall into the habit of *matching*, classifying and quantifying that are imposed by the dominant visual faculty. E.H. Gombrich's *Art and Illusion* studies the peculiar habits of matching and "realistic" correspondence that arise in the culture visually dominated. A handy demonstration of the power of sight to affect hearing and the other senses can be illustrated by reading *aloud* the following words:

> Un petit d'un petit
> S'étonne aux Halles
> Un petit d'un petit
> Ah! degrés te fallent
> Indolent qui ne sort cesse
> Indolent qui ne se mene
> Qu'importe un petit d'un petit
> Tout Gai de Reguennes.

(from *Mots D'Heures: Gousses Rames* by Luis D'Antin Van Rooten)[3]

Let Miller take two groups of people and show them the same movie, but let one group see it by front projection and one see it by rear projection through a silk screen. Each group will be unaware that the other has seen the movie at all. Then let each group write an essay on the experience. The resulting essays will show wide divergence in approach to the experience. One group will describe a

[3]A collection of pseudo French verses made up of an arrangement of French words contrived to reproduce phonetically a selection of Mother Goose rhymes in English: in this quotation, "Humpty Dumpty".

"hot" experience, and one a "cool" experience. Not even ad agencies "believe" that the same program of images seen by front and rear projection provides two totally different experiences. Movie and TV vary much more widely than mere front and rear projection of the same movie. (This experiment has been performed several times by my students in different countries.)

The study of media begins with the observation of their effects. Effects cannot be observed by concepts nor hypotheses as in conventional quantitative testing, for media are environments and inclusive processes, not products and packages. If the hot radio medium were turned off for a month in the oral cultures of the Near-East, there would be an instant cooling of the political climate. You cannot gnash your teeth on TV. If TV could be substituted, a mass revulsion for their "hot" attitudes would occur. The TV generation feels a revulsion for all centralist bureaucratic organization whether in education or politics, or in urban life.

Marshall McLuhan

University of Toronto

To *William Jovanovich*

August 12, 1971

Dear Bill:

Jonathan Miller has been continuing his anti-McLuhan crusade in the July 15th *Listener*. Having at last taken time to read his McLuhan book, I can honestly say I am amazed that he would take so much trouble to accomplish such a pitiable objective. He doesn't know what I am talking about because he has never taken a step outside the boundaries of visual space so dear to the positivist and the quantifier in these recent centuries. It all ended with Lewis Carroll and the new science of nuclear physics, to say nothing of poetry and the arts in this century. Of these things Miller has no inkling, except as mysterious, irrational mythologies that he finds extremely repugnant. In the name of 19th-century rationalism he mounts an anti-Catholic crusade against McLuhan in the spirit of the Rev. Paisley of Belfast. Even if Miller is a fanatic left-winger, it is hard to understand how he could be so provincial, or parochial. He belongs to the same vintage as Lewis Mumford who, likewise, cannot understand me at all.

Let me urgently recommend to you Jacques Lusseyran's *And There Was Light*. It is an unforgettable book.

To Pierre Elliott Trudeau

September 21, 1971

Dear Mr. Trudeau:

In the violent seas of "news" and publicity in which you have had to exist in recent months, I have refrained from saying anything whatever. I want you to know that you are in my prayers and that I have been perpetually amazed at the imaginative skill with which you have managed the utterly conflicting jobs with which you are confronted. You are immeasurably the greatest Prime Minister Canada has ever had, the first who has ever been equipped with an awareness of contemporary culture. [Edward] Heath and [Richard] Nixon are provincial school-boys beside you. With this advantage of your pre-eminence and contemporaneity is the back-lash of uncomprehending fury and envy which they elicit. Your detractors cannot imagine how humble one is made by the recognition of the scope of your problems.

Some while ago I sent Jim Davey a manuscript of my *Executive Dropout* which I have written with Barrington Nevitt. He is an electric engineer and a management consultant with long experience in Europe and South American countries. Our book is now in the press and will, I hope, be of direct aid in relating decision-making to the new fact of speed-up.

Corinne and I rejoice in your marriage and keep you and Margaret in our prayers.

In a few days our daughter, Teri, has a new book on the orations of American Indian chiefs to their tribes.[1] It will be published in the U.S. and in Canada, and you will of course receive a copy. Teri hopes that it may have some direct use in focussing the matter of Indian and ethnic minorities. The alienated ones have a natural intuition of ecology, since they are the victims of its absence.

[1]Teri McLuhan, *Touch the Earth* (1971).

To Martin Esslin[1]

September 23, 1971

Dear Mr. Esslin:

Thank you for taking the trouble to say a few words about Miller's *McLuhan*.

[1]Martin Esslin (b. 1918 in Vienna) was head of radio drama for the BBC; in 1977 he became Professor of Drama at Stanford University. He had written a long, pro-McLuhan review of Miller's *McLuhan* in *Encounter* ("Dr Miller on the Fringe", June 1971), in which he chided Miller, in his "curious little book", for his "misapplied pedantry". He describes the Miller book as a "neat demolition job expertly carried out, except that the contractors went to the wrong address and have destroyed the wrong building. McLuhan, who is an intellectual gadfly, a divine *provocateur*, a catalyst and stimulant, is treated as though he were an experimental psychologist and annihilated as such. It is as though the Ministry of Education were to remove Shakespeare from the curriculum because he placed Bohemia by the sea—for that obviously proves that he teaches the wrong geography and is therefore harmful to learning."

I have only read Miller in the last couple of weeks, having been assured the very day it arrived that it was a spoof. Since then I have discovered that some people take him seriously. Personally, I am baffled to know why he bothered to write the book at all, unless he is some kind of an idealogue fanatic. In that case, he has no intellectual life and no perceptual life that could be of the slightest interest to any intelligent person. One of the advantages of being a Catholic is that it confers a complete intellectual freedom to examine any and all phenomena with the absolute assurance of their intelligibility. Moreover, there is absolute value in intelligibility as such, to say nothing of pleasure and satisfaction. The universal cult of commitment to the wrongs of the world as a program of vehement verbalization, is hypocritical and sentimental in the extreme. Naturally, I am aware of the stupid and degraded motives of the general run of mankind. There seems to be no lack of protesters about this matter. The protests, however, come from people at least as unaware as their enemies.

May I ask you whether you think it reasonable that I should write a letter to *Encounter* concerning Jonathan Miller? In his book he refers to my work as a pack of lies, without referring to any of my percepts whatever. In what sense do you think he means "lies"? Does he imagine that I have consciously and deliberately falsified evidence?[2] Surely Miller is a clown with the habits of a sixth-form debater?

I am unaware of anyone in the U.K. who has the slightest understanding of media. The study of media begins, not with their uses or their programs, but with their *effects*. Indeed, the "cause" of any medium is its effects. Perhaps it would be a complete mistake to do anything at all about Miller? I am not concerned to have a reading public in the U.K. Please give me your thoughts, and again thanks for your piece on me.

Sincerely yours,

[2]In his friendly reply (October 2) to McLuhan's letter, Esslin wrote: "I don't think he [Miller] meant any harm in talking of 'lies'—it is merely a forceful way of saying 'matters not scientifically proven or correct'."

To J.M. Davey
Office of the Prime Minister

September 29, 1971

Dear Jim:

Naturally, Nevitt and I are watching the changing relationship between Canada and the U.S. in relation to the analysis we did on hardware and software in our *Executive as Dropout*, which I think you have. It is now in the press for early Spring publication.

A great advantage which Canada enjoys over the U.S. is the relative absence of massive installations. We enjoy many of the 20th-century opportunities of other "backward" countries. We are free to start in with the software and by-pass the hardware. That is our privilege for having missed the 19th century. Of course, areas like Montreal and Toronto, precisely to the degree to which they *did* have a 19th century, are in a bad way. The message of the electric age is to by-pass these places also, and not to make their problems those of the country at large. Highly centralist hardware and hardware areas have to be regarded as bad investments that are better forgotten. Sooner or later the U.S. will have to write off its big cities and hardware also. In this situation the U.K. is almost helpless.

I want to ask your counsel and aid in some anti-abortion strategies which I am beginning to be associated with. The abortion mill closely resembles Buchenwald. People directly engaged in it would risk their lives to save the life of a two-year-old child from a car or truck. What has happened is a complete collapse of community awareness via specialism of function. As long as an operation or process is divided into sufficiently small segments, nobody feels any responsibility for anything. Communal awareness has no chance to come into play. This was the mystery of Buchenwald and such camps. A few weeks ago I spoke with Germans and Austrians directly related to those events. They were pious Catholics, and I asked them how they could have permitted these things. Their answer was simply "We just did our bit and were unaware of the other bits." It is by this type of programming that we can calmly expect our highways to deliver a given number of dead per day or week. The really devastating programming is the destruction of perception and sensitivity by the creation of vast environments far exceeding human scale. The King Kong fantasies are direct expressions of the feeling most people have in their environments which have become monsters. Yet, the best intentioned bureaucrats in all governments are busily engaged in creating bigger and blacker King Kongs every day of the week. Meantime, the kids are repudiating the society and fleeing to small communes. Of course, the effect of current unemployment will be to reconcile many of them once more to the environment as it is.

Our anti-abortion group here at St. Mike's needs to discover ways of presenting films on national networks, if possible. These films don't have to have any pro or con slant, if they are permitted to show the actual process. If any practical program has begun anywhere that you know of, I would be happy to hear about it.

Hoping you have had a good summer, and that your family is in the best of shape,

Warm regards
Marshall

To The Listener[1]

October 8, 1971

Dear Sir:

Dr. Jonathan Miller prefers argument to enlightenment. Like a fractious pupil, he stamps his feet, sticks out his tongue, makes faces, and demands satisfaction from a patient pedagogue. Mark Twain, when challenged to a duel and asked to choose the place and the weapons, promptly replied: "You stand down a well and we'll use stones!" If Dr. Miller will stand in his "well of ignorance" undefiled by Rimbaud's *Illuminations* or any other radical insights, I will drop a few more perils, hopefully to stun him, gently, into elementary awareness.

How can Dr. Miller disagree with me, when he insists in presenting his own conventional prejudices as the "content" of my writing? The straw men ride again. Dr. Miller ignores the physical, psychic and social impact of any medium whatever simply by reducing its "message" or *effects* to "the canons of traditional thought." Dr. Miller cannot even begin to disagree with me, if he cannot understand the reasons I have given for the divergence between the pictorial movie and the iconic TV images, between "light upon" and "light through." It is as if he would urge our *listeners* that the difference between a stained glass window (light through) and a mural (light upon) "can be quite satisfactorily described in the conventional vocabulary of vision." Poor old Rouault!

It is obvious that Dr. Miller is not aware of the media researches of General Electric Company's psychologist, Herbert Krugman. As to "unified sensibility" or *synesthesia* or the difference between matching and making in human perception, Dr. Miller could obtain first aid from E.H. Gombrich who says in *Art and Illusion*:

> What is called "synesthesia", the splashing over of impressions from one sense modality to another, is a fact to which all languages testify. They work both ways—from sight to sound and from sound to sight. We speak of loud colors or of bright sounds, and everyone knows what we mean. Nor are the ear and the eye the only senses that are thus converging to a common center. There is touch in such terms as "velvety voice" and "a cold light", taste with "sweet harmonies" of colors or sounds, and so on through countless permutations. . . . representation is never a replica. The forms of art, ancient and modern, are not duplications of what the artist has in mind any more than they are duplications of what he sees in the outer world. In both cases they are renderings within an acquired medium, a medium grown up through tradition and skill—that of the artist and that of the beholder. . . . synesthesia concerns relationships.

[Relevant to the great gap between program "content" and the effect of the medium itself is the approach to the image in J[acob] Isaac's *Background of Modern Poetry* [1951]:

[1]This letter—in reply to Jonathan Miller's letter to *The Listener* of September 9, 1971—was addressed to Dr Karl Miller, Editor, and appeared in *The Listener* on October 28, 1971. *The passages in square brackets were omitted.*

"The exact word", says Mr. [Richard] Aldington, "does not mean the word which exactly describes the object [in] itself, it means the exact word which brings the effect of that object before the reader as it presented itself to the poet's mind at the time of writing the poem."]

Apropos the linguistic studies of N[oam] Chomsky, Thomas S. Kuhn, philosopher of science, was recently cited by *The Listener*, July 27, 1971, p. 142, on "what people are prepared to accept as facts at one point cease to be and new things are regarded as facts." My own studies of media as environments that alter patterns of perception and sensibility are intended to develop awareness of the process by which "new things" come to be regarded as "facts." These "new facts" concern the message or *effects* of new media as hidden environments. These effects are not the "content" of the media. The content is always the "hypocrite lecteur"[2] (or *auditeur*). This is the central fact missing from the speculations of Noam Chomsky concerning the verbal universe.[3] Languages are not programs but environments which are hidden from the young learner, and to which, like fish to water, he relates synesthetically, using all his faculties at once. After childhood the senses specialize via the channels of dominant technologies and social weaponries. Electric channels of information have the effect of reducing (or elevating) people to the discarnate status of instant information.

The first principle of evidence is that things have to be approached on their own terms if any understanding is to be attained. Edgar Allan Poe was the first to stress the need to begin with *effects* and to work backwards, in poetry and in detective fiction alike. Just as Poe provided clues for ascending from "The Maelstrom,"[4] Beckett replays, not waiting, but the *effects* of the experience of waiting, in *Waiting for Godot*. In *Four Quartets* T.S. Eliot studies effects as causes: "in my end is my beginning." And Wyndham Lewis noted that "The artist is engaged in writing a detailed history of the future because, 'older than the fish', he alone can live in the inclusive present." In Symbolist art, connections are deliberately pulled out in order to involve the public in a creative role. In Symbolist statement, the *ground* is suppressed in order to highlight the *figure*. A boot lying on a highway is a symbol, a tire is not, for the medium can reverse the roles of producer and consumer by making the reader or audience not only the "content" but the co-maker of the work. Movie and TV are antithetic.

When I say "the medium is the message", I suppress the fact that the user or audience or cognitive agent is both the "content" and maker of the experience, in order to highlight the *effects* of the medium, or the hidden environment or *ground* of the experience. The nineteenth century, as the first great consumer age, suppressed the function of the user and the public as cognitive agent and producer. The Pre-Raphaelites at least strove to overcome the passive consumer bias of an industrial time by stressing the role of *work* and crafts in art and society.

[2]See page 436, note 2.
[3]In *Syntactic Structures* (1957) and *Aspects of a Theory of Syntax* (1965) by Noam Chomsky.
[4]Poe's story "A Descent from the Maelström".

They tried to have some relevance to their time by playing down the consumer role and scorning the easy package method that had grown up in the arts and industry alike. In his time, John Donne strove for relevance to his "hypocrite lecteurs" by constructing for them a broken and discontinuous discourse. He was seeking non-lineal and non-nineteenth-century effects:

> [. . . to trouble the understanding, to displace, and discompose and disorder the judgement. . . . or to empty it of former apprehensions, and to shake beliefs, with which it had possessed itself before, and then, when it is thus melted, to poure it into new molds, when it is thus mollified, to stamp and imprint new forms, and new opinions in it.[5]]

Donne's "Attic" or "curt" and broken style not only ruffled the feathers of the seventeenth-century Establishment, but appeals to contemporary minds in our own century.

[In 1903, Mr. W.B. Yeats, meditating on the "emotion of multitude", explained that it is achieved by a *discontinuous* parallel between two actions:

> I have been wondering why I dislike the clear and logical construction which seems necessary if one is to succeed on the modern stage. . . . The Greek drama has got the emotion of multitude from its chorus . . . to witness[,] as it were, some well[-]ordered fable. . . . The Shakespearean drama gets the emotion of multitude out of the sub-plot which copies the main plot, much as a shadow upon the wall copies one's body in the firelight. We think of King Lear less as the history of one man and his sorrows than as the history of a whole evil time.[6]]

[Depth awareness is created by parallel suggestion, not by connected statement. Yeats' observation can also be found in Bacon who writes on the modes of aphorism as contrasted with "writing in Method", in his *Advancement of Learning*:

> . . . aphorisms, representing a knowledge broken, do invite men to inquire farther; whereas Methods, carrying the show of a total, do secure men, as if they were at farthest.]

Even the ad agencies know that to sell a car or a coat, they must present the satisfactions in *figure-ground* relationship that will create the desired psychic effects. They would not show a coat in relation to naked natives nor a car in a world without roads. The nineteenth-century consumer preference is not relevant to the electric age of quantum physics, even though our media bureaucracies continue to produce mainly consumer packages. Miller's "humanist" preferences are quite blatantly on the side of the consumer package: "Once a comic, always a comic." But has Dr. Miller ever stooped to below the fringe to consider that his days of lucrative clowning may have had a hidden *ground* of grievance? As Steve Allen, the entertainer, authoritatively explained: "The funny man is the man with a grievance." The catharsis of laughter may conceal and allay dangerous passions.

[5]Unidentified.
[6]Extracted from W.B. Yeats, "Emotion of Multitude" (1903) in *Essays and Introductions* (1961).

The nineteenth-century consumer bias behind Dr. Miller's mental fringe is obvious in the narrow spectrum of his concern as to what constitutes relevant effects. He does not consider media as radical environments but as easy vehicles for acceptable packages. Did Dr. Miller succeed in keeping his nose clean while dirtying his hands in modern media, or did he just blow his mind? Honest Jonathan now demands "ocular proof" of media effects. As James Joyce writes: "As for the viability of vicinals, when invisible they are invincible."[7] Does Dr. Miller believe he can gain immunity from invincible media effects by shrouding himself in "the canons of traditional thought" and by taking refuge in "the conventional vocabulary of vision"? Is Dr. Miller really suffering from motivated somnambulism, or is he merely trying to isolate and placate his own audience? He resembles a voice I recently heard from the back of a hall: "It's lies! all lies!" Up front people began to say: "McLuhan has arranged it." For every specialist has a stake in his own knowledge, just as every conventional man has the right to defend his own ignorance.

Marshall McLuhan

[7]The correct reading is given on page 369, note 1.

To Yousuf Karsh[1]

October 6, 1971

Dear Yousuf:

I was more than honoured, I was stunned to find myself in the glorious company you assembled in your new book.[2] I can only say "thank you" and hope that your art will never grow less than now when it is at its splendid prime.

Warm personal regards from
Corinne and me

P.S. Please tell me about permissions (if any) procedures for use of any of the photos you took of myself. We have some small black and white photos. There would be, automatically, acknowledgement of yourself. [*Handwritten:*] Things are much behind here since my kidney stone. That item seems clear now.

[1]Yousuf Karsh (b. 1908), the distinguished Ottawa portrait photographer.
[2]Yousuf Karsh, *Faces of Our Time* (1971).

To the Editor of Mademoiselle

Oct. 15, 1971

Dear Sirs:

In your Aug., 1971 issue, under Nancy Collins' piece,[1] you mention me and the Coach House where I direct the Centre for Culture and Technology! The 9' × 12' mural in the seminar room was not made by Buckminster Fuller, but René Cera, a French painter and architect.[2] The theme of the painting is "T. V. in Action" with the tube in the Centre and the psychedelic images surrounding it. The title is "Pied Pipers All", since Cera saw that the tube was alienating the young from a generation of elders who had no thought of paying the piper for the latest technological caper.

This is a splendid and impressive painting by a great craftsman whose prolific work has been bottled up in Canada. If you would be interested in using a copy of this colourful mural with a comment on its significance and topicality, I could supply same.

Sincerely yours,

[1]*Mademoiselle*, August 1971, pp. 333, 336.
[2]See page 230, note 1. The mural was painted in March 1969.

To Ashley Montagu

October 22, 1971

Dear Ashley:

Thank you very much for the handsome new edition of *The Direction of Human Development* [1955; 2nd edn 1970].

There are many things that I wish you were available to discuss. In recent years I've been working on causation. More and more I feel compelled to consider causation as following from effects. That is, the effects of the telegraph created an environment of information that made the telephone a perfectly natural development. In a certain sense, therefore, the effects of the telephone provided the invention of the actual hardware instrument. This, of course, is non-lineal, non-sequential causality. In fact, it suggests that causes and effects are simultaneous, if anything.

I am baffled to know why it is that in the Western world there has been no study of the effects of innovations. There is, of course, much readiness to study the inputs that are called the "content" of our technologies, but insofar as technologies create environments which alter all forms of human perception, there is a hiatus. In merely literary terms, nobody studies what sort of effect Dante or anybody else wanted to have on his time and his public. Instead, they study what they imagined the writer was saying to the public. What a man is saying is far from the effect he may wish to have, or that, in fact, he does have. Personally, I consider the effect which a writer wishes to achieve as his theory of communication. I know of no studies of anybody's theory of communication. For example, quite apart from the concepts of anthropologists, and aside from the content of their work, what is the *effect* that they seek on their time? How do they wish to change it?

To Jacqueline Tyrwhitt

November 10, 1971

Dear Jackie:

Yes, I will do a short preface to the Empedocles book, as you suggest. Do you think that relating him to the major 20th-century figures such as Yeats, Pound, Eliot, Joyce, etc. is the best approach? I would be on tricky ground if I were to attempt to relate him to the needs of classical scholarship. Please find out just how long a preface is best, and how soon it needs to be done.[1]

Thanks for your comments on the general Eastern time system.[2] It really does relate to the need to go out for privacy and to go in for community. At the present time in North America, for example, the telephone is wrecking the role of office as privacy. Result is that you can no longer reach anybody by telephone. Either they go to interminable meetings the moment they get to the office, or they leave town for frequent interruptions of their schedule. The memo and the letter are being brought back into compulsory use as protest against the telephone.

Am sending you a copy of *The Gutenberg Galaxy* as well as a bilingual New Testament. I had a Greek one but cannot find it. Perhaps they are available in Athens.

Teri's *Touch the Earth* has been getting a tremendous send-off and immediate acceptance. A copy will be on its way to you soon. She expects to go back to England in a week or so. Her English address is: 6 Aldridge Road Villas, London W. 11.

[1]McLuhan's prefatory essay, "Empedocles and T.S. Eliot", eventually appeared in *Empedocles* (1976) by Helle Lambridis, published by the University of Alabama Press in its Studies in the Humanities series, no. 15.

[2]In her letter of November 1, Tyrwhitt praised the Greek time system that allows an "off" period in the afternoon. This was in response to McLuhan's asking her about synchronizing the American 9-to-5 day with that of 8-to-1 and 6-to-9.

To William Kuhns

December 6,1971

Dear Bill:

Congratulations on your *Post-Industrial Prophets*.[1] I just wanted to help you out on a couple of matters, e.g. pages 197–9. The rear-view mirror not only shows objects rushing away from us, but also objects looming and coming up on us. You have not studied Joyce or Baudelaire yet, or you would have no problems in understanding my procedure. I have no *theories* whatever about anything. I make observations by way of discovering contours, lines of force, and pressures. I satirize at all times, and my hyperboles are as nothing compared to the events to which they refer. If you study symbolism you will discover that it is a technique of rip-off by which *figures* are deliberately deprived of their *ground*. You do not seem to have grasped that the message, as it relates to the medium, is never the content, but the corporate *effects* of the medium as an environment of service and disservice. I was grateful, therefore, to Charles Reich in *The Greening of America* (page 167) when he said: "The medium itself tends to be overlooked because it has no content." This is one of the very few times in which any of my readers has ever said what he thought I was saying.

I have always assumed that the *user* of any medium is the *content*. The person who turns on an electric light is the content of the electric light, just as the reader of a book is the content of the book. This is standard Aristotelian and Thomistic doctrine, that the cognitive agent is himself thing and content. In the same way, on page 199 you miss what to me is the very obvious fact that human consciousness is an analogical mirror far more potent than all other mirrors that merely provide a univocal or matching image.

I would be grateful to you if you could give me any examples where I have *mis-stated* any fact whatever. My canvasses are surrealist, and to call them "theories" is to miss my satirical intent altogether. As you will find in my literary essays, I can write the ordinary kind of rationalistic prose any time I choose to do so. You are in great need of some intense training in perception in the arts. To talk about my work without showing the centrality of percept vs. concept, and the totally diverse character of visual, audile, and tactile spaces, is to have no apprehension of my observations about the media. In point of fact, Harold Innis (incidentally, he was baptized Herald Innis very prophetically by a mother who was devoted to the *Family Herald!*) had no training whatever in the arts, and this was his gross defect.

Cordially Marshall

[1]William Kuhns, *The Post-Industrial Prophets* (1971), which includes chapters on five men whose books greatly influenced/interested McLuhan—Lewis Mumford, Sigfried Giedion, Jacques Ellul, Harold Adams Innis, and Buckminster Fuller—and a chapter on McLuhan himself: "The Sage of Aquarius". The reference in the next sentence is to a section in this essay entitled "McLuhan As Seen Through a Rear-View Mirror".

To Harry J. Boyle[1]

Dear Harry:

You know the expression about "things tending to find their own level." The simple fact is that the viewer, the hearer, the reader, only accepts those parts of any experience that seem meaningful to him. What he cannot relate to, he throws aside or ignores. If, on the other hand, he lives in an environment or surround of noble sights and sounds, he may gradually form habits and expectations that enable him to assimilate more than he did at first.

Your question about the great names of radio broadcasting could be approached this way: did the voices of these men constitute an environment of resonating challenges and insights?[2] If so, they probably *did* raise the level a bit. Henry Morgan was here at the Centre last Monday and spoke of his feeling that Canadians do verbalize more efficiently than Americans.[3] He is quite aware that verbal expression is rapidly declining among the young. It is the public that largely determines the style of discourse that is going to be presented to it. I find it extremely difficult to write or speak to both British and an American public in the same week. One has to "put on" the public as the garment or the "mask" which one must wear in speaking to them. In turn, this mask is the energy which one turns on when writing or speaking.

As for Canadian content, a Chinese, looking at a Canadian program, necessarily translates it into his Chinese experience, just as a Canadian faced by a Chinese experience translates it into his Canadian experience as best he can. The incoherence, the dispersed and non-focused character of the Canadian publics makes the Canadian writer or performer very uncertain about how to turn on the power that his audience potentially has.

Best wishes,

[1]Harry J. Boyle (b. 1915)—journalist, broadcaster, and the author of books of light essays and five novels—was at this time Vice-Chairman (later Chairman) of the Canadian Radio-Television Commission. He wrote three articles on McLuhan in 1967 (*Weekend Magazine*, March 18; *Stimulus*, May-June; and *Weekend Magazine*, November 11) and two profiles of McLuhan shortly after his death (*Globe and Mail*, Toronto, January 5, and *Reader's Digest*, July 1981). Boyle knew McLuhan as a "charming man who was a great conversationalist and a stimulating person. There are few occasions to rub up against such a person. I enjoyed them very much."

[2]Boyle had written McLuhan asking for his views on CBC Radio's influence on the Canadian make-up, particularly that of some of its best-known broadcasters.

[3]Henry Morgan (b. 1915) was a popular and witty American television personality (known particularly as a panelist on *I've Got a Secret*) who lived in Toronto from 1971 to 1975.

1972

To Edmund Carpenter

January 26, 1972

Dear Ted:

Thanks for your wonderful letter. Much of it will be of special interest to Elizabeth [McLuhan], who is doing her M.A. in art and anthropology at Albuquerque. She is supposed to do her M.A. here in Toronto in the next few months by studying local Indian painters. She does have a great zest and flair in these matters.

Apropos the Baedecker, [George] Steiner certainly would not do.[1] What is needed is your kind of structural awareness that goes across times, places, cultures. While talking with a Japanese recently I finally penetrated the mystery of Western inhibitions about studying the effects of technology. I had been pointing out to him our unique North American pattern of going outside for privacy and inside for community, the reverse of all other cultures in the world, and then happened to bring up this matter of Western refusal to consider the effects of technology on psyche. He volunteered at once that the fear is simply "invasion of privacy"! There it is, Ted, after all these years. The Western psyche is a fragile, specialized product of the phonetic alphabet which stands in terror of any snooping around for its credentials, whereas tribal men welcome such study. The tribal man says, "Let's see what will happen and then decide to stay away from it", whereas the Western man says, "Let's try it anyway and see what happens." When you read Thomas Kuhn's [The] Structure of Scientific Revolutions [1962; 2nd ed. 1970], it is quickly apparent that there never was a scientist in history who ever set out to make breakthroughs or discoveries. All scientists seem to have been earnest supporters of whatever establishment they could unite with. When breakthroughs occurred, they frequently were in trouble but then, as now, the last thing in the world that any scientist or scholar wants is a discovery or breakthrough.[2] In view of this overwhelming fact a question arises—how do people conclude that scientists are interested in discovery? How can people manage to pretend that scholarship exists to advance knowledge? This is [not] only not true, but never has been true. Is it the evolutionary metaphor that haunts the mind?

Have you read Shands yet?[3] How would he be for the Baedecker?[4]

---

[1]See page 361, note 1.

[2]This relates to the idea that a breakthrough makes all previous knowledge obsolete and indicates radical change, which the establishment deplores. The eventual result of Columbus' finding a new world—instead of a route to India, which his backers hoped he would find—was that Europe was reduced to a secondary power.

[3]Harley C. Shands, M.D., was associated with the Department of Psychiatry, Roosevelt Hospital, Brooklyn, and the author of Semiotic Approaches to Psychiatry (1970).

[4]See page 504, note 1.

To Thomas Langan[1]

March 2, 1972

Dear Tom:

Thanks for your note on the Greeks and the visual. Since talking to you, I have read L. Entralgo's *The Therapy of the Word in Greek Antiquity*.[2] Entralgo is a historian of medicine and his study is concerned with all the magical properties in Greek culture. Naturally these are all non-visual so it is really a study of the audile-tactile. The book came out in English in 1970 from Yale University Press. Would that I had had it years ago.

Only recently I discovered in Cicero his observation that the arts of poetry and logic began with writing. The word "poetry" does not appear in Homer, and Isocrates, founder of rhetoric, never gave a speech in his life. He wrote them, i.e. founded the *art*. In the same way, Socrates founded dialectic by writing. Those pre-Socratics had no systems and no dialectic and committed their insights to aphorisms which are figures without ground and without context. I am looking into the kinds of supposed context which have been attributed to the pre-Socratics, and I suspect that they are non-existent.

Regards,

[1]Professor Thomas Langan (b. 1929) at this time taught in the Department of Philosophy, University of Toronto; in 1978 he joined the Philosophy Department of St Michael's College. He became a friend of McLuhan's in 1969.

[2]Pedro Lain Entralgo, *The Therapy of the Word in Classical Antiquity* (1970), translated by L.J. Rather and J.M. Sharp.

To Ashley Montagu

March 6, 1972

Dear Ashley:

Am very much obliged to you for sending me *Statement on Race*.[1] It is an indispensable document. Currently Canada is taking in a good many blacks from Jamaica and such places. Since, in Wasp Toronto, none of these people will ever experience a day of unharassed existence, I ask myself why we do this. No Wasp can ever form a natural special relation with a black. He may form a supernatural relation in the order of Christian charity or he may form various social bonds, marital, or domestic employer and employee relations, but never without great self-consciousness.

Are we to suppose that there are people who feel that a great change in black-white relationships can result from propinquity? Would such an idea be the basis of the Canadian immigration policy? Is such policy, on the other hand, merely greed to exploit "cheap labour"?

[1]Ashley Montagu, *Statement on Race: An Extended Discussion in Plain Language of the UNESCO Statement by Experts on Race Problems* (1951; 3rd ed., 1972).

To Bruce P. Tracy[1]

March 10, 1972

Dear Professor Tracy:

Your letter of March 3rd came most timely. I have been doing some work on Henry James in the matter of his use of outside and inside spaces in America and in Europe in his novels. Since North Americans go outside for privacy and inside for community, whereas Europeans go outside for community and inside for privacy, Henry James was able to use these antithetic modes in many different patterns. I am not sure how much he really understood of the matter. I am also much interested in his use of cliché and schemata from the popular arts. Also, his perceptual discovery that we do not *experience* what we take in directly without transforming it, has been the basis of my media study. However, I didn't learn this from him, and have only just discovered that he was aware of it.

By all means, drop by any time you can, and you can be assured of lots of dialogue.

Very best wishes,

[1]Tracy—who was Assistant Professor of English, California State College, Dominguez Hills, California—had written his Ph.D. dissertation on Henry James and had heard McLuhan speak at the University of Southern California. He wrote to him, asking if he could spend a month at the Centre.

To Claude Cartier-Bresson[1]

July 19, 1972

Dear Claude:

Corinne and I are just back from Athens and Delos cruise which proved to be a very complex social event.[2] We were surrounded by people of world notoriety and international wealth. This is quite unlike the first Delos cruise ten years ago where the stress had been on scholarship and knowledge. As we sort out our memories of our Paris visit, we find your acquaintance and hospitality standing out very clearly indeed. We look forward to a follow-up opportunity.

[1]Claude Cartier-Bresson (brother of the famous photographer Henri Cartier-Bresson) of Maison Mame, Paris, was McLuhan's French publisher of *La Galaxie Gutenberg* (1967), *Pour Comprendre les Media: Les prolongements technologiques de l'homme* (1968), and *Counterblast* (1972)—all translated by Jean Paré; *Mutations 1990* (1969), a short paperback compilation drawn from several articles by McLuhan translated by François Chesneau; and *Cliché à Archetype* (1974), a rewritten version of *From Cliché to Archetype* translated by Derrick de Kerckhove. The McLuhans stayed with the Cartier-Bressons at their house in Chambord for a weekend in 1973.

[2]Having attended the first Delos Symposion in 1963 (see page 289), McLuhan, with his wife Corinne and his son Michael, attended the last one, "Delos Ten", held in July 1972. They were among nearly 250 other guests aboard the *Orpheus* (which cruised the Greek islands), who included Buckminster Fuller, Herman Kahn, Gyorgy Kepes, Margaret Mead, Jonas Salt, Arnold Toynbee, Jacqueline Tyrwhitt, C.H. Waddington, and Barbara Ward.

During the Paris visit my thoughts turned constantly to James Joyce, and I have been asking myself since whether it might not be a very effective international service for you, or somebody, to set up a small "James Joyce Bookshop." A great many Americans and Europeans are full-time students of James Joyce, who did much of his work in Paris. There is no place in the world where all of his writings can be found together. Shakespeare and Company used to be a centre [in Paris] for Joyce fans, but it no longer serves this function. I am sure that a small place devoted entirely to Joyce, in English and in translation, would attract very much attention and become a kind of social and intellectual centre.

I will be glad to comment further on this possible project if it interests you as a public-relations venture. Meantime, many cordial thanks for your thoughtfulness.

To Gyorgy Kepes[1]

August 1, 1972

Dear Gyorgy:

It was very good to see you again and to meet Mrs. Kepes. Corinne and I were so much under the weather that our social life was much restricted.

I hope you will get a look at my *Take Today: The Executive as Dropout* (Harcourt, Brace, Jovanovich, Inc., N.Y.) which I did with Barry Nevitt, an electric engineer. Our discussion of the great contemporary shift from hardware to software is very close to your interests, and I very much wish that it might become a basis for further dialogue between us.

You were certainly the person at the [Delos] conference most near my own interests and concerns, if only because of your understanding of the world of design. The bulk of the people there were fairly brick-and-mortar or hardware men who belong almost entirely in the 19th century. Ecology is the most they are prepared to concede to our time and their approach to that problem is almost entirely piecemeal. I think that we are already living in a new kind of world city that is far outside the ken of Doxiadis. Since we are actually living in that new city electrically, it is inevitable that the perceptual life of the young will accommodate to it in spite of the irrelevance of the concepts that they are being taught. The suddenness of the leap from hardware to software cannot but produce a period of anarchy and collapse in existing establishments, especially in the developed countries. That is our immediate prospect and our present actuality.

Looking forward to further meetings,

---

[1]Gyorgy Kepes (b. 1906) was Professor of Visual Design at the Massachusetts Institute of Technology Centre for Advanced Visual Studies and wrote *The Language of Vision* (1939), which is discussed in *The Gutenberg Galaxy*. McLuhan contributed "The Emperor's Old Clothes" to *The Man-Made Object* (1966) in the series *Vision + Value* edited by Kepes.

To Tom and Dorothy Easterbrook

August 1, 1972

Dear Tom and Dorothy:

Corinne and I have had quite a lot of flitting about, first to Dublin, then to Paris, then to Athens and Delos, and now home for the rest of the summer, we hope.

You have probably heard from Jane [Easterbrook] about our recent muggy, hot spell. Corinne and I got bad cases of bronchitis in Dublin and carried this bug throughout our trip. In spite of this, Dublin was an unexpected joy. We met wonderful people there and had a chance to feel the quality of life. There being no industry to speak of, the city is still dominated by people and their pleasure in visiting and chatting during the "working" day. The Americans are buying up the rural areas in Ireland for speculative reasons. At present one of these reasons is stud farming. We were entertained by Mr. and Mrs. McEnery who are in that business themselves, having a very large ranch on the outskirts of Dublin itself. He is an Irishman who made a fortune in Wall Street. He became a fan of my Dew Line Newsletter and that is how we made our contact. Bob O'Driscoll of St. Mike's English Department is doing a sabbatical in Dublin to work on Yeats and Irish theatre. He has rented a large house beside Joyce's Martello Tower and gives large parties. He gave one for us that went on until 5 a.m., although I remember that we got away somewhat before then.

In Dublin I had to give some lectures both on radio and TV and in public, and these turned out quite well. In Paris there were no lectures but some TV appearances, which were complicated by my inadequate French. Paris is a lot like Dublin in that the people insist on keeping the human qualities uppermost, rigorously suppressing any temptations to be efficient or punctual. The result is that at all hours of the day and night there are endless conversations in progress in restaurants and cafés. In one of these we met Professor [Jean] Duvignaud, who is a keen media man teaching this under the guise of the sociology of art at the University of Tours.[1] Teri is in Paris a good deal, and he [Duvignaud] took us all to visit a friend of his, the dramatist [Eugène] Ionesco. It was in the evening and Ionesco explained that he had to go to see the second part of his new play *Macbett* (a parody of power on the theme of *Macbeth*).[2] I boldly suggested that we might be allowed to accompany him, and he was delighted. We got there just at the intermission and we were able to see the last part of the play with him. It won't have its première in English for some months. It is a delightful spoof of power antics. After all, Macbeth was a hijacker, too.

We went to Athens in order to join the Delos seminar on shipboard. This year there were 200 people, including a huge batch of "biggies" from the World Bank, the Ford Foundation, the Mayor of Detroit, and people in power and energy

---

[1]Duvignaud taught in the Department of Sociology, Université Rabelais, Tours, France.
[2]Eugène Ionesco (b. 1912), *Macbett* (1972).

fields, oil and electronic. The theme was "Implementing the Future of the City." Naturally, these were earnest men, rather all 19th-century types, still preoccupied with bricks and mortar.

I hope you are going to enjoy *Take Today: The Executive as Dropout* and write down some thoughts about it for us.

It seems to me that you are due to be back in Toronto sometime this year. We look forward to that.

To John Culkin

August 2, 1972

Dear John:

Here it is Liz's birthday and I haven't even thanked you for the great event which you made of my birthday a week ago. Our wondrous light-sculpture machine never fails to impress our friends and visitors and to provide solace for us too.

Let me also say that I have pored over *Doing the Media* and have been much impressed.[1] You have hit upon the proper use of media as perceptual trainers. I am going to circulate it hereabouts. Perhaps you could send me another copy or two? Have also begun to put out a few feelers for aid in seeding media Centres here and there, with a view to having a Digest to assemble problems and discoveries periodically. What are your thoughts about this?

I don't seem to be able to crawl out from under all the paper on my desk, so excuse this brief one.

[1]In *Doing the Media: A Portfolio of Activities, Ideas and Resources* (1972)—edited by Kit Laybourne and Pauline Cianciolo, and published by the Center for Understanding Media, New York, of which Culkin was founder and director—contains an introductory chapter by Culkin entitled "Doing the Truth" (adapted from his "Schoolman's Guide to Marshall McLuhan", *Saturday Review*, March 18, 1967), which states that "McLuhan's major work is *Understanding Media*, and it provides much of the stimulus for *Doing the Media.*"

To David Sohn[1]

August 3, 1972

Dear David:

Ballantine Books now tell me that *From Cliché to Archetype* will not be out until the end of August. Meantime, *Take Today: The Executive as Dropout* came

[1]David Sohn (b. 1927)—a highly respected school teacher in the Evanston public school system (Illinois), who had been an education consultant for Bantam Books, the publisher of the paperback edition of *Understanding Media*—had corresponded with McLuhan since the mid-1960s and visited him in Toronto in March 1975. Sohn wrote the Preface and Introduction to the textbook *Media, Messages & Language: The World as Your Classroom* (1980) by Marshall McLuhan, Kathryn Hutchon, and Eric McLuhan—the U.S. edition of *The City as Classroom.*

out (Harcourt, Brace, Jovanovich Inc., N.Y.) and I think it would interest you greatly.

Thanks very much for the Pound item. I once spent two hours with him at St. Elizabeths hospital. For some reason that has been parlayed into a close relationship. My admiration for Pound's work increases constantly.

To John Cage[1]

September 13, 1972

Dear John:

It was good to have even a brief visit with you, but we didn't have a chance to talk about the matter I am going to mention now. During the past year or so, I have been trying to work out the relation between jazz and Rock in the English language. For various reasons, which we can discuss at length sometime, it is impossible to have a music that is not based on the rhythms of a particular tongue or speech. Speech is the "hidden" *ground* for the music as *figure* in any culture whatever. There are specific and complex reasons why the oral tradition of American Southern speech constitute the only possible ground for jazz and rock. Some of these reasons include the fact that English is almost the only language in the world that has actual feet and not mere syllables. Equally basic is the relation of English to the metropolitan patterns of industrial sound. New technological sounds and patterns are processed through the speech in order to become "music". To people who do not understand this complex of speech technology factors, it must seem very mysterious that Chinese and Norwegian alike are compelled to sing Rock in English rather than in their own tongues.

I have been doing a good deal of work on this subject, and hope to do a great deal more. That is why I am asking for any help or suggestions you can offer. For example, in your own music, have you employed speech rhythms and intervals, consciously or unconsciously? Do you know anybody who has ever worked on these lines?

The fact of "feet" in English relates to the power of English to incorporate complex dance rhythms which are excluded by the languages that have only syllables. The fact that only English has prosody among modern languages, whereas all the rest have only separate syllables, was mentioned to me by a Professor of Italian here when I asked him what was Dante's prosody. He said at once: "There is no prosody in Italian." Since then, I have checked this out. It is absolutely staggering to realize that one has been a Professor of English for decades without knowing this unique fact about the English language. It is even more appalling to realize that everybody else appears to be as ignorant as I am. I

---

[1]John Cage (b. 1912) is the avant-garde American composer who introduced chance procedures—with his *Music of Changes* (1951), a piano work that was determined by coin tosses—and "happenings" and live electronics into his musical compositions.

feel that you and Merce Cunningham might have discovered some things in this area, and I am most eager to learn about them.[2]

Most cordial good wishes,
Yrs Marshall

[2]Merce Cunningham is the distinguished American dancer and choreographer whose collaboration with John Cage has continued into the mid-1980s.

To Margaret Atwood[1]

November 22, 1972

Dear Miss Atwood:

It is good to know that you are on the University of Toronto campus as our resident writer this year. Lately, I have had the luck to read *Survival* where I found at once the answer to a question which I have been asking for some years: "Why do North Americans, unlike all other people on this planet, go outside to be alone and inside to be with people"[2] I knew that the answer would be massive, since if it were anything else, it would be easy to spot. You provide the answer in *Survival* when you indicate the North American crash program for conquering nature. Surely no other continent was ever ripped off so quickly or completely, but then Renaissance man, and afterwards, had unsurpassed technology for doing just that. Less well-equipped cultures were inclined to make a truce with nature quite early. Perhaps Western man was not prepared for the sudden capitulation of nature with Sputnik in 1957. When the planet went inside a man-made environment, nature had to yield to art and ecology.

Sometime I hope we can chat about the ways in which going outside to be alone and inside to be folksy have shaped North American genre. Meantime, congratulations on *Survival*.

[1]Margaret Atwood (b. 1939)—the well-known Canadian poet, novelist, short-story writer and critic—was at this time Writer-in-Residence at the University of Toronto. She had recently published *Survival: A Thematic Guide to Canadian Literature* (1972), in which the literature is discussed partly in terms of the victim struggling with a hostile natural environment.

[2]In her reply of November 27, Margaret Atwood wrote: "One wonders about the Eskimos especially in mid-winter but I suppose they do not go outside to be alone but rather to hunt which is quite different."

To Rollo May[1]

December 14, 1972

Dear Rollo:

Many thanks for sending *Power and Innocence*. We have been using the topic

[1]Rollo May (b. 1909) is the author of numerous books on psychology and psychiatry, including *Love and Will* (1969) and *Power and Innocence: A Search for the Sources of Violence* (1972).

of power as our special one for this year at the Centre. Last year we had looked at the satisfactions of great wealth, and found few. The theme of power proves even more elusive.

One of the themes of *Take Today: The Executive as Dropout* (Harcourt Brace Jovanovich Inc., N.Y. 1972), my latest book, is the loss of identity through sudden new electric environments, the consequence being the quest for identity via violence. As we move from the old hardware world of nineteenth-century industrialism into the new simultaneous electric environment of information, the natural tendency is inward, with complete loss of merely private identity and loss of outer goals and objectives.

I find your entire approach to the problems of power and loss of identity most helpful. But I am puzzled to know why you study these problems as *figure* minus the cultural *ground* in which they occur. There seems to be a universal inhibition in the Western world to study the *ground* of events, or structures. I have been asking myself for the past two years whether this inhibition, or subliminal reluctance, relates to the peculiar character of private identity in the West? As Eric Havelock explains in *Preface to Plato*, the private identity of Western man appears to be grounded in the peculiar effects of the phonetic alphabet in abstracting private from corporate identity. If private identity, in this sense, is an artefact, then it is easier to understand why any probing of the nature of psychic change as shaped by outer environments might breed insecurity and panic. In the Orient, and in non-phonetically literate countries where private identity hardly exists, there is no uneasiness about probing the causes of psychic change resulting from man-made or technological environments. But from Plato to the present, in the Western world, there has been no theory whatever of psychic change resulting from technological change. The exception is the work of Harold Innis (*The Bias of Communication*) and his disciples, Eric Havelock and McLuhan.

Natually, I would be most interested in your comments on this entire matter of psychic change in *figure-ground* terms. Even Freud paid no attention to the *ground* of psychic conditioning, except tangentially, in *Civilization and Its Discontents* [1930]. His Oedipus complex would be meaningless except in a highly literate environment. Historically, Oedipus himself was a product of technological change. When the oral and tribal Greek was submitted to the detribalizing action of the visually oriented alphabet, his new private identity was suddenly in violent interface with the old corporate, or incestuous, identity. Today we have an instant replay, as it were, of the Greek historical shift from oral to visual culture as we move from visual to acoustic culture, electrically.

May it be a blessed New Year for you.

1973

To Jane Bret[1]

January 3, 1973

Dear Jane:

Apropos your fascinating quote from Percy's *Moviegoer*, Harley [Parker] and I have just been discussing it and noticing that the process involved is the change of *ground* or environment into *figure* or art form by means of translation into another medium.[2] Harley mentions a time when he was painting a large old house in downtown Toronto. It turned out to be a brothel, but the inmates became absolutely fascinated by the business of being translated into a painterly medium. Harley was in the process of certifying a brothel! Perhaps language does this for everything we speak of. Until something has been named, it hardly exists. By the same token the planet, by being put inside the Sputnik or satellite medium, becomes an art form too. There's a book called *Hawthorne Revisited* which describes the Hawthorne "effect".[3] This happened at a Western Electric plant near Chicago, when the work force was subjected to a wide variety of changes of their environment—heating and lighting were made both pleasant and unpleasant, but no matter which, work performance improved steadily. It gradually dawned on the observers that the workers enjoyed being "on stage", as it were, somewhat as when a person visits a psychiatrist in order to have "a public."

Since writing the above, I have had lunch with Bob Patchel of the C.B.C. He was delighted with your quote from the *Moviegoer*, but he challenged the idea of the TV icon and the certification of placelessness. However, Harley and I explained to him that whereas the movie is a *figure-ground* pictorial form, TV is iconic in the full sense that iconic merges *figure* and *ground*. If the iconic form pushes the "place" up into dignity, it may also tend to downgrade the user or "viewer",

---

[1] Jane Bret—a teacher and writer of North Dallas, Texas—wrote a piece on liturgy and the media that attracted McLuhan, and when they met in Dallas he invited her to visit his Centre, which she did. She and her husband, William Bret, an attorney, became firm friends of McLuhan.

[2] The quotation Jane Bret provided from Walker Percy's novel *The Moviegoer* (1961) had to do with the "certification of place": residents felt their neighbourhood to be anonymous and did not identify themselves with it until they saw it in a film—when they began to feel at home there. Bret, who had participated in the filming of *The Exorcist* in the Georgetown neighbourhood of Washington, D.C., wondered if the TV image of place had the opposite effect of decertification, or of certifying placelessness.

[3] Henry A. Landsberger, *Hawthorne Revisited* (1958), published by the New York School of Industrial and Labour Relations. The "Hawthorne studies" investigated the monotonous working conditions of factory personnel at Western Electric's Hawthorne plant in Cicero, Illinois, in the late 1920s. It was found that human relations greatly affected the quantity and quality of output, that output improved not only when working conditions improved but when they were made worse, and that workers responded positively to being studied, not to changes in environment. The improvement factor was known as the "Hawthorne effect".

because the iconic is multi-sensuous. The Platonist, with his specialized and merely visual archetypes (*figures* without *ground* rather than merged with *ground*), gets a sense of divinity from his abstraction of *figure* from *ground*. The Aristotelian, with his hylomorphic *figure* and *ground* interplay, seems more earthy and rooted. In the same way the movie would seem to many to be Platonic and visual compared to TV, with its mingling of the senses in an iconic merger.

This may help to explain why TV is so predominantly a participation medium. It also is relevant to mention St. Thomas' pervasive use of the term "participation." According to Geiger, the only time Aquinas explains his use of "participate" is when he says: "Suppose that we say that air participates the light of the sun, because it does not receive it in that clarity in which it is in the sun." (This quote is from *De Hebdomadibus* Chapter 2). Aquinas seems to say that participation is a "cooling" process as well as being a *figure-ground* relationship, i.e. existence is real cool, but the Platonists are always trying to hot it up by separating *figure* from *ground*. Is not the academic seen in general to break *figure* away from *ground* for the sake of simplicity and intensity? I owe this quote to page 90 of *Saving the Appearances by* Owen Barfield (Harbinger paperback), which is a quite wonderful little book.[4] The mere fact that he focused on "participation" in Aquinas—which is, as it were, St. Thomas' theory of communication in a word— may be a sufficient indication of his quality.

Apropos the Percy quote about certification of place, you might note the passage from Shakespeare's *A Midsummer Night's Dream* about the power of the poet to give "to airy nothing a local habitation and a name." The role of language itself, as of any other medium, is to translate and to transform being by "participation" and perception. All media perform this function in some degree. My C.B.C. friend, at lunch today, was pointing out the annoyance of his friends when he mentions any "inaccuracies" in press releases about himself. They prefer the press release to the actuality, giving art priority over nature, as it were. Once an event has been recorded the recording is, mysteriously, felt to have more reality than the original. This, by the way, must be the effect of the instant replay. That is, the replay is felt in some way to be superior to the play itself, since it has translated the event into an art form.

Apropos the "content" approach to media, is it not a clear case of the Platonist need for the *figure* minus the *ground*?

Have been dipping into *Telepolitics* a good deal,[5] and enjoying it. I attach one observation to myself, namely, the remark about the Spaniard as accepting, but not approving, the developments of his time. For me the study of these events is a conscious attempt to defuse them, as it were, and certainly involves a scorn for many of their pretentions which amounts to satire.

We hope you will come back to the Centre before long, and meantime, a blessed New Year.

[4]See page 335, note 3.

[5]Frederic D. Wilhelmsen and Jane Bret, *Telepolitics: The Politics of Neuronic Man* (1972), a study of the role of television in politics and propaganda.

To Pierre Elliott Trudeau

Dear Pierre:

A one-liner that is very flexible in its uses goes: "As Zeus said to Narcissus: 'Watch yourself!' "

There is a basic political principle that may or may not be Hegelian in pattern. It follows the structure of the wheel and the axle. Between the wheel and the axle there must be "play". This play is "tough". When the interval between wheel and axle is too small, they seize up and there is neither wheel nor axle. When the interval is too large, the wheel falls off. The principle that the resonant interval between the wheel and axle is *where the action is* would seem to apply quite well to war, and politics, and many social situations. Let me illustrate: the Western world is going eastward via electricity. That is, it is going inward and abandoning its outer goals. The Eastern world, on the contrary, is going outward via our nineteenth-century technology and is acquiring outer goals and objectives. Between these two vast components moving antithetically, there is a resonant interval, a gap. As with the wheel and the axle, the gap is *where the action is*. At the moment this gap is Viet Nam.

Is it not important to understand that Viet Nam is not a component nor an objective nor a target, but only a resonant interval or "interface"? In quantum mechanics the chemical bond is referred to as the resonant interval, since there are no connections. The same principle would seem to apply to the interface between political parties. That is, the action would take place in the gap between them. By the same token Women's Lib would be the interval between masculine and feminine senses or parties. The interval would be a gap of non-sex, "where the action is."

The ordinary instinct to speak of the business game, or the political game, would seem to be rooted in the awareness of "play" as crux in all forms of social action. It is a basic feature of play that it keeps us in touch, and is also extremely involving of our faculties. Paradoxically, there is also the principle of leisure involved in play, since it is only the specialist who works. When we are using only a small part of our faculties, we are working. When we are totally involved, we are playing. The artist is always at leisure, especially when most intensely engaged in making.

To Muriel C. Bradbrook[1]

Dear Miss Bradbrook:

One of our librarians at the University of Toronto has become very much interested in my account of our library at the Cambridge English School as I knew it in the 1930's. Apart from its modest scale, one of its main features had been, for me, the display of relevant books in a variety of fields. I got the feeling, merely by examining the shelves, that these were the books regarded as of primary significance in contemporary poetry, aesthetics, history, and so on. My librarian friend would like to know what sort of selection process had gone to the making up of that library. Had it been of individual or group inspiration? As for myself, I would be most interested to know what kinds of changes have gone on in the English School library since the 1930's. The paperback had scarcely begun, although there were a few Penguin[s].

There are 39,000 new titles in America alone per annum, and so far as I know there is no longer *a* reading public anywhere. There are literally hundreds and hundreds of reading publics, with only a small amount of overlap among them. My librarian friend is eager to experiment with various means of encouraging the development of a coherent group of readers who can share a wide diversity of contemporary interests. Do you think of any periodicals currently able to achieve something of this sort in their book-review departments?[2]

We recently had William Empson to dinner.[3] He is teaching at York University here in Toronto during the current year. L.C. Knights was talking on Ben Jonson here recently.[4] These were major links with the Cambridge I knew in the 1930's.

Corinne joins me in warm regards and wishes for a splendid New Year.

[1] The Elizabethan scholar Dr Muriel C. Bradbrook (b. 1909) was at this time Principal of Girton College, Cambridge. McLuhan met her at Cambridge in 1939 and they corresponded off and on from 1940 to 1978.

[2] To this Dr Bradbrook replied: "As for periodicals, I despair of them. There is not one, no, not one, that is doing anything to make 'a coherent group of readers'."

[3] The English poet and critic (Sir) William Empson (1906–84)—who, like McLuhan, had studied under I.A. Richards at Cambridge—was the author of *Seven Types of Ambiguity* (1930; revised 1947, 1953), which greatly impressed McLuhan when he read it at Cambridge: "Found it excellent" (diary reference of December 30, 1935); "Enjoying Empson's criticism very much" (January 4, 1936). Empson extended "ambiguity" to include: (i) metaphor; (ii) "when two or more meanings are resolved into one"; (iii) two apparently disconnected meanings, as in a pun; (iv) when "alternative meanings combine to make clear a complicated state of mind of the author"; (v) an area of "fortunate confusion"; (vi) a contradictory or irrelevant statement that forces interpretation on the reader; and (vii) when two opposite meanings of a word show a division in the poet's mind. About Empson's visit to Toronto, see also the letter to Claude Bissell beginning on page 468.

[4] L.C. Knights (b. 1906), an Elizabethan scholar, was Professor of English Literature at Cambridge University, 1965–73, and is the author of *Drama and Society in the Age of Jonson* (1937), among other books.

The letter that follows concerns a newsletter that both Margaret Mead and McLuhan had received from the Pan-Hellenic Anti-Dictatorial Movement ("Kinema")—abbreviated to PAK—dedicated to ending the military junta in Greece; it was founded by Andreas Papandreou, who taught at York University, Toronto, in the early 1970s and was therefore associated with the Toronto chapter. The newsletter cited the arrest of eight Greek freedom fighters and observed that "eighty-four of you 'intellectuals, scholars and scientists' " cruised the Aegean and later called for "concerted worldwide action to build human settlements in which man could live happily". It asked for clarification, in the light of the Greek dictatorship and the arrest of the freedom fighters, of what was really meant by "concerted world action", "happy settlements", etc. In a letter to McLuhan of January 11, 1973, Mead asked him to respond to her intended reply (quoted), in which she declared her awareness of the denial of freedom worldwide; that while certain individuals deprived of freedom received much publicity, there were "voiceless peoples inside our own countries, and all over the world, who have no champions"; and that, dedicated as she was to working for the world, she had no time for the kind of "Sybarytic vacations" they had imagined the Delos cruise to be. Mead replied to PAK in a letter of March 2, 1973 that both she and McLuhan signed.

To Margaret Mead

January 25, 1973

Dear Margaret:

Thanks for the reminder about the PAK Newsletter. I had managed to overlook it in the general pile-up of mail here.

I think your suggested reply is quite masterly, and I would be happy to co-sign it with you, if that seems practical. If I were to write personally, I would have to indicate that my own role of exploring and understanding situations tends to exclude the moralistic observation or political action. In practice, Margaret, my idea of action in such matters is to consult directly and personally with people as close to the events as I can possibly get. I am not entirely sure why I choose to avoid a personal manifesto of my feelings or attitudes in such matters. This may be merely personal to myself, but I am always baffled when people ask me how I am feeling. As a form of greeting, it makes me wince with its callous and careless unconcern masquerading as good-will. Sometimes I stop these people and ask them point-blank: "Do you really want to know? Because it may take quite a while to tell you!" Perhaps some of this centers into my feelings about personal expression concerning the odious and sickening manifestations of human greed and aggression. I would wish to avoid any appearance of moral superiority in confronting human depravity. It is so easy to borrow virtue by juxtaposing oneself with viciousness. On the other hand if one has a name or a position which could be used to mitigate evils, it would be unpardonable to refrain. I may say that I consider the Delos meetings as of a very dubious quality and performance. The participants of all such gatherings seek reassurance for their convictions rather than new awareness of their inadequacy. My own concern is with the exploration of ignorance rather than the shoring-up of existing knowledge.

In the above observations I have really been exploring my own ignorance of myself. I hope you will point out for me a useful course of action or intervention in this matter if I have overlooked it.

To Hugh Kenner   February 2, 1973

Dear Hugh:

Warm congratulations on the Hopkins appointment, and also for the assignment to the Alexander Lectures.[1] I look forward to this very much.

Bill Wimsatt was here recently to give a lecture and a seminar, and I was present when he dined with William Empson and Norrie Frye, making a very strange gestalt indeed! Empson has been up at York since October, totally ignored by the University of Toronto until I brought him down for dinner with several of the staff, including Kay Coburn.[2] He is to lecture on February 7th on "The Secret Marriage of Andrew Marvell." Empson is quite delightful, and indiscreet. He was telling us that Arthur Waley knew no Chinese, much to the embarrassment of the British Foreign Office when they put him on to big assignments.[3] He also wonders whether Joseph Needham knows any Chinese whatsoever.[4]

I enclose a copy of Bill Wimsatt's parody of Yeats. It strikes me as a classic. I have not got his permission to send it to anybody, but I shall tell him that I sent you a copy.[5]

All the best,

[1]Professor Hugh Kenner (see page 189, note 3) had accepted an appointment at Johns Hopkins University, where he is Andrew W. Mellon Professor of Humanities. In March 1973 he gave the Alexander Lectures ("The Meaning of Rhyme") at University College, University of Toronto.

[2]The distinguished Coleridge scholar Kathleen Coburn (b. 1905) was at this time Professor Emeritus of Victoria College, University of Toronto.

[3]The English orientalist Arthur Waley (1889–1966) opened up Chinese and Japanese literature to the general public as a celebrated and prolific translator. His knowledge of the languages was self-taught and he never travelled to the Far East. McLuhan heard Waley read Chinese poetry on November 1, 1935 in Cambridge.

[4]Joseph Needham (b. 1900) is the author of *Science and Civilization in China* (1954) and *Clerks and Craftsmen in China and the West: Addresses on the History of Science and Technology* (1970).

[5]In a letter to McLuhan of January 29, Professor Wimsatt included his parody of William Butler Yeats's "An Irish Airman Foresees His Death", entitled "An English Chairman Foresees His End". It begins: "I know that I shall meet my fate/Some day upon this chair above./Those that I hire I do not hate./Those that I teach I do not love." On February 2 McLuhan acknowledged receipt of this to Wimsatt (telling him that he had sent a copy to Kenner) and asked some rhetorical questions about the nature of parody: e.g. "Is the comic effort of parody partly a complaint about the too perfect form? Is not all humour, at root, the expression of grievance and also catharsis for same?"

To Lawrence D. Conklin[1]   February 2, 1973

Dear Mr. Conklin:

You ask me some very hard questions about the norms of society and the relation of individuals to same. There was an item in the papers last week about a group of educated people who volunteered to pretend madness in order to get accepted into mental hospitals. They succeeded in getting accepted in twelve hospitals quite easily. The doctors who admitted them and who treated them were unable to detect the fact that they were sane people from the outside free world. However, the patients in the hospitals instantly spotted the fact that these people were sane because they could see that they were *playing*. Perhaps it is the ability to *play*, the good humour needed to enter into fun and games, which is the final mark of sanity. When people become too intense, too serious, they will have trouble in relating to any sort of social game or norm. Perhaps this is why jokes are so important. On one hand they tell us about where the troubles and grievances are, and, at the same time, they provide the means of enduring these grievances by laughing at the troubles.

I am enclosing a typical current cartoon which draws attention to the fact that the so-called social norms in the electric age of instant replays tend to dissolve very quickly. People find it very difficult to have any identity or responsibility when everything is changing and changing at electric speed.

[1]Mr Conklin, a prisoner at Leavenworth, Kansas, wrote to McLuhan on January 1 questioning the "norms" of society that would allow a person who had been "in jail, prison, reform schools, foster reform schools since he was 8½ years old, (he's now 40) with less than 90 days in the free society" to be tried for murder. He asked whether "this person" did not have a mental disorder and should have been judged insane "due to the corrupt system that had brain washed him through the years", or whether he should be tried as a normal person. He thanked McLuhan in advance for his answer.

To Barbara Ward[1]   February 9, 1973

Dear Barbara:

Many thanks for your thoughtful letter, and much commiseration for the miserable bout of flu. I read in the life of Mary Queen of Scots [Antonia Fraser's biography?] that influenza was new in the 16th century, when it was called "the new acquaintance." Now it has become like Aquinas, an old acquaintance which shall never be forgot!

I wish I had an opportunity to chat with you about the matters that you put in the letter. I think it is typical of the blessedly accomplished Delos Conferences

[1]Barbara Ward (Lady Jackson, 1914–81) had been foreign editor of the *Economist*, governor of the BBC, and was at this time completing a period of teaching at Columbia University in the School of International Affairs. She was the author of several books, including *The Rich Nations and the Poor Nations* (1962), *Nationalism and Ideology* (1966), and *Human Settlements: Crisis and Opportunity* (published by Information Canada, Ottawa, in 1974), which grew out of her attendance at the last Delos Symposion.

that their atmosphere forbade any discourse whatever. Let me begin with your concern about "the effect of visual, communal images (via television) upon the survival of literacy." In the first place, television does not present a visual image, but an X-ray icon which penetrates our entire organism. Joyce called it "the charge of the light barricade"—part of the Crimean war against mankind. Stained-glass images are not visual either, since they are defined by light *through*, as in Rouault paintings. The structure of these images is audile-tactile, as in abstract art, both of Symbolist and Cubist kind. They stand at the extreme from phonetic literacy. Today, for example, when the Japanese are about to spend six billion on a program of phonetic literacy and the abolition of their own iconic culture, it is extremely important to understand the nature of these images and their effects. The phonetic alphabet is unique in the world in that its images abstract from all semantic meanings. There is no other alphabet that is not loaded with semantic meanings and multi-sensory images. By abstracting all semantics from the signs, the phonetic alphabet also abstracted the visual faculty from all the other senses, making Euclid possible. One of the many effects of this extreme abstraction of the visual sense was to enable the Graeco-Roman world to translate all their cultures into itself, while making it impossible for other cultures to translate us into them. The Graeco-Roman man was not only extremely aggressive but has always insisted that everybody adopt his way. When the Japanese have installed the phonetic alphabet, they will behave exactly in that manner with regard to the Chinese or the Hindus.

Visual man is the most extreme case of abstractionism because he has sepa-rated his visual faculty from the other senses, giving him unlimited powers of blue-printing knowledge and experience and political programming. Only Graeco-Roman man has ever had this visual faculty in isolation, and today it is threat-ened, not by any single factors such as television or radio, but by the electric speed of information movement in general. Electric speed is approximately the speed of light, and this constitutes an information environment that has basically an acoustic *structure*. At the speed of light, information is simultaneous from all directions and this is the structure of the act of *hearing*, i.e. the *message* or effect of electric information is acoustic, even when it is read in a newspaper with a mosaic of world-wide items under a single date-line. The Symbolists long ago, and Yeats, Joyce, Pound, Eliot in this century, spent their entire lives expounding the aesthetics of the resonant intervals of acoustic space. The same resonant intervals have become the basis of modern quantum mechanics. The major factor is that the *interval* is where the action *is*. Whereas visual space is continuous, uniform, connected and static, the spaces created by all the other senses are discontinuous and dynamic. At the speed of light the simultaneous information that now enmeshes the human organisms of the planet easily dominates and erodes all visual culture with its rational bias for the connected.

I don't think that what I am saying, Barbara, would make much sense for anybody who had not spent a good deal of time studying the constitution of spatial forms. Very few people, even among scientists, recognize the fact of visual or acoustic space as such. Those who *do* recognize [it] are too specialized to relate *it* to anything. The fatal flaw of the Graeco-Roman thing has always been specialism and unrelatedness. Nobody has ever written, or even mentioned, "Plato's theory of communication." From Plato and Dante to Wordsworth and Bertrand Russell, nobody has ever noticed what the theories of communication were. A communication theory means, basically, discussion of: "What did he think had happened to him that should also happen to his public?" Newton, for example, devoted his entire life to apologetics and scriptural exegesis. He thought that mathematics would end all the problems of Christian apologetics. His main scientific endeavours were spent on commentaries on the Book of Daniel, which have never been published.

Communication theory for any *figure* requires the including of the *ground* for that figure and the study of the interplay between the *figure* and its *ground*. Graeco-Roman, or visual man, has consistently studied the *figure* minus the *ground*. When Q.D. Leavis did a study of *Fiction and the Reading Public*, there was an uproar because she had ventured to suggest that highly literate people could lead moronic lives through most of their waking hours. It is the only study ever made, in English, of a reading public. That is, the study of *ground* for the *figure* of the novel. The ordinary study concentrates on *figure* minus *ground*, i.e. the *content* of the novel is studied and the kinds of readers and their relation to the novel are ignored. Visual man likes to assume a merely neutral transportation process as between the *figure* and the *ground*, ignoring the complex changes that take place in both *figure* and *ground* during all communication [*handwritten addition*: except for H.A. Innis' Empire and Communication.]

Visual man cannot tolerate the study of the *subliminal* and the non-visual aspect of his own life. Such is not the case in the Orient or in any other non-Western culture. Panic and inhibition characterize Gracco-Roman man when his visual assumptions are either studied or threatened. (To study or to threaten are the same thing, by the way, for the visual man.) As Bertrand Russell said at the opening of his *ABC of Relativity*, "Einstein is not difficult, but he does require a total reorganization of the imaginative life." What Russell was trying to say was that Einstein had no visual components to present to his students since he was dealing entirely with an acoustic and resonating world.

What you say about the complementing of the Graeco-Roman by the Hebraic is true enough, but when the Hebraic self righteousness is added to the visual abstraction and specialism, you have the Western technocrat of yesteryear. Of course ecology is acoustic in its bias, and so is the Hebrew in *his* culture. That is one reason why the Hebrews have been so prominent in the arts of the past century. They could never be happy in an abstract visual culture since their kind of literacy is not visual at all.

The above is not intended as an attack on the visual man or a defence of acoustic man. The qualities of life attainable by each are quite different, and it is no longer necessary to be locked up in any one of these pockets exclusively. To return to the Graeco-Roman for a moment, the paradox is that whereas the Graeco-Roman, from Plato to the present, has no theory of communication at all (what is called "communication theory" today is merely the transportation of data from one machine to another machine), Christianity proclaims its communication theory loud and clear. Every aspect of the Christian thing is communication and change and transformation. As such, Christianity and the Graeco-Roman thing are antithetic, and yet Christianity has been the main means of propagating the Graeco-Roman thing, even to the extent of depriving those areas that reject Western civilization of Christianity. There is surely a great mystery about the wedding of dogma and politics. Every technological change or innovation brings in new political forms, and new dogmas are mustered to fend off the new threats. Is not the history of dogma the story of the wall built against the world? As Chesterton said: "Any stigma is good enough to beat a dogma." I have no doubt at all that *Christus Vincit*. That is why a Christian cannot but be amused at the antics of worldlings to "put us on". This, however, does not resolve the question of what kinds of strategies literate people should deploy in propping up this or that portion of worldly culture at any given time. Must not the Christian strategy be pragmatic and tentative? When the entire Western world is going inward via electric information, and the entire Orient is going outward via Western hardware and technology, how is it possible to make value judgements? We already know the qualities and satisfactions to be attained by both these modes of the visual and the acoustic. Shall we simply say "A plague on both your houses—I mean both your city house and your country house!"? We can't take either of these houses very seriously. At present, when the power to create diverse forms of space and work and residence are almost unlimited, it would seem to be a very good time to up-date vision of a Christian culture or city.

Corinne has just had extensive surgery and bone-mending for both feet. For twenty years, walking has been torment for her. Now we hope all is amended. We are both great admirers of yours, and wish to be most fondly in your thoughts.

Most Cordially—Marshall

P.S. Looking over the above, I notice one vast hiatus, i.e. visual = "civilized", and acoustic = "tribal". All non-visual cultures are tribal, in varying degrees; that is, time-bound and structured by kinship.

To Claude Bissell

February 9, 1973

Dear Claude:

Greetings to you and Christine in your new quarters.[1] Most recently, from that part of the world, William Empson has come to the Toronto campus. He gave a lecture at Sidney Smith [Hall] on "The Secret Marriage of Andrew Marvell." One overwhelming fact that emerged was that Andrew Marvell was

---

[1]After Bissell resigned as President of the University of Toronto, he and his family moved into a house on Erskine Avenue, in North Toronto.

the master of seventy-seven types of ambiguity.[2] Marvell turns out to have been a quadruple agent for various political groups, all of whom paid him for undermining all the others. He was an extremely worldly man who lived in terror of damnation, and his secret marriage to his landlady was to facilitate certain inheritances, but also motivated by his hatred of women.[3]

[Marvell's] "The Coy Mistress" poem ["To His Coy Mistress"] takes on some rather startling meanings in the light of Empson's analysis. Would that we had a video tape of his delivery. His rubicund face, bound by a drooping white moustache, had also some histronics such as I had never seen. He read aloud from a volume which he seldom saw since it was above eye level, with the spine of the book dangling by one string, while he flapped 30 or 40 pages at a time, back and forth. He recited constantly, both from the book and from a great mass of lecture notes that were distributed for several feet around him. These notes he examined with convulsive and darting movements, which were like the action of a card shark shuffling several decks simultaneously. However, I have saved the most amazing part for the last—namely, his voice. Overall it was somewhat like the sound of air escaping from a tire, punctuated by occasional sounds of words. Tiny phrases of three or four words could definitely be heard every minute or so, as he rose suddenly above the general hissing noise that came through the moustache. Several times he alluded to the contemptible P.A. mechanism that lay beside him, unused. The audience was strongly impelled to seize this equipment and wrap it around his neck, if only to strangle him. If one had heard of Marvell before, and even read a bit, the scattered stabbings of tiny phrase bits were very tantalizing indeed. For those who had not heard of Marvell, there were the histronics! It was a good show at worst, and unforgettable, at best.

We miss you hereabouts, and feel less at home in Toronto without you. Corinne has just had extensive repairs to the bones of her feet, which will keep her in casts for a month. The surgeon said: "These aren't bones—it's spaghetti!" One result is that she has had more rest than at any time since giving birth to Michael. That reminds me, Michael has just announced that he's going to be married on March 21st. It's going to be a vegetarian feast for the first day of Spring!

[2]For William Empson and his book *Seven Types of Ambiguity*, see page 462, note 3.
[3]It is now thought that Andrew Marvell (1621–78) did *not* marry his housekeeper, Mary Palmer.

To Pierre Elliott Trudeau

February 12, 1973

Dear Pierre:

Just a word about interviews on the subject of your *arrogance*. Is it not relevant to ask the interviewer for help in clarifying the problem as it affects the supposed public that is represented by the interviewer? Are there not many hidden factors that the interviewer should explicate as part of his or her job in mediating between you and the public? For example, to the Wasp world (white Anglo-Saxon

Protestant) your mere existence as head of state is arrogant presumption. That is, for a French Catholic to rule over the "superior and dominant" group represents to them a kind of reversal of nature, an upsetting of the relation between *figure* and *ground* in gestalt terms.

In a word, there is a widespread assumption that your arrogance exists in merely occupying your present role. That is, it has nothing to do with your personal image but rather with your corporate role. As long as you were content to "put on" your public by playfulness and "clowning", it was felt that they did not have to take you seriously. As soon as you "play it straight", the Wasp public feels abused, since it alone has the right to assume the mask of serious corporate power.

Note how [President] Richard Nixon has ineptly tried to mitigate his crude and harsh image of liaison with various figures in the world of entertainment. He is quite unable to combine these qualities in himself in the way that you have done. To the Wasp world the light-hearted approach to power represents aristocratic insouciance and security. The entertainer is a figure which they themselves have crowned. He is permitted to hurt them by his humour, for that is the mask of his power and relevance alike.

A great complication occurs in the matter of your image as it must be presented simultaneously to French and English. Our media totally ignore this fact. The obligations which you have to the French electorate seem to be much at odds with the forming of an image for effective relatedness to the Wasp world. Neither on radio, TV, nor in the press is there ever the slightest hint that this problem exists. You are obliged to perform a balancing act on the high wire for two conflicting publics. It is very important that these publics should see each other at the same time that they are watching you, for their responses to you and to one another are totally diverse.

> Cordially and
> Prayerfully
> Marshall

To Ernest Sirluck   February 21, 1973

Dear Ernest:

I am dictating this note to Mrs. Stewart from the lobby of the Inn on the Park during an intermission in a Management and Marketing program. I mention this by way of explaining my somewhat abrupt approach to the Sambrook manuscript, in which I can detect no improvements of consequence.[1] He is determined to

---

[1] This letter concerns a book of readings edited by James Sambrook, of the University of Southampton, that was eventually published as *Pre-Raphaelitism: A Collection of Critical Essays* (1974) in the series *Patterns of Literary Criticism* (1965–74), published by the University of Chicago Press. The General Editors of the series—which presented criticism of a literary subject or movement in the form of previously published essays, plus one new essay by the volume editor—were McLuhan, Richard J. Schoeck, and Ernest Sirluck. McLuhan had previously requested changes in the Sambrook volume; because of disagreements over this, the series was not continued.

exclude from the pre-Raphaelite thing its central preoccupation with the intimate relation between life and art and work. [Thomas] Carlyle had stressed this in his *Past and Present* [1843] and in his presentation of the life of the medieval monastery. [John] Ruskin stressed it throughout his work on art, as did William Morris in the setting up of his workshops for the arts and crafts. But some concern with the relation between the technical and craft approach to all the arts is central to [Walter] Pater and [G.M.] Hopkins and [W.B.] Yeats, all of whom were pre-Raphaelites.

> Irish poets, learn your trade,
> Sing whatever is well made, . . . [2]

The central concern with technique and skill in the arts is what gave the pre-Raphaelites their eminent right to power as healers of the wounds inflicted on the human psyche by the industrial system in which life and work and art had been fragmented and separated. The integrity of these factors was not as intensely pursued by the pre-Raphaelites as by the Symbolists in France or by the Symbolist followers in England and Ireland. Yeats and Pound and Joyce and Eliot pushed the inter-relation of craft and vision even further than the pre-Raphaelites, but to present the pre-Raphaelites without full recognition of their very large effort in this direction of unification of interests would be an extreme form of distortion of their aims and activities.

I would like to hear from Professor Sambrook his reasons for suppressing this entire central aspect of the pre-Raphaelite program. Merely in passing, it might be noted that the popular Pater phrase "to burn with a hard gem-like flame" was borrowed from the world of the plumber, whose blow-torch was seized upon as a kind of triumphant instance of the interplay of the lowest and the highest forms of life and toil and art. The phrase was used to indicate the meeting of all the senses in a moment of synesthesia. The pre-Raphaelites may have been mistaken in presuming such objectives, but the fact that it was their primary concern (that concern, incidentally, brings them closest to ourselves in the twentieth century) cannot be omitted.

Corinne has just had some extensive surgery on her feet which has left her miserable. She is in for a long convalescence. Meantime, my affairs have got considerably scrambled by trying to take care of hers. We look forward to some *happy* walking when she recovers.

Regards to you and
Lesley from us both
Marshall

Ernest Sirluck

[2]W.B. Yeats, "Under Ben Bulben".

To Jay P. Corrin[1]

March 16, 1973

Dear Mr. Corrin:

Apropos your request for information about the influence of Catholic thinkers while I was at Cambridge, I should mention *Take Today: The Executive as Dropout* (Harcourt, Brace, Jovanovich Inc., 1972, N.Y.). This study concerns the drastic decentralizing of all services resulting from electric speed-up. Insofar as Chesterton had any politics, they were called "distributist" and concerned exactly the need for decentralizing of work and human organization, which we are now beginning to witness in the post-industrial age. My interests were in art and poetry, and in these areas the models of perception are always a generation or so ahead of the practical world. I have ever since applied my art interests to the understanding of media and environments and have never had any political interests.

Insofar as Catholic thinking had any direction in England from Newman to Chesterton, it was radically unrevolutionary, e.g. Newman introduced the tutorial system to Oxford (see *The Imperial Intellect*). Chesterton and his group were pre-Raphaelites who wished to reunite art and work, restoring the worker to his abode as place of work. Naturally nobody would be a conservative in a world of mass production. It would be just as meaningful to call a hippie or a dropout a conservative today as to nominate any English Catholic for that term or role.

[1]Jay P. Corrin wrote McLuhan on March 5, 1973 from the Department of History, Boston University, saying that he was working on a Ph.D. thesis on "the influence of Catholicism on English conservative thinking during the inter-war years" and asking for "a few general reflections on Catholicism and politics in Britain during the 1930's."

To Edmund Carpenter

March 23, 1973

Dear Ted:

Would you care to do an essay on Levi-Straus' theory of communication, or [Noam] Chomsky's?[1] I think both of these men are working with *figure* minus *ground*, in the Cartesian tradition. By the way, what is called the second Copernican "revolution" was simply the pulling out of the medieval acoustic *ground* and handing over to the visual *figure* all the attributes to acoustic *ground*. That is, the individual subject was considered to possess the totality of world intellect and consciousness. Perhaps the third Copernican revolution took place when anthropologists handed this acoustic *ground* back to the tribal collectivities. Speak-

[1]Claude Lévi-Strauss (b. 1908), the French social anthropologist and central exponent of Structuralism, views human behaviour as a system of communication. Noam Chomsky (b. 1928), the American linguist and philosopher, revolutionized the study of linguistics with his theory of generative grammar, which postulates structure, not sound, as the basis for speech.

ing of the acoustic, has there been any study or mention of the relation of grammar and literacy? Do you remember when we used to talk about the impossibility of grammatical error in pre-literate societies? Today Chomsky is trying to attribute grammatical infallibility to the innate constitution of the human mind, which is to flip back to the Cartesian mode.

In the Middle Ages the scholastics tried to reduce language to logic, and today Chomsky and the linguists seem to be trying to reduce grammars to logic—logic being the visual mode of connectedness. You remember Theodore Lipps with his observation that all possible symphonies were contained in the single clang of a bell?[2] Is not the same true of language? Acoustically speaking an entire linguistic culture could be encoded acoustically in almost any phrase or pattern of that tongue.

Hope to see you soon.

Yrs Marshall

[2]Theodor Lipps (1851–1914) was a German philosopher who wrote several books (in German) on music, including *Aesthetik* (2 vols, 1903). The reference here is to the statement "The simple clang represents to a certain extent all music" in Lipps, *Psychological Studies* (1926), translated by H.C. Sandbourne, p. 223.

To Morton and Caroline Bloomfield[1]   March 26, 1973

Dear Morton and Caroline:

What a wonderful invitation to join you in Jerusalem at this time of year. It's not really feasible, but absolutely delightful just to think about it. Our youngest is being married very soon and there are a lot of preparations, but Corinne joins me in regrets that we could not visit you there.

I may have told you about our old friend, Max Rosenfeld. He is now, I believe, the mayor of El Karem, the birthtown of John the Baptist. We miss them very much. Since they left, of course, Toronto has become a swinging city which, I suppose, means it doesn't have very long to go!

I might mention, apropos communication studies, that I have begun to realize that my peculiar approach to all matters has been to enter via the *ground* rather than the *figure*. In any gestalt the *ground* is taken for granted and the *figure*

[1]Professor Morton Bloomfield (1913–87) was a distinguished medievalist in the Department of English and American Literature and Language, Harvard University; he was teaching at the Hebrew University in Jerusalem on a sabbatical from Harvard, where he had completed four years as Chairman of the Department and to which he would return as Kingsley Porter Professor of English emeritus. McLuhan first met Bloomfield on November 24, 1935, at Trinity Hall, Cambridge, through their mutual friend Guy Turgeon (see page 66, note 2). Bloomfield—who had been a fellow student of Turgeon's at McGill University, and was then on a fellowship at the University of London—was visiting Turgeon on the Christmas break. McLuhan and Bloomfield became friends when they met again in 1936 as fellow Graduate Assistants at the University of Wisconsin, and they saw each other thereafter in Cambridge, Mass., and in Toronto.

receives all the attention. The *ground* is subliminal, an area of effects rather than of causes. Some day I hope you will do a small book called "Chaucer's Theory of Communication." There should be such a book for Plato, and Virgil, and Dante, and Newton, and Darwin, but no such books exist. Nobody wants to study the sort of changes, or the sort of effects, that any of these people wanted to make in their contemporaries. If you are game for the Chaucer study, tell me because I have a series in view.

To Clare Boothe Luce[1]

April 6, 1973

Dear Mrs. Luce:

It is now a year since we met you in Honolulu and Corinne and I both wish to greet you with special blessings for your birthday and the years ahead.

Canada is beginning to look more and more edible in U.S. eyes, and this situation appears to be developing very rapidly. Thus a young Harvard student came here recently. He had received a scholarship to study Canadian resources and he elected to study Marshall McLuhan as a Canadian resource. Human insatiability knows no bounds!

[1]Clare Boothe Luce (b. 1903)—playwright (*The Women*, 1936), widow of the publisher Henry Luce, and a former U.S. Representative from Connecticut (1943-7) and Ambassador to Italy (1953-6)—was living in retirement in Hawaii. After their first luncheon meeting in 1972, she and McLuhan kept up a correspondence.

To Claude Bissell

May 10, 1973

Dear Claude:

This is the kind of day that would endear the University of Toronto to anybody! The leaves are still in that early bright-green stage, and flowers galore are sending their messages. I think it was Empson who said: "Tulips are right in doing anything that comes into their heads."

William and Heather Empson have returned to London. Unhappily we missed the going-away party for them since I was in Denver that weekend. In fact that was last weekend and I have only just begun to catch up.

Enjoyed your piece "Deep in a British Desert".[1] The current bonanza of Canadian letters is probably euphoria based on affluence. One of the advantages

[1]An essay by Bissell that had recently appeared in the *Globe and Mail*, Toronto. It was written at the University of Leeds, where Bissell was a Visiting Commonwealth Fellow, giving a graduate course in Canadian literature. The "desert" in the title alludes to the fact that in the UK at this time Canadian literature (and Canada) was virtually non-existent.

of my commitments to media study has been the relative freedom from the need to express opinions about writers. However, for some time I have been meditating a play based on media, with the media themselves and their publics present on the stage as individuals, more or less articulate. There will be ample opportunities for these individuals to explain how they made and unmade events and reputations around the world.

I think I mentioned to you about finding the reasons why North Americans go outside to be alone and inside to be social, the reason being that having "tamed" Nature, we continue to look at it as a dangerous enemy. Increasingly this broken enemy needs to be helped, somewhat in the way of the Indians. Whether the Australians have the same idea of Nature as the enemy in their literature, I do not know. Perhaps you have noticed. If so please tell me.

In revising *Understanding Media* and looking over new material,[2] I have hit upon the dynamic that occurs when private identity is rapidly dissolved by the electric surround of information. The private ego, based on visual Euclidean and alphabetic culture, wilts under the impact of the acoustic surround of information from all directions at once. "The Hollow Men" are the products of the radio age rather than the remnants of the industrial time. As private identity dims, ethical absolutes wane in the private sector while becoming much more absolutist in the corporate or public sector. The Watergate affair is a nice mix-up of these patterns, with the "bugging" being damned as an invasion of privacy and charged against the pollution of the corporate or public ethic. I am not sure that you can have it both ways at once. (Someone said recently, "An argument is when two men are trying to have the last word at the same time.")

The decline of private identity comes with the rise of committees and conferences as means of propping up the individual and of transferring the responsibilities for actions to the group. The paradox is, then, that as the individual gets weak, his demands for participation in the corporate thing get stronger and stronger. Is not this apparent in the union problem where the individual workman can only expect attention when on strike? And so with the hijacker?

Have recently been studying Pirandello. His play *To Clothe the Naked* concerns the Christian virtue seen under the aspect of newspaper coverage—maimed and wounded egos crying out for newspaper coverage and recognition.[3]

Wish you were here to discuss the matter of mounting a program for degrees in communications. It has come up lately as one means to recapture undergrads from the social-science areas, on the one hand, and on the other hand to bring

[2]The urge to revise *Understanding Media* led McLuhan to develop the text of a new book, which he called *The Laws of the Media* (this title is mentioned in numerous letters that follow). He worked on it for several years (latterly with the collaboration of his son Eric), but it was not published. Intending "to provide a ready means of identifying the properties of and actions exerted upon ourselves by our technologies and media and artefacts", it is in four short chapters plus an Epilogue, and includes in its first half discussions of acoustic space and visual space and of the two hemispheres of the brain.

[3]Luigi Pirandello, *To Clothe the Naked and two other plays* (1962), translated by William Murray; the title play is known in Italian as *Vestire gli gnudi*.

larger numbers of graduate students into the university. There is a way whereby without altering courses or instructors' activities, all existing programs can be used as communication credits. It is not unlike the new square-rig ship that the Scandinavians have invented. They now have a four-master that can be sailed by one man. Instead of having a great crew to man the ropes and sails, it is only necessary to turn the masts themselves by a central control button. In this case the "one man" would be the student who would be free to select any credit in the university for a communication degree. However, he would have to develop projects which brought his various elected subjects into rapport and interplay. Chemistry and Latin or Greek could be as easily related as mathematics and physics and poetry. Instructors would have to change nothing at all beyond recognizing that some students in their classes were taking the course for a communication credit. Regular seminars of students and faculty, on a volunteer basis, would permit the dialogue to develop.

McGill already has a Ph.D. in communications under the auspices of the English Department. They have some specific offerings for the M.A. but only projects and dissertations for the Ph.D. You see, most American universities have a Ph.D. in communication which is almost entirely slanted toward hardware expertise. Hundreds of their students want to come up here and would be thrilled to have a course available in the language area, minus the hardware.

Recently in New York, at lunch with Betty Friedan,[4] I met Alvin Toffler . . . By the way, future shock[5] is cultural lag, i.e. unawareness of what hit. Don Quixote's "What a blow that phantom gave me" refers to the windmill which was the latest technology in Spain at that time. Part of the joke was that Spain had only just got windmills, long after everybody else. Future shock is also anaesthesia administered as therapy—apprehension in place of comprehension, self-pity instead of self-help.

Barry Nevitt has been doing a good deal of travelling for me, since he knows a lot of languages and is allowed to leave his government job for these trips. He has just returned recently from the University of Mexico and he leaves today for Vienna, Venice and Rome. He was pointing out how the Church in Mexico became an easy push-over when it owned too much land and hardware, much as in 16th-century England. A too-visible church and a too-visible liturgy are equally prone to flip into the opposite mode.

P.S. Tom Easterbrook has had a bad time with his inner organs and the surgeons. He's up and around, and we are praying for the best.

---

[4]Betty Friedan (b. 1921) is the American social reformer and feminist who achieved fame with her book *The Feminine Mystique* (1963).

[5]In his book of this title (1970) Toffler defines "future shock" as "the shattering stress and disorientation that we induce in individuals by subjecting them to too much change in too short a time."

To Duke Ellington[1]

May 17–1973

Dear Duke:

Corinne and I were thrilled to read about your doctorate in music from Columbia University. We have friends there who will tell us all about it later. Meantime, we pray that you are in superb health and enjoying the wonderful music you have given to us all these many years.

Warm regards,

Written on noticing the item in the *Toronto Star* 5/14/73

[1]"Duke [Edward Kennedy] Ellington (1899–1974), the distinguished American bandleader and jazz composer, met the McLuhans, who were great admirers, at a dinner in Toronto given by a mutual friend in the late 1960s. When they attended his performance at the Imperial Room of the Royal York Hotel, Ellington dedicated one piece to Marshall and one to Corinne—a practice he repeated on other visits to the city.

To Franklin R. Gannon[1]

June 12, 1973

Dear Mr. Gannon:

The Dew-Line Newsletter was discontinued after the 24th issue. It would have been fun to continue it had I had the time. One conference in Dew-Line sub-scribers was held in the Bahamas, and it proved especially successful. An amaz-ing range of activities and interests were represented from restauranteurs and balloonists to bankers and politicians. Having had a couple of years of the Dew-Line, they had many data in common to make inter-communication quite effective. It would, of course, be quite possible to have another conference right here in Toronto, almost at any time. I have had open seminars on Monday nights from 8:00 to 10:00 and we tackle just any kind of problem whatever.

Naturally I am concerned about the information revolution which is currently ravaging our established institutions. The reason that most people are helpless in tackling such problems is that they approach them via the *figure* rather than the *ground*. These are gestalt terms which refer to the interplay between components. Thus the *ground* is always hidden or submerged, and yet it is the area of *effects* and in all situations and developments, effects come before the causes manifest themselves. I have an essay on this in *Technology and Culture* (University of Chicago Press, Vol. 14, #1, January, 1973).[2]

The fact that effects come before causes, whether in the motor of the motor car, or the telephone, or in politics, is hidden from most literate and visually

[1]Franklin R. Gannon was Staff Assistant to President Richard Nixon. He wrote McLuhan on June 6, 1973, enquiring about the *Dew-Line Newsletter* and saying that he would like to meet him because, as Gannon was involved in "the broad formulation of domestic policy", he believed it was important to understand "the media which conveys and explains it".

[2]Marshall McLuhan and Barrington Nevitt, "The Argument: Causality in the Electric World", *Technology and Culture*, vol. 14, no. 1, January 1973.

oriented people since they have an unconscious bias to approach everything in terms of its "content." Thus the Watergate affair[3] is only incidentally a political revolution and is, in fact, a change in the entire perceptual and imaginative life of our Western, and especially American, world. At electric speed of information movement, for example, the individual ego and identity is enormously reduced in proportion as it becomes deeply involved in the social lives of mankind. Paradoxically the diminishing of the private identity results, on the one hand, in a great deal of individual permissiveness and laxity, while on the other hand it leads to great intensity of demand for moral absolutism in the public sector. All of that is in the area of *figure*. The hidden *ground* of the entire development is the new speed of information movement, for it is this movement at the speed of light which not only transforms our image of ourselves but involves us in the lives of others in a completely new way.

My writings baffle most people simply because I begin with *ground*, and they begin with *figure*. I begin with *effects* and work round to the *causes*, whereas the conventional pattern is to start with a somewhat arbitrary selection of "causes" and then try to match these with some of the effects. It is this haphazard matching process that leads to fragmentary superficiality. As for myself, I do not have a point of view but simply work with the total situation as obvious *figures* against hidden *ground*.

Once it is understood that the hidden *ground* of our time is information moved at the speed of light, then it becomes easy to see why schooling is changing so drastically. It becomes possible to explain why universities really need not much concern themselves any longer with instruction. Such observations, if offered as a private point of view, would seem outrageous, but if one is working from the *ground* one discovers the new lines of force in the overall situation.

I hope that we shall have a chance to discuss some of these things sometime. I do go to New York fairly often.

[3]A series of scandals involving President Nixon, beginning in July 1972 when agents of Nixon's re-election committee were arrested in Democratic party headquarters in the Watergate apartment building in Washington. Following their conviction in 1973 suspicions of a high-level conspiracy were borne out by revelations made public when a special Senate committee held televised hearings. In July 1974 articles of impeachment were adopted by the House Judiciary Committee against Nixon, who resigned on August 9, 1974.

To Clare Boothe Luce July 6, 1973

Dear Clare:

Your excellent essay on Watergate in *The New York Times* (June 3rd) encouraged me to try my hand. I enclose a rough draft of my piece.[1]

[1]Marshall McLuhan, "Mr. Nixon and the Dropout Strategy", the *New York Times*, July 29, 1973. McLuhan also wrote "Watergate as Theatre", *Performing Arts*, vol. 10, no. 4, Winter 1973.

Many things are moving far too quickly for comprehension, but at least the large patterns are discernible. One of the peculiarities of the electric intercom is that it is the sender who is sent. Thus electronic man tends toward the disembodied or discarnate condition of "angel". I suggest that the incarnational Church has need to confront this new discarnate state of the laity under electronic conditions.

To Nicholas Johnson[1]

August 29, 1973

Dear Commissioner Johnson:

Very sorry to have missed you during your recent Toronto visit. Having recently been reading your "How to Talk Back to a TV Set" with much edification, I duly noted your wistful mention of myself and your inability to understand my work.[2] The fact is that not only is my work hard to understand, but the media are even harder to understand. My own approach to the media has been derived from many years of study of Symbolist art and poetry from Poe to Valéry, from Cézanne to Picasso. People unfamiliar with these matters have little hope of entering the electric age with any comprehension. This is no cynical observation, but a simple fact that artists are the only people who take the trouble to understand our environments. The Symbolists taught me, starting with Poe, that in all situations the *effects* come before the *causes*. That's why we can say when anything happens that "the situation was ripe". Understanding this basic principle I began to study the effects of the media as my beginning point. Very few people had ever attempted this, even for brief stretches.

Having taught media principles to many students over the years, I know that the problem in understanding media is a cultural one. The Western mind is trained to go from A to Z, but not from Z to A. This mind, which is becoming vestigial and confused, works entirely on visual principles (i.e. logic) which insist that things are connected and homogeneous. This is true for the visual sense alone, and the electric age brings all of the other senses into play, ending the dominion of the visual and the "rational". There are extremely few people who are serious enough in their mental endeavours to train their perceptions to confront new situations. The so-called "experts" are not among these. The expert, as such, is full of insecurity. That is why he specializes in order to obtain some degree of confidence.

For years now I have explained to audiences that there is a very simple way to end the régime of popular trash on the media. Our teachers have merely to conduct a weekly examination in the classroom on the programs and comic books, etc., that have been viewed during the preceding week. As you know, the effect would be as fatal to the trash as it is to Shakespeare. The rage of the commercial

[1]This letter was addressed to Commissioner Nicholas Johnson, Federal Communications Commission, Washington, D.C.
[2]Nicholas Johnson, *How to Talk Back to Your Television Set* (1970).

establishment would be beyond words. It is worth a try. As you well know, the expressions of moral indignation are of no avail and serve merely to alienate the young.

Congratulations and very best wishes on your work,

To Tony Schwartz[1]

August 30, 1973

Dear Tony:

I may have mentioned earlier that I had looked into some of the effects of the microphone in Catholic liturgy. Speaking to the Fathers hereabouts, I was told unanimously that the microphone on the altar simply eliminated the Latin Mass because the stepping up of the Latin sounds to higher intensity made them meaningless. The vernacular, on the other hand, which has long been at high intensity via the microphone and via the printed word, does not provide opportunities for meditation that the Latin Mass did. You see, the "blessed mutter" of the Mass did not prevent people meditating and praying during the Mass, whereas the vernacular does prevent them.

Another effect of the microphone is to turn the priest around to face the congregation, so that now he "puts on" the congregation rather than putting on God. Another effect is the obsolescing of the church building or fabric, since the loudspeakers in the church permit sounds to come from every direction, rendering the acoustics and the visual lay-out of the church meaningless.

If these observations prompt any further thoughts in you, I would be most grateful to have them.

Hoping all is going well with *The Responsive Chord*.

[1]Tony Schwartz (b. 1923)—a well-known communications specialist in New York who evolved the resonance theory in electronic communication and wrote *The Responsive Chord* (1973)—read *Understanding Media* with great excitement in 1965, finding that it connected with, and amplified, many of his own ideas about the predominance of auditory over visual (print) methods of communication that were functioning in the environment. He met McLuhan in New York through a mutual acquaintance, and a fast friendship developed. They spoke frequently on the phone thereafter and always met when McLuhan visited New York. Schwartz is President of New Sounds Inc.

To Edward T. Hall

September 5, 1973

Dear Ned:

It has been quite a while since we have corresponded. I have long wanted to send you this note on North American sensory spatial orientation. It all began a few years ago when I was giving a talk to some British advertisers. Wishing to explain to them the difference between the British and American publics, I started with a meditation on the American dislike of advertising in theatres and movies. Europeans and British alike accept ads in their theatres and movies without demur, although they will not accept them on radio or TV without a great deal of demur. It took me two or three years to discover that, unlike all the rest of mankind, Americans go out to be alone and go home to socialize. It was two or three more years before I discovered the reasons for this unique behaviour in North America. Cutting it short, it has to do with our having used a crash program to substitute external nature in North America. The people who came here with highly advanced technology regarded the challenge of "nature" as a wild thing to be tamed and subdued.

It was easy to check these things out in American literature and architecture, once the basic pattern had been discerned. The American novel is unique in sending its characters out to sleuth and adventure rather than to socialize. Henry James is a wonderful case and requires more space than I have so far given to the subject. Naturally I do not consider my approach as adequate to the whole matter. It is a tremendous subject and at the present time TV is reversing the American attitudes to outer and inner by bringing the outside into the home and the inside out into the public. Shortly Americans may share much more of the British and European outlook in these matters.

I would love to have some of your immediate observations about this whole spatial thing. I enclose a copy of an article I did for the *Critic* referring to some of these matters.[1]

---

[1]Marshall McLuhan, "Do Americans Go to Church to be Alone?" *The Critic*, vol. XXXI, no. 3, January/February 1973.

To Sheila Watson

September 7, 1973

Dear Sheila:

Eric has been having a wonderful time reading your Ph.D. thesis. He may slip in a word about it.

Talking to Pauline Bondy recently, she told me again the time when she asked Lewis: "What is vorticism?" He replied: "There is no such thing. For years I thought I had discovered a form that was not in nature; then one day I discovered it in looking through a catalogue of deep-sea fish."

I had forgotten this aspect of vorticism. What are your thoughts on it?

To John D. McCabe[1]

September 12, 1973

Dear Professor McCabe:

I just wanted you to know that I am very glad that you have taken on the role of editing *Renascence*, and I wish to congratulate you on your anniversary issue, in which I am happy to appear.[2]

I no longer pretend to have an over-all image of the activities of Catholic writers, but I have long had a feeling that there is no such thing as a Catholic reading public. For that matter there is no such thing as a reading public, although there are literally thousands of reading publics, with 39,000 new titles per annum in the USA and 39,000 new titles per annum in the UK. I grew up in the '20s when it was still possible to nourish the illusion of a structured public of low-brow, middle-brow and high-brow readers. These are terms which are scarcely used, it seems. Ecumenically speaking, it might be interesting to conjecture on whether there *should* be a Catholic reading public any more. Would it be useful to mount a symposium on any of these subjects?

Cordially,

[1]This letter was addressed to Professor John D. McCabe, Editor, *Renascence*, Marquette University, Milwaukee, Wisconsin.

[2]Marshall McLuhan, "Mr. Eliot's Historical Decorum", *Renascence* 25, Summer 1973—a reprint of the article that first appeared in the Autumn 1949 issue (vol. 2, no. 1).

To D. Carlton Williams

October 5, 1973

Dear Carl:

[*Handwritten*] Although I recall recommending her

I had not realized that Sister St. Michael was to be honoured at Western.[1] She will be profoundly and gratefully moved by the honour. I am always stymied by these formalities, and few people have toiled as she has in the cause of the aging.

Let me mention another remarkable instance of heroic and unflagging service. Fr. Stan Murphy (Basilian) of the University of Windsor (formerly Assumption College) has sustained the Christian Culture Series with zero staff and zero budget for more than thirty years.[2] Almost every famous writer, painter, philosopher, and head of state, to say nothing of whole symphonies, ballet troupes, and choirs of world reputation have performed for him for free. The reason is they admire Stan Murphy so much for his cultural work.

Murphy's work was made possible by the international position of Windsor

[1]For Mother St Michael, see page 336, note 1. Dr Williams (see page 129, note 1), to whom McLuhan is writing, was President of the University of Western Ontario, London, Ont.

[2]See page 129.

and of Assumption College located beside the Peace [Ambassador] Bridge. Murphy used both the Canadian and the U.S. publics simultaneously in all his events, alternating between auditoriums in Detroit and in Windsor. The publics from both countries converge each week on one side or t'other of the river. Of course, it was the wealth and size of the Detroit audience that Murphy was able to employ for the Canadian advantage. It is, to put the matter mildly, to say that there has never been anything approaching the scale of Murphy's operation in Toronto. The international greats he has brought to Windsor are not people who perform in Toronto. Strangely, Toronto is so fragmented and specialized by university and other patterns that it could not rally or focus the kind of interest needed for these events of Murphy's.

You may remember that Murphy came to Toronto when he heard of the presence of Wyndham Lewis here during the war. He rescued Lewis from absolute poverty and total neglect by Toronto and took him back to Windsor where Lewis began to teach Comparative Literature. It was when Lewis gave a lecture on the Culture Series on Rouault that my mother, who attended the lecture, wrote me in St. Louis. I could not credit the possibility that the great Lewis was actually in Windsor. After all, he was one of the greatest men of the century, both in painting and in prose. I got on a train at once and went to Windsor and met Lewis. When I got back to St. Louis, I arranged sitters and lectures for him, and he came to St. Louis for a year. One day he said: "Why don't we go back to Windsor and start up my old art magazine *The Enemy*?" I wrote Murphy at Assumption and he arranged for me to have a job at Assumption at once, so Lewis joined me in Windsor, just as the war ended. Lewis decided to go back to London and I stayed on at Assumption, whence I moved up to Toronto via the Basilians.

It would be a boon if Murphy could have some secretarial aid to help him record the history of the Series and the fantastic social and intellectual adventures associated with it. Personal anecdotes alone would make a wonderful volume. For years I have been trying to think of some way of getting some wider Canadian recognition for the achievements of Stan Murphy. I know of nobody who has done anything comparable anywhere else in the world.

[*Handwritten*] Affectionate regards to Peggy too,

Yrs Marshall

To Ronni Fiedler[1]

December 19, 1973

Dear Mr. Fiedler:

I would like to congratulate you on Mr. Stephen Darst's "Prufrock with a Baedeker" piece.[2] When I lived in St. Louis in the late thirties, I was interested

---

[1] This letter was addressed to Ronni Fiedler, Letters Editor, *Harper's Magazine*, New York. It was not published; however, Walter Ong's response to the Darst article discussed below appeared in the issue of March 1974.

[2] This article appeared in the January 1974 issue of *Harper's Magazine*.

in occasionally catching sight of trucks bearing the label "The Prufrock Brick Company." This could have been an echo in my mind engendered by the relation of Eliot's father to the "Hydraulic Press Brick Company." However, I did not then know that Eliot's father had been so employed. Had there been a rival brick company called "Prufrock", it is possible that Eliot was putting somebody on, as was his wont!

I would also like to draw attention to some remarks on St. Louis which appear in [T.S. Eliot's] *To Criticize the Critic* (Farrar, Straus & Giroux, N.Y. 1965). An address delivered by Eliot at Washington University in St. Louis on June 9, 1953 appears in this volume under the title "American Literature and the American Language." Here he states:

> . . . I am very well satisfied with having been born in St. Louis: in fact I think I was fortunate to have been born here, rather than in Boston, or New York, or London. (p. 45)

Artistically speaking, Eliot had rather impressive reasons for making this remark, and these reasons are not mentioned by Mr. Darst. Walter J. Ong, S.J., wrote a delightful essay on some of the memories of St. Louis which appear in Eliot's *Four Quartets*.[3]

What I am going to mention about Eliot in St. Louis goes very deep into the structure of the English language, and relates directly to the "St. Louis Blues". Eliot has said a great deal about jazz and blues, both in his prose and in his poetry, and he was vividly aware that the rhythms of spoken English, preserved in the oral tradition of the South, were immediately present in the structure of jazz.[4] For many reasons, which need not be cited here, both jazz and rock are forms of music which have made English a world language, since these forms cannot be sung except in English. They are so compelling that people around the world are willing to sing them in English. Further, the peculiar character of jazz derives from the South, perhaps because of the interplay between industrial and metropolitan life, on one hand, and agrarian life on the other hand. People situated on the frontiers between metropolitan and agrarian culture are naturally inclined to interplay them. The sounds of the city can be poured through the spoken idiom in such areas.

The oral tradition of the South is Elizabethan in form, as is that of Ireland. One thing that musicologists have not been very explicit about is the human need to put the sounds of the environment through the vital social process of dialogue in order to humanize the merely mechanical sounds of the environment. As a poet, Mr. Eliot was exceedingly aware of the role of the poet in "up-dating" the speech vehicle that it may serve the humanizing needs of its time. Eliot, in fact, has something to say about this matter in the speech already quoted above. Eliot

---

[3]Walter J. Ong, " 'Burnt Norton' in St. Louis", *American Literature*, vol. xxxiii, no. 4 (January 1962).

[4]See McLuhan's article, "Mr. Eliot and the St. Louis Blues", *The Antigonish Review*, no. 18, Summer 1974.

was acutely aware of the strategic location of St. Louis, culturally and psychologically speaking, mentioning:

> [the City was St. Louis—the] utmost outskirts of which touched on Forest
> Park, terminus of the Olive Street streetcars, and to me, as a child, the
> beginning of the Wild West . . . (p. 44)

The city of St. Louis, with its origin via the French fur traders who opened up
the entire North American continent, is a meeting-point of East and West and
South by virtue of its two great rivers, the Missouri and the Mississippi. In the
speech quoted, Eliot remarks on the universality of the Mississippi:

> . . . Yet the Salem of Hawthorne remains a town with a particular tradi-
> tion, which could not be anywhere but where it is; whereas the Missis-
> sippi of Mark Twain is not only the river known to those who voyage on it
> or live beside it, but the universal river of human life—more universal,
> indeed, than the Congo of Joseph Conrad. For Twain's readers anywhere,
> the Mississippi is *the* river. There is in Twain, I think, a great unconscious
> depth, which gives to *Huckleberry Finn* this symbolic value: a symbolism
> all the more powerful for being uncalculated and unconscious. (p. 54)

The strong local flavour combined with unconscious universality is what Eliot
perceived as the significance of St. Louis in his own life and work. In giving him
access to a world in which jazz and blues were formed, Eliot saw his own role as
the up-dater of the English language in our time. Up-dating is a process which
only the greatest figures can perform, and this role Eliot considered to have been
performed by Mark Twain in *Huckleberry Finn*:

> . . . Twain, at least in *Huckleberry Finn*, reveals himself to be one of those
> writers, of whom there are not a great many in any literature, who have
> discovered a new way of writing, valid not only for themselves but for
> others. I should place him, in this respect, even with Dryden and Swift, as
> one of those rare writers who have brought their language up to date, and
> in so doing, "purified the dialect of the tribe." (p. 54)

As a man from St. Louis, Eliot regarded New England as relatively local compared
to St. Louis and the Mark Twain territory which it includes. The "up-dating"
process—which Eliot notes having been performed by Dryden and Swift, on one
hand, and Mark Twain, on the other—is to be understood as a *figure-ground*
interplay. Dryden and Swift, in the age of Newton, stripped the rhetorical flowers
from English, bringing it into relation to mathematics and astronomy. Mark Twain,
in the age of the telegraph, retrieved the full tribal dialect of group speech, the
stripping away of the façade of written respectability and polish in favour of the
audile-tactile involvement which came to fruition in jazz. All this and much more
about St. Louis and its crucial role can be found in Eliot's prose and poetry.
Obviously, he regarded it [i.e. St Louis], and intended his readers to regard it, as
"no mean city."

Marshall McLuhan

To Froanna Lewis

December 21, 1973

Dear Mrs. Lewis:

We have many occasions and reasons to think of you and Wyndham, and are naturally concerned to know of your welfare. Recently the arrival of *The Roaring Queen* provided us with much joyful and festive renewal of our satisfaction and admiration for Wyndham's work.[1] Surely it would be a natural for stage or screen or TV!—a unique and uproarious exposé of the power rackets of the little art-and-letters crowds. It's really very Chaucerian, with its diverse band of noble spirits making the cultural pilgrimage to the country-house shrine. Each is given the rich iconic treatment which Wyndham shared with Chaucer. Now that there are no serious standards in art or letters anywhere, it is easier and easier to admire Wyndham's splendid perceptions and his joyful stripping of the shams. Very few, before or since, have had the absolute certitude of taste and percept which enabled Wyndham to deride the paltry crowd that ordinarily rules these matters.

At present Corinne is under the weather with a retinal tear, wilting under the prospect of the wedding of our youngest daughter on February 9th. Eric plans to marry in the spring, as well. We have only one granddaughter to date, a little girl who lives in Newport Beach.

I have just had a request from a Mr. Victor Cassidy to provide him with all the data I can about myself. He says he is writing a biography of Wyndham.[2] It will be grand if you can get your own work to press, and silence them all!

May you have a blessed and Holy Christmas and New Year.

---

[1]Wyndham Lewis's satiric novel about an authors' competition, *The Roaring Queen*, was finished in 1930, with characters modelled on Arnold Bennett, Virginia Woolf, Rebecca West, Eugene Jolas, and others. The portrayal of Bennett (Samuel Shodbutt) was considered libellous and the novel was rejected by Chatto and Windus, then accepted by Jonathan Cape in early 1935 but not published. It did not appear until July 1973.

[2]This book was not published; nor did Mrs Lewis ever publish a memoir.

1974

To John Polanyi[1]

Dear John:

Thank you for your very thoughtful comments of December 20th. I hope it will be possible to sit down and have a proper chat before too long. Lunch is not really conducive to such discourse.

I am perhaps less inclined than you are to belittle the advantages of "contemporary military manuals". The mere fact that "we are always ready to fight the last war" is itself a kind of orientation so that the state of any art or science is necessarily one of varying degrees of obsolescence.

Apropos the utility of philosophers and historians of science, I have used a number of them but am always hoping to find more and more adequate ones. I enclose a page from Platt's *Step to Man*, having found some relevance in his account of laboratory procedure at Cambridge. You will probably be amused at the somewhat romantic presentation of the laboratory gestalt. Naturally, the role of the paradigm or image borrowed from contemporary culture as a tool in organizing scientific perceptions is an area where linguistically trained people feel somewhat at home. That is, they are inclined to be critically curious of the hidden verbal assumptions in paradigms. Personally, I have always found questions more interesting than answers, and probes more exciting than products. All of my work has been experimental in the sense of studying effects rather than causes, and perceptions rather than concepts. That this is not a normal way of proceeding in the Western world, I know only too well from the public response of distrust and disbelief concerning my motives. My motives, so far as I have been able to ascertain them, are simply an intellectual enjoyment of play and discovery.

I hope it is going to be a grand New Year for you and your family.

---

[1] Dr John Polanyi (b. 1929) was at this time Professor of Chemistry, University of Toronto; later in 1974 he was made University Professor. In October 1986 he won the Nobel Prize for chemistry, sharing it with Dudley Herschbach of Harvard and Yuan Tseh Lee of the University of California at Berkeley.

To Sidney Halpern[1]

January 9, 1974

Dear Dr. Halpern:

Your request for some statement from me concerning the role of Israel, presents many aspects. As a Roman Catholic I have long employed the aid of a Hebrew maiden, the Blessed Virgin Mary. She has been a constant help to me in my studies and has been called "Our Lady of Good Studies" by Roman Catholics because of her own studies of the Scriptures in the temple as a child. To myself, as to most Catholics, a conscious debt to Israel is enormous, since we regard ourselves as being in the continuous line of Judaic development. On the other hand, the role of non-Christian Israel in the world has always been opaque and a divine mystery to the Roman Catholic. About anything so profound, it is merely irrelevant to have a personal point of view. What would appear more relevant to me is that we discuss these matters by kneeling in prayer together. The apocalyptic role of Israel has become more intensely manifest during the past few years. Many people are meditating and praying about this by way of *action*.

My own writing has been concerned with the development, in the simultaneous electric world, of the physical unity of the human family. I would be happy if you could suggest to me an effective approach to these matters that would enable me to make a forceful and convincing statement. As a Catholic who thinks of himself as a Jew spiritually, and as a student of the media, who thinks of us all politically, as members of the same family, what do you suggest I might say?

Sincerely yours,

[1]Dr Sidney Halpern of Philadelphia had written to McLuhan, enclosing a letter (dated November 28) to the Editor of the *New York Times* from an Israeli writer, Aharon Megged, the thrust of which Dr Halpern echoed when he asked, in his letter of December 20: "Could you take a few minutes to satisfy my curiosity as to why you have remained silent while the fate of the oldest and most exclusive fraternity in history, a dying species, is being decided?. . . A world that has no room for Israel does not deserve to exist. If you disagree, please let me know."

To Gerald Mason Feigen[1]

January 23, 1974

Dear Gerry:

Have you seen those items about the astronauts? Written reports, at least, have indicated considerable psychic change in all of them. Most of them have become religious "freaks". Your thoughts about new environments created by our electric

[1]Dr Gerald Mason Feigen (b. 1917), a close friend of McLuhan's, is a man of many parts. He is a surgeon, a ventriloquist (which enables him to work with disturbed children), a writer, and is at present on the Board of Directors of the Marshall McLuhan Center for Global Communications in Los Angeles. He and his associate in a consulting firm, the late Howard Luck Gossage, introduced McLuhan to the literary community and to the media of San Francisco in a McLuhan Festival, 1965. They are briefly described in Tom Wolfe's article on McLuhan, "What If He Is Right?" (see page 330, note 1).

means of moving at the speed of light may find some echoes in *Four Quartets* by T.S. Eliot. It is a poem which is entirely concerned with acoustic or simultaneous space. Acoustic space, which differs entirely from visual space, is one whose centre is multi-locational—the centre is everywhere, the margin nowhere. Is not gravity of this nature? Visual space, on the other hand, is continuous, connected, homogeneous and static. It is the only sensory mode having these characteristics. Visual space is infinitely divisible, whereas all the other senses have spaces that are quite indivisible. This is probably why the electric space of simultaneous information is transforming our entire outlook. That is, we are now using our eye as an ear, and vice-versa.

Eric [McLuhan] is to be married shortly, and so things are jammed up here. Many of the problems you raise are discussed in *Take Today: the Executive as Dropout* (Harcourt, Brace, Jovanovich Inc. N.Y. 1972). It is concerned with the effect of electic speed in reorganizing human experience and decision-making.

To John W. Mole, O.M.I.

January 29, 1974

Dear Fr. Mole:

Just a note that I have looked at *Communio et Progressio* and found it futile.[1] Does this mean that I should say so in public? Or write to the members of the [Pontifical] Communication Commission about it?

Have been paying a lot of attention to Kant, Hegel and phenomenology of late, with full realization that Kant and Hegel simply flipped out of Hume's visual determinism into acoustic subjectivism. All of their followers are still under the illusion that the acoustic world is spiritual and unlike the outer visual world, whereas, in fact, the acoustic is just as material as the visual. However, to Western man the acoustic always seems a release into another more relevant dimension. At least this was a possible hide-out until nuclear physics moved in with its acoustic structures. The "structuralism"[2] of the European phenomenologists is the audile-tactile world which I know very well, since I use it at all times myself. The logical, rational world is visual, continuous, and connected, but when pushed to its limit, flips into the acoustic form, as with Hume and Kant. What I am coming to is the question of the magisterium:[3] the Eastern church, being iconic and audile-tactile, could not tolerate the visual hierarchy of Rome with external, materialis-

---

[1] The Pastoral Instruction on the media, emphasizing its moral aspects, issued by the Pontifical Commission for Social Communication (of which McLuhan was made a member) to implement the decree of the Second Vatican Council on Communications (*Inter Mirifica*, 1963). On December 24, 1973, Father Mole had sent McLuhan Chapter VIII of a typescript of his critique of it, which later appeared in *Christian Communications*.

[2] See page 506, note 2.

[3] *Magisterium* is the technical name for the teaching authority of the Roman Catholic Church, which includes papal encyclicles and documents issued by the Holy See.

tic aspects, and today, as the Western church also is invaded by the simultaneous electric thing with its multi-locational boundlessness, the whole question of Roman authority becomes crucial.

"Process" theology[4] and the speculative theology of the descendants of Kant and Hegel is unconsciously in the grip of the merely acoustic dimension. This is the world of involvement par excellence. It is the anti-Graeco-Roman form of the pre-Socratic world of hoi barbaroi. The Third World is the world of the barbarians, of course. I do not pretend to perceive a providential plan or pattern in these matters, but I cannot see any reason for withholding intelligibility from the acoustic domain created by electric simultaneity. Have you, yourself, discovered any evidence of understanding these matters in their unique and antithetic structuralist terms? I have yet to meet a philosopher who understood what had happened to Kant and Hegal in their flight into the acoustic during their revulsion from the visual determinism of Locke and Hume.

An understanding of these factors provides an immediate release from the opacity and tension that now exists in these areas. Such understanding also permits a realistic programming of environments by media in suchwise as to relieve many psychic miseries, e.g. the current disasters in our schools and communities as we try to subject the students to the old visual disciplines of literacy, without considering that these students have been transformed by their electric environment. The electric transformation causes us to resist and to reject the old visual culture, regardless of its value or relevance. These kinds of psychic oscillation resulting from large environmental change are no longer necessary, any more than the plague. Psychic diseases can now be treated for what they are, namely manifestations of the response to man-made technologies. Environmental noise and disturbance can be controlled as readily as the unhygienic conditions that prevailed until recent times. The psychic effects of TV are no more necessary than the physical effects of polluted drinking water. As long as people persist in ignoring the subliminal and hidden effects of media on psyche and society, they will attribute these things to the "will of God".

Yours in Our Lord
Marshall

[4]A branch of dissident theology—that is, in disagreement with the *Magisterium* or official teaching—within the Church.

To Harry Skornia

February 6, 1974

Dear Harry:

Just getting around to your New Year greeting. Our youngest, Michael, married last Spring, and our youngest daughter, Elizabeth, is being married in a few days, at the coldest time of our year, and while we have a burst water main to contend with! i.e., no water in the house at all, and a house full of visitors.

By the by, did you notice *TV Guide* for September 15, 1973 with the report on the effects of turning off TV in Germany and in England? People were paid to turn off TV for as long a period as they could bear. Some went as long as three months, most wilted after one week, and *everybody* showed withdrawal symptoms as from alcohol or drugs. Naturally, this had nothing to do with program content.

Glad to hear about your going to Rome. I have been appointed to the Papal Commission on Communications, but haven't put in an appearance yet, and I'm afraid I see very little reason for doing so. I would be a very disturbing note, indeed.

Please do keep me in touch with your studies and activities, and say 'hello' to old friends.

To James W. Carey[1]

March 25, 1974

Dear Professor Carey:

It was only a few days ago that one of my students brought to my attention "The Mythos of the Electronic Revolution" from *The American Scholar*.[2] Wish you had sent me an off-print when it appeared. Perhaps you have clarified some of your thoughts since writing the paper and discovered that I have no Utopian or any other directions in my approach to technology. It must have been my training in Symbolist poetry and criticism that led me to adopt the formalist and structuralist approaches to art and technology alike. These approaches simply exclude the possibility of moralizing or value judgments except as something that might be added later as a personal confession.

One thing I have discovered about media study in general is that since the *effects* of media are subliminal, the study of these effects irritates many people as if it were an invasion of their privacy. Many people assume that if something is centralist or decentralist it is an advantage or disadvantage to some paradigm or other that they entertain. For example, I consider the instantaneous or electric as inevitably decentralizing all forms of activity, on one hand, but, on the other hand, as totally involving everybody in everybody in a way which makes private identity impossible. Merely to point this out inspires in many the idea that I am

[1]Professor James W. Carey—Director, Institute of Communications Research, University of Illinois, Urbana—had written the long essay "Harold Adams Innis and Marshall McLuhan" for the *Antioch Review* (vol. xxvii, no. 1, Spring 1967); it is the final essay in *McLuhan: Pro & Con* (1968) edited by Raymond Rosenthal.

[2]James W. Carey and J.J. Quirk, "The Mythos of the Electronic Revolution", *The American Scholar* 30, Spring and Summer 1970. This two-part article discusses the "set of notions . . . most readily associated with [McLuhan] . . . the futurist ethos that identifies electricity and electrical power, electronics and cybernetics, with a new birth of community, decentralization, ecological balance and social harmony."

for or against something or other. Personally, I don't see how it is possible to study anything if one is for or against it at the outset at least. In terms of the historical grouping of causes, material, efficient, formal and final, I realize more and more that I work mainly with formal causes, i.e., with structures. Structures I have discovered to be audile-tactile rather than visual, but that is another story. Moreover, in a simultaneous world which structures information at the speed of light, effects are simultaneous with their causes, or in a sense "precede" their causes. Even in the most mundane matters, we say that "the time was ripe" when something drastic happens, that is, the *effects* arrive before the *causes*.

Moralizing, on the other hand, is an attitude which is easily engendered by concern with material and efficient causes and once one asks, "Who owns this newspaper?" or "Who runs this newspaper?", most people are prepared to make value judgments. I hope you will have a look at my latest book *Take Today: The Executive as Dropout* (Harcourt, Brace, Jovanovich Inc. 1972) in which I study the structural effects of electric speed in decision-making and management.

I include a brief resumé of my three latest books, and also a copy of the Causality piece.[3]

I am introducing Eric Havelock to a University of Toronto audience today. He, too, was an associate of Harold Innis here years ago and his *Preface to Plato* (Oxford University Press, 1963) and his *Prologue to Greek Literacy* (University of Cincinnati, 1971) are basic books which testify to this fact, even though Innis is not mentioned by name.

You are familiar with academic timidity and respectability. You are taking your academic life in your hands when you write about Innis and McLuhan. You must be a fearless character. I have never found anybody who was really interested in anything who was also afraid to take the consequences of disapproval. Was it Hercule Poirot who, when asked "What is truth?" replied: "Eet ees whatever upsets zee applecart."

Currently here at the Centre we are doing an inventory of all the breakthroughs in all fields of art and science since 1900—a story of dumped applecarts!

Best wishes,

[3]Marshall McLuhan and Barrington Nevitt, "The Argument: Causality in the Electric World", *Technology and Culture*, vol. 14, no. 1, January 1973.

To Pierre Elliott Trudeau

March 26, 1974

Dear Pierre:

There may be some relevance in the questions that Clare Booth Luce asked recently [March 19], and my replies. First, her questions:

(1) How do you explain why Vatican II, which closed in a burst of ecumenical fervor that was expected to revive the faith of the Catholic world in the Church's institutions and teachings was, instead, followed (and so soon) by

the greatest loss of faith in them that we have seen since the Reformation? Was Vatican II the cause?

(2) Please explain why you think (or don't think) that the impeachment of R[ichard] N[ixon] is going to purify democratic politics and "restore integrity" to Government, and how this will help us control inflation, pollution, repair the breach with NATO, etc.

(3) What are your theories of money and of value? Why, for example, did those great Etruscan statues which stood for years in the Great Hall of the Met., praised by all the critics and admired by all the populace, valued in nine figures, suddenly become valueless when they were discovered to be forgeries? Are Value and Money, like Beauty, in the eye of the beholder? Or, what other than life itself (and health in life) has intrinsic value?

Now, my replies to her questions:[1]

Vatican II was a blossoming of liberal individualism and a kind of immolation of the individual in the great new involvement plunge made possible by the TV sensibility of inner-tripping. The moment that people become deeply involved they lose their private identity and their direction. If the Reformation was the tossing away of acoustic and musical hierarchies in favour of visual and private points of view, Vatican II was the burial of this individualism in the newly created swamp of electronic togetherness and total involvement, as in a skin-flick where everybody gets inside one skin. In the novel *Silence* [1969], Shusaku Endo has an introduction explaining how impossible it is for Hellenistic or Western Christianity to find a foothold in the tribal or acoustic swamp of Japan. I have written in the *Critic* and elsewhere on this subject, asking Catholic philosophers and theologians to explain what successor to the Graeco-Roman literary tradition they foresee. The mystery of how the Church was committed to this Graeco-Roman thing is quite beyond me, although I perceive it as providential, in the strict sense. Today, under electric conditions there's no way in which the Graeco-Roman tradition can survive in the West.

To use the terms of Ballandier who invented the phrase "the Third World",[2] there is the First World of 19th-century industrialism and the Second World of Russian Communism and the Third World is that which is left out of these benefits. But he forgot the Fourth World, the instantaneous global village which, since Sputnik (October, 1957), created Spaceship Earth, an ecological entity, without passengers but only crew. The First World has as much trouble relating to the Fourth World of electronics as the Third World has in obtaining benefits from the First World of industrial hardware. On the other hand, the Third World has no trouble in relating to the acoustic and electronic Fourth World.

The magisterium of the Church tends to become multi-locational and acoustic,

---

[1]From here until the end of the second-last paragraph the text duplicates most of the letter McLuhan wrote to Mrs Luce on March 25, 1974.

[2]The Supplement of the *Oxford English Dictionary* credits G. Balandier, in his *Tiers Monde* (1956), with the first use in print of "Third World", referring to the countries of Asia, Africa, and Latin America not politically aligned with either Communist or Western nations.

with central Roman authority becoming difficult to imagine. Please note that I am doing now, as elsewhere, a structural or a formal meditation on the situations we have encountered.

The Protestant strategy in the 16th century was to use the new portable book as a God-given means of escape from the Roman yoke. Rome used the book in the opposite way, as a means of standardizing and centralizing by uniformity. The law of implementation is always to use the new thing for the old purpose, while ignoring that the new thing tends to destroy the old purposes. I have discovered over the years that the *effects* of innovation are always subliminal, and people resent having this pointed out, feeling that you are invading their privacy in so doing.

Let us turn, then, to your question about the impeachment of Richard Nixon. Nixon and the U.S.A. is caught between the First World and the Fourth World. That is, while having all its commitments to the old Graeco-Roman hardware, it is totally involved in the new electronic information environment which is dissolving all the controls and all the goals of the First World. The Fourth World, or the elecronic world, reduces personal identity profiles to vestigial level and, by the same token, reduces moral commitments in the private sector almost to zero. Paradoxically, however, as private morals in the private sector sink down, new absolutist demands are made of ethics in the public or political sector. R.N. had the misfortune to bring the old private morals into the public place just when this reversal had occurred. There is also the misfortune of his image which is intensely private and non-corporate and therefore totally unsuited to TV. (Charisma is looking like a lot of other people—anything except one's self!)

The U.S., the only great country in the world based on a written Constitution, has no way of coping legally or politically with the new oral and acoustic situations created by the electronic bugging and the general X-ray procedures in the entire private sector. Man-hunting has become the biggest business on the planet in the electronic age, and is a return to the Paleolithic conditions of the hunter. The impeachment threat represents the rage of the literate media against the new electric environment which has invaded their world and corrupted all their values. I would like very much to explain in more detail the clash between written and oral patterns to commitment in society and politics and personal life alike.

You ask also about inflation and pollution and the breach with NATO, etc. I have an unpublished paper in which I try to explain that inflation also is the encounter of incompatible worlds, the clash between the old commodity markets and the new money, or information markets. Money as information, and investment, now moves at instant speeds, putting an unbearable strain and rim-spin, as it were, on the old price system with its quantified commodities. This huge disproportion between the old speeds of the hardware world and the instant electric speeds of the software Fourth World extends to our private lives as much as to our social existence. It is impossible to retain private goals in an instant world. One must flip instead into role-playing, which means submergence in corporate situations. Strange that I should be mentioning these things today when I am going to introduce Eric Havelock to a University of Toronto audience. In his *Preface to Plato* (Oxford University Press, 1963) he explains how the phonetic alphabet evoked a private image of the substantial individual. I understand this much better now than even he explains it. The unique technology of the phonetic alphabet was the fact that its components were phonemes (meaningless bits) rather than morphemes (meaningful bits). Magically, the fission of the phonetic alphabet is to isolate the visual sensory factor from all the other senses, and to constitute the image of the private person. We are now playing this drama in reverse in the electric age.

Your questions about my theories of money and value and the Etruscan forgeries would take a little while to elaborate. Let me mention, however, that we live in the age of the "genuine fake" because we understand for the first time the art process and the making process as never before, so that Picasso said long ago: "I always paint fakes". The function of art in relating us to ourselves and to our world and in freeing us from the adaptive or robot role, has changed entirely in the electric time. The art product as such becomes relatively insignificant compared to the process of making and of participation in that making. What you mention as the "value" of the Etruscan images, relates very much to their commodity character in the First World of industrial hardware. In that world they stood for the antithesis and, therefore, the ideal of industrialism. Hypocritically, the First World worshipped art as its own opposite. The Etruscans themselves would have agreed with the Balinese who say: "We have no art. We do everything as well as possible." Or, they would agree with a local junkyard sign which reads: "Help beautify junkyards. Throw something lovely away today."

You are most generous in even noticing my Civic Award, and it is quite princely of you to have written me about it.[3] Mrs. McLuhan joins me in heartiest and most cordial regards to you and your family.

P.S. In the cause of bilingualism, I enclose a new book made by a friend of mine who is a former Professor of French here at the University of Toronto. It seems to me to hold the promise of a live TV show in which French idioms are presented both acoustically and visually.[4]

[3]On March 6, 1974 McLuhan was one of nine recipients (along with his colleague at the University of Toronto, Northrop Frye) of a Civic Award of Merit from the City of Toronto.

[4]This alludes to *Daisy* (1974), a paperback book by Alta Lind Cook, who had taught French at Victoria College, University of Toronto. It is a long sequence of line drawings, one to a page, of Professor Cook's flower character Daisy in various romantic attitudes illustrating amusing bilingual captions.

To Pierre Elliott Trudeau

April 3, 1974

Dear Pierre:

I see by the papers that there is, and will continue to be, a great deal of confusion about streaking. It is just possible that I can be of some help here. The streaker is a "put on" in the same way that the stripper is. She takes off her clothes in order to "put on" her audience. Though nude, she is completely clad in her audience, as much as a model in a life class. It is when she steps backstage that she is naked, or minus her audience.

The streaker [nude runner] is putting on his audience because he wishes to be seen. He is a role-player and not a private person, therefore he hides his face and his name. His "put on" has to do with a grievance against what he feels to be a hypocritical society. The streaker and the striker are near kin, only the striker strips off the services which are the social clothing in order to "put on" his audience. It would be easy to enlarge this theme, but probably not necessary. The moral issue of decency or indecency is really irrelevant in view of streaking as essentially a political act of defiance and rebellion.

[1]In his reply the Prime Minister questioned why McLuhan thought streaking was essentially a *political* act of defiance; to him it had even greater significance as a rebellion against social values.

To York and Lela Wilson[1]

April 11, 1974

At exactly the same time that our water main at home is being replaced, and all the lawn is being dug up, at this same time, our water main at the Centre here is being replaced. What do you call that? Vibes?

A few minutes ago, Corinne learned that her only aunt had died, and she will leave at once for Fort Worth for a whole week. Now that both her mother and aunt are dead, there is a great deal of hassling with family property and papers. This morning, Eric and I were both at the Passport Office with completed forms and dossier. Now that mine has run out, it is necessary to get an entirely new passport in accordance with the new national regulations. Meantime, term papers and exam papers are stacked around us. It is a very unforgiveable time of year!

Last night at the Centre we were talking about Hamlet and his frantic efforts to achieve the conditions of violence. Somehow or other, he couldn't manage to achieve it even though he had lots of reasons to be violent. These observations

[1]York and Leila Wilson were neighbours—they lived near Wychwood Park on Alcina Avenue—and close friends of the McLuhans. York Wilson (1907–84) was a well-known painter who exhibited internationally after the late 1950s when he turned to abstraction; a work of his that is seen often by Torontonians is the mural (1959) in the foyer of the O'Keefe Centre. McLuhan wrote a Foreword to *York Wilson* (1978) by Paul Duval. The Wilsons wintered in San Miguel, Mexico.

must have inspired violence in somebody in the group, because a book I had received yesterday from André Malraux with a flattering inscription and instructions to be sure to read page 213 since it would "be of use to me in my work", simply vanished from the scene. The book was entitled *La Tête Obsidienne*.[2]

This is Corinne's birthday, and I would like to have her portrait painted as soon as possible, by somebody you would suggest. Is there an ideal person for the job?[3]

Naturally, we are looking forward to your return on May 15th, and are cheered at your news of having had a very satisfactory year.

[2]Page 213 of *La Tête d'Obsidienne* (1974) by André Malraux (1901–76)—French novelist, essayist, and Minister of Culture under President Charles de Gaulle—contains a discourse on the "Musée Imaginaire". This was presumably sent to McLuhan in recognition of his work at the Centre—described in a report entitled "Structural Museology"—on "the changing role of the museum in the new information environment of the 'Fourth World', or the electric age."

[3]Corinne McLuhan's portrait was painted in 1975 by Clarke Cunningham.

To Ray di Lorenzo[1]

May 21, 1974

Dear Ray:

Since writing to you, the U of T Press has promised to publish the Nashe book,[2] and, more important, massive breakthroughs came while working on *Finnegans Wake* with Eric. They will appear cryptically and briefly in Eric's essay on the *Wake* in the Summer issue of the *Joyce Quarterly*. In a word, the five parts played by the characters in the Wake, as well as in many 18th-century novels and writings, are the five parts of rhetoric,—the "five acts" of Horace, the five parts of *Troilus and Cressida*, the five parts of *The Prince*, the five parts of *The Wealth of Nations*, the five acts of all Renaissance plays. Without exception, the critics from Horace to the present have mistaken the five acts to mean special separation rather than functional variation.

The four books of the *Wake* are the four levels of exegesis, as also the *Four Quartets*, and the five parts of each Quartet are the five parts of rhetoric, as well as many other works of Joyce and Eliot. St. Augustine's *De Doctrina* has the five parts of rhetoric as its divisions, and Eric and I have simply not had time to check out the full range. Many of the Schoolmen must have used these five parts deliberately, since they concern the integrity of the word.

Apropos *Can Grande*, I used to know the letter by heart, and shall look at it

[1]Ray di Lorenzo, a former student of McLuhan's, was teaching a course in medieval literature at the University of Dallas.

[2]McLuhan worked on a revision of his Ph.D. thesis on Thomas Nashe for some time, but it was not published.

again.[3] Meantime, check whether Dante's three-part structures reflect the trivium. I think it can be said off the cuff that they necessarily do so. Shall check it out of course, for my Nashe re-write. Shall certainly heed your comments on light and languages.[4]

[3]Thirteen surviving letters by Dante, written in Latin, include a long letter to Can Grande della Scala which contains the first comment on the *Divine Comedy*: it states that the poem should be interpreted both literally and allegorically, explains the meaning of the title, and presents the argument of its three divisions.

[4]Di Lorenzo had commented that "in so far as every thing has both essence and an existence, every thing is light."

To Bernard and Mary Muller-Thym

June 11, 1974

My dearest Bernie and Mary:

Naturally, we are thinking of you day and night, and remembering all the wonderful times we had in St. Louis.[1] Your home was the super seiminar of all time, in which young instructors were taught the mysteries of cuisine, avant garde music, new liturgy, and metaphysics. It was a very rich and heady brew that formed and was shared by your delighted friends. I pray that other such centres exist even now, and that others will be as lucky as I in sharing them. The fact that you and Bernie had such a wonderful musical background, to say nothing about your knowledge of St. Louis University, and the Jesuits, and the city of St. Louis, was like knowing James Joyce himself! By the way, Eric has a piece coming out in the July issue of *The James Joyce Quarterly*, on the *Wake*, which must inevitably have considerable impact. He not only introduces all of the thunders, but explains that the four-book structure relates to the four levels of exegesis, and the five "characters" are presentations of the five divisions of rhetoric in action. Of course, the five divisions of *inventio, dispositio, elocutio, memoria*, and *delivery* are simultaneous in each moment of the *verbum*, or *logos*. The ten thunders are two five-act plays of the eye and the ear in reciprocal complementarity.

Even as I say these words to Mrs. Stewart, the Hart House bells are chiming merrily to celebrate the current Convocation. We are just back from Eric's wedding in England. He married an English girl named Sabina Ellis, who had been working here on the Ontario Arts Council. The wedding took place in Belmont Abbey (Benedictine) in Hereford, which is on the border of Wales. We had good weather and the country was at its best, which is saying quite a lot. We like the new in-laws, Norman and Pat Ellis, and they drove us around the country quite a bit to see their old friends and haunts. For example, they took us to The Shaven Crown, a 14th-century Inn owned by their relative, Montagu Moore. It's in the town of Shipton-under-Wychwood, where Sabina was baptized. From this town came Marmaduke Matthews, the painter, who created and named Wychwood Park were we live[2]—so Sabina has one foot in the Park now, and another foot in Shipton-under-Wychwood.

[1]The Muller-Thyms were undergoing marital difficulties. They eventually divorced.
[2]See page 375, note 3.

To Pierre Elliott Trudeau

June 13, 1974

Dear Pierre:

Just a note to indicate one very effective way of dealing with hecklers. Beckon him to come forward to the microphone and not to waste his sweetness on the desert air, as it were. There might be an occasional heckler who had a speech ready for such an occasion, but it shuts up 99% of them instantly. It is a way of turning the tables, and compels the heckler to "put on" the public instead of "putting on" the speaker. There's a great gap between using the speaker as a captive audience and using the captive audience as a public.

Apropos your query about streaking as social rather than political defiance, I agree, since I was using the word "political" to cover social forms as well.

Recently, I was in Stockholm to give some talks and I discovered that Scandinavia is the world in which North American hippies would be at home. The reason for this lies in the fact that Scandinavians have very low identity profiles. They are real "cool" in the sense of being group-oriented rather than private goal-seekers. They originated the ombudsman, and think of themselves as dedicated to helping the little people like themselves. Wouldn't you say that our own rebellious youngsters are "nobodies" who resent having to share the establishment with the somebodies of yesterday? That is, the young people with very low identity profiles find it difficult to accept jobs or roles in which high identity is expected. Is it not Nixon's carnestness and specialist goal-seeking that alienates him from the new generation?

May I venture to suggest also an approach to the women's-lib matter? Women are less specialized than men, and long accustomed to adapting to a variety of roles. In our new instant-information environment, most men who have been accustomed to specialist job and functions must now switch from role to role in the course of a day. In the big hierarchies this creates extreme discomfort and dismay, and it is increasingly obvious that women could perform many of these functions better than men. However, when a woman is compelled to assume the role of a customs or immigration official, she becomes the specialist monster, the very antithesis of role-playing. Yet we consider it natural for men to perform these specialist functions.

To King Carl Gustav of Sweden

June 18, 1974

Your Majesty:

My wife and I shall always be your debtors for the delightful experience of meeting you and dining with you.[1] As for myself, I am especially proud of the

[1] Marshall and Corinne McLuhan had attended the EBAV (Esselte Bonnier Audio Visual) Conference in Stockholm on June 5 and lunched with the King on June 6.

sculpture awarded to me personally by yourself. It's a very witty piece indeed, a pencil entwined, as it were, in a serpent form. It strongly suggested the devious writhings, even of the written word.

Sweden was a quite unexpected experience. If I had had any preconceptions, they would certainly have been outdone by the experience. My first feeling in Stockholm was: "Here is greatness consistent with human scale." The bounty of Sweden combines greatness and modesty, grandeur and playfulness, in the most unexpected ways.

We shall keep you in our prayers, and hope that you will find real joy in your American visit. Having heard that you are interested in Rock music, I am sure you will become the darling of young America. It has been said that Rock is the sound of the city, re-cycled through the language of the American South.

Heartiest good wishes for the trip, and may your reign be as joyful for Sweden as Sweden was for us.

In all homage
Marshall McLuhan

To Hugh and Winifred Lane[1]

June 18, 1974

Dear Hugh and Winifred:

It was a joy to see you at the wedding with Jennifer. To have gone back with you to your place would have been quite perfect, but quite impossible, since we were under real pressure to keep a schedule in Paris and Stockholm. Both of these occasions were fascinating, but also extremely wearing. Better in retrospect. Both daughter Teri and I had books fresh out in Paris, and these involved various interviews with press and TV. Between times we managed to see some friends, including Eric and Sabina [McLuhan] who have only now come home to Toronto.

We found Stockholm quite delightful and full of surprises. By the way, one of the peculiar aspects of my own work is that I study the *effects* of various human technologies as they relate to psyche and society. Try it sometime. Simply begin to ask about any item within range or reach, what effects it has had upon the users and on the other artifacts. If you have a Xerox at your school, simply make a brief inventory of some of the changes that have taken place in your own activities at the school as the result of Xerox. Now, the strange thing about studying effects (which, by the way, is *formal* causality) is that it alarms and angers people. For example, it is not possible to say the Latin Mass into a microphone. The moment you point this out, people assume that you are the enemy of all microphones, and perhaps the enemy of the Mass as well. Since nearly all effects of anything tend to be subliminal and hidden, it may be that studying them panics people into supposing you are invading their privacy. When studying effects it is

---

[1]Hugh Lane (see page 63, note 1) had been a fellow student of McLuhan's at Trinity Hall, Cambridge. He and his wife attended the June wedding in England of Eric McLuhan and Sabina Ellis.

very difficult, if not impossible, to make value judgements. So I have long ago given up moralizing about technology and the media. Yet, I am considered to be the deadly enemy of the printed word, simply because I notice some of the impact it had in shaping our world.

To D. Carlton Williams

July 8, 1974

Dear Carl:

You may have heard about the streaker as just a passing fanny! I enclose a couple of new jokes picked up on travels.

As you may know, I did a preface for Bill Key's *Subliminal Seduction.*[1] Bill's work offers a very natural area of study for yourself as a psychologist. When I was addressing the Headmasters of North America in New London the other day, I mentioned that it was jet travel that made it possible for such conferences to take place, the time factor, etc. One person piped up: "So you despise us. You hate conferences!" More and more I discover this kind of reaction to any attempt to feel the hidden *ground* of any service environment. It may be the result of sagging psyches and enfeebled egos which go with mass media and the mass man. I think it is generally recognized that there has been a fantastic decline in the identity profile of our Western populations. And this, of course, makes everybody much more vulnerable to the subliminal world. I think that it would be extremely interesting to have some people in the sociology division look at the responses to Key's work, both in the university and outside in the public, because it is a response which I have encountered, especially in the U.K. where the corporate ego is often tottering indeed.

The Key case is all the more remarkable in the light of the utterly gutter world that he is exposing, beside which the Watergate data are eligible in any Sunday-school paper. Dixon's book on the subliminal does report that it is the most-mentioned and least-investigated area in contemporary psychology.[2] Excuse me, Carl, if I appear to be intruding into touchy territory. I can plead that it is my own territory in a very special way, and one which I have explored at considerable cost and danger. Key too is a loner, but a man of very much integrity and courage. You will be the most able person to decide whether his adversaries are people of high quality and noble outlook.

Unlike myself, however, Bill Key has tackled the gorgon of advertising tycoons, with their twenty-two billion annual budget. There is nothing shy about a billion bucks, except that it is terrified of getting adverse publicity. Bill Key has put advertising in jeopardy. This means that all these publications that benefit from

[1]Wilson B[rian] Key, *Subliminal Seduction: Ad Media's Manipulation of a Not So Innocent America* (1972), with an Introduction by Marshall McLuhan. Key acknowledges the stimulus of McLuhan's seminars, which he attended during four years spent in Toronto.

[2]Norman F. Dixon, *Subliminal Perception: The Nature of a Controversy* (1971).

advertising will also take a dim view of Bill Key, especially newspapers and magazines. It would seem that he has chosen a very vulnerable base in the Journalism Department from which to conduct his crusade.

Am reading *The Power to Inform* by Jean-Louis Servan-Schreiber.[3] He is a newspaper owner in Paris, and he makes no bones about the total dependence of his operation on advertising.

[3]Jean-Louis Servan-Schreiber, *The Power to Inform: Media, the Information Business* (1974), a translation of *Le Pouvoir d'informer*. Servan-Schrieber was a Parisian friend of McLuhan's.

To Hans Selye

July 12, 1974

Dear Dr. Selye:

How delightful of you to send me your adventures in the bizarre![1] Have only begun to read the book, and am going very carefully. I want to ask you to check the possibility that there may be four phases in the G.A.S.[2] On page 39 you cite three stages. I wonder if there is not a second one in A? Namely, after the initial upsurge, is there not an obsolescing or pushing aside of the unneeded energy? Also on page 39, apropos childhood, is it not followed by adolescence with its peculiar "retrieval" or anticipation of old age? Does not adolescence anticipate and mimic post-maturity?

I have found in dealing with Laws of the Media that there are not three but four phases in the response to every technology: (a) enhancement or increase of activity, (b) the obsolescing or pushing aside of earlier activity, (c) the retrieval of some form of response that had been obsolesced much earlier, and finally (d) the flip into the opposite form when anything reaches its peak performance.

Shall write again soon.

[1]Hans Selye, *Stress Without Distress* (1974).
[2]The General Adaptation Syndrome (first described in 1936), which has three phases: alarm reaction, stage of resistance, and stage of exhaustion. Selye saw them as analogous to the three stages of life: childhood, maturity, and senility.

To the Editor, the Toronto Star[1]

July 24, 1974

Dear Sir:

Without rehearsing the arguments in the abortion matter, I would like to draw attention to some of the hidden *ground* of this matter. As people become more

[1]This letter was published on the editorial page of the *Toronto Star* on July 31, 1974. With a change in the opening, it was also sent to The Honourable Otto Lang, Minister of Justice, Ottawa. The first sentence of the letter to Lang reads: "I want you to know that your stand on the abortion problem is deeply appreciated by lots of people."

deeply involved in each other by the sheer speed of information which covers them, there is a very great loss of private identity, with the consequent insecurity and rage and violence. When instant information exists around the entire planet, there is, as it were, inflation of human quantity which threatens all human values whatever and eliminates the experience of private identity. When identity is weak, all constraint and social restriction become intolerable.

Paradoxically, it is the sheer involvement of everybody in everybody which creates the illusion that new life is cheap and even superfluous. Nothing could be more misleading than *trendiness* in such matters. Electric speeds of information literally create the mass man and obliterate the private man. If this can be called a trend, it is a trend to the loss of all life values whatever. At the old slow speeds of information, before the telegraph, there were habits of detachment and objectivity which don't hold up against the total involvement and immersion in the World Tank.

Abortion "thinking" has all of the characteristics of the panicky trends of the radio age in the 20's, which produced Hitler and Stalin, with their mass followings. Abortion "thinking" is taking place in an even deeper swamp of mass hysteria created by the inner trips of the TV image. It is important to realize that all of our *thinking* about abortion is taking place in the smogged-over world of TV. It is becoming monstrous even to mention the *individual* rights of the born, or the unborn. Only huge categories will serve, such as the "rights of pregnant teenagers" or the "rights of all pregnant mothers." Only very large quantities of organic material (crowds) can now command attention.

The quantity of the world population becomes a very strong argument against mankind. The current inflation itself seems to be a basic assumption behind abortion "thinking". Pregnancy becomes a kind of "inflation" and abortion becomes a happy expedient for inflation control. Pregnancy as an irresistible kind of inflation endangers the mother's psychic income, reducing her standard of "living."

Is it too late to point to our universal victimization by media in which private identity has been abolished? For trendy people, the destruction of private identity by instant information involvement is a mandate to attack all forms of private life which remain. There are many people for whom "thinking" necessarily means identifying with existing trends. If medical and laboratory science can spawn human organisms as readily as fungus, then this trend means that we must deal with all existing human organisms as expendable fungus. However, the trend to the democratization of nuclear warfare still seems to give pause to a few (now that everybody can make his own atom bomb). Perhaps trends cannot always be trusted. The trend toward increasing enlightenment by electric media has flipped us back into the world of the occult, that is, the world of horoscopes and hidden forces. Abortion "thinking" is entirely in accordance with the trend toward the mechanization of death and of birth alike. The meat-packers have got there "firstest with the mostest."

To Rollo May

July 25, 1974

Dear Rollo:

Glad to have an excuse to drop you a note. Have been working lately on an inventory of "breakthroughs" in the arts and sciences since 1900. These breakthroughs depend on changes in "models" of perception and can usually be spotted by the vortex of commotion and distress which they occasion. The primary advantages which we enjoy in this project is our awareness that there are several varieties of "space", whereas the sciences, at least, adhere to only one kind of space, namely visual space.

The big breakthrough that came with Planck in quantum mechanics and Freud in *The Interpretation of Dreams* (both in 1900) was the recognition of discontinuity in matter, and between the conscious and the unconscious.[1] The physicists identified this interval as the "resonant interval" of interface, i.e. the chemical bond. This is a complete break with visual space which came with cubism or "multi-locational space" at the same time.

Perhaps you could correct me in these matters, since I am working on the proposition that visual space is continuous, connected, homogeneous, and static. All other kinds of space—tactile, audile, osmic, kinetic—have none of the characteristics of visual space and are thus not admitted to the space category. Since we hear from many directions at once, acoustic space tends to be a "sphere" whose centre is everywhere and whose margin is nowhere. Tactile space is the space of the resonant interval recognized in physics and chemistry as the world of the "interface". In practice however, the scientists, including the sensory psychologists, attempt to deal with all space under the mode of visual space. Would you not say, however, that most of our experience of space is non-visual, just as the scientists who depend upon the electronic microscope have no longer any relation to visual space in their work? I would really welcome any leads you can give me that would supplement my "space" studies.

We recently had a delightful visit with Stephanie [McLuhan]. We are really deeply grateful to you for your friendly concern for her.

---

[1] In 1900 the German physicist Max Planck (1858–1947) discovered the quantum, which revolutionized theoretical physics (he won a Nobel Prize in 1919), and Sigmund Freud (1856–1939) published his ground-breaking study of the subconscious, *The Interpretation of Dreams*. 1900 was the starting-point of McLuhan's so-called "intellectual Baedecker", described in the first paragraph of this letter, which was not completed.

To Marshall Fishwick[1]

July 31, 1974

> I hold that it is bad as far as we are
> concerned if a person, a political party, an
> army or a school is not attacked by the enemy,
> for in that case it would definitely mean that
> we have sunk to the level of the enemy.
>
> *Chairman Mao Tse Tung*

Dear Marshall II:

What's all this guff from Everette Dennis in *Mass Comm Review?*[2] It is loaded with inaccuracies which would take quite a time to amend—or emend. I am a full time academic who has very little leisure for writing, but I took four years to do *The Executive as Dropout*. From the time I came back from Fordham I was studying the corporate and political world, and paying very little attention to media. I was also preparing my doctoral (Nashe) dissertation for the press. The academic coverage is only beginning for my stuff. Remember, I have the only communication theory of transformation—all the other theories are theories of transportation only.

Currently I am getting my *Laws of the Media* ready for the press, but much of the summer has been in Joyce and Eliot research with my son Eric, who will have a major Joyce article in *The James Joyce Quarterly* in the Fall [Summer] issue.

Dennis apparently imagines that media are my primary concern. This is far from being the case. One major misunderstanding concerns my "style" which happens to be a very *good* style for getting attention. As for getting *understanding*, that depends entirely upon the reader. The user is always the content, and the user is often very evasive, or very stupid. Nobody could pretend serious interest in my work who was not completely familiar with all of the works of James Joyce and the French Symbolists. There is a much bigger interest in McLuhan in

---

[1]The American historian Marshall Fishwick (b. 1923), who first met McLuhan in 1966, is Professor of Communications at the Virginia Polytechnic Institute and State University.

[2]Fishwick had sent McLuhan the April 1974 issue (vol. 1, no. 2) of *Mass Comm Review* (published by Mass Communications and Society Division, Association for Education in Journalism, Temple University, Philadelphia), which contained an article by Everette E. Dennis entitled "Post-Mortem on McLuhan: A Public Figure's Emergence and Decline as Seen in Popular Magazines". In it Dennis examines what he saw as the creation of McLuhan's reputation by articles on and about him that appeared in wide-circulation magazines, beginning in 1965 and reaching a peak in 1967—when 27 articles about McLuhan appeared in the *New York Times*—and 1968 (the period when McLuhan was at Fordham). Suggesting a deliberate co-operation on McLuhan's part with the mass media, Dennis relates the McLuhan phenomenon to the concept of "human pseudo-events" presented by Daniel Boorstin in *The Image; or What Happened to the American Dream* (1962). Dennis ends by ascribing what he saw as "McLuhan's decline as a symbolic leader, as a public symbol" to a breaking down of the McLuhan image caused by his "wandering over the whole psychic landscape", relaying limited messages to too many interest groups, so that "there was general confusion about who he was". In consequence, McLuhan "moved outside the range of American mass media". Dennis ends by acknowledging the importance of McLuhan's ideas in analysing communication and its processes—which, he says, had been mainly disseminated by the popular magazine.

the Latin world than in the Wasp world. My biggest following is in Mexico, and South America, and then, next, in Paris and Japan. *Understanding Media* and *The Gutenberg Galaxy* have been translated into 22 languages, and are about to appear in several other languages.

Yours Marshall

To Marshall Fishwick

August 1, 1974

Dear Marshall II:

Am enclosing some materials which you might well forward to Everette Dennis. You can check my bibliography against his. What do you know about him? He seems to have the usual anti-McLuhan animus that characterizes the schools of communication. That is, they are all information-theory people, as people. He seems to think that [the American historian] Daniel Boorstin [b. 1914] has all of my material in a proper academic form. What do you think about that? My reading of Boorstin tells me that he is a content man, and if media creates "pseudo events", likewise they create pseudo people.

Why did Dennis choose to ignore *The Mechanical Bride* (1951)? Or the fact that I was a well-known literary critic long before that? Why does he choose to ignore that my work is essentially satirical and non-moral, cf., the greatest satire is non-moral. Would it not be better for you to devise a reply to Dennis, using some of the enclosed materials?

Apropos my sudden prominence in the 60's, it happened with the dropout TV generation who were happy to discover the rage which my stuff produced in the academic bosom and to associate themselves with me on that account. Now that the TV generation is squaring up again, they no longer feel the same satisfaction in zapping the establishment via McLuhan. McLuhan continues to engender academic rage while the TV kids are running for cover. Everette Dennis is obviously an academic like Daniel Boorstin (for whom he seems to harbour admiration). The reason that I am admired in Paris and in some of the Latin countries is that my approach is rightly regarded as "structuralist". I have acquired that approach through Joyce and Eliot and the Symbolists, and used it in *The Mechanical Bride*. Nobody except myself in the media field has ventured to use the structuralist or "existential" approach. It is a highbrow approach, and the schools of communication are uniformly hardware and flatfoot in their training and activities.

Please tell me what you think should be done in order to make the best possible use of this beach-head.

---

[1]Structuralism is a European movement in the human sciences (which influenced English-language literary theory and criticism, beginning in the 1960s) that conceives of any cultural phenomenon as the product of a system, or codes, of "signification", and tries to identify a "grammar" of culture—the rules and constraints by which meaning is generated and communicated.

To Malcolm Muggeridge[1]

September 19, 1974

Dear Malcolm:

We are still enjoying the backlash of your charity! It was a grand visit and chat we had. Now and then I get comments from acquaintances who seem to be under the impression that you see me as an enthusiastic promoter and exponent of electric technology who is dissolving the values of Gutenberg culture. This is very far from being the case, and all of my life has been devoted to teaching and cultivating literary values. When I published *Gutenberg Galaxy* I was entirely mystified about the response which assumed it to be an attack on the printed word. I felt like a person who had turned in a fire alarm only to be branded as an arsonist. It took me years to discover that many people are upset when they encounter situations which they must share and which are also beyond their conscious control. Since nearly all the *effects* of what we do are beyond conscious control, people often panic in the presence of subliminal features of their daily experience when these matters surface. Since my work is entirely devoted to studying subliminal effects of technology (that is, nearly all of the effects), I begin to understand why I am mistaken for an exponent of the things I abominate. My training in Symbolist art and poetry has long made me familiar with subliminal life in art and poetry and language in general. It has been my procedure to apply this knowledge to popular culture. My first book was on the subliminal effects of advertising.

Since the study of effects relates to the matter of form and structure, it is not possible to moralize these things. The formal structure of a virus eludes moral value as much as the form of a sculpture, but that need in no way blind us to the effects of these things. I am sure you have had many opportunities to observe perverse subliminal responses to your own work.

[1] Malcolm Muggeridge (b. 1903), the famous English journalist and author of many books, was at this time Writer-in-Residence at the University of Western Ontario. He had recently made an appearance at a Monday-night seminar of McLuhan's Centre for Culture and Technology.

To R. Murray Schafer[1]

December 16, 1974

Dear Murray:

Naturally I approve entirely your approach in soundscape. We are living in an acoustic age for the first time in centuries, and by that I mean that the electric

[1] Ronald Murray Schafer (b. 1933)—author and educator and a Canadian composer of international reputation—was a member of the Department of Communication Studies at Simon Fraser University, Burnaby, British Columbia from 1965 to 1975. In 1969 he founded the World Soundscape Project, a research and educational endeavour concerned with all aspects of sound environments. Schafer—who met McLuhan in 1955 when he was a student—had sent him on November 19, 1974, his article "The Music of the Environment", which he was expanding into his book *The Tuning of the World* (1977), a draft of which he asked McLuhan to read.

environment is simultaneous. Hearing is structured by the experience of picking up information from all directions at once. For this reason, even the telegraph gave to news the simultaneous character which created the "mosaic" press of disconnected events under a single date-line. At this moment, the entire planet exists in that form of instant but discontinuous co-presence of everything.

One hidden dimension of the soundscape is to be found in Rock music, which pours the sounds of the city through the rhythms of the English language as a means of humanizing metropolitan cacophony. The role of music as humanizing technological noise by processing it through the regional dialects, seems to have been ignored by all musicologists. Rock can only be sung in English, and for that reason the Chinese and the Africans and the Hindu learn English so they can sing Rock. The radio soundscape, earlier, had brought forth jazz, which also depends entirely on the rhythms of the English language, especially its Southern and oral manifestations.

In a magazine called *Listening* (University of Chicago Press, vol. 9, nos. 1 & 2, Winter/Spring, 1974, p. 9–27), I have a recent essay explaining in what senses the medieval period was acoustic right up to the edge of the Gutenberg, or visual revolution.[2] [Johan] Huizinga, in *The Waning of the Middle Ages* [1954], explains some of it, and Siegfried Giedion in *Mechanization Takes Command* has a section on medieval comfort, in which he explains that a medieval space was furnished even when empty, because of its acoustic properties.

If you can manage to interest psychologists in the nature of acoustic space, you would be doing a good work. What they, and all scientists, call "space" is simply visual space, which is continuous and connected and static. Scientists and architects alike refer to this as "physical" space. It is the space which can be divided and quantified, measured and tabulated. Acoustic space cannot be divided or connected, and it is certainly not static but dynamic. Clinging to the remnants of visual space in this new acoustic age has become a kind of a paranoiac state. Personally, I think I prefer visual to acoustic space, but this should not be a matter of either/or. In his *Responsive Chord*, Tony Schwartz explains how the TV image uses the eye as an ear (on page 14). (Incidentally the book was published by Doubleday, N.Y. in 1973.) The rapid disappearance of literature is directly related to this factor.

Had you ever thought of surveying the poets for some of their awareness of the soundscape, starting with the opening of Chaucer's Prologue to the *Canterbury Tales*, and onwards? I think you will find direction and perception in this matter. Let me urge you to put some of this material into your *Tuning of the World*. Would be glad to help.

---

[2]This article was entitled "The Medieval Environment: Yesterday or Today?".

1975

To Pierre Elliott Trudeau

January 22, 1975

Dear Pierre:

Apropos my inflation piece, which you mentioned you might show to John Turner,[1] two articles on multi-national corporations in the *New Yorker* for December 2nd and 9th drew attention to some of the ways that they avoid the equilibrium operations of our own commodity by direct "transfer trading" among themselves. Computerized book-keeping enables them to "cook the books" in such a way as to accommodate them to a wide range of needs. A separate set with unique "bottom line" is kept for each government and each government department, so that there is no question of their ever paying any income tax.

It is computerized book-keeping that by-passes the structure of the old industrial markets of nineteenth-century hardware, rendering Keynesian strategies helpless. That is, the computer is an electric form that is able to transcend the structure of the "First World" arrangements. (I.e., the "First World" = the Western industrial set-up, the "Second World" = Russian socialism, the "Third World" = all those countries without a nineteenth century, and the "Fourth World" = the electric information world which goes around all of them, having quite different effects on each.)

We shall persist in our prayers for you and Margaret.

[1]The Right Honourable John Turner (b. 1929) was at this time Minister of Finance in the Trudeau government. He resigned in September 1975. He was Prime Minister of Canada from June 30 to September 17, 1984, when he became Leader of the Opposition. The "inflation piece" was doubtless the McLuhan/Nevitt article in *The New York Times* (September 21, 1974), "A Media Approach to Inflation".

To Hugh Lane

March 5, 1975

Dear Hugh:

The winter has begun to enter that seemingly endless phase, although we have had some very warm weeks earlier. Corinne and I have been in the Bahamas recently, but only for two days of balm and sun. It was a work trip for IBM.

Something that I have often thought of asking you, is to obtain a copy of *The Latin Grace* from the [Trinity] Hall. When I was there I had intended to obtain one of these from each of the Colleges. Perhaps there is a volume or brochure containing such? I am currently on my second run through the *New Testament* in Greek, but only do a few verses a day. My Latin has improved greatly since doing a bit of Greek. Is this commonly recognized? I mean that Latin depends heavily on Greek for its structure?

Another item: have been doing a good deal in Ovid's *Metamorphoses* since discovering that Joyce's *Dubliners* uses them, one for one, as sub-plots. Nobody whatever has suspected the Ovid parallel, so it is rather exciting to open up this territory. Joyce gets some very comic effects out of the parallels and introduces the parallel mainly in his metaphors and symbols rather than in the story-line.

My work on the history of rhetoric which I did for my Cambridge Ph.D. has suddenly opened some new doors, thanks to studying *Finnegans Wake* along with my son, Eric. The five divisions of rhetoric stressed by Cicero and Quintilian (*inventio*, *dispositio*, *elocutio*, *memoria* and *delivery*) were what Horace was referring to when he said: "Every play must have five acts." (Again, this has been missed by the classical scholars.) In the history of Christian theology the five parts were considered to be simultaneous rather than sequential. These five divisions are not only used everywhere by Joyce in structuring all of his books, but are used with the utmost care by Ovid as well. Dante and Chaucer used them everywhere and always, as do all the major writers of the Renaissance and afterwards. It turns out to be a huge unexplored territory of luminous form, and I would be happy to hear your comments from any angle whatever.

To John Culkin

June 19, 1975

Dear John:

I just did a note to my friend, Fritz Wilhelmsen, Thomist at the University of Dallas. He is interested in working on St. Thomas' theory of communication, and I have pointed out to him that Aquinas designates his audience, the people he wants to influence and alter, in the Objections of each article. Then I realized that the audience is, in all matters of art and expression, the formal cause, e.g., fallen man is the formal cause of the incarnation, and Plato's public is the formal cause of his philosophy. Formal cause is concerned with effects and with structural form, and not with value judgments.

My own approach to the media has been entirely from formal cause. Since formal causes are hidden and environmental, they exert their structural pressure by interval and interface with whatever is in their environmental territory. Formal cause is always hidden, whereas the things upon which they act are visible. The TV generation has been shaped not by TV programs, but by the pervasive and penetrating character of the TV image, or service, itself.

Imagine my amazement on picking up *Art and Scholasticism* [*and the Frontiers of Poetry*, 1962] by [Jacques] Maritain the other day to discover that he has nothing whatever to say about formal cause. He is a complete Cartesian subjectivist in by-passing the entire world of rhetorical *elocutio*. If you study Eric's piece on classical rhetorical structure in *Finnegans Wake*, you will see how basic classical rhetoric is in Joyce. It is equally relevant to T.S. Eliot, and Eric is the first to point this out. (By the way, he is going to the University of Dallas for a couple of years to work on his Ph.D. in that rather ideal academic environment where we both taught this Spring for a few weeks.) This matter of formal causality and the environments created by the media is so big that I hope your new academic set-up will be able to take hold of some of it.

To Marion Hammond[1]

June 20, 1975

Dear Marion:

This is just a note about the ordination of women which concerns "formal causality", i.e, structural form which is inseparable from "putting on" one's public. The writer's or performer's public is the formal cause of his art or entertainment or his philosophy. The *figure/ground* relation between writer and public or between the artist and his making is an interplay, a kind of intercourse. This interplay is at its peak in all performance before the public and is characteristic of role-playing in general. There is, as it were, a sexual relation between performer and public, which relates specifically to the priest or minister. The congregation is necessarily feminine to the masculine role of the priest. (This is characteristic also in medicine, of the surgeon who is only exceptionally a woman.) It is, therefore, this inherent sexual aspect of the priesthood that makes the ordination of women impractical and unacceptable to a congregation in their feminine role.

Perhaps there has been insufficient thought given to the nature of role-playing in its metaphysical or formal causality. This is apropos the local headlines about [the] Anglican synod OK-ing the ordination of women.

Praying that you are all well, and hoping to hear from you,

[1] The Reverend Marion J. Hammond was rector of the Parish of St. Thomas (Episcopal) Church, Denver, Colorado.

To Pierre Elliott Trudeau

July 2, 1975

Dear Pierre:

I think this may be a rather important note, and its brevity should be no indication of its significance. Apropos the problem of hanging and capital punishment, there seems to be a universal assumption that hanging is punitive, retaliation for misdeeds.[1] I suggest that this is a very minor aspect of the matter. The central significance of capital punishment is the ritual that it entails, and this ritual serves primarily to enhance the significance and importance of human life by drawing attention to the decisive and infinite implications of the moment of death. If this is taken to concern capital punishment as *figure*, let us consider the *ground* that supports that figure or procedure.

We live in a time when the coalescing of all people on earth into a single mass-public has diminished human private identity almost to the vanishing point. Anybody at a ball game, for example, is a nobody, and the entire planet has become our ball park. Under electric conditions of our inter-involvement of all mankind, the information environment has blanketed and smothered private identity. This effect has made human life appear very cheap indeed. The TV generation cannot *feel* very much importance attaching to the private person. On the other hand, the loss of private identity which has come rather suddenly upon Western man has produced a deep anger at this rip-off of his private self.

There are thus two kinds of violence relating to the same situation: first, the kind that comes from the unimportance of everybody; and second, the kind that comes from the impulse to restore one's private meaning by acts of violence. On the frontier everybody is a nobody and violence is the order of the day. Electronic man lives on such a frontier at all times, doubting his identity and his survival alike. Psychologically considered, violence is an attempt to restore order to achieve identity.

With prayers for you and Margaret
Yrs Marshall

[1]In the spring of 1975 René Vaillancourt of Montreal was under sentence of death by hanging for the killing of Toronto policeman Leslie Maitland on February 1, 1973. His fate and the issue of capital punishment were hotly debated in Parliament and in the Canadian press until he and two other prisoners on death row were granted stays of execution by Cabinet on October 22, 1975. Prime Minister Trudeau and Solicitor-General Warren Allmand were determined to bring about the abolition of capital punishment in Canada, and on July 14, 1976 the House of Commons enacted a bill that did just that. In fact no one had been executed in Canada since 1962.

To Pierre Elliott Trudeau

July 30, 1975

Dear Pierre:

When you reply to my letters, I feel extremely selfish for taking any of your time at all. However, I feel obliged to clarify the theme of violence and capital punishment, if possible. Rollo May has a book—*Power and Innocence*—in which the theme is my own, namely, that violence in its innumerable modalities is typically a response to loss of identity or to a threat against one's self, or one's thought. Technical innovations, simply by creating new environments, upset people's images of themselves. The bigger the technology, the bigger the upset, and the bigger the threat to one's image. The image can be private or corporate.

All this relates to the other situation I mentioned, namely, that one's image of one's self at a ball game is minimal. The most important figure in the world is a nobody at a ball game. Electronically, however, all of us are attending the same ball game in the same ball park, namely, Spaceship Earth. Our involvement in each other has become so intense that our private image has been reduced to the minimum. The universal response is one of anger and violence, which is not made the less by the mysteries and unexpected rip-off of the private self which has taken place. Violence is a natural attempt to re-establish and to re-discover the nature of one's being. The Scripture tells us that "the King of Heaven doth suffereth violence, for there the least shall be the most."

My other thought in this matter concerned capital punishment as a *means* of re-establishing the importance and dignity of individuals. I am not advocating capital punishment, but I am pointing to its effects in enhancing the significance of the human drama of life and death. At present the legal procedures of trial and incarceration for murder seem to multiply the sheer quantity of bureaucratic activity, while withdrawing all dignity from the participants. When you say: "I would rather subscribe to the following explanation: material comfort, social conformity, monotonous and repetitive jobs generate frustrations and aggressions for which our culture (or social organization) does not provide enough creative outlets, and destructive behaviours are the result", I certainly agree with you. However, this situation is itself a monstrous rip-off of private identity. I also agree with your idea of the problem as one which demands creative outlets. However, I seem to be saying that the ritual of capital punishment, carried out in the most public possible way, is itself an intensively creative outlet for the entire society.

Our daughter Teri, whom you met, has spent the last three weeks at the Moscow Film Festival. Her picture on [Edward G.] Curtis [*The Shadow Catcher*], the photographer of North American Indians, having been one of three North American films chosen by the Russians for their Festival. She has certainly found her creative outlet, though it has entailed some very vicious competition and frustration.

One of the strange things I have discovered about my own work is that Westerners in general resent having the effects of any technology brought to their attention. That print, or the telephone, or TV should have any effect on them at all, is taken to mean that they have been manipulated and degraded. The person who is blamed for this, is the person who points it out to them.

I enclose two or three jests which I hope you will find usable.

To Clare Westcott[1]

November 26, 1975

Dear Clare Westcott:

Martin O'Malley's piece in the [Toronto] *Globe* on censorship prompted me to contact Don Sims and the Censorship Board.[2] A visit to 1075 Millwood Road proved quite traumatic. Don Sims and his Board are subjected daily to a barrage of violence and horror that makes the front lines of the first war seem quite ordinary. The word "censorship" no longer applies. The Don Sims role is that of directing operation *Survival*.

What I had in mind when I first contacted Don Sims was to explain to his group that the problem of pornography and obscenity related to fragmentation and specialism, much in the same way that sentimentality consists in playing up one emotion in isolation to all the others. Pornography and obscenity, in the same way, work by specialism and fragmentation. They deal with *figure* without a *ground*—situations in which the human factor is suppressed in favour of sensations and kicks. In the same way, the individual can be separated out from the society, Robinson Crusoe style. I first began to explain to Sims that pornography and violence are by-products of societies in which private identity has been scrubbed or destroyed by sudden environmental change, or unexpected confrontations which disrupt the image which the individual or the group entertains of itself. Any loss of identity prompts people to seek reassurance and rediscovery of themselves by testing, and even by violence. Today the electric revolution, the wired planet, and the information environment involve everybody in everybody to the point of individual extinction. The TV image, for example, has the power to dissolve the private identity almost entirely, quite apart from any program content. Discussions with Don Sims revealed that even the program content of the pictures they deal with is such as to raise the possibility of anaesthesia. That is, sensationalism so spectacular inevitably leads to numbing and loss of awareness. Even the popular *Exorcist* or *Jaws* raise this possibility, while seeming to offer the possibility of catharsis or relief from real situations by means of fictional violence.

However, the scope and scale of the non-human sensationalism with which the Don Sims group must deal points not so much at a situation in which people need catharsis, as [at] a situation in which an entire society is in its death-throes. For centuries before radio and TV, Western man had steadily eroded and fragmented his personal and social life by means of specialism in his senses and in his emotions. The advent of electric technology, especially TV, brought about an instant merging of the senses which had previously been abstracted and fragmented. Centuries

---

[1]This letter was addressed to Clare Westcott in the office of William Davis, Premier of Ontario.

[2]Don Sims (b. 1914), a former radio broadcaster, was appointed Chairman of the Board of Censors of the Theatre Branch of the Ministry of Consumer and Commercial Relations, Ontario, on September 30, 1974.

of intense individualism had prepared the way for a sudden group merger. All men at a ball game are nobodies. At the speed of light, everybody is a nobody. There is a further dimension at the speed of light—everybody is discarnate, a nervous system without a body. Anger and frustration resulting from such sudden inexplicable situations and loss may well account for the extremities of violence and obscenities manifest in the new floods of pornography.

After a bit of chat with the Don Sims group, it became obvious that they were engaged in trying to hold together some semblance of the human image. Unexpectedly, and environmentally, they have been nominated to perform a heroic task calling for superhuman sanctity. The term "censorship" is ludicrously inadequate for such a function. A resounding and positive term is needed. The violence that Don Sims tries to stem is matched on other fronts by the strikes performed by people conscious of huge loss of private identity. To understand how this has happened is a primary and urgent need.

Sincerely yours,

P.S. By way of stressing the positive feature in the work of censors, why not call them "Centre for Human Rights and Entertainment"?

To Edward T. Hall

December 8, 1975

Dear Ned:

Have found *Beyond Culture* a rich experience. On page 110 you mention "five surprisingly different but apparently related activities in the frontal part of the brain. These "five" correspond exactly to the five classical divisions of rhetoric, which were associated with the *Logos* or the *Verbum!* Have been doing quite a bit of work on these of late. Of course I am unhappy about page 135, where you accuse me of unacknowledged borrowing. How happy I would have been to give you full credit had I recognized the source at the time of writing![1]

I have recently done another book on *The Laws of the Media* (not yet published), explaining the linguistic character of all human artifacts, hardware or software. Are you familiar with any investigators who explore the characteristics of the various kinds of sensory space; e.g., touch, the sensory interval; and visual space, the only space that is continuous, connected and static; and acoustic space, the sphere whose centre is everywhere and whose margin is nowhere? I cannot find psychologists who are interested in the characteristics and components of space.

---

[1]In note 4 to Chapter Two, "Man as Extension", on page 215 of E.T. Hall's *Beyond Culture* (1976—McLuhan was sent page proofs by Hall), Hall writes: "Marshall McLuhan used to talk about innering and outering (processes he could see at work in man), and few people knew what he meant until he began speaking in terms of extensions—a term he borrowed from the author—in *The Gutenberg Galaxy* (1962)." In his reply of December 19 to this letter, Hall said that McLuhan was not to be "unhappy" about the note, that the matter of acknowledgement was not mentioned, and that "We all get things from each other".

1976

To Sheila Watson

January 26, 1976

Dear Sheila:

While moving forty or fifty books from the sofa last night, your volume of stories and essays surfaced![1] I have gotten into it again, after weeks. I shall get some copies from the Coach House Press. It is really a wonderful collection and should be in more commercial publication. Have you done anything about this recently? Would you be agreeable to my promoting it a bit?

Today we are about to take off for Dallas and New Orleans for a visit with Eric and Sabina and for some talks.

One of the many thoughts I had as I read your Lewis essays was how stupid of people with our interests to scatter to the four winds. There is no way in which serious work can be promoted without team effort. In isolation, it is ground to powder. My own position here at the University of Toronto is no better than yours at the University of Alberta. Total isolation and futility! However, thanks to my publications, I can have serious and satisfactory relations with people off campus and abroad, leaving the local yokels to gnash their molars!

[1]This refers to an issue of *Open Letter*, a journal of experimental writing, devoted to Watson and entitled "Sheila Watson: A Collection" (series 3, no. 1), published in 1974 by the Coach House Press, Toronto.

To Michael Hornyansky[1]

February 3, 1976

Dear Professor Hornyansky:

A student in a seminar recently cited some comments of yours concerning my supposed views on the printed book.[2] I recently sent a piece on this matter to *Newsweek*, a copy of which I enclose.[3]

[1]Professor Michael Hornyansky (b. 1927) is a member of the English Department of Brock University, St Catharines, Ont.

[2]In his reply of March 2, 1976 Hornyansky quoted the passage McLuhan was referring to, from Hornyansky's essay "Is Your English Destroying Your Image?" in Joseph Gold (ed.), *In the Name of Language!* (1975). It reads in part: "The man who deplores a return to the 3 R's as a step back toward the cave . . . belongs to the McLuhanite fringe who scream that print is dead, the book is buried and citizens of the global village must be expert in the new mysteries of film and tape and incantation. I never know how much to blame on the ancient sage himself, because I'm never sure what he means or how serious he is." McLuhan's reply of April 21 began: "Yours is a very typical problem of the merely visual man."

[3]On December 8, 1975 McLuhan wrote a long letter (which was not published) to the Editor of *Newsweek*, about an article, "Why Johnny Can't Write", that appeared in the issue of that day.

Working out of Symbolist studies, I long ago began to study the *effects* of human artifacts. Flaubert's work, for example, is entirely concerned with these effects as they shape psyche and society. Since the effects of any form are always subliminal, many literary people seem to resent the idea that they have been manipulated unconsciously by their favourite medium. Since, however, there are many media today competing with literature for the manipulation of consciousness, it becomes mandatory to sort out the friends and enemies of the book. I discovered, in doing this, that merely to suggest that the book has any subliminal effects whatever is to be considered an enemy of the book. (The so-called content of the book is the reader, as Baudelaire pointed out in his "hypocrite lecteur, mon semblable, mon frère.") Those people who think that I am an enemy of the book have simply not read my work, nor thought about the problem. Most of my writing is Menippean satire,[4] presenting the actual surface of the world we live in as a ludicrous image.

Sincerely yours,

[4]The *Satire Ménippée* (ref. the Greek satirist Menippus) was a French political lampoon that circulated in Paris in the 1590s.

To David Staines[1]

March 15, 1976

Dear David:

Just back from a couple of weeks in Mexico where we had excellent weather and fascinating friends and acquaintance. The return from Harvard was just a few hours before leaving for Mexico and left no opportunity to drop you a note of thanks. Now, I have read Douglas Bush's essay on Leacock and enjoyed it immensely,[2] and have also been snatching moments with the [Stephen] Sondheim songs from the disc you generously gave me. It isn't likely that I shall get to New York in time to take advantage of your offer to get tickets for [Sondheim's] *Pacific Overtures*. The two weeks in Mexico have left me with a formidable backlog.

I'm thrilled with the idea of your being able to get *The Irish Homestead* versions of *Dubliners*, and I am duly impressed and grateful for your discovery of where *The Irish Homestead* hides out![3] Slokum and Cahoon's *A Bibliography of James*

[1]Canadian-born David Staines (b. 1946)—who at this time was Assistant Professor of English at Harvard University (1973–8) and is now Professor of English at the University of Ottawa—had organized a series of six public lectures at Harvard on "The Literature & Culture of Canada", under the auspices of the Department of English and American Literature and Language, for which McLuhan, Margaret Atwood, Northrop Frye, and Hugh MacLennan were among the speakers. McLuhan's address, "Canada: The Borderline Case", was given on February 25 and was rewritten for inclusion in the book that grew out of this series: *The Canadian Imagination: Dimensions of a Literary Culture* (1977) edited by Staines.

[2]Douglas Bush's essay, "Stephen Leacock", was included in *The Canadian Imagination*.

[3]McLuhan was interested in examining those stories in James Joyce's *Dubliners* (1914) that first appeared in the periodical *The Irish Homestead*, and Staines obtained photocopies of these original versions from the Harvard Library and sent them to him.

Joyce (Yale University Press) provide the data about the first appearances of the *Dubliners* stories.

You remind me about my piece on "The Borderline Case" as being due by mid-May. I have forgotten about your thoughts on optimum size of this piece. My spirits droop at the mere thought of tackling it. I am still suffering from the drop in altitude from Mexico City. Apropos John Kelleher [Professor of English, Harvard] do you think it might be proper to send him a complete list of the names in *Dubliners*? This would be tantamount to asking him to write a monograph on the same! Please advise. Of course any expenses you incur apropos the *Dubliners* source materials I shall be happy to take care of.

More soon

Yrs

Marshall

To Hans Preiner[1]

May 7, 1976

Dear Hans:

Look forward to hearing from you shortly. This is just a quick request that you do a short note for me on the cooling effect that TV had on the neo-Nazi thing on the Czech border. Remember about the signs that excited a fracas, and how TV cooled it in a day or two?[2]

What I have further in mind is that South Africa has had TV for three months and I want to contact somebody in South Africa who will begin to pay attention to the *effects* of TV, since it offers a superb ground for media study.

Am just back from South America where radio still creates great instability politically.

---

[1]Hans Preiner—a Viennese friend of Teri McLuhan's who was active in young people's television in Vienna was associated with the Institut für Informationsentwicklung (the Centre for Understanding Media) there—brought McLuhan to Vienna for lectures when he was on his way to Salzburg, in the summer of 1971. (See page 430, note 8).

[2]In a letter of June 8, 1976, Preiner described the incident alluded to (which took place on Austria's Yugoslavian border in 1972): the destruction, by German-speaking inhabitants of the province of Carinthia, of road-signs printed in the language of the local Slavonic majority. The tension was subdued when Austrian TV decided to do a live program on the dispute, inviting audience participation in a panel discussion. According to Preiner, "nothing happened. The combattants retired into baroque statements and demonstrated reason & wisdom . . ."

To Robert Cowan[1]

May 7, 1976

Dear Mr. Cowan:

Congratulations on your excellent Lewis Newsletter. I have sent you $3.00 for a subscription, and would be happy to pay for any of the back numbers.

An excellent theme for your Letter would be *Windy at Rugby*. He was exceedingly proud of having been the rare recipient of "the sixth licking", i.e., in one day he received six separate lickings. He said that having received the fifth, he suddenly realized he was near immortality, and hastened around to the prefect's door and proceeded to smash his tennis ball against it until he qualified for the sixth licking.

Once, when I was recording his voice in St. Louis on a little home recorder, he was amazed to hear his voice: "I sound like a bloody Englishman, and thought that I had a good American accent!" It must have been the first time he had ever heard a recording of his own voice. On that occasion he read passages of "One-Way Song", and, by the way, "One-Way Song" is carefully and classically divided according to the five divisions of rhetoric. However, this was first pointed out to me by my son, Eric, who is an expert in classical rhetoric in modern literature. He could write you a little piece on the five divisions in "One-Way Song". He has a quite complete essay on "The Rhetorical Structure of *Finnegans Wake*" in the *James Joyce Quarterly* (Volume 11, #4, Summer, 1974).

My first meeting with Wyndham Lewis occurred as a result of a letter I received from my mother who had heard him on the Christian Culture Series. His theme was "Rouault, Painter of Original Sin." Lewis had delivered this lecture at the Book Cadillac Hotel in Detroit—it must have been in 1944 [1943]. Having checked that he was *the* Wyndham Lewis, the ogre of Bloomsbury, I got on a train with my friend, Felix Giovanelli, of the Modern Language Department at St. Louis University. We found Lewis in a basement apartment in the heart of Windsor, and he told us of how lucky he had been to find it. He had simply stood on the street, asking passers-by if they knew of any available space for rent. Lewis accepted us at once, with no kind of formality, and we gradually formed the project to bring him to St. Louis where we hoped to find him some painting commissions and some lectures. We were sufficiently successful in this to justify his coming to St. Louis with Froanna. One bit of luck occurred when I discovered through a neighbour in St. Louis (Mrs. Gelhorn, mother-in-law of Ernest Hemingway) that Erlanger, the Nobel Prize winner in physics at Washington University in St. Louis, was to have a portrait done. When speaking to Mrs. Gelhorn, I proposed Lewis as a worthy painter to do the Erlanger portrait and she at once phoned Hemingway in Cuba and asked him directly about whether she should commission Lewis for the job. Hemingway promptly said "yes" and gave Lewis an enthusiastic build-up, with the result that Lewis did the painting

---

[1] This letter was addressed to Mr Robert Cowan, The Wyndham Lewis Society, Pollokshields, Glasgow.

for $1,500.00. This act of Hemingway's is not insignificant in view of the rage that he had felt when "The Dumb Ox" essay appeared in *Men Without Art*.[2]

Mrs. Lewis has been engaged in a memoir of her husband for many years, and it might be possible to get some bits of it for your Letter. I will be happy to supply other things from time to time concerning Lewis.

All best wishes with your enterprise.

Marshall McLuhan

[2]See page 141.

To Eric Havelock
May 10, 1976

Dear Professor Havelock:

It is a joy to have *The Origins of Western Literacy* from O.I.S.E.[1] It put me in mind of the fact that you are one of the few people in the Western world who ever studied the *effects* of human innovation. Effects belong to formal causality, and one of the effects of the alphabet had been to create a pervasive visual *ground* which involves the commitment to efficient causality. From Parmenides onward, connected space and logical reasoning supplanted analogy and formal causality. It has become very apparent to me that the formal cause resides in the public, or audience, of the speaker or writer.

Would that there were many of you in the field.

[1]Eric Havelock, *The Origins of Western Literacy: Four Lectures Delivered at the Ontario Institute for Studies in Education, March 25–8, 1974* (1976).

To Woody Allen[1]
August 25, 1976

Dear "Alvy",

It was fun getting into the new (for me) medium. You made me aware of the phenomenal amount of work and skill that is involved in making a film. Naturally it was delightful meeting you and working with you.

The preliminary precaution concerning mention of my being in one of your films just didn't register adequately with me. Of course, I did not mention the matter to any publication source. One's friends pass the word quickly among themselves, so that I cannot imagine it remaining a secret. Of course, I would never dream of having an interview about it, or making a statement at any time, so that the most that could possibly come out would be a passing gossip reference. Most probably, however, this will not occur.

With heartiest good wishes for the future of this film.[2]

[1]The famous American film director, actor, and writer Woody Allen (b. 1935) invited McLuhan to appear in a scene in his film *Annie Hall* (1977), which became very successful and received an Academy Award as Best Picture. "Alvy" is the name of the character Allen played in the film.

[2]On September 26 Woody Allen replied: "You were a wonder in the film and it was a real treat working with you."

To John M. Dunaway[1]

September 1, 1976

Dear Professor Dunaway:

It was in 1934–6, when I was an undergraduate at Cambridge in England, that I encountered the writings of Jacques Maritain. *Art as Scholasticism* was featured on the shelves of our English department library, and I had a glorious time discovering that art and the art process were essentially intellectual in character. In those years I was deeply interested in things Catholic, having started in that direction under G.K. Chesterton whose *What's Wrong with the World* I had read in 1932. From that time I read everything I could get my hands on by Maritain, and have kept fairly well up on all of his works.

Part of the excitement in reading Maritain was the awareness that he was saying something new about something very old, so that there was the excitement of discovery and of sharing this discovery with one's contemporaries. I discovered Maritain simultaneously with the work of I.A. Richards, and T.S. Eliot, and Ezra Pound, and James Joyce, and Wyndham Lewis. All of these people seem to relate to each other in many different ways, and each seems to enrich the other. Along with the works of contemporary painters and ballet and the world of Sergei Eisenstein and music, one had the experience of a very rich new culture, in which the great intellectual Maritain was a notable ornament. Maritain helped to complete the vortex of significant components in a single luminous logos of our time.

[1] The letter is addressed to Professor John M. Dunaway, Department of Modern Foreign Languages, Mercer University, Macon, Georgia. His letter to McLuhan is not extant.

To Ruth Nanda Anshen[1]

September 2, 1976

Dear Nanda:

The enclosures may help you to follow my work more easily. For thirty years at least I have been using the two-hemisphere approach under the names of the *written* and the *oral*, the *visual* and the *acoustic*, the *hot* and the *cool*, the *medium* and the *message*, *figure* and *ground*, and so on. Now it turns out that medicine has been building a great beach-head for this approach with its new understanding of the two hemispheres of the brain. If you look at the traits of the left hemisphere, you will discover the lineaments of the First World—the literate and industrial world,—and, on the other hand, in the right hemisphere you will perceive the characteristics of the Third World—the world without the phonetic alphabet.

During the past century, while the knowledge of the two hemispheres has been

[1] Ruth Nanda Anshen planned and edited the World Perspective series (Harper & Row) in which *Through the Vanishing Point: Space in Poetry and Painting* (1968), by McLuhan and Parker, was volume XXXVII.

growing, there has also been a new electronic milieu or environment which automatically pushes the right hemisphere into a more dominant position than it has
held in the Western world since the invention of the phonetic alphabet. The two
hemispheres naturally respond to the milieu or total surround in which people
live and work. My work has been a dialogue between the two hemispheres in
which the characteristics of the right hemisphere are given so much recognition
that I have been unintelligible to the left-hemisphere people. It happens that the
left-hemisphere people are completely out of touch with the results and the formal
characteristics of their own new electric technologies.

Tomorrow Corinne and I leave for Paris for a week at a UNESCO Conference
on "The Place of the Artist in Society." Corinne's hearing is still a great worry.
Will catch you up on some of the goings-on of the rest of the family when I get
back.

To Sheila Watson

September 14, 1976

Dear Sheila:

I wonder whether Wyndham Lewis had these hemispheres in mind when he
talked about the "split man"? As you can see, the right belongs to the artist, and
the left to the bureaucrat—Shem the penman, and Shaun the cop.[1]

The reason that Hans Dronker's letter of 1967 did not arouse any special interest
in me was, of course, the fact that these hemisphere people are left hemisphere
only. They talk about both, but live in the left only. I talk about both, and live in
the right hemisphere. However, they have had no training in the right hemisphere,
even though they talk about it. Further, the point they don't understand is the
fact of environmental interface with the hemispheres. The literate lineal environment for 2500 years has given dominance to the left hemisphere, whereas the
simultaneous and discontinuous electric environment gives sudden dominance
to the right hemisphere for the first time in 2500 years. Here is a generation gap
indeed!

---

[1]McLuhan was referring to "Part VI: The Split-Man" and "Part XI: Mr. Zagreus and the
Split-man" in Wyndham Lewis's *The Apes of God* (1930)—the figure of the "split-man" also occurs
in some of Lewis's drawings—and to Shem and Shaun, twin presences ("the each's other") in
Joyce's *Finnegans Wake*. McLuhan used the term "split-man" in his essay "Edgar Poe's Tradition"
(*Sewanee Review*, Winter 1944).

To President-Elect Jimmy Carter[1]

November 4, 1976

A TOAST AND A PRAYER TO THE KING OF OUR HEARTS TODAY.

MARSHALL McLUHAN

[1]McLuhan was hospitalized for a slight heart attack when he sent this telegram. Jimmy Carter replied on November 10: "I deeply appreciate your congratulations and your prayers. Please let me continue to benefit from your support, advice and prayers as I assume the office of the Presidency. Sincerely, Jimmy."

To the Editor, The Globe and Mail, Toronto

December 7, 1976

Dear Sir:

Blaik Kirby's review of *The Money Changers* (Monday, December 6th) missed a wonderful opportunity to explain Arthur Hailey as "a fabulously successful commercial novelist." *Airport*, *Hotel*, and *Wheels*, like *The Money Changers*, are not based on a story-line. Rather, they follow the path of development and social process. They offer a kind of mimesis or dramatization of the human learning process itself. The process which Arthur Hailey has hit upon is like the documentary technique, itself a kind of repeat of the stages by which men experience their world. That is why the documentary, as such, whether in the news reel or in John Grierson's famous *Night Mail* or his *Milk Route*, fascinates readers and viewers alike.[2] The incidental ornaments which Hailey adds, and which Kirby finds "slick" and "shallow", in no way disturb the basic genetic or development pattern of social action and experience which are involved in the mass of themes of *Airport* and *The Money Changers*. There are dozens of similar themes which Hailey has not touched, and his audience will be delighted if, and when, he gets around to them.

Sincerely yours,

(dictated by Prof. McLuhan and signed in his absence)

[1]This letter—which was published in the *Globe* on December 11—refers to the books of the popular novelist Arthur Hailey (b. 1920), of which *The Money-Changers* (1975) was then the latest. Hailey was sent this letter, as it appeared in the *Globe*, and wrote a note of thanks to McLuhan on January 27, 1977.

[2]John Grierson (1898–1972) was head of the Empire Marketing Board Film Unit when it made the documentary *Milk* in the late 1920s; the Unit was transferred to the General Post Office, with Grierson still head, when *Night Mail* (1936) was made. In 1939 Grierson became the first commissioner of the newly formed National Film Board of Canada.

To Bob Hittel[1]

Dear Bob:

Enclosed is the revised bibliography which I think is in a much more publishable state than the one you worked from. Since there is likely to be a continued and perhaps increasing demand for this bibliography, and since it is mostly to be used by scholars and researchers, would you not say that it deserves a fairly rigorous and precise ordering? There is not likely to be any other bibliography, though there may be appendixes and additions to this one.

The enclosed list is in a form acceptable to scholars and bibliographers, having the uniformity and consistency they expect. It affords a solid basis for the subsequent appendixes and additions, which could be put on in the form you have already used. However, it seems that it is best to have a more solid and uniform basis on which to build the appendixes.

You indicated that this would be expensive to re-do. I agree, and I think it's only fair that I should contribute to the cost in any degree that you suggest.

Have been recovering quite quickly from my small heart attack, and naturally regard it as a timely warning to ease up a bit. However, the amount of mail and day-to-day jobs (in addition to my teaching) are continuing to increase. The teaching load, however, is to get quite a bit lighter after this year.

We think of you and Pat fondly, and very often.

Love,

(dictated by prof. McLuhan and signed in his absence)

[1]Bob Hittel compiled a useful bibliography—first published in 1975 by Wake-Brook House, Fort Lauderdale, Florida—entitled *The Writings of Marshall McLuhan: Listed in Chronological Order from 1934 to 1975: with an appended list of reviews and articles about him and his work*. It was reissued in an expanded edition in 1977.

To Sheila Watson

Dear Sheila:

As I mentioned, I really had managed to swing Scott [Taylor] over to left hemisphere.[1] Once there, he performs quite well. As for my health, it seems to be almost back to normal.

Naturally, I am most interested in the work you have been doing on Joyce, and

[1]Scott Taylor had been a graduate student of both Sheila Watson at the University of Alberta and of McLuhan at the University of Toronto. McLuhan was his supervisor for his MA thesis on Gertrude Stein. His essay "By Design Gertrude Stein" appeared in *white pelican* (Autumn 1973).

very grateful for the reference to the Vico book.[2] Have never seen it. The quote you provide about Marx is most helpful. Nobody has ever attempted to write up Marx's theory of communication (I call it TOC). To do a TOC for anybody involves the study of the public they wish to transform. Aquinas puts his public in the front window. It is the list of objections which he has to other people's views on any particular subject. The study of publics is really the study of formal causality, since nobody can write without imagining a group of people who need his help. Is that not the Canadian problem? We cannot imagine anybody needing our help intellectually. Our problems are so similar to those of the U.S. that we use them as the answer to our problems as well.

As you know, my studies of *Dubliners* and Ovid have revealed that Joyce had a continuous parallel going between each story and one or more of the *Metamorphoses* of Ovid. This parallel is not a connection, and I think that most of the problems about "sources" over the centuries has been complicated by the assumption that a source is not a parallel but a connection. The parallels between Homer and *Ulysses* are never connections, and I don't think the scholars would have done anything about it apart from the title of *Ulysses*, plus the direct aid that Joyce provided. I have now forgotten whether Joyce ever discussed these parallels with Stanislaus.[3] Certainly he never discussed Ovid and *Dubliners* with anybody that I know of. Also, he never discussed the parallels between the ten thunders and the various human technologies with anybody either.

If you come across any clues in the matter, please give a signal. Would there be any opportunity to see the thesis on *Finnegan*, or the work of *Ulysses*, or the abstracts of same? Apropos the "McLuhan canon", I am working fairly steadily now on *The Laws of the Media*, which deal with all human technologies as completely metaphorical in structure and effect. This means that the most human thing about us is our technologies, as Sir Peter Medwar said whimsically, not knowing how utterly true it is.

I hadn't realized that Wilfred was also retired, but I can imagine that he has much to work on. Give him our regards.

Eric mentions that he may well do his doctoral dissertation on *Tristram Shandy*. There are many things to tell you about, but shall save them for the next letter.

Christmas love and greetings from us all,

(dictated by phone and signed in Professor McLuhan's absence)

---

[2]*Giambattista Vico: An International Symposium* (n.d.) edited by Giorgio Tagliacozzo. The quotation referred to was from an essay in the book, "Vico and Marxism", by Eugene Kamenka.
[3]James Joyce's brother, John Stanislaus Joyce (1884–1955).

1977

To Mike Gravel[1]

January 17, 1977

Dear Mike:

I am enclosing the very item that you may be looking for, and which you can certainly make use of, in any event. What the brain surgeons have discovered about the two hemispheres of the brain tells us that the First World is left hemisphere, and the Third World is right hemisphere. For decades I have been trying to expound this difference in terms of the eye and the ear orientation of cultures. The Greeks and the Romans gave special salience to the eye via the phonetic alphabet and the invention of Euclidean space. With the alphabet, the lineal and connected character of space became apparent to literate man alone. The "barbarians" went on living in acoustic space, in a world dominated by oral culture. Logic belongs to the left hemisphere alone, but the simultaneous world of the right hemisphere is given new dominance by the electric-information environment. This fact is not known to the hemisphere analysts.

The sudden new dominance of the right hemisphere is what turns the young away from reading and from goal-seeking. The right hemisphere is concerned with quality of life, and the left hemisphere is concerned with quantity. As our electric age goes East, the Orient is going West by means of our old industrial hardware. My latest book (*Take Today: The Executive as Dropout* New York: Harcourt, Barce, Jovanovich Inc., 1972) is entirely concerned with the changing patterns of decision-making and management in a world of instantaneous information. (You may have to order the book directly from Harcourt, Brace, Jovanovich.) The flip in American politics from policies to images is characteristic of the dominance of the right hemisphere.

[1]Mike Gravel, U.S. Senator for Alaska, had written McLuhan on December 14, 1976, commiserating on his recent illness and asking to see a study he had heard of on the learning patterns of Eskimos. McLuhan sent him an article by Robert Trotter—"The Other Hemisphere", *Science News*, April 3, 1976—which deals with the learning patterns of the Inuit.

To Marc Lalonde[1]

January 21, 1977

Dear Mr. Lalonde:

The following problem is one that not only I have encountered, but some of my colleagues as well. It concerns the matter that Canada Pension Plan payments should be automatically payable at age sixty-five, so that even when applications

[1]The Honourable Marc Lalonde (b. 1929) was then Minister of National Health and Welfare. There was apparently no reply to this letter.

are received late, all back payments would be retroactive. Many people operate under the illusion that the government intends to increase benefits for those who stayed in the Plan after age sixty-five. However, at present this is not so. Thus, some people did not apply at age sixty-five because they were still employed. The people affected are: (a) those who are *not* legally minded, and who don't know *anything* about it (this includes the great majority of people), and (b) those who *are* legally minded, thinking that if they continued to pay into the CPP, benefits would accrue.

In my particular case, I was sixty-five in July, 1976, and knew nothing about the need to make special application until the subject happened to come up during a conversation with friends. I have now been advised by the Toronto District Office of the CPP that my benefits will not begin until this month, January, 1977, even though I am entitled to have had them since August, 1976.

It would appear that your intentions to achieve social justice are being perverted into a travesty through the obscurity of the legal procedures.

Sincerely yours,

To Pierre Elliot Trudeau

February 24, 1977

Dear Pierre:

Everybody I know has been deeply thrilled by your recent performance and reception in the U.S. That was a really imaginative and masterly approach, which you brought off superbly.

It was while I was trying to explain *charisma*, as manifested by Jack Kennedy and also by Jimmy Carter, that I raised the fact of *your* very powerful charisma. Jack Kennedy looked like the all-American boy, the corporate, inclusive image of American ideals. Nixon, on the other hand, looked like himself alone, a private image, fatally defective in the TV age. In contrast, Jimmy Carter has the charisma of a Huck Finn, a Southern boy, and he also has the vocal rhythms and corporate power that got him the black vote. It was while I was explaining these things that the interviewer asked: "What about Pierre Trudeau?" I replied that your corporate mask, your charisma, is both powerful and very popular with the young, in part because of the subtle hint in your image of "mask" of the native Indian. As you know, the Red man is very powerful with the TV generation since he is Third World, and they are also Third World. He was *always* Third World; but they, the young, are having their first experience of it. Naturally, pulled out of the context of this image discussion it sounds very different, and even derogatory. You know me well enough to know that I would never say anything derogatory about you.

In the case of Carter, it became clear during the election that the image has supplanted the policy. A political point of view is not practical on TV since it is a resonating, multi-positional image, so that any moment of arrest or stasis permits the public to shoot you down. Maybe that is the meaning of the old gangster quote: "Talk fast, Mister!", and also, "*Smile* when you say that!" I have yet to find a situation in which there is not great help in the phrase: "You think my fallacy is all wrong?" It is literally disarming, pulling the ground out from under every situation! It can be said with a certain amount of poignancy and mock deliberation.

I am doing a piece about separatism and media in collaboration with Barrington Nevitt. He's the management consultant with whom I did the book on *The Executive as Dropout*. Our piece draws attention to the hidden *ground* that underlies all the many forms of separatism in our time. I refer to the *ground* of instant information that extends to the entire planet, and the effect of which is not centralism but decentralism. Any form pushed to its limit, as is pointed out by Aristotle and Aquinas, flips into the opposite form. Whereas hardware communication is a kind of transportation which centralizes organizational structures, electric communication is simultaneous and confers autonomy on every part of a structure. That is why the executive drops out of the old organization-chart patterns at electric speed. At electric speed, which is the speed of light, we are disembodied beings. On the phone, or "on the air", we are instantly present, but minus our bodies. Politically, discarnate man may have an image, but not a physical body. There is a corresponding loss of personal identity and responsibility which creates separatism in private life and family life and in all institutional existence. When one becomes aware of this hidden *ground* and its effects, one should be better prepared to cope with, and to counteract, these effects. Ours is surely the first human generation that has ever encountered such an undermining disease which afflicts us at all levels of church and state.

To Cleanth Brooks[1]

March 21, 1977

Dear Cleanth:

There's a wonderful man here by the name of Roger Poole.[2] He's been visiting from England for the past few months. Roger knows more about French phenomenology than anybody I have ever met, having known many of them personally, and having worked with Levi-Strauss for years, and lectured at the Sorbonne. He's a Cambridge critic who takes a very dim view of phenomenology as it is currently in vogue at Yale and elsewhere. The pattern used by all phenomenology began with Descartes in selecting *figures* without *ground*, the Norrie Frye style of classification without insight. Of course, the whole thing

[1]Cleanth Brooks (b. 1906), whom McLuhan had known since the 1940s, was Professor of English at Yale University from 1947 to 1975. He wrote the well-known critical work *The Well-Wrought Urn* (1947).

[2]Roger Poole (b. 1939)—who had written *Towards Deep Subjectivity* (1972) and now teaches at the University of Nottingham—was a Commonwealth Fellow at York University, Toronto (1976-7).

has happened over and over again, beginning with the Schoolmen in the 12th century, but the Puritans pushed it into a methodism of spiritual purification. This aspect of dialectic as a spiritual mystique gets some treatment in *Surprised by Sin* by Stanley Fish.[3] In fact, however, it is identical with the Cartesian thing and the Port-Royal grammar of 1660[4] which established the direct line of linguistic development which is involved in all phenomenology even today. You recall that Descartes eliminated all the parts of rhetoric except method or *dispositio*, and how this continues in unbroken line to Hegel, and then onward.

This entire development is at present reaching a kind of terminus which is brought about by the development of a completely new awareness of *ground*, prompted by the twin-hemisphere studies. Since Poole is interested in doing a serious critique of the entire thing, I would appreciate any suggestions from you about bibliography or incidental readings.

I only became aware of phenomenology recently when some French people like Barthes[5] took an interest in my work— the study of *effects*. This puzzled me and led me to look into their position, which I should have done long ago. My media studies work entirely by *figure* and *ground*, both the input and the consequences, and this has created great disapproval of my work in all manner of quarters. I never understood what happened to Bill Wimsatt when he went chasing after Beardsley and phenomenology. Perhaps you know the story there. I very much look forward to having a word from you.

Cordially,

[3]Stanley Fish, *Surprised by Sin: The Reader in "Paradise Lost"* (1967).

[4]Port-Royal was a French Cistercian convent near Versailles, founded in the thirteenth century. When the abbey moved to Paris in 1626 it became a centre of Jansenism; its "little schools", and textbooks, became famous. It was suppressed in the early 1700s.

[5]See page 539, note 1.

To Malcolm Muggeridge

March 29, 1977

Dear Malcolm:

Let me reassure you that the University of Dallas is a wonderful spot, a university which has retained human scale, honour-course traditions and rich dialogue.[1] My son Eric is working on a Ph.D. there. He and his wife Sabina are expecting a baby any day, and we may be there for the christening. This would overlap with your visit, and it would be delightful to get together. Meantime, we look forward to your being in Toronto before too long, in any event.

[1]Muggeridge was about to fill the McDermott Lectureship, which McLuhan held in 1975.

To Karel Appel

March 30, 1977

Dear Karel:

It was good news about your coming back here in the Fall.[1] Meantime, I enclose a sample of the new book on *The Laws of the Media*. My discovery in this book is that all human artifacts have a basically verbal structure, as testified to by the four-part metaphor manifested by each.

Am now racing to that class I told you about on the phone.

[1]An exhibition of Karel Appel's "Complete Graphic Works", sponsored by the Art Gallery of Hamilton, was opened in Hamilton, Ontario, by McLuhan on November 4, 1977. Not long after this letter was written, on April 20, Walter A. Moos, Appel's Canadian representative, sent McLuhan a lithograph of Appel's "Happy Child", which was inscribed to him.

To Karel Appel

May 5, 1977

Dear Karel:

Your picture is placed proudly in the place of honour in our sitting-room, and is a delight to everybody, including me![1] It has a wonderful figure/ground structure which compels a great deal of attention and meditation, as well as humour and delight.

Am just running out of town for a bit, and shall write to you when I get back.

Cordially,

(dictated by Professor McLuhan and signed in his absence)

[1]See previous letter.

To Woody Allen

May 19, 1977

Dear Woody:

Heartiest congratulations on *Annie Hall*! Having been out of town a great deal, Corinne and I have not yet been to see the picture. As a matter of fact, we are trying to round up the family and friends to go as a party. However, there's no mistake that people have responded most enthusiastically about the whole thing, even about my wee bit![1]

[1]On June 1 Woody Allen replied: "*Annie Hall* doing very well so far. Hope you get a chance to see yourself in it soon. You were great!"

To Robert H. Eringer[1]

August 30, 1977
May 30, 1977

Dear Mr. Eringer:

I attended the Bilderberg Conference in 1969 and was nearly suffocated by the banality and irrelevance. My "foul language" consisted in explaining to such big names as Bob MacNamera, George Ball, Dean Rusk, and many from the U.K. that they had not a single clue concerning a world in which information moved at the speed of light. They were uniformly nineteenth-century minds pretending to relate to the twentieth century. My book *Take Today: The Executive as Dropout* (Marshall McLuhan and Barrington Nevitt, N.Y. Harcourt, Brace, Jovanovich Inc., 1972) explores some of the effects on decision-making in an electronic environment. Nothing has changed since then, and all conferences in all parts of the world are still conducted on those nineteenth-century principles.

Best wishes,

[1]Mr Eringer, a student at the London School of Economics, was researching the Bilderberg Conferences (see page 372) and had heard that McLuhan had not been invited back because of his "foul language". He asked for comments.

To Jimmy Carter

August 10, 1977

Dear President Carter:

In California recently I had an opportunity to discuss with Governor Brown some of the problems of learning disabilities in the young generation. He has become deeply concerned about the growing rate of non-literacy in California schools. This is a matter that I have worked on here at the Centre for many years. We have come up with what may be a new and helpful approach which relates to the peculiar character of electric media in general, and to television in particular. "On the phone" or "on the air" we do not experience our physical bodies. When abstracted from our physical bodies in this way, we cease to relate to "Natural Law" and the consequent sense of morality and social responsibility. The numerous forms of separatism and dropoutism that are experienced in our time may well derive from this *discarnate* state of electronic man. With special attention to the act of reading the printed word, a key fact would seem to be that the TV watcher makes little or no motor response to the sensory experience. The act of reading requires a great deal of visual motor activity which has become difficult for the TV generation to perform.

I enclose a copy of my statement to Governor Brown which includes both a brief diagnosis and outline of positive therapy.[1] My own interest in the nature of

[1]On August 4, 1977 McLuhan and Hurst (see page 534, note 2) submitted to Governor Edmund G. Brown, Jr, of California—whom McLuhan had met on July 12 (see page 545, note 1)—a two-page statement headed "Dyslexia or Learning Disability within our present-day society".

electronic media has often been taken as evidence of my indifference to the visual and literate values of our society. The enclosure will, I hope, dispel that fallacy.

Believe me, dear Sir, your most concerned and committed supporter, [2]

Marshall McLuhan

[2]This letter was acknowledged by Landon Kite, Staff Assistant to President Carter. The President asked that McLuhan approach the Department of Health, Education, and Welfare.

To André Kostelanetz[1]

August 11, 1977

Dear Andre:

We pray that you have enjoyed *Bertram's Hotel.*[2] By the way, the 9 o'clock [TV] Sunday show, *The Duchess of Duke Street*, has quite a few overtones of the Agatha Christie world, since the Duchess is a scullery maid who becomes the proprietress of the posh "Bentinck Hotel".

Thanks very much for the clipping of Richard's piece. It raises a matter which I don't think I ever discussed with you. For years now I have been noticing the way in which language plays a role in music by mediating between audience and environment. In a word, language processes the man-made sounds of the community by moving them through the structure of human speech. In other words, all forms of music are a wedding of communal speech and environmental sounds. However, without language there could be no music whatever.

I enclose a note that was published in *Rolling Stone* back in April, 1976.[3]

[1]André Kostelanetz (1901–80) was a Russian-born American conductor—the uncle of Richard Kostelanetz (see page 415)—who gained wide popularity for the luscious sound of his own orchestra and of his arrangements of light music.

[2]Agatha Christie, *At Bertram's Hotel; Featuring Miss Marple, the Original Character as Created by Agatha Christie* (1965).

[3]"Jazz and Rock—Electric Environment".

To Sister St John[1]

[August 12, 1977]

[No typed complimentary opening]

Corinne and I are back after a seven or eight week tour of Australia, New Zealand, Fiji and Hawaii. We also visited Mary and our grand-daughter Jennifer in Newport Beach, both going and coming home. Australia was a lot of fun, although it was mainly a work trip. It is colourful and vivid, place and people alike.

[1]Sister St John O'Malley, C.S.J. (1889–1986) graduated from St Michael's College, University of Toronto, in 1921 and taught Classics in the university for over fifty years.

Also, they have wonderful seafood! Corinne and I especially enjoyed Fiji, which is exactly what one dreams of its being—exotic, unspoiled, with native costumes only in evidence:—the men large and athletic, in knee-length skirts (cf. kilts, but the kilts are pleated in order to provide ample length of cloth in which the wearer can wrap himself on cold nights). The Fijian men also wear bright hibiscus flowers behind the ear. If they wear the flower behind the right ear, they are *not* married, and if behind the left ear, they *are* married.

The Fijians have managed to keep industry out of their islands. Hawaii, of course, is completely Americanized, but still has its charm. We were especially taken by large parrots sitting on trapezes in hotel lobbies and squawking "Hello", with broad American accents. Frequently, they would sway the trapeze sideways, while screaming "Hello"!

Corinne and I both got in quite a lot of swimming, although Corinne is the natural water-baby while I tend to be hydrophobic!

Australia proved to be quite fascinating, and we had a kind of crash course by way of introduction through our acquaintance with Alfred Byrne who had been our friend for years in Toronto before he went to become head of General Electric in Australia. Having been head of G.E. in Australia for eighteen years, he knows everybody, and introduced us to all of them! We had the red carpet treatment, beginning with a luncheon with the Cardinal and the Mayor of Sydney. I was surprised to find the Australians to be more English than Canadians, and also more American than Canadians. They are a vivid, aggressive group who don't worry about the problem of national identity. The novels of Jon Cleary and of Colleen McCullough afford a good image of the Australian life and character.

Since I was mainly the guest of the radio broadcasters of Australia, my main talks took place in Brisbane, Sydney and Melbourne, where I had large and attentive audiences. We got to see *The Tales of Hoffman* at the Sydney Opera and were told that the architect had designed those fascinating ornaments at the top of the building to resemble whales' teeth. It's a bit like our own City Hall which consists of two concave and adjacent shells. The winner of the design contest, Revell,[2] told me on the night he was given the prize that he had shaped the building to resemble the white and yolk of an egg. This fact seems to be as little known here as the whale-teeth story.

Am trying to get caught up on my backlog of mail at present.

Love in Our Lord
Marshall
and Corinne

[2]Viljo Revell (1910–64) was the Finnish designer of Toronto's New City Hall (1958–65). Revell's winning design was announced on September 28, 1958.

To Clare Boothe Luce

August 29, 1977

Dear Clare

We were indeed most disappointed to have missed you, there being so many things to discuss.

Dyslexia is a direct result of TV watching, since it is the peculiar nature of the TV image to prevent motor response in the eyes.[1] The eyes are immobilized, hence the soporific effect. This does not happen with the movies, and there was little said about dyslexia in the age of the movies. No studies have been made, so far as I know.

My friend, Art Hurst, has been studying this for many years, and I have been working with him.[2] Directly related to TV and dyslexia is the fact that 90% or more of learning-disability problems are exclusively male. Hurst and I have discovered the reason for this, and it is correctable. Hurst has designed a stereo-scopic head-camera (existing head-cameras are one-eye only) which would enable the user to determine coming dyslexia problems instantly from the age of six months onward. When he presented this design to a Chicago firm some years ago, they said it would cost $50,000 to make. A great deal of our delinquency problem results from the rage of dyslexic victims who are unable to cope with our learning procedures. Typically, a delinquent tends to be a very bright person who is naturally aware that he *is* bright, and hence the more frustrated. The cost of Hurst's head-camera is minute compared to the cost and suffering and loss due to quite corrigible dyslexic conditions.

As for restricting the use of TV, it surely should be part of a media ecology program. If people became aware that TV watching diseased the young, physi-cally, and independently of programming, there would be no problem about restricting its use. TV is as radioactive as radium.

If you had not had more explanation of why boys are more often the victims of dyslexia, it is, in a word, that boyish sports do not require delicate muscular coordination such as is necessary for reading. Sewing, cooking, cosmetics, etc. develop these coordinations in girls rather than boys.

There will be nothing done about these matters among psychologists and soci-ologists, since they cover too much ground and therefore do not accommodate themselves to the specialized and quantitative methods of science. I hasten this off to you because of its urgency, and you are in a position to trigger effective action.

[1]Mrs Luce had complained in a letter of August 19 that TV had a "dyslectic" effect: she watched it after 8 p.m., and even though it bored her she was somewhat hypnotized and could not turn it off. Dyslexia is an impairment of the ability to read.

[2]W.A. Hurst, O.D., of Gravenhurst, Ontario, had developed the "Binocular Eye Marker Head Camera".

To James McGrath[1]

September 19, 1977

Dear Mr. McGrath:

Apropos the dyslexia thing in relation to TV, Dr. Arthur Hurst and I have been moving ahead on the stereoscopic head camera which he designed years ago and which still does not exist at the present time. This instrument is indispensable for the study of dyslexia in many of its forms. That is, the pattern of eye movements, particularly at the near-point or reading distance, may be ascertained quickly by this instrument. What this camera is able to do quickly cannot be done at all by the existing methods in studying the viewing habits. We are proceeding to obtain a patent for this instrument at the present time.

The TV child in the last fifteen years has been subjected to an immobilizing experience of TV imagery which, unlike the movie, innundates without evoking any motor response. The fact that almost all dyslexia is found among boys and not girls, merely points to the counter-action of typical female activities as compared with the typical physical activities of boys. Reading requires delicate motor coordination, and does not develop among the ball players and hockey players. The typical female activities of sewing, skipping, cooking, cosmetics, etc. elicits delicate coordinations which are favourable to the visual motor activities involved in reading. Of course there are auditory factors that come into play even in visual dyslexia, but here too the vocal and more subtle auditory experience of girls is entirely an advantage over that of the boys. However, this is a separate matter. While 20% of the entire population suffers from some form of dyslexia, it is interesting to note that 90% of these sufferers are male.

I hope that we can follow up on this.

Sincerely yours,

[1]The Honourable James McGrath M.P. was Official Opposition Spokesman for Consumer Affairs, Housing and Urban Affairs, Ottawa.

To Sheila Watson

October 3, 1977

Dear Sheila:

While in Venice last week, I looked up Olga Rudge, Pound's old friend.[1] She's

[1]Olga Rudge (b. 1895) was Ezra Pound's friend for half a century and the mother of his daughter Mary (de Rachewiltz). Born in Youngstown, Ohio, Miss Rudge grew up in Paris and became a concert violinist. Pound reviewed a concert by her in London on November 25, 1920, and a few months later they met in Paris. She assisted Pound in the completion of his opera Le Testament—in the first abbreviated concert performance of which, in 1926, she was the featured violinist. Their daughter Mary had been born the year before. Pound lived with Miss Rudge for the last ten years of his life in Sant' Ambrogio and Venice, where he died in 1971. (See Peter Dale Scott's "A Conversation with Olga Rudge" in Poetry Flash, Berkeley, California, November 1985.)

eighty and vigorous, and has a home in Venice which she has owned since the late twenties. It was bought for her by her parents. It is quite roomy—three or four stories. In her sitting room she has the Gaudier-Brzeska sculpture. It is a splendid piece. She also has a large amount of unsorted correspondence covering many years and people, and she would like to get some help in editing the material for publication. It seemed an ideal situation for some Ph.D. student, or some young faculty person on leave of absence. I promised her to look into the matter. Please send your suggestions.

[*Handwritten*] backlog always vast after these absences

Yrs Marshall

To James O'Roark[1]

November 15, 1977

Dear Dr. O'Roark:

It is a strange coincidence that I should be reading Wyndham Lewis' first novel as your letter arrived! His first novel is one hitherto unpublished and it is called *Mrs. Duke's Million*. It is now being published here in Toronto by the Coach House Press, 301 (rear) Huron Street, Toronto, Ont. Canada M5S 2G5. The manuscript for this novel came from the Cornell University Library collection of Wyndham Lewis. It may be of some help to you to know that there is a complete Wyndham Lewis collection at Cornell University. My own Lewis collection is fairly complete, but I don't think that there are any duplicates in the collection. I enclose copy of a little piece I did for Bernard Lafourcade's special issue of *Les Cahiers de l'Herne* in *L'Herne* (27 rue de Bourgogne, Paris 7, France) in 1970.

I saw a great deal of Lewis during the 2nd war, but having followed his suggestion that I join him in Windsor, Ontario at Assumption University, I had no sooner done so than the war was over and he went home. His plan had been that we begin to put out once more his journal *The Enemy*.

Of course you know about the *Wyndham Lewis Newsletter* (published by The Wyndham Lewis Society, 148 Bellahouston Drive, Glasgow. Acting Secretary: Frank Fitzpatrick)

I can readily understand your enthusiasm about this man. Having studied him a great deal, I realize how much I owe him. Some of my students have done doctoral dissertations on him, and at least one of these should have been published long ago.

Very best wishes in your Lewis procedures,

[1]James O'Roark, M.D.—of Santa Barbara, California—was a Wyndham Lewis enthusiast.

To Pierre Elliott Trudeau

December 13, 1977

Dear Pierre:

We deeply enjoyed your princely hospitality at the "Three Little [Small] Rooms", and your presence at our seminar left a very deep impression of your cordial and lively person.

One of the things we have been working over in the seminar has been the problem of inflation and joblessness, two closely related things. To put both matters very briefly, the nature of work has changed drastically since we have begun to live in a simultaneous information environment. By the same token, the nature and function of money has been greatly altered by the electric information environment. Apropos work, the repetitive nine-to-five job has shifted into a new pattern of *role*-playing, which means a variety of functions, e.g., a mother doesn't have a job, she has *fifty* jobs, i.e., a role. The major form of work in the electronic age has become "keeping an eye on other people", whether audience research or public relations or simply espionage. It is sometimes called "data processing". On the other hand, apropros money, it was long ago obsolesced by "credit" whose natural tendency is towards debt and poverty. When given the speed of the computer, the credit card covers a lot of ground.

The main verb in all this is the speed of light, which also alters the role of politician from a party representative to a charismatic image. This image obsolesces parties and policies alike. This is very compressed, but I know you are busy—perhaps not too busy to hear a joke that has just turned up. It concerns a traveller returning from the U.K. with a dozen bottles of whiskey. At the Customs he is asked: "What have you got here?" He replies: "Holy water." The Customs officer opens one of the bottles and takes a swig, and says: "That's not holy water—that's whiskey!" At this the traveller exclaimed rapturously: "It's a miracle!"

Corinne and I pray that your Christmas and New Year will be liberally strewn with miracles!

1978

To Eric Havelock

February 2, 1978

Dear Havelock:

"The Pre-Literacy of the Greeks" is a gem, and the revelation that literacy rises from the craft level to the literate level is a delightful paradox, full of implication.[1] On page 375 your illustrations of the object uttering itself to the observer became the very popular figure of Prosopopoeia,[2] which gave rise to the whole literature in the Renaissance.

My son Eric had earlier mentioned the break-up of the Logos into the three trivium branches. Since I wrote my dissertation back in the late 30's, the literature on rhetoric has grown enormously. However, there is very little on *grammatica* or on *dialectica*. Your own work would seem to fall quite naturally into the world of classical *grammatica*.

We look forward very much to any follow-up essays.

[1]E.A. Havelock, "The Preliteracy of the Greeks", *New Literary History—A Journal of Theory and Interpretation*, vol. VIII, no. 3, Spring 1977.

[2]*prosopopoeia*, the rhetorical introduction of a pretended speaker or the personification of an abstract thing.

To Clare Boothe Luce

April 7, 1978

Dear Clare:

Once again birthday greetings, for which I enclose an unpublished essay on the twin hemispheres of the brain and the media,[1] and a short article on discarnate man.

Had you noticed the opening page of Peter Drucker's *The Unseen Revolution*?[2] His theme is that, thanks to the pension financing in North America, ordinary pensioners own 60% of the equity capital, and that makes us the most socialistic area on the planet! Russians own 12% compared to our 60%. This is one of the hidden effects of the computer. This past year has been a very exciting time intellectually.

Have you come across the work of Michael Davies? e.g., *The Liturgical Revolution* and *Cranmer's Godly Order* and *Pope John's Council* (Arlington House Publishers, New Rochelle, N.Y. 1976). He is a young school teacher in the U.K., and has done a lot of homework.[3]

May it be a wonderful year for you!

[1]See page 541, the end of note 1, bottom.

[2]Peter Drucker, *The Unseen Revolution. How Pension Fund Socialism Came to America* (1976).

[3]Michael Davies, *The Liturgical Revolution*, in two volumes: Part One, *Cranmer's Godly Order: The Destruction of Catholicism Through Liturgical Change* (1976); Part Two, *Pope John's Council* (1977).

To Larry Henderson[1]

May 24, 1978

Dear Larry:

I notice in the current [*Catholic*] *Register* the reference to uncertainty about the nature of pornography. May I suggest that it is basically, and always, an aggressive assault on the private person, as well as being a violation of decorum. That is to say that anything that is done with the intention of doing violence to the individual or to group decorum can be both pornographic and obscene. This implies that matters which one time or one company one would regard as pornographic or obscene, might appear harmless at another time or to another company. An ordinary four-letter word from daily use might be felt as violent and aggressive and obscene if used in the public presence of the Queen of England. The word *porn* refers to *prostitute*, and hence to the language and behaviour associated with prostitutes. The word *obscene* refers to something off-stage in Greek drama; i.e., something unfit to appear in the public part of the stage.

There is the further fact that the user is always the content of any situation. (Aristotle's way of putting it was to say that "the cognitive agent is and becomes the thing known"—*De Anima.*)

This matter, which concerns our everyday experience, happens to be also an abstruse philosophical problem which concerns all knowledge and identity. I think I have mentioned on other occasions that electronic man is discarnate and therefore a mass man, or one minus any private identity. For the electronic man the classic doctrine about the cognitive agent is either meaningless or unacceptable.

Cordially,

[1]Larry Henderson (b. 1917)—a pioneer in international reporting to Canada, broadcaster, and author—became a convert to Roman Catholicism in 1965 and in 1973 editor of *The Catholic Register*, a position he held until his retirement in 1986.

To the Editor of the Toronto Star

[July 4?, 1978]

Robert Fulford's article "Meet France's Marshall McLuhan" was very flattering; he placed me in the company of Roland Barthes, who once asked me to collaborate with him on a book.[1]

Fulford sees Barthes as impenetrable as myself.[2] He explains: "In the English-

[1]This letter, which was published on July 6, 1978, was in response to an article by Robert Fulford in the *Toronto Star* (June 17, 1978)—bearing the title McLuhan gives—on Roland Barthes (1915–80), the French writer-critic and teacher who published many books on culture and semiology (the analysis of language as a sign system) that combine dazzling ideas with a basic impenetrability, but that nevertheless made him what Fulford called "a major intellectual hero of France in the 1970s".

[2]Fulford did not refer to McLuhan's "impenetrability". Apart from the title, the only mention he made of McLuhan in this article was in the sentence: "Like Marshall McLuhan, he [Barthes] sees the way that you express yourself as potentially more important than what you actually say."

speaking world, an intellectual becomes a success almost always because he can produce a few quite simple ideas and market them efficiently."

It is true that my "impenetrability" results from the fact that I do not use any ideas at all, but perceptions only. The untrained intellectual deals only with concepts and theories, and has little skill in the study of effects and consequences. This condition extends to the journalistic world.

As for Barthes, he is a "phenomenologist"—that is, one who tries to see the patterns in things while also playing along with the dominant theory of his world.

Personally I prefer to study the pattern minus the theory. This is what confuses Fulford.

Marshall McLuhan
Centre for Culture and Technology
Toronto

To Pierre Elliott Trudeau   6th December, 1978

Dear Pierre:

Seeing a headline about the "Unity Task Force", I was suddenly struck by the incongruity of relating bilingualism to unity. If all Canadians spoke both languages there would be great enrichment of our culture, but there would be a much greater tendency towards plurality and diversity rather than unity. Surely to reach unity as a desired effect of a bilingualism programme requires imposition from above. On the other hand a bilingual pattern could be *acceptable* if it grew up naturally from below. But again, such an idea would lead not to unity, but rather to diversity. Somehow a non-sequitur has entered the rationale of the bilingualism programme. The federal idea of free association is not the same thing as unity. Do not English Canadians speak American and feel at home in the U.S.A. without the slightest thought of unity? Many French Canadians must likewise feel quite at home in English Canada linguistically without supposing that they have any commitment to unity. I am trying to discover the line of reasoning that led to the adoption of a bilingualism policy as a means of unity, when it almost certainly has the opposite effect.

Just as a possible parallel, Governor Brown in California was originally flatly opposed to Proposition 13, but managed to switch horses in midstream and to take on Number 13 as his personal policy and as his primary election issue. This switch proved to be completely successful. In other words, might it not be entirely practical to modulate the bilingual programme as a means of fostering enrichment rather than unity?

[1]The Prime Minister replied on December 18 that surely unity would be greatly increased "if we could all communicate with each other", and that far from being divisive the Official Languages Act was not intended to make people bilingual but to ensure that "*both* the principal languages of the country would be fully respected at the federal level." If each group feels that the other is not being favoured by the government, unity will be promoted.

[2]Proposition 13: in 1978, in California, a citizens' initiative brought about a 57% cut in property taxes (thus severely limiting government spending). The bill was passed by a 65% majority.

1979

To B. Ann Vannatta[1]

8th January, 1979

Dear Ms Vannatta:

Apropos your inquiry about the effects of the hemispheres of the brain on journalism, let me point out the current development of extensive punning in headlines. This points to a real shift to acoustic values over against literate values. The iconic and resonant character of headlines is adjacent, as it were, to the acoustic. Nevertheless the wide-open use of puns in headlines is one of the effects of the new ascendancy of the right hemisphere. Open *Finnegans Wake* at random and sample the "all-night's newsery-reel". Joyce was doing futuristic journalism in every line. Notice that the puns promote a kind of sneaky editorializing by way of interlacing of themes. Further, this points to a whimsical and fanciful treatment of news, indicating a switch of the real world into science fiction. The right hemisphere is not only holistic and inclusive, but is the area of body language and the entire world of sports and games. Wish I had time to chat about this further, but must conclude here.

With all good wishes for a happy New Year,

[1]B. Ann Vannatta, a graduate student in journalism at the University of Tennessee, wrote McLuhan on November 10, 1978 asking him to comment on the role of the right hemisphere of the brain in journalism.

To Ivan Illich[1]

11th January, 1979

Dear Ivan:

May it be a grand New Year for you!

Glad to hear that you have begun to consider the hemispheres of the brain. I am happy to enclose some useful bibliographical material for you.

[1]Ivan Illich (b. 1926) was born in Vienna, received his Ph.D. from the University of Salzburg in 1951 (the year he was ordained a Roman Catholic priest—he resigned the priesthood in 1969), and co-founded, and became director of, the Centro Intercultural de Documentacion in Cuernavaca, Mexico. Among his books is *De-schooling Society* (1971), which warns that institutional instruction "smothers the horizons of the imagination". He had written McLuhan on New Year's day, recalling that "a couple of years ago", sitting "around the fire" in McLuhan's home, "you spoke to me about the right/left hemispheres" of the brain, and he requested bibliographical information about the research that had been done on this subject. McLuhan included in the enclosures with the letter below his article "The Brain and the Media: The 'Western' Hemisphere", which appeared in the *Journal of Communication* in 1978.

To Pierre Elliott Trudeau

1st February, 1979

Dear Pierre:

Your thoughtful reply to my query about what line of thinking lay behind the bilingual policy brought to my mind the familiar phrase of Baudelaire in his *Envoi* to *Les Fleurs du Mal*, "Hypocrite lecteur, mon semblable, mon frère". The "lecteur" is the reader of the poem who "puts it on" as a mask through which he looks at the world. (The hypocrite is a mask-wearer.) When the reader "puts on" the poem, he inevitably distorts it, and this is reciprocated by the poet, who "puts on" the reader as his "semblable" and his "frère". The poet has a natural grievance against the reader's distortion of his poem, and so he enjoys the activity of distorting the reader in turn by putting on the reader as his mask. (Behind the idea of the "put-on" is the metaphysical idea of the cognitive agent who is, and becomes, the thing *known* in classical philosophy.

If a poem has the natural and inevitable power of altering both the reader and the poet and their inter-relationship, how much more is this true of our two languages! The speaker of any language assumes it as a medium or a mask by which he experiences the world in a special way, and by which he relates to people in a very special way. The French tongue as a mask or medium at the federal level has a quite different meaning and function from the same tongue at the private level. A language in the hands of a lawyer or a judge or a bureaucrat has a quite different significance from the same language used by friends or enemies. I suggest that your approach to bilingualism as a means of "language equality" is abstract and objective, but not related to the experiential, subjective level. That is not to say this is a misguided attitude, but it merely indicates that the *effects* of languages as media are quite different from the input or intended meanings. All inputs have side effects which are usually considered irrelevant by the speaker or sender.

You are probably familiar with the Shannon-Weaver model of communication theory.[1] (I enclose a copy of it in an article on the two hemispheres of the brain.) Shannon and Weaver were mathematicians who considered the side-effects as *noise*. They assumed that these could be eliminated by simply stepping up the charge of energy in the circuit.

The left hemisphere, the one developed in our Western world by phonetic literacy, is the lineal and visual mode of objective awareness, whereas the right hemisphere is the acoustic and involved mode of awareness. The Third World is almost entirely right hemisphere, and the First World is tending, under electric-information environments, to transform itself into a new kind of Third World. The Third World, on the other hand, is frantically trying to develop the attri-

[1]The Shannon-Weaver model of communication—from Claude E. Shannon and Warren Weaver, *The Mathematical Theory of Communication* (1964)—is illustrated in Chapter 2 of *The Laws of the Media* by a chart depicting a message's being transmitted over a communication channel from a transmitter to a receiver, with all unwanted additions to the signal being called noise.

butes of the left hemisphere by lineal and quantitative education and production. The confusion and loss of identity in the First World is one of the results we experience as we acquire Third World characteristics (loss of private identity and loss of goals, etc.). Should China be effective in acquiring phonetic western literacy, the explosion in that ancient culture would be total. The ancient Greeks did not long survive their own acquisition of phonetic literacy. The explosion within our own world is telling enough, and is the occasion for much prayer from us for you and your great responsibility.

Corinne and I thought that the Christmas card photo of you and the boys was and is most eloquent and delightful.

To Clare Boothe Luce

5th April, 1979

Dear Clare:

A happy and blessed birthday to you! I enclose by way of greeting a little memo that I did some time ago, and to which I would now add some further notes.

On the telephone, or on the air, man is in every sense discarnate, existing as an abstract image, a *figure* without a body. The Cheshire cat in *Alice in Wonderland* is a kind of parallel to our state. When discarnate, man has no identity, and is not subject to natural law. In fact he has no basis for morals of any sort. As electric information moved at the speed of light, man is a nobody. When deprived of his identity, man becomes violent in divers ways. Violence is the quest for identity. In Canada there is pending a large body of nihilistic legislation dedicated to the ideal of freedom. No-fault divorce is being succeeded by no-fault murder!

Discarnate man is not compatible with an incarnate Church. I would welcome your thoughts concerning a possible response to this situation. I cannot see that the physical existence of man is compatible with the speed of light. There is no lack of evidence of both physical and metaphysical violence as a response to this situation. T.S. Eliot has a line which seems to indicate awareness of the discarnate state of electronic man: "We all go into the silent funeral; nobody's funeral, for there is nobody to bury."[1]

Loving regards,

---

[1] "And we all go with them, into the silent funeral,/Nobody's funeral, for there is no one to bury." L1. 110–11, "East Coker", in T.S. Eliot's *Four Quartets* (1940).

To Stanley J. Murphy, C.S.B.

12th April, 1979

Dear Father Stan:

Today is the forty-second anniversary of my reception into the Catholic Church.

We also heard word today from England that Mrs. Wyndham Lewis has just died. Her friends would be grateful if you could offer Mass for her.

By coincidence I had my passport pictures taken again today and at the photographer's shop there was a large portrait of Paul Martin, whose relation to Lewis you know so well.[1]

---

[1]The Honourable Paul Martin (b. 1903) was a Member of Parliament for Essex East from 1935 to 1968, when he was appointed to the Senate. His family home is in Windsor, Ontario. Lewis did a black chalk drawing of Mrs Martin in 1944 and a portrait in oils in 1945.

To Pierre Elliott Trudeau

16th April, 1979

Dear Pierre:

I have been following the election campaign and wish to make a brief note; namely, that since the issues are tending to get "hot", it would be a huge advantage to shift the main broadcast coverage to radio. Radio is a "hot" medium and is indispensable when the issues get hot. TV is a fantasy medium and has good reason to be called "cool" or all-involving. The current issue of *Business Week*, I have been told, carries comments on the surprise return of Bill Clement as Governor of Texas, the first Republican in many years. He did it by radio—radio spots. The best man in the world for such spot coverage is my friend Tony Schwartz in New York City. He put Carter in by some inspired spots at the last moment. Tony is basically a sound or radio man, although he has a little book on television called *The Responsive Chord*. I tried to get in touch with Bill [Jim] Coutts about this but failed to reach him.[1]

Radio charisma is a completely different thing from TV charisma. TV charisma means looking like a lot of nice people, e.g. the [Walter] Cronkite image. Radio charisma merely consists of sounding dedicated.

---

[1]James Coutts (b. 1938) was Principal Secretary to the Prime Minister.

To Edmund G. Brown Jr[1]

24th April, 1979

Dear Jerry:

We have an election under way here in Canada and the issues include separatism, as well as jobs and inflation. All of these are hot issues. That is to say, they are completely unsuited to the TV medium. With TV political clout is via charisma; i.e. looking like a lot of other people—acceptable people. Richard Nixon looked only like himself and committed suicide on TV. By the same token policies are best not mentioned on TV, since they tend to be points of view. TV does not present the possibility of a point of view, if only because it works by rear projection.

Senator [Eugene] McCarthy, who had hot issues to sell was phased out of the scene on his first TV appearance. It is quite otherwise with policies that are urgent and sharply defined. They belong on radio, the hot medium and the medium for the hard sell.

Warm good wishes in your endeavours.

You may not have come across this![2]

[1]Jerry Brown was Governor of the State of California, whom McLuhan visited in his office in Sacramento on July 12, 1977—a visit that was well covered by the California press. (McLuhan was accompanied by his daughter Mary McLuhan Colton, who was later appointed by Brown to the State Board of Education.) Their conversation—McLuhan discoursing on TV, the politician's image, the twin hemispheres of the brain, work, the destruction of Greece by the alphabet, Christianity, 1900 and the beginning of modern man, the possibility of harmonizing our lives through the power of electronics, and the end of capitalism; Brown interrupting with a brief question or statement—was transcribed in the *Los Angeles Times* (March 12, 1978) with the heading "The Medium Brings His Message to the Governor: Marshall McLuhan Meets Jerry Brown and the Results Are Indescribable". It was reprinted from *The CoEvolution Quarterly*, Winter 1977/8, edited by Stewart Brand, who was present.
[2]Enclosed was a "Doonsbury" cartoon sequence about Brown's candidacy for governor, with its heavy TV coverage, ending: "Governor, if we were to turn off the camera, would you exist?"/"I don't want to speculate on that."

To Pierre Elliott Trudeau

7th September, 1979

Dear Pierre:

I think there is no question but that your beard has cooled your image many degrees! There may be a time when you would wish to hot it up again. This, by the way, reminds me of a factor that relates to our Centre here: we have a monopoly on the study of the effects of media and technology. I wish this were not so but the monopoly is very real. The Greeks did not even study the effects of the alphabet on themselves, or its relation to the rise of Euclid and rationalism.

Another matter is that this is the last year for the Centre as it is presently related to the University of Toronto. This is mainly a financial matter, although there is also the fact that they cannot find anybody to replace me. I personally know of some possible replacements and this could be one of the matters I would like to discuss with you when we get together.

Our own study of the relations of media and politics might be an aspect that would favour some support. Hutchins once set up a Center for the Study of Democratic Institutions in California, which is still functioning. It would be easy to improve on their programme. There is, incidentally, a basic reason why we have this monopoly on the study of the effects of media and I would be happy to discuss that with you also when we get together.

Jimmy Carter, by the way, is the first American President from the Deep South, and many of his problems arise from a culture-clash between his oral tradition and the bureaucratic world of modern politics and government. I have often said that he is, as it were, Huck Finn in the White House. Since he is coming up here in November, it might be feasible to be of some help to him!

On September 26, 1979—shortly before he was to depart for Sao Paulo, Brazil, where he was to speak at a large communications conference—McLuhan suffered a massive stroke. (In hospital, coming out of an anesthetic after a brain scan, he said: "Eric, Brazil"—Eric McLuhan went in his place.) He survived this stroke, but the left hemisphere of his brain had been damaged and he lost the ability to read and write and most of his powers of speech. After six weeks of therapy he gradually became able to live each day with some normality and learned to meet constant frustration with patience. He could not verbalize ideas but he could utter single words, or occasionally something he had long ago memorized. In the spring, looking out the window at the rain in the company of his friend Patrick Watson, he recited "April is the cruellest month . . ." from The Waste Land. *He enjoyed seeing friends—being talked to and read to. In the summer of 1980 Corinne and Marshall McLuhan had a short holiday with Ted Carpenter on Long Island, and towards the end of September they went to Sidney, Cape Breton Island, to attend the première of Teri McLuhan's film* The Third Walker. *On December 30 they were visited by a New York friend of McLuhan's, Father Francis Stroud. On New Year's Eve, McLuhan enjoyed a celebratory dinner with Stroud at home. That night he died in his sleep.*

The funeral was held at Holy Rosary Church, Toronto, on January 3, 1981. Marshall McLuhan's life and accomplishments were honoured at a Memorial Service in Convocation Hall, University of Toronto, on January 29.

1981

From Prime Minister Trudeau to Corinne McLuhan

PRIME MINISTER • PREMIER MINISTRE
January 7, 1981
Ottawa, K1A 0A2

My dear Corinne

It is with great sadness that I write to express my sympathy to you and your family. Despite the setback which Marshall suffered more than a year ago, the news of his death was still a terrible shock.

Much will be said and written, and rightly so, about his marvellous intellect, his years of teaching, his global eminence as a social theorist, as a seminal scholar and writer. But the dominant thoughts in my own mind are of you and your children, and of my own sense of loss.

I have long valued his friendship, and have warm memories of our stimulating conversations. His letters were a constant delight, even when they included those terrible puns he used to urge me to use in political debate.

Marshall's life and work increased my sense of pride in being a Canadian. His crackling mind provided me with much pleasure and many lasting insights. His work, I am sure, will live on to challenge thoughtful men and women of future generations.

At this time, perhaps what is of most consolation to you is your knowledge of his great faith, and of the goodness of his life. He was a man whose fame did not dilute his profound awareness that our destiny in life is to love and to serve.

In the name of the government and people of Canada, I want to express the sympathy of a nation which is saddened by his death, and grateful for his life. For my part, I simply pray that God will grant strength, lasting peace and serenity of spirit to you and your family.

Yours sincerely,
Pierre

Index

Italicized page numbers denote letters written to the indexed subject.
McLuhan's writings and ideas are listed under McLuhan, Herbert Marshall.